DISCARDED

S0-BJM-548

SHELTON STATE COMMUNITY
COLLEGE
JUNIOR COLLEGE DIVISION
LIBRARY

DD   Pflanze, Otto.
218
•P44   Bismarck and the
        development of
        Germany

DATE			
FEB 18 1987			
AUG 24 1989			
JUN 02 1990			
APR 25 1996			
MAR 12 2001			
MAY 1 2018			

© THE BAKER & TAYLOR CO

DISCARDED

BISMARCK

AND THE DEVELOPMENT OF GERMANY

THE PERIOD OF UNIFICATION, 1815-1871

Historisches Bildarchiv

BISMARCK IN 1863

DISCARDED

BISMARCK

AND THE DEVELOPMENT

OF GERMANY

THE PERIOD OF UNIFICATION, 1815-1871

BY OTTO PFLANZE

PRINCETON, NEW JERSEY

PRINCETON UNIVERSITY PRESS

DISCARDED

Copyright © 1963 by Princeton University Press
ALL RIGHTS RESERVED
L.C. Card: 63-7159
ISBN 0-691-00765-9

First Princeton Paperback Edition, 1971
Second Printing 1973
Publication of this book has been aided by
the Ford Foundation program to support publication,
through university presses, of works in the
humanities and social sciences

Winner of the McKnight Foundation
Humanities Award for 1962

Printed in the United States of America
by Princeton University Press, Princeton, N.J.

This book is sold subject to the condition that
it shall not, by way of trade, be lent, resold, hired out,
or otherwise disposed of without the publisher's consent,
in any form of binding or cover other than
that in which it is published.

ABBREVIATIONS USED IN THE FOOTNOTES

APP   Historische Reichskommission, *Die Auswärtige Politik Preussens, 1858-1871* (Vols. I-VI, VIII-X, Berlin, 1932-1939)

DPO   Heinrich Ritter von Srbik, ed., *Quellen zur deutschen Politik Österreichs, 1859-1866* (five vols., Oldenburg, 1934-1938)

GW   Herman von Petersdorff and others, eds., *Bismarck: Die gesammelten Werke* (fifteen volumes, Berlin, 1923-1933)

HW   Julius Heyderhoff and Paul Wentzcke, eds., *Deutscher Liberalismus im Zeitalter Bismarcks, Eine politische Briefsammlung* (two vols., Bonn, 1925-1927)

OD   Ministère des Affaires Étrangères, *Les origines diplomatiques de la guerre de 1870/71, Recueil de documents officiels* (29 vols., Paris, 1910-1932)

RKN   Hermann Oncken, ed., *Die Rheinpolitik Kaiser Napoleons III. von 1863 bis 1870 und der Ursprung des Krieges von 1870/71* (three vols., Berlin, 1926)

SBHA   *Stenographische Berichte über die Verhandlungen des Landtages, Haus der Abgeordneten*

SBHH   *Stenographische Berichte über die Verhandlungen des Landtages, Herrenhaus*

SBR   *Stenographische Berichte über die Verhandlungen des Reichstags des Norddeutschen Bundes*

CONTENTS

Maps on pages 37 and 304
by R. L. Williams

BISMARCK

AND THE DEVELOPMENT OF GERMANY

THE PERIOD OF UNIFICATION, 1815-1871

INTRODUCTION

THE BISMARCK PROBLEM

WITH the exception of Napoleon, no other figure in modern European history has attracted as much interest as Otto von Bismarck. Since the first serious studies of the man and his career appeared sixty years ago, the size of the bibliography has reached staggering proportions.[1] Still the flood of books and articles continues with no sign of abatement. Bismarck and national unification have as great a fascination for Germans as do Lincoln and the civil war for Americans.

To non-Germans as well, the personality and achievement of the Junker genius have a magnetic attraction. His political career of almost half a century was one of the longest in the annals of statecraft. For nearly three decades of that time he was the dominant figure in German and European politics. Unexplored nooks and crannies, even whole rooms, are still being discovered in the edifice of his career. The wide range of his interests, the complexity of his mind, and his almost incredible skill at political invention and maneuver have made the subject difficult to exhaust.

By far the most important reason for continued interest, however, is the need to reassess the German past in view of the terrible tragedy of the twentieth century. In a book of essays dedicated to this theme Hans Kohn remarked that "the process of rethinking German history centers rightly around the appreciation of Bismarck's work." Reviewing the "German catastrophe," Friedrich Meinecke, the dean of German historians, wrote sadly in 1945, "The staggering course of the first, and still more the second world war no longer permits the question to be ignored whether the seeds of later evil were not already present in the Bismarckian Reich."[2]

---

[1] Hajo Holborn, *The Political Collapse of Europe* (New York, 1951), p. 200. The best general survey of the literature is Walter Bussmann, *Das Zeitalter Bismarcks* in Leo Just, ed., *Handbuch der deutschen Geschichte*, III/3 (Constance, 1955).

[2] Hans Kohn, ed., *German History: Some New German Views* (London, 1954), p. 30; Friedrich Meinecke, *Die Deutsche Katastrophe* (Wiesbaden, 1946), p. 26. For reviews of the "Bismarck controversy" see Kohn, *op.cit.*, pp. 11-43, and An-

During the last decade and a half, leading German historians have given their answers to the question Meinecke raised. No other issue has aroused such intense, even impassioned, interest among scholars in postwar Germany. But the replies have been mostly negative. In 1946 S. A. Kaehler set the tone by denouncing as "legend," "prejudice," "propaganda" the view that any connection existed between Frederick the Great, Bismarck, and Hitler. Without taking the opposite viewpoint, Franz Schnabel questioned the wisdom of the solution which Bismarck provided for the problem of German unity. A more lasting solution, he argued, would have been the federated central Europe advocated at the time by Constantin Frantz. By forcing Austria out of Germany in 1866, Bismarck prepared the way for the disintegration of the Hapsburg monarchy and hence the ultimate isolation and decline of Germany itself. Gerhard Ritter and Wilhelm Schüssler were quick to rebut this "surprising thesis." The pressure of German nationalism, they assert, was "irresistible"; only the little-German Reich of 1871 was acceptable to the German people. In reply the Austrian historian, Heinrich Ritter von Srbik reiterated once more his lifelong defense of the concept of a united central Europe.[3]

Ritter, Schüssler, and Schnabel agree, nevertheless, that the great chancellor was the last master of the art of eighteenth-century "cabinet diplomacy" in an age increasingly dominated by national passions and crusading ideologies. According to Ritter, "Bismarck had nothing to do with the nationalism of the nineteenth and twentieth centuries and its blind fanaticism. One cannot possibly stress that fact sharply enough." Schnabel is equally emphatic, maintaining that the Junker "had nothing in common with the dictators of the nationalistic period" and was completely devoid of that "*moderne Vaterländerei*" typical of the new na-

---

dreas Dorpalen, "The German Historians and Bismarck," *Review of Politics*, xv (1953), 53-67.

[3] S. A. Kaehler, *Vorurteile und Tatsachen* (Hameln, 1949), pp. 27-35; Franz Schnabel, "Bismarck und die Nationen," *La Nouvelle Clio*, i-ii (1949-1950), 87-102, also in *Europa und der Nationalismus, Bericht über das III. internationale Historiker-Treffen in Speyer—17. bis 20. Oktober 1949* (Baden-Baden, 1950), pp. 91-108; Gerhard Ritter, "Grossdeutsch und Kleindeutsch im 19. Jahrhundert," in Walther Hubatsch, ed., *Schicksalswege deutscher Vergangenheit, Festschrift für Siegfried A. Kaehler* (Düsseldorf, 1950), pp. 177-201, and "Das Bismarckproblem," *Merkur*, iv/1 (1950), 657-676; Wilhelm Schüssler, "Noch einmal: Bismarck und die Nationen," *La Nouvelle Clio*, i-ii (1949-1950), 432-455, and *Um das Geschichtsbild* (Gladbeck, 1953), pp. 102-122; Heinrich Ritter von Srbik, "Die Bismarck-Kontroverse," *Wort und Wahrheit*, v/2 (1950), 918-931.

tional patriotism. "Bismarck was not at all a man of national or popular ideas," writes Schüssler, but "a man of state and the reason of state . . . the man of pure *Staatsräson*."[4]

This is also the position of Hans Rothfels, who has long denied that the Bismarckian Reich could validly be called a "national state." He believes this description applicable only to the western, not the eastern frontier, which included many Poles and excluded millions of Germans. He quotes with approval the view of a British historian, Sir Lewis Namier, that "German aggressive nationalism derives from the much belauded Frankfurt parliament rather than from Bismarck and 'Prussianism.' " While the great chancellor has been most frequently criticized for having created the German state in defiance of the dominant ideas of his age, this was in Rothfels' opinion his greatest virtue. He is significant for our times precisely because he was alien to his own century and sought to disarm and confine those revolutionary forces which have since threatened our destruction. Walter Bussmann, author of the most recent general survey of the Bismarckian period, sees in Rothfels' writings the most penetrating analysis of the subject.[5]

On the other hand, such lifelong students of Bismarck's career as the late A. O. Meyer and Otto Becker persisted in identifying him as a German patriot whose primary aim from the outset was national unification. To them the national character of the second Reich was self-evident. In this they followed the views of two earlier historians, Heinrich Friedjung and Erich Brandenburg, both of whom saw evidences of national purpose very early in his career. Another older school believed that he began as a Prussian patriot

---

[4] Gerhard Ritter, *Europa und die deutsche Frage* (Munich, 1948), pp. 69-108, "Bismarckproblem," p. 673, *Staatskunst und Kriegshandwerk, Das Problem des "Militarismus" in Deutschland* (Munich, 1954), I, 302-329; Franz Schnabel, "Bismarck und die Klassische Diplomatie," *Aussenpolitik*, III (1952), 635-642, and "Das Problem Bismarck," *Hochland*, XLII (1949), 8-9; Schüssler, *Geschichtsbild*, pp. 120-121.

[5] Hans Rothfels, *Bismarck und der Osten* (Leipzig, 1934), "Bismarck und die Nationalitätenfragen des Ostens," *Ostraum, Preussentum und Reichsgedanke* in *Königsberger Historische Forschungen*, VII (Leipzig, 1935), "Bismarck und das neunzehnte Jahrhundert," in Hubatsch, ed., *Schicksalswege*, pp. 233-248, *Bismarck und der Staat* (Stuttgart, 1954), pp. xvii-xlviii, "Zeitgeschichtliche Betrachtungen zum Problem der Realpolitik," in Richard Dietrich und Gerhard Oestreich, eds., *Forschungen zu Staat und Verfassung: Festgabe für Fritz Hartung* (Berlin, 1958), pp. 526-529, "Problems of a Bismarck Biography," *Review of Politics*, IX (1947), 362-380; Lewis Namier, *1848: The Revolution of the Intellectuals*, in *Proceedings of the British Academy*, XXX (1944); Bussmann, *Zeitalter Bismarcks*, p. 247.

and made the transition to German nationalism fairly late. Richard Fester chose the year 1865, Erich Marcks 1866, Erich Eyck 1867. In the most recent biography Wilhelm Mommsen argues that Bismarck had no other purpose than establishment of Prussian hegemony over northern Germany and that the little-German Reich was the consequence of French imperialism. Its founder was an adherent of the national state only "in a very limited sense."[6]

Only upon one point is there near unanimity: German scholars reject the interpretations of Erich Eyck and A. O. Meyer, authors of the most detailed scholarly biographies. Completed during the second world war, the two works are widely divergent in viewpoint. An émigré from the Hitler regime, Eyck wrote from the outlook of the nineteenth-century liberal opposition. While marvelling at Bismarck's genius, Eyck criticized his actions at almost every turn of his career. Meyer's view, on the other hand, is that of a conservative German nationalist, to whom Bismarck was the apex of German political achievement. There is a significant difference in the tone and temper of the German reaction to these works. While Eyck's interpretation has aroused a sharp, even irritated, response, the "old-fashioned," "outmoded" view of Meyer has generally been treated with tolerance.[7]

Most German scholars have been equally adamant in repudiating the view of Bismarck commonly held abroad: that of the "iron chancellor" or "man of blood and iron." Schüssler, Otto Vossler, Leonhard von Muralt, and Gustav A. Rein have emphatically stressed that Bismarck, in stark contrast to Hitler, was moved by a sense of ethical responsibility, grounded in an intense religious

[6] Arnold Oskar Meyer, *Bismarck: Der Mensch und der Staatsmann* (Stuttgart, 1949); Otto Becker, *Bismarcks Ringen um Deutschlands Gestaltung* (Heidelberg, 1958); Heinrich Friedjung, *Der Kampf um die Vorherrschaft in Deutschland, 1859 bis 1866* (10th ed., Stuttgart, 1916), I, 141; Erich Brandenburg, *Die Reichsgründung* (2nd ed., Leipzig, 1922), II, 30-35, 78-79; Richard Fester, "Biarritz, eine Bismarck-Studie," *Deutsche Rundschau*, Vol. 113 (1902), p. 236; Erich Marcks, *Der Aufstieg des Reiches* (Stuttgart, 1936), II, 274-275; Erich Eyck, *Bismarck, Leben und Werk* (Zurich, 1941-1944), I., 367; Wilhelm Mommsen, *Bismarck, Ein politisches Lebensbild* (Munich, 1959), pp. 167-168.

[7] Rothfels, "Problems," pp. 362-380; Schüssler, *Geschichtsbild*, pp. 101-102, 142-143; Schnabel, "Problem," p. 406; Ritter, "Bismarck-problem," pp. 659 ff.; Emil Franzel, "Das Bismarck Bild in unserer Zeit," *Neues Abendland*, V (1950), 223-230; Wilhelm Mommsen, "Der Kampf um das Bismarck-Bild," *Universitas*, V/1 (1950), 273-280; Leonhard von Muralt, *Bismarcks Verantwortlichkeit* (Göttingen, 1955), 218-220; Maximilian von Hagen, "Das Bismarckbild der Gegenwart," *Zeitschrift für Politik*, VI (1959), 79-83; Joachim H. Knoll, "Werk und Methode des Historikers Erich Eyck," *Neue deutsche Hefte*, Part 64 (1959), pp. 729-736.

faith and earnest submission to a personal, all-powerful God. This inner piety preserved him from the "demonism of power."[8] In an important work Ritter has striven to cleanse his reputation from the taint of militarism. Contrary to Moltke, the chancellor was opposed to "preventive war." During the conflicts of 1864, 1866, and 1870, he insisted upon the supremacy of diplomatic over military strategy. His "greatest service," Schüssler declared, was the erection of "firm barriers" against demands of the military for supremacy over political policy in wartime.[9]

With but few exceptions, therefore, Germany's leading scholars have rejected the view that there was any direct relationship between the Bismarckian and Hitlerian Reichs.[10] Later Meinecke himself appeared to retreat from his position of 1945. The Bismarckian *Machtstaat*, he concluded, was a geopolitical necessity for Germany. Ritter has detected an upsurge of "Bismarck veneration"; Bernhard Knauss writes of a "certain tendency to re-popularize Bismarck" by picturing him as the George Washington of German history; and Wilhelm Mommsen rejoices that a "much more positive judgment" of Bismarck has developed in recent years, while cautioning against "too much of a good thing."[11] Comfort is found in the fact that the first German

8 Schüssler, *Geschichtsbild*, p. 139; Otto Vossler, Bismarcks Ethos," *Historische Zeitschrift*, Vol. 171 (1951), pp. 263-292; Muralt, *Verantwortlichkeit*, pp. 65-140; Gustav Adolf Rein, *Die Revolution in der Politik Bismarcks* (Göttingen, 1957), pp. 307-354. In 1943, however, Rein wrote of Hitler as "the rescuer and benefactor of Europe." *Europa und das Reich* (Essen, 1943), p. 87.

9 Ritter, *Staatskunst*, i, 238-329; Schüssler, *Geschichtsbild*, p. 80; also Muralt, *Verantwortlichkeit*, p. 34.

10 Notable exceptions are the articles by Karl Buchheim, Alfred von Martin, Johann Albrecht von Rantzau, and Walter Hofer translated in Kohn, *New German Views*, pp. 44-64, 94-107, 157-174, 187-205, Werner Richter, "Das Bild Bismarcks," *Neue Rundschau*, Vol. 63 (1952), pp. 43-63, and the brilliant but neglected article of Herbert Michaelis, "Königgrätz, Eine geschichtliche Wende," *Die Welt als Geschichte*, xii (1952), 177-202. See also the remarkable work of Heinrich Heffter, *Die deutsche Selbstverwaltung im 19. Jahrhundert* (Stuttgart, 1950), whose scope is considerably greater than its title. The criticism of Robert Saitschick, a Swiss literator, is one-sided and misses the mark, *Bismarck und das Schicksal des deutschen Volkes, Zur Psychologie und Geschichte der deutschen Frage* (Basel, 1949). In a series of courageous articles Ludwig Dehio, editor of the *Historische Zeitschrift*, censured government policy and public temperament in the period of William II, but only by implication did his criticism extend to Bismarck and his work. *Deutschland und die Weltpolitik im 20. Jahrhundert* (Munich, 1955), translated as *Germany and World Politics in the Twentieth Century* (New York, 1959).

11 Friedrich Meinecke, "Irrwege in unserer Geschichte?" *Der Monat*, ii (1949-1950), 3-6, and the replies of Hajo Holborn and Geoffrey Barraclough, pp. 531-538, the former translated in Kohn, *New German Views*, pp. 206-212; Ritter,

chancellor was not highly regarded by Nazi ideologists. Conservative historians have been inclined to trace the origins of the Nazi revolution to the breakdown of the old aristocratic society and bureaucratic state under the impact of liberal and democratic ideas and the emergence of the masses as a factor in politics. There is also a tendency to see these ideas and movements as importations from abroad, foreign influences which had a cancerous effect upon the sound organism of German society. It is assumed that the German Reich created by Bismarck and overturned in the revolution of 1918 was essentially a healthy institution whose destruction eliminated the most effective obstacle to the rise of totalitarianism.[12]

One of the purposes of this book is to question this assumption on grounds more valid than those previously advanced by critics of Bismarck. The history of Scandinavia, western Europe, and the Anglo-Saxon world shows that there is no necessary causal relationship between popular sovereignty and the rise of totalitarianism. It cannot be denied that Germany has been influenced for the worse by some unfortunate trends common to the whole of European civilization. But it is also true that during the last two centuries a cultural cleavage opened along the Rhine. In the development of her political attitudes and institutions Germany followed a course largely independent of the west.

The unique development of Germany began, of course, long before Bismarck. Its origin lay in the character of the Prussian political and military system, the late appearance of the German middle class, the subjection of church to state in the Lutheran faith, the link between authority and freedom in German political thought, the victory of historical over natural law, the idealization

---

"Bismarckproblem," p. 658; Bernhard Knauss, "Neue Beiträge zum Bismarckbild," *Politische Studien*, x (1959), 266-267; Wilhelm Mommsen, "Der Kampf um das Bismarck Bild," *Neue Politische Literatur*, iv (1959), 210. Typical of the trend toward rehabilitation are the popular biography of Ludwig Reimers, *Bismarck* (two vols., Munich, 1956-1957), the diplomatic "textbook" of Friedrich Haselmayr, *Diplomatische Geschichte des zweiten Reichs von 1871-1918* (3 vols., Munich, 1955-1957), the dramatized story of the dismissal by Richard Sexau, *Kaiser oder Kanzler* (5th ed., Berlin, 194?), and the similar, though not uncritical, work of Rudolf Baumgardt, *Bismarck: Licht und Schatten eines Genies* (Munich, 1951).

[12] Rothfels, "Bismarck und das neunzehnte Jahrhundert," pp. 236 ff.; Ritter, *Deutsche Frage*, pp. 41 ff. This is also the general tendency of Muralt, *Verantwortlichkeit* (pp. 187-217) and Rein, *Revolution in der Politik Bismarcks*.

of the state and its power, and the German view of nationality as a matter of common culture rather than common citizenship.[13]

Because of Bismarck the gap widened still more. He compounded a new synthesis in German political attitudes between German nationalism, Prussian militarism, and Hohenzollern authoritarianism. Through the moral power of the German national idea he constructed a new and firmer basis for traditional autocratic and militaristic institutions in the emergent age of mass democracy. He legitimized and preserved for Germany the political system of "mixed powers" (that is, an authoritarian executive combined with a popular legislature) which elsewhere in western Europe was but a transitional stage in the growth of a liberal-democratic order. His career heightened the already dangerous adulation of power in Germany and accentuated the popular belief that what matters in the employment of power is success. He perpetuated in a far different age the Frederician tradition of the genius-statesman, unlimited in the last analysis by any constitutional restrictions and responsible alone to his own inner conscience for his conduct of public affairs.

Undoubtedly there was much in Bismarck's statesmanship reminiscent of the political style of the eighteenth century. The diplomatists of the age of reason did not seek to remake the world in the image of their own religious or political faiths, but to strengthen the power and security of their states within the framework of the European equilibrium. The latter was regarded as the precondition of political stability and the protective mechanism which preserved the independence of the powers. Bismarck's motives were those of *raison d'état* and *arrondissement* typical of eighteenth-century statecraft. His aim was not to unify the German cultural nation, but to expand the Prussian state within the limits of the European balance of power. Like Frederick the Great, he insisted upon the supremacy of political over military strategy.

[13] See Ernst Troeltsch, "The Ideas of Natural Law and Humanity in World Politics," in Otto Gierke, *Natural Law and the Theory of Society, 1500-1800* (Cambridge, 1934), I, 201-222; Fritz Fischer, "Der deutsche Protestantismus und die Politik im 19. Jahrhundert," *Historische Zeitschrift*, Vol. 171 (1951), pp. 473-518; Hajo Holborn, "Der deutsche Idealismus in sozialgeschichtlicher Beleuchtung," *Historische Zeitschrift*, Vol. 174 (1952), pp. 359-384; Leonard Krieger, *The German Idea of Freedom* (Boston, 1957); Jacques Droz, "Concept français et concept allemand de l'idée de nationalité," in *Europa und der Nationalismus*, pp. 111-133; Hans Rothfels, "Grundsätzliches zum Problem der Nationalität," *Historische Zeitschrift*, Vol. 174 (1952), pp. 339-358.

With Clausewitz he believed that war is properly but a continuation of diplomacy "by other means."

The "cabinet diplomacy" of the eighteenth century was possible, however, only because of the relative homogeneity of social and political conditions in that age. Europe possessed a common political structure, a common political outlook, and a common ruling class. Monarchical government, the concept of divine right, and aristocratic rule were universal. While the status of the nobility depended upon the survival of the monarchical order, no international crusade was necessary to rescue that vested interest. England was the only exception to the general consensus, but the English revolution was not accompanied by a violent social upheaval, and furthermore it was not deliberately exported.

The French revolution and Napoleonic conquests disrupted this harmony and introduced a new era of crusading idealism in European politics. But the old order, while severely damaged, was by no means destroyed, and its restoration in the settlement of 1815 created the possibility of a return to classical diplomacy. For a time conservative doctrine and the fear of revolution delayed its reappearance. During the fifties, however, the drift toward realism in the European psyche brought about a revival of the eighteenth-century diplomatic style. In many respects Bismarck, Buol, and Gorchakov were closer to Kaunitz, Choiseul, and Frederick the Great than to Metternich, Alexander I, and Frederick William IV.

Nevertheless, it is utterly incorrect to depict Bismarck as a man out of his age, belonging more to the past than the future. The practice of cabinet diplomacy in the nineteenth century became increasingly difficult because of the erosion of its social and political foundation. Bismarck was one of the first to grasp that the emerging age of popular movements required a new kind of politics. No longer could the masses be ignored in the conduct of either domestic or foreign affairs. Whatever the ends of the statesman, war and foreign conquest required the moral approbation of a righteous cause. At home the doctrines of legitimacy and divine right no longer sufficed to justify authoritarian rule. If monarchical institutions were to endure in an age of dynamic economic and social change, they had to be rooted in the more fertile soil of national sentiment.

Bismarck was the political surgeon who amputated nationalism

from liberalism and conservatism from legitimism. Following
Louis Napoleon, he comprehended that nationalism and liberalism
were not necessarily compatible and that the former might actually be converted into an anti-liberal force. "It was only through
Bismarck," Bertrand Russell shrewdly observed, "that German
patriotism became respectable and conservative, with the result
that many men who had been liberal because they were patriots
became conservative for the same reason." In the process German
nationalism lost what remained of that humanitarian and cosmopolitan outlook which was its endowment from Herder and the
ages of reason and romanticism.[14] His exploitation of nationalism
for imperialistic and authoritarian purposes is what makes Bismarck, like Napoleon III, a transitional figure between the politics
of the eighteenth and twentieth centuries, between the age of aristocratic absolutism and that of authoritarian nationalism.

Moral forces provided Bismarck with means rather than ends,
with objects to be manipulated rather than with guides for political action. What moved him was not the ideal of German national unity, but the quest for greater internal stability for the
Hohenzollern monarchy and greater external power for Prussia
in Europe. Had Austria been willing to continue the dual domination of Germany on a basis more favorable to Prussia, or had
the constellation of European politics been less favorable for
Prussian expansion, he would have followed a conservative course
in foreign policy, co-operating with Austria and Russia against
popular forces in Germany and Europe. Within Prussia he would
have endeavored to outflank the liberal opposition by appealing
to the artisan and proletarian classes through a policy of state
socialism.

Nevertheless, it is doubtful that Bismarck would have been
permanently satisfied to follow the conservative course. The radical, even revolutionary, one of alliance with German nationalism
was more in keeping with his volcanic temperament and, furthermore, it promised the greater gains. At one stroke it provided a
common solution to the double crisis he faced at home and abroad.
It gave him the moral means with which to justify simultaneously
the expansion of Prussia and the retention of Hohenzollern au-

[14] Bertrand Russell, *Freedom versus Organization, 1814-1914* (New York, 1934),
pp. 362, 368; Michaelis, "Königgrätz," pp. 190 ff.

thority. Finally it enabled him to travel with the "stream of time" by steering into a current of great potential strength.

In stealing the national plank from the liberal platform Bismarck had a number of precedents to follow. Since 1806 the Prussian government had either preempted or appropriated much of the liberal program. The Stein-Hardenberg reforms, the Zollverein, the Prussian constitution of 1848-1850, and the free-trade treaty of 1862 pointed the way for his action. But the theft of the cause of national unity was the most persuasive act of all in reconciling the German liberals to authoritarian rule. It demonstrated with finality the truth of Bismarck's statement to Napoleon that "only the kings make revolution in Prussia."[15]

He owed his success in raiding the liberal program in large part to the absence of any genuine popular movement in Germany. Despite the remarkable changes in the economic and social structure of Germany during the late fifties, there was as little mass support for the liberal cause in the constitutional conflict of 1862-1866 as there had been during the later stages of the revolution in 1848. This weakness arose from the inadequate penetration of liberal ideals into the lower strata of German society, but also from the deliberate unwillingness of the liberals to look after the material needs of the working class. The alliance of the aristocratic and middle classes consummated by Bismarck in 1866 left the working class no other recourse than to find in proletarian socialism its spiritual home.

As an autonomous movement German nationalism was also patently lacking in vitality before 1870. For six decades German nationalists had been confronted with the challenging task of uniting a badly divided people, but only once, in 1848, did the ideal of national unity generate sufficient popular support for the attempt. Within weeks, however, the patriotic fervor evaporated. By May 1849 only a few were still willing to sacrifice for the cause. At other times only the external stimulus of a crisis with France (1813-1815, 1840, 1859, 1867, and 1870-1871) succeeded in bringing any life to the national movement. Only on two of these occasions (1813-1815 and 1870-1871) was anything accomplished, and this was due entirely to the leadership provided by the Prussian state, whose ministers exploited German nationalism for their own political ends. The achievements of 1864 and 1866 were at-

15 *GW*, viii, 459.

tained by the Prussian state over the bitter opposition of the national movement. In 1864 the efforts of the Nationalverein through popular agitation to push through the claims of the Prince of Augustenburg to Schleswig-Holstein ended in complete failure, and in 1866 the nationalists could not prevent civil war over issues believed in the beginning to be alien to the national cause.

The common view of German nationalism as an irresistible current sweeping down the decades to fulfillment in 1870 is a fiction of nationalistic historians, derived from the hopes and aspirations of those *kleindeutsch* leaders, like Sybel and Treitschke, who were their intellectual forebears. Only under the stimulation provided by Bismarck for his own political ends did German nationalism begin to move the masses. It is a fact of fateful significance that German national sentiment could gain sufficient momentum to overcome the particularistic loyalties of the German people only in combination with Prussian militarism and Hohenzollern authoritarianism.

The lethargy of German nationalism before 1870 does indeed leave open to doubt the assumption that the Bismarckian Reich was the only possible solution to the German question. At Königgrätz, however, the concept of a unified national state, represented by Prussia, was completely victorious over the older concept of universal empire, represented by the Hapsburg monarchy. Under the Holy Roman Empire and the German Confederation the German people possessed no precise frontier delimiting the area of their political and cultural influence. For centuries their fate had been joined with that of the peoples of central Europe. By restricting their horizon, the decision of 1866 greatly accelerated the growth of that inverted national sentiment which was to devastate Europe in the twentieth century. The achievement of national self-determination by Italy and Germany accentuated the ambitions of the subject peoples of the Hapsburg monarchy to divest themselves of German leadership and assert their cultural and political autonomy. The ultimate consequence was the disintegration of central Europe into its many national components.[16]

Throughout Europe the constitutional system of "mixed powers" underwent changes in the nineteenth century which call into question its inherent stability as a governmental form. Either the power of the legislature penetrated the executive creating parlia-

16 Michaelis, "Königgrätz," pp. 179-185.

mentary government, or the reverse occurred with a consequent devitalization of parliamentary life. England, France, Italy, the Netherlands, and the Scandinavian countries experienced the former process. In Prussia the possibility of such a development arose during the constitutional conflict of the sixties. Owing to Bismarck's genius the chance was lost and the contrary current set in. Through the victories of 1866 and 1870 the essential features of the Prussian system, with some diminution of parliamentary authority, were extended over the rest of Germany. Another important consequence was the disorganization of the major political parties. Bismarck's manipulations fragmentized the party structure and reduced the possibility of stable majorities. His stark realism weakened the attraction of political ideals and exalted in German political attitudes the prestige of power at the cost of principle.

His undeniable sense of ethical responsibility is inadequate as a justification for Bismarck's arbitrary actions. The possession of an active conscience, grounded in religious faith, is never a sufficient substitute for legal and institutional checks on the use of power. Although he deplored absolutism, Germany's first chancellor demonstrated by his willingness to break the constitution that he recognized in the final analysis no higher authority than the expediency of power. The priority he gave to might over right in both domestic and foreign affairs established an unfortunate precedent in German history upon which men of other aims and other conscience were eventually to capitalize. It was the precedent of the man of titanic will, to whom success is the major criterion, who appears in a time of chaos and weakness to lead his people over seemingly insuperable obstacles to the promised land of internal stability and external power.

Bismarck himself was deeply skeptical of the capacity of individuals to shape history. But his own career shows that his pessimism was unjustified. To be sure, he did not create the forces with which he dealt. By manipulating, however, he altered them. The combinations he achieved became a historical influence of the first magnitude. Bismarck belongs to that category of men whom Hegel called "world-historical individuals" because through them the world is changed.

BOOK ONE

THE YEARS OF PREPARATION

1815-1858

*"One cannot possibly make history, although
one can always learn from it how one should
lead the political life of a great people
in accordance with their development and
their historical destiny."*—BISMARCK in 1892

CHAPTER ONE

THE STREAM OF TIME

HE stream of time flows inexorably along. By plunging my hand into it, I am merely doing my duty. I do not expect thereby to change its course." This was the thought with which Bismarck began his career in the Prussian foreign service in 1851.[1] Four decades later, his view was still the same. To his many visitors in Friedrichsruh he was fond of saying: "Man can neither create nor direct the stream of time. He can only travel upon it and steer with more or less skill and experience; he can suffer shipwreck and go aground and also arrive in safe harbors."[2] His political career was one of the most effective of all time. Yet he felt to the end comparatively helpless before the push of historical forces. Only by examining the character of those forces can one understand the course he steered and the destinations for which he aimed. What was the stream of time upon which Bismarck set sail?

In the early nineteenth century the currents of historical evolution in Europe were many and swift. The great cultural synthesis of the enlightenment was in rapid dissolution. Under the influence of economic change the traditional social order began to be replaced by new and antagonistic social classes. The clarity and unity of rationalist thought gave way to the murky depths and swirling eddies of romanticism. New centers of political and intellectual orientation appeared in liberalism, conservatism, nationalism, and, ultimately, socialism. Everywhere men grappled desperately for new principles in which to believe and new forms of organization with which to contain the growing complexities of modern life.

Like the Atlantic nations, Germany was affected by the movement of these many forces. But here they appeared in a different order and strength, and tended to flow in different channels. Through Bismarck, furthermore, they were to be molded and

---

[1] *GW*, xiv, 249.

[2] *GW*, xiii, 558. For other similar remarks see *GW*, xi, 46; xiii, 304, 468; xiv, 751-752, 879-880.

transformed, their relationships split apart and recombined. The power with which he accomplished this was that of the Prussian state.

1. THE PRUSSIAN STATE

Prussia was largely the creation of a series of long-lived, energetic, and talented rulers. The character of both the state and its people was determined by the effort to create under difficult circumstances a power capable of asserting itself in European politics. The land was poor, sparse in resources and population, and without easily defensible frontiers. Security and growth alike required a standing army large in proportion to the population. Once created, this force was also useful for the suppression of feudal liberty within the state. During the same half century which saw the triumph of absolutism in France and its defeat in England, Elector Frederick William I suppressed the feudal estates in all his possessions. Whatever possibility there might have been for their development into modern representative institutions vanished.[3]

The growth of the army led inevitably to the creation of a state bureaucracy. Beginning with the conscription of soldiers and the collection of taxes, the agents of the monarchy assumed the function of building up the general economy. In a country possessing little commerce and urban life the state was compelled, if the financial burden of the army was to be borne, to play a positive role in raising the productive capacity and living standard of the population. During the century after 1640 the power and influence of the bureaucracy penetrated every aspect of Prussian society.

The character of this bureaucracy was permanently influenced by the nature of its origin. It was a rigorously trained and disciplined instrument for the transmission of royal authority. Until the end of the reign of Frederick the Great the king was the sole executive, acting through state secretaries whose function was not to formulate policy but to execute it. The system discouraged individual initiative and rewarded strict conformity. As early as the eighteenth century, university training and state examinations

---

[3] See F. L. Carsten, *The Origins of Prussia* (Oxford, 1954); also Fritz Hartung, *Deutsche Verfassungsgeschichte vom 15. Jahrhundert bis zur Gegenwart* (5th ed., Stuttgart, 1950), pp. 100 ff.

were required of civil servants; advancement came not through patronage, but through service. Dishonesty, disobedience, and independent action were strictly punished. The employment of retired generals and disabled or over-aged soldiers infused habits of military discipline.[4]

The machine-like character of the Prussian army and civil service had a lasting and unfortunate effect upon the mentality of the people. In an age of mercenary forces the Prussian army was much more closely identified with the population than in other countries. Although many foreigners served in all ranks, the officer corps was drawn largely from the Prussian nobility and the foot-soldiers from the native peasantry. Hence the spirit of "cadaver obedience" (*Kadavergehorsam*) drilled into the army carried over into the civilian population. The bureaucracy had a similar influence. The ex-soldiers in the lowest ranks, most frequently in contact with the public, added that harshness of tone and authoritarian manner thereafter typical of officialdom in Prussia and ultimately in Germany. The influence of army and bureaucracy upon the popular mind was all the greater because they lacked competition. There were no other organizations of comparable size in Prussian society. The day of big business lay in the future. Far from being a rival, the Lutheran church was actually part of the state administration.

The doctrines of Luther greatly increased the power of the authoritarian state in Germany. In his view the state was ordained by God to maintain order in an evil world, to protect the Christian few from the sinful majority. Luther was highly conscious of the corrupting nature of power and considered the state a worldly institution. But he denied the right of popular resistance against a tyrannical, even pagan, ruler. By placing its administration under the state, he made the church a vital prop of princely authority. By assigning to the state the functions of education and social welfare, he limited the role of the church to the propagation of faith.[5]

After Frederick the Great monarchical absolutism evolved into

[4] On the Prussian bureaucracy see Walter Dorn, "The Prussian Bureaucracy in the Eighteenth Century," *Political Science Quarterly*, Vol. 46 (1931), pp. 403-423, and Vol. 47 (1932), pp. 75-94, 259-273.

[5] On the political views and consequences of Luther, see Hajo Holborn, *A History of Modern Germany: The Reformation* (New York, 1959), pp. 186-194; also Fischer, "Protestantismus und Politik," pp. 473 ff.

bureaucratic absolutism. None of his successors was able to monopolize the executive function. While the final power remained with the king, the actual administration of government gravitated into the hands of ministers. In military matters a similar migration of function was evident. During peacetime routine military administration came to be handled by officers immediate to the king. Even in wartime Frederick's successors assumed only nominal command of the army.[6]

With the growth of an administrative apparatus the state came to be regarded as something apart from the person of the monarch. Frederick the Great contributed to this development with his famous dictum, "I am the first servant of the state." By refusing to interfere in the judicial process in matters of private law he also helped create an independent judiciary. Thus he founded the important tradition that, if absolute, the Prussian government ought not to be arbitrary. Those who wield power must themselves be subject to the laws of the state and the natural norms of justice. This was the beginning of the German concept of the *Rechtsstaat*, the state governed by the rule of law.[7]

Socially the Prussian system was an alliance between the monarchy and Junker aristocracy. While subjecting them to the state, the Great Elector made important concessions to the nobles. In Brandenburg and Prussia they were permitted to carve out latifundia through the enserfdom of the peasants. They were largely exempt from taxation, and commoners were forbidden to purchase noble estates. The alliance was also evident in local government. Rural Prussia was governed by royal agents (*Landräte*) nominated by the county nobility, though responsible only to Berlin. On the latifundia Junker landlords retained the feudal right to govern peasants and burghers. They lived like "kings in miniature," exploiting their powers of local government for their own economic advantage.[8]

More important still, the Junkers were the reservoir from which the Hohenzollern staffed the positions of command in both army and bureaucracy. Feudal vassalage was converted into the obligation and privilege of serving in the officer corps of the new

6 Hartung, *Verfassungsgeschichte*, p. 252; Hugo Preuss, "Verwaltungsreform und Politik," *Zeitschrift für Politik*, ɪ (1907-1908), 109.

7 Gerhard Ritter, *Friedrich der Grosse* (2nd ed., Leipzig, 1942), pp. 232 ff.

8 Franz Schnabel, *Deutsche Geschichte im neunzehnten Jahrhundert* (4th ed., Freiburg, 1948), ɪ, 99.

princes against the emperor rather than of the natural rights of man. The progress of the princes toward absolutism passed as but an aspect of the assertion of their aristocratic rights in the empire. In this way the German idea of freedom became associated with the absolute state. Despite the many social and political changes which subsequently occurred, this association was never really dissolved.[14]

The stagnant character of the German middle class also had its influence upon German intellectual life. The period 1770-1830 was, to be sure, one of tremendous intellectual activity on the part of the German bourgeoisie. It was the age of Kant, Herder, Goethe, Schiller, and Hegel. The German "idealists" broke away from the ideas and models of the French and German enlightenment in search of a new philosophy and new forms in which to express it. Dissatisfied with the limits of rationalism, they sought to penetrate the secrets of existence through artistic intuition and imagination as well as reason. Characteristic of the movement was an intense humanism, a vital absorption in problems of individual growth and self-development.

Nevertheless, the German intellectuals were not the spokesmen of the middle-class from which they came, nor even closely identified with its interests. As academicians, many were state officials and hence part of the bureaucratic system. Others were rentiers with the leisure for intellectual pursuits. For the most part, the German idealists were non-political. Intent on cultivation of their intellectual and spiritual faculties, they ignored the mundane matters of politics and statecraft. While they valued freedom, it was freedom of spirit they had in mind, not the social and political freedom of the citizen.[15]

Among Germans, therefore, the word "freedom" acquired a double meaning: in the realm of the intellect it meant the freedom of the human spirit and in that of politics the freedom of absolute states. The fusion of these concepts was achieved in the organic theory, the foundations of which were laid by Herder. Revolting against the atomistic view of man and society in the enlightenment, Herder pointed out the organic individuality of national cultures. Each possessed a unique character (*Volksgeist*) determined by the peculiarities of its historical growth.[16] What could

14 Krieger, *German Idea*, pp. 3 ff.; Valjavec, *Strömungen*, p. 40.
15 *Ibid.*, pp. 41 ff.   16 Schnabel, *Deutsche Geschichte*, I, 185 ff.

23

be said of national cultures, it soon was realized, could also be said of the state. As a traditional institution, constructed by successive generations of the race, it too was an organism endowed with personality. As such it also had the power and right of self-realization. In exercising this right, the state asserted its freedom.

The final consequence of this development was the idealization of the state and its power. Since the state was an organism, it was believed to possess, like human beings, a spiritual essence and moral worth. Hence Hegel could describe it as "the actually existing, realized moral life" or "the divine idea as it exists on earth." "Christ died not only for men," declared the philosopher Adam Müller, "but also for states."[17] The consequence of this conception upon German political thinking was disastrous. In their search for a new religious orientation, the German idealists "changed the arena of ethical and spiritual decisions in human history." The state replaced the church as the repository of moral values. Elsewhere in western Europe moral authority continued to reside in the Christian faith and the ethical norms of natural law, but in Germany it came to be identical with the state and the ruling power.[18]

3. THE SPECTRUM OF GERMAN LIBERALISM

Because of the late development of her bourgeoisie, Germany did not have a liberal "movement" in the genuine sense of the word until the 1840's. Not until the industrial revolution first began to affect the traditional social structure could a popular force develop to challenge, in some degree, the existing arrangements of society and government. Before that time liberalism was monopolized by intellectuals and progressive bureaucrats. The former sought to explicate it in the form of political philosophy and the latter to give it practical effect in the field of statecraft. The stamp which they gave to liberal thought through two generations of political life left an enduring mark upon the German conception of the free society.

The schizoid nature of German liberalism was apparent in the

17 Hegel, *The Philosophy of History* (New York, 1944), pp. 38-39; Jakob Baxa, ed., *Adam Müller: Die Elemente der Staatskunst* (Jena, 1922), II, 178-195.
18 Holborn, "Der deutsche Idealismus," p. 370; Troeltsch, "Ideas of Natural Law and Humanity," pp. 201-222.

4. THE VARIETIES OF CONSERVATISM

After 1789 the European nobility, attacked by the democratic doctrine of equality, was compelled to find an ideological justification for powers and privileges which had previously been taken for granted. In Germany the defenders of the aristocratic order found a convenient starting point in Edmund Burke's view of the social contract as a partnership which may not be dissolved at the fancy of the living generation, for it is a partnership between the living, the dead, and the unborn. "Each contract of each particular state," he wrote in *Reflections on the Revolution in France*, "is but a clause in the great primeval contract of eternal society, linking the lower with the higher natures, connecting the visible and invisible world, according to a fixed compact sanctioned by the inviolable oath which holds all physical and all moral natures, each in their appointed place." This concept harmonized very well with the organic theory, which since Herder had become one of the central doctrines of romantic thought. Out of their union came the political philosophy of romantic conservatism.[28]

The true law of nature, the conservatives maintained, was not based upon rational norms, but upon historical development. The valid structure of German society and government was the corporate one inherited from the middle ages, not the atomized society of liberalism or the centralized government of absolutism. State and society were integrally joined in a living body whose members were estates and corporations working together for the welfare and continued vitality of the whole. In the place of equality and individual freedom the conservatives praised the feudal system with its contractual rights, services, and dependencies. Whereas the rationalists had completed the divorce of theology from political theory begun by Machiavelli, the conservatives accomplished their remarriage. The traditional institutions of society were God's handiwork and to do them violence was blasphemy. If the state was a vital organism, then it was, like all living beings, a creation of the divinity. Far from being merely the creation of men for the nega-

[28] On Prussian conservatism in general, see Sigmund Neumann, *Die Stufen des preussischen Konservatismus, Historische Studien*, Vol. 190 (Berlin, 1930), and Gerhard Ritter, *Die preussischen Konservativen und Bismarcks deutsche Politik, 1858-1875* (Heidelberg, 1913); on Burke's influence see Schnabel, *Deutsche Geschichte*, I, 194 ff.; on the eighteenth-century origins of the conservative movement Valjavec, *Strömungen*, pp. 255 ff.

tive purpose of warding off evil, the state was instituted by God for the improvement of man's moral virtue.[29]

Like the liberals, however, the conservatives had an ambivalent attitude toward the state. While the absolute state had absorbed their independent political rights, its monarch was still the apex of the aristocratic social pyramid and its power the chief bulwark of the nobility against the rising pressure of new social classes. Hence the romantic conservatives were faced with the problem of reconciling the feudal system they admired with the absolute state which was its natural foe.

The philosophy of Karl Ludwig von Haller provided a solution. In contrast to the Jacobins, Haller maintained that the natural and therefore God-ordained condition of man was one of inequality and dependence, the stronger over the weaker. The microcosm of society was the family. As the father rules over wife and children, the master governs his servants, the landowner his peasants, the teacher his pupils, the leader his followers, the prince his subjects. The entire social fabric was woven from such dependent relationships based upon mutual duty and service more than upon force. The prince alone was independent, subject only to God. The state he ruled was simply the highest in a pyramid of contractual relationships, which were matters of private, not public law. Haller's denial of the existence of public law was, in effect, a rejection of the modern state itself.[30]

The models for Haller's system were the patrician order of his native Berne and the patriarchal governments of the smaller principalities in Germany. But his most devoted following appeared in Prussia, for whose "military state" he had less sympathy. Two influential noblemen, the brothers Ludwig and Leopold von Gerlach, formed the "Christian-Germanic circle" to study and propagate his doctrine. In his *Restauration der Staatswissenschaft* they found an arsenal of ideas with which to defend the aristocratic order against absolutism and bureaucratic liberalism. Ludwig objected, however, to his "deistic-naturalism," maintaining that legitimate

[29] See Reinhold Aris, *History of Political Thought in Germany from 1789 to 1815* (London, 1936), pp. 251-265, 288-319.

[30] Haller's chief work is *Restauration der Staatswissenschaft oder Theorie des natürlich-geselligen Zustands* (six volumes, Winterthur, 1816-1834); for an analysis of his political philosophy see Wilhelm Hans von Sonntag, *Die Staatsauffassung Carl Ludwig v. Hallers* (Jena, 1929); on Haller personally Ewald Reinhard, *Karl Ludwig von Haller, der "Restaurator der Staatswissenschaft"* (Münster, 1933).

monarchs governed by the grace of God, not by the right of the stronger. As the ruling caste, the nobility were carrying out God's will, not merely acting according to a functioning natural law. The patrimonial state was a "Christian state," its constitution the ten commandments.[31]

In the Stein-Hardenberg period an internal opposition began to develop in Prussia for the first time since the seventeenth century. It was not a bourgeois-liberal, but an aristocratic-conservative opposition, dedicated to the defense of specific aristocratic rights rather than general human rights. Its power and its chance rested, moreover, upon influence rather than numbers. The Gerlachs were close friends and advisers of the crown prince. When the latter ascended the throne in 1840 as Frederick William IV, Leopold, a general, became his personal adjutant and Ludwig, a career civil servant, was appointed president of the superior court of appeals in Magdeburg. In accord with romantic doctrine Frederick William finally summoned an estates general, the ill-fated "united diet" of 1847. Except for their attempt to recreate the *Ständestaat* of the middle ages, however, the romantic conservatives tended to avoid political change. Law was regarded as the expression of God's will. To try to "make" it, rather than "find" it, was to violate the divine order.[32]

Other Prussian conservatives, however, found Haller's rejection of the modern state unrealistic and sought a doctrine more in harmony with the facts of political life. Ultimately one appeared in the philosophy of Friedrich Julius Stahl. A converted Bavarian Jew, Stahl was given a chair in the University of Berlin by Frederick William IV. In search of a way to harmonize unity and diversity in the world and to find absolute values in the flux of history, Stahl found his solution in the concept of personality. The "highest principle of the world" was a personal, creative being, the single source of all diversification and change. With this concept he was able to draw a parallel between the universe and the state. The supreme being expressed the unity of the world, the state that of its subjects. In monarchical systems the prince personified the

31 On the views of the Gerlachs see Hans Joachim Schoeps, *Das andere Preussen* (2nd ed., Honnef, 1957), pp. 11-92.

32 Schnabel, *Deutsche Geschichte*, ii, 32; iv, 486. Actually the influence of the Gerlachs upon Frederick William was always limited. The king was convinced that, as a divine-right monarch, he possessed insights superior to other mortals. Herman von Petersdorff, *König Friedrich Wilhelm der Vierte* (Stuttgart, 1900), pp. 1 ff., 35 ff., 60 ff.

state. The personal relationship between sovereign and subject was as necessary as that between God and man. Following Luther he believed the state was instituted by God to maintain order in a sinful world. To this end power was properly concentrated in the hands of the prince and not decentralized in a feudal hierarchy. In the Lutheran tradition he allowed only the rights of protest and passive resistance against tyranny.[33]

No more than the romantic conservatives was Stahl an absolutist. While rejecting the organic theory as such, he believed in the necessity of an assembly of estates. By *Stände*, however, he meant the existing occupational groups into which society was "naturally" divided, not the medieval corporations of which the romanticists dreamed. In 1848 he was willing to include even the unpropertied urban proletariat.[34] The powers of the assembly were to be purely "moral" and "consultative." Having no control over the executive and no firm financial authority, it was to act merely as a "watchman" to guarantee the supremacy of law.[35] Later he realistically accepted the wider powers of the Prussian Landtag granted in the constitutional law of January 31, 1850. During the 1850's he argued for representation only by the "higher classes"; i.e., landowners and industrialists, with the former predominant.[36] Ultimately his conception, rather than Haller's, became the foundation of conservative thought in nineteenth-century Prussia. After 1848 it enabled the conservatives to become reconciled to the constitutional system. But it also paved the way for their eventual acceptance of the Bismarckian Reich.

5. CROSS-CURRENTS OF NATIONALISM

In western civilization the idea of the nation has been reached from two directions. Among the Atlantic peoples the molding force was that of the state. Here the awareness of nationality developed

[33] *Die Philosophie des Rechts* (1st ed., 3 vols., 1830-1837). On Stahl's early career and intellectual development see Gerhard Masur, *Friedrich Julius Stahl, Geschichte seines Lebens* (Berlin, 1930); also Schnabel, *Deutsche Geschichte*, iv, 539-547, Erich Kaufmann, *Studien zur Staatslehre des monarchischen Prinzips* (Leipzig, 1906), and Herbert Marcuse, *Reason and Revolution, Hegel and the Rise of Social Theory* (2nd ed., New York, 1954), 360-374.

[34] *Die Revolution und die constitutionelle Monarchie* (2nd ed., Berlin, 1849), pp. 58-59; Bernhard Michniewicz, *Stahl und Bismarck* (Berlin, 1913), p. 101.

[35] Friedrich Julius Stahl, *Das monarchische Prinzip* (Heidelberg, 1845), pp. 25-26.

[36] *Philosophie des Rechts* (3rd edition, Heidelberg, 1854-1856), iii, 317-334, 389 ff., 443-449; Michniewicz, *Stahl und Bismarck*, pp. 101-107.

from a common political allegiance and experience. But in central and eastern Europe the awareness of nationality preceded and even helped in the creation of the nation-state. Here national consciousness grew from the chrysalis of individual cultures. This difference in historical timing and direction drove another of those divisive wedges into the center of European civilization. The Atlantic peoples have tended to regard nationality as a matter of the subjective will of the individual (*un plébiscite de tous les jours* in the extreme formulation of Ernest Renan). But on the other side of the Rhine nationality came to be determined by such objective factors as language, folkways, and ethnic origin. After the appearance of social Darwinism in the late nineteenth century it also became a matter of "blood" and racial stock.[37]

As Friedrich Meinecke demonstrated in a classic study,[38] the idea of German nationalism was born within the older cosmopolitan sentiment of the eighteenth century from which it separated itself only gradually. By emphasizing the individuality of national cultures Herder's concept of the *Volksgeist* helped to awaken national consciousness not only in Germany but throughout central and eastern Europe. At the same time it accentuated that individuality by encouraging German authors to abandon the slavish imitation of French literary and intellectual models. The great outpouring of literary and philosophical effort known as German idealism provided a new and richer content to German culture which made Herder's concept all the more meaningful to the educated class. From a mere recognition of the individuality of the German spirit the intellectuals proceeded to the assertion of its superiority. "Every people had its day in history," Schiller declared, "but the day of the German is the harvest of all time."[39] The conviction grew that German culture had a world mission to perform. Even after the liberation of the German national idea from cosmopolitanism this element of its universalism remained.[40]

In the beginning, nevertheless, this attitude was non-biological, and even non-political. It did not mean national exclusiveness. In Herder's view civilization was many-sided and the encouragement

37 Droz, "Concept français et concept allemand," and Rothfels, "Problem der Nationalität."

38 *Weltbürgertum und Nationalstaat, Studien zur Genesis des deutschen Nationalstaates* (5th ed., Munich and Berlin, 1919); see also Joachimsen, *Vom deutschen Volk zum deutschen Staat.*

39 Quoted in Schnabel, *Deutsche Geschichte*, I, 289.

40 *Ibid.*, pp. 283-315.

of the development of all national cultures could but enrich the whole. Among German idealists the growing conviction of a national mission actually signified a retreat from politics, rather than a politicization of cultural ideals. In a period of French military domination they found a haven in the empire of the spirit. Here they felt a sense of superiority as the heirs and synthesizers of what was best in the nordic and classical traditions.[41]

In other minds, however, the French imperium soon produced a nationalistic reaction of political significance. The overthrow of the republic and the substitution of Napoleonic absolutism disillusioned those who had accepted the cosmopolitan message of the revolution as a fulfillment of the age of reason. The defeat of Prussia and the completion of the French conquest of Germany aroused in some the same kind of fiery national sentiment which the French themselves had experienced after 1789. For the first time the cry for a closer political union of the German nation was raised. As we have seen, however, the galvanizing energy for the war of liberation came from the Prussian bureaucracy rather than from a spontaneous movement of citizens. Through social, political, and military reforms liberal officials sought to tap the same reservoir of national power which had enabled the French to conquer most of Europe.[42]

For the German nobility it was as necessary to counteract the persuasive pull of the ideal of German unity as it was to refute liberalism. Although Haller had largely ignored the question of the nation, his followers found it increasingly difficult to do so. Ultimately they recognized, moreover, that the concept of the *Volksgeist* was even better suited to their purposes than to those of a Fichte. The true content of the German spirit, they argued, was the historic form of the nation: that is, political multiplicity rather than unity. Traditionally Germany was a collection of principalities, ruled by legitimate princes, and presided over by the Hapsburg monarchy. Although the Holy Roman Empire was gone and many principalities had disappeared, the basic structure of the German community had been preserved in the German Confederation. The romantic Frederick William IV even toyed with the idea

---

[41] See Robert R. Ergang, *Herder and the Foundations of German Nationalism* (New York, 1931).

[42] See Friedrich Meinecke, *Das Zeitalter der deutschen Erhebung 1795-1815* (4th ed., undated).

of placing the imperial crown once more on a Hapsburg head.[43]

Cultural nationalism was not the only form of the national idea in Germany. Within the larger German states the growth of monarchical power had produced in the eighteenth century a "state nationalism" based on a common dynastic allegiance and political experience. In Prussia the penetrating activity and power of the monarchy made the citizenry in their daily lives acutely aware of the state. Service in the wars of Frederick the Great generated in the officer corps and Junker caste feelings of patriotic loyalty which extended to the state as well as the dynasty. Frederick sought to inculcate in them an *"esprit de corps et de nation."* Although he demanded from ordinary subjects nothing but hard work and obedience, some of this same national patriotism blossomed among the masses as well. The genius and fame of the philosopher-king and the glory of his victories were persuasive. They gave to many subjects a feeling of pride and, even in the absence of political rights, a sense of identification with and participation in a powerful national community.[44]

After 1815 the homogeneity of the Prussian nation was disrupted by the incorporation of the Rhineland. More urban than the rest of Prussia, the area possessed a larger middle-class, fewer landed noblemen, and more peasant free-holders. Its inhabitants were Catholic and in the beginning more favorable to Austria than Prussia. Under the French imperium they had acquired the Napoleonic code, the French system of communal government, and the concept of civil equality. With some success the Rhinelanders resisted the efforts of the Berlin government to impose the Prussian legal, political, and even social structure upon the west. But after 1840 Rhenish particularism began to dissolve. A new leadership appeared, composed of moderate liberals willing to collaborate with the regime. The best way to protect Rhenish interests, they maintained, was to work for a constitutional government in Berlin. Significantly they thought of German unity chiefly in terms of Prussian hegemony and a Hohenzollern Kaiser.[45]

43 Meinecke, *Weltbürgertum*, pp. 223 ff.; Schoeps, *Das andere Preussen*, pp. 76 ff.

44 Meinecke, *Weltbürgertum*, pp. 30 ff.; Ritter, *Friedrich der Grosse*, p. 199; Ernst Rudolf Huber, "Der Preussische Staatspatriotismus im Zeitalter Friedrichs des Grossen," *Zeitschrift für die gesamte Staatswissenschaft*, Vol. 103 (1943), pp. 430-468. See also the famous passages in *Dichtung und Wahrheit* (Books Two and Seven) in which Goethe described the influence of Frederick upon Germany as a whole.

45 See Droz, *Le libéralisme Rhénan.*

While both conservative and state nationalism opposed the centripetal pull of German liberal nationalism, they were not necessarily in harmony. Conservative nationalism was essentially quietistic, regarding political change of any sort (especially the destruction of sovereignties) as a blasphemous tampering with God's handiwork. But state nationalism of the Prussian kind with its militaristic tradition was potentially a disruptive force. Its inherent chauvinism was reinforced by the romantic view of the state as an organism requiring growth for self-realization and possessing an individuality which could be developed only in conflict with other states.[46]

In southern Germany state nationalism took yet another form. Although the medium states—Baden, Württemberg, and Bavaria —were in varying degrees the artificial creation of Napoleonic statesmanship and the Congress of Vienna, all three succeeded after 1815 in building a sense of national identity. In Bavaria the task was easiest, for the Wittelsbach dynasty was the oldest ruling house in Germany and the Bavarian *Stamm* alone among the ancient German tribes had, down through the centuries, retained some degree of political homogeneity. Under the statesman Montgelas the integration of the new territories was accomplished through the techniques of enlightened despotism. But in Baden and Württemberg it was achieved by the grant of constitutions providing for popular representation. Here an association developed between liberalism and state nationalism.[47]

While limited by these competitive forms of nationalism, the ideal of German national unity grew in appeal for the German professional and intellectual class. After 1815 the wartime enthusiasm was kept alive in the universities by patriotic student organizations, the Burschenschaften. Suppressed after the Wartburg festival of 1817, the national movement was resuscitated by the revolution of 1830 and the Hambach festival of 1832. In 1840 French pressure on the Rhine and the elevation of Frederick William IV to the Prussian throne provided new stimuli. During the 1840's industrial growth produced economic pressures for unity.

[46] The best illustration of this viewpoint is the *Gegensatzlehre* of Adam Müller, *Elemente der Staatskunst*, I, 67-88. On Müller see Jakob Baxa, *Einführung in die romantische Staatswissenschaft* (Jena, 1931), pp. 164-200, Schnabel, *Deutsche Geschichte*, I, 309 ff., and Meinecke, *Weltbürgertum*, pp. 121-151.

[47] Erich Brandenburg, *Die Reichsgründung* (2nd ed., Leipzig, 1922), I, 43-45.

North Sea

Baltic Sea

Jutland

Kolding

Düppel
Flensburg
Alsen
Dannevirke
Kiel

Schleswig

Holstein
Lübeck

Königsberg

East P.

West P.

Mecklenburg

Pomerania

La.

Hamburg

Oldenburg

Bremen

Hanover

Schönhausen
Berlin
Potsdam
Brandenburg

Posen

Hanover

Westphalia
Prussia

Br.

An.

Göttingen

Kassel

Cologne

El.
Hesse

Gotha

Erfurt

Dresden

Silesia

Oder

Aachen

Ducai

Thuringian
States

Saxony

Koblenz

Nassau

Frankfurt

Rhineland

Moselle

Darmstadt

Hesse

Bohemia

Olmütz

Palatinate

Karlsruhe

Bavaria

Moravia

Baden-Baden

Stuttgart

Württemberg

Rhine

Baden

Sigmaringen

Munich

Vienna

Danube

Salzburg

Empire of Austria

Buda

Pest

Tyrol

Gastein

Carinthia

Hungary

Rhone

Lombardy
(Lost 1859)

Venetia
(Lost 1866)

Carniola

GERMANY
1815-1866

German Confederation
of 1815

Br.   Brunswick
An.   Anhalt
La.   Lauenburg

French
Boundary
Changes

Moselle

Prussia

Luxem-
burg

Trier

Palatinate

Tholey

Saarlouis

Boundary of 1814

France

Landau

Rhine

Metz

Boundary of 1815

Vistula

Elbe

The narrow circle of German national sentiment appeared to widen.[48]

These were the years in which the ideas of liberalism and nationalism welded their alliance in the common struggle against the forces of particularism and reaction. As has been shown, however, German liberalism was not a single, but a divided, movement. Upon these divisions German nationalism acted as a welcome synthetic force. In the Burschenschaften it created a bridge over deep political fissures. For moderate liberals it provided a new solution for the problem of combining authority and freedom. Among the radicals it seemed to offer a convenient "moral lever" with which to set the masses in motion in the interest of democratic ideals.[49] Whatever their disagreements on political theory and program, moreover, moderates and radicals could at least unite on the necessity of German unification. In his *Briefwechsel zweier Deutschen* of 1831 Paul Pfizer analyzed this common bond, but pointed out a residual difference of prophetic significance. The moderate argued that Germany must be "first united and then free," the radical that freedom was the prerequisite of unity.[50]

Whatever their views on the alternative paths toward freedom and unity, moderate and radical alike were attracted by the chimera of national power. German liberalism had its birth as a political force in a period of national humiliation. It was a child of the war of liberation and the crucial issue of its earliest years was more that of national prestige and force than of freedom. Pride of intellectual achievement was not enough to appease indefinitely the growing national ego. The conviction grew that without political unity the cultural mission of the German *Volksgeist* could never be fully achieved. The growth of industry and commerce created in the business community the desire for a greater economic unity than the Zollverein afforded and that only political unity could achieve. It is quite likely, nevertheless, that the primary motivations behind the awakening desire for national unity were neither military nor economic, but political and psychological.[51]

[48] Droz, *Le Libéralisme Rhénan*, pp. 346-361.

[49] Krieger, *German Idea*, pp. 263, 329; R. Hinton Thomas, *Liberalism, Nationalism and the German Intellectuals, 1822-1847* (Cambridge, 1951), pp. 124 ff.

[50] In *Deutsche Literaturdenkmale des 18 und 19. Jahrhunderts*, Vol. 144 (Berlin, 1911), pp. 270-271.

[51] Andreas Dorpalen, *Heinrich von Treitschke* (New Haven, 1957), p. 59. As

Equally fateful was the growing conviction that Prussian leadership was essential to German unity. Frederick the Great had elevated the prestige of the Hohenzollern monarchy throughout Germany. Under Stein and Hardenberg Prussia undertook the task of national regeneration and liberation. The territorial settlement of 1815 left her largely German in population. By organizing the Zollverein she started Germany on the path toward economic unity. In the crisis of 1840 her army appeared to be the chief bulwark against foreign attack. While still unprepared to demand the exclusion of Austria, liberal nationalists began to regard Prussia as the future nucleus of a united Germany. They longed for her liberalization, but the reality was reaction. Hence they took refuge in the Hegelian myth of her liberality. In the "ideology of Prussianism" the Frederician state became the haven of spiritual freedom and intellectual cultivation. The assignment of a "national mission" to Prussia reinforced the traditional synthesis of freedom and authority in the German mind.[52]

6. THE REVOLUTION OF 1848

The propulsion behind the German revolution of March 1848 was not the liberal-national movement. The revolutionists had no central aim or direction. The source of their discontent was not doctrine or principle, but specific grievances and vague feelings of injustice. Without the February uprising in Paris and the revolutionary mood it produced in Europe the attack would probably not have occurred in Germany. Liberalism, however, had become the conventional language of protest, and through its terminology, often imperfectly understood, the dissatisfied gave voice to their resentments. The spontaneous violence of the masses elevated to power the moderate liberals who had never approved of revolution but were now called upon to lead one.[53]

late as 1864 the Bavarian statesman and future German chancellor, Hohenlohe-Schillingsfürst, observed in a letter to Queen Victoria that German unity would mean some material sacrifice in the German medium states, but that this was outweighed by "the need for honor and prestige." Friedrich Curtius, ed., *Denkwürdigkeiten des Fürsten Chlodwig zu Hohenlohe-Schillingsfürst* (Stuttgart, 1907), I, 142.

[52] See Scharff, *Gedanke der preussischen Vorherrschaft*, Droz, *Le Libéralisme Rhénan*, pp. 250 ff., Heffter, *Selbstverwaltung*, p. 254, and Hans Rosenberg, *Rudolf Haym und die Anfänge des klassischen Liberalismus, Beihefte der Historischen Zeitschrift*, Vol. 31 (Munich, 1933), pp. 90 ff.

[53] On the general character of the revolution see Rudolf Stadelmann, *Soziale*

In Berlin the revolutionary cabinet was composed of the leaders of the moderate opposition from the united diet of 1847. From the outset they were compelled to mediate between the king, backed by the army, and the Prussian national assembly, elected by universal and equal suffrage. As the months passed, the extremes grew ever farther apart and the task of mediation increasingly difficult. Frederick William listened more and more to the "camarilla" of reactionary generals and officials who wished to overthrow the revolution, and the national assembly fell under the domination of radicals critical of the moderate policies of the cabinet.[54]

In Frankfurt on the Main a revolutionary parliament assembled to draft the constitution for a united Germany. Here the moderates faced a similar problem of reconciling the interests of the German governments, which they did not wish to liquidate, and the wishes of the radicals, who wanted a more far-reaching revolution. Ultimately the spirit of compromise prevailed. The final draft provided for a federal structure with a monarchical head and a parliament elected by universal suffrage.[55] Essentially, however, the structure was one of mixed powers, for the cabinet was to be appointed by the Kaiser and its "responsibility" was not defined.

While the deputies debated, the foundation beneath them crumbled. Throughout most of Germany the revolutionary enthusiasm of March evaporated with astonishing speed. The burghers were shocked by the vigor with which artisans and workers manned the barricades and by the social goals they voiced. The lower classes, on the other hand, were disappointed by the inadequate social program of the bourgeois elements they had boosted into power. During the summer and autumn there was renewed fighting in Berlin, Baden, and Frankfurt. This pressure from below forced the moderates to turn increasingly to the right for support.[56] But suddenly this prop too was removed. At the end of October the

---

und politische Geschichte der Revolution von 1848 (Munich, 1948), Hamerow, *Restoration, Revolution, Reaction*, Jacques Droz, *Les Revolutions allemandes de 1848* (Paris, 1957), and the older work of Veit Valentin, *Geschichte der deutschen Revolution* (two vols., Berlin, 1930-1931).

[54] *Ibid.*, II, 42 ff.; Jordan, *Entstehung der konservativen Partei*, pp. 192-194, 297 ff.

[55] On the origins of this clause see Hamerow, *Restoration, Revolution, Reaction*, pp. 120, 131.

[56] *Ibid.*, pp. 122 ff., 137 ff., Stadelmann, *Geschichte der Revolution*, pp. 145 ff.

remaining moderates in the Berlin cabinet were turned out of office and a reactionary cabinet under Count Brandenburg appointed. The army disarmed the citizen guard without incident. The national assembly was removed from the capital and dissolved on December 5. As a last act of defiance, the deputies called upon the public to refuse taxes to the reactionary government. But the response was weak.[57]

Having discarded the moderates, the monarchy proceeded to steal their program by promulgating on December 5 a constitution with many liberal features. By this act the crown returned to the Stein-Hardenberg tradition of bureaucratic liberalism, but with the vital difference that the reform had its origin in the strategy of a reactionary government rather than in the genuine convictions of liberal civil servants. On May 30, 1849, a second decree substituted for equal suffrage the famous three-class suffrage law, which divided and weighted votes according to income. Other conservative features were added in the "constitutional charter" of January 31, 1850.[58] Even so, the final result was a constitutional monarchy of mixed powers not unlike what the moderates had long advocated. Out of lumber burglarized from the liberal program the Prussian crown constructed a constitutional facade behind which the old order remained essentially intact.

Even before the restoration of monarchical authority in Prussia, the cooperation between Berlin and Frankfurt had been limited. Although Frederick William IV had promised the merger of Prussia within Germany and the Frankfurt constitution provided for Prussia's dismemberment, neither the moderates of the Prussian cabinet nor the radicals who dominated the assembly were willing to abandon the Prussian state. Their Prussian patriotism competed with their German nationalism. But the radicals also hoped to make good in the Prussian constitution what they had sacrificed in the German one.[59] By refusing the imperial crown offered by the Frankfurt parliament in April 1849, Frederick

[57] Karl Obermann, *Einheit und Freiheit, Die deutsche Geschichte von 1815-1849 in zeitgenössischen Dokumenten* (Berlin, 1950), pp. 652 ff.

[58] See Friedrich Frahm, "Entstehungs- und Entwicklungsgeschichte der preussischen Verfassung," *Forschungen zur brandenburgischen und preussischen Geschichte*, Vol. 41 (1928), pp. 248-301, and Hans Walter, *Die innere Politik des Ministers von Manteuffel und der Ursprung der Reaktion in Preussen* (Berlin, 1910), pp. 38 ff.

[59] Meinecke, *Weltbürgertum*, pp. 374 ff.; Jordan, *Entstehung der konservativen Partei*, pp. 191-197.

William merely completed the withdrawal begun by the liberals themselves.

In Frankfurt the consequence of this refusal was the collapse of the moderate-radical alliance. While the moderates tamely departed for home, the radical minority chose to resist. In Bavaria, Württemberg, and the Rhineland demonstrations occurred, but only in Dresden and the Palatinate did serious fighting develop. It was suppressed by the Prussian army assisted by the popular militia. For the most part the fate of the Frankfurt parliament and its constitution met with general apathy; the popular movement had long since recoiled from its initial support. On all fronts and levels the revolutionary synthesis had dissolved.[60]

In spite of its defeat the Frankfurt parliament brought into focus for the first time some of the major problems of German nationalism. Like revolutionists everywhere the German liberals were dazzled by the mirage of power. The prevailing mood in Frankfurt was evident in Friedrich Dahlmann's famous words: "The path of power is the only one which will satisfy and satiate the swelling desire for freedom (*Freiheitstrieb*), because it is not merely freedom which the German has in mind. For the most part it is the power which he has hitherto lacked for which he lusts."[61] During the first months of the revolution the drive for power expressed itself in the demand for war against Russia and Denmark. Some genuinely believed the revolution threatened by Russia, but others, like Max and Friedrich von Gagern, desired war in order to give "the highly excited nation . . . an object for its hostility; thus alone would unification be possible."[62] When the Russians did not attack, the liberals found a better issue and easier target in Denmark, which since 1846 had been attempting to incorporate Schleswig. The Prussian army was commissioned for the attack, but in September 1848 it withdrew before the threat of British intervention. This failure, which the Frankfurt parliament was impotent to prevent, left a livid mark on the liberal soul.

The chauvinism inherent in the national idea was also evident in the attitude of the revolutionists toward neighboring peoples.

[60] Stadelmann, *Geschichte der Revolution*, pp. 174 ff.; Valentin, *Revolution*, II, 448 ff.

[61] Quoted in Friedrich Meinecke, *Die Idee der Staatsräson in der neueren Geschichte* (Munich, 1924), p. 493.

[62] Quoted in Namier, *Revolution of the Intellectuals*, p. 54.

Like nationalists everywhere in 1848, the Germans started with the assumption that self-determination was a general human right valid for all peoples. Within weeks, however, they commenced to deny to the Poles, Danes, and Czechs what they demanded for themselves.[63] Nevertheless, the Frankfurt parliament ended by accepting realistic limits to the nation-state they planned.

All of the future problems of German unification were foreshadowed in the debates. Should Austria be included or excluded? Did inclusion mean the whole of the Hapsburg monarchy or just the German segment? The former solution would have defeated the whole concept of national unity, while the latter raised the difficult practical question how the German segment could be built into two sovereignties, Austrian and German, without creating insoluble problems for one or both. Upon these issues the deputies soon divided, for and against Austria's inclusion, into two parties: the "great-Germanists" and "little-Germanists." In the end the majority decided for the little-German solution. By this act they deliberately excluded part of the German cultural nation and established the future frontiers of the German state.

The inroads of the Prussian government on the liberal program did not cease with her conversion into a constitutional monarchy. After rejecting the "pig crown" offered by the Frankfurt parliament, Frederick William IV, counselled by Josef Maria von Radowitz, proposed a federal union of little-Germany under a conservative constitution. Although excluded from the federation, Austria would have been joined to it on a higher level, the "German union," which would have guaranteed the frontiers of the entire Hapsburg empire. Rather than impose this solution, Frederick William sought the approval of the other German rulers, the Prussian Landtag, and a new German parliament which met in Erfurt. While princes and parliaments deliberated and delayed, the opportunity slipped away. In August 1849, the Austrian government succeeded, with the aid of Russian troops, in crushing the Hungarian revolt. Fully recovered from the ordeal of revolution, Vienna could again look after her interests in Germany.[64]

Prince Schwarzenberg, the new prime minister, was in no mood to surrender the paramount position which Austria had for cen-

63 *Ibid., passim*; see also Thomas, *Liberalism, Nationalism*, pp. 81 ff.
64 On the crisis leading to Olmütz see Friedrich Meinecke, *Radowitz und die deutsche Revolution* (Berlin, 1913), pp. 233 ff.

turies enjoyed in Germany. He was determined, in fact, not only to revive the German Confederation, defunct since the revolution, but to strengthen Hapsburg primacy in that body. Once the domestic crisis was over in Austria, he summoned the lesser states in Germany to return to the diet in Frankfurt and demanded the inclusion of the whole of the Hapsburg monarchy in the confederation.[65] During 1850 friction between Austria and Prussia, each heading an organization which asserted authority over all Germany, steadily increased. In November both sides claimed the right to send troops into Hesse-Kassel to quell a disturbance in that troubled principality. The armies of Austria and Prussia mobilized. At Bronzell near Fulda there was a skirmish on November 8. Germany wavered on the precipice of civil war.

Under pressure from the ultra-conservatives, Frederick William dismissed Radowitz. But this was not the end of the matter. The new cabinet, led by Otto von Manteuffel, advanced in place of the German union the demand for parity between Austria and Prussia in the government of the confederation. Prussia, however, was unprepared for war and within the government there was great confusion and difference of opinion. From Russia came admonitions against a breach of the peace.[66] At Olmütz on November 29, Frederick William agreed to permit confederate occupation of Hesse-Kassel and to demobilize the Prussian army. In return the Austrians promised to discuss confederate reform at a conference in Dresden. No agreement was reached there, and in the summer the confederation was restored unchanged.

Outwardly Germany was as before the cataclysm of 1848. But this was an illusion. Beneath the surface changes of great significance were underway in political outlook and political relationships. The age of romanticism was fast being replaced by that of realism and materialism.

7. THE DRIFT TOWARD REALISM

The mid-nineteenth century was a watershed between the great ages of philosophy and science. Abstract speculation gave way to

---

[65] Rudolf Kiszling, *Fürst Felix zu Schwarzenberg* (Graz-Köln, 1952), pp. 129 ff., and Adolph Schwarzenberg, *Prince Felix zu Schwarzenberg* (New York, 1946), pp. 112 ff.

[66] On the Russian part in the Olmütz crisis see Willy Andreas, *Die Russische Diplomatie und die Politik Friedrich Wilhelms IV. von Preussen, Abhandlungen der preussischen Akademie der Wissenschaften*, Jahrgang 1926, Philosophisch-Historische Klasse, Nr. 6 (Berlin, 1927), pp. 45 ff.

empirical research, metaphysical systems to scientific theories. In the 1820's and 1830's the towering synthesis of Hegel dominated western thinking, in the 1860's and 1870's the evolutionary theory of Darwin. Whereas Hegel had sought to unite in a single philosophical system the realms of reason and reality, his successors—Marx, Comte, Mill—concentrated on the latter.[67] The romantic style was superseded in art by impressionism and in literature by realism; the world of nymphs and knights was abandoned for that of Madame Bovary and Jean Valjean. In politics faith in the supremacy of principle began to yield to the belief that the great issues are decided by power alone.

To romantic conservatives the conflicting forces in European politics were opposed principles, not interests. As a matter of dogma they believed that the three great eastern monarchies had but a single cause: the maintenance of conservative order against France, the home of Jacobinism and Bonapartism, and against the forces of liberal and national subversion everywhere. But after 1849 motives of self-interest, never entirely absent from European politics, began to dominate. In Germany the conflicting plans of Radowitz and Schwarzenberg brought the dual powers close to conflict. In 1854-1856 the Crimean war shattered beyond repair the fragile structure of the holy alliance. Instead of aiding Russia against England and France, Austria, while officially neutral, actually sided with the western powers. Schwarzenberg's successor, Count Buol, prided himself on having accomplished "nothing less" than a revolution in the foreign relations of Austria. But he had done more than that. He had inaugurated a new era in diplomacy in which the interests of power were to take precedence over the principle of conservative solidarity.[68]

This development in the sphere of practical politics had been foreshadowed by several decades in German political thought. Hegel accomplished the moral legitimation of power politics. In the eighteenth century a distinction had been drawn between the state as it was and the state as it ought to be. By discovering a dialectical process in history, Hegel was able to overcome this dualism by identifying the rational with the real. In expanding its power,

[67] See Herbert Marcuse, *Reason and Revolution* (2nd ed., New York, 1954).
[68] See Gavin B. Henderson, "The Diplomatic Revolution of 1854," *American Historical Review*, Vol. 43 (1937), pp. 22-50, and S. A. Kaehler, "Realpolitik zur Zeit des Krimkrieges—Eine Säkularbetrachtung," *Historische Zeitschrift*, Vol. 174 (1952), pp. 436-445.

the state merely acted out its role in the grand dialectic of history and hence fulfilled a moral end. Unlike the rationalists, Hegel recognized no conflict in statecraft between the egoistic pursuit of power and the demands of universal law and morality. War was not an absolute evil, but a logical necessity.[69]

In the organic theory German conservatives found a similar means of legitimizing power politics. The historical school was never able to accept the political quietism of romantic conservatism. The most essential characteristic of an organism, they argued, was that of growth and development. Since that which existed was the product of change, it could itself have no permanence. The state-personality, moreover, could achieve self-realization only through conflict. Hence Adam Müller maintained that the power struggle could not be judged from the standpoint of individual morality. The wars of the eighteenth century had their origin, not in the caprice of rulers and cabinets, but in "an inner pressure toward vital growth stemming from the push of past generations and completely unapparent to the present."[70] While critical of wars fought for total domination at the cost of the European community (e.g., the Napoleonic wars), Müller's philosophy came close to the moral approbation of war as such.[71]

With the passing of the great age of philosophy the concept of the organic power-state was perpetuated in German thought by the historians. While rejecting the larger structure of Hegelian thought, Leopold Ranke accepted the view that the state was an organic personality whose vitality and individuality were determined by the "idea" which was its inner motive force. The shaping of this innate idea, however, did not occur in isolation, but in conflict with the ideas of other states. Hence war was not a scourge, but the final and necessary test of the moral and spiritual fibre of the state.[72]

Before 1848 German liberals had relied primarily upon the force of idealism to achieve their goals. The tide of liberalism, they believed, would inevitably sweep over the cracking sea-wall of the

---

[69] Meinecke, *Staatsräson*, pp. 427-460; Hermann Heller, *Hegel und der national Machtstaatsgedanke in Deutschland* (Berlin, 1921), pp. 57 ff.; and Franz Rosenzweig, *Hegel und der Staat* (2 vols., Munich, 1920).

[70] Quoted in Meinecke, *Weltbürgertum*, p. 141.

[71] Adam Müller, *Elemente der Staatskunst*, I, 80-81; Schnabel, *Deutsche Geschichte*, I, 312-315.

[72] Theodore H. von Laue, *Leopold Ranke, The Formative Years* (Princeton, 1950), pp. 80, 86; Heller, *Machtstaatsgedanke*, pp. 147-155.

Metternich system. Through the failure of 1848, however, their trust in the power of principle suffered a terrible blow from which it was never fully to recover. The collapse of their hopes had varying effects upon the lives and views of the participants. Many radicals, like Carl Schurz, emigrated to lands where their ideals had already been realized; some, like Wilhelm Liebknecht and Ferdinand Lassalle, gravitated into socialism; others, like Johann Karl Rodbertus and Lothar Bucher, became converts to conservatism; a few, like Franz Ziegler and Johann Jacoby, clung to their positions, isolated and impotent; most, like Benedikt Waldeck and Hermann Schulze-Delitzsch, capitulated to the spirit of compromise. When they re-emerged in Prussian political life after 1859, very few of the left-wing liberals still demanded a revolutionary transformation of the Prussian constitution. While desiring greater social and political equality, the majority had relinquished the goal of parliamentary government and even universal suffrage. Thereafter they are best designated as "democratic" rather than "radical" liberals.[73]

Among moderates the reaction was more uniform. To be sure, two important figures, Robert von Mohl and Georg Gervinus, turned toward radicalism, the former to a belief in the necessity of popular sovereignty, the latter to the conviction that only a republic could guarantee human rights. But the great bulk of the moderates moved toward a position which they regarded as "realistic" and "practical" in contrast to their "doctrinaire" viewpoint of the pre-March period.

The first signs of this development came but a few weeks after the dissolution of the Frankfurt parliament. In late June the moderates, summoned by Dahlmann and the Gagern brothers, assembled in Gotha to conclude that the aim they had sought in Frankfurt was more important than the "form" of its attainment.[74] They agreed to go to Erfurt and cooperate with the Prussian government in establishing the German union. Thereafter this group, in which the "classical liberals" of the pre-March period predominated, were to be known as the *Gothaer* or "old liberals." These "political professors" were repelled by the excesses of the

[73] Krieger, *German Idea*, pp. 341-397; Hans Neumann, "Franz Ziegler und die Politik der liberalen Oppositionsparteien von 1848-1866," *Forschungen zur Brandenburgischen und preussischen Geschichte*, Vol. 37 (1925), pp. 280-281.

[74] Georg Witzmann, *Die Gothaer Nachversammlung zum Frankfurter Parlament im Jahre 1849* (Gotha, 1917), pp. 71-73.

radicals in Dresden and Baden, greatly impressed by the durability of the old state structure, and deeply discouraged by the impotence of the revolution. They set their hopes for the future upon the use of Prussian power to accomplish German unity under a constitution which, while preserving traditional authority, might at least leave open the way for the realization of the *Rechtsstaat*.

This increased respect for power found its philosopher in August Ludwig von Rochau. A journalist who had begun as a radical but had gravitated before 1848 to the moderate position, Rochau distinguished sharply between philosophical speculation and practical politics (*Realpolitik*). While the former had to do with what principles ought to rule, the latter recognized that power alone rules. The subjection of power to law was "unreasonable"; the strong cannot let themselves be ruled by the weak. "Neither a principle, nor an idea, nor a treaty will unite the splintered German forces, but only a superior force which swallows up the rest." He concluded that the state could generate the power to unify Germany only in alliance with the bourgeoisie.[75] In view of what had just occurred, however, the conclusion was *non sequitur*.

Although Rochau's position was perhaps more extreme than most, his work had considerable influence. Among right-wing liberals there spread the conviction that even "despotism" was acceptable if it were but the instrument of unification. The youthful Heinrich von Treitschke declared, "I'll go with the party which shows the strongest national initiative"; methods were secondary; what mattered was the goal.[76] In many minds the romantic cult of genius and the general discouragement over the efficacy of popular movements combined to produce a vague longing for a new Siegfried who would brave the flames to awaken the German nation from her sleep of centuries.[77]

[75] *Grundsätze der Realpolitik, angewendet auf die staatlichen Zustände Deutschlands* (2nd ed., 1859), pp. 2-3, 224. In this work Rochau coined the word *Realpolitik*, soon to become common currency in German political literature. On his relationship to the liberal movement see Krieger, *German Idea*, pp. 353-6.
[76] Andreas Dorpalen, *Treitschke*, pp. 16, 31.
[77] Brandenburg, *Reichsgründung*, I, 342-343.

CHAPTER TWO

THE INTERNAL FUNCTIONS OF POWER

1. FAILURE OF A FORMAL EDUCATION

N April 1, 1815, as the allied armies gathered for the final campaign against Napoleon, Otto von Bismarck was born on the estate of Schönhausen in Brandenburg. His heritage was both bourgeois and aristocratic. Through his father he belonged to a Junker family which for five centuries had owned noble estates on the banks of the Elbe. His mother was Wilhelmine Mencken, descendant of a long line of distinguished German academicians and daughter of an able civil servant who had risen to the post of cabinet secretary to Frederick the Great and Frederick William II. A woman of beauty and spirit, Wilhelmine was ambitious for her children and gave them a more enlightened education than was usual among the gentry. Instead of hiring a tutor, she sent Otto at the age of six to the rigorous Plamann boarding school in Berlin and later to a *Gymnasium* in the same city. Here he received the best humanistic education available.[1]

While his marks were fair, the student was little affected by what he learned. The classical ideal, which was its foundation, appears to have played no part in molding his intellect and character As for so many, classical languages were formal intellectual exercises rather than avenues for the discovery of a philosophy of life. His later writings, speeches, and conversations show none of the classical interests in the fully developed man or the famous Greek "style." The unique clarity and force of his speech and writing did not derive from classical models. Always a person of manifold inner conflicts and tensions, Bismarck never understood the Greek admonition, "Be harmonious!" He retained some knowledge of Latin, the language of law and government, but forgot his Greek, the language of philosophy and aesthetics. His practical

[1] On Bismarck's early years see the first volume of Erich Marcks' uncompleted biography, *Bismarcks Jugend, 1815-1848* (Stuttgart, 1909). For a perceptive interpretation of his material see Wilhelm Lütgert, *Die Religion des deutschen Idealismus und ihr Ende* (Gütersloh, 1923-1930), Vol. IV.

mind never acquired the habits of reflection and abstract speculation. He never felt the urge to penetrate to the essence of life or to acquire a metaphysical system capable of containing and explaining its phenomena. Nor did the classical tradition in its later forms appeal to him. He had no interest in the art and culture of the Renaissance or in the philosophy of German idealism.[2]

During his years in the *Gymnasium* (1827-1832) the productive period of German idealism was nearing its end. He was aware of the greatness of Goethe and Schiller and read their works with enjoyment. Although Goethe's realism was close to his own nature, the stirring drama and historical interest of Schiller attracted him more. But, again, the powerful humanistic impulse, which was the essence of idealism in its classical phase, left no impression upon him. What he read provided him with quotations which later adorned his speech and writing but did not change his way of looking at life. It did not mold his character or form his mind.

The foreign languages he learned were French and English. Although he spoke the former from childhood and became completely fluent, he had little real sympathy for French culture. In his schools anti-French sentiment, dating from the war of liberation, was still very much alive. Like many Germans of this epoch, he formed a lasting sympathy for things English.[3] Byron and Shakespeare were probably the authors he most preferred. In Byron he found a kindred spirit: bold, grandiose, and restless. Yet his favorite quotation was from Shakespeare—significantly, not the deluded Othello, conscience-ridden Macbeth, or indecisive Hamlet, but the autocratic Coriolanus ("Go, get you home, you fragments!"). In music he was drawn to the exciting chords and crescendos of Beethoven rather than the classicism of Haydn and Mozart, or, later, the somber romanticism of Wagner. Although these interests are perhaps symbolic of his nature, it is too much to

[2] *Ibid.*, pp. 3 ff.; Otto Graf zu Stolberg-Wernigerode, "Unbekannte Gespräche mit Bismarck," *Süddeutsche Monatshefte*, Vol. 27 (1929-1930), p. 312. Later he criticized his primary education as oriented more toward the head than the heart and condemned it as responsible for the moral and political degeneration of his time. Letter to Wilhelm Harnisch, February 16, 1849. Hans Rothfels, ed., *Bismarck-Briefe* (Göttingen, 1955), p. 121.

[3] *GW*, xiv, 469. This had no influence upon his political outlook. While he admired the English political system (as it was before the reform bills), he thought it impossible to duplicate in Germany because of the uniqueness of its social foundation. Horst Kohl, ed., *Die politischen Reden des Fürsten Bismarck* (Stuttgart, 1892-1905), i, 125. See Eva Maria Baum, *Bismarcks Urteil über England und die Engländer, Münchener Historische Abhandlungen*, xi (Munich, 1936).

say that he "abandoned himself to the spirit of Lord Byron, Shakespeare, and Beethoven."[4] Music he liked for background, rather than serious listening, and his reading of literature was confined largely to the leisure years of his youth. Neither provided him with a vital, molding, inner experience.

Nor did the study of mathematics and the natural sciences influence the formation of his mind. His love of nature, both deep and abiding, was for the meadows, forests, and rolling hills of rural Pomerania, the land of his childhood. For nature as science he had no interest. He was skeptical of the results of scientific theory and experiment.[5] Nevertheless, there can be little doubt that he was affected by the growing scientific spirit of the age. Often he described himself as a natural scientist determined to discern the phenomena of politics as they are, rather than as they ought to be. Like Ranke, he had little knowledge of the subject matter of science, but he was influenced by its spirit of objective inquiry. The practice of politics, however, he always regarded as an "art," not as a science.

No more than the humanistic *Gymnasium* did the university influence the basic structure of his mind and thought. In Göttingen (1832-1833) he very quickly took up the rowdy, duelling, beer-drinking life of the corps student, and in Berlin (1834-1835) he crammed for the law exam which was the gateway to a career in the civil service. At the time both universities were intellectual centers of importance. In Göttingen were Friedrich Dahlmann and Jakob Grimm and in Berlin Friedrich von Savigny and the scholars of the Hegelian school. During their student years many future leaders of Germany—for example, Delbrück, Bennigsen, Mevissen, Freytag, Sybel, Treitschke, and Duncker—received in the university an intellectual stimulus which lasted a lifetime. But Bismarck's formal education had little apparent effect.[6]

In Göttingen his only scholarly interest was history. Yet the historian who appealed to him most was the old-fashioned Heeren rather than the eminent Dahlmann. In Berlin his greatest intellectual stimulation came from his American friend, John Lothrop Motley, and the Baltic aristocrat, Alexander Keyserling. He prof-

4 Gustav A. Rein, *Die Revolution in der Politik Bismarcks* (Göttingen, 1957), p. 75; also pp. 45 ff.

5 Lütgert, *Idealismus*, IV, 5.

6 Marcks, *Bismarcks Jugend*, pp. 83 ff.

ited much from their discussions of Shakespeare, Goethe, and Byron. Through Keyserling, a gifted pianist, he gained his appreciation of Beethoven. The two essays with which he completed his degree—one in philosophy, the other in political economy—were works of no originality. They were mere hurdles to be leaped on the way to a career.[7] Like many of his social class, he acquired in the university, not an appreciation of intellectual disciplines, but a certain contempt for the academic mind. In his vocabulary "professor" was an epithet. Ideas which he found unrealistic he always dismissed as *"Doktorfragen"* or *"Professorenweisheit."*

During the years he spent in Kniephof and Schönhausen (1839-1847) Bismarck found the time and inclination to read. This was the period of frustration, of isolation and loneliness, after the failure of his attempt at a civil service career and before his marriage and first appearance in public life. Here he cultivated his interest in history and stored up in a highly retentive memory the material with which he leavened many a speech and document in later years. What he acquired, however, was a purely factual knowledge; he had no interest in historical synthesis or in the philosophy of history. Although he read Hegel, he admitted that he did not understand him. He also read Spinoza and the young Hegelians, but it was their religious rather than their philosophical viewpoints which interested him. He was attracted by Spinoza's pantheism and by the biblical criticism of Strauss, Bauer, and Feuerbach. But this also he soon rejected.[8]

In childhood Bismarck received no firm religious foundation. He could not remember a single discussion with his father on the subject of faith.[9] Not a very religious man, the elder Bismarck was content with a simple, naïve trust in God's love and mercy. His wife had been raised in the rationalist tradition and was not a churchgoer. None of the watered-down religious formulas of the enlightenment, however, satisfied her. She took up the popular occultism of the time, interested herself in mesmerism and clairvoyance, and read the works of Swedenborg, Schubert, and Kerner.[10] Although confirmed by Schleiermacher in the *Dreifaltigkeitskirche* in Berlin, Bismarck maintained in later years that he had learned

[7] *Ibid.*, pp. 104 ff. For the *Referendar* essays see Horst Kohl, ed., *Bismarck-Jahrbuch*, ii (1895), 3-47.
[8] Marcks, *Bismarcks Jugend*, pp. 126-127, 246-247.
[9] *GW*, xiv, 67.
[10] Marcks, *Bismarcks Jugend*, pp. 72-73.

nothing from the great theologian.[11] Soon thereafter he decided
to give up the nightly prayer which had been his habit since childhood. In later years he described the religious views with which
he graduated from the *Gymnasium* variously as "deistic," "athe-
istic," and "pantheistic."[12] His very confusion on this point shows
that, although a skeptic, he had arrived at no theoretical position
even with regard to his skepticism. Similarly the religious faith
which he finally acquired was largely lacking in theological content.

Scholars have differed concerning the nature of Bismarck's religious conversion.[13] Yet there can be little doubt of its sincerity,
for it altered his personal conduct. During the 1840's the young
bachelor at Kniephof acquired a reputation for impropriety
among the pious gentry of the neighborhood. He was a reckless
rider, hard drinker, persistent hunter, and expert marksman, who
liked to play jokes with his pistol. By his own admission he fell
into "bad company" and "thought every sin permissible."[14] In
local society he was usually referred to as the "wild" or "crazy"
Bismarck. Beneath the carefree exterior, however, lay a persistent
discontent. This stemmed partly from the frustrations of his career, but the deeper cause was a conviction that life is "shallow
and fruitless." In this mood he began to debate religious questions
with two devout Pomeranian neighbors, Moritz von Blanckenburg
and Marie von Thadden, Blanckenburg's fiancée.[15]

Although Bismarck regarded most of the gentry with a mixture
of humor and contempt, Moritz was a respected friend and Marie

[11] *GW*, vii, 100. A similarity in their attitudes toward prayer leaves open the
possibility that Schleiermacher actually influenced his pupil. Neither believed it
possible to move God through prayer. See Friedrich Meinecke, *Preussen und
Deutschland im 19. und 20. Jahrhundert* (Munich, 1918), pp. 301-303, and Hajo
Holborn, "Bismarcks Realpolitik," *Journal of the History of Ideas*, xxi (1960), 85.

[12] *GW*, vii, 11, 224; xiii, 463; xv, 5; Lucius von Ballhausen, *Bismarck-Erinnerungen* (Stuttgart, 1920), p. 492.

[13] For the older literature see: Friedrich Meinecke, "Bismarcks Eintritt in den
christlich-germanischen Kreis," *Historische Zeitschrift*, Vol. 90 (1903), pp. 56-92,
reprinted in *Preussen und Deutschland*, pp. 296-337; Marcks, *Bismarcks Jugend*,
pp. 244 ff.; Otto Baumgarten, *Bismarcks Stellung zu Religion und Kirche* (Tübingen, 1900) and *Bismarcks Glaube* (Tübingen, 1915); Hans von Soden, *Bismarcks
Glaube* in Ernst Jackh, ed., *Der deutsche Krieg*, xl (1915); A. O. Meyer, *Bismarcks Glaube im Spiegel der "Loosungen und Lehrtexte,"* in *Münchener Historische Abhandlungen*, Erste Reihe, i (Munich, 1933); Max Buchner, "Bismarck
und die Religion," *Gelbe Hefte*, xi (1935), 541-561. For the more recent literature
see note 46.

[14] *GW*, xiv, 46.

[15] Marcks, *Bismarcks Jugend*, pp. 183 ff.

a person of wit and charm. Her father was Adolf von Thadden, an important rural leader of the Prussian religious revival and a close friend of the Gerlachs. It was Marie who introduced Bismarck to Johanna von Puttkamer, his future wife. Both women worked diligently for his conversion. Marie's death in October 1846 was a shattering personal tragedy. The news of her approaching end wrenched from his tortured mind the first prayer he had uttered in sixteen years, and from that day onward prayer and devotion became an intimate part of his existence. In December he wrote the famous *Werbebrief* to Heinrich von Puttkamer in which he declared both his religious conversion and his love for Johanna.[16]

The revival movement to which Bismarck now adhered had begun primarily as a lay movement within the Lutheran church. It was a resurgence of eighteenth-century pietism, which had declined among the educated classes during the high tide of German idealism. Although led by Junkers, many of them veterans of the war of liberation, the movement sought to reach the lower classes. Like the mystics of the pre-reformation epoch, the pietists sought to achieve a sense of union with God. Where the regular clergy was unsympathetic to their cause, their devotions were conducted by lay preachers in private dwellings. They rejected the rational, unemotional element which had penetrated the clergy during the enlightenment. In place of reason they emphasized feeling; for theology they substituted divine and brotherly love.[17]

This was also the pattern of Bismarck's religious life. In future years he rarely went to church and cared little for the ministry and pastoral sermons. His devotion was limited to prayer, Bible reading, and the daily verses of the Moravian Brethren. While influenced by the Lutheran tradition, his faith was essentially untheological. Later we shall see that it gave him a personal orientation and sense of purpose in life which he had previously lacked. Contrary to his pietistic friends, however, he did not find in religion a doctrinal basis for his politics.[18]

In his memoirs Bismarck related that he graduated from the *Gymnasium* with the belief that a republic was "the most sensible form of the state." He was, he observed ironically, a "normal product of our public instruction." Having heard "so many bitter

---

[16] *Ibid.*, pp. 251 ff.; *GW*, xiv, 46-48.

[17] Meinecke, *Preussen und Deutschland*, pp. 296-337; Schnabel, *Deutsche Geschichte*, iv, 383 ff.

[18] Lütgert, *Idealismus*, iv, 12.

or denigrating criticisms of the ruler from grown-ups," further-more, he wondered what it was that "could cause millions of people continually to obey one individual." From his years in the Pla-mann school (six to twelve), where the Jahn tradition predomi-nated, he also "brought away German-national impressions." But these "observations," he continued, were purely "theoret-ical" and "not strong enough to uproot inborn Prussian-monarchical feelings." "My historical sympathies remained on the side of authority." As a child he regarded Harmodius, Aris-togeiton, and Brutus as "criminals" and grew indignant at every German prince who "before the thirty years war" had opposed the Holy Roman Emperor. From the Great Elector onward, how-ever, he stood with the Hohenzollern against the Kaiser.[19]

Bismarck was a royalist.[20] Although both sides of his family had served the Hohenzollern dynasty, it was the Junker side which was the origin of his monarchist sympathy. Perhaps this arose from his rejection of his mother. "It often seemed to me," he once wrote, "that she was hard, cold toward me."[21] He never grew to like the urban world into which she sent him at such a tender age, determined that he should "learn much and become much." In childhood he was filled with nostalgic longing for the country and in later years it never left him. The fields and forests for which he longed were indelibly associated with his Junker heritage. "As the pictures in house and church show," he once wrote of Schön-hausen, "my fathers have been born and have lived and died in the same rooms for centuries. . . ."[22] The symbols of the Mencken line were academic books and documents of state; those of the Bis-marcks were land, home, portraits, gravestones and a thousand other visible and tangible things. Through the Bismarck name, moreover, he belonged to a privileged caste. His marriage and religious conversion completed his sense of identification with it.

Bismarck, however, was never a romanticist. To be sure, he pre-ferred the vocabulary of feudalism to that of the modern state: "subject" instead of "citizen," "royal servant" instead of "civil servant." In later years he often referred to himself as the "vassal"

19 *GW*, xv, 5.
20 See G. Adolf Rein, "Bismarcks Royalismus," *Geschichte in Wissenschaft und Unterricht*, v (1954), 330-349.
21 *GW*, xiv, 67.   22 *Ibid.*, p. 74.

of his "liege lord," the king. Once he wrote, "He has the right to receive homage from every single subject and every corporation in the country when and where it pleases him."[23] Nevertheless, this attitude was directed more toward the person of William I than toward the institution of kingship. Although he served no less than four successive rulers, his chosen epitaph ("A loyal German servant of Kaiser William I") gave homage to only one. Nor was his vassalage unconditional. Throughout their relationship he often used the threat of resignation to overcome the king's reluctance on critical policies.

With a frequency which carries conviction Bismarck maintained that the Hohenzollern dynasty reigned by divine right ("by the grace of God"). From this it cannot be assumed that he had any theoretical position with regard to the institution of monarchy as such. Later we shall see from both his words and actions that the argument of "legitimacy" had little meaning for him. Once he wrote of the claim to sovereignty by the German small states as an "unhistorical, Godless, unjust swindle."[24] Much is usually made of his "organic" view of the state. But the proof consists of only a few brief quotations, such as the phrase "permanent-identic personality" which he used only once.[25] Certainly the organic concept as understood by the romantic conservatives was alien to his thinking. He described his political attitude before 1847 as "*ständisch-liberal.*" This meant that he sided with the aristocratic opposition to absolute monarchy.[26] His reasons, however, were practical rather than doctrinaire.

In Stahl he found a viewpoint much closer to his own than those of Haller and the Gerlachs. Stahl and Bismarck began their active political careers in the Prussian Landtag and Erfurt parliament. They were associated in the founding of the Prussian Conservative Party. How much Bismarck was influenced by his learned colleague is difficult to determine.[27] From Erfurt in 1850

23 *Ibid.*, p. 571; also III, 147, and Robert von Keudell, *Fürst und Fürstin Bismarck, Erinnerungen 1846-1872* (Berlin, 1901), p. 110.

24 *GW*, XIV, 578. On another occasion he spoke to Gerlach of the "abstract sovereignty" of the lesser states. *Ibid.*, VII, 106.

25 Hans Rothfels, *Otto von Bismarck: Deutscher Staat* (Munich, 1925), p. xxi, and Egmont Zechlin, "Bismarck und der ständische Gedanke," *Nationalsozialistische Monatshefte*, V/1 (1934), 562.

26 *GW*, XV, 16.

27 See Erich Marcks, *Bismarck und die deutsche Revolution, 1848-1851* (Stuttgart, 1939), pp. 154 ff., and Michniewicz, *Stahl und Bismarck*, pp. 108 ff.

he wrote of "our dear Stahl, who casts his pearls here before the swine. He still has pearls for me, although with the years the time will yet come . . . when our ways will separate."[28] Probably he was attracted by Stahl's realism and his solution to the problem of combining monarchical and representative institutions. It is safe to say, nevertheless, that he passed over the theoretical structure by which the philosopher justified monarchical power. In one of his early speeches Bismarck announced his adherence to the concept of the "Christian state" and remarked that the basic purpose of political institutions was "the realization of Christian doctrine." But this appears to have been a convenient argument of the moment rather than a deep-seated conviction. He was debating against a measure to permit Jews to enter the civil service.[29]

Bismarck believed that the state, like all else, was part of the divine world-plan. His subordination of church to state and the dualism of Christian morality and political necessity in his thought were characteristic of Lutheranism. Nevertheless, it cannot be proved that he actually shared with Luther and Stahl the conviction that the state had been instituted by God to protect the virtuous few from the sinful majority.[30] His attitude toward the state was pragmatic, not theological. What impressed him was not its divine, legal, idealistic, or cultural nature, but its power.

In this he was by no means unique. We have seen that he appeared as an actor on the political scene at a time of transition toward political realism. And yet there was a vital difference between his view and that of most of his contemporaries. In contrast to Ranke and Treitschke, for example, he was incapable of thinking of the state as a "moral personality" or of its power as a "spiritual essence." For him the state was primarily a device for

---

[28] *GW*, xiv, 157-158. Years later he remarked to Lothar Bucher, "Do you believe that Stahl and company were sympathetic to me. Most certainly not! But at least they had a tangible goal, and I could go a way with them; yet I knew very exactly where our ways separated." Quoted in Michniewicz, *Stahl und Bismarck*, p. 162. The high point of the relationship was their joint authorship of an amendment to the Radowitz constitution in Erfurt. Kohl, *Reden*, i, 232 ff.

[29] *Ibid.*, pp. 21-31. Stahl's *Der Christliche Staat und sein Verhältnis zu Deismus und Judentum* (Berlin, 1847) appeared after Bismarck's speech and shows some difference in viewpoint. Michniewicz, *Stahl und Bismarck*, pp. 56 ff. Others detected the influence of Ludwig von Gerlach. Ernst Ludwig von Gerlach, *Aufzeichnungen aus seinem Leben und Wirken, 1795-1877* (Schwerin, 1903), i, 477.

[30] Leonhard von Muralt, who takes a contrary position, admits that there is no direct evidence to support it. *Bismarcks Verantwortlichkeit* (Göttingen, 1955) p. 106.

governing and its power but a means to concrete, practical ends. What were those ends?

Throughout his career Bismarck was fond of describing himself to political opponents as a statesman above all personal and partisan interest, whose sole concern was *salus publica*.[31] Like the historian, however, the statesman is part of the historical process and not above it. His conception of what constitutes the public welfare is formed in the crucible of the mind, where it is inevitably alloyed with personal aims and social biases. Bismarck was no exception. His thought about the state was compounded of both subjective and objective elements. Internally its power was the means of his own self-fulfillment and of survival for the aristocratic order in a century of dynamic change; externally its power was the means of common protection against foreign aggression and of the expansion and aggrandizement of the Prussian nation-state.

2. THE WILL TO POWER

In a youthful novel, *Morton's Hope*,[32] Motley painted a lively portrait of the young Bismarck he knew as a student in Göttingen. Unlike its protagonist, "Otto von Rabenmark," his Junker friend was not a skilled musician, "excellent classical scholar," or remarkable linguist. Like Rabenmark, however, he was a roistering student and constant duellist. Beneath his "fools-mask" Motley's hero was a man of serious purpose. "I have a certain quantity of time on my hands," he confessed. "I wish to take the university as a school for action. I intend to lead my companions here, as I intend to lead them in after life."[33] Like Bismarck, he planned a career in diplomacy. But unlike him he got involved with a countess, slew two men, fled, was captured, stabbed his accuser in the courtroom, and ended it all by taking poison.

Motley's picture of Bismarck is that of a self-assured young man, conscious of unusual talents, of an aggressive and combative nature, driven by a dynamic urge to lead and dominate. According to another reminiscence, he was a natural leader in the play-battles of the children in the Plamann school. He advertised his

[31] Rothfels, *Deutscher Staat*, pp. 71-72, 80, 84.
[32] *Morton's Hope, or the Memoirs of a Provincial* (2 vols., New York, 1839). Whether Bismarck ever read the novel is difficult to say. In 1850 he reported to their mutual friend, Sharlach, "Motley writes very popular novels." *GW*, xiv, 162.
[33] *Morton's Hope*, i, 164.

arrival in Göttingen by challenging an entire student corps.[34] Bismarck was well over six feet tall, powerfully built, and a terror on the duelling floor. During three semesters he fought no less than twenty-five *Mensuren* and was wounded only once—by his account a foul stroke.[35] In 1852 he exchanged shots in a duel with Georg Vincke. Neither was struck and, while their seconds rejoiced, Bismarck lamented that duelling etiquette did not allow him, being the challenged, to demand another round. In 1866 an assassin fired five times at him on a Berlin street. As the pistol exploded, the Junker turned upon his attacker and seized him by the throat. He had, he once remarked, a "natural lust for combat."[36]

The will to power was the central characteristic of Bismarck's personality. Political power was the only means by which he could attain self-fulfillment.[37] Had he been of the middle class, he might have satisfied this need as an entrepreneur. His was the great age of industrial and corporate expansion in which were founded Germany's largest fortunes and business empires. But Bismarck was born a Junker to whom a business career was taboo. The only reservoir of power open to him was that of the state. He was highly attracted by the idea of a military career. In later years he liked to refer to himself as a royal officer, despite the fact that he experienced only one year of military training and his commission was in the militia, not the regular army. After promotion to the rank of major-general in 1866, he wore the uniform as his normal dress.[38] In a Christmas letter to William I in 1872 he regretted that it had been his lot to serve the royal house behind the writing desk rather than on the front. He would much rather have won battles than diplomatic campaigns.[39] Yet it was not true, as he asserted, that the decision to enter the diplomatic service was entirely the work of his parents. Although his mother wished it, Otto for once concurred.[40]

[34] Marcks, *Bismarcks Jugend*, pp. 55-56, 87.

[35] Heinrich von Poschinger, ed., *Bismarck und die Parlamentarier* (Breslau, 1894), I, 30.

[36] *GW*, xiv, 258; vii, 90, 116-117.

[37] See the analysis of Helmuth Wolff, *Geschichtsauffassung und Politik in Bismarcks Bewusstsein* (Munich, 1926), pp. 57 ff.

[38] One may doubt that the sole reason was the better protection the high collar gave against colds. Keudell, *Fürst und Fürstin Bismarck*, p. 386.

[39] Horst Kohl, ed., *Anhang zu den Gedanken und Erinnerungen von Otto Fürst von Bismarck* (Stuttgart, 1901), I, 232-233; see also *GW*, vii, 137.

[40] Marcks, *Bismarcks Jugend*, pp. 83 ff.

On application he met his first frustration. Ancillon, the foreign minister, thought the rural gentry too rustic to master the arts of diplomacy and politely discouraged him. Hence Bismarck began his career as a *Referendar* in the provincial administration at Aachen (June 1836). Within a few months he found the subaltern life of an apprentice civil servant intolerable. Next summer he went on leave, overstayed it to pursue (vainly) his courtship of an English girl, and afterward never returned to Aachen. In the winter he managed to get transferred to Potsdam, where some months later he resigned.[41]

In a remarkable letter he gave his reasons. The bureaucracy, he complained, had no place for an independent and critical spirit. The civil servant is like a musician in an orchestra, who must perform regardless of what he thinks of the melody or its interpretation. "But I want to play the tune the way it sounds good to me or not at all. . . . My pride bids me command rather than obey." In general, statesmen are motivated, not by patriotism, but by "pride, the desire to command, to become admired and renowned. I confess I am not free from these passions." Unsubmissive by nature, he could see only one way to scale the heights of his ambition: through a Prussian parliament. He envied states with "free constitutions" where the individual could make his influence felt and his views effective. His imagination was fired by the examples of Peel, O'Connell, and Mirabeau.[42]

Political power was ultimately the means by which Bismarck fulfilled and realized himself, and yet it would be unfair to assume that he wielded it only for personal aggrandizement. From the beginning to the end of his career he keenly felt the obligation he had undertaken. While granting freedom to act, power subjected him to its own necessity, imposing goals and purposes more important than the mere satisfaction of personal conceit. Such a sense of responsibility has led others into the morass of self-doubt and self-criticism, but upon Bismarck the effect was different. It made him hypersensitive to criticism and opposition, for his confidence in the superiority of his own judgment was absolute. The

---

[41] *Ibid.*, pp. 131 ff.

[42] *GW*, xiv, 13-17, 31. Years later Keyserling reminded him of a comment made in these years: "constitution unavoidable; this the path to outward fame; one must also be inwardly pious." Kohl, *Anhang*, ii, 246 ff.

very qualities which prevented him from being a dutiful subordinate made him in later years an autocratic superior.

His highly developed sense of duty was reinforced by his religious faith. At the beginning of his diplomatic career in 1851 he wrote, "I am God's soldier and I must go where he sends me, and I believe that he sends me and fashions my life as he needs it."[43] Nevertheless, he did not conceive himself as the mere passive tool of God's will. Unlike Frederick William IV he did not feel compelled to wait upon divine inspiration. What he received from God, he believed, was the obligation to act according to the dictates of his reason and conscience. God was not the instigator of his actions, but their judge. It was not utterly impossible, however, for man to perceive God's will in the direction of human events. "I am happy," he remarked, "when I discern whither our lord God is going and can hobble after him."[44]

While he did not believe it possible to invoke divine intervention, he found sustenance in prayer and a feeling of subjection to a higher power. In times of great stress, like the war of 1870-1871, his faith fortified him in the titanic struggle to gain his will over great odds. In times of political frustration he found solace in the assumption that what he could not prevent or make otherwise was God's doing. As a young man, separated for months from wife and family, his religion helped him to keep to the path of sexual morality.[45] It gave to his natural self-confidence a moral underpinning and added to the certitude with which he asserted his will over others.

It is highly doubtful, nevertheless, that Bismarck's religious conversion can be considered a decisive turning point in the development of his character.[46] His determination to dominate and direct did not spring from a sense of divine mission, but from an earlier, more elemental force in his personality. Conversion did not fundamentally alter his attitude toward his fellowman. His

---

[43] *GW*, xiv, 208, also 227.   [44] A. O. Meyer, *Bismarcks Glaube*, p. 9.
[45] Muralt, *Verantwortlichkeit*, pp. 89-90.
[46] The contrary viewpoint is held by S. A. Kaehler, "Zur Deutung von Bismarcks 'Bekehrung,'" in Heinrich Runte, ed., *Glaube und Geschichte, Festschrift für Friedrich Gogarten* (Giessen, 1948), pp. 189-209; Wilhelm Schüssler, *Um das Geschichtsbild* (Gladbeck, 1953), pp. 122-141; Otto Vossler, "Bismarcks Ethos," *Historische Zeitschrift*, Vol. 171 (1951), pp. 263-292; Muralt, *Verantwortlichkeit*, p. 97. While accepting the general viewpoint of these authors, Pastor Franz Pahlmann is critical of their theology, "Der Stand des Gesprächs über Bismarcks Glauben," *Geschichte in Wissenschaft und Unterricht*, vii (1956), 207-222.

cynical view of minds and motives, his frequent hatred and malevolence toward those who opposed him, his willingness to exploit and use others show that the Christian doctrine of love and charity had no great influence upon him. His faith provided the reinforcement, not the foundation, of his sense of responsibility. From feudal times the gentry had preserved the tradition of an aristocratic status group dedicated to the functions of government and defense in the interest of the whole. Through Frederick the Great the tradition was deliberately transformed into patriotic service to the Prussian nation-state. In relying solely upon the voice of conscience, Bismarck discarded the possibility of an objective moral code and was willing to disregard the limitations of law in his conduct of public affairs. Hence his religion was compatible with much of his earlier skepticism. It helped him put his personal life in order, but it produced no basic change in his social attitudes.[47]

3. THE FORTRESS OF ARISTOCRATIC INTERESTS

The squire from Schönhausen began his political career in the united diet of 1847 as an effective and partisan champion of conservative interests. From the tribune he opposed every reform which meant the least sacrifice to the aristocratic class, whether proposed by the crown or the liberal opposition. On hearing (March 19, 1848) of the uprising in Berlin, he armed the villagers in Schönhausen and hastened to Potsdam to promote a counterrevolution by the army backed by loyal peasants. But the Prussian generals refused to act without the king's command, and Prince William of Prussia, whom he thought to use for the conspiracy, had left for Britain.[48] In a speech on April 2 the Junker tearfully accepted the revolution on the grounds that he could do no other now that "the crown had buried its own coffin." During the following weeks he hesitated to attack the new regime publicly. Like many of the nobility, he was temporarily demoralized by the force

[47] See Holborn, "Bismarck's Realpolitik," pp. 87-90. Holborn has revived the older viewpoint of Meinecke, Lenz, and Brandenburg. One of the descendents of the circle of Pomeranian pietists has recently raised afresh the doubts of nineteenth-century conservatives as to the genuineness of Bismarck's conversion. Reinold von Thadden-Trieglaff, *War Bismarck Christ?* (Hamburg, 1950).

[48] G. Adolf Rein, "Bismarcks gegenrevolutionäre Aktion in den Märztagen 1848," *Die Welt als Geschichte*, xiii (1953), 246-262; Max Lenz, "Bismarcks Plan einer Gegenrevolution im März 1848," *Sitzungsberichte der preussischen Akademie der Wissenschaften*, Jahrgang 1930, Philosophisch-Historische Klasse, pp. 251-276; Marcks, *Bismarck und Revolution*, pp. 19 ff.

of the revolutionary tide and the failure of the monarchy to defend itself.[49]

This hesitation came to an end when the liberal cabinet announced its fiscal program. To pacify the urban masses it substituted for the grist tax a direct tax paid only by the well-to-do. Recalling the united diet, the ministers asked for the power to issue extensive credits for the relief of business enterprises which had suffered from the revolution. Bismarck denounced both measures as a "gift from the treasury to the cities," which would eventually have to be paid for by the "country and the small towns." The minister of finance, he charged, saw all the needs of the public "through the spectacles of industrialism." It was the first attempt to arouse the rural areas against an urban government, soon to become a familiar technique of the counter-revolution.[50]

In May he failed of election to the Prussian national assembly, which replaced the united diet. Impotently he watched while the new parliament drafted a constitution which would have abolished the formula of divine right and titles of nobility. Furthermore, the deputies ended the exclusive hunting rights of the Junkers; progress was made on a measure to eliminate their feudal judicial powers in the manorial courts; and bills were introduced providing for the abolition of aristocratic exemptions from the real estate tax and of certain payments and services still owed by the peasantry to Junker landlords.[51]

Bismarck was angry and alarmed, particularly over the financial measures. "A real estate tax," he wrote in the *Kreuzzeitung* "is not a tax, but a confiscation of capital." It was a conspiracy of the city against the country, of the capitalists against the Junkers. In the name of "order and justice" the liberals had be-

---

[49] Kohl, *Reden*, i, 45-46. At the end of March he amended the text of a proposed conservative proclamation submitted to him by Ludwig Gerlach by inserting the promise, "No reaction, and readiness to sacrifice." Hans J. Schoeps, "Unveröffentlichte Bismarckbriefe," *Zeitschrift für Religions- und Geistesgeschichte*, ii (1949), 2-3; Ludwig Gerlach, *Aufzeichnungen*, i, 518-523. His moderation aroused bitter criticism from his ultra-conservative friends. Later he apologized. *GW*, xiv, 103-104, 109; Hermann Witte, "Vom Nachlass Ludwig von Gerlachs, mit ungedruckten Briefen Bismarcks," *Archiv für Kulturgeschichte*, xxxi (1943), 140-141. For the attitudes of other conservatives see Jordan, *Entstehung der konservativen Partei*, pp. 130-132, 154 ff.

[50] Kohl, *Reden*, i, 51-56; also *GW*, xiv, 105; Jordan, *Entstehung der konservativen Partei*, pp. 128, 159.

[51] Alexander Bergengrün, *David Hansemann* (Berlin, 1901), pp. 507 ff.

gun to "plunder one class of citizens to reward another."[52] The issue, he believed, was "literally one of the existence of a large part of the conservative party."[53]

Equally alarming was the program of the Frankfurt parliament. Bismarck feared for the continued "social and political existence of Prussia."[54] In a speech of 1849 he maintained that the Frankfurt program was more "social than national" in character. "If the revolution had been restricted to the national issue, the movement would have been limited to a few prominent people. Only by raising the social question were they able to cut the ground from under us. By misrepresentation they excited the greed of the unpropertied for the possessions of others, and the envy of the less well-to-do against the rich."[55]

What most excited his wrath was the conviction that the king himself had been responsible for the defeat of the old regime. In March the army had never swerved in its loyalty to the crown. The troops would have crushed the revolution at the barricades, had Frederick William not ordered a premature withdrawal.[56] During the summer Bismarck joined the Gerlachs in a "camarilla" of ultra-conservatives whose aim was to persuade the king to stage a *coup d'état*. For the time being, however, Frederick William refused to act. Bismarck fumed over his impotent behavior, which was so costly to the nobility. In August he drafted a threatening petition for the signature of his conservative friends. The new financial legislation, it declared, was "a confiscation of private property" unequalled in history except by "conquerors and dictators." For this neglect of their rights "the great majority of the Prussian people will hold your majesty responsible before God and the hereafter." Frederick William should understand, in other words, that where Junker rights and privileges were con-

---

[52] Kohl, *Jahrbuch*, I, 475-483; III, 399-400; VI, 10-16; Ludwig Gerlach, *Aufzeichnungen*, II, 20. Until 1851 Bismarck was a constant contributor to the columns of the *Kreuzzeitung*. Only a few of his articles can be identified with certainty. The claim of Bernhard Studt to have identified 125 contributions is insecure. See his *Bismarck als Mitarbeiter der Kreuzzeitung in den Jahren 1848 und 1849* (Bonn, 1903), and Hans J. Schoeps, "Der junge Bismarck als Journalist," *Zeitschrift für Religions- und Geistesgeschichte*, III (1951), 1-12.

[53] *GW*, XIV, 111-112.

[54] *GW*, XV, 26-27; XIV, 103. Apparently the final version of the letter was somewhat different. Marcks, *Bismarck und Revolution*, p. 26. On the social reforms to which he objected see Hamerow, *Restoration, Revolution, Reaction*, pp. 168 ff.

[55] Kohl, *Reden*, I, 111.

[56] *GW*, XV, 47-48; also XIV, 160-162; X, 16.

cerned there was a limit to royalism. On August 18-19 the squire from Schönhausen participated in the "Junker parliament" in Berlin, which organized the nobility for the defense of their interests.[57]

In Bismarck's eyes this was not mere self-seeking. As a candidate for parliament he was probably sincere in describing himself to the voters as "independent and non-partisan" in contrast to a merchant or industrialist. Without a sense of greed he could openly declare, "I am a Junker and want the advantage of being one."[58] The privileges of his caste, he believed were justified by its unique contribution to the general welfare. In 1849 he devoted a speech to this subject. History proved that only those states with an hereditary aristocracy attained "lasting prosperity and power." The great victories of the Prussian army had been purchased with their blood. Opposed to both monarchical and democratic absolutism, they were the greatest bulwarks of freedom in Prussian society. They were the keel and rudder which counterbalanced the raging winds of the *Zeitgeist*.[59]

In a letter of 1849 Bismarck argued that it was the patriotic duty of the Junkers to look after their own material interests. Without independent means this class could no longer continue to serve the state.[60] To the end of his days he held steadfastly to the view that the agricultural classes were the backbone of society. The endurance for victorious campaigns came from the cultivation of the land, rather than the tending of machines. While the soil nourished the healthy instincts of patriotism and dynastic loyalty, the city bred the loathsome diseases of treason and revolution. The producing classes of German society were the farmers and rural nobility, not the capitalists, factory workers, bureaucrats, court nobility, and *Geldadel*. They were the "worker bees" whose culture should be the main interest of political economy.[61] His defense of the nobility, in other words, was not romantic, but realistic. He did not speak of the sacred trust of time, but of the utilitarian services of the nobility in the present.

Most important for his future conduct were the practical conclusions Bismarck drew from his experiences of 1848. As he had

[57] *GW*, I, 1-2; Marcks, *Bismarck und Revolution*, pp. 58-60. In June he had remonstrated personally to Frederick William, but was disarmed by the king's friendly candor. Petersdorff, *Friedrich Wilhelm IV*, pp. 13-14.
[58] *GW*, x, 22; vii, 15; xiv, 123-124.   [59] Kohl, *Reden*, i, 144-153.
[60] *GW*, xiv, 112.   [61] *GW*, ix, 90 ff., 196 ff.; xii, 611.

predicted, once Frederick William resolved on force, the revolution proved but a "spook." Out of respect for public opinion the king had deceived himself about the "real relationships of power." In his memoirs the Junker concluded that the *Realpolitiker* need concern himself with the clamor of press and parliament only insofar as it affects loyalty of the troops.[62] This was also his view in 1849. In a speech he declared that the struggle between popular sovereignty and divine right would never be settled by parliamentary debate. The final arbiter between bourgeois and Junker, liberal and conservative, was force, not oratory. Victory lay not with the parliamentary majority, but with the mailed fist of the state.[63]

This must not be taken to mean that Bismarck regarded popular opinion as unimportant. No more than Machiavelli did he ignore moral forces in politics. Like the Florentine, however, he regarded them as objects of exploitation and manipulation, rather than as determinants of political action. They must be permitted neither to influence the conduct of policy, nor to corrode the vital instruments of state power. Throughout the rest of his career Bismarck's first purpose in domestic politics was to preserve monarchical control over the means of force. We shall see, in fact, that this was precisely the issue which brought him to office in 1862. Behind his rigidity on this point lay the memory of the events of 1848 and the recognition that the remaining autocratic powers of the monarchy were the fortress without which the nobility would lie naked and exposed to the assaults of its enemies.

4. THE REJECTION OF ABSOLUTISM

Bismarck was never an absolutist. Like most conservatives he regarded the state as a source of danger as well as safety. In the past the greatest threats to aristocratic interests had come from royal absolutism and bureaucratic liberalism. But in Bismarck's case the dislike of the bureaucratic machine was also personal. As we have seen, he was repelled by his brief experience as a civil servant and frustrated by the lack of any other path to political power.

The united diet of 1847 offered both a means of personal advancement and an opportunity to continue his old feud against

62 *GW*, xv, 47-48; also xiv, 161.   63 Kohl, *Reden*, i, 77-78.

the governmental apparatus. In that body he was as forthright against reforms proposed by the bureaucracy as against those stemming from the liberal opposition. With other conservatives he was angered by some of the liberal features of the constitution decreed on December 5, 1848.[64] Elected to the new Landtag, he argued vociferously against the efforts of the Manteuffel government to complete the liquidation of manorialism and put an end to peasant unrest.[65] So severe were his attacks that he was nearly expelled from the conservative faction.[66] When summer came, his rancorous pen scratched out a bitter denunciation. "The bureaucracy is cancerous from head to foot; only its mouth is healthy, and the excrement it issues in the form of laws is the most natural filth in the world." On other occasions he described the civil service as the embodiment of "Bonapartism" and "heathen-republicanism." The germ of this "disease" was a false education which inculcated habits of skepticism and criticism. Low salaries and slow promotions encouraged civil servants to promote innovations which might lead to their own advancement.[67]

It was Bismarck's sincere conviction that a parliament was required to counterbalance the "revolutionary" tendencies of bureaucratic liberalism. But what kind of parliament? How was it to be chosen and what were to be its powers?

Bismarck began as an advocate of the corporate state (*Ständestaat*). His ideal parliament was one chosen by estates and equipped only with the power of "public criticism." Under the influence of Stahl he saw in 1848 the wisdom of adding to the three traditional estates (nobility, peasantry, and middle class) a fourth representing the urban proletariat.[68] His motive was practical, rather than romantic. What he wanted was not the resurrection of

[64] *GW*, xiv, 120-121; Ludwig Gerlach, *Aufzeichnungen*, ii, 36 ff.; Leopold von Gerlach, *Denkwürdigkeiten* (Berlin, 1891), i, 259 ff.; Walter, *Innere Politik Manteuffels*, pp. 44 ff.

[65] Kohl, *Reden*, i, 162 ff.; *GW*, xiv, 144, 164; Kohl, *Jahrbuch*, iii, 400-408. On the Manteuffel reforms see Hamerow, *Restoration, Revolution, Reaction*, pp. 219 ff., and Walter, *Innere Politik Manteuffels*, pp. 73 ff.; Georg Friedrich Knapp, *Die Bauern-Befreiung und der Ursprung der Landarbeiter in den älteren Theilen Preussens* (Leipzig, 1887), i, 217 ff.; ii, 411 ff.

[66] Ludwig Gerlach, *Aufzeichnungen*, ii, 93, 98.

[67] *GW*, i, 375; xiv, 159-160, 244, 328; Kohl, *Reden*, i, 303.

[68] Richard Augst, *Bismarcks Stellung zum parlamentarischen Wahlrecht* (Leipzig, 1917), pp. 6 ff.; Leopold Gerlach, *Denkwürdigkeiten*, i, 244. It is also possible that Bismarck's views on an assembly of estates were influenced by the writings of his Pomeranian neighbor, Ernst von Bülow-Cummerow. Marcks, *Bismarcks Jugend*, pp. 222 ff.

a medieval institution, but the creation of a representative body based upon occupational and interest groups in which landowners would have the dominant voice. Universal, direct, and equal suffrage he condemned because of its emphasis upon numbers, rather than intelligence and understanding. Their greater skill at party organization and political agitation would enable the liberals to elect their candidates even though they represented a minority of the voters.[69]

Nor was he satisfied with the three-class system established by royal decree on May 30, 1849. It divided the electorate artificially according to wealth rather than interests and occupations. "We do not represent the people," he told the deputies, "Let's climb down from this pedestal upon which we have placed ourselves."[70] He denied that *any* system could accurately reflect the popular will. Since this was the case, it was folly to speak of parliamentary representation as a natural right of the individual. The rest of this address was a spirited defense of the aristocratic order and of its right to govern in the public interest.[71]

During the first two years of its existence he hoped to see the Prussian lower chamber replaced by an assembly of estates.[72] In a letter of 1851 to Leopold Gerlach he argued that this could be done without violating the constitution. The crown should simply summon a new united diet, which would assume the legislative functions of the Landtag. The latter would wither on the vine.[73] Soon, however, he came to the conclusion that such a maneuver was unnecessary. Because the liberals boycotted the election, the first chamber chosen under the three-class system was dominated by conservatives. In a memorial of 1853 to Prince William of Prussia Bismarck asserted that "as long as times are peaceful the same persons reappear in the chamber whatever the election law." The best "guarantee" for the conduct of parliament was not a particular "recipe for its composition," but the limitation of its powers.[74]

[69] Kohl, *Reden*, I, 88-89; *GW*, XIV, 124.
[70] Kohl, *Reden*, I, 302.   [71] *Ibid.*, pp. 149-153.
[72] Augst, *Bismarcks Stellung*, p. 15; Ludwig Gerlach, *Aufzeichnungen*, II, 180-181; Schoeps, "Bismarckbriefe," pp. 5-6. In 1851 Frederick William IV also wanted to reconstruct the lower chamber on a corporative basis, but Otto Manteuffel and others opposed the necessary *coup d'état*. Heinrich von Poschinger, ed., *Unter Friedrich Wilhelm IV, Denkwürdigkeiten des Ministers Otto Freiherrn von Manteuffel 1848-1858* (Berlin, 1900-1901), II, 24, 47-51; III, 97 ff.
[73] *GW*, XIV, 223-224. For Leopold Gerlach's view see *Denkwürdigkeiten*, I, 585 ff.
[74] *GW*, I, 375-376.

Here he faced a crucial problem which was to bother him for the rest of his career. If its powers were too feeble, parliament would be ineffective as a counterweight to the bureaucracy; if too strong, the chamber would become a threat to the crown. In either case the interests of the nobility were in danger. Where should the line be drawn?

The constitution decreed on December 5, 1848 and revised in the charter of January 31, 1850 gave the crown and both chambers an equal voice in the passage of legislation. Since the upper chamber was ultimately converted into a hereditary house of lords, this meant that crown and nobility possessed an absolute veto. As a deputy in the lower chamber Bismarck vigorously opposed all attempts to increase its power. For the first time he expounded the famous "gap theory" (*Lückentheorie*), which was to be the crown's legal defense in the constitutional conflict of the 1860's. The constitution made no provision for settling serious disagreements between crown and parliament. In such cases, Bismarck argued, the will of the former must prevail.[75]

In the memorial of 1853 to Prince William he amplified his views. "[Parliament] must be equipped with the means to ward off new laws and new taxes and to exercise a controlling criticism over the governmental system, namely over the financial housekeeping and the inner administration." But that was all. "It must never have the power to force the crown to act against the will of the king, or to coerce the king's ministers; otherwise, it will unfailingly misuse that power." To prevent this evil the crown must be able to prohibit any changes in the laws of the country undertaken without its consent. Parliament must be allowed no final control over the budget "or any part thereof." Pending approval of a new budget, the previous one must remain in effect. The crown must have the authority to continue levying taxes, once granted, without the further approval of parliament.[76]

From the beginning the Junker believed in the importance of parliament as an institution. It was the means by which he had launched his own career. In 1858 he decried the "servility" and "inertia" which threatened the Landtag with "insignificance and oblivion" and encouraged "bureaucratic coups" by the cabinet.

75 Kohl, *Reden*, I, 312-321. See also his article in the *Kreuzzeitung*, Jan. 23, 1850. Kohl, *Jahrbuch*, III, 411-413.
76 *GW*, I, 375-376.

To remain healthy, the state required some "freedom of movement."[77] More than three decades later in retirement, he uttered similar complaints about the German Reichstag. But the impotence of the Prussian and German parliaments was the natural consequence of the largely negative functions he gave them. They were conceived for the "defensive" purpose of protecting the nobility from the encroachments of the bureaucracy and the crown.[78] In any serious struggle for power he favored the monarchy over the legislature. While both royal absolutism and parliamentary government were hazards to the interests of the nobility, the latter was decidedly the greater.

His utterances are notable in that age for their lack of philosophical reasoning. In sharp contrast to most of his contemporaries, whether liberal or conservative, his thinking about political questions was limited almost solely to practical considerations. What interested him in constitutional matters was not the validation of theoretical rights or of a historical theory, but the representation of concrete interests and the distribution of powers.

[77] To Leopold Gerlach, March 2, 1858. *GW*, xiv, 485-486. The purpose of the letter was to oppose Ludwig's attempt to extend the parliamentary term to six years in the hope of warding off the reforms expected of the approaching "new era" cabinet.

[78] *GW*, i, 375.

CHAPTER THREE

THE EXTERNAL FUNCTIONS OF POWER

1. A PRUSSIAN NATIONALIST

AMONG German historians and political scientists the most common justification for authoritarian government has been geopolitical. Located on the open plains of northern Europe with no adequate geographical barriers, the Prussians had to develop a governmental system capable of reacting quickly and effectively against foreign attack. Ranke gave this view its classic statement in his *Dialogue on Politics*: "The position of a state in the world depends on the degree of independence it has attained. It is obliged, therefore, to organize all its internal resources for the purpose of self-preservation. This is the supreme law of the state."[1] In German political literature this principle is known as the *Primat der Aussenpolitik*. While Ranke was its philosopher, Bismarck is generally considered to have been its greatest practitioner.[2]

Although a secondary theme, the concept of the *Primat der Aussenpolitik* does appear in Bismarck's recorded thoughts during the early period of his career. In February 1851 he delivered a harsh speech opposing extension of the financial powers of parliament on the grounds that the proper conduct of foreign policy would be impossible in a government dominated by the second chamber. In a body composed of five to six parties, majority decisions were the "unsteady result of a very complicated diagonal of forces." The composition of the British house of commons, on the other hand, was far different. Here there were only two parties, one of which had a secure majority subject to the "iron discipline" of leaders who were at the same time cabinet ministers.[3]

---

[1] Theodore H. von Laue, *Leopold Ranke, The Formative Years* (Princeton, 1950), p. 167.

[2] See Max Lenz, "Ranke und Bismarck," *Kleine Historische Schriften* (Munich, 1910), pp. 383-408. Despite their seeming affinity in viewpoint, Ranke was very critical of Bismarck's actions after 1862. See Otto Diether, *Leopold von Ranke als Politiker* (Leipzig, 1911), pp. 518 ff., and Stephen Skalweit, "Ranke und Bismarck," *Historische Zeitschrift*, Vol. 176 (1953), pp. 277-290. For a criticism of Ranke's concept see Heinrich Heffter, "Vom Primat der Aussenpolitik," *ibid.*, Vol. 171 (1951), pp. 1-20.

[3] Kohl, *Reden*, I, 300-301.

This praise of the British system cannot be taken at face value.[4] The house of commons was the great model of the Prussian liberals, and Bismarck liked to irritate the deputies by pointing out the inadequacy of the parallel. A passage in his memorial of 1853 to Prince William shows that he was opposed to parliamentary government whatever the composition of the chamber: "Prussia's greatness was by no means achieved through liberalism and free-thinking, but through a series of strong, resolute, and wise rulers who carefully nourished and saved the military and financial resources of the state. They held those resources, moreover, in their own unshackled hands until the favorable moment came to cast them with reckless courage into the scales of European politics. . . . The demand is undoubtedly justified that every Prussian should enjoy the degree of freedom which is consonant with the public welfare and with the course which Prussia has to take in European politics, but no more. One can have this freedom without parliamentary government. . . ."[5]

Bismarck's use of the *Primat der Aussenpolitik* differed from that of Ranke and other apologists for Prussian authoritarianism. While their argument was defensive, his was offensive. He maintained that monarchical control over the vital functions of government was necessary, not to defend Prussia from the threat of foreign aggression, but to take advantage of the opportunities that might arise for her expansion. His motive for expansion was not geopolitical, but nationalistic—for the greater glory and power of Prussia and the Hohenzollern dynasty.

Bismarck's nationalism was of the type formed by the state rather than by a common culture.[6] Only in his old age, and rarely even then, did he speak of the nation as a cultural phenomenon. To the end he regarded the "mediation" of dynastic loyalty as necessary for the creation of national sentiment. His family heritage made it natural for him to take this view. For centuries the Bismarcks had served in the armies of the Hohenzollern. Prussian patriotism was his birthright.[7]

---

[4] On other occasions he wrote of the "incalculability" of English policy because of her party system. *GW*, ii, 143, 221; xiv, 429, 436, 440.
[5] *GW*, i, 375.   [6] See pp. 32 ff.
[7] See my "Bismarck and German Nationalism," *American Historical Review*, lx (1955), 559 ff. In replying to this article Hans Rothfels not only failed to deal with the new issues it raised, but attributed to the author a view ("Wendung Bismarcks zum grossdeutschen Nationalstaatsgedanken") diametrically opposed to that which the article actually develops: *Bismarck, der Osten und das Reich*

This is not to say that the young Bismarck was devoid of German feeling. At school he was exposed to German national sentiment. In Göttingen he flirted briefly with the Burschenschaft, but was repelled by the "extravagance of their political views" and their unwillingness to "give satisfaction" by duelling.[8] His German patriotism was limited to the "spirit of 1812," as the conservative nobility had understood it. Most of the Junkers who went to war in 1812 did so to liberate German soil from the foreigner, not to unify Germany. What men of this conviction wished was the solidarity of Germany's princes, rather than the sovereign union of its peoples.[9]

Bismarck's opposition to the revolution of 1848 was, in part, owing to its threat to the integrity of the Prussian nation. He was outraged by the liberal plan for an autonomous Poland.[10] But an even greater danger came from the Frankfurt parliament and the proposal to merge Prussia into Germany. In the Landtag debate on the Frankfurt constitution (April 1849), he declared it self-evident that "everyone . . . who speaks German wants German unity. . . ." But this remark was pure embellishment, for he continued in another vein. The proposed constitution "seeks to undermine and demolish that house of state constructed by centuries of glory and patriotism and cemented throughout by the blood of our ancestors." The Prussian government, he declared, should put forward its own plan for German unity.[11]

The German union plan, nevertheless, also excited his opposition. In September he denounced the intention to surrender Prussian independence to this "phantom." The powers given the Hohenzollern king in the little-German federation were not enough

---

(Darmstadt, 1960), p. 64 (n. 69). The confusion over Bismarck's nationalism (see introduction) has arisen because of the failure to identify his type of national sentiment. Otto Becker's view that Bismarck was from the beginning a German nationalist is based, not on contemporary evidence, but upon his words and writings after 1866. *Bismarcks Ringen*, pp. 33 ff., 63. Becker's denial of the existence of a "Prussian nation" (pp. 47, 103) is belied by Bismarck's own frequent use of the term. For a few examples see *GW*, II, 383; IV, 31; X, 38, 43; XIV, 160, 666-667.

[8] *GW*, XV, 5 ff.

[9] Kohl, *Reden*, I, 9-10; *GW*, XIV, 89; Meinecke, *Weltbürgertum*, pp. 298 ff.

[10] Kohl, *Reden*, I, 49-51; *GW*, XIV, 104-106; Marcks, *Bismarck und Revolution*, pp. 43-44.

[11] Kohl, *Reden*, I, 92-94. The occasional expressions of German national sentiment which Bismarck voiced in this period (another example: *GW*, XIV, 106) were obviously tactical, intended to dazzle the opposition and outdo them at their own game. The references to his Prussian patriotism are far more frequent and convincing.

to compensate for the fact that Prussia could be outvoted in its governing body. The scheme meant the dissolution of Prussia, "the best pillar of German power." During the year of revolution she alone had saved Germany from foreign danger: "What preserved us was that which constitutes the real Prussia. It was what remains of that much stigmatized *Stockpreussentum*, which outlasted the revolution: that is, the Prussian army, the Prussian treasury, the fruits of an intelligent Prussian administration of many years standing, and that vigorous spirit of cooperation between king and people which exists in Prussia. It was the loyalty of the Prussian people to their hereditary dynasty. It was the old Prussian virtues of honor, fidelity, obedience, and bravery, which permeate the army from its nucleus, the officer corps, outward to the youngest recruit. This army harbors no revolutionary enthusiasm. You will not find in the army, any more than in the rest of the Prussian people, any need for a national rebirth. They are satisfied with the name Prussia and proud of the name Prussia. . . . Prussian we are and Prussian we wish to remain."[12] In this passage appear all the elements which composed Bismarck's conception of the nation: dynastic loyalty, autocratic paternalism, military discipline, and patriotic sacrifice. During the following debate an opponent branded him "a lost son of the great German fatherland," to which Bismarck replied, "My country (*Vaterhaus*) is Prussia, and I have never left my country and I shall never leave it."[13]

2. AGGRESSIVE NATIONALISM

Both forms of the national idea are potentially aggressive. The cultural nationalist regards national unity, or national independence, as a moral right which transcends existing international law and the established distribution of power between states. The concept of national self-determination is easily transformed into a belief in national superiority and the right of dominion over alien cultural groups. Bismarck, on the other hand, was inclined to look upon Prussian expansion more as a matter of opportunity than of moral necessity. He found his model in the career of Frederick the Great rather than in the French revolution and the wars of libera-

---

[12] Kohl, *Reden*, I, 113, also 235-241; *GW*, xiv, 152 ff.; Schoeps, "Bismarck als Journalist," pp. 2-12.
[13] Kohl, *Reden*, I, 117.

tion. Personal ambition and Prussian pride, the need for self-fulfillment through political power and the desire for Prussia's aggrandizement in German and European politics, sprang from the same elemental force in his personality.

Bismarck's earliest recorded judgment on the subject of international politics indicates the direction of his thinking. During his Kniephof period he once remarked in a gathering of rural gentry that "the chief aim of the mighty upon earth is to widen their borders and extend the area of their dominion. 'I am of the opinion that the time will again come when the kingdom of Prussia will undergo a significant expansion.' "[14] That this remark was remembered and later recorded suggests that it aroused antagonism at the time. Among pietistic Junkers the Frederician tradition was regarded with strong distaste. The conquest of Silesia had been a violation of the principle of legitimacy and of a solemn compact between princes.

During the spring and summer of 1849 Bismarck believed Prussia's great moment had arrived. At home the Hohenzollern monarchy was again firmly in the saddle; abroad there was no coalition capable of blocking her growth. England was apparently favorable to the idea of a little-German union under Frederick William IV. France was involved in internal difficulties. That power which had the most to lose, Austria, was still crippled by the revolt of Hungary. With the possible exception of Russia, no major power would have opposed Prussian hegemony in Germany. In his April speech against the Frankfurt constitution, Bismarck recommended that Prussia "give laws to Germany rather than receive them from others."[15]

The German union plan[16] excited his contempt not only because of its content, but because of the method chosen for its adoption. Frederick William eschewed violence and took the path of negotiation and parliamentary approval. In August Bismarck grasped immediately that the collapse of the Hungarian revolt had transformed the situation. The issue would be decided, he wrote, not by parliamentary procedure, but by diplomacy and war. "What we chatter and resolve about it has no more value than the moonlight reveries of a sentimental youth, who builds castles in the air and

[14] *GW*, VII, 4.
[15] Kohl, *Reden*, I, 93.
[16] See pp. 43-44.

believes that some event for which he hopes will make him into a great man."[17]

In the Landtag on September 6 he subjected the king to a scathing comparison. What would Frederick the Great have done had he been alive and ruler at such a moment? There were two possibilities. He might have allied Prussia with Austria, "the old comrade-in-arms," and aided her in the destruction of the "common enemy"—liberal and national revolution; this would have given to the Prussian king the "brilliant role" played in Europe by Czar Nicholas I; or at the risk of war he might have dictated a constitution to the German people "with the same right with which he conquered Silesia. . . . This would have been a truly national policy for Prussia." Either alone or in cooperation with Austria, Prussia would have gained for Germany "the power which is her due in Europe." "All of us want the Prussian eagle to spread his wings, to protect and rule from Memel to the Donnersberg." But these wings must remain free, unpinioned by a new Holy Roman Empire and unclipped by a liberal constitution of the Frankfurt type.[18]

This was no mere oratorical flourish. In his famous "blood and iron" speech of 1862 Bismarck reminisced about the "favorable moment" which had been allowed to "slip by." When he composed his memoirs in the 1890's the subject still teased him. Again he speculated over what a resolute monarch might have accomplished during that auspicious spring of 1849.[19] Even more striking is the fact that the two alternatives in the speech of September 6 were again uppermost in his mind during the years of crisis which ended in the civil war of 1866; should Prussia expand her power in Germany in agreement with Austria or alone and, if necessary, even against her?

3. A CONFLICT IN VALUES

We have learned that the power of the state represented for

---

[17] *GW*, xiv, 134-136; Kohl, *Reden*, i, 78.

[18] *Ibid.*, pp. 110-114. If he read this speech, Frederick William probably took no offense. When Hermann von Beckerath urged him to take the Frankfurt crown, he had replied, "If you could have directed your eloquent words to Frederick the Great, he would have been your man; I am no great ruler." Alexander Scharff, "König Friedrich Wilhelm IV, Deutschland und Europa in Frühjahr 1849," in *Geschichtliche Kräfte und Entscheidungen, Festschrift zum Fünfundsechsigsten Geburtstage von Otto Becker* (Wiesbaden, 1954), p. 145.

[19] Kohl, *Reden*, ii, 29-30; *GW*, vii, 422; xv, 46.

Bismarck: first, the only available means of self-expression and self-fulfillment; second, a fortress for the protection of the interests and values of his social class in a time of dynamic change; and, third, an instrument for advancing the Prussian national interest in foreign affairs. These last two functions were, however, not necessarily harmonious. While rejecting the ideological and religious reasons of the romantic conservatives against an egoistic policy of state, Bismarck was well aware that such a policy might prove very hazardous to aristocratic interests. The fate of the Junkers could not be completely separated from that of the European nobility as a whole; nor could the Hohenzollern dynasty hope to outlive for long the collapse of monarchical government in central and eastern Europe. Yet a policy of self-interest could also be severely handicapped by the necessity of upholding the holy alliance and observing the sovereign rights of the German princes. During the crisis which led to Olmütz, this conflict in values caused Bismarck to follow a zigzag course. When confronted by a choice between the interest of state and the conservative cause, he could not at this point make up his mind.

In November 1850 his initial reaction to the dismissal of Radowitz and the shift of Prussian policy from the German union to the issue of parity was exuberant and bellicose. "Now let war come, regardless where or with whom. Every Prussian sabre will glisten high and joyfully in the sun."[20] But after his arrival in Berlin from Schönhausen, where he had heard the news, he joined the Manteuffel clique in the cabinet to rally the conservative party for peace. Certain practical considerations influenced this shift in attitude: from August von Stockhausen, the minister of war, he heard that the army had been so deployed to deal with the revolutionary uprisings of the preceding year that now it could not even defend Berlin; two of Radowitz's supporters were still in the cabinet, and it was possible that the German union might yet become the Prussian war aim.[21] Nevertheless, his about-face was also

---

[20] *GW*, xiv, 179-180.

[21] *GW*, xv, 52-53; xiv, 181-182. Unknown to Bismarck, Stockhausen himself was chiefly responsible for Prussia's unpreparedness. The minister was opposed to the war, moreover, on political grounds. Friedrich Meinecke, *Radowitz und die deutsche Revolution* (Berlin, 1913), pp. 513-515; Ludwig Dehio, "Zur November-Krise des Jahres 1859," *Forschungen zur brandenburgischen und preussischen Geschichte*, xxxv (1923), 134-145. Apparently Bismarck was employed by Manteuffel as an agent in the diplomatic negotiations which led to Olmütz. *GW*, i, 2; xiv, 182-183, 185.

owing to a confusion in values. This is shown by his fluctuating attitudes over the occupation of Hesse-Kassel and the problem of parity between the dual powers in the confederation.[22]

As previously explained, the dual powers came close to war in November 1850 over whether Prussia, acting for the German union, or Austria and Bavaria, acting for the German Confederation, had the right to quell an internal disturbance in Hesse-Kassel. The issue was vital to Berlin, for across this principality ran the military roads connecting the eastern and western halves of the Prussian monarchy. One evening during the crisis, Bismarck had a heated argument with Leopold Gerlach. While the general maintained that conservative monarchies must at all costs avoid conflict, Bismarck replied that Prussia could not tolerate "too much Austrian impertinence." "We cannot permit 100,000 Bavarians and Austrians to take up positions between our eastern and western provinces." Gerlach took the view, however, that the issue was "purely juridical." In occupying Hesse-Kassel, Austria was simply acting for the confederation, whose constitution was still valid law in Germany. According to Gerlach's daughter, Bismarck made a shocking rejoinder: "He recognizes no law in foreign affairs, only convenience; Frederick II, 1740, is his example."[23]

Three days later, at the height of the crisis, however, he expressed views in a letter to his wife which were remarkably close to those of Gerlach. Radowitz, he declared, had sent Prussian troops into Hesse-Kassel "in violation of international and confederate law." Agreement had now almost been reached on the terms of a joint occupation. The question was "only a matter of military etiquette." How could anyone want to lay waste Europe over such a "petty issue"? "There is the greatest danger that for the sake of such bagatelles conservative armies, which love and respect each other, will slaughter one another and place the fate of Germany in the hands of foreigners." France lusted for the Rhineland. England would do nothing to aid Prussia. Her only allies would be the democrats of the national revolution. Should

[22] Concerning these issues and the climax of Olmütz, see pp. 43-44.

[23] *GW*, xiv, 182; Ludwig Gerlach, *Aufzeichnungen*, ii, 116. Leopold Gerlach's version of the debate is less revealing. *Denkwürdigkeiten*, i, 559, also 584. Years later a close friend remembered that in 1849 Bismarck had remarked, "What do I care about the [German] small states; my only concern is the security and increased power of Prussia." *GW*, vii, 18.

Prussia be victorious, they alone would profit. Had the understanding of Prussian honor sunk so low that it could be used for revolutionary purposes?[24]

But was the demand for parity worth a war? On November 19 Bismarck published an article in the *Kreuzzeitung* through which the public first learned of this demand. If Prussia were refused, it warned, "we also want war." The Junkers would raise the cry of their ancestors, "Dat walde Gott un kold Isen!"[25] Despite some suspicion, Bismarck seems to have been fairly confident that Austria would agree to this "reconciliation . . . at the expense of the small states."[26] Yet he noted with approval his government's intention to continue military preparations until the negotiation was concluded. If war came, he wrote on the 18th, it would be fought "only against Austria and Bavaria and, God helping us, we are equal to the test."[27]

On December 3 Bismarck delivered a major speech in defense of the Olmütz agreement of November 29. By this time it was apparent that Russia too had to be numbered among Prussia's potential foes. He began by pointing out the futility of war against "two of the three greatest continental powers, while the third mobilizes on our frontier, eager for conquest."[28] But then he admitted, "I would not shrink from such a war, nevertheless; in fact, I would advise it, if someone could prove to me that it is necessary, or could show me a worthy goal . . . which cannot be attained in any other way. Why do large states go to war nowadays?" His reply to this rhetorical question has become one of the most famous of Bismarck's quotations: "The only sound basis for a large state is its egoism and not romanticism; this is what distinguishes a large state necessarily from a small one. It is not worthy of a large state to fight for a thing which is not in its own interest. Just show me an objective worth a war, gentlemen, and I will agree with you."[29]

[24] *GW*, xiv, 182-183. The letter could scarcely have been more orthodox had it been written by Leopold Gerlach himself. See his *Denkwürdigkeiten*, i, 556 ff.

[25] Kohl, *Jahrbuch*, iii, 414-415.

[26] *GW*, xiv, 181, also 180, 183.

[27] *GW*, xiv, 181-182.

[28] This was a reference to France, which had mobilized an observation corps of 40,000 men on the Rhine frontier.

[29] What Bismarck had in mind was not the romantic cosmopolitanism of the Gerlachs, but the romantic sentimentalism which prompted Radowitz and Frederick William IV to embrace the national cause. This is shown by his letter to Sharlach, July 4, 1850. *GW*, xiv, 160-161. See also his article of November 19 in the *Kreuzzeitung*. Kohl, *Jahrbuch*, iii, 414-415.

The German union, he continued, was not such an objective, for it meant the mediatization of Prussia. A war to preserve the integrity of the Hessian constitution would be just as quixotic. Furthermore, the passage of Austrian troops across the military roads gave no cause for alarm. As long as Prussia had the use of their length, Austria could be permitted to cross their width! "Wars of principle" were to be decried; the only true criterion of foreign policy was the interest of state. The Prussian interest, he insisted, lay in the "avoidance of every shameful alliance with democracy" and in the attainment of parity with Austria. "We do not wish to make conquests. I do not want to discuss here how much this fact is to be deplored, nor how willingly perhaps one might conduct a war simply because his king and commander says, 'This country strikes my fancy and I want to have it.' . . . At the moment this question does not concern us." He admonished those eager for war to await the outcome of the conferences to be held in Dresden. Until a "positive result" was achieved there, Prussia ought not to demobilize. "Then there will still be time to go to war, if we actually cannot avoid it with honor, or do not wish to avoid it."[30]

Apparently he had not been told that at Olmütz Frederick William had already agreed to demobilize. We have no evidence of his immediate reaction to this information, but later sources suggest further ambivalence. In a *Kreuzzeitung* article published on April 20, 1851 he described the Olmütz agreement and the prevention of war as "very fortunate."[31] Certainly the reasons he had advanced for avoiding war over Hesse-Kassel were equally valid for the issue of parity. In order to fight a war against Austria and her German allies, possibly supported by Russia, Prussia would have been forced to enter a "shameful alliance" with the popular forces of liberal nationalism. In his memoirs, nevertheless, Bismarck was still critical of the government's failure in the Dresden conferences of January-May 1851 either to obtain concessions from Austria or to find grounds for war.[32]

During his early years in politics Bismarck wavered between the seemingly opposite poles of the interest of state and the inter-

---

30 Kohl, *Reden*, I, 261-279.

31 Schoeps, "Bismarck als Journalist," p. 10. Luckily for Bismarck's future career the king, angered by an accusation of treason against Radowitz in the article, never learned the author's name. *Ibid.*, p. 9.

32 *GW*, xv, 57.

est of conservative order. Faced by the necessity of choice, he was indecisive, but tended to give priority to the latter. During the next stage of his career the conflict was resolved and the priority reversed.

4. THE INTEREST OF STATE

The squire from Schönhausen was due a reward for his recent services to the monarchy. But what was suitable? Aside from his abortive service in Aachen and Potsdam, his experience in state administration was that of an assistant *Landrat* and dike captain on the Elbe. The tiny duchy of Anhalt-Bernburg needed a prime minister. Bismarck liked the idea: "the duke is a fool and the minister duke." But then it was proposed to make him a *Landrat*, which pleased him less. The final decision was startling. In April 1851 Frederick William, acting on Leopold Gerlach's advice, appointed him Prussian delegate to the diet of the German Confederation. His youthful dream had been fulfilled. Success as a deputy had vaulted him high over the laboring files of bureaucrats into the rank of the powerful. His was the most important post in the Prussian foreign service.[33]

Established in 1815 at the Congress of Vienna, the German Confederation was intended to provide security against the dangers of external attack and internal revolution. It was not a sovereign body, but a miniature United Nations composed of thirty-eight independent states of varying size and influence. Austria and Prussia, the "dual powers," were by far the largest and most powerful. By tradition Austria was the leading state and occupied the "presidency," a position of no executive authority other than that which her delegate was able to assume as presiding officer of the diet. After the dual powers came the "medium states": Bavaria, Saxony, Württemberg, Hanover, and Baden.[34] The "small

---

[33] *GW*, xiv, 190, 193, 202, 206-207; vii, 17, 31; Leopold Gerlach. *Denkwürdigkeiten*, i, 616, 618, 620, 637, 648; Hans J. Schoeps, "Neue Bismarckiana, 1851-1854," *Zeitschrift für Religions-und Geistesgeschichte*, iv (1952), 167-168. Incredulously Prince William asked, "And this militia lieutenant is supposed to be envoy to the confederation?" Heinrich von Poschinger, ed., *Preussens auswärtige Politik 1850 bis 1858, Unveröffentlichte Dokumente aus dem Nachlasse des Ministerpräsidenten Otto Freiherrn von Manteuffel* (Berlin, 1902), i, 208. Ludwig Gerlach, *Aufzeichnungen*, ii, 124. Because of his inexperience he was apprenticed for three months to a career diplomat, Theodor von Rochow.

[34] Denmark and Holland were also members, the former for Holstein and Lauenburg, the latter for Limburg and Luxemburg. Neither exercised much influence upon confederate affairs.

states" ranged from the two Hesses, of moderate size, to the "free cities" and the Thuringian states, whose tiny dimensions were a cartographer's nightmare. Like the UN general assembly, the diet was not a legislature, but a congress of diplomats whose votes were instructed by their respective governments. The most vital questions could be passed only by unanimous vote, matters of less moment by simple majority.

Until 1848 the confederation had been a relatively stable organization. In the interest of their entente with Russia in European affairs, the dual powers avoided friction in Germany. While protecting the prerogatives of the presidency, Metternich made no effort to increase its authority. Before Radowitz the Prussian government had no serious desire to alter the structure of the confederation or to challenge Austrian leadership in its affairs. The rare cases of positive action taken by the diet were the result of prior agreement between Vienna and Berlin.

After the revolution neither power was inclined to return completely to this state of affairs. While Manteuffel hoped to attain parity between Austria and Prussia, Schwarzenberg desired to strengthen Austrian primacy in the diet by increasing the powers of the presidency and reducing the number of matters requiring unanimity in the actions of that body.[35] In the struggle which ensued, the lesser states played an important role. The dual powers had in the past combined to dominate them, but now each needed their support against the other. Until the climax of 1866, therefore, the contest between Austria and Prussia was essentially one for control over the other members of the confederation.

The lesser states tended to side with that power which, at the moment, was feared the least.[36] This was usually Austria. Because of the events of 1848-1850 the German princes were alarmed over the possibility of Prussian expansion in Germany. The parliaments of Frankfurt and Erfurt had shown, moreover, that the hopes and ambitions of the little-German nationalists were cen-

[35] Arnold O. Meyer, *Bismarcks Kampf mit Österreich am Bundestag zu Frankfurt, 1851-1859* (Berlin, 1927), pp. 19 ff., 66 ff.; Heinrich Ritter von Srbik, *Deutsche Einheit, Idee und Wirklichkeit vom Heiligen Reich bis Königgrätz* (Munich, 1935-1942), i, 385 ff.; ii, 92 ff.

[36] On the policies of the medium states see Sigmund Meiboom, *Studien zur deutschen Politik Bayerns in den Jahren 1851-1859, Schriftenreihe zur bayerischen Landesgeschichte*, Vol. vi (Munich, 1931), and Walther P. Fuchs, *Die deutschen Mittelstaaten und die Bundesreform 1853-1860, Historische Studien*, Vol. 256 (Berlin, 1934).

tered upon the Hohenzollern monarchy. The victory of this form of the national idea would mean mediatization and perhaps dispossession of the lesser dynasties. Hence they usually supported Austria on any issue of moment. Prussia found herself the minority party in the diet.

Under these circumstances any Prussian delegate would have faced an uphill struggle in Frankfurt. Bismarck's temperament, however, aggravated the quarrel. In later years he described himself as having been in a "state of political innocence" and a "rather good Austrian" when he entered the diet in May 1851.[37] But this was hardly the case. On informing his wife of the appointment on April 28, he wrote: ". . . I cannot refuse to accept, although I foresee that it will be a fruitless and thorny office. In spite of my best efforts I shall lose the good opinion of many people. But it would be cowardice to decline."[38] Whose esteem did he fear to lose? Was it that of Gerlach, who expected him to support at all costs the cause of conservative solidarity with Austria? To others he is said to have remarked that the German small states were but a "hindrance" to Prussia; Austrian "arrogance" must be checked "at any price."[39]

His first letters and reports from Frankfurt show that even before the diet had undertaken any serious business Bismarck was sharply critical of his Austrian counterpart, Count Thun, and of the confederation as such. One week after arriving he wrote, "No one, not even the most evil-intentioned skeptic of a democrat, would believe what charlatanry and pomposity lie hidden in this diplomacy." On the same day he wrote Hermann Wagener that he had "little hope for favorable results" from the diet. Once the

---

[37] *GW*, II, 23; III, 239; VII, 113, 121-122; XIV, 441, 558; XV, 198. Most historians have accepted these statements at face value. Proof is also seen in the fact that on March 6 he had defended the diet in the chamber of deputies as the most successful protector of Germany's unity and power since the Hohenstaufen. Kohl, *Reden*, I, 327-328; A. O. Meyer, *Bismarcks Kampf*, pp. 22-25. But this was his parliamentary duty as a spokesman of his party. Throughout the period leading to Olmütz his attitude toward Austria had been charged with hostility and suspicion, softened at times by concern over the forces of revolution. In later years he exaggerated the change which occurred in his attitude at Frankfurt in order to heighten his case against Austria as the sole source of the friction which rent the confederation. More accurate is what he wrote to Otto Manteuffel at the end of his first month, "When I came here, my expectations of results from the diet's deliberations were not high, but since then they have decreased." *GW*, I, 17.

[38] *GW*, XIV, 206-207.

[39] Richard Schwemer, *Geschichte der freien Stadt Frankfurt a. M., 1814-1866* (Frankfurt a. M., 1918), III/2, 61.

two men had set up a channel of communication safe from espionage, he was more explicit. "The Austrians intrigue under the mask of jovial good fellowship; they lie, steal dispatches (even the most upright among them), gamble, whore, and seek to get the better of us in the small formalities which have thus far been the whole of our activity."[40]

As the quarrel in the diet developed, he reached the conclusion that the primary motive in the conduct of foreign policy is self-interest. Like a "natural scientist," his sole aim was to see things as they actually are.[41] "In politics no one does anything for another, unless he also finds it in his own interest to do so."[42] This is the one fundamental rule of all political behavior. Such causes as the "principle of legitimacy" and the "interest of Germany" are moral camouflage with which statesmen conceal the egoistic aims of their countries.[43] "Alliances between large states," he wrote, "are of value only when they express the actual interests of both parties."[44] Conflicts, on the other hand, are the inevitable result of contradictory interests. The clash between Austria and Prussia was not arbitrary. History and geography were its source, not the whims of monarchs and ministers.[45] "In the middle of Europe it is impossible to wait passively upon the march of events or to try to stay removed from them." "If we do not prepare for ourselves the role of the hammer, there will be nothing left but that of the anvil."[46]

The quest for political advantage, he concluded, must be pursued with complete objectivity. For the statesman, as for the natural scientist, the only trustworthy guide is reason. Reward, revenge, and punishment have no place in politics. "Not even the king himself has the right to subordinate the interests of the fatherland to personal feelings of love or hatred toward foreigners."[47] Since the pursuit of rational self-interest seems natural to the conduct of states, he presumed that it is, like all things in

40 *GW*, xiv, 213-214, 217, 228; i, 17, 22; xv, 198. See the letters of June 22 and July 4 to Leopold Gerlach and Kleist-Retzow. "The Austrians are and remain card sharpers." *GW*, xiv, 219-224, 230-231. Note also the sense of injury with which he reacted to his first interview with Thun. *GW*, vii, 23-24.

41 *GW*, i, 40, 70, 104; iii, 190; vii, 38; xiv, 441.

42 *GW*, ii, 231; xiv, 473. Although written in 1857, this judgment was already implicit in one of the first letters written from Frankfurt. *GW*, i, 17.

43 *GW*, i, 401-402, 404, 456; iii, 147-148; xiv, 327, 332, 335. See Rechberg's report of his talk with Bismarck on June 19, 1857. A. O. Meyer, *Bismarcks Kampf*, pp. 551, 558.

44 *GW*, i, 515; iii, 382; xiv, 465.   45 *GW*, i, 70, 119-120; ii, 311; xiv, 441.

46 *GW*, ii, 231; xiv, 474, also 465, 467.   47 *GW*, xiv, 465.

nature, a part of the divine plan. The duty of the statesman is to discern that interest and dedicate himself to its fulfillment. This was for Bismarck, the devout Christian, a moral compulsion from which there could be no escape.[48]

The necessities of state, however, inevitably conflict with other values likewise sanctified by religious faith. In contrast to the Gerlachs, Bismarck held that the ordinary codes of human conduct are inapplicable to the statesman. He was highly critical of the "chivalric" attitude of Frederick William, who disdained "to exploit the embarrassments of other states" for the benefit of his own.[49] In his eyes this was a neglect of duty and of the responsibility imposed by the deity. His letters to Berlin complain bitterly of the lies told by the Austrian delegates; nevertheless, he was aware that truth could sometimes be very dangerous to the interest of state.[50] One of his most striking talents was the capacity to mold an argument and create conviction by emphasizing the partial truth. But where an outright lie seemed essential he did not hesitate. What he detested was the unnecessary lie told out of habit, incaution, or personal malice. Looking backward at the end of his career, the sage of Friedrichsruh recognized the double standard of the statesman-cavalier and expressed the hope that in the hereafter his conduct as a Prussian officer would compensate for his sins as a diplomat.[51]

But what of the social and political viewpoint of conservatism? Must this value likewise be sacrificed on the altar of the interest of state? By no means did Bismarck abandon his belief that the protection of conservative institutions was a proper function of foreign policy. Where the Prussian interest did not interfere, he participated in the witch-hunts of the diet against liberal laws and constitutions in the lesser states.[52] In two letters, written to Gerlach and Manteuffel in 1857-1858 he made his viewpoint clear:

"I also recognize as my own the principle of struggle against revolution, but . . . in politics I do not believe it possible to follow principle in such a way that its most extreme implications always take precedence over every other consideration. . . ."

---

[48] *GW*, I, 238; II, 125-126; III, 148; XIV, 468-469, 549. Vossler, "Bismarcks Ethos," pp. 263 ff.

[49] *GW*, I, 435.

[50] *GW*, I, 389. "If I can't lie, I can't accomplish anything," he once remarked. Ludwig Gerlach, *Aufzeichnungen*, II, 273.

[51] *GW*, IX, 161; also VIII, 594.   [52] Augst, *Bismarcks Stellung*, pp. 29 ff.

"In representing Prussia abroad one cannot be partisan to the same extreme degree as in domestic affairs. . . ."[53]

Both motives remained, in other words, but priority now belonged to the interest of state.[54]

This change did not occur solely because Bismarck, in his new occupation as a diplomat, was in closer contact with the realities of foreign affairs and more aware of its problems. Even more important was the fact that he had a better perspective of the events of 1848. After Gotha it was apparent that moderate liberals had recoiled from their momentary alliance with the radical left. Shocked by the subterranean forces exposed in the revolution, they were forced into greater dependence than ever upon established authority. After the failure of the revolts in Saxony and Baden, the radicals were in a state of disintegration. By boycotting the first elections held under the three-class system in Prussia (1849), they delivered parliament into the hands of the conservatives.

Most striking of all, however, was the political apathy into which the mass of the population had fallen. Scarcely a ripple remained of the tidal wave which swept Germany in March 1848. In the Prussian election of 1855 only one-sixth of the eligible voters went to the polls. By a program of agrarian reform and guild protectionism, the regime of Otto Manteuffel did its best to appease the peasant and artisan classes. As the decade progressed, the tempo of industrialization and economic activity increased. Germany was caught in the grip of a great material revolution which for a time completely absorbed the energies of the bourgeoisie. Politics were left to the government and the Conservative Party.[55]

[53] GW, xiv, 470; ii, 323, also 227.

[54] It has generally been assumed that his experience in Frankfurt converted Bismarck from a "partisan politician" into a "statesman," that he lost his one-sided interest in the aristocratic-monarchical cause and thereafter devoted himself to the interest of state. What occurred, however, was an important shift in emphasis, not a fundamental conversion. See Hans Mombauer, *Bismarcks Realpolitik als Ausdruck seiner Weltanschauung, Historische Studien*, Vol. 291 (Berlin, 1936), pp. 37-38.

[55] See the excellent description of Prussia at mid-century by Ferdinand Fischer, *Preussen am Abschlusse der ersten Hälfte des neunzehnten Jahrhunderts* (Berlin, 1876); also Heinrich Heffter, *Die deutsche Selbstverwaltung im 19. Jahrhundert* (Stuttgart, 1950), pp. 349 ff.; Theodore S. Hamerow, *Restoration, Revolution, Reaction: Economics and Politics in Germany, 1815-1871* (Princeton, 1958), pp. 219 ff.; Hans Walter, *Die innere Politik des Ministers von Manteuffel und der Ursprung der Reaktion in Preussen* (Berlin, 1910), pp. 52 ff.

CHAPTER FOUR

THE STRATEGY OF *REALPOLITIK*

1. THE ART OF THE POSSIBLE

N HIS years of retirement after 1890 Bismarck had the leisure and occasion to express his views more fully than before on the nature of politics. These reflections were based, of course, on his entire political experience of nearly five decades. They have validity, nevertheless, for his early years, for they show toward what conclusions he was heading when he forged the techniques of political strategy which were to make him the most effective statesman of his century.[1]

His skepticism concerning the chances of the statesman in the stream of time was a recurrent theme. "By himself the individual can create nothing; he can only wait until he hears God's footsteps resounding through events and then spring forward to grasp the hem of his mantle—that is all."[2] In a person of other temperament this awareness of the smallness of man and the inadequacy of his best efforts would have ended in resignation and apathy. But, as we have seen, Bismarck was driven by a vital compulsion to seize the helm and steer. If man could do little, it was at least his moral duty to accomplish what he could.

The statesman's task is complicated not only by the over-powering flow of the time stream, but by the unceasing clash of contradictory forces: "It is a principle of creation and of the whole of nature that life consists of strife. Among the plants—as a forester I experience this in my cultures—through the insects to the birds, from birds of prey up to man himself: strife is everywhere. Without struggle there can be no life and, if we wish to continue living, we must also be reconciled to further struggles."[3] He described these struggling forces as states, nations, social classes, political parties, economic and sectional interests, and even feuding individuals. The conflict of opposites he believed to be a condition of

---

[1] O. Pflanze, "Bismarck's 'Realpolitik,'" *The Review of Politics*, xx (October, 1958), 492-514.
[2] A. O. Meyer, *Bismarcks Glaube im Spiegel der "Loosungen und Lehrtexte,"* in *Münchener Historische Abhandlungen*, Erste Reihe, i (Munich, 1933), 9-10.
[3] *GW*, xiii, 555.

human progress and hence an intentional part of the divine plan.[4]

The unending clash of contradictory forces and the sweep of the time-stream make the tasks of the statesman forever inconclusive and beset his course with grave uncertainties: "My entire life was spent gambling for high stakes with other people's money. I could never foresee exactly whether my plans would succeed. . . . Politics is a thankless job, chiefly because everything depends on chance and conjecture. One has to reckon with a series of probabilities and improbabilities and base one's plans upon this reckoning. . . . As long as he lives the statesman is always unprepared. In the attainment of that for which he strives he is too dependent on the participation of others, a fluctuating and incalculable factor. . . . Even after the greatest success he cannot say with certainty, 'Now it is achieved; I am done with it,' and look back at what has been accomplished with complacency. . . . To be sure, one can bring individual matters to a conclusion, but even then there is no way of knowing what the consequences will be. . . . In politics there is no such thing as complete certainty and definitive results. . . . Everything goes continually uphill, downhill."[5]

Since this was the nature of political life, Bismarck concluded that its phenomena could not be systematized: "There is no exact science of politics, just as there is none for political economy. Only professors are able to package the sum of the changing needs of cultural man into scientific laws. . . . Already many have spoken of my political principles. The professors and their imitators in the newspapers constantly decry the fact that I have not revealed a set of principles by which I directed my policies. . . . Politics is neither arithmetic nor mathematics. To be sure, one has to reckon with given and unknown factors, but there are no rules and formulas with which to sum up the results in advance."[6]

"Professor" was a very nasty word in Bismarck's vocabulary. Whom did he have in mind? Adam Smith, Malthus, Ricardo, Sismondi, Say, and Bastiat were the names he mentioned. The "scientific laws" to which he referred, then, were such as *laissez-faire*, the "iron law of wages," and the Malthusian theory. The economic doctrines of liberalism, he argued, were formulated in the interest of industrial capitalism by "English clergymen," "Jewish bank-

---

[4] *GW*, xiii, 559, 570; ix, 8 ff. During the conflict of 1870, he described war as the "natural condition of mankind." *GW*, vii, 388.

[5] *GW*, ix, 397 ff.   [6] *GW*, ix, 90, 93, 420.

ers," and "French merchants and jurists." "The whole political economy given us by the academicians and the press is a political economy for commerce and not for agriculture as well." It ignores "the actual relationships and overriding circumstances," and "speaks only of one-sided, private interests where general interests are primarily at stake."[7]

What Bismarck objected to, however, was not merely the partiality of the economic doctrines of Manchesterism, but the whole rationalistic belief in the existence of natural laws in society equivalent to those in the structure of the universe. The natural world he knew, as the owner of fields and forests, was the disorderly one of growing things and not that of algebraic equations and physical laws. In the popular biology of social Darwinism he found a better parallel between science and society. His views reflected the revolt of the nineteenth century against the seventeenth and eighteenth centuries, the period of biological discovery against that of astronomy and physics, the age of romanticism against that of rationalism, and, last but hardly least, the outlook of the conservative against that of the liberal.

If not a scientific discipline, what was politics in Bismarck's view? He gave his answer on several occasions:

"Politics is less a science than an art. It is not a subject which can be taught. One must have the talent for it. Even the best advice is of no avail if improperly carried out."

"Politics is not in itself an exact and logical science, but it is the capacity to choose in each fleeting moment of the situation that which is least harmful or most opportune."

"Because they have as yet scarcely outgrown the political nursery, the Germans cannot accustom themselves to regard political affairs as a study of the possible."[8]

The art of the possible—this was Bismarck's conception of the craft of the statesman. Every great artist, however, is a compound of genius and advanced knowledge in the techniques of his medium. Hence we have a right to ask: what were the essential techniques of the wizard of the Wilhelmstrasse in his quest for the possible?

If the study of the past could yield no science of politics, Bis-

---

[7] *GW*, ix, 90.

[8] *GW*, ix, 399; xiii, 468; ix, 93; also xiii, 177. "Politics," he remarked on another occasion, "is a science of relatives." *GW*, iii, 251.

marck was far from thinking that it had no value for the statesman: "For me history existed primarily to be learned from. Even if the events do not repeat themselves, at least circumstances and characters do. By observing and studying them one can stimulate and educate one's own mind. I have learned from the mistakes of my predecessors in the art of statesmanship and have built up my 'theory,' although one ought not to speak of such in the narrow sense of the word."[9] From the mistakes of Napoleon I he learned to exercise "wise moderation after the greatest successes," from those of Napoleon III not to "confuse slyness with falsehood." "I spoke the stark truth. That they often didn't believe me and then afterward felt very surprised and disillusioned is not my fault."[10]

Deceptive frankness and moderation in victory were important weapons in Bismarck's tactical armory. It is doubtful, nevertheless, that he depended much on historical precedent as a guide to political action. While he may indeed have learned from the fate of the first Bonaparte, Napoleon III was after all not a historical figure, but a contemporary opponent on the chessboard of European politics. Although well versed in recent European history, Bismarck used its facts primarily as a reservoir of argument to support decisions made on other grounds.[11] His knowledge of political tactics stemmed more from his own personal experience and intuition than from historical example:

"More than anything else politics demands the capacity to recognize intuitively in each new situation where the correct path lies. The statesman must see things coming ahead of time and be prepared for them. . . . An indispensable prerequisite is patience. He must be able to wait until the right moment has come and must precipitate nothing, no matter how great the temptation."

"From childhood I have been a hunter and fisher. In both cases waiting for the right moment has been the rule which I have applied to politics. I have often had to stand for long periods in the hunting blind and let myself be covered and stung by insects before the moment came to shoot."

"Correct evaluation of the opponent is also indispensable to

[9] *GW*, IX, 90. [10] *GW*, IX, 93-94.

[11] Bismarck's use and conception of history have been critically analyzed by Helmuth Wolff, *Geschichtsauffassung und Politik in Bismarcks Bewusstsein* (Munich, 1926). See also Maria Fehling, *Bismarcks Geschichtskenntnis* (Stuttgart, 1922).

success. This means the exercise of caution. In chess one should never base a move on the positive assumption that the other player will in turn make a certain move. For it may be that this won't happen, and then the game is easily lost. One must always reckon with the possibility that the opponent will at the last moment make a move other than that expected and act accordingly. In other words, one must always have two irons in the fire."

"Many paths led to my goal. I had to try all of them one after the other, the most dangerous at the end. It was not my way to be single-handed in political action."[12]

Patience and careful timing, the intuitive recognition of the correct path, and the accurate evaluation of his opponents—these were all typical characteristics of Bismarckian statecraft. But his "two irons" and "many paths" were the most important revelation of all. They are clues to a general technique of political strategy which he developed in the diplomatic quarrels of the 1850's and later applied in many other situations in both domestic and foreign affairs.

Essentially, his method was the constant provision for alternative courses of political action. "In major domestic and foreign affairs and questions," wrote a contemporary, "Prince Bismarck likes to provide himself with an alternative in order to be able to decide the same in one of two opposed directions."[13] Frequently these alternatives were multiple solutions to political problems which could be simultaneously explored until the moment of final choice. Often they were multiple possibilities of alliance with opposed political forces between which a final choice had to be avoided as long as possible.

In its many variations the strategy of alternatives provided Bismarck with a means of navigation amid the shifting currents and treacherous eddies of the time-stream. It enabled him to gain and retain the initiative. The knowledge that his quiver held more than one arrow gave him the confidence and sureness that most of his opponents lacked. If one bolt fell short of the mark, another was ready to follow. By this means he minimized the risk, if at the last moment the most desirable objective appeared too costly. But the availability of an alternative could also be used to remove

12 *GW*, ix, 400, 50; xiii, 468.
13 Max Freiherr Pergler von Perglas, Bavarian envoy in Berlin, quoted in Fritz von Rummel, *Das Ministerium Lutz und seine Gegner, 1871-1882* (Munich, 1935), p. 2; also Srbik, *Deutsche Einheit*, iii, 70.

obstacles along the way. By candidly revealing the availability of a course more disadvantageous to his opponents than to himself, he might force them to yield. His alternatives were seldom bluffs. No matter how drastic, they were usually practical threats which he was ready to carry out if so compelled. By monopolizing the alternative possibilities which the situation afforded, he often severely restricted his adversary's sphere of action.

His awareness of a world animated by the constant clash of competing forces made Bismarck sensitive to the possibility of exploiting their mutual antagonisms for the benefit of his own cause. Usually he sought the middle ground between conflicting interests, the point from which alliance with either was possible. By attaining and preserving freedom of choice between opposed interests he was often able to bring them into an equilibrium of mutual frustration. Through the static immobilization of hostile interests he gained the liberty to promote his own. The position for which he constantly strove was that of the fulcrum in a balance of power. By seizing the position of greatest mobility, he maneuvered others into those of least latitude.

Sometimes Bismarck's alternatives were actually successive stages through which he hoped to pass toward the achievement of a desired objective.[14] The immediate arrangement with which he met a particular situation was often intended to be but the beginning point from which to progress toward a hidden goal of more drastic character. What could not be brought into existence by an independent act of creation might eventually be achieved through the principle of organic growth. Today's acorn was tomorrow's oak. He sought to utilize the motion of social and political forces by placing in their paths the objects of his interest to be pushed into positions beyond his own strength to attain.

These related patterns of strategy are evident in the recommendations of the 1850's and 1860's with which Bismarck urged his government into a more aggressive policy toward Austria.

2. THE FULCRUM OF POWER

Like Bismarck, Otto von Manteuffel was a realistic, not a romantic, conservative. Yet the two men differed greatly in political temperament and technique. While determined to surrender noth-

---

[14] This is the general theme advanced recently by Otto Becker, *Bismarcks Ringen um Deutschlands Gestaltung* (Heidelberg, 1958).

ing to Austria, the foreign minister refused to take the initiative against her and strove to avoid a public quarrel. A pessimist, he feared the consequences of war for the conservative order. He favored reason and persuasion over threat and force. But Bismarck's "lust for combat," his personal ego and Prussian pride, soon brought him into open conflict with Count Thun, the Austrian delegate.[15]

At stake were petty issues of protocol as well as matters of high policy. In the diet chamber, where previously only the presidential envoy had smoked, the Junker drew out a cigar and asked Thun for a light. When the count received him in shirt-sleeves on a hot day, he pulled off his own jacket. Forced to wait a few minutes in the presidential antechamber, he stalked out. Neither Thun, nor his successor, Prokesch-Osten, had the nerves to endure this kind of rancor. Count Rechberg, who arrived in 1855, had more endurance. But even he came close to a duel with the Prussian delegate.[16]

Back of this personal friction lay for Bismarck a serious political purpose: the determination to exact from Austria full recognition of Prussia's equality of status in the confederation. The Austrians had to realize that prior agreement with Berlin was necessary on any important business to be transacted by the diet. From another standpoint his aim was establishment of the Prussian right of veto; votes had to be "weighed as well as counted."[17] While he acted under orders from Berlin, the character which the struggle assumed in Frankfurt was determined by the Prussian delegate. From his busy brain poured a steady stream of adroitly worded reports and letters designed to influence the decisions of Manteuffel and, through Leopold Gerlach, the king as well.

In Frankfurt his first tactic was obstruction. "When Austria hitches a horse in front, we hitch one behind."[18] With clever amendments he vitiated the importance of measures backed by the Hofburg. In cases of the least doubt he denied the jurisdiction of

[15] Gunther von Richthofen, *Die Politik Bismarcks und Manteuffels in den Jahren 1851-1858* (Leipzig, 1915), pp. 31ff.; Srbik, *Deutsche Einheit*, II, 174-175.

[16] Meyer, *Bismarcks Kampf*, pp. 41 ff.; Eduard von Wertheimer, *Bismarck im politischen Kampf* (Berlin, 1930, pp. 9-10).

[17] *GW*, II, 259; also I, 114 ff., 128 ff., and Manteuffel's instruction in Heinrich von Poschinger, ed., *Preussen im Bundestag, 1851 bis 1859* (Leipzig, 1882-1884), I, 1-3.

[18] Quoted in Srbik, *Deutsche Einheit*, II, 175.

the diet or insisted that voting be by unanimity rather than by majority. Traveling from court to court in southern Germany, he endeavored to win the confidence of rulers and statesmen in the hope of splitting apart the opposing coalition. Where persuasion failed, he incited the fear of retribution and sowed the seeds of mutual jealousy and discord. As a last resort he threatened Prussia's secession.

These tactics were entirely negative. Naturally they were unsatisfactory to a person of Bismarck's temperament. He wanted not only to halt the Austrian, but to launch the Prussian offensive. In one of his first reports to Manteuffel he doubted that the confederation could ever meet the needs of the Prussian state. In the Zollverein he saw a useful precedent. Through similar treaties he proposed to expand Prussian influence "within the geographical area made dependent upon us by nature." By promoting the material interests of the population Prussia could make the confederation superfluous—a useless shell which would drop away from the growing kernel.[19] We shall see this possibility constantly recurring in his calculations down to the year 1870.

From the beginning, however, his main reliance was upon the coercive rather than the evolutionary approach. What Prussia required, he concluded, was a new source of power capable of forcing the opposition either to bend or buckle. Isolated in Germany, she must seek in Europe allies with which to threaten the security of Austria and the lesser states. "Fear and fear alone, that is the only thing which has any effect in the palaces from Munich to Bückeburg."[20]

This meant that the Prussian alliance with Austria must be abandoned in European as well as in German politics. In the past the eastern coalition between the dual powers and Russia had served two purposes: it had been the fortress of conservatism in Europe and had prevented the German medium states from seeking to escape the domination of Austria and Prussia by allying themselves with France. Bismarck maintained that the coalition no longer served either of these functions. Internally Germany now appeared fairly safe from a repetition of the events of March 1848, and abroad in Paris the second republic had yielded to the second empire, which he regarded as less menacing to the Euro-

19 GW, i, 17, 99, 140; ii, 321; iii, 268; vii, 24-25; xiv, 223.
20 GW, xiv, 372.

pean order. Hence Prussia could afford to loosen her tie with Austria and create the specter of alliance with France.

During January 1853 Bismarck commenced to advocate such a policy in a series of letters to Gerlach and Manteuffel. It was wrong, he argued, for conservatives in Berlin to treat the imperial pretensions of Napoleon with public contempt. The sneers of the *Kreuzzeitung* at the coming marriage of Louis to Eugénie de Montijo were needlessly provocative. "I am convinced that it could be a great misfortune for Prussia if her government should enter an alliance with France, but, even if we make no use of it, we ought never to remove from the consideration of our allies the possibility that under certain conditions we might choose this evil as the lesser of two." By wiping out the impression that Prussian antagonism toward France was irrevocable, it would be possible to regain that "freedom of position which our illustrious ruling house has in the past used so successfully for the expansion of its power."[21]

These documents are among the most significant of Bismarck's Frankfurt period. Here he revealed for the first time his conviction that Prussia must find *outside* Germany the sources of power with which to dominate the lesser states and force Austria into submission. A few years later he gave his most succinct statement of what he had discovered at this time: "In the last analysis the influence of a power in peace depends upon the strength which it can develop in war and on the alliances with which it can enter into the conflict. . . . The conquest of influence in Germany depends entirely upon the belief among the confederate states in the possibility, probability, or certainty that Prussia can count on foreign alliances in the event of war."[22] France appeared to be the only major power available for this purpose. Shunned because of his

21 *GW*, I, 285-287; XIV, 289-291; also I, 291. The view that Bismarck changed his attitude toward the eastern entente after the Crimean war is inaccurate. Thus A. O. Meyer, *Bismarcks Kampf*, pp. 308-309; Mombauer, *Realpolitik*, pp. 49 ff.; Egmont Zechlin, *Bismarck und die Grundlegung der deutschen Grossmacht* (Stuttgart, 1930), pp. 102-103. The change began in the winter of 1852-1853 before the eastern crisis arose. The first sign was a letter of November 24, 1852 to Manteuffel deploring the anti-Bonapartism of the king. *GW*, I, 261. To Leopold Gerlach, on December 4, he still maintained that friction with Austria must be restricted to Germany. But the letters of January 27, 1853 criticizing the attitude of the *Kreuzzeitung* show a complete reversal in viewpoint. Later he used the consequences of the Crimean war to justify a policy actually arrived at on other grounds. *GW*, II, 141, 167, 217; III, 266; XIV, 352.

22 *GW*, II, 221, also 231; XIV, 465.

name and revolutionary origin, Napoleon III was a pariah in the society of European monarchs. He needed allies.

The very policy which Bismarck now advocated for Prussia was precisely that for which he never tired of condemning Austria and the medium states. He often accused Austria of a willingness to come to terms with Napoleon III in order to exert pressure on Prussia in Germany. In tones bordering on righteous indignation he frequently warned that the medium states of the south would at the slightest opportunity return to the *Rheinbundpolitik*.[23] This term was the equivalent of "traitor," for it harked back to the time when the southern dynasties sold out to Napoleon I in return for their own aggrandizement.

At this time, nevertheless, Bismarck was sincere in disclaiming any wish to see Prussia actually allied with France. His intention was not to substitute one coalition for another, but to adopt a strategy of alternative pressures. He desired a mobile policy unencumbered by a firm commitment to any power, free to form a temporary intimacy when and where the situation demanded. Prussia should seek to hold a mediate position between Austria and France. Unbound to either, she could exploit the one against the other, making a definite choice only in the extremity of war.[24]

Here Bismarck hoped to find the coercive force which he so vainly sought within the confederation. Such a policy, he believed, would strike terror in the ranks of the lesser states, for a Franco-Prussian alliance might be the prelude to a series of annexations such as had so often changed the political geography of Germany. Fright would bring them under the influence of Prussia and reverse the situation which had hitherto existed in the diet. Pressed into the minority, Austria would now be forced to respond to the Prussian will.

At the time it was conceived this tactical scheme had a major shortcoming. As long as the Austro-Russian segment of the eastern alliance remained intact, a Prussian flirtation with France might not have the effect Bismarck desired. With backing from Russia, Austria could still make a firm stand in Germany. Even while Bismarck wrote, however, a new crisis was developing on the

23 *GW*, xiv, 246, 284-286, 292, 295.

24 In Berlin Legation Councilor Küpfer also advocated such a policy. Heinrich von Poschinger, ed., *Unter Friedrich Wilhelm IV, Denkwürdigkeiten des Ministers Otto Freiherrn von Manteuffel 1848-1858* (Berlin, 1900-1901), ii, 268 ff.

eastern horizon which soon dissolved the bond between Vienna and Petersburg.

3. THE CRIMEAN WAR

In May-July 1853 Turkish resistance to Russia's demand for a protectorate over the Christian population in the Ottoman empire led to Russian occupation of the Danubian principalities. Encouraged by Britain and France, the sultan declared war in October. Six months later Europe stumbled into a major conflict which its statesmen neither wanted nor had the wisdom to avoid. Inevitably the conflict placed Austria and Prussia under severe pressure. The geographical difficulty of attacking Russia made their participation on the western side seem vital to England and France, while the Czarist government confidently expected their assistance as conservative powers and members of the holy alliance.

In Vienna, Count Buol, foreign minister since the death of Schwarzenberg in 1852, was alarmed by the appearance of Russian troops on the lower Danube. He also saw in the affair a golden chance to shut Russia permanently out of the Balkans and establish Austrian power in the area. But conservative ministers opposed him, and Franz Joseph was dubious. At first Buol steered down the middle, seeking both to avoid antagonizing Petersburg and to win the friendship of the western powers. During 1854-1855 he moved dangerously close to war against Russia. For this he needed the backing of Prussia and the German Confederation.[25]

To Bismarck the proper course seemed obvious: Prussia should exploit the Austrian need to satisfy her own. Early in 1854 he advised Manteuffel to wait until Austria was thoroughly involved in the east. Once her troops were deployed on the Balkan front, Prussia should suddenly present the Hofburg with the alternatives of Prussian support or hostility. The price of the former ought to be a secret treaty establishing separate spheres of influence, "partly geographical, partly topical," between the dual powers in the German Confederation. In the diet the Austrians must respect the Prussian veto. If refused, Prussia could attack the exposed Bo-

25 On Austrian policy see Heinrich Friedjung, *Der Krimkrieg und die österreichische Politik* (Stuttgart, 1907); Kurt Borries, "Zur Politik der deutschen Mächte in der Zeit des Krimkrieges und der italienischen Einigung," *Historische Zeitschrift*, Vol. 151 (1934-1935), pp. 294 ff.; S. A. Kaehler, "Realpolitik zur Zeit des Krimkrieges—Eine Säkularbetrachtung," *ibid.*, Vol. 174 (1952), pp. 436 ff.

hemian frontier. "The great crises provide the weather for Prussia's growth." She was not a "satiated state."[26]

In Berlin there was no unanimity of opinion or purpose. The ultra-conservatives were pro-Russian, Prince William and his coterie pro-western. Buffeted by many counsels, Frederick William steered an erratic course, alternately drawn by the desire for neutrality and driven by the fear of isolation. His conservative soul was tortured by the prospect that the eastern alliance might collapse; above all he wished to preserve Austro-Prussian solidarity in European politics. Hoping to control Austria, he granted a renewal (April 1854) of the defensive alliance which had bound the dual powers since 1851. In addition to a mutual territorial guarantee, it was established that Austria might act in the east only in agreement with Prussia. But if she should become involved with Russia, Berlin would mobilize 100,000 troops on the eastern frontier—200,000 if the situation should worsen. Immediately the Hofburg took advantage of the compact. In June Buol delivered an ultimatum, forcing the Czar to withdraw his troops from the Danubian principalities, which Austria herself now proceeded to occupy.[27]

Bismarck's reaction to the April treaty illustrates again his conception of political strategy. If Austria invoked the treaty, he advised Frederick William, Prussia ought to assemble her troops "not in the neighborhood of Lissa, but in Upper Silesia." Here they would be in a position "to cross either the Russian or the Austrian borders with equal facility." Since the forces of all other nations were now deployed in the east, this was the true fulcrum of European power. "With 200,000 men your majesty would at this moment become the master of the entire European situation, would be able to dictate the peace and win for Prussia a worthy position in Germany." Although receptive, Frederick William was mostly just amused by this bold idea. "A man of Napoleon's sort," he replied, "can commit such acts of violence, but not I."[28]

[26] GW, i, 427-430; xiv, 347, 368 ff.

[27] On the Prussian course see Kurt Borries, Preussen im Krimkrieg, 1853-1856 (Stuttgart, 1930) and Reinhold Müller, Die Partei Bethmann-Hollweg und die orientalische Krise, 1853-1856 (Halle, 1926). The source of the confusion lay in the inability of Frederick William to govern through his ministers and his willingness to permit the interference of his many camarilla and "kitchen cabinet" advisers. See Fritz Hartung, "Verantwortliche Regierung, Kabinette und Nebenregierungen im konstitutionellen Preussen, 1848-1918," Forschungen zur brandenburgischen und preussischen Geschichte, Vol. 44 (1932), pp. 2-17.

[28] GW, xv, 72-73; vii, 221; xiii, 337.

Instead he proceeded to cooperate with Austria in a rather tentative fashion through most of 1854. Bismarck found this policy "cowardly" and "shameful." Must Prussia, he asked, ever play Leporello to the Austrian Don Juan?[29] Fearing that Prussia might be dragged into a war against Russia for purely Hapsburg interests, he worked desperately to keep her neutral. In this there was chance of assistance from the medium states which also had nothing to gain from such a conflict. Meeting in Bamberg they formed a coalition to look after the interests of the "third Germany."[30] It now appeared possible for Prussia to split Austria from her German allies.

Again Bismarck came forward with a characteristic proposal. He urged that Prussia threaten to move in any one of three directions: (1) alliance with Russia ("it is senseless to swear continually that we would never go with Russia"); (2) alliance with France ("and indemnify ourselves at the cost of our perfidious comrades in the confederation"); or (3) alliance with German liberalism ("a new cabinet oriented toward the left . . . so partial to the western powers that Austria would be outdistanced and forced to hold vainly to our coat tails"). By these means he hoped to press the medium states into joining Prussia in a league of armed neutrality which would also include Holland, Sweden, and Denmark.[31] But if the German states should "desert" her, neutrality would be impossible for Prussia. She must either go with Russia and execute a surprise attack upon the Bohemian frontier, or "with the west" and "divert the water of German public opinion into our own sluices" rather than let it flow to the "Austrian mill." "My policy," he declared, "would be the first named."[32]

Although Frederick William ignored this advice, he was finally compelled to change his attitude toward Austria. In December Franz Joseph overtaxed his friendship by signing a treaty with France and England which appeared to be the prelude to war. Next the Hofburg proposed mobilization of the confederate armies against Russia. But this move was frustrated in the diet by Prussia and the lesser states. Throughout 1855 Bismarck enjoyed

---

29 *GW*, I, 446-447; II, 143; XIV, 365-367, 375, 380, 514.

30 Meiboom, *Politik Bayerns*, pp. 77 ff.; Fuchs, *Mittelstaatten*, pp. 36 ff.

31 *GW*, I, 503; II, 42; XIV, 334-335. Originally he included only the German middle states, Belgium, and Sardinia. *GW*, XIV, 310. Apparently the idea for such a league originated in Russia. Christian Friese, *Russland und Preussen vom Krimkrieg bis zum Polnischen Aufstand* (Berlin, 1931), p. 75.

32 *GW*, XIV, 370.

the unaccustomed luxury of heading the majority. A brake was applied upon Austrian policy which prevented her from entering the conflict. But when peace came the coalition dissolved. Austria resumed her leadership of the lesser states, and Prussia returned to isolation. In Germany all was as before.[33]

4. THE CHESSBOARD OF POLITICS

Europe, however, was not the same. The eastern alliance, which since 1815 had been the most important constellation in European politics, was now in a state of dissolution. By her *Realpolitik* in the Crimean War, Austria had severed the conservative bond which for decades had united her with Russia without gaining a substitute in France and Britain. In Petersburg her ultimatum was regarded as treachery and in the west her failure to join in the war was a disappointment. Prussia on the other hand had established a fund of good will in the Russian capital which in future years was to grow in value. But for the time being the greatest gainer was Napoleon, who emerged from the Congress of Paris as the dominating figure in European politics.[34]

The war had scarcely commenced before Bismarck began to calculate what new combinations might be erected over the wreckage of the old. In December 1853 his letters to Gerlach already speculated over the possibility of rapprochement between France and Russia. While arguing against Prussian support of Austria, he warned Manteuffel that cooperation between the dual powers in the east would force Russia to make peace and seek the alliance of Bonaparte. The czar would find this "the most natural way out, if we make hell too hot for him." Such a combination would have irresistible attraction for the medium states. Austria too would seek to join it. In order to forestall her foes and avoid isolation, Prussia would be compelled to become the "third in this repulsive alliance."[35]

But he spoke differently to others. Moustier, the French minister to Prussia, heard him say that a firm alliance with France

---

[33] Borries, *Preussen im Krimkrieg*, pp. 250 ff.; Friedjung, *Krimkrieg*, pp. 132 ff.; Charles W. Hallberg, *Franz Joseph and Napoleon III, 1852-1864* (New York, 1955), pp. 72 ff.

[34] Kaehler, "Realpolitik," pp. 443-444; Zechlin, *Grundlegung*, pp. 453-454; Werner E. Mosse, *The European Powers and the German Question, 1848-1871* (Cambridge, 1958), pp. 49 ff.

[35] *GW*, xiv, 334, 346, 351-352, 405; i, 407, 426, 444, 490. Apparently Manteuffel was influenced by the argument. Borries, *Preussen im Krimkrieg*, p. 226,

and Russia was most in accord with Prussia's interests. In October 1854 Glinka, a Russian diplomat in Frankfurt, reported that the Prussian delegate had described such a coalition as his "political ideal," "the only combination which could satisfy the political needs of the three countries."[36] At the court of the czar this suggestion was taken seriously, and Glinka inquired whether Frederick William IV could be won for such a plan. With astounding self-assurance Bismarck replied that he could promise success, "if your government wishes to intrust me with the task of convincing him." He left no doubt about the purpose he had in mind: "If we foresee the necessity for war against Austria, we must be in a position to attack her while she is still unprepared and before she can concentrate her troops on our frontiers."[37] At the moment French and Russian troops were locked in fatal combat in the Crimea, and Berlin was busy negotiating with Vienna over a fresh agreement to supplement the treaty of April 1854!

And yet Bismarck's project was not lacking in realism. During the summer and early fall French spokesmen had assured him that the war against Russia was but an expedient for Napoleon; that there was no lasting source of conflict between the two countries; that France intended to expand into Italy rather than Germany; that Prussia could become the bridge for a tripartite alliance against Austria.[38] In Russia Britain was regarded as the real enemy; toward France there was little hostility and some speculation about the possibility of future alliance.[39] But Czar Nicholas shuddered at the idea of dealing with a Bonaparte. On hearing of his refusal through Glinka, Bismarck sent the laconic reply: "Necessity will compel you to do it." The troubled Nicholas wrote, "That is just as sad as it is possible." Within a few months he was dead. His successor, Alexander II, was more accessible to the idea. In April 1856 he replaced Foreign Minister Nesselrode, advocate of the eastern alliance, with Prince Gorchakov, to whom the French coalition was a near obsession.[40]

[36] F. de Martens, *Recueil des traités et conventions conclus par la Russie avec les puissances étrangères* (St. Petersburg, 1874-1909). VIII, 444; Friedrich Frahm, *Bismarcks Stellung zu Frankreich bis zum 4. Juli 1866* (Kiel, 1911), p. 32.

[37] Martens, *Recueil*, VIII, 453-454. On Frederick William's viewpoint see Borries, *Preussen im Krimkrieg*, p. 227.

[38] *GW*, I, 465, 485-486, 494, 505.

[39] "Ein russisch-französisches Allianzprojekt von 1855," *Deutsche Revue*, XXI/4 (1896), 292-300.

[40] Martens, *Recueil*, VIII, 454; Friese, *Russland und Preussen*, pp. 8 ff. Concern-

At this time Bismarck evidently regarded the Franco-Russian alliance as not only probable but desirable. While still careful to conceal his opinion from Gerlach, he confessed to Manteuffel in February 1856, "I hope for more than fear such an alliance, provided that we jump into it with both feet." For Bismarck this was a very unusual judgment; it meant that he no longer sought for Prussia the middle position in European politics. Apparently this decision arose from his despair over the Prussian situation in the diet. From the outset he had been under no illusion concerning the permanence of his majority during the Crimean crisis. In view of its approaching dissolution he believed Prussia must "accentuate [her] European more than [her] German relationships." A triple alliance was "the only means with which to escape the Austrian snare and domination by the medium states."[41]

When he discussed the problem again, however, Bismarck was more cautious. During 1856-1857 he addressed to both Gerlach and Manteuffel a long series of letters, among the most famous of his career, in which he analyzed thoroughly the Prussian position in German and European politics. In none of these documents did he again describe the alliance as one to be joined so impetuously. Perhaps he wished to sweeten a pill difficult for Gerlach and the king to swallow. But it is more probable that Bismarck himself had come to appreciate better the dangers which his policy involved. While improving Prussia's position in Germany, it would have made her the least influential member of the most powerful coalition in European politics.

Hence Bismarck returned to the policy of the fulcrum. There was a strong possibility, he argued, that Europe would divide into two opposed power blocs, each desirous of Prussian support. A need for mutual support against common foes made a Franco-Rus-

---

ing rapprochement between the two powers during and immediately after the war see: V. Bourtenko, "Un projet d'alliance franco-russe en 1856," *Revue historique*, Vol. 155 (1927), pp. 277-325; W. E. Mosse, "The Negotiations for a Franco-Russian Convention, November 1856," *Cambridge Historical Journal*, x/1 (1950), 59-74; François Charles-Roux, *Alexandre II, Gortchakoff, et Napoleon III* (Paris, 1913), pp. 112 ff.; Ernst Schule, *Russland und Frankreich vom Ausgang des Krimkrieges bis zum italienischen Krieg 1856-1859, Osteuropäische Forschungen*, Neue Folge, Vol. 19 (Königsberg, 1935), pp. 4 ff.

41 *GW*, II, 120; also I, 456, 516; XIV, 425. This document was overlooked by Lenz in his controversy with Schiemann. Theodor Schiemann, "Bismarcks Audienz beim Prinzen von Preussen," *Historische Zeitschrift*, Vol. 83 (1899), pp. 447-458, and Max Lenz, "Ein Apologet der Bismarck-Memoiren," *ibid.*, Vol. 84 (1900), pp. 39-71.

sian alliance probable; this would summon into existence a counter-coalition composed of Austria and England. As long as the cleavage between these blocs remained infirm, Prussia should ally with neither. She should "hold open every door and every turning." By exploiting this pivotal position she could extract favors from both sides.[42]

But if the Franco-Russian alliance should develop "warlike purposes," neutrality would become impossible for Prussia. Since the collapse of the eastern entente, the German Confederation was no longer a viable instrument for German security. In a war against France and Russia neither Austria nor the medium states would be trustworthy allies; England, moreover, could give Prussia little assistance on the continent. In this extremity Prussia would have to abandon her middle position in favor of alliance with the probable winners. It was wise to prepare this option in advance. The alliance would not be desirable for Prussia, if she should become the "third member *after* its creation." Hence Prussia should hedge by keeping alive the French desire for a "more intimate understanding." This appeared to be "the best means of hindering, delaying, or minimizing the harm" of a Franco-Russian alliance.[43]

This argument was, of course, but a façade. Bismarck sought to persuade his superiors in Berlin that rapprochement with France and Russia was a necessity of European politics, when in reality it was for him primarily a necessity of *German* politics.[44] As before, his aim was to coerce Austria into granting the expansion of Prussian influence. Only by tapping a new reservoir of power outside Germany could Prussia consolidate her position within. The first step must be to cultivate good relations with France. Merely by responding to the desire of Napoleon to make a state visit in Berlin, Prussia could create consternation in the rest of Germany. Even if an actual alliance were never signed, it was foolish to throw away the advantages which the dread of such an event would bring.

42 *GW*, XIV, 473; II, 150, 223.   43 *GW*, II, 144, 222-223.

44 In the views Bismarck expressed during the Crimean war Muralt has seen the origins of his "policy of the European middle" in the 1870's and 1880's. While accurate, this fails to consider the important distinction that Bismarck's purpose in the earlier period was offensive, in the latter period defensive. Muralt ignores the many documents of the 1850's in which the aggressive purpose of the policy is evident. Leonhard von Muralt, *Bismarcks Verantwortlichkeit* (Göttingen, 1955), pp. 141-217.

While affected by the argument, Frederick William could not be brought to take any step which might lead to a breach with Austria.[45] The tradition of Austrian leadership and conservative solidarity were too deeply embedded in his thinking. Gerlach was highly shocked over the radical proposals of his "pupil." The two men argued the matter out in an exchange of letters famous for their illustration of the differences between the romantic and realistic views on foreign policy.[46] Basically the dispute was one of relatives, not of absolutes. While the interest of state and the struggle against revolution were important to both, Bismarck gave precedence to the former, Gerlach to the latter.[47]

As was his wont, Gerlach opposed rapprochement with Napoleon on the ground that the Napoleonic dynasty, having been founded on revolution, could have no place in the respectable family of European monarchs. Nevertheless, he buttressed this argument with another of different character. Because it was in the interest of France to do so, he believed, Napoleon would inevitably ally himself with the popular forces of liberal and national revolution. Using Bismarck's own words, he wrote that *this* was the "reality" which it was folly to "ignore."

Only the second of these arguments was capable of impressing Bismarck. Even so he thought it false. His interviews with Napoleon in 1855 and 1857 had convinced him that the emperor was of a far different calibre than his dreaded uncle. Where the latter had been bold, aggressive, and calculating, the former was sly, limited, and sentimental. There was no danger of a resurgence of French imperialism on a revolutionary scale; the founder of the second empire had neither the instincts of a conqueror nor the talents of a field commander. Nor was he impelled by the necessity of propagating revolution. On the contrary, liberalism was as

[45] Friese, *Russland und Preussen*, pp. 134 ff.

[46] For the entire exchange see *Briefwechsel des Generals Leopold von Gerlach mit dem Bundestagsgesandten Otto von Bismarck* (Berlin, 1893). See also *GW*, xv, 110 ff.; xiv, 460 ff.; Ludwig Gerlach, *Aufzeichnungen*, ii, 209; Manteuffel, *Denkwürdigkeiten*, iii, 193-194; Richard Augst, *Bismarck und Leopold von Gerlach* (Leipzig, 1913).

[47] For discussions of this problem see Friedrich Meinecke, *Weltbürgertum und Nationalstaat* (5th ed., Munich and Berlin, 1919), p. 315, *Preussen und Deutschland im 19. und 20. Jahrhundert* (Munich, 1918), pp. 279-295, and Otto Vossler, "Bismarcks Ethos," *Historische Zeitschrift*, Vol. 171 (1951), pp. 271 ff. The recent work of Kurt Bigler, *Bismarck und das Legitimitätsprinzip bis 1862* (Winterthur, 1955), goes too far in picturing Bismarck, in contrast to Gerlach, as a man of pure expediency.

great a threat to his own power as to that of any other European monarch. His imperialistic ambitions were centered on Italy, rather than on the Rhine, where French expansion would certainly recreate the coalition which had crushed the first Napoleon.[48]

Bismarck also refused to be impaled on the first prong of Gerlach's fork. The whole conception of "legitimacy" he dismissed as out of accord with historical fact. Analyzing the origins of the so-called "legitimate" dynasties of Europe, he exposed the fact that the ultimate source of all authority, even that of the Prussian monarchy itself, was revolution. The Napoleonic regime had as good a claim to legitimacy as any other.[49] "As a romanticist I can shed a tear for his fate," he wrote of the deposed Louis Philippe. "As a diplomat I would be his servant, were I a Frenchman. Being what I am, however, I count France only as a piece and to be sure an unavoidable one in the chess game of politics, no matter who happens to be her ruler. In this game it is my business to serve only *my* king and *my* country."[50]

5. THE ALTERNATIVES OF COERCION

Since the beginning of the Crimean crisis Bismarck's attitude toward Austria had become increasingly belligerent. In January 1855 the Austrian ambassador in Berlin reported that on visits to the capital the Junker had been heard to say that Austro-Prussian dualism could no longer be tolerated in Germany. Through the centuries it had always been productive of war. One more was needed to eject Austria from Germany. Three months later Rechberg reported from Frankfurt that Bismarck had been doing some loose talking "about the necessity for Prussia to expand not in Poland, but in Germany, namely in Saxony and Hanover." During a visit to Paris in August the Junker told a Prussian diplomat, Prince von Reuss, that war with Austria was unavoidable.[51]

In April 1856 he informed Gerlach and Manteuffel of his belief that "we shall have to fight for our existence against Austria in the not-too-distant future." Nevertheless, he disavowed any desire to precipitate such a conflict. It would come, he believed, in the

---

[48] For Bismarck's view of Napoleon see Frahm, *Stellung zu Frankreich*, pp. 37 ff., and Herbert Geuss, *Bismarck und Napoleon III, Kölner Historische Abhandlungen*, Vol. I (Köln, 1959), pp. 23 ff.
[49] *GW*, II, 226 ff.; XIV, 470 ff.   [50] *GW*, XIV, 465.
[51] Meyer, *Bismarcks Kampf*, pp. 239-240, 261-262; Erich Marcks, *Otto von Bismarck, Ein Lebensbild* (Stuttgart, 1915), p. 40.

natural course of events. "The Viennese policy being what it is, Germany is too small for the two of us." "We shall both plow the same disputed acre as long as no honorable arrangement has been made and executed concerning the influence belonging to each in Germany." Such an arrangement, he argued, should be a "political or geographical line of demarcation."[52]

More than a year later he spoke just as bluntly to his Austrian colleague in Frankfurt. Without any authorization from Berlin he told Rechberg, "The existing situation cannot continue and must lead either to an understanding or a decisive break." It was a delusion for Austria to assume that she could count on Prussian aid in the event of war. The imperial government must reckon with the "reality" that, if no settlement had been reached with Prussia, the latter would be found in the ranks of the enemy. Concerning the details of such a settlement he was again vague. The two powers, he said, must avoid holding any "point in common."[53] What he appears to have had in mind was the division of Germany into separate spheres along the Main.

Despite his bellicose utterances, it would be a mistake to assume that Bismarck believed war the only means of accomplishing this end.[54] What he had decided upon was the necessity, not of war, but of coercion. There were two possibilities: coercion by threat followed by a negotiated settlement, or coercion by violence and a settlement dictated by the fortunes of war. The first course would result in the peaceful division of Germany into two spheres of influence, but the second meant that Prussia would seek to drive Austria out of Germany, expand her frontiers to link her eastern and western provinces, and reorganize the rest of Protestant Germany into a federation under her own domination. These were the alternative goals of the Prussian state, as Bismarck now conceived them. Both were to be considered and prepared. Being the less dangerous, the former was preferred, but in view of the nature of the conflict with Austria, the latter was more likely.

[52] *GW*, II, 142; XIV, 441.
[53] Meyer, *Bismarcks Kampf*, pp. 549-553. Naturally Bismarck made no mention of this unauthorized threat in his report of the interview. *GW*, II, 232 ff.
[54] Those who recorded his remarks obviously remembered only their sensational import and forgot or ignored the qualifying phrases which appear everywhere in the documents which came from his pen during these years. His attitude is best expressed in a letter to Leopold Gerlach of June 1855. "We must hold open the bridge to Austria, but not cross it ourselves." *GW*, XIV, 406. During the Italian war of 1859 he told Gerlach, "We must go either with or against Austria." *GW*, VII, 39.

As has been shown, Bismarck sought the necessary means of coercion in the potential combinations of European politics. Through the separation of Austria and Russia, the Crimean War had given Berlin the possibility of seizing the fulcrum in the European balance of power. By placing herself in the pivotal position from which alliances in at least two directions were possible, Berlin could arouse fears in Vienna and the lesser capitals which might break their resistance to the expansion of Prussian power.

Brilliant though it was, this strategy had a serious shortcoming. If, as Bismarck anticipated, the mere threat of an alliance with France and Russia proved insufficient, Prussia might be compelled to promote such a combination in order to make war on Austria. Should she fight alone, Prussia would at least be compelled to stay close to these powers in order to prevent their coming to Austria's assistance. Or if they should conspire to make war on Vienna for their own ends, Prussia would have to join them as a secondary partner. In any event the abandonment of the favored position of the fulcrum was likely. Whatever gains she achieved in a successful war might be offset by restrictions imposed upon her in victory by her two mighty allies, both of whom had a traditional interest in a weak and divided Germany.

Toward the end of the 1850's, however, certain developments in German and European politics, when coupled with changes in Bismarck's own thinking, enabled him to readjust the pattern of strategy by which he hoped to promote the Prussian interest. By adding yet another force to his system of pressures he increased its flexibility and reduced its hazards. This force was that of German nationalism.

BOOK TWO

THE YEARS OF DECISION
1858-1863

Komm, Einzger, wenn du schon geboren,
Tritt auf, wir folgen deiner Spur!
Du letzter aller Diktatoren,
Komm mit der letzten Diktatur!
—JOHANN GEORG FISCHER in 1848

CHAPTER FIVE

THE UTILITY OF GERMAN NATIONALISM

1. A MODERN RICHELIEU

N HIS earliest reports from Frankfurt, Bismarck pointed out the value of mobilizing German public opinion as a Prussian weapon against the diet majority. The dynasties of the lesser states were compelled to seek alliance with Austria because the interests of their subjects ran parallel to those of Prussia. The experiences of 1848-1850 had revealed the potential affinity between German nationalism and Prussian imperialism. Should these two forces ever combine, crowns would topple and sovereignties be destroyed. Bismarck urged his government to exploit the fear of such an alliance by actively promoting the material interests of the German commercial and industrial classes.[1]

In the diet he engaged Count Thun in a hot contest for public favor.[2] Both posed hypocritically as champions of the national welfare. By means of "front" organizations and a heavily subsidized press Bismarck's legation in Frankfurt became an effective center for the dissemination of Prussian propaganda in central and southern Germany.[3] From his experiences he drew the conclusion that Prussia could easily outdistance Austria and the medium states in any conclusive struggle for popular opinion.[4]

For the time being, nevertheless, he sought the coercive power

---

[1] *GW*, I, 17, 114; II, 321; VII, 24-25, 38; XIV, 223.

[2] Arnold O. Meyer, *Bismarcks Kampf mit Österreich am Bundestag zu Frankfurt, 1851-1859* (Berlin, 1927), pp. 355-356.

[3] *GW*, I, 52 ff., 63, 121, 246 ff. Also Friedrich W. Lange, *Bismarck und die öffentliche Meinung Süddeutschlands während der Zollvereinskrise, 1850 bis 1853* (Giessen, 1922).

[4] *GW*, II, 239. His appreciation of the value of a popular reinforcement for foreign policy is also shown by his desire to encourage the Landtag to take a stand on the issues dividing Austria and Prussia. *GW*, I, 116; II, 299, 320-321, 323-324; III, 70-71; XIV, 487, 544. He advised against the overzealous harrying of democrats by the Berlin police as harmful to Prussia's foreign relations, but advocated the suppression of journals which opposed or failed to support her policy. *GW*, I, 317, 515-516; XIV, 390.

111

with which to break apart the opposing coalition in the combinations of European politics, rather than in the movement for German national unity. But he continued to speculate on the potential utility of the latter for Prussia. During the Crimean crisis, as we have seen, he listed "a new cabinet oriented toward the left" as one of the three alternative courses open to Prussia. In Frankfurt he experimented with the possible effect of such a change: "With the tone of one who has had nothing to do with it and is not pleased by the prospect I have described this to several of my colleagues as the probable development of Prussian policy. In each case my hearers became very excited and upset about it. They fear such a possibility more than cholera and concede that Austria would be immediately outdistanced and forced into the defensive on the question of hegemony in Germany."[5] In his memorial of 1853 to the Prince of Prussia, he stated his belief that "parliamentary liberalism" might be exploited as a "temporary means" with which to gain for the Hohenzollern monarchy a satisfactory solution of the German question.[6]

This shows how far the fear of revolution had receded in Bismarck's mind. He judged it possible for the king to appoint a liberal cabinet, use it to carry out a stroke in foreign affairs, and then dismiss it without jeopardizing his own authority. The "liberals" whom he had in mind, of course, were the moderates. From their actions in the revolution and their conduct at Gotha and Erfurt it was evident that they were not fundamentally antipathetic to authority and that their interest in national unity far outweighed their dedication to liberal principle. In November 1853 Bismarck wrote to Gerlach: "We are in the same position with regard to the *Gothaer* as were Louis XIII and XIV to the German Protestants; at home we have no use for them, but in the small states they are the only elements which want anything to do with us."[7] At the dawn of the age of classical diplomacy, Richelieu, cardinal of the church, had exploited the ideological force of Lutheran Protestantism in the interest of state against the Hapsburg monarchy. In its twilight Bismarck, the Prussian conservative, proposed to exploit the ideological force of German nationalism to a similar end.

The career of Louis Napoleon was a persuasive example. This

[5] *GW*, I, 505-506.   [6] *GW*, I, 375.
[7] *GW*, xiv, 329.

latter-day Bonaparte combined the qualities of Mazzini and Machiavelli. He was a curious mixture of crusading idealism and realistic self-interest. By promoting the cause of national self-determination in Europe he hoped to upset the settlement of 1815 and open the way for French expansion. Through the elevation of France's power in Europe he expected to identify his regime with the French nation and perpetuate the dynasty.[8]

While in Frankfurt Bismarck followed with keen interest what transpired beyond the Vosges. As always it is difficult to say how much he acquired from others. In later years he spoke of having learned from Napoleon's mistakes, but he said nothing of having profited from his successes. It is more probable that what happened in France merely reinforced his own observations about the tactical possibilities inherent in the German political situation. Events had shown that nationalism was not necessarily hostile to authoritarian institutions. Far from being the inseparable companion of liberalism, it might easily be converted into an anti-liberal force. The foreign policy of Napoleon demonstrated that the ideal of national self-determination, when applied to the divided and submerged cultural nations of central and eastern Europe, was capable of supplying a vital *élan* and moral approbation to an aggressive foreign policy executed in the interest of state.[9]

During the 1850's Bismarck came to appreciate the potential utility of German nationalism as a strategic weapon for the reinforcement of Prussian foreign policy. Not until later, after the commencement of the Prussian constitutional conflict, did it come to have a similar function in domestic affairs. In the beginning his purpose was not to weaken a domestic opposition by the theft of the national cause, but to find in the ideal of national unity a point of contact, as in 1848-1850, between the Hohenzollern monarchy and the German liberal movement. The economic, social, and political development of Germany in the late 1850's could only have encouraged him in the conviction that such a policy was practical.

[8] Concerning the influence of Napoleon see H. Gollwitzer, "Der Cäsarismus Napoleons III. im Widerhall der öffentlichen Meinung Deutschlands," *Historische Zeitschrift*, Vol. 173 (1952), pp. 23-75.

[9] In refuting Bismarck's "Bonapartism," G. A. Rein came to the surprising conclusion that, while using some "Bonapartist means and methods," Bismarck in the last analysis rejected Napoleonism in choosing a national basis for his policy. This would seem to be precisely the element of greatest similarity between the two men. *Die Revolution in der Politik Bismarcks* (Göttingen, 1957), pp. 131-132.

2 . GERMANY'S SECOND REVOLUTION

After twenty years of preparation there occurred in Germany during the last part of the fifth decade a spurt of economic activity which brought her overnight into the age of industrial capitalism. Between 1850 and 1860 coal production in Germany doubled from six to twelve million tons; pig iron production increased from 215,000 to 529,000 tons. The number of steam engines in use rose from 1,416 in 1846 to 10,113 in 1861 (26,354 to 184,649 horsepower). Similar expansions occurred in the construction of railways and "metalled" roads.[10] During this period the foundations of modern German capitalism were laid. Before 1850 only 118 joint stock companies were established in Prussia; during the next twenty years 295 were formed. The capital of the former was 672,400,000 marks as against 2,404,800,000 for the latter.[11] With the crash of 1857 Germany began for the first time to experience the cyclical pattern of modern capitalism.

Radical changes also occurred in the size and structure of the population. Despite a decline in birth rate and the emigration of about one million citizens, the population of Germany increased from 35,900,000 to 38,000,000 between 1850 and 1860. While the rural areas remained fairly static, the new millions poured into the cities which grew up about the smoking factories at a dizzy pace.[12] The older entrepreneurs retained and strengthened their positions, and were joined by a whole new class of businessmen, many of whom rose to wealth and economic power within a few years. For the first time Germany had a numerous and prosperous bourgeoisie. Working in the grimy factories and mining pits and living in crowded and sordid dwellings of the new industrial towns, moreover, was a new proletarian class as yet scarcely aware either of its fate or its potentiality.[13]

[10] A. J. P. Taylor, *The Struggle for Mastery in Europe, 1848-1918* (Oxford, 1954), p. xxix; W. Bowden, M. Karpovich, and A. Usher, *An Economic History of Europe since 1750* (New York, 1937), pp. 468-472. On the general development of German industry see Pierre Benaerts, *Les origines de la grande industrie allemande* (Paris, 1933), pp. 373 ff., and August Sartorius von Waltershausen, *Deutsche Wirtschaftsgeschichte, 1815-1914* (2nd ed., Jena, 1923), pp. 156 ff.

[11] Jürgen Kuczynski, *A Short History of Labour Conditions under Industrial Capitalism*, Vol. iii/1, *Germany, 1800 to the Present Day* (London, 1945), p. 67.

[12] Taylor, *Struggle for Mastery*, p. xxv. On the subject of demographic movement and change see Benaerts, *Industrie allemande*, pp. 131-161, and Werner Sombart, *Der Moderne Kapitalismus* (Munich, 1927-1928), iii/1, 390.

[13] See the statistics in Benaerts, *Industrie allemande*, pp. 573-580.

Agriculture kept pace for a time with industry. In 1840 Justus Liebig published his revolutionary work on the application of chemistry to agriculture and introduced the age of scientific farming. The German customs union and the new means of transportation stimulated agricultural as well as industrial production. Although total production figures are lacking, the yearly export of the Zollverein countries increased from an average of 9,600,000 bushels in 1836-1840 to 20,300,000 in 1861-1864.[14] Among the leaders in the use of new techniques were owners of the latifundia east of the Elbe. Many became the owners and operators of agricultural industries such as breweries, distilleries, saw mills, and sugar refineries. Both the rationalization of agricultural production and the founding of these enterprises required the use of modern business accounting and management. Hence the gap between rural land-owner and urban businessman began to narrow. The economic basis for their future political collaboration was being formed. In the liberal doctrine of *laissez-faire* they were soon to find a common bond of ideology and interest.[15]

Not all Junker landowners were able to adjust to the new and alien world of capitalistic agriculture. Debts and mortgages, bankruptcies and foreclosures forced a startling number to sell their estates. By 1859 thirty-four percent of all latifundia in the province of Prussia were held by commoners and in Brandenburg and Pomerania the figures were actually sixty-four and sixty-two percent. Among the peasants another transformation was underway. Nearly 1,500,000 had become free-holders as a result of the reforms and were likewise compelled to cultivate business instincts and "assume some of the characteristics of the urbanite."[16]

The political consequences of these economic and social devel-

14 Gertrud Hermes, "Statistische Studien zur wirtschaftlichen und gesellschaftlichen Struktur des zollvereinten Deutschlands," *Archiv für Sozialwissenschaft und Sozialpolitik*, Vol. 63 (1930), pp. 121-162; Sartorius von Waltershausen, *Wirtschaftsgeschichte*, pp. 160-165; Friedrich Lütge, *Deutsche Sozial- und Wirtschaftsgeschichte* (Berlin, 1952), pp. 358-360.

15 The landowners of eastern Prussia were the first converts to the doctrine of "Manchesterism" in Germany. Julius Becker, *Das deutsche Manchestertum, eine Studie zur Geschichte des wirtschaftspolitischen Individualismus* (Karlsruhe, 1907), pp. 24-25, 33.

16 Eugene N. Anderson, *The Social and Political Conflict in Prussia, 1858-1864* (Lincoln, 1954), pp. 12-15; Theodore S. Hamerow, *Restoration, Revolution, Reaction: Economics and Politics in Germany, 1815-1871* (Princeton, 1958), pp. 219 ff.; Sigmund Neumann, *Die Stufen des preussischen Konservatismus, Historische Studien*, Vol. 190 (Berlin, 1930), pp. 35 ff.

opments, however, were inconsiderable. Had the great expansion of the middle class occurred in the pre-revolutionary period, class egoism, material interests, and liberal idealism might have combined to change the course of German politics. But the timing was otherwise, and, when the new entrepreneurial class finally appeared, the revolutionary force of German liberalism had already spent itself. Despite the remarkable change in economic and social life, the same social groups continued to supply political leadership in Prussia. In the chamber of 1848 7.5 percent of the seats were held by businessmen; in 1862 the figure was 7.2 percent. Within the chamber of deputies liberal party leadership was largely in the hands of civil servants and landowners. The "young Lithuanians" who founded the Progressive Party were country squires from East Prussia who had found their way to liberalism via the doctrine of free trade and Kantian ethics.[17]

This is not to say that the business community was of no political influence. Merchants and entrepreneurs took part in the political process on the local level by participating in election committees and other party activities, but very few had either the time or inclination to run for parliament. What occurred after 1859 was simply the election of liberal rather than conservative deputies from the same social groups which had traditionally provided political leadership. Before and after that date more than sixty percent of the lower chamber was composed of that academically trained elite which by virtue of education, office, or occupation was regarded by the electorate as best suited for political leadership. They were "notables," men of social prestige, but without independent status, more concerned with political discussion than political success.[18]

[17] Anderson, *Social and Political Conflict*, p. 445. See also Nikolaus von Preradovich, *Die Führungsschichten in Österreich und Preussen, 1804-1918* (Wiesbaden, 1955), pp. 154 ff., and Reinhard Adam, "Der Liberalismus in der Provinz Preussen zur Zeit der Neuen Ara und sein Anteil an der Entstehung der Deutschen Fortschrittspartei," in Verein für die Geschichte von Ost- und Westpreussen, *Altpreussische Beiträge* (Königsberg, 1933), pp. 145-181. A notable exception, Victor von Unruh, who was a wealthy industrialist, remarked to Hermann Schulze-Delitzsch (October 12, 1864), "The well-to-do bourgeoisie are politically stunted." He deplored their lack of "political nerve" and "energy" when faced by a man like Bismarck. Friedrich Thorwart, ed., *Hermann Schulze-Delitzschs Schriften und Reden* (Berlin, 1909-1913), IV, 256-257, also 18-19; V, 133-134.

[18] Anderson, *Social and Political Conflict*, pp. 283 ff.; Hansgeorg Schroth, *Welt- und Staatsideen des deutschen Liberalismus in der Zeit der Einheits- und Freiheitskämpfe, 1859-1866, Historische Studien*, Vol. 201 (Berlin, 1931), pp. 59-74.

Had the state completely ignored their needs or openly harmed their interests, the new bourgeoisie might have drifted into political radicalism, but this was not the case. Although the government often took an active part in the development of basic industry, this was owing to the inadequate accumulation of private capital as well as to the continuing tradition of state paternalism. In Germany Berlin promoted free trade as a political weapon against Austria and because it served the needs of an expanding industrial and agricultural export. On the whole, the state encouraged the entrepreneurial class to become absorbed in business activity and to leave the affairs of government to established authority.[19]

What the new business interests objected to was not the system, but some of its features and many of its practices. The Junker control over the bureaucracy, officer corps, and local rural government was galling.[20] The extensive regulatory powers of the "police state" over affairs affecting the daily lives and activities of most citizens was considered burdensome and unnecessary. The individual was believed to have inadequate protection against the abuse of these powers by bureaucratic officials. On the one hand, businessmen complained of too much bureaucratic paternalism and, on the other, of inadequate assistance in the construction of railroads and waterways. Perhaps the greatest annoyance of all was the handicap placed upon the expansion of trade and the growth of industry by German disunity. Although the Zollverein had created a single market for little-Germany and the adoption of a common code had produced order in the field of commercial law, German businessmen were still plagued by the confusion in currencies, weights, measures, and freight rates, the discrepancies in business laws and regulations, the restrictions on domicile and residence, and the lack of support and protection in world trade.[21]

As yet there was no sign of a proletarian radicalism capable of taking the place left vacant by the decline of radical liberalism.

[19] Leonard Krieger, *The German Idea of Freedom* (Boston, 1957), pp. 342-343; Heinrich Heffter, *Die deutsche Selbstverwaltung im 19. Jahrhundert* (Stuttgart, 1950), pp. 350-351; W. O. Henderson, *The State and the Industrial Revolution in Prussia 1740-1870* (Liverpool, 1958), pp. xix ff.

[20] The number of middle-class officials and officers in the Prussian service in the nineteenth century was, however, higher than commonly assumed. Preradovich, *Führungsschichten*, pp. 160-168.

[21] Anderson, *Social and Political Conflict*, pp. 18 ff., 148 ff.

117

In 1848 the communist manifesto and the agitation of Marx and Engels in the Rhineland had little effect. Marx's chosen people, the factory laborers, were but a very small segment of the German working class and they were better paid and employed than the older class of handicraftsmen. Distressed artisans and peasants had provided the chief popular force behind the revolution, but no Moses came to lead them out of the wilderness. During the 1850's the Manteuffel regime made a determined bid for the support of both groups against the middle class. Agrarian reforms completed the economic emancipation of the rural laboring class from manorialism. The re-establishment of craft guilds under state protection nourished the interests of the artisans. Child labor was limited, the truck system abolished, and welfare associations subsidized.[22]

By the end of the decade significant changes were evident. Inflation had robbed the worker of much of his gain in wages. The crash of 1857 produced for a time widespread unemployment. The remorseless advance of the factory system and the doctrine of *laissez-faire* exposed the artisans to new disasters.[23] But it also produced a factory proletariat of significant size. Among 17,-000,000 Prussians in 1863 there were estimated to be 770,000 factory workers, 1,090,000 handicraftsmen, and 3,430,000 farm laborers.[24] At last there had begun to appear the social material for which Marx had vainly searched in 1848.

Nevertheless, the line of demarcation between urban workers and lower middle class was still vague. Among the former, class-consciousness was only weakly developed. Those who were politically aware looked to the democratic wing of the liberal movement for the advocacy of their interests. Although the first rays of light had pierced the horizon, the day of their disillusionment had not yet dawned.[25]

[22] Hamerow, *Restoration, Revolution, Reaction,* pp. 137-172, 207-237.

[23] *Ibid.,* pp. 209 ff.; Kuczynski, *Short History,* pp. 74-82; Benaerts, *Industrie allemande,* pp. 544 ff., 580 ff.

[24] Estimate of the *Neue Frankfurter Zeitung* quoted in Ernst Schraepler, "Linksliberalismus und Arbeiterschaft in der preussischen Konfliktszeit," in Richard Dietrich and Gerhard Oestreich, eds., *Forschungen zu Staat und Verfassung, Festgabe für Fritz Hartung* (Berlin, 1958), p. 388. Benaerts estimated the industrial labor force of the whole Zollverein in 1860 at about 450,000 persons. Counting their families he calculated the number of persons subsisting from factory wages between 1,300,000 to 1,400,000. *Industrie allemande,* pp. 573-575.

[25] Schraepler, "Linksliberalismus und Arbeiterschaft," pp. 387 ff.

For a person of Bismarck's views and aims there was no reason therefore to be alarmed about the general character of German economic and social development in the late 1850's. Neither bourgeoisie nor proletariat were as yet fundamentally opposed to the existing order. There were signs that the former would welcome any Prussian initiative in the problem of German unification. All that was needed to mobilize this force in the interest of Prussian foreign policy was the establishment of a nexus between the monarchy and liberal national movement. As the decade closed, it appeared attainable.

3 . THE NEW ERA

After Olmütz, Prussia had entered into a period of reaction; court and government were dominated by extreme conservatives. Although the constitution was retained, the upper house of the legislature was converted by royal decree into a largely hereditary "house of lords." Popular apathy and governmental pressure at election time enabled the conservatives to control the lower chamber. In local government the liberal reforms of the revolutionary period were liquidated; even the administrative powers of the Junkers (*Gutspolizei*) were restored. Church affairs were handed over to the extreme orthodox, and the administration and curricula of the schools were under their influence. But the most obnoxious aspects of the reaction were the measures of political repression: espionage, denunciation, discrimination, and arbitrary arrest. Not even Prince William, heir to the throne, and his circle were safe from police surveillance.[26]

In October 1857, Frederick William IV was incapacitated by a stroke. For a year Prince William acted as his deputy, and, when it became apparent that the king would not recover, the prince established a regency. In 1861 the ailing monarch died and William succeeded to the throne. In many respects the two brothers contrasted sharply. Frederick William was a romantic personality. A man of sensitivity and imagination, of keen artistic interest and understanding, he was prone in governmental affairs to impractical dreaming, sudden enthusiasms, and easy disillusion-

---

[26] Research on the period of reaction after 1850 has been sparse. On the general character of the regime see Hans Walter, *Die innere Politik des Ministers von Manteuffel und der Ursprung der Reaktion in Preussen* (Berlin, 1910), pp. 152-158, and Neumann, *Stufen des Konservatismus*, pp. 119 ff.

ment. Until it became apparent that the king would be childless, William had not expected to rule. Like most younger sons of the royal family he received an entirely military education. In bearing and outlook he remained to the end a soldier—sober, realistic, and accustomed to command.[27]

On matters of principle the brothers were in basic agreement. Both were divine-right monarchists, firmly convinced that to rule was both a right and duty imposed by God. While Frederick William had vague ideas about restoring the feudal *Ständestaat*, William firmly adhered to the absolutist tradition of his house. Repeatedly Frederick William considered tearing up that "scrap of paper" he had granted in 1850. In his political testament he urged his heir to do so. But after some deliberation William declined to begin his rule with such an unpopular step.[28]

During the 1850's the Prince of Prussia strongly disapproved of the repression and chicanery of the Manteuffel regime. His disgust was reinforced by the moderate liberal views of his wife, Augusta, a Weimar princess of talent and enlightened spirit. From their residence in the Rhineland city of Koblenz the royal pair maintained contact with the moderate conservatives of the opposition led by Moritz von Bethmann-Hollweg. Through the journal which expressed their views this faction was known as the *"Wochenblatt* party," in contrast to the *"Kreuzzeitung* party" which dominated cabinet and court in Berlin.[29]

The royal brothers were also in disagreement on foreign policy. While critical of its constitution, William had supported the Radowitz plan in 1850. Unlike the romantic conservatives, he considered the Olmütz capitulation a shameful defeat. He found it hard to forgive the czar for siding with Austria in the crisis. During the Crimean war he favored cautious cooperation with Austria in order to avoid isolation; Bismarck's advice he dismissed as that of a "schoolboy." His interest in German unity was more positive and lasting than that of his brother. In May 1849 he wrote: "Whoever wishes to rule Germany, must conquer it. . . .

[27] See the comparison of the two personalities in Petersdorff, *Friedrich Wilhelm IV*, pp. 1 ff., and Erich Marcks, *Kaiser Wilhelm I* (9th ed., Berlin, 1943), pp. 65 ff.

[28] Petersdorff, *Friedrich Wilhelm IV*, pp. 165 ff.; Marcks, *Wilhelm I*, pp. 127 ff.; *GW*, xv, 132-133.

[29] Walter Schmidt, *Die Partei Bethmann—Hollweg und die Reaktion in Preussen, 1850-1858* (Berlin, 1910); Justus von Gruner, "Rückblick auf mein Leben," *Deutsche Revue*, xxvi/2 (1901), 180-193; Müller, *Partei Bethmann-Hollweg*.

THE UTILITY OF GERMAN NATIONALISM

That Prussia is destined to lead Germany is shown by our whole history, but it is a matter of when and how." During the 1850's he regarded "moral" rather than "physical" conquest as the "how" of Prussian policy. "Wise legislation" and "elements of unification like the Zollverein," rather than violence, were the proper course. He was firmly convinced of the Prussian right to parity in the confederation and fundamentally suspicious of Austrian aims. As a soldier he deplored the inadequacy of Germany's military defenses. He came to power with the determination to reorganize both the Prussian and confederate armies. His aim was the division of confederate forces during wartime into two commands, Prussian and Austrian, operating on a common plan of campaign.[30]

His program for Germany required a fresh beginning in Prussia, a new regime with greater popular support. Hence one of William's first acts on becoming regent was to dismiss Manteuffel. The new cabinet was drawn from the *Wochenblatt* party and the old-liberal opposition in the Prussian chamber of the 1850's. Three of its members—Rudolf von Auerswald, Baron von Patow, and Count von Schwerin—had served in the liberal government of 1848. The minister-president was William's distant relative, Prince Charles Anthony of Hohenzollern-Sigmaringen. At the foreign ministry was Alexander von Schleinitz, like Charles Anthony and Auerswald a close friend of the regent and Augusta. From these ministers William expected a new moral tone, obedience to the constitution, reforms of a moderate nature, but no fundamental changes and no sacrifice of royal authority. With brutal frankness Bismarck warned him that the new cabinet did not contain "a single individual of statesmanlike calibre."[31]

To shrewd observers the change did not appear very drastic. Instead of the feudal conservatives the aristocratic "whigs" were

30 Ernst Berner, ed., *Kaiser Wilhelms des Grossen Briefe, Reden und Schriften* (Berlin, 1906), I, 203, 230-234, 269-275, 449, 479-482; Heinrich von Poschinger, ed., *Preussens auswärtige Politik 1850 bis 1858, Unveröffentlichte Dokumente aus dem Nachlasse des Ministerpräsidenten Otto Freiherrn von Manteuffel* (Berlin, 1902), I, 44-45, 72-73, 107-111; II, 349; Horst Kohl, ed., *Anhang zu den Gedanken und Erinnerungen von Otto Fürst von Bismarck* (Stuttgart, 1901), I, 47; *APP*, II/1, 266; Marcks, *Wilhelm I*, pp. 98 ff.
31 *GW*, xv, 141. Budberg, the Russian envoy, was of like opinion. *APP* I/1, 55. On the political complexion of the cabinet see Alexander Bergengrün, *Staatsminister August Freiherr von der Heydt* (Leipzig, 1908), pp. 247 ff.; Gruner, "Rückblick," pp. 333 ff.; Heinrich von Poschinger, ed., *Erinnerungen aus dem Leben von Hans Viktor von Unruh* (Stuttgart, 1895), pp. 198-199.

now in power.[32] To the general public, however, any change from the previous regime was progress. The ministers began their work amid great popular enthusiasm. It was believed that a fresh page had been turned in Prussian and German history. Their government was hopefully dubbed "the new era."

Immediately the cabinet received a resounding endorsement from the electorate. The chamber chosen in 1855 had contained 218 supporters of the government, opposed by 116 moderate liberals. In November 1858 the Manteuffel conservatives withered to 57, facing 263 backers of the new era. The liberals were all too conscious that the change had come through no act of their own. "Just don't press!" was the motto of the democratic wing. Leading former radicals of 1848—Waldeck, Jacoby, Schulze-Delitzsch, Unruh, and Rodbertus—took no active part in the election and even instructed their followers to vote for moderates. Although a few aspired to form an independent party of the extreme left, Waldeck refused to cooperate, and without him there was no chance. The radical tradition was nearly extinct.[33]

For the first time in Prussian constitutional history, monarch, cabinet, chamber, and people appeared united and harmonious. From the unhorsed conservatives of the *Kreuzzeitung* party came the only dissent. Without support from the crown they were powerless. But William was already suspicious of the popular response his actions had aroused. "What have I done," he asked querulously, "to merit praise from that crowd?"[34]

4. THE ''BOOKLET''

In March 1858 Bismarck made an effort to influence the foreign policy of the coming regime in a memorial known as the *Booklet* because of its length.[35] He predicted that in the near future Austria would seek a decision in the struggle against Prussia. She would maneuver Berlin into the position of having to

---

[32] See Neumann, *Stufen des Konservatismus*, pp. 130 ff.

[33] Thorwart, *Schulze-Delitzsch*, IV, 18-19; V, 133-134; Schmidt, *Partei Bethmann Hollweg*, pp. 219-245; Wilhelm Biermann, *Franz Leo Benedikt Waldeck, Ein Streiter für Freiheit und Recht* (Paderborn, 1928), pp. 253-255, 290. On Waldeck see particularly Ludwig Dehio, "Benedict Waldeck," *Historische Zeitschrift*, Vol. 136 (1927), pp. 25-57.

[34] Friedrich von Bernhardi, ed., *Aus dem Leben Theodor von Bernhardis* (Leipzig, 1893-1906), III, 156-157; Ernst II, Herzog von Sachsen-Coburg-Gotha, *Aus meinem Leben und aus meiner Zeit* (Berlin, 1887-1889), II, 393-394.

[35] *GW*, II, 302-322.

choose between the violation of the confederate constitution and the surrender of Prussian independence. Since Prussia must choose the former, this would expose her to a war of "execution" intended to end her resistance for all time.

It is highly doubtful if Bismarck actually believed this an imminent possibility. But his exaggeration of Austria's intentions enabled him to give a sense of urgency to the question which now followed: with what means could Prussia defend herself against such a development? The medium states, he believed, were the key to the situation. The effectiveness of Austrian policy in Germany depended upon their support; only by gaining control over them could Prussia recover the initiative. It was futile to try to win them by acts of friendship. They must be coerced.

In the *Booklet* there is no mention of the combinations of European politics which for five years had played the primary role in Bismarck's calculations on this point. He now took the view that the only suitable source of power with which to buttress Prussian foreign policy was the moral pressure of German public opinion. In contrast to their governments, the interests of most Germans outside Austria coincided with those of the Prussian state. In order to make this fact apparent, Berlin need only encourage the Prussian press and parliament to take a more active interest in questions of foreign policy. Bismarck had no doubt that the general symphony of public opinion would follow the score composed by the government. Outside Prussia the theme would be taken up by the press and legislatures of the lesser states. The few chords of dissent would be lost in the swelling harmony. Before such a demonstration the other German governments must inevitably give way.

Whatever promoted the interest of Prussia, he declared, added to the welfare of the German nation. For Bismarck this was a new and significant argument. The first hint of it had appeared in a memorial to Manteuffel of May 1857. Here he accused the princes of the lesser states of being aware that their "exaggerated sovereignty" was an "evil for Germany." "They know very well that Prussia's disunited situation is difficult enough in itself to bear and that the unnatural compulsion of the small intervening states to assert their independence has become a severe handicap for us and for German life and development." Arguing for rapprochement with France, he wrote, "Only outside Germany are the means available to consolidate our position in the interest of Germany itself."[36]

In the *Booklet*, however, Bismarck found these means *within* Germany, and hence his contention was all the more persuasive. The true representative of the national welfare, he declared, was Prussia, "the pure German state," rather than the confederation, whose majorities were "dependent upon non-German interests." "There is nothing more German than precisely the development of the particularistic interests of Prussia rightly interpreted."[37]

These phrases have a strange and discordant sound coming from the arch-reactionary of 1848 and even from the diplomatic realist of the 1850's. Since 1851 he had consistently derided those of his colleagues who appealed to the "German" interest. He had scornfully rejected the criticism that his filibustering in the diet had harmed Germany by preventing any united action on the part of the confederation. In Frankfurt and Vienna he had challenged his opponents to abandon the hypocritical phrases of German patriotism and negotiate realistically on the basis of self-interest. However inconsistent his arguments, Bismarck's purpose was undeviating. His aim was to expand the power of the Prussian state and he was willing to consider all possible means to that end. This was the narrow bridge leading across the chasm which had previously separated him from the German national cause.

By March 1858 Bismarck had conceived a revolutionary plan for Prussian expansion, the execution of which would one day startle Europe. He proposed that Prussia exploit the moral power of German nationalism in the interest of the state, that a conservative monarchy deliberately employ the sentiment for national unity to reinforce its foreign policy at the cost of a conservative foe. For the time being, however, he had little success with his proposals. During the summer he conferred with William in Baden-Baden, but apparently got nowhere. When the new cabinet took office in the fall, William and Schleinitz decided on rapprochement with Austria and Britain. It was a popular decision in Prussia. In liberal dogma friendship with Britain was a basic tenet. But even the conservatives (including Gerlach) approved because of their alarm over French and Russian "Caesarism."[38] Naturally

36 *GW*, ii, 217-223.   37 *GW*, ii, 317-322, also 370-371.
38 *APP*, i/1, 52-54, 60-62, 67; Boris Nolde, *Die Petersburger Mission Bismarcks, 1859-1862, Russland und Europa zu Beginn der Regierung Alexander II* (Leipzig, 1936), pp. 1-2; Friese, *Russland und Preussen*, pp. 152 ff.

this choice meant that the bellicose Junker from Schönhausen had to be recalled from Frankfurt. In March 1859 he traveled for seven days across drifted plains and frozen streams to his new post in St. Petersburg. With bitter irony he wrote of having been "put in cold storage on the Neva."[39]

[39] *GW*, xiv, 495. As usual, he blamed his political misfortune upon feminine intrigue, maintaining that his replacement's wife, Countess Usedom, hankered for the society and climate of Frankfurt. *GW*, xv, 135 ff.

CHAPTER SIX

PETERSBURG AND PARIS

1. THE REVIVAL OF THE NATIONAL CAUSE

"REGRET," Napoleon told the Austrian ambassador at a new year's reception, 1859, "that our relations are not as good as I wished, but please report to Vienna that my personal feelings toward the Kaiser are unchanged."[1] This ominous remark presaged a new revolutionary epoch in European politics. At Plombières in July the emperor had plotted with Cavour for the unification of Italy. On March 3, 1859 he secured the benevolent neutrality of Russia. On April 23 the blundering Buol precipitated the struggle by an ultimatum against Sardinia. Once more the forces of national revolution, quiescent since 1849, were in motion. Ultimately they were to escape the control of the man who evoked them. The sorcerer on the Seine proved to be but an apprentice, whom no master came to save.

With remarkable prescience Bismarck had anticipated the new epoch and its potentialities for Prussia. From Petersburg he urged his government to seize its opportunity. "Ours will be the winning card in the present situation," he wrote to Gustav von Alvensleben, the regent's adjutant, "if we let Austria become deeply involved in the war with France and then burst out with our entire army to the southward, taking our boundary stakes in our knapsacks and planting them again on the Bodensee or where the Protestant faith ceases to predominate." The divided segments of the Prussian state must be united. Within twenty-four hours the incorporated peoples would fight for their new master, "especially if the prince regent will do them the favor of rebaptizing the kingdom of Prussia as the kingdom of Germany."

This was the "safest play" Prussia could make. If "too adventurous," Berlin should at least exploit the situation "either to change our relationship to the confederation or to release our-

[1] Joseph A. von Hübner, *Neun Jahre der Erinnerungen eines österreichischen Botschafters in Paris unter dem zweiten Kaiserreich, 1851-1859* (Berlin, 1904), II, 150-151.

selves from it."[2] To Schleinitz he wrote that "Prussia would soon be able to construct better and more natural relations with her German neighbors," once the confederation were dissolved. "I would like to see the word 'German' instead of 'Prussian' inscribed on our banners only when we are more closely and more suitably united with our countrymen than previously; it loses some of its charm when used as it is now in connection with the confederate diet."[3]

But again Bismarck's counsel was ignored in Berlin. Like his brother in the Crimean war, William was unable to arrive at a clear and decisive policy. While sympathetic toward Austria, he deplored Buol's ultimatum which cut short his efforts to preserve peace. The revolutionary implications of Napoleon's attack alarmed him, but so did the national indignation in Germany against France. He wished neither to ally with Austria nor to exploit her distress for the expansion of Prussian power in Germany. After the Hapsburg defeat at Magenta on June 4 he mobilized six army corps and proposed in London and Petersburg "armed mediation" to halt the struggle. In Vienna he demanded the right of command over the confederate contingents.[4]

Bismarck was outraged at the prospect that his government would "draw the Hapsburg chestnuts out of the fire." Zealously he reported the threats of Alexander and Gorchakov that Russia would never permit France to go down to defeat under the weight of Austrian and Prussian arms; from the moment of Prussian entry into the conflict, Germany, rather than Italy, would be the main theater of war.[5] In the Russian capital he made no secret of his disagreement with the policy of William and Schleinitz. Word of his disloyalty filtered back to Berlin. For a time William considered either a reprimand or recall.[6]

But suddenly the fighting stopped. Shocked by the bloodshed,

2 The contents of this letter must be pieced together from two sources: *GW*, xiv, 517, and Meyer, *Bismarcks Kampf*, pp. 480-481.

3 *GW*, iii, 38. See also iii, 33-34, and Leopold von Gerlach, *Denkwürdigkeiten* (Berlin, 1891), ii, 652.

4 *APP*, i/1, 172-176, 274-284, 421-424, 467-468, 546-555, 646-647, 654-657, 749-756; Berner, *Kaiser Wilhelm*, i, 453-461, 497-501; Hans Kentmann, "Preussen und die Bundeshilfe an Österreich im Jahre 1859," *Mitteilungen des österreichischen Instituts für Geschichtsforschung*, Ergänzungsband xii (1933), pp. 297-415.

5 *GW*, iii, 22-23, 33, 58, 61; vii, 40-41; xiv, 516, 519; Nolde, *Petersburger Mission*, pp. 62 ff.

6 Johannes Schultze, ed., *Kaiser Wilhelms I. Weimarer Briefe* (Berlin, 1924), ii, 15-16; Gruner, "Rückblick," p. 78; Nolde, *Petersburger Mission*, p. 67.

alarmed over the pace of Italian unification, and uncertain of Prussian policy, Napoleon negotiated the peace of Villafranca. None of the major powers was satisfied with the results: Austria lost a province; Prussia had antagonized all and gained nothing; Russia and France had some grounds for satisfaction, but both were soon alarmed at the speed with which Italian unification proceeded and the form it assumed. Sardinia devoured the chestnuts, while the rest came away with scorched fingers.

The appointment of the new-era cabinet and the French attack upon Austria produced startling changes in the whole political climate of Germany. Throughout the country the fall of the feudal party in Berlin was greeted with enthusiasm. Since William and several of his ministers had supported Radowitz in 1850, those German nationalists who looked to Prussia for leadership were filled with fresh hope. It was chiefly the war of 1859, however, which aroused the question of German unity from a decade of uneasy slumber. Romantic conservatives and liberal nationalists alike were disturbed by the French attack upon a member of the confederation. In Italy the first Napoleon had begun the career of conquest which brought the borders of France to the Rhine. The crisis refreshed the memory of 1812-1813 and produced a demand for war. Over the course of the conflict there was general disappointment. The failure of Austria and Prussia to come to terms demonstrated again the incapacity of the German Confederation. Fresh rumors of an entente between France and Russia kindled the fear of a hostile coalition against which Germany had no adequate defense.[7]

These anxieties produced the demand for a German state capable of defending the nation against foreign attack. In turn this brought up the further question of the inclusion or exclusion of Austria. Once again the politically conscious public began to divide upon the issue of a great- or little-German unification. The strength of the great-Germanists lay mostly in the south among the farmers and rural nobility, the middle class of the small towns,

---

[7] On the development of German national sentiment see Heinrich Ritter von Srbik, *Deutsche Einheit, Idee und Wirklichkeit vom Heiligen Reich bis Königgrätz* (Munich, 1935-1942), ii, 297 ff., 377 ff.; also Kurt von Raumer, "Das Jahr 1859 und die deutsche Einheitsbewegung in Bayern," in Herman Haupt, ed., *Quellen und Darstellungen zur Geschichte der Burschenschaft und der deutschen Einheitsbewegung*, viii (Heidelberg, 1925), 273-327; and Annie Mittelstaedt, *Der Krieg von 1859, Bismarck und die öffentliche Meinung in Deutschland* (Stuttgart, 1904).

and the politically active Catholics, that of the little-Germanists among the bourgeoisie of the great towns, the industrial, commercial, and capitalistic interests, Protestants, and many intellectuals (especially the more popular historians).

From the beginning the little-German movement attained the greater momentum. Its leaders dominated the Nationalverein founded in September 1859 to agitate for German unity. For the first time German liberals of many political viewpoints coalesced in a common organization which transcended their differences. Although many southern liberals remained aloof, the Nationalverein succeeded by virtue of the vagueness of its first platform in uniting moderates and democrats who had split in 1848-1849 over the decision to invite Frederick William IV to become the constitutional monarch of a united Germany. The inclusion of former radicals produced internal tensions which lasted throughout the organization's history, but leadership remained in the hands of moderates and "realistic" democrats willing to accept the unification of Germany under a constitution preserving the autocratic authority of the Hohenzollern monarchy. At a second congress in 1860 they succeeded in establishing this as the association's program.[8]

The Nationalverein was not a mass movement, but an elite body of only a few thousand members led by a Hanoverian nobleman, Rudolf von Bennigsen. To be sure, the journalists, deputies, professors, and other notables who belonged had a public influence greater than their actual number. Nevertheless, the membership was largely middle-class and intentionally so. Repeatedly the association refused to lower its dues to encourage workingmen to join.[9] The primary purpose of its founders was to put the governments rather than the masses in motion. They did not intend to attack the ruling system, but to gain its cooperation for national ends. Their immediate hopes were placed on the new-era cabinet.

[8] See Srbik, *Deutsche Einheit*, III, 3 ff., and Adolf Rapp, *Grossdeutsch-Kleindeutsch*, in *Der deutsche Staatsgedanke* (Munich, 1922); Hermann Oncken, *Rudolf von Bennigsen* (Stuttgart, 1910), I, 346 ff., 435 ff.; Paul Herrmann, *Die Entstehung des deutschen Nationalvereins und die Gründung seiner Wochenschrift* (Leipzig, 1932); Walter Grube, *Die Neue Ära und der Nationalverein, Ein Beitrag zur Geschichte Preussens und der Einheitsbewegung* (Marburg, 1933); Kurt Bachteler, *Die öffentliche Meinung in der italienischen Krisis und die Anfänge des Nationalvereins in Württemberg 1859* (Tübingen, 1934).

[9] Hermann Oncken, "Der Nationalverein und die Anfänge der deutschen Arbeiterbewegung 1862-1863," *Archiv für die Geschichte des Sozialismus und der Arbeiterbewegung*, II (1912), 120-127.

2. BISMARCK, SCHLEINITZ, AND THE "NATIONALVEREIN"

In July 1859 Bismarck returned to Germany in wretched health. A quack doctor in Petersburg had treated his rheumatic knee with a mustard plaster which ate into the flesh and destroyed a vein. An eminent Russian surgeon advised amputation. In Berlin he lay for two weeks in a hotel consulting other doctors and considering other cures. But even in this condition his mind was politically active. From the press he learned of the intent to form the Nationalverein and grasped immediately its significance for his plans. A chance contact gave him the opportunity to establish liaison between its leaders and the Prussian cabinet. One day Victor von Unruh called upon him at the Hotel Royal.[10]

An industrialist and leading liberal, Unruh had first met Bismarck in the united diet. Although politically in strong disagreement, the two men held each other in high personal regard.[11] Unruh was completely unprepared for what he now heard. "Prussia is completely isolated," Bismarck told him. "There is but one ally for Prussia, if she knows how to win and handle them . . . the German people!" Laughing at Unruh's astonishment, he hastened to reassure him. "I am the same Junker of ten years ago . . . but I would have no perception and no understanding, if I could not recognize clearly the realities of the situation."[12]

The response to this parley was gratifying. On September 12, three days before the meeting in Frankfurt which created the Nationalverein, Unruh composed a letter to Bismarck. The leaders of the national revival, he declared, were waiting "with great suspense" to see how Prussia would react to their movement. Austria had already announced her vigorous opposition. By "ener-

10 *GW*, xv, 158-159; Robert von Keudell, *Fürst und Fürstin Bismarck, Erinnerungen 1846-1872* (Berlin, 1901), p. 72.

11 Unruh had been the last speaker of the Prussian national assembly before its dissolution in December 1848. During 1856 Bismarck had tried to protect him from persecution by the Manteuffel regime. *GW*, xiv, 560; Unruh, *Erinnerungen*, pp. 194 ff.

12 *GW*, vii, 37-39. The date of this interview is uncertain. Unruh's account was written sometime after the event and the circumstances he describes do not fully correspond with any of Bismarck's visits to Berlin during this period. Willy Andreas dated it "mid-March." *Ibid.* Erich Eyck accepted this view. *Bismarck, Leben und Werk* (Zurich, 1941-1944), i, 296. But Egmont Zechlin chose September 24. *Bismarck und die Grundlegung der deutschen Grossmacht* (Stuttgart, 1930), p. 155. Boris Nolde appears to have picked the more likely time, the latter half of July. *Petersburger Mission*, p. 204.

getic action in the national question" Prussia could win many hearts in Germany. But if she failed to give forthright support, "we will not be able to do anything in the Prussian interest." Zeal for the national cause was their only motive. "We, including Herr von Bennigsen, would be sincerely pleased if you should be named minister of foreign affairs."[13]

Bismarck received this note in Baden-Baden, whence he had been called for consultation with the regent. Here he discussed the liberal overture freely with Schleinitz. Returning to Berlin in late September, he reported another conference with the liberal leader. According to Unruh the general mood of the Frankfurt meeting was highly favorable to Prussia. "Rather the most severe Prussian military government than the misery of petty disunion," the democrat August Metz had cried to great applause. Years later Unruh admitted that he had discussed with Bismarck on this occasion the possibility of a "temporary military despotism," insisting he had meant the dictatorship of a revolutionary government, rather than that of a legitimate monarchy.[14] But at the time Bismarck understood otherwise.

Schleinitz found Unruh's information "noteworthy—gratifying." Nevertheless, he was suspicious of popular forces and sought to steer a middle course, neither hostile toward nor allied to the national movement. While sympathetic to the cause of national unity, he had too great a respect for law and legitimacy to follow a revolutionary policy.[15] He was a man of suavity and charm, but lacking in energy and decision. Even the supporters of the new-era cabinet complained of his "vacillating weakness, his way of saying nothing in his dispatches which he does not retract in the next sentence, this constant 'to be sure—but—yet—indeed—nevertheless.' "[16] So great was his fear of France that he wished to accept an Austrian offer of alliance. But his colleagues in the cabinet were inclined toward a national policy in opposition to Vi-

---

13 Horst Kohl, ed., *Bismarck-Jahrbuch*, IV (1897), 154-157.

14 Unruh, *Erinnerungen*, pp. 209 ff.; *GW*, III, 64; VII, 129; XIII, 155.

15 L. Raschdau, ed., *Bismarcks Briefwechsel mit dem Minister von Schleinitz, 1858-1861* (Stuttgart, 1905), p. 47; Kohl, *Anhang*, II, 304; Grube, *Neue Ära und Nationalverein*, pp. 36 ff. Certainly he was not encouraged by Bismarck's disclosure of Unruh's desire to see Bismarck as foreign minister. Unruh, *Erinnerungen*, p. 209.

16 Heinrich von Sybel quoted in *Aus dem Leben Bernhardis*, III, 313. See also *APP*, II/1, xi.

enna.[17] In March 1860 Charles Anthony and Rudolf Auerswald persuaded the regent to look for another foreign minister. Bismarck was an obvious candidate.[18]

By chance he was still in Germany. During the winter he had lain desperately ill of pneumonia and rheumatic fever at Hohendorf in Pomerania—by his diagnosis "an explosion of all the anger I accumulated during eight years in Frankfurt."[19] In March he was better and returned to Berlin at the height of the crisis over Schleinitz. The ubiquitous Theodor von Bernhardi wrote in his diary on the 29th that the Junker was "seeking contact with the liberals and telling everyone willing to listen that he has been misunderstood, even slandered, and that he is actually a man of liberal outlook."[20]

Early in April the regent summoned Bismarck and Schleinitz to present their opposing views. As usual the former argued for the revision of Prussian policy toward Austria and for rapprochement with Russia. Apparently he made no mention of his desire for close relations with France. But he did present his case for the drastic revision of the confederation and the creation of a German parliament. Schleinitz, on the other hand, maintained that France, rather than Austria, was Prussia's foremost foe. Solidarity with Austria against this hazard was the traditional policy of the Hohenzollern monarchy. In view of a possible Franco-Russian combination, the danger from across the Rhine was more acute than ever. Popular opinion was opposed to an alliance with Russia.[21]

No sooner had Schleinitz finished than the regent announced his decision against any change in the foreign ministry. To Bis-

[17] *APP*, ii/1, 63-64, 80-83, 259-266; Rudolf Haym, *Das Leben Max Dunckers* (Berlin, 1891), pp. 211 ff.; *GW*, xiv, 545.

[18] *GW*, xv, 161 ff.   [19] *GW*, iii, 67.

[20] *Aus dem Leben Bernhardis*, iii, 305, also 309. In the Landtag Bismarck heard Georg von Vincke, his old opponent, praise him as an opponent of Austrian hegemony in Germany. There were even rumors of a coming Vincke-Bismarck cabinet. Eyck, *Bismarck*, i, 350.

[21] *GW*, xv, 161-162; vii, 113. The date of this conference is uncertain. On March 26 the ministers debated the issue in a crown council and William made his decision for a middle course. On April 5 Schleinitz presented his resignation, which was refused. *APP*, ii/1, 282-285. On April 10 Bismarck wrote that, had there actually been a crisis over the position of foreign minister "ten days ago," it was "now" over, although the question of policy was still unsettled. Eight days before the Regent had granted him permission to return to Petersburg, but his pass had not arrived. *GW*, xiv, 545. The press reported Bismarck's presence in the palace on April 3 and 11. Horst Kohl, ed., *Bismarck-Regesten* (Leipzig, 1891), i, 166.

marck this meant that William had previously made up his mind and staged the conference merely to appease Charles Anthony and Auerswald. Yet for many weeks he refused Bismarck's request for permission to return to Petersburg. Apparently William was still uncertain what use to make of this talented, volatile man. In June the order finally came; the Junker returned to the Neva for another winter. The Hohenzoller, said Charles Anthony, had declined to "give billy goat the job of gardener."[22]

3. BISMARCK IN ISOLATION

William's decision had indeed already been made. In a crown council on March 26 he had listened to the conflicting views within the cabinet and afterward composed for Schleinitz a directive dictating a policy of rapprochement, though not alliance, with Austria against France.[23] Despite his weakening confidence in Schleinitz, there appeared to be no other practicable policy. Recent events had made the minister to Russia a highly dubious choice as foreign minister. At the moment Europe appeared on the verge of a fundamental readjustment in power relationships which would end the chaos produced by the Crimean war. This readjustment threatened Bismarck's plans and, even worse, his career.

In May 1859 the rash Buol, architect of disaster, had been replaced by Rechberg, disciple of Metternich and advocate of the holy alliance. At the Quai d'Orsay Walewski, conservative and russophile, lost his position as foreign minister (January 1860) to Thouvenel, radical and russophobe. During the same month came the first reports of Napoleon's intention to annex Nice and Savoy; in March he claimed them as his reward for permitting the unification of central Italy under Sardinia. In the tense atmosphere created by the recent war this event was interpreted as the beginning of a new era of Bonapartist expansion. His next target was expected to be the "natural frontier" of the Rhine. From the Thames to the Neva a wave of anxiety swept Europe. Palmerston and the British cabinet lost what remained of their faith in Napoleon. Czar Alexander and his advisers were shocked by the consequences of their bargain of the preceding year. The cost of revenge against Austrian perfidy was high. In Rumania, Hungary, and Poland the cause of national self-determination

[22] Haym, *Duncker*, p. 213.　　　　[23] *APP*, ii/I, 259-266, 282-285.

made new progress. During May came the dramatic landing of Garibaldi in Sicily followed by the collapse of the Neapolitan kingdom. The specter of revolution hovered over Europe. In July William and Franz Joseph met at Teplitz and in October they assembled at Warsaw with Alexander. The holy alliance appeared close to its day of resurrection.[24]

These developments placed Bismarck in a difficult situation. In recent years he had made no secret of his disagreement with the anti-French policy of his government. Naturally his views were distorted. Among liberals and conservatives alike he was reputed to be a "Bonapartist," the unprincipled advocate of alliance with Napoleon whatever the cost. As he neared the vortex of power these rumors circulated with increased velocity.[25]

In May 1860 he sought to counteract this "nonsense" among the ultra-conservatives by explaining his point once more to Leopold Gerlach. Formerly the two men had differed on both policy and principle, but now they disagreed on principle alone. "Fundamentally," wrote Bismarck, "you want nothing to do with Bonaparte and Cavour; I do not want to go with France and Sardinia— not because I hold it to be morally wrong, but because I consider it harmful to the interest of our security." It was a matter of "complete indifference" who ruled France. Considerations of law, justice, and legitimacy could never be used as criteria for foreign relations; the one and only consideration was "political utility." "I am a child of other times than yours, but just as true to mine as you to yours." "To me France would be the most dubious of all allies, although I must hold open the possibility of such an alliance, because one cannot play chess if 16 out of 64 squares are excluded from the game."[26]

After returning to Petersburg, Bismarck came under sharp attack in the nationalist press. Since September 1859, the leaders of the Nationalverein had given up the idea of alliance with the Hohenzollern monarchy. They were disappointed by the flabby policy of Schleinitz and had lost confidence in Bismarck, the agent through whom they had hoped to consummate the union. His reputed willingness to sacrifice German soil to Napoleon made the

---

[24] Werner E. Mosse, *The European Powers and the German Question, 1848-1871* (Cambridge, 1958), pp. 87 ff.; Nolde, *Petersburger Mission*, pp. 135 ff.

[25] Leopold Gerlach, *Denkwürdigkeiten*, II, 718-719; Haym, *Duncker*, p. 213; *Aus dem Leben Bernhardis*, III, 328-329, 337-339; IV, 14, 32, 294, 306.

[26] *GW*, XIV, 548-549; also VII, 39.

latter a convenient target.[27] In the conservative press no voice was raised in his defense. Bismarck felt betrayed by these men with whom he had so often "eaten from the same bowl." "One ought not to rely upon men," he commented bitterly. "I am thankful for every impulse which draws me within myself."[28]

The man from Schönhausen was isolated. His views on foreign policy had alienated his old friends among the Prussian conservatives, but had failed as yet to gain him the support of German liberals. He fought back by directing an old associate in Frankfurt, Carl Zitelmann, to show trusted journalists certain documents which would refute the accusations made against him. Furthermore, he asked Zitelmann to seek out Unruh. "Perhaps he can explain to you why the Nationalverein attacks me despite the fact that for nine years I have steered against wind and weather a course which, although for conservative aims and purposes, was nevertheless parallel to theirs."[29] But still the attacks continued.

The greatest hazard to Bismarck's future, however, was that the charges might be believed by those close to the regent. In desperation he requested of Gorchakov an official Russian denial that the Prussian envoy had ever proposed a three-power alliance against Austria involving the cession of German soil. But the vicechancellor refused: "Qui s'excuse, s'accuse."[30] Next Bismarck wrote to Auerswald: "Since 1856, I have characterized the alliance of France and Russia in my official reports to his majesty, the king, as an eventuality whose realization we must hinder with all our resources, because our position, as a member of such an alliance, will be a subordinate one and, as an opponent, a weak one." Because of the friction between Austria and Prussia, nevertheless, the German Confederation was not a viable institution for the defense of Germany in a dangerous war: "If, in spite of all our efforts, a Franco-Russian alliance cannot be prevented, we must in good time either ally ourselves closer with Russia than with France or come to such a fundamental understanding with Aus-

---

[27] Oncken, *Bennigsen*, I, 341 ff., 364 ff., 377-378, 521-522; Otto Westphal, *Welt- und Staatsauffassung des deutschen Liberalismus, Historische Bibliothek*, Vol. 41 (Munich, 1919), pp. 141 ff. Typical was a pamphlet by Karl Twesten which asserted, as though it were a matter of general knowledge, that the Junker envoy had sought during his stay in Germany in 1860 to bring about an alliance with France and Russia at the cost of German soil. *Was uns noch retten kann, ein Wort ohne Umschweife* (Berlin, 1861), p. 47.

[28] *GW*, XIV, 561-562.   [29] *GW*, XIV, 560.

[30] *GW*, III, 100-101.

tria that we can count on an honorable collaboration between the two powers and thereby upon an inner strengthening of the Austrian monarchy. I have always had the courage of my convictions, and, if I considered advantageous the furtherance of the Franco-Russian alliance and our union with the same, I would openly say so." In the existing situation the promotion of such an idea would be "proof of inconsequence and lack of judgment." He feared that such rumors would reflect upon the "soundness of my political understanding." "If I have desired an alliance in recent years, it has been one with England and Russia, but this is easier to talk about than to bring about."

Auerswald should know, he maintained, from their conversations of the previous spring "that I am neither Austrian, nor French, nor Russian, but Prussian, and that I see our welfare only in trust in our own strength and that of the German national movement."[31] In a letter to Alexander von Below-Hohendorf, his host during the long illness of the preceding winter, he reiterated this point. "During the entire period of my visit in Germany," he wrote, "I never advised anything else but reliance upon our own strength and, in event of war, upon that evoked by us from the German nation."[32]

4. A REVISION IN STRATEGY

From his defense of 1860 against the attacks of the National-verein and ultra-conservatives it is evident that Bismarck's views had undergone a considerable change since 1857. The shift was one of strategy rather than of conviction. As before, his basic aim was to further the interests of Prussia. He was not a convert to the cause of German nationalism, but he had come to appreciate its potential utility for the expansion of Prussian power. This was now, in fact, the primary force with which he hoped to coerce Austria and the lesser states into granting the Prussian demands. No longer did he count upon a Franco-Russian alliance to achieve

[31] *GW*, xiv, 558-560. In November he again wrote Auerswald, "In the long run we have actually but one reliable support, the national strength of the German people (if we do not intentionally reject it). This will be true as long as they see the Prussian army as their defender and their hope for the future and do not see us conducting wars for the benefit of other dynasties than the Hohenzollern." *GW*, xiv, 564-565.

[32] *GW*, xiv, 561-562. Concerning Bismarck's influence on Below see Ernst Ludwig von Gerlach, *Aufzeichnungen aus seinem Leben und Wirken, 1795-1877* (Schwerin, 1903), ii, 233.

this end. He conveniently forgot that in 1856 he had wanted to jump "with both feet" into such an alliance. Now he even maintained that this coalition must be prevented if at all possible. What were the reasons for this revision?

Since the Crimean war, events had shown that, despite its apparent logic, there were grave obstacles in the path of a Franco-Russian alliance. To be sure, neither of the powers could succeed in its major objectives without support from the other: France in the revision of the settlement of 1815 and Russia in the revision of that of 1856. Without Russia's benevolent neutrality Napoleon would have hesitated to move against Austria in 1859 and without French assistance Russia had little chance of liquidating the restrictions placed on her sovereignty in the Black Sea. Yet Napoleon was reluctant to part company with London; he feared British sea power, for which Russia could supply no substitute. Furthermore, Czar Alexander was much too conservative to relish entering into a genuinely revolutionary compact with Napoleon. After the annexation of Nice and Savoy he became increasingly cool to the idea.[33] But Gorchakov was incorrigible. Even in the midst of the conservative rapprochement of 1860 he continued to hold out an arm to Paris, eager for the most feeble handshake.[34]

In Petersburg, Bismarck had the chance to study at close hand the mind and character of the Russian vice-chancellor. Superficially brilliant, fluent of thought and adept at phrases, he was more political technician than statesman. Bismarck recognized that France offered the only possible "maneuver terrain" for Russian policy. Nevertheless, after observing for some time the prince's "repetitive game of advance and withdrawal" he began to doubt its seriousness. Russia was absorbed in internal problems and could give little time or energy to foreign affairs. For reasons of prestige Gorchakov maintained the appearance of an active policy,

[33] The desire for alliance with France and Prussia, which Alexander expressed to Bismarck in June 1860, was based on the belief that the two conservative powers might in this way keep a close rein on Napoleon. Ludwig Raschdau, ed., *Die politischen Berichte des Fürsten Bismarck aus Petersburg und Paris, 1859-1862* (Berlin, 1920), I, 115-116. A few days later Bismarck reported evidence of growing antipathy on the part of Alexander against France. *Ibid.*, pp. 128-129.

[34] On the general problem of rapprochement between Paris and Petersburg see Schüle, *Russland und Frankreich*, pp. 141-149; Christian Friese, *Russland und Preussen vom Krimkrieg bis zum Polnischen Aufstand* (Berlin, 1931), pp. 13 ff., 88 ff., 124 ff.; Mosse, *European Powers*, pp. 87-93; also Alfred Stern, "Ein russisch-französischer Bündnisplan 1858," *Europäische Gespräche*, IX (1931), 30-39.

but it was "basically just a sham fight having neither aim nor result, a gymnastic performance which is executed with elegance and distinction by this brilliantly capable artist and then repeated."[35]

It was never Bismarck's way to cling to outworn possibilities. When the alliance failed to develop, he ceased to base his plans upon it. But he was probably honest in disclaiming any desire for such a coalition. As his letter to Auerswald shows, he now fully appreciated its dangers for Prussia. During recent years Napoleon's policies had shown a general shiftiness which inspired caution. "It is Napoleon's great talent," Bismarck wrote Schleinitz, "to conceal himself in a cloud of vapor in such a way that no one knows where or whether he will emerge. Perhaps he will remain within and steam leisurely away *ad infinitum.*" His hidden ambitions and slippery character made the gray-eyed man in the Tuileries indeed a "dubious" ally.[36]

Nevertheless, it would be false to assume that France and Russia had ceased to play important roles in the system of pressures by which Bismarck hoped to gain his ends in Germany. On the contrary, he continued to argue that Prussia must constantly dangle the possibility of alliance with France before the eyes of Austria and the medium states. In 1860-1861 he did his best to soften the suspicions of Schleinitz and William that Napoleon would attempt to annex the Rhineland as he had Nice and Savoy. The emperor was well aware, Bismarck maintained, that such a move would seriously upset the European balance and bring into existence a counter-coalition similar to that which had defeated his uncle. Furthermore, he would be inclined to attempt it only if assured of the active cooperation of the German medium states. In order to prevent this, Prussia need only preserve a more intimate relationship than the medium states with France. The function of a Franco-Prussian rapprochement in Bismarck's altered

---

[35] *GW*, III, 305; also 390; Friedrich Frahm, *Bismarcks Stellung zu Frankreich bis zum 4. Juli 1866* (Kiel, 1911), pp. 50 ff. On Gorchakov see Nolde, *Petersburger Mission*, pp. 25 ff., and François Charles-Roux, *Alexandre II, Gortchakoff, et Napoleon III* (Paris, 1913), pp. 115-116.

[36] *GW*, III, 207; XIV, 549; VII, 39. To Bernstorff in January 1862 he wrote, "France and Austria are each in their own way, destined as a rule to be opponents of Prussia, not through the arbitrary will of their momentary rulers, but by the weight of enduring historical circumstances." *GW*, III, 315.

strategy was to isolate Austria and the medium states, rather than to prepare a military alliance against them.[37]

His purpose in promoting good relations with Russia was similar. In Petersburg he worked constantly and with success to ingratiate himself with Gorchakov and the royal family.[38] His reports to Berlin left out what might harm and emphasized what might improve relations between the two powers. Nevertheless, it is grotesque to maintain that the contact with Russia, which proved so useful in future years, was entirely of his manufacture.[39] Its foundation had been laid in the Crimean war and in the close family tie between the Romanovs and Hohenzollern (Alexander's mother was William's sister). The failure of Gorchakov's French policy and of the attempt to renew the holy alliance left Russia no other potential ally than Prussia. After the Warsaw conference in October 1860 the fear of revolution receded and Austro-Russian rivalry in the Balkans increased. It was apparent, nevertheless, that Russian policy had entered a dormant stage. By 1861 Bismarck had little to report from Petersburg other than domestic conditions.[40] The most that could be expected of Russia in any future clash with Austria was benevolent neutrality.

Great Britain had also been drawn into his scheme. Previously he had discounted altogether the importance of London for Prussian policy. In 1857 he had told Leopold Gerlach that Britain could never be regarded as a reliable ally. The reform bill had placed her foreign policy at the mercy of shifting majorities in parliament. His purpose at the time, however, was to dissuade Manteuffel and the king from ever joining Britain and Austria to counteract a Franco-Russian alliance. Even then he recognized that Britain was Prussia's "unnatural enemy." There was no conflict between their interests; only the momentary combinations of European politics threatened to force the two countries into opposed camps. When the danger of an Austro-British coalition passed, the "unnatural enemy" became a "natural ally."[41]

37 *GW*, III, 69-70, 220, 251, 289-290; also I, 505.

38 *GW*, III, 291; Friese, *Russland und Preussen*, pp. 238-239; Gerhard Heinze, *Bismarck und Russland bis zur Reichsgründung* (Würzburg, 1939), pp. 25-26. Long before arriving in Petersburg he was known to the czar as a "useful and very devoted friend." F. de Martens, *Recueil des traités et conventions conclus par la Russie avec les puissances étrangères* (St. Petersburg, 1874-1909), VIII, 453.

39 Mosse, *European Powers*, pp. 93-101.

40 *GW*, III, 174, 305, 327; Friese, *Russland und Preussen*, pp. 247-248.

41 *GW*, XIV, 436, 440, 468.

Nevertheless, Bismarck's statement to Auerswald concerning his desire for alliance with Britain and Russia must be treated with caution. The government of the new era was partial toward London. Britain had long been the mecca of German liberal opinion. During and after the Crimean war, William had favored a pro-British policy. Albert, the prince consort, had been his friend and adviser. By adding Britain to his list of Prussia's potential allies, Bismarck brought his own policy, with no sacrifice to its essential purpose, a little nearer to the dominant current in the Prussian court.[42] As he indicated to Auerswald, however, a union between Britain and Russia was most improbable. Throughout the nineteenth century the interests of these two powers were in conflict from the Balkans to India; no other cleavage among European powers was more difficult to bridge.[43]

Even if attainable, an alliance with Britain and Russia could never have performed the function which Bismarck had originally expected of a coalition with France and Russia. Russia had to be discounted for reasons already analyzed, and Britain was not a land power capable of effective military assistance against Austria. Throughout the century London had steadily avoided entanglement in continental struggles in which she had no direct, tangible interest; only a French attack upon the Rhineland or a renewal of the Russian drive toward the Mediterranean would have created such a situation. Bismarck's purpose in promoting an understanding with Britain and Russia was, therefore, to isolate Austria rather than create a dynamic alliance for her military coercion.[44]

In 1860 yet another piece was added to Bismarck's diplomatic chessboard. To Schleinitz he described the enlarged Sardinia as "our natural ally against France, if the occasion should arise, as well as against Austria. The French alliance would cease to be dangerous and dictatorial for Piedmont if she could gain support

---

[42] Lord Bloomfield, British ambassador in Berlin, believed Bismarck's motive was that of ingratiating himself with Prince William. Veit Valentin, "Bismarck and England in the earlier period of his career," *Transactions of the Royal Historical Society*, 4th series, xx (London, 1937), 28.

[43] He recognized that Gorchakov's interest in such a combination was insincere. His aim was to disrupt the Anglo-French entente and thus force France to seek an understanding with Russia. *GW*, iii, 158; Friese, *Russland und Preussen*, p. 240. For Bismarck's efforts to improve relations with Russia and Britain see *GW*, iii, 30-33, 156-158, 247, 264, 315; Raschdau, *Berichte aus Petersburg und Paris*, i, 74, also 96-97.

[44] Heinze, *Bismarck und Russland*, p. 16.

from Prussia."[45] After Napoleon's incorporation of Nice and Savoy he shifted his policy, though not his principle. In the letter of May to Leopold Gerlach, already quoted, he wrote, "In my opinion this is not the time to stiffen Sardinia's back against France; the moment is either behind or ahead of us. I believe the prospect remote in view of the personal situation at home, but I do not consider it impermissible."[46] The "personal situation" was the attitude of the regent who was shocked by the overturning of so many thrones and sovereignties in Italy and alarmed at the apparent inclination of Napoleon to round out the French frontiers to their "natural boundaries."

European legitimists were angered even more when the house of Savoy continued to spread its rule over the rest of Italy (except for Rome and Venice). Czar Alexander was especially outraged by the conquest of Naples in which his dynasty had a long-standing interest. Through Bismarck, Gorchakov sought to persuade the regent, who was both indignant and undecided, to join Russia in severing relations with Turin.[47] In Berlin the *Kreuzzeitung* romanticists agitated for the same cause. On this subject Bismarck was a poor intermediary. He used the opportunity to explain to Schleinitz how greatly his own views now differed from those of the *Kreuzzeitung*.[48] "Our sword of justice cannot reach over the whole world." The only criterion of Prussian policy was "consolidation" of Prussia's interest. "Although I can be wrong, I am convinced that the creation of a strong Italian state in the south between France and Austria is beneficial to Prussia"— beneficial abroad, because the creation of a potential ally would add to Prussian security, and beneficial at home, because a friendly policy toward Italian national unity would make a favorable impression upon German liberal nationalists. During 1861 Bismarck urged his government to recognize the new state. "In my opinion we would have had to invent the kingdom of Italy, had it not come into existence on its own."[49]

45 *GW*, III, 70.

46 *GW*, XIV, 549.

47 *GW*, III, 115, 118; *APP*, III/1, 653-655, 663-669. Cavour answered conservative protests with the argument that in supporting Garibaldi he had saved the monarchical principle in Italy by stealing the national cause from the republicans! *Ibid.*, pp. 683-685.

48 Nolde, *Petersburger Mission*, pp. 127-128, 135 ff., 148 ff.

49 *GW*, III, 147-148, 179, 314, 319.

141

Italy was a useful pawn. As long as Venice lay in Austrian hands, the new state would inevitably be found in the ranks of the Hapsburg foes. In peace or war, Italy could be used to exert a pressure on Austria's southern flank which would weaken her resistance to Prussia in the north. Nevertheless, this "natural ally" had only limited value for Prussia. Her diplomatic and military strength was not great, and her geographical position made her of little use in the diplomatic struggle for hegemony over the German medium states.

5. A GERMAN PARLIAMENT

It is now apparent that in Bismarck's strategic plan the Franco-Russian coalition had been replaced by the movement for German national unity:[50] The function expected of the latter was that previously assigned the former: to supply a means of pressure with which to gain the initiative in the struggle against Austria and the medium states. This vital substitution was made possible and in some degree dictated by the changing conditions of Prussian and European politics. But Bismarck also saw that an alliance with German nationalism had none of the drawbacks of a coalition with France and Russia. Having lost their revolution, the German liberals were a controllable ally. In this combination the Hohenzollern monarchy had the best chance of remaining the dominant partner.

But how was the national movement to be mobilized against Austria and her German allies? As early as 1858, at the time of the composition of the *Booklet*, Bismarck believed that this could best be done by raising the demand for a German parliament. The proposal appears for the first time in a letter of that year to Below-Hohendorf. In it Bismarck foresaw that in 1865, when the customs treaties were to expire, Prussia might be forced to dissolve the Zollverein and begin anew. It would then be necessary "to adopt one of the features of the union project of 1849 by establishing a kind of customs parliament with provision for *itio in partes*, if the others demand it." Such an institution would give to the German taxpayer a way in which to counteract the particularistic economic policies of the lesser states. Through this channel the most important economic interests of the nation could be

---

[50] Zechlin takes a similar view, but seeks the accompanying motives in a somewhat different light. *Grundlegung*, pp. 157-158.

brought to the support of Prussian policy in Germany. Because of congruent interests the two were obvious allies.[51] Two years later he raised this proposal again in a memorial addressed to Schleinitz. The chief issue of the moment was again that of Hesse-Kassel. Backed by Austria and the majority in the diet, the elector had once more attempted to subvert the liberal constitution of his principality. Although Schleinitz was inclined to give way, Bismarck argued that Prussia should instead seize the opportunity to subvert the German Confederation. At the minister's request he drafted a Prussian declaration which roundly condemned the diet for interfering in the domestic affairs of its members. The confederation was incapable, it declared, of realizing the national aspirations of the German people. The common feeling of national unity was the "only cement which can make the confederate contract into something more than an ordinary treaty of state between neighboring sovereigns." In an accompanying note to Schleinitz he proposed that the declaration also include the call for a "representative assembly in the confederation."[52] It was the most radical statement yet to come from Bismarck's pen. As he anticipated, Schleinitz made no use of it.

In the summer of 1861 the opportunity came to advance his plan once again under more favorable circumstances. A year had passed since William had made his choice between Bismarck and Schleinitz. The latter had been generally unsuccessful in his attempt at alliance with Britain and Austria. Lord Russell, the British foreign secretary, had shied away from any policy which might force France to combine with Russia. In the autumn, the British press raised a clamor over the alleged mistreatment of a traveler named MacDonald arrested by the Prussian police. During the winter the British public reacted critically to news of the growing conflict in Berlin between king and parliament. The climate of opinion, once seemingly favorable to such an alliance, appeared to be growing cold.[53]

Schleinitz's policy toward Austria had been equally calamitous. The rapprochement begun so hopefully at Teplitz in July 1860 collapsed when the attempt was made to negotiate concrete terms. No more than in 1859 were the Austrians willing to concede the

51 *GW*, xiv, 486-487. For Below's letter see Kohl, *Jahrbuch*, iii, 127-129.
52 *GW*, iii, 71-76.
53 Friese, *Russland und Preussen*, pp. 243 ff.

dual division of command over confederate forces during wartime, or the Prussianization of the lesser contingents through their adoption of the Prussian military system. William was gravely disappointed. In this mood he was open to suggestions for a Prussian diplomatic offensive in the German question.[54]

Since 1859 it had become more and more difficult for German rulers to ignore the issue of German national unity. Among professional groups—lawyers, historians, physicians, theologians, school teachers, and book dealers—it had become common to hold national conventions with political overtones. Even more significant were the ever larger national festivals of choral, hunting, and gymnastic societies. Their meetings sparkled with nationalistic oratory, their banquets with patriotic toasts. On Bastille day 1861, a fanatic named Becker fired several shots at William in Baden-Baden because he had not "done enough for German unity." All that the Hohenzoller suffered was a contusion and stiff neck. When the reactionary Hessian minister, Baron Dalwigk, tried to exploit the incident by urging suppression of the Nationalverein, William replied sharply that the wiser course was to satisfy the just demands of the German people.[55]

In Baden-Baden William was surrounded by liberal-national influences. His son-in-law, Grand Duke Frederick of Baden, and the latter's foreign minister, Franz von Roggenbach, had been warned by their old-liberal correspondents in Berlin that the ailing new-era cabinet could be rescued only by a strong initiative in foreign affairs.[56] To William they presented a plan for the federal union of little Germany with a national parliament and Prussian executive, to be made acceptable to Austria by a constitutional guarantee of the entire Hapsburg empire. But the conservatives were also active. Summoned from Petersburg by Minister of War Albrecht von Roon,[57] Bismarck was asked for his

[54] Paul Bailleu, "Der Prinzregent und die Reform der deutschen Kriegsverfassung," *Historische Zeitschrift*, Vol. 78 (1897), pp. 385-402.

[55] Grube, *Neue Ära und Nationalverein*, pp. 119-120; Friedrich Curtius, ed., *Denkwürdigkeiten des Fürsten Chlodwig zu Hohenlohe-Schillingsfürst* (Stuttgart, 1907), I, 111; Wilhelm Schüssler, ed., *Die Tagebücher des Freiherrn Reinhard von Dalwigk zu Lichtenfels aus den Jahren 1860-1871* (Stuttgart, 1920), pp. 39 ff.

[56] Hermann Oncken, ed., *Grossherzog Friedrich I. von Baden und die deutsche Politik von 1854-1871* (Stuttgart, 1927), I, 115-153, 251 ff.

[57] The cabinet crisis which occasioned Roon's message was over domestic rather than foreign policy. The new-era ministers had opposed William's ambition to receive from the "estates" of the realm an oath of fealty at his coronation in Königsberg as out of place in a constitutional monarchy. Roon and Edwin Man-

views on the matter. The result was his famous "Baden-Baden memorial."[58]

In it he argued once more that Prussia's role in the existing confederation was not adequate in view of the burden she bore for the defense of Germany. The confederation was incapable of satisfying the popular aspiration for national unity. Hence Prussia should publicly announce her support of "a national assembly of the German people." By insisting that its members be chosen by the state legislatures Prussia could make certain of their "intelligence and conservative outlook." In such an organ Bismarck saw "the only unifying force which can supply an adequate counterweight to the tendency of the dynasties to adopt separate and divergent policies."[59]

Since Austria and the lesser states would certainly never voluntarily consent to such a program,[60] Prussia ought to strive for the same objective by way of an alternative course. Following the plan he had once outlined to Below, Bismarck advocated that Prussia work for the establishment of a Zollverein parliament. By "skillful leadership" of such an organ she could force the lesser states into agreements similar to the Zollverein treaties but dealing with military affairs. The ultimate goal was: (1) a common military organization supported by income derived from tariffs and related taxes, and (2) a representative assembly made up of the combined legislatures of the member states and equipped with the power to legislate in matters dealing with trade and commerce.

While the king pondered this proposal Bismarck urged it upon

---

teuffel saw in the crisis the possibility of splitting the cabinet and driving out the remaining liberal ministers. By the time Bismarck arrived in Germany, however, William had given in and the crisis had passed. Zechlin, *Grundlegung*, pp. 194-195.

[58] There are two versions of this document: one drafted in July for the king and another in September for leaders of the Conservative Party. The earlier draft has the more radical phrasing, for it had to compete with a similar plan by Roggenbach, while the later version was intended to convert the conservatives to a new policy in the German question. Hermann Oncken, "Die Baden-Badener Denkschrift Bismarcks über die deutsche Bundesreform (Juli, 1861)," *Historische Zeitschrift*, Vol. 145 (1931), pp. 106-130. Oncken prints the July version; the September version is in *GW*, III, 266-270.

[59] In the July version the wording is a little different: "the most effective, perhaps the only and the necessary unifying force. . . ."

[60] The July draft argues that acceptance of the proposal in non-Austrian Germany was "not outside the realm of the politically possible," but that Austria was the stumbling-block to its universal acceptance. In both versions he recognized that acceptance by Austria would be possible only if she divided her German and non-German provinces so drastically that the only remaining link would be "personal union" under the emperor.

the leaders of the Conservative Party as a party platform. In a letter to Below he deplored the purely "negative" and "defensive" attitude of the Prussian conservatives. It could never conquer "terrain and adherents" and even jeopardized the existence of the party. The idea of conservative solidarity in foreign affairs was a "dangerous fiction." Such "quixotry" was incompatible with the primary task of the Hohenzollern monarchy: "the protection of *Prussia* against injustice." The "sovereignty" of the lesser states was an "unhistorical, Godless, and unjust swindle" dangerous to the future of Prussia and Germany. The conservatives should declare for a confederate or Zollverein parliament. "Until now very modest concessions to the national cause have always been considered worthwhile. One could create a very conservative national assembly and still reap the thanks of the liberals."[61] In other words, the conservatives should capture the national cause from their foes. Far from harmful to the interests of the conservative aristocracy, it might well be the means of survival in this dynamic century, a life preserver on the raging flood of the "time stream."

In German nationalism Bismarck had found a new "moral basis" for the expansion of Prussian power. Even though the plan for a confederate parliament would certainly be rejected in the Frankfurt diet, he believed its announcement alone would bring Prussia a resounding victory in the fight for public opinion. As his memorial in the Hesse-Kassel affair shows, Bismarck conceived such a declaration as a tactical gambit which would give Prussia the initiative in the struggle against the diet majority. It might shock the opposition into concessions. Even if it did not, Prussian manipulation of the Zollverein would soon convince them that the threat was no bluff. Should pressure in this direction lead to conflict, Berlin would have the best possible moral ground upon which to go to war.[62]

If successful either by peaceful or warlike means, Prussia would have laid the cornerstone of a new structure in Germany favorable to her interests. In the national parliament she would find an in-

---

[61] *GW*, xiv, 578-579. The letter was a criticism of the platform of the conservative Volksverein being founded by Hermann Wagener. See Felix Salomon, *Die deutschen Parteiprogramme* (3rd ed., Leipzig, 1924), pp. 104-105.

[62] Since the 1850's the idea of a Zollverein parliament had been under public discussion. In 1861 it was approved by the first German Handelstag, a convention of businessmen under the chairmanship of David Hansemann. W. O. Henderson, *The Zollverein* (Cambridge, 1939), pp. 285 ff.; Oncken, *Bennigsen*, i, 499; *HW*, i, 113.

strument with which to counteract the pressures of particularism. But the parliament too had to be held in check. According to Roggenbach, Bismarck also planned an upper chamber composed, like the confederate diet, of delegates from the state governments which would debate and vote in secret. In short, centripetal and centrifugal forces would counterbalance each other, while the decisive power remained in the hands of the "holder of the balance." Like Europe, Germany was to have its balance of power with the Hohenzollern monarchy in the pivotal position of greatest control.[63]

By no means did Bismarck regard an alliance with German nationalism as the only possible course. In accordance with his general views on political strategy he considered it but one of the alternative combinations available to Berlin. As before, Prussia must hold open every door and every turning. In applying pressure against Austria and the medium states she must preserve the choice of rapprochement with either German national opinion or France and Russia. As the situation permitted, either weight (or both) might be used to depress the scales.

Should war against Austria be necessary, Prussia must rely primarily upon her own strength and that of the German national movement. The former would supply the punching power for victory and the latter the moral cause for which to fight. If France should threaten to intervene, the pact with German nationalism would also be a useful means of pressure against the Tuileries.[64] Against Austria, Italy alone among the European powers was a prospective ally. She could be rewarded with Italian rather than German soil, and there was little prospect that in victory she would ever become an uncomfortable rival for Prussia. The friendship of the other European powers was to be cultivated, not as a source of military assistance, but as a means of isolating Austria and her German allies.

6. THE CONFLICT JOINED

The revolution in Prussian foreign policy, however, was not to commence with Bismarck. William was afraid of this "red reactionary" with his formidable talents and daring plans. Instead he chose as his new foreign minister Count Bernstorff, ambassador at London. While conservative, the count was acceptable to the

---

[63] Zechlin, *Grundlegung*, pp. 164-165.   [64] *GW*, xiv, 555.

remaining new-era ministers. He favored rapprochement with France and a strong Prussian initiative in the German question. At Ostend on September 7, 1861, William and Bernstorff conferred with Roggenbach and accepted in general the Baden program for confederate reform.[65]

Those German nationalists who learned of these negotiations were hardly satisfied with the results. When Roggenbach submitted the details of his program, the Prussians objected to its more liberal features, such as ministerial responsibility and a parliament chosen by direct election. Grand Duke Frederick and his minister readily consented to drop these points. Nevertheless, they grew timid about submitting the plan to the other German states.[66] When finally advanced by Bernstorff on December 20, it came, not as a demand, but as a rebuttal to another proposal by Baron Beust of Saxony. In rejecting Beust's plan for a tripartite reorganization of the confederation under Austria, Prussia, and the lesser states, Bernstorff declared that only a little-German federation within the existing great-German confederation could satisfy the German need for national unity. Although the language was mild, the Austrians were shocked. Prussia had revived the Radowitz plan.[67]

In 1862 the tempo of popular agitation quickened again. Leading members of the ailing Nationalverein gathered at Easter and agreed to promote periodic congresses of nationalist deputies from German diets and parliaments. The event was reminiscent of the Offenburg assembly of 1847 and the pre-parliament of 1848. But the most dramatic occurrence of the year was a gigantic hunting festival held in Frankfurt. In July ten thousand men armed with hunting rifles paraded through the Eschenheimergasse before the confederate diet. The hunters had nothing but pasteboard targets in mind, but even the Prussian and Austrian embassies thought it best to display that day the red-black-gold tri-color of 1848.[68]

[65] Kurt Promnitz, *Bismarcks Eintritt in das Ministerium, Historische Studien*, Vol. 60 (Berlin, 1908), pp. 19-32.

[63] Oncken, *Grossherzog Friedrich I*, I, 278-312; Karl Ringhoffer, *The Bernstorff Papers* (London, 1908), II, 90 ff.; Gruner, "Rückblick," p. 159. During his year in office Bernstorff made no real attempt to establish liaison with the Nationalverein. Grube, *Neue Ära und Nationalverein*, pp. 128 ff.

[67] Ludwig Aegidi and Alfred Klauhold, eds., *Das Staatsarchiv, Sammlung der officiellen Aktenstücke zur Geschichte der Gegenwart*, II (1862), 1-21; *DPO*, II, 53-55; Srbik, *Deutsche Einheit*, III, 375-376.

[68] Oncken, *Bennigsen*, I, 566-567; Zechlin, *Grundlegung*, pp. 263-265.

Although little-German sentiment predominated at such affairs, the great-Germanists were by no means inactive. They gained encouragement and added strength from contrasting political developments in Berlin and Vienna. While the Hohenzollern monarchy fell ever deeper into the pit of reaction, the Hapsburg empire seemed on the ascent toward constitutional government. The defeat of 1859 had revealed the bankruptcy of the old policy of centralized absolutism inaugurated by Schwarzenberg and Bach. In the "October diploma" of 1860 provincial diets were restored and in the "February patent" of 1861 a central parliament was created for the whole empire. The reform was nothing but a "constitutional overcoat" beneath which lay intact the absolute powers of the crown. For the time being, nevertheless, the German liberals were impressed.[69]

These basic laws also made it easier for Vienna to approach the problem of reform in Germany. Through the device of a "narrow" parliament, which excluded Hungary, reform minister Anton Schmerling created the possibility of dissociating for some purposes the Austrian half of the empire, which belonged to the German Confederation, from the eastern half, which did not. This opened the possibility of consolidating the confederation on a great-German basis. There were good reasons for such a policy. The Schmerling system was based on the German population of the empire. To be successful it required the backing of forty million confederate Germans against the ambitious Czechs and troublesome Magyars. In the foreign ministry he found a willing ally in Biegeleben, the influential secretary for German affairs and advocate of an aggressive German policy. Together they pressured the reluctant Rechberg into a policy of confederate reform.[70]

The Austrians based their plan on that of Beust as modified by Baron Dalwigk of Hesse-Darmstadt. To the existing structure of the confederation there was to be added a chamber of delegates drawn from the parliaments of the member states, an executive committee representing their governments, and a high court with the power to interpret confederate law. In such a system Prussia

69 On the Austrian reforms see Josef Redlich, *Das österreichische Staats- und Reichsproblem* (Leipzig, 1920-1926), also A. J. P. Taylor, *The Hapsburg Monarchy* (London, 1941), pp. 112 ff.

70 Enno Kraehe, "Austria and the Problem of Reform in the German Confederation, 1851-1863," *American Historical Review*, LVI (1951), 274-294.

could be permanently outvoted by Austria and her middle-state allies. The method of adoption was clever—overly so. Instead of proposing an organic change in the confederate constitution, which was sure to encounter a Prussian veto, Vienna planned to present a bill calling for the chamber of delegates purely as an advisory body for consultation on the law codes currently being considered by the diet. Once in existence, the Austrian coalition would see to it that the chamber remained in session and became an organic part of the confederate government. By the same route the high court and executive committee would also appear.[71]

In January 1862 a secret envoy from Vienna went from capital to capital in Germany seeking support for the plan. With some reservations the middle states agreed to assist in the Austrian power-play. If the confederation fell to pieces in the ensuing struggle, they even agreed to form a new organization without Prussia. But when it came to action the lesser states dragged their heels. Not until July did the ministers assemble to draft the details. As always they were reluctant to take a decisive step, fearing to cut their ties with Berlin and yet prodded by their greater fear of Prussian imperialism and the swelling agitation for national unity. Finally the wavering ended. Bavaria, Württemberg, Hesse-Darmstadt, Saxony, and Hanover joined Austria in presenting the bill to the diet.

On August 14, the diet assembled in the Eschenheimergasse at Frankfurt for the first vote—on a motion to refer the bill to committee. No one was sure how Usedom, the Prussian delegate, would vote. Would Prussia, wracked by internal conflict and desperately in need of popular favor, actually vote against a measure which promised a greater degree of unity? Usedom "surprised even the least hopeful with the vehemence of his denunciation." Not only did he reject the idea of confederate reform by majority vote; he loudly challenged the assembled delegates to undertake a *real* German reform including a strong executive and a national parliament. Only thus could the national longing for greater power and respect abroad be satisfied. By overwhelming majority, nevertheless, the chamber voted for committee consideration. Austria had crossed the first hurdle.[72]

[71] *DPO*, II, 67 ff.; Srbik, *Deutsche Einheit*, III, 376 ff.
[72] Kraehe, "Problem of Reform," p. 287; *DPO*, II, 444 ff.; *Staatsarchiv*, III (1862), 154-159.

While the Austrian offensive gathered momentum, Bernstorff had already begun a Prussian counterattack in the economic field. Negotiations with France for a tariff treaty based on free trade were hurried to conclusion in March. Since 1860 the French empire had negotiated a series of such treaties with England, Belgium, and Switzerland. If this one were ratified, Prussian industry would gain access to a steadily widening European free market. But for Austria the prospects were disastrous. If she tried to follow suit, her infant industries would be suffocated by foreign competition. The move threatened to block for good the Austrian ambition to enter the Zollverein.[73]

Prussia's success in organizing little Germany into a customs union had always been considered dangerous to Austrian interests. It lent credence to the argument that Berlin was the natural nucleus of the little-German atom. For this reason Schwarzenberg's attempt to consolidate Austrian power in Germany had been accompanied by Ludwig Bruck's plan for the expansion of the Zollverein into a great central-European economic union. But in 1853 Berlin had succeeded in negotiating treaties with the lesser states for renewal of the Zollverein. All Vienna received was the promise that before the next renewal in 1865 Prussia would negotiate for Austrian entry into the union. Now the French treaty even nullified this promise, for Austria could never enter a customs union based on free trade. By granting France "most favored nation" status, the treaty destroyed Austria's special relationship to the Zollverein.[74]

For a time it appeared as though Austria might even benefit from the Prussian move. Under the rules of the Zollverein all members had to agree to any changes in the tariff laws of a participating state. Most medium states were incensed by the far-reaching character of the agreement and its consequences for their Austrian ally. But they hesitated to abandon the Zollverein. Its economic advantages were too great, its popular support too apparent. Although industrial and agricultural interests in Bavaria and Württemberg were opposed, most German businessmen favored the French treaty. After the expansion of the late 1850's

[73] See Eugen Franz, *Der Entscheidungskampf um die wirtschaftspolitische Führung Deutschlands (1856-1867)*, *Schriftenreihe zur bayerischen Landesgeschichte*, Vol. 12 (Munich, 1933), pp. 34 ff., 145 ff.; Henderson, *Zollverein*, pp. 273 ff.; Ringhoffer, *Bernstorff Papers*, ii, 143 ff.

[74] Franz, *Entscheidungskampf*, pp. 3 ff., 169 ff.

the entrepreneurs felt confident of their ability to meet foreign competition at home and avidly desired a greater share of the European market. Under the leadership of John Prince-Smith the movement for free trade had made many converts in Germany.[75]

Desperately Austria maneuvered to meet the Prussian challenge. In April Rechberg promised to guarantee the lesser states against economic loss if they should unite with Vienna in a new customs union. In July he proposed a central-European union which would have joined the whole of the Hapsburg monarchy to the Zollverein. Together the dual powers would then negotiate a new treaty with France and England. Bernstorff counterattacked on July 21 by recognizing the kingdom of Italy and on August 2 by signing the March agreement with France. All that remained to put the latter in effect was an exchange of ratifications, which was delayed while Prussia rounded up the votes of the Zollverein states. At stake, Karolyi told Bernstorff, was Austria's very existence. "Likewise for Prussia," was the reply. Should Austria persist, the result would be a "struggle of life and death."[76]

7. PARIS INTERLUDE

With Bernstorff's appointment the curtain went up on a drama whose *dénouement* was to be reached on the battlefields of Bohemia in 1866. Bernstorff, however, was just a minor character who prepared the scene and set the mood, while the leading actor waited impatiently in the wings for his cue. In ill health, the count had accepted the foreign ministry with the greatest reluctance. During his year in the Wilhelmstrasse he repeatedly asked to be allowed to return to London. For Bismarck it was a time of uncertainty and depression. After attending William's coronation in Königsberg (October 18, 1861) he took the weary road back to Petersburg for another winter in the frozen north. "Three years ago," he complained, "I would still have made a useful minister, but now, when I think about it, I feel like a sick equestrian facing a series of jumps."[77]

[75] *Ibid.*, pp. 159 ff.; Becker, *Manchestertum*, pp. 26 ff. Born in London, Prince-Smith spent his career in Germany as a publicist and agitator for the doctrines of Adam Smith, Malthus, Ricardo, and Bentham.

[76] Franz, *Entscheidungskampf*, p. 220; Kohl, *Jahrbuch*, vi, 155-156; *Staatsarchiv*, iii (1862), 228 ff.

[77] Ringhoffer, *Bernstorff Papers*, ii, 83 ff.; *GW*, xiv, 581.

In March 1862 a sudden crisis in the developing struggle with parliament prompted his recall to Berlin. Still William could not bring himself to accept the ministerial candidate urged upon him by Roon. The post of minister without portfolio was discussed. But Bismarck had no wish to mount the horse unless given the reins. To end the quandary he demanded either dismissal or appointment to a new diplomatic post. On May 23 he was sent off to Paris, newly decorated with the order of the red eagle, first class. It was recognized, however, that his services would soon be needed in Berlin. In their parting audience William told him to remain *au qui vive*. Bismarck was deeply vexed by this indecision.[78] Nevertheless, Paris offered him the opportunity to probe once more the mind of the man who was so vital to the success of his whole scheme of foreign policy.

During his last visit in 1857 Napoleon had made proposals of alliance so far-reaching that Bismarck had been unwilling to report them to Berlin, knowing how they would shock Gerlach, Manteuffel, and Frederick William IV. On that occasion the emperor had denied any ambition to expand toward the Rhine (except for a "small rectification" of the frontier). Such a move would arouse the whole of Europe against France. Instead he confessed his intention to promote the cause of Italian unification and obtain for France territory on the Mediterranean. In return for Prussia's benevolent neutrality in a war with Austria, France would favor her acquisition of Hanover and Schleswig-Holstein. This would enable her to develop a navy. Europe was lacking in sea powers of second rank capable, in combination with France, of opposing the oppressive naval supremacy of Great Britain.[79]

Since the nadir of 1860 relations between Prussia and France had improved. As his attitude toward Austria stiffened, William was not averse to some degree of rapprochement. In October 1861 he made a state visit to Compiègne. A few months later the commercial treaty followed. Hence it was natural that Napoleon should again speak frankly to the Junker diplomat who for years had been the reputed advocate of a French alliance. On June 5, 1862, Bismarck dined in the Tuileries and afterward listened to

[78] Promnitz, *Bismarcks Eintritt*, pp. 33-36; Kohl, *Bismarck-Regesten*, I, 175-176; *GW*, xv, 163 ff.

[79] See Frahm, *Stellung zu Frankreich*, pp. 53-74; Richard Fester, "Bismarcks Gespräche mit Napoleon III. im April 1857," *Historische Zeitschrift*, Vol. 84 (1900), pp. 460-465.

Napoleon advise that a German national policy was the best solution to Prussia's internal difficulties.[80] Three weeks later envoy and emperor conferred again at Fontainebleau. Suddenly Louis posed the crucial question, "Do you believe that the king would be disposed to conclude an alliance with me?" Bismarck parried, "For an alliance there must be an aim or a motive." What he intended, Bonaparte replied, was not an "adventurous project," but an "intimate and durable entente" based on common interests. "You could never imagine what singular overtures were made to me by Austria a few days ago."[81]

In reporting this episode Bismarck was careful to stress that he did not advise a formal treaty with France. His major emphasis was upon the fresh evidence of Austrian perfidy. Nevertheless, his dispatch touched William in a sensitive spot. In the press rumors of a French-Russian-Prussian alliance mingled with those of Bismarck's coming appointment to the foreign ministry. "Tell him," he instructed Bernstorff, "that I shall never consent to an alliance with France."[82]

Except for these interviews there was little to report from Paris. This was the dead season in European politics when rulers and ministers took time out to nurse their ailments at the baths. On an excursion to London the Junker conferred at length with Palmerston and Russell, listened to their advice on the introduction of a parliamentary system in Prussia, and replied that liberal opposition to military appropriations would vanish, should the government adopt the aims of the Nationalverein.[83] At a formal dinner he had the chance to speak to Disraeli. Revealing his coming appointment, he frankly told the conservative leader of his intent to find a pretext for war against Austria and to suppress the lesser states in the name of German unity. "Take care of that man!" the shrewd Englishman warned. "He means what he says."[84]

80 *GW*, III, 366-368.   81 *GW*, III, 381-383; xv, 173-174.

82 Promnitz, *Bismarcks Eintritt*, pp. 44-49; Kohl, *Jahrbuch*, VI, 155; Otto Nirrn-heim, *Das erste Jahr des Ministeriums Bismarck und die öffentliche Meinung, Heidelberger Abhandlungen zur mittleren und neueren Geschichte*, Vol. 20 (Heidelberg, 1908), pp. 38 ff., 57 ff., 281 ff. This episode probably heightened William's distrust of Bismarck. On September 12 he dismissed the suggestion of his appointment to the cabinet with the remark, "Bismarck is pressing for an alliance with France, which I will never accept." Promnitz, *op.cit.*, p. 103.

83 *GW*, III, 384-386.

84 Carl Friedrich Vitzthum von Eckstadt, *St. Petersburg und London in den Jahren 1852-1864* (Stuttgart, 1886), II, 158-159.

Daily the Junker expected word from Berlin and daily he was disappointed. His nerves were on edge. His letters home complained of William's indecision, the ambiguity of Bernstorff's position, and the unsettled nature of his own existence. "My things are still in Petersburg and will be frozen in there; my carriages are in Stettin, my horses in the country near Berlin, my family in Pomerania, and I on the highway."[85] In disgust he departed southward on an extended leave. From late July to early September he bathed at Trouville and Biarritz, climbed in the Pyrenees, sampled the local wines, and fell platonically in love with a Russian princess, the vivacious Katherina Orlow.[86]

As the vacation idyll neared its end, his mind turned again to politics. In Toulouse on September 12 he resolved to force the issue, even if it meant being minister without portfolio. Returning to Paris he received coded telegrams of reply from Bernstorff and Roon. "Periculum in mora. Dépêchez-vous," read the latter. Early on the morning of September 19 the Junker boarded the train for Berlin. Twenty-four hours later he arrived to confront the most severe domestic crisis of the Hohenzollern monarchy since that fateful day in March 1848 when the revolutionists manned the barricades.[87]

[85] *GW*, xiv, 619.
[86] See Nikolai Orloff, *Bismarck und Katharina Orloff, Ein Idyll in der hohen Politik* (Munich, 1936).
[87] *GW*, xiv, 619; xv, 177; Zechlin, *Grundlegung*, pp. 287-291; Promnitz, *Bismarcks Eintritt*, pp. 105-116, 155-198.

CHAPTER SEVEN

GERMANY AT THE CROSSROADS

1. FAILURE OF THE NEW ERA

ISMARCK first conceived his plan for the exploitation of German nationalism in 1858-1859, when conditions for its execution appeared particularly ripe. The prince-regent was intent on reconciling the crown with its subjects; all Germany was enthusiastic for the new-era cabinet; the Nationalverein appeared willing to act as a bridge between the Hohenzollern monarchy and German nation. When he came to power, however, these conditions had disappeared. In Prussia the period of harmony had passed; by 1861 crown and parliament were bitterly at odds over the issue of military reform. Repulsed by Schleinitz and virtually ignored by Bernstorff, the Nationalverein had turned away from the Prussian state to seek its ends through the liberal movement. At Coburg in October 1862 the association raised a demand for the Frankfurt constitution of 1849.[1]

From the outset the new era was an illusion. Not for a moment did William waver from his belief in divine-right absolutism. The moderate liberals he chose as ministers were never in full control of the governmental apparatus. Occupying the important posts of justice and commerce were two ministers, Ludwig Simons and August von der Heydt, held over from the previous regime. The three closest advisers of the regent—Gustav von Alvensleben, Edwin von Manteuffel, and Albrecht von Roon (appointed minister of war in 1859)—were all men of absolutistic and anti-liberal conviction. Beneath the cabinet the key administrative officials responsible for carrying out ministerial decisions were mostly ultra-conservatives appointed during the period of reaction. The house of lords remained a stronghold of reactionary power possessing

[1] Grube, *Neue Ära und Nationalverein*, pp. 128-143; Oncken, *Bennigsen*, I, 580 ff. On the development of the conflict see Fritz Löwenthal, *Der preussische Verfassungsstreit, 1862-1866* (Munich, 1914), pp. 1-108.

the veto with which to kill any legislation of which the conservatives disapproved.[2]

When the first reform bills stumbled against these obstacles, there began within the liberal factions a general shift to the left culminating in the founding of the "German Progressive Party" in 1861. As the title indicates, its program was both liberal and national. Like the Nationalverein, in which many of its leaders were active, the new party embraced both moderate and democratic liberals, the former predominating.[3] Throughout Germany parties of similar name and program began to appear in the smaller states. In Prussia the progressives opened an attack intended to force the government into a more liberal program at home and a more national policy in foreign affairs. In December they scored a surprising victory at the polls, capturing 109 seats. With other oppositional groups they controlled 161 votes in the chamber, opposed by 164 conservatives and old-liberals.[4]

By now it was quite evident that Prince William and the liberal deputies had completely different conceptions of the role which the new-era cabinet was to perform. The latter looked upon the cabinet as an instrument of liberal reform, while the former considered it merely a means for reconciling parliament and popular opinion to the royal will. The consequence was that by the end of 1861 the cabinet lay spread-eagled between monarchy and parliament, able neither to progress, retreat, nor stand upright.

The liberal ministers themselves had no clear idea of the part they ought to play. Their ability was as limited as their liberalism. Caught in an embarrassing dilemma, they could make no positive decision for either monarchy or parliament. To bend to the will of the regent meant betrayal of their political convictions and popular support. But to follow the dictates of parliament meant dismissal, loss of power and position, and the triumph of the conservatives. Like the liberal ministers of 1848, they were embarrassed by the drift to the left in the chamber. If they broke

2 On the complexion of the cabinet see Alexander Bergengrün, *Staatsminister August Freiherr von der Heydt* (Leipzig, 1908), pp. 247 ff. As a matter of "principle" the new-era ministers refused to remove lesser officials for political reasons. Friedrich von Bernhardi, ed., *Aus dem Leben Theodor von Bernhardis* (Leipzig, 1893-1906), III, 271, 275.

3 Oncken, Bennigsen, I, 564-565; Martin Philippson, *Max von Forckenbeck, Ein Lebensbild* (Dresden, 1898), pp. 61 ff.

4 Ludwig Bergsträsser, "Kritische Studien zur Konfliktszeit," *Historische Vierteljahrschrift*, XIX (1919), 353-354.

with the king, they would have no other choice than to join forces with those democratic liberals to whom they were fundamentally opposed.[5]

For that matter Prince William and the liberals in parliament were impaled on the horns of a like dilemma. Divided by factions, wavering in determination, uncertain of their popular following, and lacking in experienced leadership, the liberals hesitated to open an irreparable breach between themselves and the crown. Even the progressives had no real desire to bring about the fall of the cabinet which had begun its labors with so much hope and promise and with which they had earlier identified themselves. Despite growing mistrust, William also found it difficult to dispense with his moderate liberal ministers. He did not want to return to the Gerlach-Manteuffel school of politics and could see no alternative source from which to draw a new government.[6]

The consequence of these antagonistic motives and vacillating attitudes was a series of crises and compromises in the years 1860-1861, the most important of which concerned the bill for reorganization of the Prussian army.

2. THE MILITARY CONFLICT

Under the great military reform of 1814-1815 Prussian citizens were obliged to serve three years in the regular army (called the "line"), followed by two years in its reserve and thereafter fourteen years in the militia (*Landwehr*). The latter was divided into two levies of seven years each. In war the fighting army consisted of the line, reserve, and first levy of the militia. Because of economies in the military budget the size of the army had not kept pace with the rapid expansion of the population. Of those youths who were eligible, only one-half could actually be drafted. For the same reason the usual term of service in the line had come to be two years; increased to three years in 1856, it had been reduced again to two and one-half in practice. The ranks of the reserve and militia were filled out by recruits who received but a few weeks training. Instead of being an extension of the regular army, as originally intended, the militia had practically become a separate

---

[5] *Aus dem Leben Bernhardis*, III, 272-273, 285-286; IV, 159-160.

[6] *Ibid.*, IV, 107, 160; Philippson, *Forckenbeck*, p. 36; Ludwig Dehio, "Die Taktik der Opposition während des Konflikts," *Historische Zeitschrift*, Vol. 140 (1929), pp. 287 ff.; Oncken, *Grossherzog Friedrich I*, I, 323.

organization. Most of its officers had received only one year of formal military training.

On coming to power in 1859 William was fully determined to change this system which he had long considered defective. Three years of training for infantry and four years for other branches, he insisted, were necessary to inculcate the habits of discipline and obedience essential to an effective fighting force. By raising the number of draftees, lengthening by six months their period of service, and increasing service in the reserve to five years (later reduced to four), he proposed to double the size of the army. But he also wished to introduce radical changes in the militia. Most of his life he had been distressed by the sight of those "dirty militiamen" who marched past at military reviews in ragged ranks and moth-eaten uniforms. He doubted that even a reformed *Landwehr* could be expected to fight side by side with, and as competently as, the line. Hence he proposed that during wartime the fighting army consist only of the strengthened line and its reserve. The militia, in other words, was to be separated altogether from the regular army and relegated to the rear.[7]

The regent and his generals were not alone in the belief that serious reforms were necessary. After the Italian war all political factions in Prussia recognized that the army was inadequate in size and organization. Flushed with renewed enthusiasm for the national cause, the liberals expected Prussia, headed by a liberal cabinet, to become the nucleus of a little-German unification for whose achievement the use of force, or at least its threatened use, would be necessary. Under these circumstances their suspicion of the army as the traditional instrument of autocratic power diminished.[8]

But the old fears returned as soon as the regent's plan became known. The enlarged army meant an increase in taxation of twenty-five percent, which alarmed the commercial classes just recovering from the depression of 1857. The primary objection, however, was not financial, but social and political. Behind the changes planned for the militia and the lengthened period of military service, the liberals detected a plan of the Junker military caste to

[7] Gerhard Ritter, *Staatskunst und Kriegshandwerk, Das Problem des "Militarismus" in Deutschland* (Munich, 1954), I, 144 ff.; Gordon A. Craig, *The Politics of the Prussian Army, 1640-1945* (Oxford, 1955), pp. 138 ff. See particularly William's remarks to the cabinet on December 3, 1859. Berner, *Kaiser Wilhelm*, I, 461-478.
[8] Zechlin, *Grundlegung*, pp. 173 ff.

strengthen the authority of the monarchy and buttress its own position in Prussian society at the cost of the bourgeoisie.[9] This was, in fact, the case.

Like the introduction of local self-government and universal military service, the militia system had originally been intended by the reformers of 1807-1815 to give the general public a vested interest in the Prussian state and the success of its army in wartime. This had been lacking in the largely mercenary army of the eighteenth century, which was the personal instrument of the monarch. Through the militia and general conscription, Scharnhorst and Boyen wished to put forces in the field animated more by patriotism and willingness to sacrifice for the commonweal than by professional efficiency, loyalty to the king, and that "cadaver obedience" which was the pride of Prussian militarism. Although the reform was incomplete, their conception of the army as a partly civilianized force became as important to the liberals as the *Rechtsstaat*, constitutionalism, and the rights of man.[10]

William and his military advisers were hostile toward the militia system for the very reasons that the liberals were attracted to it. In a famous memorial of 1858, through which he won the confidence of the regent, Roon condemned it as a "politically false institution." The militiaman, he declared, was not a soldier, but a civilian in thought and attitude. There was no proof that in war patriotic enthusiasm was an adequate substitute for the iron discipline and *esprit de corps* imparted by years of formal military training. In domestic politics, moreover, the militia was a positive hazard to royal authority. As long as a vital part of the army consisted of "civilians in uniform" whose wishes had to be considered, the king would never be master of his own house. One purpose of William's reform, therefore, was to get rid of Boyen's compromise between a royal and popular army. The army was to become again what it had been in Frederician times: the personal and "non-political" instrument of the royal will.[11]

Unlike some of the reactionary absolutists of the two previous reigns, William and Roon had no intention of abolishing universal

9 Eugene N. Anderson, *The Social and Political Conflict in Prussia, 1858-1864* (Lincoln, 1954), pp. 109 ff.; *Aus dem Leben Bernhardis*, III, 284-285; Craig, *Prussian Army*, pp. 145-146.

10 Ritter, *Staatskunst*, I, 125 ff.

11 Waldemar von Roon, *Denkwürdigkeiten aus dem Leben des General-Feldmarschalls Kriegsministers Grafen von Roon* (4th ed., Breslau, 1897), II, 521-572; also I, 345 ff.

conscription in favor of a purely mercenary army. Quite the contrary, it was their deliberate purpose to employ the three years of military training as a means of implanting habits of loyalty and obedience to the monarchy which would make the conscript for the rest of his days a staunch supporter of the crown and its political authority. The army was to become the "school of the nation." Whereas Scharnhorst and Boyen had wished to revive the Prussian army with an injection of civic patriotism, William and Roon desired to use the draft to inject military attitudes into civil life.[12]

From the purely military-technical side there was no real need for a three-year training period. In April 1862 a board of fifteen generals (including Helmuth von Moltke), appointed by William to study the problem, agreed on the adequacy of two and one-half years with furlough during the winter months. Under certain conditions they granted that two years would not impair military efficiency. Three decades later during the reign of William II the term of service was actually reduced to two years with the approval of the army command, despite the more complicated weapons and tactics which had to be taught. In 1914 the shortened term stood the test of war.[13]

The liberals sensed the ulterior political aim of the military reorganization. In reacting against it, the democratic progressives themselves developed an offensive purpose. Speaking to the hunters' festival in Frankfurt (July 1862), Hermann Schulze-Delitzsch openly declared that constitutional development would never be assured until "parliament is backed by a people's army standing amid an armed people." Later he maintained he had meant a future German parliament, not the Prussian Landtag. But his speech confirmed William's belief that the progressives aimed at the establishment of parliamentary control over the armed forces. While this was not the case, the deputies ultimately did open an attack upon important aspects of the Prussian military state. In April 1863 the military committee of the chamber of deputies recommended limitation of the jurisdiction of military courts to military offenses, liquidation of cadet schools and military courts of honor, selection and promotion of officers according to ability

12 Ritter, *Staatskunst*, I, 154 ff.
13 Bergsträsser, "Kritische Studien," pp. 349-350.

rather than social caste, and equality of pay between the elite *Gardekorps* and the regular troops.[14]

Another vital issue was the relationship between political and military authority. In 1852 Otto Manteuffel had modified the collegial structure of the Prussian cabinet by obtaining from Frederick William IV an order limiting the right of access to the king by his fellow ministers.[15] An exception was made in the case of the minister of war. Invariably a general and a career officer, he had the privilege of taking matters to the king without prior approval of the minister-president. This meant that there was no intermediate civil authority between himself and the monarch. Although he was officially responsible only to the king, the minister of war was required by the constitution to appear in parliament to explain and defend government bills dealing with military affairs. This necessity did at least subject his actions to a degree of popular review.[16]

This was not true, however, of the chief of the military cabinet. Under the Prussian system the king was technically the acting commander of the armed forces, a duty and prerogative which could not be delegated to a minister. To assist them in this function the Hohenzollern had turned to the division of personnel in the war ministry, which thereby acquired a dual character. As a division of the war ministry, its members were concerned with such matters as the selection and promotion of officers, but, as aides and advisers to the commander-in-chief, they formed an unofficial "military cabinet." Their chief had direct access to the king and hence the opportunity to by-pass the minister of war and the whole civil cabinet. Through this channel men of purely military training and outlook could influence the entire course of the government. "To ambitious and power-hungry personalities it presented an opportunity for uncontrollable political influence 'behind the scenes.' "[17]

14 Friedrich Thorwart, ed., *Hermann Schulze-Delitzsch's Schriften und Reden* (Berlin, 1909-1913), IV, 106-107, 128-131; V, 224-225; *SBHA* (1863), IV, 656-658.

15 For the cabinet order see Otto Küsel-Glogau, *Bismarck: Beiträge zur inneren Politik* (Berlin, 1934), p. 70. To reach the king the other ministers had to go through the minister-president, who had the privilege of being present during the audience.

16 Ritter, *Staatskunst*, I, 207 ff.; Rudolf Schmidt-Bückeburg, *Das Militärkabinett der preussischen Könige und deutschen Kaiser* (Berlin, 1933), pp. 46 ff.

17 Ritter, *Staatskunst*, I, 223. On the development of the military cabinet see Heinrich O. Meisner, *Der Kriegsminister, 1815-1914* (Berlin, 1940), pp. 7 ff., and Schmidt-Bückeburg, *Militärkabinett*, pp. 57 ff.

In 1848 an attempt was made to abolish this position which menaced any kind of democratic government. Although the military cabinet was reintegrated into the ministry of war, an informal "camarilla" of military advisers took its place. During the rest of the reign of Frederick William IV this shadow cabinet, headed by Leopold Gerlach, directed the reactionary measures which emasculated the work of the revolution and sealed the daily conduct of the government against the infection of liberal ideas.[18]

One of its members, Edwin von Manteuffel, remained behind to serve the regent in the dual role of chief of military cabinet and head of the personnel division. A man of uncompromising absolutistic views, the general was determined to reconstruct the power of the military cabinet at the cost of the ministry of war and hence of constitutional government. Although this was ultimately to bring him into conflict with Roon, who entered the cabinet in late 1859, both men shared the objective of securing the army from every constitutional restriction. In January 1861 Manteuffel succeeded in getting William's approval of a cabinet order which removed from the signature of the minister of war all military orders except those dealing with purely administrative matters and those requiring legislation or dealing with the budget.[19]

In a pamphlet published in 1861 Karl Twesten, a prominent progressive, painted Manteuffel as a highly sinister figure. The general, he charged, was primarily a courtier, long out of contact with the army, where he was little liked. His power to dispose over military personnel was conducive to whim and nepotism; his usurpation of functions of the ministry of war complicated military administration. What crisis would be required to "remove this unwholesome man from an unwholesome position"?[20] Manteuffel demanded that the deputy retract not only the personal attack, which was indeed slanderous, but his entire criticism of

---

[18] Meisner, *Kriegsminister*, pp. 16 ff.; Fritz Hartung, "Verantwortliche Regierung, Kabinette und Nebenregierungen im konstitutionellen Preussen, 1848-1918," *Forschungen zur brandenburgischen und preussischen Geschichte*, Vol. 44 (1932), pp. 2 ff.

[19] On Manteuffel see Gordon Craig, "Portrait of a Political General: Edwin von Manteuffel and the Constitutional Conflict in Prussia," *Political Science Quarterly*, LXVI (1951), 1-36; Ludwig Dehio, "Manteuffels politische Ideen," *Historische Zeitschrift*, CXXXI (1925), 41-71, and "Edwin von Manteuffel und der Kaiser," *Deutsche Rundschau*, CCVI (1926), 40-48, 149-157; a more favorable view is given by Wilhelm Gradmann, *Die politischen Ideen Edwin von Manteuffels und ihre Auswirkungen in seiner Laufbahn* (Düsseldorf, 1932).

[20] Twesten, *Was uns noch retten kann*, pp. 81-82.

the military cabinet, much of which was accurate. When Twesten refused, the general sent a challenge and shot him through the arm. Manteuffel's purpose, Twesten believed, was to silence all public criticism of the army.[21]

The Prussian army was often called a "state within a state." Through Roon and Manteuffel most of its vital affairs were removed from any kind of political control, whether by cabinet or parliament. Of its higher officers ninety percent were carefully chosen from the Junker caste. After the purges conducted by Manteuffel, they were mostly of conservative and absolutistic views. The oath they swore was to the person of the king, not to the constitution or civil government. They were a pressure group which the king himself could not ignore, even if he desired. They were the one fully dependable support for his own authority.[22]

3. LORD AND VASSAL

In the beginning both cabinet and parliament sought to avoid a head-on collision over the military bill. Many members of the old-liberal majority in the chamber of 1860 believed, in fact, that the measure should be accepted, distasteful though it was, in order to avoid embarrassing the new-era ministers. But the liberal press was critical and the deputies responded to its pressure. While approving the proposed expansion, the committee on military affairs insisted on certain economies and rejected the regent's plans for the militia and the three-year period.

To the relief of the deputies the government then withdrew the bill and asked for a "provisional appropriation" to enable it to proceed with the expansion alone. This was granted, but only after the minister of finance, Baron Patow, had given verbal assurances that those parts of the general plan to which parliament objected would not be put into effect. On Edwin Manteuffel's urging William chose to ignore this promise, which apparently he had not authorized. By royal command thirty-six infantry regiments of the militia were separated from the army and replaced by a like number of new regiments of the line. On January 18, 1861

21 *HW*, I, 62-65. On Twesten see Dehio, "Taktik der Opposition," pp. 294 ff. Regretfully William had to go through the formality of confining Manteuffel, deploring the temporary loss of his services as a "triumph of democracy." Berner, *Kaiser Wilhelm*, II, 15; also Roon, *Denkwürdigkeiten*, II, 21.

22 "I know," remarked Frederick William IV, "that my army is the condition for the existence of my throne." Quoted in Meisner, *Kriegsminister*, p. 18. See also Wilhelm I, *Weimarer Briefe*, p. 64.

their standards were ceremoniously dedicated over the tomb of Frederick the Great.[23] This high-handed action outraged liberal opinion, but still the moderates who controlled parliament hesitated to precipitate an open break. When the matter came up again in 1861, they granted a second provisional appropriation. In December came the rousing electoral victory of the progressives, already mentioned, which greatly strengthened the opposition in the chamber of deputies. During March 1862 the deputies forced the issue by passing the "Hagen bill." By requiring the itemization of the military budget for 1862, the bill would have made it impossible for the government to continue shifting funds to purposes not authorized by parliament. William reacted by dissolving the chamber and replacing the remaining new-era ministers with conservatives. Despite severe bureaucratic pressure on the voters, the election in May was catastrophic for government candidates. Conservative strength shrank to ten seats; the old-liberals were severely reduced. But the opposition grew to 223, of whom 135 were progressives. The government's critics were now clearly in control of the chamber.[24]

These developments created a sense of emergency in the royal palace. For more than a year Edwin Manteuffel had predicted revolution. With his associates he drafted a detailed plan for the remorseless conquest of the city, street by street, should the opposition take to the barricades. There was to be no repetition of the capitulation of March 1848. From his ready talk of "bloody heads" it seems certain that Manteuffel not only expected but even desired an uprising. Its ruthless suppression would permit the crown to abolish parliament and the constitution. He pictured himself as the Strafford who would purge the political opposition and rescue the monarchy from its enemies.[25] Roon too was thinking of Strafford, but more of his fate than his achievement. Someone had once prophesied that the general would die "by the neck."[26]

[23] Craig, *Prussian Army*, pp. 146 ff.; Eugen Frauenholz, *Das Heerwesen des XIX. Jahrhunderts, Entwicklungsgeschichte des deutschen Heerwesens*, v (Munich, 1941), 250-254.

[24] Bergsträsser, "Kritische Studien," pp. 353-368; Ringhoffer, *Bernstorff Papers*, II, 180 ff.; Philippson, *Forckenbeck*, p. 82.

[25] Ludwig Dehio, "Die Pläne der Militärpartei und der Konflikt," *Deutsche Rundschau*, CCXIII (1927), 91-100.

[26] Roon, *Denkwürdigkeiten*, II, 107.

Manteuffel's chance never came. Not even the democratic liberals had any serious thought of revolution.[27] In the summer and early fall came a final attempt at compromise. Since 1860 the moderates had abandoned their opposition to the militia part of the government's program; hence the one demand upon which the liberal factions were still united was the reduction of the service period from three to two years. Rather than risk open conflict with parliament, the cabinet advised William to concede the shorter term. Even Roon was unnerved by the determined attitude of the chamber. With Heydt, the minister of finance, he was in contact with the moderates in search of a compromise. Before parliament on September 17 he openly spoke of his willingness to come to terms. But two days later he was compelled to reverse himself, for William had flatly refused to budge. On the evening of Roon's first speech the king bluffed his ministers by dramatically summoning Crown Prince Frederick William. This was a threat of abdication, a prospect that conservatives had every reason to dread.[28]

Those who are teased by what "might-have-been" in history have always found the character of Frederick William a fascinating study. In 1862 he was strongly opposed to the course which his father was taking. Through his mother, a Weimar princess, and his wife, a daughter of Queen Victoria and an earnest advocate of the English system, he had been exposed to liberal influences. Among his friends and associates were men close to the old-liberals and progressives. While believing in the necessity of military reform, he was willing to compromise on the length of service. Had he ascended the throne, the issue would have been settled.

But would German history have taken a radically different course? As with most "ifs" in history the answer is not wholly clear. Frederick William was not a resolute personality with a

[27] Outside Prussia a few radicals—Wilhelm Rüstow, a renegade Prussian officer, Ludwig Schweigert, a former captain in the Austrian army, and Fedor Streit, prominent on the extreme left of the Nationalverein—seriously speculated on the possibility of organizing rebellion. But their illusions were not shared by most radical refugees, including Marx. Gustav Mayer, *Ferdinand Lassalle, Nachgelassene Briefe und Schriften* (Stuttgart, 1921-1925), v, 15 ff.

[28] On the September crisis see particularly Wilhelm Treue, "Wollte König Wilhelm I. 1862 zurücktreten?" *Forschungen zur brandenburgischen und preussischen Geschichte*, Vol. 51 (1939), pp. 275-310; also Promnitz, *Bismarcks Eintritt*, pp. 67-99, 117-154; Zechlin, *Grundlegung*, pp. 291 ff.; Ringhoffer, *Bernstorff Papers*, II, 193 ff.; Bergengrün, *Von der Heydt*, pp. 301-306; Johannes Schultze, ed., *Max Duncker: Politischer Briefwechsel aus seinem Nachlass* (Stuttgart, 1923), p. 334.

clearly reasoned political philosophy. His liberalism was of the compromising sort common to the old-liberals, who were his chief political advisers. By rebuilding the government of the new era he wished to steer a mediate course between absolutism and parliamentary democracy. Basically the prince was "more Hohenzollern than Coburg." There was an "authoritarian tendency" in him which leaves open to doubt whether, had he become king in 1862, he could have maintained the delicate balance of liberal and conservative forces which was his political ideal.[29]

Nevertheless, the possibility existed that without a political genius such as Bismarck to help him (and there was none in the old-liberal camp) Frederick William might have been swept along by the liberal tide from one compromise to another. But there was yet another possibility. The army too was a political force. After openly clashing with the Bismarck government in 1863 the crown prince suspected that the generals were conspiring to replace him as heir to the throne with his reactionary uncle, Prince Frederick Charles, or the latter's son.[30] Had he become king during these vital years of decision, the Prussian conservatives would hardly have let their royalism stand in the way of their interests. Who can say what might have come out of the collision of popular and reactionary forces which would then have ensued?

In any case William certainly had no intention of giving way to Frederick William, unless it proved impossible to find ministers willing to carry out his military policy and rule the country without a legal budget. On the evening of September 17, the threat of abdication was sufficient to drive the shocked cabinet into line, but two days later Heydt and Bernstorff handed in their resignations. After a futile attempt to mediate between the king and his defecting ministers Frederick William hurried off on the 20th to rejoin his family in Thuringia. From his father's final remarks he assumed that Bismarck's appointment was not imminent. Three days later he was shocked to learn from a telegram that he had been misled.[31]

29 Heinrich O. Meisner, ed., *Der preussische Kronprinz im Verfassungskampf 1863* (Berlin, 1931), pp. 47-62; Heinrich O. Meisner, ed., *Kaiser Friedrich III., Tagebücher von 1848-1866* (Leipzig, 1929), pp. xiv ff., xliv ff.; Martin Philippson, *Friedrich III., als Kronprinz und Kaiser* (Berlin, 1893), pp. 77-78.

30 Friedrich III, *Tagebücher 1848-1866*, pp. xxvii-xxviii; Meisner, *Kronprinz im Verfassungskampf*, pp. 161-162; *Aus dem Leben Bernhardis*, v, 339.

31 Treue, "König Wilhelm I," pp. 291 ff.; Friedrich III, *Tagebücher 1848-1866*, pp. 160-161; *Aus dem Leben Bernhardis*, iv, 334; Philippson, *Friedrich III*, p. 97.

Since May, William had held the Junker in reserve for just such a crisis. Yet he was still apprehensive of this man who wanted to "turn everything upside down." Queen Augusta and Frederick William had vigorously protested his qualifications. As late as September 7 William remarked to Roon that Bismarck was impossible, for he favored alliance with France. On the 16th, nevertheless, he let Bernstorff summon him to Berlin. Three days later the dissolution of the cabinet left the king with no other choice. But still he could not fully make up his mind. Would even this daring and resolute man accept the conditions refused by the retiring ministers?[32] William's uncertainty grew when he learned that the Junker had conferred with the crown prince immediately on arriving from Paris. Had Bismarck come only to serve his son?

On September 22 Bismarck drove to the gothic summer palace at Babelsberg for the fateful interview which was to decide his and Germany's future. Pointing to the draft of his abdication proclamation, William explained the situation. In good conscience he could no longer reign unless ministers could be found who would "conduct my government without subjecting me to the will of the parliamentary majority." When he paused, Bismarck asserted his willingness to serve with Roon in a new cabinet and his confidence that other ministers could be found to replace any who might resign.

But the king was still uncertain and pressed him with specific questions. Would Bismarck carry through the military reorganization? The answer was "Yes." Against the will of the majority in parliament? Once more came an emphatic affirmative. William was impressed. He had expected reservations, conditions, arguments. But Bismarck judged man and mood with complete accuracy. Despite his doubts about the wisdom of the course William was following, he assumed the role of a feudal vassal come to learn his lord's will. The king made up his mind, "Then it is my duty to try to continue the struggle, and I will not abdicate."[33]

Bismarck's appointment is the best possible demonstration of the authoritarian power of the Hohenzollern monarchy. He

[32] Ernst II, *Aus meinem Leben*, II, 497; Promnitz, *Bismarcks Eintritt*, p. 27; Zechlin, *Grundlegung*, pp. 252-256, 279-280; Ludwig Gerlach, *Aufzeichnungen*, II, 248; Roon, *Denkwürdigkeiten*, II, 120-121.

[33] *GW*, xv, 177-180. For William's brief account of the interview and the draft of his abdication proclamation see Friedrich III, *Tagebücher 1848-1866*, pp. 497-500.

gained his position by the personal decision of the king and he was to retain it through varying vicissitudes for nearly a quarter of a century for the same reason. In 1862 he did not have the full support of a single faction in the Prussian Landtag. Even the conservatives were dubious of this "democrat in disguise."[34] The king himself was tortured by doubt. Only Roon resolutely desired his appointment. To the general he was the final hope of rescue. William's abdication appeared to mean surrender of the army to parliamentary control and the end of the Prussian military state.[25]

Bismarck judged the situation in similar terms. The central issue, he told the king in Babelsberg, was not one of "liberalism or conservatism of one shading or another," but of monarchical or parliamentary government. The latter had to be avoided at all costs—even if it meant a "period of dictatorship." "In this situation I shall be quite open in giving you my opinion, if your majesty should request of me things which I do not consider right, but if you insist on your own judgment I would rather go down with the king than desert your majesty in the contest against parliamentary government." Undoubtedly this argument was *ad hominem*, designed to inspire confidence and whip up the fighting mood of his soldier-monarch. Nevertheless, Bismarck often repeated it under other circumstances during the years which followed.[36]

Whether or not Bismarck and William thought so, it is not certain that in 1862 Germany actually stood on the dividing line between monarchical and parliamentary government. It will be shown that none of the liberal parties or factions consciously aimed at the latter result. Had William abdicated, nevertheless, it is likely that the Prussian chamber of deputies would have attained a greater degree of influence over state policy and German parliamentary life in general a far greater vitality. As has

---

[34] *GW*, vii, 140; Herman von Petersdorff, *Kleist-Retzow* (Stuttgart, 1907), pp. 366 ff.; Promnitz, *Bismarcks Eintritt*, pp. 99-101. On September 24 Wilhelm Dilthey wrote to Hermann Baumgarten, "Not a single party is for Bismarck; all of the vague hopes which have been placed on him vanish with his entry into the present cabinet." Not even the most "fantastic" politician could attempt a stroke in foreign policy without solution of the military question. *HW*, i, 117.

[35] On September 21 the cabinet warned William that abdication would mean "self-destruction" for the crown. Friedrich III, *Tagebücher 1848-1866*, pp. 494-497. On the long personal relationship between Roon and Bismarck see Roon, *Denkwürdigkeiten*, ii, 19-20, 27-28; *GW*, xv, 206.

[36] For example, Horst Kohl, ed., *Die politischen Reden des Fürsten Bismarck* (Stuttgart, 1892-1905), ii, 78, 285.

been suggested in the introduction, there was something inherently unstable about the system of mixed powers. Elsewhere in Europe parliaments gained in power at the cost of the executive, and under Frederick William such a development might have occurred in Prussia. But the longevity of William and the genius of Bismarck assured that the actual course was to be the reverse.

CHAPTER EIGHT

THRUST, PARRY, RIPOSTE

1. AN ATTEMPT AT COMPROMISE

N THE day after Bismarck's first visit to Babelsberg the parliament, with but eleven dissenting votes, struck out of the budget for 1862 the funds already expended by the government for military reorganization.[1] By this act the deputies finally ended the temporizing with which, since 1860, they had sought to avoid an open breach with the crown. It was expected that the government would now be compelled either to concede to their wishes with regard to the two-year service period or restore the army to its status as of 1859. With this ultimatum the question of military reform retreated into the background and the more fundamental issue of the constitutional powers of king and parliament came to the fore. The "army conflict" was transformed into a "constitutional conflict."[2]

Despite his fighting words in Babelsberg, Bismarck was not at all pleased by the prospect of a final test of strength between crown and parliament, nor reconciled to its necessity. Although he had come to power because of the internal crisis, his primary interest was still foreign affairs. In the "Baden-Baden memorial" of 1861 he had advised William to avoid conflicts with parliament because of their damaging effect upon external policy. If she were to achieve her ends in Germany, Prussia must give the impression abroad that "all organs and forces of the country" were united

[1] Indicative of the immaturity of parliamentary practice in Prussia was the fact that there was no deadline for the passage of budget bills. Hence the deputies were still debating the budget for 1862 while the funds it was to grant were being expended. Since the government had presented the budget for 1863 in May, the chamber actually had before it simultaneously two budget bills. Waldeck even had to convince the deputies that the two measures should be considered individually rather than lumped together in a single debate. H. B. Oppenheim, *Benedikt Franz Leo Waldeck, der Führer der preussischen Demokratie, 1848-1870* (Berlin, 1880), p. 163.

[2] On the parliamentary situation leading to the September crisis see Kurt Promnitz, *Bismarcks Eintritt in das Ministerium, Historische Studien*, Vol. 60 (Berlin, 1908), pp. 25-38, 50 ff., 117 ff.; Löwenthal, *Verfassungsstreit*, pp. 75-108; Ritter, *Staatskunst*, I, 188.

behind the government.[3] But now the situation was worse than ever. With his usual flexibility Bismarck determined upon a final attempt to reconcile the conflicting parties.

The maneuver was highly dangerous. If awkwardly carried out, it could have destroyed the impression he had made in Babelsberg and given weight to the demands of the extremists for a reactionary cabinet under Edwin Manteuffel. On the night of October 3, Bismarck dined with an old associate of Petersburg days, Kurd von Schlözer, and told how he intended to get away with it:

"We drank a lot of champagne, which loosened even more his naturally loose tongue. He exulted about pulling the wool over everybody's eyes. Partly by himself and partly through others, he is seeking to get the king to concede the two-year service period. In the house of lords he paints the reaction he plans in colors so black that, as he puts it, the lords themselves are becoming anxious about the conditions he says he will bring about if need be. Before the gentlemen of the second chamber he appears at one moment very unbending, but in the next hints at his desire to mediate. Finally he intends to make the German cabinets believe that the king is hard put to restrain the Cavourism of his new minister. There is no denying that until now people are impressed by his spirit and brilliance. *C'est un homme!*"[4]

Where parliament was concerned there was some reason to believe that these tactics would be successful. Far from firmly united against the government, the deputies were divided into parties, caucuses, and factions with differing aims. On the right was a caucus known as the "Constitutionalists," the remaining core of the old-liberals who had recently dominated the chamber. Although dissatisfied with the course chosen by the king and unhappy about the fate of their colleagues in the cabinet, they were deeply suspicious of those further to the left who had taken over control of the chamber. One wing under Georg von Vincke wished to come to terms with the government at whatever cost, while the other under Wilhelm Grabow was reluctant to break the bonds of liberal solidarity by such a surrender.[5]

The bulk of the opposition came from the Left Center and Pro-

[3] *GW*, II, 320-321.
[4] Kurd von Schlözer, *Petersburger Briefe, 1857-1862* (Stuttgart, 1921), p. 261.
[5] For the general viewpoint of this party see Otto Westphal, *Welt- und Staatsauffassung des deutschen Liberalismus, Historische Bibliothek*, Vol. 41 (Munich, 1919).

gressive parties, which together controlled two-thirds of the chamber. Sometimes called the "Bockum-Dolffs Caucus" from the name of its leader, the Left Center was composed of moderate liberals largely from the Rhineland. Most hoped for a government surrender on the term-of-service issue; otherwise they were willing to cooperate with the progressives to force the Junker cabinet out of office. From its inception the Progressive Party was plagued by internal tensions which forecast its ultimate division in 1866. Many moderates, like Karl Twesten and Viktor von Unruh, dreaded the prospect of a fruitless conflict with the government. Fearing that either the crown or liberal majority might be driven to extremes, they sought an acceptable basis for compromise. But the democratic wing, led by such men as Baron Hoverbeck, Rudolf Virchow, and Hermann Schulze-Delitzsch, was inclined to hold its ground. On the extreme left a democratic faction of about forty deputies led by Benedikt Waldeck was determined to force the issue. Waldeck's influence was on the rise. His was the measure passed on September 23 to compel the government to restore the army to its condition as of 1859. The coalition of left centrists and progressives was a marriage of convenience rather than of love. Once the common objective was achieved, the followers of Bockum-Dolffs hoped to split apart the progressives, of whose democratic wing they strongly disapproved. The Left Center would then become the nucleus of a party of moderates which would supply the ministers for a new cabinet.[6]

By finding the right formula Bismarck hoped to precipitate this cleavage. First he withdrew the budget bill for 1863 and called for an "armistice." Next he sought out influential liberals of all parties to point out why every effort should be made to come to terms. The internal conflict was a "serious handicap to our prestige and actions abroad." In German politics his aims were those of the opposition; the army reform was "indispensable" for their achievement. Liberals ought to cooperate with the new cabinet, for its appearance had saved the country from complete reaction. The two-year term was "harmless" and might even be "advantageous." But time was required. Like a horse, he told Twesten, William balked at anything new; force made him all the

6 On the tensions within and between the liberal parties see Promnitz, *Bismarcks Eintritt*, pp. 64 ff.; Dehio, "Taktik der Opposition," pp. 288 ff.; *HW*, i, 75 ff.; Philippson, *Forckenbeck*, pp. 77 ff.

more stubborn. Through persuasion and the influence of the generals, he could ultimately be brought around. Meanwhile, the liberals must not complicate the task.[7]

On September 30 he presented his case to the budget committee of the lower chamber. It was his first crucial test as minister-president. Some found him "pleasant" and "conciliatory." Others got the impression he was nervous and uncertain. His hands shook and his speech, always uneven in tempo, was very abrupt. But for a "Mark Junker" he had considerable wit. Ideas and suggestions cascaded from his lips. One person who was there described the swift pace of Bismarck's mind as "kaleidoscopic"; the colors changed almost too quickly for the eye to follow. The effect was dazzling. Only later did the listener conclude that he had tasted "not wine, at the most soda."[8]

Bismarck fed the committee a sharp blend of threat, blandishment, and appeasement. His was a difficult task. Unable to promise publicly the two-year period, he had to hint that it was in prospect. Speaking of reconciliation, he had to leave the impression that he had no urgent need of concession or compromise. For dramatic effect he drew from his cigar case an olive branch, his precious souvenir of Avignon and Katharina Orlow. But the deputies were neither cowed, diverted, nor mollified. After two years of waiting and compromising they had lost all confidence in the commitments of the government.[9]

Luckily for Bismarck, William apparently did not hear of his secret promises to the liberal leaders. Nevertheless, his open remarks to the budget committee produced the first great crisis in his relationship with the king. In the opposition press his veiled threats aroused a sharp reaction; even Roon disapproved of the "witty digressions" with which he had entertained the deputies.

[7] *GW*, vii, 55-62; Friedrich III, *Tagebücher 1848-1866*, pp. 500-503; Eduard von Simson, *Erinnerungen aus seinem Leben* (Leipzig, 1900), pp. 354-355; Heinrich von Poschinger, ed., *Erinnerungen aus dem Leben von Hans Viktor von Unruh* (Stuttgart, 1895), pp. 214-215; Keudell, *Fürst und Fürstin Bismarck*, p. 112. There were reports that he had even offered cabinet posts to certain old liberals. Heinrich von Sybel, *The Founding of the German Empire by William I.* (New York, 1891), ii, 511-512; Ludolf Parisius, *Leopold Freiherr von Hoverbeck* (Berlin, 1897-1900), ii/1, 87-88. The ultras were shocked. Petersdorff, *Kleist-Retzow*, pp. 341-342.

[8] Otto Nirrnheim, *Das erste Jahr des Ministeriums Bismarck und die öffentliche Meinung, Heidelberger Abhandlungen zur mittleren und neueren Geschichte*, Vol. 20 (Heidelberg, 1908), pp. 89, 91; Kohl, *Reden*, ii, 37-38.

[9] *Ibid.*, pp. 16-36.

At Baden-Baden, whence he had gone after appointing the new minister-president, William was surrounded by those who disagreed with his choice—Augusta, Frederick William, and Grand Duke Frederick of Baden. Bismarck surmised that there was talk of Louis XVI, Strafford, and Polignac.

Anxiously he hurried out to meet the royal train returning from the south on October 4. Boarding at Jüterbog, he found William alone and morose in an ordinary first-class compartment. "I foresee exactly how all this is going to end," the Hohenzoller declared. "Out there in the Opernplatz under my windows they will cut off your head and a little later mine." Carefully Bismarck chose his ground. What better fate than to die for such a cause—"I in the struggle for the cause of my king and your majesty for the rights which are yours by the grace of God?" William should think of the noble death of Charles I, not the ignominious end of Louis XVI. "Your majesty is faced with the necessity of fighting. You cannot capitulate. You must oppose tyranny, even if you incur bodily danger."[10]

As Bismarck saw him, William had both the virtues and failings of a Prussian officer: indifferent to danger, unquestioningly obedient to command, driven by an exalted sense of duty, but uncertain when acting on his own responsibility, over-sensitive to the criticism of superiors, and fearful of the judgment of history. With words of duty and courage Bismarck pumped confidence into William's veins. When the train pulled into the Berlin station the Hohenzoller was again in a fighting mood.[11] But this tactic rendered even more difficult the task of getting William's consent to the plan recommended by Roon and his associates on October 10.

Modelled after the system of Napoleon III, the plan would have permitted conscripts to purchase their release from military service after two years. Those unable or unwilling to pay were to serve a third year. The money raised would be used to attract volunteers. In this way the king would have been provided with a

---

[10] *GW*, xv, 194-195; also xiv, 622-623. Bismarck's surmise concerning what had taken place in Baden-Baden was incorrect. The subject of the Prussian crisis was avoided. When the nationalist demand for the constitution of 1849 was discussed, William exploded with anger, yelling at his son-in-law so loudly that he could be heard in the street. Hermann Oncken, ed., *Grossherzog Friedrich I. von Baden und die deutsche Politik von 1854-1871* (Stuttgart, 1927), i, 337.

[11] *GW*, xv, 195.

skeleton of professional soldiers within the body of a conscript army, while the bourgeoisie were to be allowed to buy their way into the reserve. Left out of the deal were those who lacked the capital to buy their releases. In addition, the plan would have established the size of the army at one percent of the population and its support at a fixed sum per soldier. Henceforth these matters were to be beyond the challenge of the chamber of deputies. By appealing to the cupidity of the liberal bourgeoisie, in effect, Roon wished to entice them into jeopardizing the basic principle of the *Volksheer*, that of equal and universal service, and the most fundamental power of any parliament, that of annual control over military appropriations.

But William disapproved. He studded the margins of the document with such comments as "ruin of the troops," "death warrant of the army." He was encouraged in his refusal by Edwin Manteuffel, to whom any law delimiting the powers of the monarchy in military matters was anathema. One after another, the offending clauses were struck out of the draft. When finally presented to parliament in 1863, the bill had no chance of accomplishing Bismarck's purpose of splitting the opposition.[12]

Throughout these negotiations Bismarck apparently remained on the sidelines. But certainly Roon acted with his approval, and it may be that some of the ideas in the draft came from him. Five years later he was to incorporate its method of setting the size and financial support of the army in the German constitution. For the present, however, he was in no position to insist. To Bernstorff, now Prussian envoy in London, he explained: "For the infantry two years, with volunteers, would be satisfactory. But if the king insisted on ten years, I would not refuse obedience in such matters. In my opinion there are more important questions than that of purchasing momentary peace with the present chamber of deputies by this concession. Peace with such people would not be lasting. As far as I'm concerned, therefore, no surrender."[13]

2. THE ATTRACTION OF POWER

Since reconciliation had failed and capitulation was unthinkable, ways had to be found to overcome the parliamentary opposi-

---

[12] Ludwig Dehio, "Bismarck und die Heeresvorlagen der Konfliktszeit," *Historische Zeitschrift*, Vol. 144 (1931), pp. 31-47; Kriegsministerium, *Militärische Schriften weiland Kaiser Wilhelms des Grossen Majestät* (Berlin, 1897), II, 479-488.
[13] *GW*, XIV, 628.

tion. More than a year before his appointment as minister-president Bismarck had outlined to Roon what his tactic would be in this situation. The crown, he wrote, could disengage itself within only by a successful diversion without. "For fourteen years we have cultivated the taste of the nation for politics without satisfying its appetite, and hence it seeks nourishment in the gutter. We are almost as vain as the French. If we can persuade ourselves of our importance abroad, we are willing to let many things at home go by the board."[14]

In his appearance before the budget committee he tried to dazzle its members with the possibility of a revolutionary use of Prussian power. The Nationalverein, he declared, had no true appreciation of the importance of the Prussian army for the attainment of its ends. The Prussian people had always had a liking for more armor than the slim body of the state could bear. Now the time had come to use it. Prussia's leadership in Germany did not depend upon the degree of her liberalism, but upon the extent of her power: "Prussia must build up and preserve her strength for the favorable moment, which has already come and gone many times. Her borders under the treaties of Vienna are not favorable for the healthy existence of the state. The great questions of the day will not be settled by speeches and majority decisions—that was the great mistake of 1848 and 1849—but by blood and iron."[15] Seen in context, this famous quotation, so often misinterpreted, was a crude attempt to distract the deputies from the domestic quarrel by dangling the prospect of foreign conquest. But the overly dramatic phrase he chose was immediately singled out for attack by the liberal press and gave him the reputation of an unprincipled man of violence which has haunted him and his memory ever since.

Although he overdid it, there were good reasons for believing in the persuasive appeal of national power and prestige for the liberal mind. Since 1859 the Nationalverein had tended to languish. Disappointed by the Prussian government, its leaders had turned to popular agitation. But the movement lagged, despite the surface activity of the sporting and professional groups, the many rallies, conventions, and floods of oratory. With the exception of Baden, voters everywhere failed to elect deputies devoted to

14 *GW*, xiv, p. 571; see also iii, 367, 381, 385-386.
15 Kohl, *Reden*, ii, 29-30.

the cause. The moderates were despondent. How could the governments and people of Germany, they repeatedly asked themselves, again be set in motion toward national unity?[16]

Some hoped for another great national crisis like those of 1812, 1840, and 1859—for a great "national war" which would dissolve the hard crust of German particularism and close the fissures of the Prussian internal conflict.[17] A generation steeped in Hegelian thought longed for the "world-historical personality" who would unleash the latent power of the Prussian state. "The German question," wrote Max Duncker, historian and adviser to the crown prince, "is a question of power and will never be solved without the deployment of Prussian power, without proofs of the national use of power and success of power." For the sake of a German national policy he was willing to accept a "military dictatorship" in Prussia. The Karlsruhe historian Hermann Baumgarten yearned for the appearance in Berlin of "the great and firm man," "a great genius or mighty tyrant" capable of "quick and decisive action."[18] Soon after Bismarck's appointment the journalist Constantin Rössler wrote that "a bold, lasting, irrevocable deed in the German question" would make the liberals forget "within days" what the Junker had previously said and done. "Then the reaction would be at an end, but likewise the opposition." A jubilant nation would shout, "Eine Diktatur für einen Mann!"[19]

On Bismarck's assumption of power there was no immediate outcry from the liberal press. For a time the editors and politicians waited and watched. "Bismarck is a chameleon," wrote Duncker to the crown prince on September 22, "to whom every party lays claim." While the moderate liberals hoped for a Bismarck-Vincke-Bonin-Sybel cabinet, the *Kreuzzeitung* expected a ministry of ultras. Not until his appearance before the budget committee and his first repressive acts in domestic affairs did the liberal assault commence.[20]

[16] Hermann Oncken, *Rudolf von Bennigsen* (Stuttgart, 1910), I, 477 ff.; Johannes Schultze, ed., *Max Duncker: Politischer Briefwechsel aus seinem Nachlass* (Stuttgart, 1923), pp. 315-321; *HW*, I, *passim*.

[17] Dehio, "Pläne der Militärpartei," p. 99; Rudolf Haym, *Das Leben Max Dunckers* (Berlin, 1891), pp. 261-262; Friedrich III, *Tagebücher 1848-1866*, pp. xxvi-xxvii; Aus dem Leben Bernhardis, IV, 314, 325-326; Duncker, *Briefwechsel*, pp. 301, 304; *HW*, I, 160-163; Hans Rosenberg, ed., *Ausgewählter Briefwechsel Rudolf Hayms* (Stuttgart, 1930), pp. 193-194, 199, 208, 211.

[18] *HW*, I, 39, 59, 61, 71; Duncker, *Briefwechsel*, p. 317.

[19] Constantin Rössler, *Ausgewählte Aufsätze* (Berlin, 1902), p. xviii.

[20] Nirrnheim, *Bismarck und die öffentliche Meinung*, pp. 71-73, 91; Duncker, *Briefwechsel*, p. 340.

The attitude of German liberals toward the Hohenzollern monarchy, in short, was still ambivalent. They were attracted by the potential utility of its power for national purposes, but repelled by its autocratic form, militaristic tradition, and reactionary policies. Those of the moderate school placed the greater emphasis upon the attraction, those of the democratic viewpoint upon the repulsion. But there was also a perceptible difference in the attitudes of Prussian and non-Prussian liberals. While the former were now embittered by the constitutional conflict and determined to fight it through, the latter tended to deplore the whole affair and hope for its settlement. Removed from the immediate scene, uninvolved in its personal feuds and passions, the non-Prussians were far more concerned about what they regarded as the greater issue of national unity. Into these fateful cleavages Bismarck hoped to drive the wedges which would split the liberal movement asunder.

The opposition parties in the Prussian chamber were aware of his Bonapartism, but doubted that he would be successful. Despite the discouragement which many felt about the strength of the popular movement, most were inclined to believe that unity could never be achieved under any other than liberal auspices. The first step toward this end, they reasoned, must be the liberalization of Germany's most powerful state. Once this had been achieved by peaceful means, a liberal government in Berlin would launch the national revolution which would put an end to dualism, destroy the German Confederation, and unify little Germany. In the thinking of democratic liberals, at least, the necessity and inevitability of this procedure was axiomatic.[21]

The axiom had its corollary: any attempt on the part of a conservative Prussian government to undertake a warlike venture in foreign policy was foredoomed to failure. How could this Junker, whose reputation reeked of reaction and who had been summoned by the king as a last resort in his struggle with parliament, possibly tap the reservoir of German national patriotism for his ends? Bred in the rationalistic tradition, the liberals could not believe that Bismarck was correct in his cynical view of the primitive instincts of the masses. They could hardly grant that the German people were "as vain as the French."

The deputies were inclined, furthermore, to speed Bismarck's

21 On the attitudes and strategy of the Prussian liberals see Dehio, "Taktik der Opposition," pp. 280 ff.

failure. In their eyes German nationalism was a holy cause not to be profaned by the unclean hands of a Junker reactionary. Many expected to weaken the force of Prussian diplomacy in the German question by remaining firm in their opposition to the new cabinet and by denying the credits necessary for military reorganization. In good times, to be sure, the government might be able to defy the powers claimed by parliament in budgetary matters and to finance the administration of the state from sources of income previously authorized. But the story would be different when Bismarck attempted his "grand action." At the crucial moment the population would refuse its moral support, and parliament would reject the extraordinary credits necessary for war.[22]

Like Bismarck, in other words, many liberals expected to find in foreign affairs the means to internal victory. Their choice of this road to power, however, was a confession of weakness. Even at the height of the constitutional conflict none of the liberal factions were willing to demand parliamentary government. Not even the democratic wing of the Progressive Party raised the cry for a politically responsible cabinet, although this was probably for many a theoretical goal. When Bismarck accused the opposition in parliament of having such an aim, the reply was an indignant chorus of denial. Many shared the opinion of the historian and left-center deputy Heinrich von Sybel that parliament without "an understanding royal leadership" was "not yet equal to the task" of governing. "The issue between the liberal and feudal parties," Duncker explained, "is essentially this: Which can win the monarchy? Which can move the monarchy over to its side?" The liberal aim was not to overthrow royal authority, but to influence its policy.[23]

Having chosen a moderate end, they were restricted to moderate means. Pressure was to be applied, but violence eschewed. The house of conservative power was not to be blown into the air, but permitted to buckle from within. By resorting to the barricades the liberals feared to loose forces beyond their control. They desired to replace the political power of the Junkers with that of the educated middle class, but not to awaken the political ambi-

22 *Ibid.*, pp. 300 ff. See also Thorwart, *Schulze-Delitzsch*, III, 192, 207.

23 Kohl, *Reden*, II, 365; *HW*, I, 105; Duncker, *Briefwechsel*, p. 284; Bergsträsser, "Kritische Studien," pp. 370-372. See also the penetrating critique of the liberal outlook by Hansgeorg Schroth, *Welt- und Staatsideen des deutschen Liberalismus, Historische Studien*, Vol. 201 (Berlin, 1931).

tions of the masses. Furthermore, the strategy they chose offered a convenient rationalization for a purely negative policy. By their reasoning the ultimate victory could be prepared, not by advancing a positive program, but merely by rejecting time and again what the government proposed. Thus the deputies could continue, moreover, to pose as the defenders of the *Rechtsstaat*, a pleasing prospect for the many lawyers, jurists, academicians, and civil servants in the liberal ranks. Good strategy seemed to coincide with good law.[24]

But there were other reasons for a negative policy. The structure of the liberal majority was shaky, incapable of supporting a policy of action. As we have seen, it was an uneasy coalition of factions whose mutual distrust had been bridged only by the necessity of common struggle. None of the liberal groups, moreover, was sure of its own internal cohesion. Not even the progressives had an adequate party organization. Hence the primary concern of the deputy was the electorate which had sent him to Berlin, meaning the small group of local magnates who had the important votes. In parliament he tended to assert his independence of party ties and decisions. Any attempt by the members to bind the party to a definite program was likely to endanger its existence. For this reason the reshuffling of party groupings was a constant phenomenon.[25]

The final and probably decisive reason for a negative policy, however, was the uncomfortable suspicion of the liberals that they had no firm popular following. Eugene Anderson has recently concluded, from an analysis of election statistics, that Prussia was "overwhelmingly" liberal in 1862—or "potentially" so! Those who participated in the struggle did not share this conviction. As the conflict neared its climax in the summer of 1862 Max von Forckenbeck, a spokesman of the moderate progressives, expressed his fear that, if the deputies should force a fresh dissolution, it would "drive the undecided people—and that is the great majority—to the other side and thus make victory doubtful for the near future."[26] The liberals had the uncertainty of frontline

[24] Dehio, "Taktik der Opposition," p. 298, and "Benedict Waldeck," *Historische Zeitschrift*, Vol. 136 (1927), pp. 50-57.

[25] Dehio, "Taktik der Opposition," pp. 287-288; Anderson, *Social and Political Conflict*, pp. 243 ff.; Unruh, *Erinnerungen*, pp. 231-232.

[26] Anderson, *Social and Political Conflict*, p. 440; Philippson, *Forckenbeck*, pp. 84-85. See also Ernst Schraepler, "Linksliberalismus und Arbeiterschaft in der

troops thinly deployed before a determined foe and backed by no reserves.

Filled with doubt and timidity where domestic issues were concerned, they hoped to find their salvation in foreign affairs. They waited for a fresh tidal wave of national sentiment to engulf the reactionary cabinet and provide a crest upon which to coast to victory. Far from regarding Bismarck's appointment as a disaster, some thought it a positive gain.[27] Eagerly they waited for him to launch the spear of Prussian power into the melee of German politics. Theirs was the fatal illusion that the liberal and national causes were inseparable and that what promoted the latter must certainly benefit the former.

3. ADVANCE AND RETREAT IN GERMANY

Although Bismarck often made domestic policy serve the needs of foreign policy, the reverse was seldom true. His quarrel with Austria arose from his view of the interest of state, rather than the need for a solution to the constitutional conflict. Nevertheless, the growing intensity of the latter undoubtedly added to the urgency of a successful stroke in the German question. A single blow might bring a double victory. But his first year in office was one of frustration and near disaster.

At the moment of his appointment the struggle between the dual powers neared a climax in both the confederation and Zollverein. During the fall the Austrian drive for a favorable reform of the confederation gained momentum.[28] On October 28 a convention of great-Germanists created the German Reformverein to combat the Nationalverein. Although in dissension about the details of the reforms proposed in August, Austria and her allies agreed in November to press for their adoption "in principle" by the diet. On the Zollverein front the Prussian case appeared to be gaining ground among manufacturers; two businessmen's conventions held in Weimar and Munich voted for the free trade treaty with France. With the exception of Saxony, nevertheless, Vienna was able to hold most of her allies in line.[29]

---

preussischen Konfliktszeit," in Richard Dietrich and Gerhard Oestreich, eds., *Forschungen zu Staat und Verfassung, Festgabe für Fritz Hartung* (Berlin, 1958), pp. 385-401.

[27] *HW*, I, 135.   [28] See above, pp. 149-150.

[29] Eugen Franz, *Der Entscheidungskampf um die wirtschaftspolitische Führung*

Following the strategy he had planned for nearly a decade, Bismarck moved first to seize the pivotal position of alternative choice. On a trip to France he apparently received assurances that Napoleon and his new foreign minister, Drouyn de Lhuys, would maintain "unconditional neutrality" in the event of war between Austria and Prussia.[30] Before leaving Paris the Prussian delivered his first stroke. Calling on Richard Metternich, he openly told the Austrian ambassador that his aim was to establish Prussian leadership in the economic, political, and military affairs of northern Germany. He preferred to attain it "through understanding and close union with Austria," but if opposed he would use "every means . . . without special scruple" to gain his ends.[31] In early December he repeated this grim warning to Karolyi, the Austrian minister in Berlin. He advised the Hapsburg monarchy to locate its sphere outside Germany in the east, ruling Hungary not as an appendix but as a vital part of the empire. As inducement he offered a "firm alliance" in European politics and a promise of "unconditional" support for Austrian interests in Italy and eastern Europe. If spurned, Prussia would "go with" Paris in any future crisis.[32]

Nevertheless, his first aggressive move in Germany came to naught and then the whole offensive miscarried. In November he dispatched an ultimatum to the Elector Frederick William of Hesse-Kassel, ordering him to end his quarrel with the Hessian parliament or risk the consequences. By marching troops into Kassel, Bismarck expected to alter the balance of forces among the lesser states in favor of the French customs treaty and renewal of the Zollverein. But the sinister prince evaded him by responding to the ultimatum, and the Hessian pawn remained in play.[33]

Deutschlands (1856-1867), *Schriftenreihe zur bayerischen Landesgeschichte*, Vol. 12 (Munich, 1933), pp. 241 ff.; W. O. Henderson, *The Zollverein* (Cambridge, 1939), pp. 294 ff.; Heinrich Ritter von Srbik, *Deutsche Einheit, Idee und Wirklichkeit vom Heiligen Reich bis Königgrätz* (Munich, 1935-1942), iii, 399, 428 ff.; Erich Zimmermann, *Der deutsche Reformverein* (Pforzheim, 1929).

30 *GW*, iv, 10-11; xiv, 627; vii, 65-67. The replacement of Thouvenel by Drouyn de Lhuys as foreign minister had aroused apprehension that Napoleon was bent on rapprochement with Austria. *APP*, iii, 41-43.

31 *GW*, xiv, 628; Freiherr von Hengelmüller, "Graf Alois Karolyi, Ein Beitrag zur Geschichte der österreichisch-ungarischen Diplomatie," *Deutsche Revue*, Vol. 38/4 (1913), pp. 35-36. Rechberg was not impressed by the threat. *Ibid.*, Vol. 38/3 (1913), p. 304.

32 *GW*, vii, 69-72; iv, 14-16, 22-25; *APP*, iii, 145-146; *DPO*, ii, 635-637. Again Rechberg's reply to Karolyi was uncompromising. *Ibid.*, pp. 623-626, 649-653.

33 *GW*, vii, 62-65; iv, 13-14; xiv, 630-631.

In December the Frankfurt diet neared a vote on the Austrian reform plan, and Bismarck began to prepare for war. "What would France do if things got hot in Germany?" he asked Talleyrand, the French ambassador. The reply was not what he expected. If the struggle remained local, France would be a spectator, but if the destruction of the confederation and a shift in the European balance were threatened, "the emperor would then seek the combination offering the greatest guarantees for the security of his state and the peace of Europe."[34] A few days later this straw in the wind from Paris was followed by another.

As was his custom, Bismarck was moving forward simultaneously on a second front. In the course of negotiations with Paris on the implementation of the free-trade treaty, he had asked the French for a guarantee that they would not make similar agreements with other Zollverein states. His aim was to make the Brandenburger Tor the "only door" through which the latter could enter the European system of free trade. Thus armed, he hoped that in 1866, after the expiration of the Zollverein treaties, Prussia could force the lesser states to accept procedure by majority vote and a parliament capable of counterbalancing the "political divergencies of the governments." In place of a reformed diet, equipped with a great-German assembly under Austrian control, he intended a reformed customs union, equipped with a little-German parliament under Prussian hegemony. But on December 30 Drouyn refused the Prussian stipulation.[35]

Undoubtedly the French shift was a severe disappointment to Bismarck. Nevertheless, his system of strategy allowed for such situations. From the pivotal position it was now necessary to draw away from Paris and closer to Vienna. The French had to be shown that the Wilhelmstrasse could be reconnected with the Ballhausplatz.[36] But this posed a difficult task. Even while seeking rapprochement with Vienna, he had to defeat the Austrian reform plan and convince the Austrians of the futility of attempting another. But Bismarck was adept at squaring the circle. In his interviews with Thun and Karolyi in early 1863 the themes of

[34] *APP*, III, 131-132, 143. The Italian ambassador was asked bluntly whether Prussia could depend upon military assistance in a conflict with Austria. Although mistrustful, the Italians were interested. *APP*, III, 129-130, 134.

[35] *GW*, IV, 16-19, 28-33; *APP*, III, 140-142; Franz, *Entscheidungskampf*, pp. 259 ff.

[36] The danger was made acute by the fact that Gorchakov was again considering the possibility of alliance with France. *APP*, III, 108-109, 120, 128; *GW*, XIV, 633-634.

appeasement, threat, enticement, and diversion appear in rapid succession. One minute he talked of the desirability of an "offensive-defensive alliance" and in the next stressed Prussia's self-sufficiency; he spoke of the dangers of the European revolution and then disclosed plans to exploit revolutionary forces for Prussia's advantage; while denying any intention of dividing Germany into two spheres, he proposed plans which would ultimately have had this effect. Finally he suggested that the dual powers "abstract" their European from their German relationships, cooperating in the one area while disagreeing in the other. Karolyi found it "truly astonishing with what rapidity Herr von Bismarck goes from one extreme to another diametrically opposed."[37]

As the vote in the diet neared, he employed the tactic of "fear and fear again" toward the lesser states, warning them that, if voted down, Prussia would immediately declare herself no longer bound by the confederate constitution. Until the last minute some of the smaller states wavered, torn between fright and hatred of Prussia. But when the votes were counted on January 22, 1863, the Austrian plan had lost, nine to seven. The sensation of the day, however, was the message which accompanied the Prussian vote. "The German nation," it declared, "can find a competent organ through which to influence the course of common affairs only in a representative body chosen directly by the people of each confederate state according to its population." To be workable such a "German parliament" would have to be equipped with a "legislative power" sufficient to make it an effective "counterweight" to the diet.[38] What the shocked delegates heard was a powerful warning that, if the Austrian coalition continued on the path of great-German reform, Prussia would ally herself with the forces of little-German nationalism. In such a competition Berlin could offer far more than Vienna.

While the Prussian delegate spoke, events were taking place in the east which again badly disrupted Bismarck's scheme and soon even brought him close to disaster. On the night of January 21 the Poles arose once more in revolt against Russian domination. Although Prussian Poland was not affected, Berlin immediately

[37] DPO, II, 719-721, 738-746, 750-758, 791-797, 809-814; APP, III, 186-187, 194, 198-199, 203-204. Thun was convinced of Bismarck's change of heart, but not Karolyi. DPO, II, 762.

[38] GW, IV, 38-40; Enno Kraehe, "Austria and the Problem of Reform in the German Confederation, 1851-1863," American Historical Review, LVI (1951), pp. 291-294.

ordered four army corps into the area and their commander issued a proclamation tantamount to martial law. In February General von Alvensleben was sent to Petersburg to consult on "common measures." It may be that he exceeded his instructions by wiring back to Berlin the draft of a convention providing for the possibility of military cooperation in pursuit of rebels across the Prussian frontier. But Bismarck quickly accepted it, for the convention appeared to signify the end of Russian attempts to appease the Poles.[39]

Bismarck's opposition to the Polish cause was primarily political rather than racial or cultural. An independent Poland, he feared, would inevitably strive for the frontiers of 1772, including Posen and west Prussia. Because of these ambitions a Polish state would be a "natural ally of France." Within the Russian government, moreover, those who favored Polish autonomy were also supporters of the French alignment.[40] But his view of the Polish question was also charged with emotion. Toward no other people did he express himself with such violent antagonism. "Harry the Poles so that they despair of their lives," he wrote to his sister in 1861, "I have every sympathy for their plight, but if we are to exist we can do nothing other than exterminate them." Undoubtedly this was written in an exuberant moment. At no time did Bismarck ever officially advocate or follow a policy of extermination against a national minority. But a letter to Bernstorff of the same year was nearly as savage. "Every success of the Polish national movement is a defeat for Prussia; we cannot carry on the struggle against this element according to the rules of civil justice, but only according to those of war."[41]

[39] APP, iii, 222-224, 231 ff. On the problem of the origins of the convention see Egmont Zechlin, Bismarck und die Grundlegung der deutschen Grossmacht (Stuttgart, 1930), pp. 430 ff.; Gerhard Heinze, Bismarck und Russland bis zur Reichsgründung (Würzburg, 1939), pp. 29-37; Robert H. Lord, "Bismarck and Russia in 1863," American Historical Review, xxix (1923), 24-48; Hellmuth Scheidt, Konvention Alvensleben und Interventionspolitik der Mächte in der polnischen Frage 1863 (Würzburg, 1937).

[40] GW, iv, 59-61; xv, 210 ff.; APP, iii, 400; Zechlin, Grundlegung, pp. 421 ff.; Srbik, Deutsche Einheit, iii, 470 ff.; Christian Friese, Russland und Preussen vom Krimkrieg bis zum Polnischen Aufstand (Berlin, 1931), pp. 269 ff., 295 ff.

[41] GW, xiv, 568; iii, 298-299. For Bismarck's general attitude toward the Polish question see Joseph Feldman, "Bismarck et la question polonaise," Revue Historique, Vol. 173 (1934), pp. 540-588, summarized in "Bismarck und die Polnische Frage," Ostland-Berichte, v (1931), 222-230; Heinze, Bismarck und Russland, pp. 21-25, 27-46; Hans Wendt, Bismarck und die polnische Frage, Historische Studien, ix (Halle, 1922).

Since 1861 he had advised the Russians against all concessions to the Poles. Now he became obsessed by the fear that the reform party in Petersburg, led by Gorchakov, might actually withdraw Russian troops and abandon the Poles to themselves. He determined to occupy the vacated region and attach it to Prussia. In a rare lapse of judgment he sounded out the governments in London and Paris on the matter.[42] One evening at a court ball he spoke to Behrend, vice-president of the chamber of deputies, about the possibility of "Germanizing" Russian Poland.[43]

Whatever the future value, there can be little doubt that the Alvensleben convention, judged by its immediate consequences, was a bad mistake. Both London and Vienna protested Prussia's intervention. But the most dangerous reaction came from Paris. The convention rescued Napoleon from a severe dilemma. He had need of rapprochement with Russia to relieve his dependence upon Britain, but the doctrine of national self-determination dictated support of the rebels, and the French public was intensely interested in their fate. Now he was able to train his diplomatic artillery on Berlin rather than on Petersburg. On February 21 he proposed identic notes from Paris, London, and Vienna censuring Prussian intervention.[44]

When the two powers refused, Napoleon turned to another scheme even more dangerous for Prussia. In early March he asked Vienna for an alliance. If events should require the surrender of Galicia to an independent Poland, Austria would receive "material compensations" and "exclusive preponderance" in the Balkans. If she would surrender Venetia to Italy, the two powers could join in dismembering the Italian kingdom into three segments (Piedmont, Papacy, Naples); Austria would receive "material compensation" in Germany, where her "preponderance" would be assured.[45] Earlier Eugénie, waving her dainty hand over a map, had revealed to Metternich the fantastic scope of the

[42] *APP*, III, 237-238, 256-259. Bernstorff's reply was discouraging. *Ibid.*, pp. 280-282.

[43] Zechlin, *Grundlegung*, pp. 470-472; *APP*, III, 354; Poschinger, *Bismarck und die Parlamentarier*, II, 24-25. In his own recital of this conversation Bismarck did not mention "Germanization." *GW*, IV, 70-71. The reports of the Saxon and British ambassadors likewise fail to mention it. *APP*, III, 271-272, 278. Two years later, however, he wrote to Bodelschwingh about the "political" wisdom of gradually "Germanizing" Posen. *GW*, V, 69-70.

[44] Zechlin, *Grundlegung*, pp. 450 ff.; Lord, "Bismarck and Russia," pp. 31 ff.; *APP*, III, 286-287.

[45] *RKN*, I, 10-16.

mirage which hovered over the Tuileries. In a general exchange of territories France was to gain the Rhine; Austria to gain Silesia, Bosnia, and Herzegovina, and "all that she wished south of the Main"; Prussia to gain Saxony, Hanover, and the duchies north of the Main; Russia to gain Asiatic Turkey, Poland to gain Posen and part of Galicia; the dispossessed princes would be used to "civilize and monarchize" the American republics on the pattern of Mexico. Metternich believed that Louis shared the "phantasmagoria" of his impetuous wife. "His language recalls the great epochs of his reign, those which preceded the Crimean and Italian wars."[46] Nevertheless, much of his army was committed in Mexico, where the decisive battle was yet to be fought; France was in no condition to fight a major continental war. Hence everything depended upon the success of the insurrection on the Vistula, which was to inaugurate the long chain of sacrifice and compensation. But the rebel cause faltered, and the Austrians declined. The mirage evaporated.[47]

Napoleon's actions, however, forced Bismarck into hasty retreat. In London, Vienna, and Paris he maintained that the convention was of "no practical importance"; having never been ratified, it did not "formally" exist; Russia's success in Poland had made it a "dead letter." Toward Austria and Russia he spoke the language of the holy alliance, pleading for a common front against revolution and vigorously denying any thought of alliance with small-German nationalism or of "any kind" of German parliament. "Given a choice between two evils, the lesser is preferable; concern for the security of a country takes precedence over plans for its growth."[48]

It was Britain, however, which finally routed the French offensive. In rejecting the French proposal of February 21, Lord Russell proposed that the powers send identic notes to Petersburg rather than Berlin, recommending a more liberal treatment of Poland. This transformed the issue. Russia and her Polish policy came to the center of the stage, while Prussia and the Alvensleben convention retreated to the wings. During the months which followed, French policy gyrated desperately from one plan

[46] *RKN*, i, 3-10.
[47] See Gustav Roloff, "Napoleon und der polnische Aufstand im Jahre 1863," *Historische Zeitschrift*, Vol. 164 (1941), pp. 49-65, and Hallberg, *Franz Joseph and Napoleon III*, pp. 314 ff.
[48] *APP*, iii, 299-304, 316 ff.; Zechlin, *Grundlegung*, pp. 487 ff.

to another. Finally Napoleon joined Britain and Austria in a series of *démarches* to Petersburg in the vain hope of coercing Alexander to liberate Poland. Twist and turn though he might, Gorchakov was compelled to reject the notes with increasing sharpness. Since Vienna and London now let the matter rest, Napoleon was impotent. His Polish intervention had failed and with it, as time was to prove, the last chance for alliance with Russia. In the future Alexander and his government leaned increasingly on Prussia in European politics.[49]

No sooner had one threat subsided than Bismarck was faced by another. Through the Polish affair Austria had acquired the pivotal position in European politics. Schmerling and Biegeleben now insisted that Vienna exploit this situation by renewing the struggle for a confederate reform consonant with her own interests. Although their plan showed some advances over the previous one, the provision for a collective executive in which Prussia would have been permanently "majoritized" made it equally unacceptable to Bismarck. The method of adoption was again exceedingly guileful. Instead of trying to pass over the Prussian veto, the Austrians stoked the fires of a steam roller with which to flatten every obstacle. While William was taking his yearly cure in Bad Gastein in early August, Franz Joseph suddenly presented the plan and invited him to a "congress of princes" to consider the matter. The date was August 3, and the congress was to meet in Frankfurt already on the sixteenth.[50]

Only with the greatest effort was Bismarck able to persuade his king not to attend. The idea of such a conclave of reigning monarchs appealed to the Hohenzoller. Since all other princes accepted, he feared the discourtesy of a refusal. In his memoirs Bismarck describes that dramatic midnight argument in Baden-Baden which ended with William in tears; the minister relieved his feelings by smashing a wash basin to bits on the floor. With it shattered the last real attempt at a great-German solution to the German question. Ridden by fears and jealousies, the lesser

49 Srbik, *Deutsche Einheit*, III, 480 ff.; Friese, *Russland und Preussen*, pp. 309 ff.
50 *APP*, III, 683-684, 688-701; *DPO*, III, 229-234; Zechlin, *Grundlegung*, pp. 566 ff.; Srbik, *Deutsche Einheit*, IV, 39 ff.; Max Lenz, "König Wilhelm und Bismarck in Gastein, 1863," *Kleine Historische Schriften* (Munich, 1910), pp. 429-474, and "Die Begegnung König Wilhelms I. mit dem Kaiser Franz Joseph in Gastein am 3. August 1863," in Alfred Doren et al., *Staat und Persönlichkeit, Festschrift für Erich Brandenburg* (Leipzig, 1928), pp. 169-213.

princes agreed to the Austrian proposal only on condition that Prussia again be invited to give her consent.[51]

For three weeks Bismarck delayed his reply. Finally on September 22 he delivered a slashing counterattack. Only a central parliament elected directly by "the entire nation" and sharing legislative power, he declared, could adequately counteract dynastic particularism; in contrast to Austria the interests of Prussia were identical with those of the German people.[52] Such a parliament would have split the German from the non-German parts ·of the Hapsburg empire—precisely what Schmerling wished to avoid. For the second time within a year Bismarck halted the Austrian diplomatic offensive by pointing out that Prussia had within reach an alternative compatible with her own interests but poisonous to those of Austria. It was a threat to ally the Prussian state with the forces of German nationalism.

Originally the Prussian note had an even more radical clause providing for "eventual" agreement with the "popular assembly" on a constitution. Perhaps on William's objection this was left out of the final draft.[53] Outwardly the Prussian note looked like an offer of universal and equal suffrage. When the British objected to a German national parliament as conducive to revolution, Bismarck replied that the "smallest property qualification" would offer a "better guarantee against revolutionary excesses" than most German electoral laws, including the Prussian. For that matter even a "high property qualification" could be satisfactory. William, furthermore, was thinking in terms of a "conservative franchise."[54] But these reservations were hidden from the public.

Standing amid the ruins of their attempt at great-German reform, Rechberg and his colleagues suddenly found themselves under attack from Paris. On November 5 Napoleon declared that the treaties of 1815 had "ceased to exist." Only a European congress could preserve the peace by drafting a fresh settlement. More than any other country in Europe, Austria had reason to fear such a congress, for it would certainly raise the question of national self-

---

[51] GW, xv, 227-241; Horst Kohl, ed., Anhang zu den Gedanken und Erinnerungen von Otto Fürst von Bismarck (Stuttgart, 1901), I, 74; Johannes Schultze, ed., Kaiser Wilhelms I. Weimarer Briefe (Berlin, 1924), II, 38-51. For a detailed study of the Fürstentag affair see Hans Scheller, Der Frankfurter Fürstentag 1863 (Leipzig, 1929).

[52] Staatsarchiv, VIII (1865), 206-213; GW, IV, 174-176.

[53] APP, III, 764-765, 779-786.

[54] Ibid., pp. 813-814; IV, 53-54; DPO, III, 239-240.

determination. Austria, rather than Prussia, now seemed to be the target of French imperialism. Vainly Rechberg pleaded for a concerted answer of the four great powers. On Bismarck's advice William's reply to Napoleon was "friendly in tone," but "held open every path." As he undoubtedly anticipated, the British cabinet torpedoed the congress plan with a brusque rejection. Queen Victoria thought it an "impertinence."[55]

After a year of crisis and disappointment Bismarck now had reason for satisfaction. Once more Prussia had the middle position in European politics. Napoleon's fumbling had poisoned his relationships with St. Petersburg and London. His policy on Poland and his talk of revising the settlement of 1815 had ended the threat of a Franco-Russian alliance and had destroyed the working entente with Britain established in the Crimean war. Rebuffed by Austria, the emperor had no other choice than to resume his courtship of Berlin.[56] But in Vienna as well there was a change in attitude. Very discouraged by the negative results of their attempt at confederate reform and frightened by the dangerous turn in Napoleonic policy, the Austrians were now ready to cooperate with Prussia. Within a few months Bismarck was to lead them deep into the morass of the Schleswig-Holstein question.

[55] George E. Buckle, ed., *The Letters of Queen Victoria*, 2nd Series, I, 114; *APP*, IV, 119-120, 135-137, 148-150, 170-172.

[56] As early as June, reports from Paris had shown that the weathercock on the Tuileries was again shifting toward Berlin. *APP*, III, 633-635, 647-648. In September Napoleon and Drouyn hinted broadly of their desire for an alliance. *APP*, III, 751-755, 757-758; IV, 40. But Bismarck was wary. *APP*, III, 633-634, 765-766; IV, 109. At the moment he was probing Petersburg over the prospect of alliance against Austria. Should France interfere, "the line of the Weser is more important to us than that of the Rhine." *APP*, III, 758-762, 786-793. But the Russian reply was negative. *APP*, III, 802, 804, 807-809.

CHAPTER NINE

A PERIOD OF DICTATORSHIP

1. A CONVENIENT CONSTITUTION

HE collapse of his attempt at reconciliation at home and his failure to achieve a coup abroad left Bismarck with no popular foundation for his policies either in foreign or domestic affairs. Since 1858 the Conservative Party had suffered a series of catastrophic defeats. Not even vigorous bureaucratic interference in the election of March 1862 had been able to halt the decline. Part of the fault lay in an inadequate party organization and press. Among the rural gentry the tasks of practical politics were considered denigrating and distasteful. While proud of their traditional function as the ruling caste, they were not yet reconciled to the necessity of appealing to the popular will.[1]

A conservative who did understand this necessity was Bismarck's old friend and associate of the revolutionary period, Hermann Wagener. In September 1861 he helped found the Prussian Volksverein, the conservative answer to the Nationalverein and Progressive Party. Socially the organization was an alliance of landowners and artisans to protect what remained of manorialism and the guild system against middle-class liberalism, *laissez-faire* capitalism, and the factory system. With official patronage it achieved minor success, reaching a membership of 26,000 in 1862 and 50,000 in 1865. During Bismarck's first months in office the Volksverein promoted a flood of "loyalty declarations," which arrived at the royal palace from the provinces almost daily. Many were borne by delegations which included peasants and handicraft workers. In October a companion organization, Die Patriotische Vereinigung, was formed under the leadership of Moritz von Blankenburg. A monster petition was launched denouncing the "unpatriotic" and "revolutionary" attitude of the opposition. By January it had accumulated a half million signatures.[2]

[1] Eugene N. Anderson, *The Social and Political Conflict in Prussia, 1858-1864* (Lincoln, 1954), pp. 352 ff.

[2] See Hugo Müller, *Der preussische Volks-Verein* (Berlin, 1914); (Ludwig

Still there was no disguising the fact that the cabinet had no significant popular support. Where the masses stood was uncertain, but the organs of public opinion, both press and parliament, were overwhelmingly on the side of the liberal opposition. Hence Bismarck had no other choice than to introduce that "period of dictatorship" whose possibility he had foreseen in Babelsberg.

For this purpose the Prussian constitution was an ideal instrument. There was more than a little truth to Edwin Manteuffel's assertion that in Prussia the old monarchy was the reality and the constitution "as yet mere theory."[3] The vital clauses were phrased with a careful ambiguity which left open the possibility of authoritarian interpretation. As early as 1851 Bismarck had stated his views on the viability of the Prussian system: "When crown and ministers are in agreement, governmental authority is stronger and firmer in Prussia than in any country in the world. There will always be an inclination to obey, as long as his majesty does not lose the will to command. . . . Through the manner in which it has been reshaped and interpreted during the last two years the constitution has ceased to restrict the process of governing and is becoming more and more just the receptacle whose content is determined by those who rule."[4]

In withdrawing the budget bill for 1863 on September 28, 1862, Bismarck had promised to reintroduce it, along with a new bill on compulsory military service, in the next session of the chamber. Under the constitution the king was obligated to summon parliament between early November and mid-January. This left open the possibility that the deputies would not receive the bill in time to take action before January 1 of the year to which it applied. Hence Forckenbeck introduced a resolution calling on the government to conform to the law by summoning parliament early enough to avoid this possibility.[5]

In his appearance before the budget committee on September

Hahn, ed.), *Die Innere Politik der preussischen Regierung von 1862 bis 1866* (Berlin, 1866), pp. 128-131; Fritz Löwenthal, *Der preussische Verfassungsstreit, 1862-1866* (Munich, 1914), pp. 136-137. The liberals spoke of the "petition swindle" because of the way in which many signatures were obtained. Nirrnheim, *Bismarck und die öffentliche Meinung*, pp. 100 ff.

3 Heinrich O. Meisner, ed., *Der preussische Kronprinz im Verfassungskampf 1863* (Berlin, 1931), p. 106.

4 *GW*, I, 62.

5 Martin Philippson, *Max von Forckenbeck, Ein Lebensbild* (Dresden, 1898), pp. 104 ff. On October 7 the resolution passed, 251 to 36.

30, Bismarck revealed how little indeed the constitution limited the crown. He quoted article 99: "All revenues and expenditures of the state must be estimated in advance for each year and must be entered in the state budget. The latter is to be established each year by law." Since the phrase "in advance" was in the first, but not the second, sentence, he maintained that the budget need not be established by law before the beginning of the year to which it was to apply. During twelve years of the constitution's existence, this had usually been the practice. The budget for 1862, from which the chamber had just stricken the funds for military reorganization, was a case in point.

Forckenbeck's resolution also called upon the government to cease making expenditures of public funds for purposes not authorized by the chamber. Turning to this issue Bismarck accused the deputies of seeking exclusive power in financial matters. Under the constitution the crown, the house of lords, and the chamber of deputies had equal voices in the passage of legislation. To the crown, however, were reserved all rights not expressly granted by the constitution to the two chambers. If the three organs could not agree on a budget, the monarchy must follow the "law of necessity" and allocate expenditures as it saw fit. "The question of law easily becomes a question of power."[6]

In a later speech Bismarck elucidated the point. Compromise, it had been asserted, was the essence of constitutional government. But if one side insisted dogmatically upon its point of view the series of compromises was broken. "In their place conflicts appear, and, since the life of the state cannot stand still, conflicts become a question of power. Whoever holds the power then proceeds according to his own will, for the life of the state cannot remain still even for a second." This was the famous *Lückentheorie*, the theory of a constitutional hiatus.[7] Against the legal side of the argument the liberals had no good defense, for it was indisputable that the constitution did not provide for the settlement of differences be-

---

[6] Horst Kohl, ed., *Die politischen Reden des Fürsten Bismarck* (Stuttgart, 1892-1905), II, 19-38.

[7] *Ibid.*, pp. 76-87. As Bismarck confessed, the theory was not his invention, but a loophole deliberately intended by those who drafted the constitution. *Ibid.*, pp. 83-84. It had been defended in the *Sternzeitung* on August 14 and 19 and advanced by the king in his debate with the cabinet. (Hahn), *Innere Politik*, pp. 26-32; Kurt Promnitz, *Bismarcks Eintritt in das Ministerium, Historische Studien*, Vol. 60 (Berlin, 1908), pp. 67-99; Alexander Bergengrün, *Staatsminister August Freiherr von der Heydt* (Leipzig, 1908), pp. 301-304.

tween crown and parliament. The deputies were compelled to take their stand less on the constitution itself, which was purposefully inadequate, than upon the constitutional practices of other countries, which were irrelevant. Nevertheless, Bismarck's use of the theory was not legalistic, but realistic. He argued the case less from the standpoint of law than of power. At one point he even maintained that it was an open question whether in cases of irreconcilable conflict the constitution itself did not become inoperable and the right of absolute government return to the crown.[8]

With this statement of the crown's position there began a duel of endurance between cabinet and parliament which was to stretch out over four years to the climax of 1866. From France in June 1862 Bismarck had outlined to Roon the tactics to be used. "The longer the affair is drawn out the more the chamber will sink in public esteem, for they have committed the mistake, and will commit it again, of involving themselves in petty details and have no speakers who do not increase the boredom of the public." While the cabinet continued to rule the country, the deputies must be engaged in "trifling" disputes over the constitution. Ultimately they would tire, vainly hope the government would "lose its wind," and long for a settlement.[9]

Early in October the house of lords rejected the amended budget bill for 1862 and exceeded its authority by accepting the original bill proposed by the government. As intended, this embroiled the two chambers in controversy over the powers of the upper house. Amid the uproar Bismarck strode to the rostrum and prorogued the Landtag.[10] For three months the hall was vacant and the liberals deprived of a forum to propagate their views. Meanwhile, Bismarck strove to put pressure on the deputies from other directions. He appealed to the provincial diets to take a stand in favor of the government's position and endeavored to split the small catholic faction from the opposition by alternately support-

8 Kohl, *Reden*, II, 84. See Rudolf von Gneist, *Die Militärvorlage von 1892 und der preussische Verfassungskonflikt von 1862 bis 1866* (Berlin, 1893), pp. 19-32. After Bismarck's victory students of constitutional law conceded the validity of his legal position on all points except that of expenditures for military reorganization unauthorized by legislation. Nirrnheim, *Bismarck und die öffentliche Meinung*, p. 82.

9 *GW*, XIV, 601. See also Friedrich von Bernhardi, ed., *Aus dem Leben Theodor von Bernhardis* (Leipzig, 1893-1906), V, 5, 12; *DPO*, III, 193.

10 Kohl, *Reden*, II, 50 ff.; Löwenthal, *Verfassungsstreit*, pp. 131-134.

ing the papacy against the Italian state and threatening Rome with reprisals against the Catholic church in Prussia.[11]

On January 14 the deputies reassembled as determined as ever. First they tried the tactic of appealing to the king about the misconduct of his ministers. But Bismarck refused to communicate their petition. "There is a limit to what a king of Prussia can hear." Reached through another channel, William replied sharply that the liberal deputies, not his ministers, were violating the constitution.[12] Soon the Polish insurrection raised a new issue to disturb the chamber. Although the threat of war hung over the land, the only source of public information was the foreign press. Bismarck refused to answer interpellations concerning the Alvensleben convention, denying the right of parliament to inquire into diplomatic negotiations. Unruh, Waldeck, Sybel, and others fiercely attacked his competence. The convention, they charged, had gratuitously elevated the Polish rebellion from a local to a European crisis and shifted the odium of the "man hunt" in Poland from Petersburg to Berlin. In reply the Junker accused the deputies of siding with the Poles and inviting foreign attack. Called to order by the speaker, he contemptuously denied that ministers were subject to parliamentary discipline. During April the chamber was further agitated by the Schleswig-Holstein issue. In the event of war against Denmark, Twesten warned, the chamber would not support the government. "I can assure you and I can assure the world," Bismarck lashed out, "that, if we find it necessary to carry on a war, we shall do so with or without your consent." The deputies roared with anger.[13]

While Ludwig Loewe replied for the progressives, the Junker ostentatiously got up and left the chamber. The deputies protested, and he returned amid a gale of laughter, which changed to fury after he spoke. The speaker, he declared, could be heard well enough behind closed doors; the minister-president had more important matters to attend to. Actually he was writing a letter to his old friend Motley. The pen scratched across the paper vibrat-

[11] Parisius, *Hoverbeck*, II/1, 107; Herman von Petersdorff, *Kleist-Retzow* (Stuttgart, 1907), p. 349; *HW*, I, 120; *GW*, IV, 4-5; *APP*, III, 50-51. On the conduct of the Catholic faction see Zechlin, *Grundlegung*, pp. 345 ff.

[12] Kohl, *Reden*, II, 63-69, 99-103; *GW*, IV, 48; Kohl, *Anhang*, I, 47-48.

[13] *SBHA* (1863), I, 255-265, 327-353, 358-389, 397-419; II, 898-906. On the Polish debates see Irmgard Goldschmidt, *Der Polnische Aufstand von 1863 in den Verhandlungen des preussischen Abgeordnetenhauses* (Köln, 1937).

ing with rancor and contempt: "I hate politics. . . . At this moment my ears are full of it. I'm compelled to listen to unusually silly speeches from the mouths of unusually childish and excited politicians . . . *querelle d'allemand*. You anglo-saxon yankees have something of that too . . . but your battles are bloody, ours verbose; the babblers cannot rule Prussia. . . . They have too little wit and too much self-satisfaction, are stupid and impudent."[14]

To the spice of anger was added the oil of patriotism. On March 17 occurred the fiftieth anniversary of the founding of the Prussian militia. Bismarck and William saw the chance to remind the public of a time when all had "rallied enthusiastically to the king" and sacrificed "for throne and country." Veterans were invited to garrison banquets, bearers of the iron cross to dine with the king in Berlin and view the great parade down Unter den Linden.[15] But the effect was cold. In parliament a Polish deputy made everyone uncomfortable by referring to the Polish revolt as a "war of national liberation." The Berliners could find no space in their homes for the 2,000 knights of the iron cross. The workers refused to parade because they were asked to march behind the troops. The sparse crowd cheered the crown prince and let the king ride by in "icy silence."[16]

At the end of February the deputies had passed a resolution condemning the Alvensleben convention. Bismarck wished to reply by proroguing parliament. But only Roon came to his support in the cabinet. To Ludwig Gerlach, Bismarck vented his anger. He could neither educate his colleagues nor get rid of them; invariably they rejected his proposals; never did they have any of their own. In May the matter was decided by a turbulent scene in the chamber. Like Bismarck, Roon refused to recognize the right of the presiding officer to call him to order. The authority of the speaker, the cabinet insisted, extended "up to the ministers' bench and no further." When the king backed his ministers, the chamber resolved that the matter could be settled only by a "change of persons and, even more important, a change of system." On May 26

---

14 *SBHA* (1863), II, 907-910; *GW*, XIV, 639.

15 *GW*, IV, 19-20; XIV, 631-632; Kohl, *Anhang*, I, 43-44, 49; Kohl, *Reden*, II, 69-73.

16 Goldschmidt, *Polnischer Aufstand*, p. 22; *Aus dem Leben Bernhardis*, V, 41-42; *HW*, I, 138; Martin Philippson, *Friedrich III, als Kronprinz und Kaiser* (Berlin, 1893), pp. 72-73; Nirrnheim, *Bismarck und die öffentliche Meinung*, pp. 195-196.

parliament was prorogued. No action had been taken on either the military or budget bills.[17]

Throughout the session Bismarck had been deliberately provocative, his manner haughty, his words scornful and derisive. He had a tactical purpose. Some of his colleagues disapproved of the Alvensleben convention; the romantic conservatives were still dubious about his appointment; foreign governments plotted his downfall. On February 25 Theodor Bernhardi reported, "Every one thinks Bismarck's government finished and is convinced that he can't hold out any longer."[18] By irritating the deputies into taking sides with the Polish rebels, however, the man from Schönhausen convinced William afresh that he was struggling against the forces of revolution in Europe. Years later he confessed having deliberately played the "Junker reactionary." "In the palace the king heard from every side insinuations to the effect that I was a democrat in disguise. I could gain his complete trust only by showing him that I was not afraid of the chamber."[19]

His tactic aroused among the opposition deputies a burning resentment. In the press doubts were raised as to his sanity. To Karl Samwer he seemed "always in half-drunken condition." "He is a gambler," observed Max Duncker, "who doesn't hesitate to risk the existence of Prussia and the dynasty." "Bismarck's end," predicted Prince Charles Anthony, "will probably be frightful."[20]

2. "DISCIPLINING" THE BUREAUCRACY

While the quarrel with parliament intensified, Bismarck and his fellow ministers launched a series of repressive measures against the opposition. The first were aimed at liberal civil servants. Both the state administration and judiciary contained many officials who identified themselves with the liberal movement. Having survived the Manteuffel regime, they had enthusiastically served the new-era government and now deplored its passing. Many had seats in the chamber of deputies.

---

[17] *GW*, VII, 73; *SBHA* (1863), II, 1189-1190, 1207, 1247-1248, 1262, 1306. Three ministers, among them Eulenburg, were still in doubt about the wisdom of prorogation. Kohl, *Anhang*, I, 67-71.

[18] Zechlin, *Grundlegung*, pp. 526 ff.; *Aus dem Leben Bernhardis*, V, 37; Fritz Hartung, "Verantwortliche Regierung, Kabinette und Nebenregierungen im konstitutionellen Preussen, 1848-1918," *Forschungen zur brandenburgischen und preussischen Geschichte*, Vol. 44 (1932), pp. 29-30.

[19] *GW*, VII, 140; Unruh, *Erinnerungen*, pp. 220-223.

[20] Nirrnheim, *Bismarck und die öffentliche Meinung*, pp. 142 ff.; *HW*, I, 134; *Aus dem Leben Bernhardis*, V, 107.

Since 1847 parallel careers in bureaucracy and parliament had been common in Prussia. The principle of separation of powers and functions was weakly developed in a system so recently evolved from absolutism. Fifty percent of the chamber elected in 1855 were "political officials," forty percent in 1862. Only the landowners with twenty-four percent approached the civil servants in strength. During the reaction the cabinet had encouraged *Landräte* to stand for election. They were the royal officials most often in contact with the voting public, and they had been hand-picked for loyalty and subservience. After 1859 an increasing number of judges entered the chamber. Their occupation, security of tenure, and largely bourgeois origin inclined them toward liberalism. Constituting but sixteen percent of the chamber in 1855, they increased to twenty-six percent in 1862.[21]

Bureaucratic liberals had always been an anathema to Bismarck. Liberal political officials were doubly so. They were both a source of dissension within the government and the core of the opposition in parliament. To a person of his autocratic temperament this was intolerable. Previously, he argued, the bureaucracy had acted as a counterweight to the crown, but since 1847 the parliament had assumed this function. Consequently the bureaucracy must now support the crown against parliament.[22]

The political officials, however, represented opportunity as well as danger. By turning the screws of bureaucratic pressure, the government might coerce them into silence or even into reversing their stand in parliament. But Prussian regulations on civil service tenure were among the most stringent in the world. Only cabinet ministers, provincial governors, *Landräte*, and state's attorneys could be dismissed outright by administrative action. Bismarck would gladly have done away with these restrictions. But short of this extreme there were many other possibilities of reprisal.[23]

Acting on the advice of Hermann Wagener, he proposed in mid-October a series of measures which even his reactionary colleagues found too punitive. Officials serving in the chamber were to be billed for the cost of substitutes, whether necessary or not. Per

21 Anderson, *Social and Political Conflict*, pp. 25-26, 445; see also Fritz Hartung, "Zur Geschichte des Beamtentums im 19. und 20. Jahrhundert," *Abhandlungen der deutschen Akademie der Wissenschaften zu Berlin*, Jahrgang 1945/46, Philosophisch-historische Klasse, Nr. 8 (Berlin, 1948), pp. 21 ff.

22 Horst Kohl, ed., *Bismarck-Jahrbuch*, I (1894), 16 ff.

23 Zechlin, *Grundlegung*, pp. 348-349.

diem payments to deputies were to be stopped, except for those paying the substitution expense. But the ministers of commerce and interior, Heinrich von Itzenplitz and Gustav von Jagow, were critical, and most of their colleagues sided with them. All that Bismarck obtained was the dismissal of one *Landrat* and three state's attorneys; eight other officials who possessed tenure were transferred to less desirable posts. The most prominent victim was Bockum-Dolffs, the outspoken leader of the Left Center.[24]

These steps were taken despite the constitutional guarantee (article 84) against reprisals for attitudes expressed in parliament. It was a reversion to the practices of the Manteuffel era, to which William himself had once so strongly objected. In approving the decision he eased his conscience by declaring that officials who opposed the government in parliament out of "conviction" should "in no way" be punished; those concerned, however, had done so for "personal considerations." Bismarck justified the action on the grounds that by their attitudes in parliament the officials misled the voters concerning the real desires of the king.[25]

The deputies were not alone in feeling the heavy hand of official displeasure. Bismarck was determined to "restore discipline at any cost" throughout the civil service. His aim was to convert the bureaucracy into an effective instrument for influencing the electorate. To this end the difficult Jagow was replaced in December by Count Eulenburg in the vital ministry of interior, which controlled the bulk of the civil service. Eulenburg's first act was to inform his subordinates that their primary duty was "unconditional" support of the crown. "Unreserved and energetic cooperation" was "demanded" of all royal officials. They were expected to enforce the same upon their inferiors.[26]

The most difficult problem was the ministry of justice. Since Frederick the Great the independence of the judiciary had been a cherished principle in Prussian law. Although the minister of justice, Count Lippe, refused Bismarck's demand that political orientation, rather than seniority, be made the basis of promotion,

24 Wolfgang Saile, *Hermann Wagener und sein Verhältnis zu Bismarck, Tübinger Studien zur Geschichte und Politik*, Vol. 9 (Tübingen, 1958), p. 67; Kohl, *Anhang*, I, 31-33.

25 Zechlin, *Grundlegung*, pp. 349-350.

26 *GW*, xiv, 627, 629; (Hahn), *Innere Politik*, p. 132. It was not easy to find a candidate willing to take the resolute action desired. Heinrich O. Meisner, ed., *Kaiser Friedrich III., Tagebücher von 1848-1866* (Leipzig, 1929), pp. 506-507.

he did establish this as the criterion for elevating state's attorneys to judgeships. Use was made, furthermore, of the regulation that for unbecoming conduct judges might be transferred or dismissed by a special disciplinary court.[27]

How many officials were affected by Bismarck's "sharp *Razzia*" is difficult to determine. A liberal deputy, himself a victim, estimated that during the entire period of the conflict at least one thousand were subjected to reprisals for their political opinions and activities. Twenty were deputies, including nine judges. A "national fund" was established to assist those in need and was deposited in Britain beyond the reach of the Prussian police. Collectors were prosecuted, and officers of the militia who signed the appeal dismissed.[28]

Apparently steps were also taken to eradicate liberal influence in the armed forces. While never as divided as the bureaucracy, the army also contained some officers of liberal viewpoint. From a correspondent Bernhardi heard of a resurgence of "spying and terrorizing" within the ranks. "They have fear of the people and are afraid they can't be certain of the army any more." "It is generally accepted," he wrote, "that in a certain quarter they want to arouse a spirit of animosity between military and civilians." While the "older and wiser group of officers" disapproved, they hesitated to speak out against what obviously had the support of Edwin Manteuffel and the military cabinet. In the election of September 1863 the troops were forbidden to vote. Roon and William regarded the election campaign as hazardous to military discipline.[29]

3. THE PRESS EDICT

Another object of concern during Bismarck's first months in office was the newspaper press. Long ago during the revolution he

---

[27] *Aus dem Leben Bernhardis*, v, 160-161; Parisius, *Hoverbeck*, II/1, 171-172; Ludwig von Roenne, *Das Staatsrecht der Preussischen Monarchie* (2nd ed., Leipzig, 1864), I/1, 247 ff. On the political attitudes of the county judges see Anderson, *Social and Political Conflict*, pp. 289-291.

[28] Ludolf Parisius, *Deutschlands politische Parteien und das Ministerium Bismarcks* (Berlin, 1878), p. 68; Walter Reichle, *Zwischen Staat und Kirche, Das Leben und Wirken des preussischen Kultusministers Heinrich von Mühler* (Berlin, 1938), p. 129; Zechlin, *Grundlegung*, pp. 350-351.

[29] Anderson, *Social and Political Conflict*, p. 438; *Aus dem Leben Bernhardis*, IV, 329-330, 338-339; v, 30-31, 98; Philippson, *Friedrich III*, p. 106; Waldemar von Roon, *Denkwürdigkeiten aus dem Leben des General-Feldmarschalls Kriegsministers Grafen von Roon* (4th ed., Breslau, 1897), II, 166-167.

had learned its political value as a collaborator of the *Kreuzzeitung*. In 1862 the conservative press was hopelessly outclassed. By one estimate it had a daily printing run of about 40,000 copies and a reading public of 200,000, while the liberal journals published 250,000 copies seen by perhaps 1,250,000 readers. In conference with Wagener, the most important conservative journalist of the day, Bismarck considered ways to dam this liberal stream and expand the conservative trickle into a torrent.[30]

One of his first acts was to end government support of the *Sternzeitung*, a journal of poor circulation long compromised by official connections. Secretly he bought the services of the *Norddeutsche Allgemeine Zeitung*, whose editor was August Brass, a revolutionary of 1848 and former exile. One of his colleagues was the Marxian socialist, Wilhelm Liebknecht, who indignantly resigned when he learned the source of Brass's new income. Camouflaged by its left-wing editor, the *Allgemeine* became the government's consistent defender. The minister-president himself often dictated or corrected articles for its columns. Nourished by this kind of patronage, its circulation steadily increased.[31]

The *Allgemeine* was but one of many newspapers which began to benefit from the public treasury. The financial records of the ministry of state list an impressive number of journalists and publications in the secret pay of the government.[32] Another form of subsidy was news itself. Beginning in November 1862 all public information was channeled into the columns of the official *Staatsanzeiger* and friendly publications. Under Bismarck's leadership the government began a thorough reorganization and expansion of the official press. For this purpose an embryonic newspaper chain was already in existence. In years past the state administration had established relations with private local newspapers, espe-

---

[30] Anderson, *Social and Political Conflict*, p. 343; Saile, *Wagener und Bismarck*, pp. 73-78. On the earlier efforts of Wagener and the Volksverein to build up the conservative press see Müller, *Volks-Verein*, pp. 58 ff.

[31] *GW*, xiv, 628; Franz Mehring, *Karl Marx, The Story of His Life* (London, 1936), pp. 331-332; Irmgard Loeber, *Bismarcks Pressepolitik in den Jahren des Verfassungskonfliktes, 1862-1866, Zeitung und Leben*, xxiv (Munich, 1935), 16-17; Parisius, *Hoverbeck*, ii/1, 125-126, 144-145. For Bismarck's later relationship to the *Allgemeine* see Kurt Forstreuter, "Zu Bismarcks Journalistik, Bismarck und die Norddeutsche Allgemeine Zeitung," *Jahrbuch für die Geschichte Mittel- und Ostdeutschlands*, ii (1953), 191-210.

[32] Loeber, *Bismarcks Pressepolitik*, pp. 18 ff., 64 ff. Subsidies were passed to south German newspapers and French journalists through the legations in Frankfurt and Paris.

A PERIOD OF DICTATORSHIP

cially in rural areas, for the purpose of transmitting official information to the public. Where such journals were lacking they had been founded and edited by the county governments. Under orders from Berlin these *Kreisblätter* were now enlarged, given a political character, and made nominally independent. Later they carried the "provincial correspondence," a feature edited by the press bureau of the ministry of interior. On occasion Bismarck himself directed what they were to print. The entire system was supported by the public treasury and the taxpayer, but it propagated the partisan views of the Bismarck cabinet and the conservative party.[33]

Meanwhile, various measures were considered for checking the opposition press. Bismarck proposed a "correction system," which would have compelled editors to print rectifications of purportedly inaccurate statements. But he was persuaded that such "chicanery" was unworthy of the Prussian government. Then he considered either prohibiting or hindering the distribution of liberal journals through the mails. But Eulenburg objected that this was of doubtful legality and too underhanded for the Hohenzollern monarchy. Instead the minister favored use of the press law of 1851.[34]

Although article 27 of the constitution forbade censorship and guaranteed freedom of expression, the framers had been careful to add an escape clause: "Every other restriction upon freedom of the press shall be made only by way of legislation." The press law of 1851 gave the government the power to license and control all media of printed expression. Issues might be confiscated and editors fined or imprisoned for propagating falsehoods, slander, distortions of fact, and incitement to hate or contempt. Under this statute the Manteuffel cabinet had introduced a rigid censorship. Even Wagener's *Kreuzzeitung* was repeatedly confiscated. Since the new-era cabinet had failed to repeal the law, Bismarck and his colleagues were able to put this weapon once more to use. In late 1862 the number of confiscations and prosecutions were stepped up, particularly in Berlin.[35]

[33] *Ibid.*, pp. 23 ff.; Anderson, *Social and Political Conflict*, pp. 360 ff. In January 1864 Bismarck told the chamber of deputies, "There is no official press; my first task on becoming a minister was to abolish it." Kohl, *Reden*, II, 300.
[34] Loeber, *Bismarcks Pressepolitik*, pp. 14-17.
[35] *Gesetz-Sammlung für die Königlichen Preussischen Staaten* (1851), pp. 273-287, also pp. 121-122; Anderson, *Social and Political Conflict*, pp. 64-65; Zechlin, *Grundlegung*, pp. 351-353.

But the ministers were dissatisfied with the results. Liberal judges persisted in viewing truth as a factual rather than a political matter. Furthermore, the cabinet became impatient with the judicial process itself. Before the bench the state's attorney had to prove his case with specific quotations from the publication in question. The liberal press, it was complained, had long since learned how to make the "most hateful attacks and insinuations against the government, against the crown itself" without providing evidence which could be used in court. Even when the government obtained a favorable decision, it affected the individuals accused, but not the newspaper itself, which might continue publication in other hands.[36]

On June 1, 1863, five days after parliament had been prorogued, the king signed an edict silencing the opposition press as well. It provided that a newspaper or periodical could be banned after two warnings because of a "general attitude" considered "dangerous to the public welfare." To the bureaucracy, rather than the courts, was given the power to decide what constituted the "public welfare." Appeals could be heard only by the cabinet, not by any judicial body. Political agitation, it was asserted, had created an "impassioned and unnatural excitement." Journalists misused their freedom to "undermine every foundation of orderly government and of religion and morality as well."[37]

Bernhardi recognized that the edict had been modelled after the press laws of Napoleon III. But Bismarck had gone even further than the dictator across the Rhine. In France a newspaper could be suppressed only for a "specific, judicially provable reason," in Prussia for its "general attitude." The diarist felt that the minister-president had crossed the critical dividing line between legitimate rule and arbitrary government. He had arrogated to the crown the right to legislate, interpret, and enforce the law.[38]

The edict was issued under article 63 of the constitution, which granted the king the right to issue decrees while parliament was not in session, but only when "urgently" required to do so "for the preservation of public safety or the settlement of an unusual emergency." Furthermore, such edicts might not be contrary to

---

36 Loeber, *Bismarcks Pressepolitik*, pp. 32-33; (Hahn), *Innere Politik*, pp. 196-197; Anderson, *Social and Political Conflict*, pp. 205-208.

37 *Gesetz-Sammlung* (1863), pp. 349-351; (Hahn), *Innere Politik*, pp. 195-198.

38 *Aus dem Leben Bernhardis*, v, 110-111.

any other provision of the constitution. Nothing had happened which could be construed as a state of emergency; the public safety was in no apparent danger; the decree had obviously been prepared before the Landtag adjourned; the constitution guaranteed freedom of speech. Unanimously the law faculties of Kiel, Göttingen, and Heidelberg declared it unconstitutional.[39]

The king himself was very uneasy about the matter. In the crown council of June 1 Bismarck, backed by the other ministers, assured him that there was "no reasonable doubt" about constitutionality. Although not immediately apparent, a threat to public safety would most certainly arise once a "bad press" had corrupted those "classes of the population which are incapable of independent political judgment." The loyalty of the army might be affected. Finally the prickling of William's conscience was soothed by the desire to be convinced. On the protocol he wrote that he had signed the decree "under the assumption" that no violation of oath or constitution was involved and after assurances that measures would be considered which "now or later" would soften its effect upon public opinion.[40] Bismarck could be content. The protocol went into the files for the benefit of the historian, the edict into the statutes for immediate use.

The conscience of the crown prince was less easily appeased. For months he had been deeply troubled by the course of the new government. During cabinet meetings he maintained an icy silence. Bismarck's efforts to win him had been in vain. His back was stiffened by his strong-willed English wife and their relatives in the distant palaces of Coburg, Brussels, and London. As the breach between crown and parliament widened, he began to fear for the Hohenzollern the fate of the Stuarts and Bourbons. Before leaving Berlin for East Prussia on May 31, he advised his father against "violation or circumvention of the constitution." Now he learned of the press edict in the cold type of a provincial newspaper. Deeply offended, he publicly stated in Danzig that he had had "no part" in the matter.[41]

---

[39] Roenne, *Staatsrecht*, I/2, 167.

[40] Meisner, *Kronprinz im Verfassungskampf*, pp. 66-67.

[41] *Ibid.*, pp. 10-22, 65-73; Frederick Ponsonby, ed., *Letters of the Empress Frederick* (New York, 1930), pp. 40-48; Philippson, *Friedrich III*, pp. 73 ff. In a letter to Itzenplitz on June 14 Count Dönhoff reported that Frederick William, to whom he had recently talked, was chiefly resentful about not having been told of the impending decree. Itzenplitz file, *Friedrichsruh Archive*. But in his diary the

William was shocked and wrathful. He forgot that once during the Crimean war he had contemplated a similar step against his brother, Frederick William IV. For a time he considered court-martial and confinement, the punishments meted out to Frederick the Great as crown prince.[42] But Bismarck persuaded him that the "reason of state" must take precedence over "paternal anger." The affair should be "blunted, ignored, and hushed up."[43] So it would have been had not copies of the letters which passed between father and son leaked into the foreign press. Once again tempers flared. Yet Frederick William lacked the nerves, resolute will, and filial impiety to conduct an open struggle against the king. They reached an uneasy reconciliation. But the relationship between crown prince and minister-president was worse than ever. Like Queen Augusta, Frederick William hated and feared the "Catiline" in the Wilhelmstrasse who seemed to be leading the monarchy into the abyss.[44]

Energetic use was made of the powers granted by the press edict. On June 5 the first warnings were issued in Berlin against six leading newspapers which had published a joint protest. By August 19, according to one estimate, eighty-one warnings had been delivered throughout the country, of which fourteen were in Berlin. Attempts at subterfuge were fruitless. The *Berliner Reform* received its second warning for reprinting passages from Lamartine on the press laws of Charles X. Most editors and publishers bowed to the inevitable. Rather than risk suppression and financial loss they outwardly conformed to the law. A "graveyard stillness" spread through the liberal press, over which could still be heard the strident voices of the conservative newspapers and the bought journals of the government.[45]

---

crown prince wrote that his intent was to make himself "publicly known as an opponent of Bismarck and his evil theories." Friedrich III, *Tagebücher, 1848-1866*, p. 198.

[42] Heinrich von Poschinger, ed., *Unter Friedrich Wilhelm IV, Denkwürdigkeiten des Ministers Otto Freiherrn von Manteuffel 1848-1858* (Berlin, 1900-1901), II, 419, also 443. Field Marshal Wrangel favored court-martial, and Edwin Manteuffel advised that such was the king's prerogative. Meisner, *Kronprinz im Verfassungskampf*, pp. 19-29, 74, 107. The prince offered to resign his military command and accept any place of exile "where I can remain entirely away from politics." *Ibid.*, pp. 74-75.

[43] *GW*, xv, 218; Meisner, *Kronprinz im Verfassungskampf*, pp. 77-82.

[44] Meisner, *Kronprinz im Verfassungskampf*, pp. 23 ff., 75-77; Kohl, *Anhang*, II, 349-352.

[45] Loeber, *Bismarcks Pressepolitik*, pp. 34 ff.

4. POWER OR LAW?

In the great debate of January 1863 on the *Lückentheorie* Bismarck vigorously defended himself against the charge of having asserted that "power takes precedence over law."[46] There can be no doubt, however, that this was his actual position. His willingness to go beyond the law is evident in the measures he proposed against liberal officials and newspapers. The press edict stretched even the rubbery Prussian constitution beyond the breaking point. But the most conclusive proof is to be seen in his thoughts about the possibility of a *coup d'état* during 1863.

On November 11, 1862, Ludwig Gerlach spent an hour in the Wilhelmstrasse and came away deeply disturbed by Bismarck's "absolutism." "One can accomplish a great deal even under a constitution by such ordinary means as fear, enticement, and the like," the Junker had told him. "If nothing avails, one can still resort to a *coup d'état*." A few months later, after the deputies had dared to attack the Alvensleben convention, Bismarck remarked that such "injuries" could not be suffered indefinitely or "all authority would be undermined." Decrees against the press and for the suspension of officials might be necessary "and as a last resort abolition of the election law." To the crown prince he confessed that the greatest obstacle to "changes in the constitution" was the king, who took his oath seriously. The ministers too had sworn to uphold it "conscientiously." "What if conscience bids me not to respect it?"[47]

In a crown council on June 16, 1863 the Junker clashed with those of his colleagues who wished to dissolve parliament and appeal to the electorate afresh. He preferred to rule the country as long as possible without parliament and an opposition press. To hold an election would be a confession of weakness, an admission that in order to govern, the crown needed a majority in parliament. To dissolve would inaugurate a "chain of dissolutions"

---

[46] Kohl, *Reden*, II, 86-88.

[47] Ernst Ludwig von Gerlach, *Aufzeichnungen aus seinem Leben und Wirken, 1795-1877* (Schwerin, 1903), II, 249-250; Friedrich III, *Tagebücher, 1848-1866*, pp. 510-511. This long-established evidence contradicts the view of Leonhard von Muralt that Bismarck "loyally subjected" himself to the constitution. *Bismarcks Verantwortlichkeit* (Göttingen, 1955), pp. 197, 228. The same is true of Gerhard Ritter's statement that "he actually had nothing in common with the *Staatsstreich* plans of the military cabinet and reactionary hotspurs." *Staatskunst und Kriegshandwerk, Das Problem des "Militarismus" in Deutschland* (Munich, 1954), I, 203.

which could be broken only by a *coup d'état*. The crown, he maintained, was not obligated to summon the Landtag before mid-January. In view of the "state of war" which existed in Prussia it was vital that the monarchy use "all the means within its power which do not run counter to the constitution."

But other ministers disagreed. Karl von Bodelschwingh, the minister of finance, pointed out that under article 99 the budget was "to be established each year by law." The Landtag must be given a chance to finish the deliberations interrupted in May, if the crown was to show its loyalty to the constitution. William found the argument convincing. It was beneath the dignity of the government to deal further with this chamber which had openly refused its cooperation.[48]

In August at Bad Gastein William confessed to the crown prince (their first meeting since the Danzig episode) that he too foresaw the likelihood of a series of dissolutions and elections. "Above all obedience must be re-established in the country." Bismarck painted a similar picture. A "constitutional regime" was "untenable" in Prussia; under parliamentary government the monarchy would inevitably fall apart. Frederick William replied that this was "peculiar talk" coming from a Prussian minister-president. If this were his attitude, why did he continue to govern under the constitution at all? Bismarck replied that he would observe the existing laws as long as he could, but the time would yet come when it would be "otherwise!"[49]

Because of these remarks Frederick William understood the true meaning of the royal rescript of September 2 which dissolved parliament. He sat through the crown council which made the formal decision in silence. But next day he had it out with his father. A cryptic entry in his diary records the conversation:

C.P.: I didn't want to express my doubts yesterday in front of the ministers. But what about the future?

King: Repeated dissolutions, one after the other.

C.P.: But to what end shall these measures finally lead?

King: Obedience in the country, scaffold, possibly a rupture of

---

[48] Meisner, *Kronprinz im Verfassungskampf*, pp. 86-87, 150. Roon and Itzenplitz sided with Bismarck, Eulenburg with Bodelschwingh. *Itzenplitz to Bismarck*, August 28, 1863. Itzenplitz file, *Friedrichsruh archive*.

[49] Friedrich III, *Tagebücher, 1848-1866*, p. 209; Meisner, *Kronprinz im Verfassungskampf*, pp. 135, 171-172.

the constitution by barricades in the streets and then naturally suspension of the same.

C.P.: In Gastein Bismarck spoke of the untenability of the constitution and of the coming necessity of its abandonment.

King: The Kaiser of Austria and I are both convinced that in twenty years there will be no more constitutions.

C.P.: What then?

King: I don't know. I won't be alive then. But this abominable constitutional system can't continue; it will only bring about the destruction of royal authority and the introduction of a republic with a president as in England [sic!]. The scoundrels of the opposition, like Schulze-Delitzsch, have to be shown who is king of Prussia.

This angry exchange of views produced a new crisis in the royal family. Encouraged by wife and mother, Frederick William refused to attend further sessions of the cabinet. But the Danzig episode was not repeated; the crown prince decided upon "passive resistance."[50]

In his personal dealings with cabinet members, however, he was far from passive. "When I see him," Roon reported, "he looks like a thundercloud." For a few days after September 2 Bismarck was absent from Berlin, and Roon had the feeling that this alone prevented a "catastrophe." Finally they met. In his memoirs Bismarck wrote that he would never forget that "hostile expression and olympian dignity" with which the prince, his face red and head thrown back, rejected the idea that the Junker could ever expect to enter his own service. Bismarck spurned the suggestion just as sharply: "That I shall never do!"[51] For many reasons, personal and political, he dreaded the day when this young Hohenzoller would ascend the throne. The possibility was not remote. William was sixty-six.

"Now begins the election swindle," Bismarck commented on September 4. During the campaign he attempted to influence the voting public by an appeal to both Prussian patriotism and Ger-

---

[50] Friedrich III, *Tagebücher, 1848-1866*, p. 213; Meisner, *Kronprinz im Verfassungskampf*, pp. 44-47, 160-161. The prince continued to attend crown councils. For a time William feared he intended to force the issue by publicly breaking with the regime. *Ibid.*, pp. 150-151, 161-162. From Windsor castle Queen Victoria wrote her "dear brother" William, trying to mediate between father and son. *Ibid.*, pp. 152-153.

[51] *GW*, xv, 222.

man nationalism. The congress of princes and the Austrian reform plan were treated as an attack upon Prussia's existence and their failure as a triumph of Prussian policy. The call for a popularly elected national parliament was an appeal to little-German sentiment. Silenced on the domestic crisis, the liberal journals were compelled to concentrate on foreign news. The Austrian plan was severely criticized and its rejection by Prussia acclaimed. Nevertheless, the liberals were not impressed by Bismarck's reply. While the moderate right ignored it, the progressive journals indignantly refused an offer of national unity from such a source. They took solace in the assumption that it was a purely tactical move of no consequence. They were determined to fight the election on the domestic issue.[52]

During the campaign the government relied heavily upon the system of bureaucratic intervention which William had decried during the 1850's.[53] Efforts were made to discourage liberal officials from standing for election. By royal decree they were assessed the cost of substitutes appointed by the government during absences in parliament. A directive from Eulenburg informed them that, if elected, they were bound by oath of allegiance to follow the "constitutional way" pointed out by the crown. Government employees were commanded to give energetic support to conservative candidates.[54] William informed the voters that "an inimical attitude toward my government is incompatible with loyalty to my person." Liberals were thereby branded as unpatriotic and even treasonable.[55]

Otto Manteuffel's rubber-stamp parliament had been elected largely through the efforts of the *Landräte*. Thirteen out of nineteen million Prussians lived in rural areas governed by these royal appointees. It was their duty to draw up voting lists, delineate

[52] *GW*, xiv, 652-653; (Hahn), *Innere Politik*, pp. 221-234; Nirrnheim, *Bismarck und die öffentliche Meinung*, pp. 568 ff.

[53] On the character of the campaign see the report of the special investigating committee of the chamber of deputies. *SBHA* (1863-1864), iv (Anlagen), Nos. 90 and 95.

[54] Anderson, *Social and Political Conflict*, pp. 386-387; *SBHA* (1863-1864), iv (Anlagen), pp. 604-605. Apparently other cabinet members (except the minister of justice) issued similar rescripts. Beneath the cabinet level the heads of bureaus and governors of provinces and districts followed suit. *Ibid.*, pp. 606 ff. See also Bismarck's directive to Ernst von Senfft-Pilsach, *GW*, xiv, 653-654. According to one authority, twenty officials were punished under these directives. Parisius, *Hoverbeck*, ii/1, 176, 183.

[55] (Hahn), *Innere Politik*, p. 241; Löwenthal, *Verfassungsstreit*, pp. 203-204.

precinct boundaries, and generally supervise the election. With their assistants they could travel about the country and electioneer at government expense. Under the Prussian "police state" they possessed extensive powers to regulate local affairs; hence many citizens were dependent upon their favor. In the election of 1863 tavern keepers were threatened with a loss of license for permitting the opposition to assemble or distribute political literature on the premises. Since taverns were the usual place of political assembly, this was an attempt to interdict the liberal campaign.[56]

Village mayors were threatened with fines and loss of position for voting against government candidates. In some cases they were ordered to stand for the electoral college, where they were to cast votes for the conservative candidate, perhaps the *Landrat* himself. Teachers were told to show "piety toward the king and authority" by voting conservative. Pastors preached the Christian virtue of voting as the king desired. Junker landlords put pressure on their tenants and other dependents. Renters of public property were instructed to support the government or suffer the consequences. Employees of government-owned railways were likewise coerced. Bismarck was responsible for the suspension of a group of railway workers who failed to prevent a hostile demonstration against himself at the Pomeranian station of Belgard.[57]

This remorseless use of the governmental apparatus for partisan purposes was not without effect on October 20. When the votes were in, the conservatives could count thirty-six deputies in the chamber as against their previous ten. In many cases liberal deputies were re-elected by greatly reduced majorities. With 258 out of 350 seats, however, they were still by far the most powerful group in the chamber. Once again the migration toward the left was apparent. While the progressives and left centrists gained a few seats, the old-liberal constitutionalists were seriously reduced; even Georg Vincke went down to defeat.[58]

The result was about what Bismarck had expected. The only cause for gratification was that the elected conservatives included some "greater capacities" than before, notably Wagener and Blanckenburg. But the great issue between crown and parliament remained undecided and Bismarck's doubts about the viability of

---

[56] Anderson, *Social and Political Conflict*, pp. 386 ff.

[57] *Ibid.*, p. 395; *GW*, xiv, 656.

[58] Anderson, *Social and Political Conflict*, p. 412; Parisius, *Hoverbeck*, ii/1, 180-181.

the Prussian system unchanged. "The Prussian monarchy and our present constitution," he told Schleinitz on October 26, "are irreconcilable things." Many obstacles, he confessed, stood in the way of the "complete and unconditional elimination" of the latter. The chief of these was the king.[59] But experience had shown that William's conscience was malleable.

[59] Meisner, *Kronprinz im Verfassungskampf*, pp. 171-172.

CHAPTER TEN

THE LIBERALS AND THE MASSES

1. THE FINAL TEST OF GERMAN LIBERALISM

 URING Bismarck's first year in office German liberalism underwent the greatest test it was to experience between the revolutions of 1848 and 1918. Since September the Prussian opposition had been subjected to a steady crescendo of dictatorial measures. The press law, an obvious breach of the constitution, was the climax. How did the liberals react?

Twenty-three liberal newspapers published a common protest, branding the edict as unconstitutional. First warnings were immediately issued by the ministry of interior, and the journals lapsed into silence on the domestic crisis rather than incur financial ruin. On June 4 the Berlin city council voted to send a delegation to the king protesting the arbitrary actions of the government. Other city councils followed suit. But the cabinet reacted swiftly. On June 6 Eulenburg issued an order forbidding city governments to take any notice of national politics and threatening mayors and other municipal officials with disciplinary action in the event of disobedience. The movement subsided. On the proposal of Schulze-Delitzsch the "society for the preservation of the constitutional freedom of the press in Prussia" was founded. It procured the legal judgments of the law faculties in Kiel, Göttingen, and Heidelberg and published the warnings issued by the government to the press in order to demonstrate their tyrannical character. But, otherwise, the society appears to have accomplished little.[1]

Reports of the crown prince's speech appeared in most German newspapers and aroused considerable comment. But the effect was

[1] (Ludwig Hahn, ed.), *Die Innere Politik der preussischen Regierung von 1862 bis 1866* (Berlin, 1866), pp. 199-200; Ludolf Parisius, *Leopold Freiherr von Hoverbeck* (Berlin, 1897-1900), II/1, 170-171; Otto Nirrnheim, *Das erste Jahr des Ministeriums Bismarck und die öffentliche Meinung, Heidelberger Abhandlungen zur mittleren und neueren Geschichte*, Vol. 20 (Heidelberg, 1908), pp. 204-205, 216 ff.

dulled, as Bismarck hoped, by the fact that there were no outward consequences. Frederick William was not summoned back to Berlin and summarily stripped of his rank and command. Instead he continued his inspection tour, while the king departed for Karlsbad and his annual cure. The "indiscretion" of the letters was the sensation of the European press in July, but no Prussian newspaper dared print the story. Those who heard about the matter got their information through the uncertain media of leaflets and rumor. Because of the source there was general skepticism.[2]

"The spirit here on the Rhine is excellent," Sybel reported on June 17. In Bonn "liberals and clericals" combined to hold a "great celebration" for the returning deputies. Forbidden by the police to demonstrate, the students drafted a declaration of support. In Krefeld, Sybel's constituency, "the entire town was in motion." A series of petitions and delegations were to be dispatched to king and cabinet.[3] But Prince Charles Anthony judged the mood "anti-ministerial," rather than "anti-royal." The least act of reconciliation by the king would reverse the situation. In Prussia "it is never too late." In July Karl Friedenthal informed Duncker that the farmers had lost interest in the quarrel. The urban agitation, which had earlier aroused them, was exhausted; the promise of a reduced military service remained unfulfilled. There was a general feeling that in military and political questions the king's judgment was authoritative. From Silesia the deputy Vincke-Olbendorf reported (June 9) that there was almost no talk of politics in the country. The general attitude was: "Nothing comes of it; better let the king rule by himself once more."[4]

Originally the deputies planned to distribute from Berlin a flood of leaflets to substitute for the suppressed journals. But in mid-July Schulze-Delitzsch complained of a dearth of manuscripts. "The best talents are away traveling; the whole press is on vacation."[5] But so were the deputies. Baron Hoverbeck, a

[2] Heinrich O. Meisner, ed., Der preussische Kronprinz im Verfassungskampf 1863 (Berlin, 1931), pp. 38-39.

[3] HW, I, 155-156.

[4] Johannes Schultze, ed., Max Duncker: Politischer Briefwechsel aus seinem Nachlass (Stuttgart, 1923), pp. 347, 356, 365.

[5] HW, I, 161; also Ludwig Dehio, "Die Taktik der Opposition während des Konflikts," Historische Zeitschrift, Vol. 140 (1929), p. 322, and Friedrich Thorwart, ed., Hermann Schulze-Delitzschs Schriften und Reden (Berlin, 1909-1913), III, 198-200.

leader of the democratic progressives, returned home so weary of politics that he could hardly bring himself to visit his constituents. He was overcome by a sense of futility, inclined to believe that the ministers whom the deputies fought were mere "tools" of "unresponsible" personalities beyond their reach.[6] On July 14, Rudolf Haym, editor of the *Preussische Jahrbücher*, wrote to Eduard Simson: "The conduct of the lot is as miserable as was to be expected. Whoever can, seeks a pretext to withdraw, saying, 'After all we can't push our way through, we must let the storm blow over,' and the like. He who is involved, fancies himself uninvolved, spares his strength, relaxes from the strain and leaves the struggle to others. Later he will reappear and be all the louder when the friends of the constitution have been victorious, or when some favorable event in foreign affairs has turned the page." But Haym's bravery was confined to letters. Wishing to avoid even a first warning from the government, he published in the June issue of the *Jahrbücher* two editorials so conciliatory to the Bismarck cabinet that they provoked a furious denunciation from his former collaborator, Heinrich von Treitschke.[7]

Outside Prussia leaders of the Nationalverein were highly disturbed by the feeble reaction to the edict. From Heidelberg the journalist August Ludwig von Rochau complained bitterly to Rudolf von Bennigsen about "the pflegm, the indolence, the indecision" of the Progressive Party. But Schulze-Delitzsch calmly replied that outsiders could hardly realize the difficulties of transacting business in a country as large and dispersed as Prussia. He went on to insist that "at this moment" there be "no hurrying, no excessive haste which could rob us of the fruits gained in the struggle."[8] To Gustav Freytag, who was also impatient, he wrote: "The present pause is both natural and necessary. . . . It is a pause not of indolence or exhaustion, but for gathering strength." Over one and a half years the deputies had engaged in unrelenting struggle. On vacation they were now "repairing the damage, reprovisioning themselves, in order to be able to renew the contest

6 Parisius, *Hoverbeck*, II/1, 169.

7 *HW*, I, 162-163; *Preussische Jahrbücher*, XI (1863), 627-653; Karl M. Schiller, ed., *Heinrich von Treitschke: Aufsätze, Reden, und Briefe* (Meersburg, 1929), III, 182-189; Hans Rosenberg, ed., *Ausgewählter Briefwechsel Rudolf Hayms* (Stuttgart, 1930), pp. 213 ff.

8 Hermann Oncken, *Rudolf von Bennigsen* (Stuttgart, 1910), I, 595-597. See also Nirrnheim, *Bismarck und die öffentliche Meinung*, pp. 182-186, 219-222.

in the autumn with new strength." Anyone seeking under these circumstances "to force any kind of real agitation" would most certainly fail and in the process do considerable damage to the liberal cause. If the masses were to be brought into motion, it could only be through some "internal calamity" or "great event abroad."[9]

His letter to Bennigsen, however, contained a challenge. It did little good to insist that *something* be done, "when one does not know one's self what."[10] Indeed this was the crux of the matter. In his attack on Haym, published in Freytag's *Grenzboten*, the vitriolic Treitschke wrote darkly of the possibility of revolution in Prussia. "It must be dared," he wrote privately, "as soon as there is prospect of success." But even he complained of the "cowardice" and the "unwillingness to sacrifice" of the "great mass of the liberals."[11] "In the whole of Prussia," Sybel informed Baumgarten, "you will not find a single person who does not hold open violence to be an act of folly and a crime."[12] Riots occurred in the streets of Berlin in early July, but the eviction of a saloonkeeper was the cause, not the prorogued parliament or muzzled press.[13] On September 11 Sybel reported again from Berlin, "No one here wants to precipitate revolution."[14]

Even if the Prussian liberals had been inclined toward violence, there were good reasons for doubting success. The secret plans of the army for dealing with a popular uprising were still in readiness. In February General Wrangel had increased the number of battalions to be used from fifty to eighty. When the Prussian army of 37,000 men marched against Denmark a year later, one of nearly equal size (35,000) remained behind in the neighborhood of Berlin.[15] At no time during the constitutional conflict did

---

[9] *HW*, i, 160-161.   [10] Oncken, *Bennigsen*, i, 595.

[11] Treitschke, *Aufsätze, Reden, Briefe*, iii, 185; v, 546-548. In the letter in which he broke with Haym, Treitschke asserted that the editor's attitude could only weaken still further "the unfortunately all too feeble indignation of the country." *Ibid.*, v, 552. Treitschke's call for revolution was more an expression of personal temperament than a judgment of the actual state of affairs in Prussia. See Hildegard Katsch, *Heinrich von Treitschke und die preussisch-deutsche Frage von 1860-1866, Historische Bibliothek*, Vol. 40 (Munich, 1919), pp. 27 ff.

[12] *HW*, i, 156.

[13] Parisius, *Hoverbeck*, ii/1, 171; *HW*, i, 162. Bismarck saw in the affair a possible pretext to banish political agitators, especially writers and journalists, from the city. *GW*, xiv, 644-645; Horst Kohl, ed., *Anhang zu den Gedanken und Erinnerungen von Otto Fürst von Bismarck* (Stuttgart, 1901), ii, 352-353.

[14] *HW*, i, 171, also 98, 102.

[15] Ludwig Dehio, "Die Pläne der Militärpartei und der Konflikt," *Deutsche Rundschau*, ccxiii (1927), 95-96.

the liberals question that the army, both officers and men, would stand behind the crown against an uprising. In a letter of May 26 Sybel wrote that he knew of no occasions in history where "a people had ever been able to accomplish anything by force" when opposed by a trained and disciplined army of 200,000 men loyal to the regime.[16]

Since revolution was out of the question, what possibilities remained? The best weapon of any parliament against the executive is financial. By finally denying the funds needed to carry out the military reorganization, the deputies had taken the first step. Under the *Lückentheorie*, nevertheless, the crown continued to expend funds as it saw fit. The constitution provided that taxes, once granted, might be levied indefinitely without further parliamentary approval. It was the misfortune of the deputies that the period of the constitutional conflict was one of steadily rising national income and increasing tax yields. While the deputies struggled against the crown, their political supporters were piling up the profits and paying the taxes which were to bring about their defeat.

The only possibility of robbing the state of this income was to organize a taxpayer's boycott. There was precedent for such a step. Before their dispersal in November 1848 the liberals of the Prussian national assembly had vainly called upon the public to refuse taxes for the reactionary government. According to Sybel and Twesten, there was much talk in June 1863 of a similar step. "Nevertheless," the former added, "it is clear that, if this is to be effective, it must begin with the upper bourgeoisie and among them the matter must ripen somewhat." Twesten wrote that "everyone agreed" it was impossible to summon a widespread boycott suddenly into existence. Ludolf Parisius remarked that in any case such a measure was unconstitutional! In Essen and its neighborhood some cases of resistance did actually occur, but the government's reaction was vigorous and the movement collapsed.[17]

Having rejected revolution and discarded a tax boycott, the Prussian liberals were bankrupt of ideas. Their ears were closed to the strategy proposed by Ferdinand Lassalle. A radical revolutionary in 1848, the gifted Lassalle now belonged to the left wing of the Progressive Party. In speeches of 1862 he had proposed a

16 *HW*, I, 153.
17 *HW*, I, 156, 159, 175-176; Parisius, *Hoverbeck*, II/2, 1-2.

kind of parliamentary strike. Undisguised absolutism, he argued, was no longer possible in an increasingly industrialized society with an expanding middle class. Consequently, authoritarian monarchies had been forced to resort to sham constitutionalism. To be victorious, the deputies need only rip away this veil of deception by adjourning the lower chamber until the government yielded. Under modern conditions, he asserted, no monarchy could rule indefinitely without parliament. "A government which has its hands continually in everyone's pocket must assume at least the appearance of having everyone's consent."[18]

By this proposal Lassalle, who had already taken the first step toward founding a socialist movement, probably intended to challenge the liberals and demonstrate their unwillingness to enter upon any decisive action which might have a revolutionary outcome. If so, he was soon proved right. His suggestion was immediately attacked by the whole liberal press. Only one deputy came out for it, but was so isolated that he resigned his seat in parliament.[19]

Even after the election of October 1863 the deputies were disinclined to force the issue by taking any positive step. To be sure, they re-elected the presiding officers (Grabow and Bockum-Dolffs) who had clashed so bitterly with Roon and Bismarck in the preceding session. They exercised their right under the constitution to vote down the press edict, which thereby became inoperative. A committee investigated and recorded the abuses of the government in the election.[20] The army bill was again rejected and the funds for military reorganization struck out of the budget for 1864. Nevertheless, the deputies turned down once more the motion that the latter bill be rejected outright without debate or amendment.[21] Nothing came of the proposal that the chamber pass a series of "striking resolutions," which would culminate in a demand for the resignation of the cabinet and the call for a tax boycott.[22]

[18] Ludwig Maenner, ed., *Ferdinand Lassalle, Reden und Schriften* in Friedrich Meinecke and Hermann Oncken, eds., *Klassiker der Politik*, Vol. 15 (Berlin, 1926), pp. 177-207.

[19] Hermann Oncken, *Lassalle, eine politische Biographie* (4th ed., Stuttgart, 1923), pp. 280-282; Philippson, *Forckenbeck*, pp. 109-110; Löwenthal, *Verfassungsstreit*, pp. 197-198.

[20] *SBHA* (1863-1864), I, 75-111.

[21] *Ibid.*, II, 713 ff. The debate on this subject is most illuminating for the conflicting views on tactics within the liberal movement.

[22] Meisner, *Kronprinz im Verfassungskampf*, pp. 171-172.

The supine attitude of the Prussian liberals in 1863 was not merely a fault of inadequate leadership. Behind their unwillingness to engage in any decisive action—whether revolution, taxpayers' boycott, or parliamentary strike—was the crippling uncertainty of popular support. In the midst of the election campaign Bernhardi noted signs that the public was "completely fed up with politics."[23] Even the slender gains made by the conservatives on election day had a depressing effect. The journalist Wilhelm Wehrenpfennig estimated that another election might increase threefold the number of conservative deputies, while Haym judged that repeated dissolutions would produce a ministerial majority. Twesten, who favored the proposal for outright rejection, reported that most believed it "would ruin us with the voters, particularly the rural ones." From Berlin Karl Mathy, a prominent Baden liberal, wrote to Freytag on November 13, "The longing for compromise hovers in the air. . . . The progressives are tame; they no longer feel so certain in their trust in the perseverance of the voters."[24]

The liberal fort was built on sand, and, while the deputies anxiously watched for the first cracks, Bismarck was considering ways and means to rip away the whole foundation.

2. THE SEARCH FOR A POPULAR FOUNDATION

Contrary to what the crown prince assumed, the Junker had not made up his mind to abandon the Prussian constitution. Undoubtedly the king was nearer the truth when he wrote his son in October. "You always come back to Minister v. Bismarck's utterance that we could reach the point of dispensing with the constitution. In his conversation with you at Gastein he presented this as *one* of the eventualities which lie within the range of possibility, while you make it out to be the goal of his efforts."[25] As in the struggle against Austria, many paths had to be explored, of which the most dangerous was the last. But none of the routes tried during Bismarck's first year in office had led anywhere. Hence the possibility of a *coup d'état* became increasingly real.

What form ought it to take? Here apparently Bismarck was not in agreement with the king. William was still troubled by his

23 *Aus dem Leben Bernhardis*, v, 121.
24 *HW*, I, 177-178, 181, 185-186; Haym, *Briefwechsel*, p. 225.
25 Meisner, *Kronprinz im Verfassungskampf*, pp. 176-177.

oath to uphold the constitution. Rather than openly violate it, he preferred to wait until the hatred of the opposition boiled over into rebellion. By resorting to the barricades the liberals would themselves break the law and release him from the obligation he found so repugnant. While his generals crushed the revolt, following the plan long since prepared, William would scrap the constitution and return to the type of personal rule which existed before 1848.

For Bismarck this was not a pleasing prospect. Although willing to accept it as a last resort, he had never been sympathetic to the idea of absolutism. Such a move would be tantamount to an admission that the monarchy's only secure foundation was the army. Bismarck wished to enlarge rather than restrict the base of the government's support. By returning to absolutism Prussia would further isolate itself in Germany; German nationalists would regard as an utter farce the Hohenzollern proposal for a national parliament. Furthermore, Bismarck saw no reason for discarding the whole constitution. On the contrary, the document designed by Manteuffel and his reactionary colleagues had proved sufficiently elastic to meet the needs of the monarchy in the constitutional conflict. The only gap of embarrassing size had been covered by the *Lückentheorie*. The fault lay not with the constitution itself, but with one of its details, the electoral law.[26]

In Bismarck's opinion the political complexion of the chamber of deputies was the artificial consequence of the three-class voting system, rather than the actual state of Prussian opinion. The law of May 30, 1849 divided the voters into three categories according to the amount of taxes paid. In the beginning this enabled the aristocratic owners of the eastern latifundia to concentrate their strength in classes I and II, which paid two-thirds of the taxes and chose two-thirds of the electors. By the late 1850's, the increased tempo of industrialization had created a new plutocracy with incomes greater than the Junkers. Many who had previously voted in the first division were forced into the second, others from the second into the third. By 1861 there were only 159,000 voters in class I and 454,000 in class II, while class III contained 2,750,000. Although they achieved majorities in all three divisions in the

---

[26] Revision of the electoral law was the last resort mentioned to Gerlach in their talk of March 4. *GW*, VII, 73. See Augst, *Bismarcks Stellung*, pp. 42 ff.

elections of 1861-1863, the liberals were strongest among the men of new wealth who now dominated the first two.[27]

Theoretically universal, the Prussian suffrage was actually very limited because of its inequality. Despite the great agitation in chamber and press, 65 percent of those eligible to vote did not do so in the election of 1862, nearly 70 percent in 1863. The number of delinquents was highest in the two western provinces, which were the traditional strongholds of liberal influence; in Westphalia 80 and in the Rhineland 82 percent of the electorate failed to vote in 1863. Most significant of all is the fact that throughout Prussia the greatest proportion of absentees belonged to class III. In 1863, 43 percent of class I, 56 percent of class II, and 73 percent of class III did not go to the polls. In the new industrial towns of western Germany the percentage of proletarian delinquents was often above 90.[28]

What were the reasons for this failure? The poor man knew that his vote was worth only one-seventeenth that of a wealthy person. Voting was indirect and by voice rather than ballot. The procedure of open voting was time-consuming and might even be hazardous for those financially dependent upon others of contrary political views. For the proletarians, moreover, the problem of daily bread was more immediate and pressing than what went on in the Landtag. On the land the peasantry had been accustomed for centuries to the idea that political questions were the proper concern of someone higher up. The Stein reforms and the revolution of 1848 had made some inroads upon this lethargy, but both had been followed by long periods of political stagnation. One may suspect that the constitutional conflict had the appearance of a quarrel between the upper classes, between those who had the power and those who had the votes. Those who had neither busied themselves with other matters.

[27] Johannes Ziekursch, *Politische Geschichte des neuen deutschen Kaiserreiches* (Frankfurt a.M., 1925-1930), I, 59-61. On the Prussian electoral system in general see Eugene Anderson, *The Social and Political Conflict in Prussia 1858-1864* (Lincoln, 1954), pp. 255 ff. For Bismarck's view of it see Hans J. Schoeps, "Unveröffentlichte Bismarckbriefe," *Zeitschrift für Religions- und Geistesgeschichte*, II (1949), 15; Horst Kohl, ed., *Die politischen Reden des Fürsten Bismarck* (Stuttgart, 1892-1905), II, 94-95; Ludwig Gerlach, *Aufzeichnungen*, II, 255.

[28] Ziekursch, *Politische Geschichte*, I, 61-62; Anderson, *Social and Political Conflict*, pp. 413 ff.; Löwenthal, *Verfassungsstreit*, p. 147. Bismarck estimated that only one-seventeenth of the eligible voted, with the consequence that those who reached the chamber were "the distilled bourgeoisie . . . the organized revolution." Gustav Mayer, *Bismarck und Lassalle, Ihr Briefwechsel und ihre Gespräche* (Berlin, 1928), pp. 34, 36.

In this untapped reservoir Bismarck hoped to find new sources of support for the monarchy. His strategy was the same as on previous occasions. In 1853 he had sought outside Germany a political force capable of exerting pressure against the Austrian coalition in the Bundestag; after 1858 he saw in German nationalism a potential ally of similar utility; now he found in the lower classes a new reserve which could be set in motion against the liberal bourgeoisie. Unlike William, he was not content merely to retreat behind the moated and bristling battlements of the Prussian military state. He much preferred to maneuver in open country, mobilizing new forces with which to turn the flanks of the foe and, if possible, strike him in the rear.

The idea of exploiting the lower classes against the bourgeoisie was not a sudden one for Bismarck. Never had he doubted the loyalty of the peasantry to the monarchy; liberalism and rebellion were in his view the natural products of cities and urban social classes. In 1848 he first became aware of the "bitter tension" between burghers and workers in Berlin and of its potential value for the nobility. While the former supported the revolution, the latter were partial to "king and military" and wanted the crown to regain its authority.[29] The democratic radicals of the extreme left, moreover, had a certain fascination for him. During the years of reaction he often sought their company and conversation, finding them more congenial than the moderates. In 1851, he reported receiving "the most respectful greetings" from the "reddest of the red here and abroad." Their press was "flattering." "They love us of the extreme right in contrast to the way they feel about the Gothaer."[30]

After 1849 he watched the government of Otto Manteuffel seek through social reform to win the support of the peasants and artisans against the middle class. Originally he shared the conservative prejudice favoring the artisans ("the backbone of the burgher

---

[29] *GW*, xiv, 114. Josef Maria von Radowitz pointed out to Frederick William IV that workingmen were the logical ally of the conservatives against the liberal bourgeoisie. Friedrich Meinecke, *Radowitz und die deutsche Revolution* (Berlin, 1913), pp. 77-78, 531-532; Theodore S. Hamerow, *Restoration, Revolution, Reaction: Economics and Politics in Germany, 1815-1871* (Princeton, 1958), pp. 72 ff., 174 ff. There is some evidence of a deliberate effort on the part of conservatives to arouse the working class of Berlin against the revolutionary government in 1848. Erich Jordan, *Die Entstehung der konservativen Partei und die preussischen Agrarverhältnisse von 1848* (Munich, 1914), pp. 285-296.

[30] *GW*, vii, 15-16, 24; xiv, 150, 189, 192.

class") and the guild system which protected their interests. During his years in the great commercial city of Frankfurt, however, he became convinced of the inefficiency of the guilds and of the virtues of mass production; he became a convert to the cause of industrial freedom. His conversion removed a major obstacle to a future alliance with the liberal bourgeoisie.[31] But it also marked his realization that the spread of the factory system was inevitable and that the factory proletariat was destined to replace the handicraftsmen as the working class of the future. This was the first step toward the recognition of its social interests—and its political potential.

3. THE SOCIAL PROBLEM

Once the depression of 1857 had been overcome, Germany entered another decade of rapid industrial progress. New clusters of smokestacks belched their soot into the air; humming machines demanded the presence of more and more workers; the social cleavage between owner and worker deepened. Once more the artisan class was in retreat before the inexorable advance of factory production. Their proletarian rivals, on the other hand, suffered many of the typical evils of early industrialism: long hours, rising prices, uneven employment, poor housing, and penury in sickness and old age. Except for some efforts to provide decent lodging, most entrepreneurs were smugly content not to worry about the social consequences of their business activities. Liberal economics required them to believe that any artificial interference with the "natural laws" of supply and demand in the labor market would have disastrous consequences for employer and employee alike. Under the influence of Manchesterism, the new-era government began to strip away guild protectionism, but did nothing to repeal the law prohibiting trade unions.[32]

The liberals were little conscious of the wisdom of binding the urban workingmen to the bourgeoisie in a common struggle against the monarchy. At most they desired only their moral and passive support. In the absence of an independent proletarian movement

[31] Kohl, *Reden*, I, 130 ff.; *GW*, XIV, 302; Hamerow, *Restoration, Revolution, Reaction*, pp. 248-251.

[32] Hamerow, *Restoration, Revolution, Reaction*, pp. 238 ff.; Julius Becker, *Das deutsche Manchestertum, eine Studie zur Geschichte des wirtschaftspolitischen Individualismus* (Karlsruhe, 1907), pp. 79 ff.; Pierre Benaerts, *Les origines de la grande industrie allemande* (Paris, 1933), pp. 573 ff.

in Germany it was assumed that this could be had without any effort to satisfy the social needs of labor. Liberal interest in the lower classes was limited to the founding of workers' educational societies (*Arbeiterbildungsvereine*). The attitude of the National-verein was typical. Though willing to finance a workers' delegation to the industrial fair in London in 1861, the association repeatedly refused to lower its dues to encourage proletarian membership. While critical of the three-class system, most liberals favored restrictions of some kind on the suffrage. Since they were prospering under the three-class system, moreover, they were unwilling to agitate against it. The issue was left unmentioned in the progressive platform of 1861. Even Waldeck, leader of the extreme democratic faction, believed that the time had not yet come to strive for equal suffrage. The liberals were repelled by the very example which inspired Bismarck: Napoleon's sinister exploitation of universal suffrage for autocratic purposes. Only a few individuals on the outer fringe of the movement, like Ziegler and Lassalle, favored an equal franchise for the masses.[33]

A major exception was Schulze-Delitzsch. With some success he sought to bind the working class to the liberal cause by promoting its economic interests within the limits of liberal economic doctrine. His program was one of "self-help" through the founding of workers' cooperatives with the aid of private capital. But the chief beneficiaries were the artisans and lower middle-class, not the industrial workers. Credit, raw material, storage, and consumer cooperatives strengthened their ability to survive the calamities of an increasingly big business economy. For indigent proletarians he had only the limp advice that by saving they might accumulate enough capital to join the cooperative system. Nor did he suc-

[33] Ernst Schraepler, "Linksliberalismus und Arbeiterschaft in der preussischen Konfliktszeit," in Richard Dietrich und Gerhard Oestreich, eds., *Forschungen zu Staat und Verfassung, Festgabe für Fritz Hartung* (Berlin, 1958), pp. 385-401; Hermann Oncken, "Der Nationalverein und die Anfänge der deutschen Arbeiterbewegung 1862-1863," *Archiv für die Geschichte des Sozialismus und der Arbeiterbewegung*, II (1912), 120-127; Paul Herrmann, *Die Entstehung des deutschen Nationalvereins und die Gründung seiner Wochenschrift* (Leipzig, 1932), p. 113; Walter Gagel, *Die Wahlrechtsfrage in der Geschichte der deutschen liberalen Parteien 1848-1918* (Düsseldorf, 1958), pp. 22 ff.; Hans Neumann, "Franz Ziegler und die Politik der liberalen Oppositions-parteien von 1848-1866," *Forschungen zur brandenburgischen und preussischen Geschichte*, Vol. 37 (1925), pp. 280-281; Wilhelm Biermann, *Franz Leo Benedikt Waldeck, Ein Streiter für Freiheit und Recht* (Paderborn, 1928), p. 296.

ceed in winning the Progressive Party to the principle of equal suffrage.[34]

This was the heart of Lassalle's program. Disgusted by the impotence of the progressives in the constitutional conflict, the fiery agitator turned to the industrial workers for the realization of his ideal of a democratic Germany. In April 1862 he called upon the proletarians to recognize themselves as the "fourth estate" to whom the future belonged. Attacking Schulze-Delitzsch's "self-help" cooperatives as futile, he demanded factory cooperatives based on "state-help." To obtain this assistance, labor must first gain political power through the grant of universal, direct, and equal suffrage. On March 1, 1863 Lassalle issued the manifesto which led to the creation of the "General German Workers Association" to agitate for this end. By their obtuseness on the social and political needs of the emerging proletarian class, the German liberals opened the way for its estrangement.[35]

In this they were not entirely alone. Prussian conservatives were almost equally blind to the potentialities of the social question. Their rural background was no preparation for an understanding of the social upheaval produced by the industrial revolution. The social relationship to which they were accustomed was that between noble landowner and submissive peasant. Their blindness was also owing to the character of their religious belief. Social welfare was never regarded as the concern of the Lutheran church, but only the propagation of the faith. Christian morality was primarily a matter of inner piety rather than service to one's fellow-man. In conservative thought the idea persisted that proletarians should regard themselves as a new estate, functioning like the nobility and middle class within the organic body of society. That many refused to conform to this romantic pattern and aspired to equality was regarded with irritation and impatience.[36]

While sharing these prejudices, Victor Aimé Huber and Hermann Wagener had a better understanding than most conserva-

---

[34] Thorwart, *Schulze-Delitzsch*, v, 186-187, 201.

[35] Oncken, *Lassalle*, pp. 293 ff.; Lassalle, *Reden und Schriften*, pp. 209-245; Schraepler, "Linksliberalismus und Arbeiterschaft," pp. 393-401; Gustav Mayer, "Die Trennung der proletarischen von der bürgerlichen Demokratie in Deutschland, 1863-1870," *Archiv für die Geschichte des Sozialismus und der Arbeiterbewegung*, II (1912), 1-67.

[36] See William O. Shanahan, *German Protestants Face the Social Question* (Notre Dame, 1954), and Fritz Fischer, "Der deutsche Protestantismus und die Politik im 19. Jahrhundert," *Historische Zeitschrift*, Vol. 171 (1951), pp. 473-518.

tives of the social developments in their time. A teacher and publicist, Huber was troubled by the deterioration of religious faith in working class families. The reason lay, he believed, in their social circumstances. Through cooperatives of various kinds, particularly housing, he hoped to raise living standards and integrate the proletarian estate into a stable Christian society. Like Schulze-Delitzsch, he believed in "self-help" rather than state assistance. An independent and disputatious soul, Huber had no talent for practical politics and never sought to found a movement.[37]

For Wagener, the political aspect of the social problem was all-important. Failure to grasp the social issue, he predicted, would lead to the ruin of the monarchy and the aristocratic order. With others of similar opinion he published the *Berliner Revue*, whose columns favored agrarianism, anti-Semitism, and "social realism." To the state, Wagener argued, belonged the primary responsibility for social welfare. While rejecting the plans of Huber, Lassalle, and Schulze-Delitzsch, he proposed that the government foster model productive associations as yardsticks for determining wages, hours, and working conditions in different industries. This would be a guide to future legislative action and government control.[38]

Wagener's social view had some of the characteristic limitations of the conservatives. While interested in promoting the interests of factory workingmen, he understood best the artisan class. His *Volksverein* was an alliance of landowners and handicraftsmen. While favoring the right to organize, he was against strikes and believed that unions should take their place, like the guilds, in the corporative structure of society. Opposed to the three-class voting system, he wished to organize the electorate by estates.[39] Despite these limitations, he was convinced that the monarchy could easily win any serious contest for the allegiance of the working class. "This is the sore spot which the Progressive Party carries around on its body." The monarchy must establish itself as the protector of the masses. "This is the secret of the popularity of Bonapartism."[40]

37 Shanahan, *German Protestants*, pp. 382 ff.
38 *Ibid.*, pp. 362 ff. See also Adalbert Hahn, *Die Berliner Revue, Ein Beitrag zur Geschichte der konservativen Partei zwischen 1855 und 1875, Historische Studien*, Vol. 241 (Berlin, 1934).
39 Müller, *Volks-Verein*, pp. 22 ff., 114, 117-120; Hahn, *Berliner Revue*, pp. 96 ff.
40 Adolf Richter, *Bismarck und die Arbeiterfrage im preussischen Verfassungskonflikt* (Stuttgart, 1935), p. 26.

Throughout Europe conservative politicians found the political system of Napoleon III an enlightening phenomenon. Nationalism, democracy, and socialism were the three principal ingredients of his political recipe. Universal suffrage preserved the fiction of popular participation; the Bonapartist tradition stimulated national pride; state socialism eased the material wants of the lower classes. Through public works, particularly the reconstruction of Paris, the dictator in the Tuileries temporarily reduced unemployment and improved wages. Some progress was made in public housing for workers. Government support was provided for private cooperatives and health insurance undertakings. By issuing government bonds in small denominations an effort was made to give people of moderate means a sense of identification with the state.[41]

4. THE TALKS WITH LASSALLE

These ideas and experiments were grist for Bismarck's mill. During the 1850's he had studied the structure of the Napoleonic system and had already borrowed parts of it. Wagener was an old friend and collaborator. After a period of eclipse he had re-emerged under the new era as the organizer and leader of the conservative party apparatus. It was only natural that Bismarck should consult him soon after coming to power.[42]

At the minister-president's request the publicist wrote three memorials outlining ways and means of "destroying" the Progressive Party. His advice concerning the disciplining of officials, organization of an official press, and the suppression and subornation of the opposition journals may well have influenced the first actions of the cabinet. His chief recommendation, however, was to base the monarchy upon the masses by promoting their material interests against the "domination of finance capital." Implicit in his argument was the assumption that divine right and aristocratic support were no longer an adequate foundation for monarchical authority. To command the future, the crown must

[41] H. Gollwitzer, "Der Cäsarismus Napoleons III. im Widerhall der öffentlichen Meinung Deutschlands," *Historische Zeitschrift*, Vol. 173 (1952), pp. 23-75; Walter Vogel, *Bismarcks Arbeiterversicherung* (Braunschweig, 1951), pp. 16-19.

[42] Saile, *Wagener und Bismarck*, pp. 65 ff.; Hermann Wagener, *Erlebtes* (2nd ed., Berlin, 1884), II, 17. As in the case of his political outlook, it is doubtful that Bismarck's interest in the social problem can be traced to the influence of Stahl. Karl Thieme, who asserts this, does not mention Wagener or even consider the tactical side of the problem. Karl Thieme, "Bismarcks Sozialpolitik," *Archiv für Politik und Geschichte*, IX (1927), 382 ff.

"place itself at the head of the movement" by promoting the "moral and material interests of the masses." In the new age there were only two possibilities: parliamentary government or the imperial system of Napoleon III.[43]

With his pencil Bismarck underlined the more significant passages in Wagener's memorials. But during the winter of 1862-1863 he was apparently much too busy to launch such a program. In March he asked Eulenburg to look into the possibility of private old-age pension funds under state supervision. A month later he prodded Itzenplitz to consult Huber for suggestions on social reform. "For political reasons" the government must "act with vigor." But nothing came of it. Both ministers were too much under the influence of liberal economic doctrine to believe in the wisdom of state action in such matters.[44]

Perhaps through Wagener Bismarck became aware of the split among the progressives signified by the founding of the General German Workers' Association. In May 1863 he took the extraordinary step of summoning Lassalle for a secret talk. Over the next ten months the radical agitator and minister-president conferred repeatedly. Years later Bismarck testified that Lassalle was "one of the most clever and attractive men with whom I have ever talked. . . . Our conversations went on for hours and I was always sorry when they came to an end." For all that divided them, they had much in common. Both were bold, outspoken, realistic, brilliant, and they shared the same foe.[45]

While frankly admitting the "revolutionary" nature of his movement, Lassalle maintained that he had no dogmatic ideas about governmental forms. "The working class," he declared, "is instinctively inclined toward dictatorship," but it must first be convinced that "this power will be exercised in its own interest." The proletarians would shed their republicanism and willingly accept a "social dictatorship" of the crown, if the latter would only "strike out in a truly revolutionary and national direction and transform itself from a monarchy of the privileged classes into a social and revolutionary people's monarchy."[46]

In the end the discussion centered upon the crucial subject of

[43] Saile, *Wagener und Bismarck*, pp. 133-144.
[44] *GW*, IV, 84-85, 94-95; Richter, *Arbeiterfrage*, pp. 87-90.
[45] *GW*, XI, 606.
[46] Mayer, *Bismarck und Lassalle*, pp. 60-61.

the election law. According to Lassalle, Bismarck declared his intention "some day" to ally the monarchy with the people through the proclamation of equal suffrage. But how was it to be introduced? The opposition majority would vote against it, and the king was against a *coup d'état*. Lassalle had the answer. Since the three-class system had come into existence by decree, it could be repealed the same way. This would automatically resuscitate the law of 1848, which had provided for universal, direct, and equal suffrage.[47]

The king's unwillingness openly to break the law was not the only reason for Bismarck's reluctance. He was unconvinced that universal suffrage would in itself produce a governmental majority. What if the lower classes continued to stay away from the polls even if given the equal vote? Once more the facile Lassalle found a "magic formula." Able-bodied citizens who failed to vote in two successive elections should be made to lose their civil rights for ten years. But still the Junker was not impressed. He wanted assurance that the voters would not only go to the polls, but vote conservative when they got there.[48] For all his talk about the "instinctive" royalism of the masses, he was not fully certain of their support. Later he described what he had in mind to his colleagues in the cabinet. One way to assure the "influence of the government on the spot" would be to send election commissioners to poll the population house by house. Or the existing election law might be changed so that government candidates would automatically receive the ballots of those who failed to vote.[49] Such were the terms in which Bismarck thought of universal suffrage at the time of his talks with Lassalle.

The drift of events discouraged the latter. Within weeks after their first meeting came the press edict. Such measures, the radical warned, would make impossible the proposed alliance.[50] During the fall of 1863 his speeches and writings brought him into conflict with the police and bureaucracy. His appeals to Bismarck had no effect. Apparently the Junker preferred to keep him under restraint. Early in 1864 a note of desperation appeared in Lassalle's messages. The imminence of war with Denmark caused him to fear that the minister-president had chosen the path of foreign adventure over internal reform. When the conflict came, Bismarck

47 *Ibid.*, pp. 28-29, 41, 61.   48 *Ibid.*, pp. 42-43, 81-84.
49 *Ibid.*, pp. 35-36.   50 *Ibid.*, p. 61.

did sever their relationship.[51] In August Lassalle fell in a duel over a love affair.

The reasons for Bismarck's decision against an alliance with the proletarian left in 1863 are not difficult to discern. Despite the exertions of its dynamic leader, the workers' association enjoyed only limited success. When he died, there were 4,600 members, of whom 3,000 were Prussian. In Berlin, where Schulze-Delitzsch reigned supreme, the followers of Lassalle were just thirty-five. "What could Lassalle offer and give me?" Bismarck asked in 1878. The "poor devil" had "nothing behind him."[52]

[51] *Ibid.*, pp. 80, 87-88; *GW*, vii, 94-95; Hermann Oncken, "Bismarck, Lassalle und die Oktroyierung des gleichen und direkten Wahlrechts in Preussen," *Historisch-Politische Aufsätze und Reden* (Munich, 1914), ii, 195-196.

[52] Oncken, *Lassalle*, p. 440; *GW*, xi, 606.

BOOK THREE

THE YEARS OF TRIUMPH, 1864-1867

*"Exalt his self-esteem toward foreigners and
the Prussian forgets whatever bothers him
about conditions at home."*—BISMARCK in 1858

*"Woe to the unfortunate devotee of principle
who thinks of the past, who is so naïve and so
unrealistic to assert that right is still right
and wrong still wrong, that success can create
power, but never right!"*—WILHELM LIEBKNECHT in 1866

CHAPTER ELEVEN

THE CONQUEST OF SCHLESWIG-HOLSTEIN

1. THE PROBLEM OF THE DUCHIES

N THE surface the Schleswig-Holstein question appeared to present Bismarck with a fine chance to strike at the domestic opposition through an impressive coup in foreign affairs. Since 1848 the "North Mark" had been a *cause célèbre* of German nationalism. In that year the government in Copenhagen had first attempted to incorporate Schleswig within Denmark. With Holstein and tiny Lauenburg, Schleswig was a possession of the Danish crown, but unlike them it did not belong to the German Confederation. By tradition, nevertheless, the two larger duchies were inseparable, and the Danish action threatened to split them apart. The Germans in the duchies rose in revolt, and the Frankfurt parliament commissioned Prussia to intervene in their behalf. But after a short campaign Berlin withdrew under pressure from the European powers, and the parliament was impotent to succor the rebels. More than any other event of 1848, this episode revealed the powerlessness of the assembly in the Paulskirche. The failure in Schleswig-Holstein presaged the failure of the German revolution itself.[1]

The Danes also suffered frustration. Although Austria and Prussia agreed with the other great powers in the treaty of London (May 1852) to respect the integrity of the Danish monarchy, Denmark was compelled to promise the dual powers (treaty of December 1851) never to incorporate Schleswig or take any steps toward that end; in addition, the king promised to consult the ducal estates concerning any future constitutional union with Denmark. This left the ambitions of Danish nationalists unsatiated and the practical problem of ruling the duchies unsolved. During the 1850's the issue remained alive, and in 1863 King

[1] On the problem of the duchies see the classic study of Lawrence D. Steefel, *The Schleswig-Holstein Question* (Cambridge, 1932).

Frederick VII issued his "March Patent," which established a new constitutional arrangement without the required consultation and augured a fresh attempt to incorporate Schleswig. During the next six months the Frankfurt diet ponderously ground out an order of execution against Denmark. But the Danes were not discouraged. Europe was preoccupied with the Polish question; the diet was quarreling over confederate reform; Prussia was troubled by an internal conflict; England and France seemed friendly to Denmark; and from Sweden came vague promises of military assistance.[2]

Suddenly, on November 15, 1863, the Danish case was thrown into confusion by the unexpected death of King Frederick. He had no direct heir. In the treaty of London the powers had sought to take care of this problem by recognizing in advance the claims of Prince Christian of Glücksburg to both the Danish kingdom and the duchies. Nevertheless, the German Prince Frederick of Augustenburg, on hearing the news from Copenhagen, immediately proclaimed himself "Frederick VIII, Duke of Schleswig-Holstein." At Gotha, under the protection of Duke Ernst of Coburg, he immediately began to assemble a government. Within a short time his sovereignty, although of doubtful legality, had been recognized by most of the German lesser states.

The Augustenburg cause was also quickly taken up by liberal nationalists throughout Germany. The fate of the duchies was regarded as a critical test of the vitality of German nationalism. If unable to meet the challenge of tiny Denmark, Germany could hardly expect to generate the power necessary to create a nation-state. For many the issue was also a test of the German will to political freedom. On hearing the news from Copenhagen, Gottfried Planck, professor of law at Kiel, wrote to his old friend Bennigsen, "Upon the outcome depends not only the rescue of the duchies for Germany and the entire position of the latter abroad, but also the course of our inner development for many years to come." Failure would result either in revolution or, more likely, a general relapse into the crudest kind of reaction.[3] To men of his conviction unity and freedom were still synonymous; progress toward one meant progress toward the other.

The Augustenburg cause appeared to embody both. Prince

2 *Ibid.*, pp. 55 ff.
3 Oncken, *Bennigsen*, i, 621; Ziekursch, *Politische Geschichte*, i, 129-130.

Frederick was known to be of liberal and nationalistic conviction. His good friend, Duke Ernst, was the patron of the National-verein. In 1848-1850 the prince had served with his father in the revolutionary army of Schleswig-Holstein.[4] Nevertheless, support of his claims placed the German liberals in the anomalous position of upholding the principle of legitimacy and seeking to increase the number of lesser states. On both points they had reversed themselves.

Immediately after the death of the Danish king, the leaders of the Nationalverein hastened to exploit the new situation. On November 18 Bennigsen summoned the executive committee to meet in Berlin. There it was quickly decided to give Prince Frederick every possible assistance. A highly inflammatory appeal was released to the public. Schleswig-Holstein, it asserted, must not be allowed to suffer the fate of Alsace-Lorraine. Just as their ancestors reconquered East Prussia from Poland, Pomerania from Sweden, and the Rhineland from France, the Germans must reclaim the northern duchies from Denmark. As "sons of the common fatherland," the German princes must take note of their responsibilities. While willing to "pardon and forget many wrongs," the people would never forgive "betrayal of their honor and freedom to foreigners." Patriotic associations were called upon to hold in readiness men, money, weapons, and materiel. A coordinating committee was set up in Göttingen under the Hanoverian politician, Johannes Miquel.[5]

But soon the Nationalverein reduced its activity in favor of a new organization with a broader base. On the subject of Schleswig-Holstein and the claims of Augustenburg the association found itself in agreement with its rival, the Reformverein. Combining their efforts, the little- and great-German organizations summoned the deputies of all German parliaments to rally in Frankfurt on December 21. Nearly five hundred came and voted unanimously to make the cause of Augustenburg that of Germany itself. Although the great Germanists objected, a permanent "committee of thirty-six" was created to act as a "center of legal activity" in marshalling support for the duchies. Intoxicated by their new-found unity of purpose, the nationalists proposed to exploit

4 On the Augustenburgs, father and son, see Johann H. Gebauer, *Christian August, Herzog von Schleswig-Holstein* (Stuttgart, 1910), and Karl Jansen and Karl Samwer, *Schleswig-Holsteins Befreiung* (Wiesbaden, 1897), pp. 103 ff.
5 Oncken, *Bennigsen*, I, 621 ff.

popular indignation to sweep the German governments into action. Here was their opportunity to demonstrate the existence of a national movement of overwhelming power, which in the future no German statesman dare ignore.[6]

Hatred of the foreigner is the best possible cement for a divided nation. Even the Prussian conservatives joined the swelling chorus of moral outrage. Where the rights of German principalities against outsiders were concerned they were not immune to national sentiment. Many were impressed by the argument of legitimacy. Since 1848 the Danish experiments with liberal constitutions had been a thorn in the flesh of conservative Europe. Impressed by these arguments, King William himself favored recognition of Augustenburg. The crown prince, who had known Prince Frederick as a student in Bonn, was his warm supporter.[7]

Amid the general enthusiasm a ripple of uneasiness spread through the minds of the Prussian liberals. What if the cunning Junker in the Wilhelmstrasse turned the situation to his own advantage? Would he seek to head the great national crusade against Denmark? Dared they carry out their threat to refuse credits for such a war? If so, what would be the consequence for their own prestige in Germany? Would they be tortured by the necessity of choosing between national unity and political freedom?[8]

Their equanimity was soon restored. On November 28, 1863, Prussia and Austria publicly based their case against Denmark on the treaties of 1851-1852, rather than on the claims of Augustenburg. A month later they branded the committee of thirty-six as "revolutionary" and called upon the states of the confederation to suppress it.[9] Throughout Germany these actions were regarded by liberals as a "betrayal" of the national cause. In Prus-

[6] Erich Zimmermann, Der deutsche Reformverein (Pforzheim, 1929), pp. 75-88; Theodor Schieder, Die kleindeutsche Partei in Bayern, Münchener historische Abhandlungen, Vol. 12 (Munich, 1936), pp. 41 ff.; Adolf Rapp, Die Württemberger und die nationale Frage, 1863-1871, Darstellungen aus der Württembergischen Geschichte, Vol. 4 (Stuttgart, 1910), pp. 59 ff.; Liselotte Konrad, Baden und die schleswig-holsteinische Frage, 1863-1866, Historische Studien, Vol. 265 (Berlin, 1935), pp. 44 ff.

[7] Gerhard Ritter, Die preussischen Konservativen und Bismarcks deutsche Politik, 1858-1875 (Heidelberg, 1913), pp. 89 ff.

[8] Dehio, "Taktik der Opposition," pp. 325-327; Parisius, Hoverbeck, II/1, 195; Oncken, Bennigsen, I, 630-631; HW, I, 183, 187. Bernhardi and Max Duncker hoped Bismarck would exploit the Schleswig-Holstein affair in order to end the domestic crisis. Friedrich von Bernhardi, ed., Aus dem Leben Theodor von Bernhardis (Leipzig, 1893-1906), v, 146, 154-155.

[9] APP, IV, 148.

sia the leaders of the opposition returned to the attack. Apparently they had been absolutely right in believing that a Junker reactionary could never act for the good of the nation.[10] Denmark and Bismarck could now be condemned in the same breath.

Bismarck had good reasons for passing up such a favorable opportunity. Despite outward appearances, the Augustenburg cause did not fit his purposes. To have backed it would have ruined his own secret plans for the duchies and aroused diplomatic complications of a dangerous kind.

2. THE STRATEGY OF ALTERNATIVES

Bismarck had long been familiar with the Schleswig-Holstein problem and alive to its possibilities for Prussia. In 1856 he confessed to Bülow, the Danish minister in Frankfurt, that "he was no friend of a sentimental or national policy and much too Prussian to make any distinctions in his feelings between Spaniards, Bavarians, or Danes. His only concern was whether Prussia had an interest in quarreling with Denmark or disrupting the Danish monarchy. For the time being this was not the case."[11] Hence he advised his government to pose before the public as the defender of German national honor in the duchies, but to make no earnest attempt to solve the problem. Instead Prussia should delay a settlement until such time as she might extract some "practical gain" from it.[12]

By "gain," of course, he meant an increase in power. In his opinion, the solution desired by German nationalists would not add to Prussia's might. Quite the contrary, it would create another medium state like Hanover and Hesse, which would inevitably fear Prussia and flirt with Austria. What Bismarck wished, long before he could openly say so, was incorporation of the duchies into Prussia. His mind brimmed with thoughts of expansion. "Prussia's mission," he declared, "is to extend itself."[13]

The odds against success were enormous. In Europe, Germany,

---

[10] Dehio, "Taktik der Opposition," pp. 327 ff.

[11] Arnold O. Meyer, "Die Zielsetzung in Bismarcks schleswig-holsteinischer Politik von 1855 bis 1864," *Zeitschrift der Gesellschaft für Schleswig-Holsteinische Geschichte*, LIII (1923), 112-113. In mid-February 1864 he told Ludwig Gerlach, "I am a Prussian, not a German." What he ought to say, Gerlach replied, was, "I am a Prussian and therefore a German—or vice versa." Ernst Ludwig von Gerlach, *Aufzeichnungen aus seinem Leben und Wirken, 1795-1877* (Schwerin, 1903), II, 262.

[12] *GW*, II, 240.   [13] *OD*, IV, 118.

and Prussia itself there was scarcely an important person or interest sympathetic to Bismarck's purpose. Among the great powers England and Austria were completely opposed to Prussian annexation, Russia mildly so. Although Napoleon encouraged it, his support was costly and possibly treacherous. All of the German lesser states backed Augustenburg. The king and crown prince had no thought of utilizing the situation for Prussia's growth. Bismarck's own subordinates in the foreign service, some of whom had direct access to the royal ear, were against his policy. In the chamber of deputies all parties were inclined toward or committed to Augustenburg. Only the left-liberal Waldeck, completely unaware of Bismarck's intention, came out immediately for annexation. With him, no more than with Napoleon, could there be any thought of compact.

After three difficult years, nevertheless, Bismarck got what he wanted. That he was able to maneuver his way through and over these many obstacles is one of the most amazing feats in the history of politics. In later years he spoke of it as his "proudest" achievement.[14] His approach to the problem was characteristic. In the beginning he was only sure of what he wanted. He knew neither how, when, nor whether it would be attained. At the close of the war in 1864 he wrote, "This trade teaches that one can be as shrewd as the shrewdest in this world and still at any moment go like a child into the dark." That Prussia had been successful he attributed to divine aid, for God had not left him alone in his blindness.[15] Bismarck's faith, however, was not one of resignation. God helps those, he firmly believed, who know how to help themselves.

In typical fashion he analyzed the situation in terms of its alternative possibilities. They were three: (1) annexation to Prussia, (2) the "personal union" of the duchies with Denmark under the Danish crown, or (3) their independence under the house of Augustenburg and inclusion in the German Confederation. If the first alternative were unattainable, which of the other two was to be preferred? German scholars have long disputed this point. His partisans have been quick to deny, his critics to affirm, that Bismarck was willing to leave Germans under alien rule rather than

14 Moritz Busch, *Bismarck: Some Secret Pages of His History* (London, 1898), I, 130.
15 *GW*, IX, 49; XIV, 672.

accept a solution disadvantageous to Prussia.[16] What he himself said about the matter varied according to his political purpose. While seeking to coerce Augustenburg into concessions in return for Prussian aid (early 1864), he gave the second alternative as his preference. After concluding his alliance with German nationalism (late 1866), he maintained that Augustenburg had been his second choice. This was also the order listed in his memoirs.[17]

To insist that Bismarck made a choice in 1863-1864 is to misunderstand his whole approach to politics. Everything depended upon the circumstances of final decision. If England and France had intervened and Austrian support failed, he would have had no other choice than to leave the duchies under Danish sovereignty. Certainly a limited Danish sovereignty was preferable to a fully independent Schleswig-Holstein under Augustenburg. The latter solution would probably have been permanent, the former temporary. The issue could have been re-opened at some future date under circumstances more favorable for Prussian conquest. If compelled to accept Augustenburg, on the other hand, Bismarck intended to exact a heavy price, which would have been tantamount to Prussian annexation.

Bismarck's great opportunity lay in the fact that the forces which opposed his primary aim were disunited. Their conflicting interests and ambitions enabled the nimble Junker to occupy his favorite position of the pivot. Again and again he used the availability of choice to frustrate the maneuvers of his opponents. Pressure was met by counterpressure in a precarious balance which for months oscillated back and forth in imminent threat of upset. That it did not was owing to the almost inhuman skill of the wizard in the Wilhelmstrasse.

In the beginning this strategy was possible only because his opponents were ignorant of his intention to annex. Otherwise they might have united long enough to wreck his chance of success. Like a hunter crossing a marsh, he remarked to Wagener, "I never advance a foot until certain that the ground to be trod is firm and safe." First he clung to the treaties of 1851-1852; then he raised the idea of personal union; finally he appeared to accept Augustenburg. Each project was dropped or permitted to collapse once

[16] Meyer, "Zielsetzung," pp. 103-104; Erich Eyck, *Bismarck, Leben und Werk* (Zurich, 1941-1944), i, 550.
[17] Meyer, "Zielsetzung," pp. 105-106, 128-130; *GW*, xv, 254.

its usefulness was over, until eventually the only practical alternative remaining was that of annexation. His conduct of the war shows the same step-by-step progression: first the confederate execution in Holstein, then Austro-Prussian occupation of Schleswig, finally the invasion of Jutland. Either excessive delay or precipitate haste could have brought disaster. Years later he explained to Lothar Bucher, "The individual actions were, in themselves, trifles; to see that they dove-tailed was the difficulty."[18]

3. BISMARCK'S MASTERPIECE

The twists and turns of Bismarckian diplomacy in the Schleswig-Holstein affair are much too intricate to be related here in detail. For that matter, no one will ever fully comprehend the incredible dexterity of his performance without reading the several documentary collections which record, as well as any written record can, his daily decisions and actions. Here it will suffice to trace the broad outline of the story.

Long ago Bismarck had concluded that the duchies could not be acquired without war.[19] Militarily Denmark and Prussia were no match. While the Prussian population was 16,000,000, that of Denmark was 2,500,000, of whom thirty percent were Germans of doubtful loyalty. Bismarck's task was to see to it that the Danes fought alone. From Great Britain came the greatest threat of intervention. Any weakening of the Danish monarchy was regarded as dangerous to British interests in the Baltic. Without another great power as an ally, however, Britain could not easily engage in a continental war. Since Russia was almost out of the question, Austria and France were the likely candidates. It was necessary then to bind Austria securely to Prussia and keep France and Britain apart.[20]

To this end Bismarck first adopted a policy of outward moderation and strict legality. All that Prussia asked, he declared, was that Denmark live up to her obligations to the German powers under the agreements of 1851-1852. For its part Berlin would hold to the treaty of London and had no intention of threatening

---

[18] Heinrich von Poschinger, *Fürst Bismarck und die Parlamentarier* (Breslau, 1894-1895), II, 24; Steefel, *Schleswig-Holstein*, p. 95. His success, he remarked to Ludwig Gerlach, was a "matter of luck and circumstances." *Aufzeichnungen*, II, 267.

[19] *APP*, III, 133; see also pp. 90-91.

[20] On British and Russian policy see Werner E. Mosse, *The European Powers and the German Question, 1848-1871* (Cambridge, 1958), pp. 146 ff.

the integrity of the Danish monarchy. Within the Prussian government the pressures against such a policy were considerable. Although disturbed by the liberal character of the Augustenburg movement, William was partial to the prince's cause and anxious to get rid of the treaty of London. From every quarter he was bombarded with advice by people of similar views: his fellow princes, the queen and crown prince, his friends in the old *Wochenblatt* party, and some of Bismarck's own subordinates in the foreign office. At crucial moments the minister-president was able to hold the king in line only by marshalling the support of his cabinet colleagues and threatening to resign.[21]

The London treaty was the rope with which Bismarck took the Austrian government in tow. Because of popular clamor over the duchies Franz Joseph and Rechberg could scarcely pursue a purely negative, "do nothing" policy in the Danish affair, and yet any "national solution" to the problem would have been a highly dangerous precedent for Vienna. The Hapsburg monarchy could not easily support the cause of national self-determination abroad and continue indefinitely to deny it at home. Hence the Austrians were relieved to learn that Bismarck was willing to turn his back upon Augustenburg and the German national movement.[22] After November 1863 the men in the Ballhaus and Hofburg were afflicted by a curious apathy. It was as though, exhausted by the futile struggle of recent years, they had lost the will and energy to protect their interests.[23]

Certainly they realized that there was only one way to avoid the perils of liaison with the wily Junker: by binding Prussia firmly to the principle that under no circumstances would Christian's succession to the duchies be open to question. This alone would have made it impossible for Berlin to acquire the duchies or create a small state under her own influence. With each successive step of the dual powers in the Danish affair Rechberg and his colleagues sought to put the Prussians into this restraining

[21] *APP*, IV, 188-190, 242-245, 259-262, 264-265, 291-292; Kohl, *Anhang*, I, 86-87; Alfred Stern, *Geschichte Europas seit den Verträgen von 1815 bis zum Frankfurter Frieden von 1871* (Stuttgart, 1899-1924), IX, 582-584; *GW*, XV, 250 ff.

[22] *DPO*, III, 443-444; *APP*, IV, 163-164, 186.

[23] "One can say," wrote Moritz Blankenburg to Ludwig Gerlach on December 4, 1863, "that the Vienna cabinet is now located in the Wilhelmstrasse in Berlin." Ludwig Gerlach, *Aufzeichnungen*, II, 259. In April Bismarck remarked to Keudell that it was "incomprehensible" why the Austrians had followed Prussia into Schleswig. *GW*, VII, 85.

harness: before the confederate execution in Holstein, before the Austro-Prussian invasions of Schleswig and Jutland, and finally during the London conference in May.

On each occasion, Bismarck evaded them by the use of his balancing technique. As far as he was concerned, so he said, the Austrians could have their guarantee, but, alas, William would never accept it. Week after week he tortured the nerves of Karolyi and Rechberg with the details of his struggles against the Augustenburg faction at the Hohenzollern court. By pressing their demands too far, he warned, the Austrians would push William in a radical direction. It was a convincing performance. Even Karolyi, usually less than gullible, concluded that Bismarck had undergone a genuine conversion. All that the Austrians succeeded in extracting was a vague commitment, made before the invasion of Schleswig, that, if Danish resistance should lead to war and abandonment of the treaty of London, the question of the succession would be decided "in no way other than through mutual agreement."[24]

In Frankfurt the dual powers joined forces to insist that the treaties of 1851-1852, not the claims of Augustenburg, must be the basis for action against Denmark. If voted down, they warned, Berlin and Vienna would proceed on their own in defiance of the diet.[25] For years Austria had led the confederate majority against Prussia; now she accepted *de facto* Bismarck's old position that the diet could not outvote the great powers. The effect was electrifying. "So they put a knife to our throats!" shouted the Bavarian minister-president. From Frankfurt the Austrian delegate reported that the loss in Austrian prestige among the lesser states was catastrophic.[26]

But again, the *trias* states showed themselves incapable of maintaining a solid front against the dual powers. In December 1863 they accepted, by a majority of one, the treaties of 1851-1852 as the basis for intervention in Holstein and Lauenburg. Once Saxon and Hanoverian troops had occupied the southern duchies in the name of the confederation, however, they rejected a proposal of the dual powers that the same motivation be used to justify an invasion of Schleswig. As a consequence, Austria and

24 *DPO*, III, 436-438, 454-458, 598-606, 616 ff., 629-634, 666 ff.; IV, 36-37, 47-48, 79 ff.; *APP*, IV, 439 ff., 477, 491, 501-502, 737-741.

25 *APP*, IV, 255-257.   26 *DPO*, III, 476-479, also 449-451.

Prussia made good their threat. In late January their forces began to cross Holstein in the direction of Schleswig, ready to fight either the Danes or the Saxons and Hanoverians. Sullenly the confederate troops gave way. The high-handed manner in which the Prussians took over the strategic towns and military quarters in Holstein excited fresh indignation. Meeting in Würzburg, the ministers of the lesser states resolved to press again for confederate recognition of Augustenburg. Bismarck's reaction was severe. He let the "sheen of the blade show above the scabbard" by mobilizing an army corps on the Saxon frontier. In Vienna Edwin Manteuffel obtained a commitment from Rechberg to participate, if necessary, in an "armed action against Germany." The revolt subsided.[27]

His profession of loyalty to the London treaty was also useful to Bismarck in the British capital. For a time it helped him lull the suspicion of the British cabinet concerning his intentions.[28] The controversy over Schleswig-Holstein was very embarrassing to Russell and his colleagues. Their interests and sympathies, as well as those of the British public, lay with Denmark, and yet the government in Copenhagen appeared to be in the wrong. Repeated attempts at mediation by the British shattered against the persistence of the Danes in clinging to the March patent. Only the adoption by Germany of the Augustenburg cause would have provided Britain with a satisfactory case for intervention.

Repeated warnings from London on this score provided Bismarck with another weapon. They helped him dampen William's enthusiasm for the prince and gave weight to his insistence that the course advocated by the lesser states could result in a major war. On the other hand, his difficulties with the Augustenburg movement were also useful in London. Pressure from this direction, he argued, compelled Prussia to make her adherence to the London treaty dependent upon Danish fulfillment of her agreements of 1851-1852 with the dual powers. Whenever Russell tried to pin him down as to what constituted fulfillment, the Junker grew vague.[29]

The crucial moment in British policy came when the dual pow-

27 DPO, III, 720-722. Heinrich Ritter von Srbik, Deutsche Einheit, Idee und Wirklichkeit vom Heiligen Reich bis Königgrätz (Munich, 1935-1942), IV, 104 ff.
28 APP, IV, 327-328. See also Steefel, Schleswig-Holstein, p. 132.
29 APP, IV, 188-190, 194-197, 213, 219-221, 252-255, 268-270, 286-287, 292-293, 300 ff., 357-359, 369-372.

ers announced their intention to invade Schleswig. Palmerston and Russell were not convinced by Bismarck's argument that a choice had to be made between "invasion of Schleswig and revolution in Germany." But the queen and most of the cabinet were unwilling to go to war over the issue. In any case Britain could not act without the support of France, and in Paris Drouyn told the British envoy with some satisfaction that "the question of Poland had shown that Great Britain could not be relied upon when war was in the distance." The Anglo-French entente was completely finished.[30]

Had they known what was transpiring between Berlin and Paris, Palmerston and Russell would have been even more perturbed. Since November 1863 Napoleon had been trying to entice Prussia into a policy of annexation. He held out the possibility of her acquiring both the German population of Schleswig-Holstein and the "crowd of small states" hampering Prussian power. "If you now have something to whisper into our ears," Drouyn told Count von der Goltz, the Prussian ambassador, "we shall listen attentively."[31] By encouraging Prussia to destroy the German Confederation, the French apparently hoped to give the *coup de grace* to the settlement of 1815. Without making any commitments Bismarck kept the suitor hopeful. The "favorable disposition" of the emperor, he explained to Goltz, was necessary as "a means of pressure on England."[32] To keep him in the proper mood the Prussian repeatedly indicated his willingness to sacrifice the Rhine frontier.[33]

As the invasion neared, he resorted to a typical maneuver. Prussia had a choice, he warned Britain and Russia, "between two

[30] *APP*, IV, 361; Steefel, *Schleswig-Holstein*, pp. 166-167; Mosse, *European Powers*, pp. 159 ff.

[31] *APP*, IV, 197-201, 207-209, 223-224, 344-346.

[32] *APP*, IV, 334-337.

[33] To Talleyrand and Karolyi (December 16) and Fleury (December 24) he declared that, if faced with a choice between Prussia's Polish possessions and the left bank of the Rhine, he would advise surrendering the latter. *APP*, IV, 324; *DPO*, III, 505. Fleury reported, "As for the Rhine frontier, the word has been spoken; should it be stressed?" "Don't speak of the Rhine," Napoleon replied, "and play down Poland." OD, I, 4. On the significance of these remarks see Herbert Geuss, *Bismarck und Napoleon III., Kölner Historische Abhandlungen*, I (Köln, 1959), pp. 97-98, and Gerhard Ritter, "Bismarck und die Rheinpolitik Napoleons III.," *Rheinische Vierteljahrsblätter*, XV-XVI (1950-1951), 353-354. Geuss and Ritter are probably correct in considering the enticement a mere "maneuver" intended to keep Napoleon's favor. But this may not be dogmatized into the assertion that the sacrifice of German soil was unthinkable to Bismarck.

alternatives": she could maintain the London treaty and preserve the recent entente between the four great powers against France, or she could abandon the treaty and "make common cause with the rest of the confederation and perhaps with the French cabinet." While the second course "would facilitate our position considerably," Berlin preferred to continue upon the first. To Sir Andrew Buchanan, the British ambassador, he expressed the hope that Great Britain "would not give a signal for the commencement of a steeplechase to Paris."[34]

This strategy sufficed to isolate the battlefield in Schleswig, but soon the problem arose again in connection with the projected invasion of Jutland. Retreating from the fortified line of the Dannevirke, made vulnerable by thick ice over the Schlei, the Danes had withdrawn northward into Jutland and behind the trenches of Düppel in eastern Schleswig. While Bismarck was secretly negotiating with the Austrians to extend the war beyond the Schleswig frontier, a detachment of Prussian troops unexpectedly crossed into Jutland and occupied the town of Kolding. Once more the British contemplated intervention. On the Seine there were ominous signs that Napoleon might reverse his policy and join them.[35] But the majority in the London cabinet voted against the venture, and the emperor appears to have reconsidered. Bismarck reinforced the French decision in characteristic fashion. Opposition from France, he warned Talleyrand, would force Prussia to halt the Jutland operation. London, Vienna, and Petersburg were already making difficulties. Berlin could not afford to alienate all of these powers. "From the moment that you show us *faccia feroce*, we must put ourselves on good terms with Austria."[36]

The diplomatic struggle of the Danish war reached a climax in the international conference which began to assemble in London on April 20, 1864, two days after German troops had stormed and taken the trenches at Düppel, the last Danish foothold on the mainland. In summoning the conference, Russell had hoped to find a way to end the conflict with as little change as possible in the *status quo ante bellum*. Bismarck saw in it a chance to get rid of

---

34 *APP*, iv, 466, 482-483; also 438, 458-465, 651-652.

35 Steefel, *Schleswig-Holstein*, pp. 186 ff.; Mosse, *European Powers*, pp. 179 ff. The Austrians were shocked by Bismarck's suggestion that rapprochement with France would provide a means of pressure on Great Britain. *DPO*, 716-720, 772; *APP*, 592-597.

36 *OD*, ii, 15, 49. Later he claimed to Gorchakov that the threat had been effective, *APP*, iv, 622.

the treaty of London, which, after screening the German advance up the Danish peninsula, had now outlived its usefulness. After informing the conference on May 12 that they no longer regarded the treaties of 1851-1852 as binding, the dual powers left open the possibility of "personal union" between the duchies and Denmark under King Christian. To the great distress of the Austrians the Danes obstinately refused to consider such a proposal. Even if they had, no agreement would have been likely. Bismarck had already succeeded in getting Austrian consent to a number of "essential conditions" too onerous for the Danes to accept.[37]

The failure of the "personal union" exposed the bankruptcy of Austrian policy. The London treaty and the principle of the integrity of the Danish monarchy were dead. With them had expired the only possibility of a satisfactory outcome of the war for Vienna. There remained only a choice between Augustenburg and Hohenzollern rule, between a "national solution" to the German question and a significant expansion of Prussian power in Germany.

4. THE DANISH CAPITULATION

On February 3, 1864, only two days after the invasion of Schleswig, Bismarck began to shove forward the alternative of annexation. In a crown council he openly confessed that this was his ultimate goal. "I reminded the king that each of his immediate forebears, except his brother, had won for the state an increase in territory . . . and encouraged him to do the same." But the Hohenzoller was troubled. To the protocol which recorded the discussion he added that annexation was not the objective of Prussian policy, but merely a possible outcome of the affair. Honest William needed time to get accustomed to the idea and more arguments to square it with his conscience.[38]

During the following months Bismarck carefully prepared the ground. Under Baron Zedlitz, the Prussian commissioner, the civil administration of occupied Schleswig began to assume a Prussian character. In the duchies a petition was circulated demanding close union with Prussia. In Prussia the conservative

---

[37] *APP*, iv, 755-756; *DPO*, iv, 80 ff.

[38] Stern, *Geschichte Europas*, ix, 584-586; *GW*, xv, 254. On the problem of dating the council see Steefel, *Schleswig-Holstein*, pp. 108-109, and R. Sternfeld, "Der preussische Kronrat von 2./3. Jan. 1864," *Historische Zeitschrift*, Vol. 131 (1925), pp. 72-80.

leader, Arnim-Boitzenburg, launched with Bismarck's connivance a petition bidding the king to seek either a Prussian protectorate or annexation. Conservative members of the Schleswig-Holstein estates appealed to William against Augustenburg.[39]

The wind from Paris was fair. In March Napoleon proposed that the London conference consult the "wishes of the population" concerning their future. While the other great powers abruptly refused, Bismarck was more subtle. He agreed to the division of Schleswig on national lines, but asserted that the will of the German population could best be ascertained by consulting the ducal estates rather than by popular referendum. Rechberg was shocked by Bismarck's agreement to such a revolutionary proposition.[40] His agitation would have been even greater had he known what else had been agreed upon in Berlin and Paris. On April 9 Drouyn consented to Bismarck's view, adding that France would "deplore" a vote for Augustenburg, but support a decision for Prussia. In return she wanted no territory, just a "frank and vigorous entente in other areas." Bismarck's reply was favorable, but cautious. Even so it cost William a sleepless night. Annexation, the king feared, would leave Prussia alone in Europe with her "arch enemy and its inscrutable leader." Would Bonaparte demand "rectification" of the Rhine frontier?[41]

His chief minister was fully aware of the hazard of falling into dependence upon France. Once the threat of British intervention had passed, the main concern of Bismarck's diplomacy—one which was to last until the climax of 1866—was to maintain the delicate balance in Prussia's relations with France and Austria. Napoleon's objective, he well knew, was to sever the line between Berlin and Vienna and fashion the one from Paris to Berlin into a leash.

The easiest way out was to get the Austrians to agree voluntarily to Prussian annexation. In January 1864 he began to plant the idea in the minds of Rechberg and his colleagues that this, after all, might be the best solution to the problem. On the 14th he casually told Karolyi that annexation was being discussed in Berlin, adding that he had "firmly" rejected the idea. If the course of events should make it a serious possibility, Austria would be given a *quid pro quo* in Italy. When Biegeleben visited Berlin in April, the minister-president told him that by giving

[39] Srbik, *Deutsche Einheit*, IV, 149-150.
[40] *OD*, II, 144-145; *APP*, IV, 667, 688, 700-701, 716-717.
[41] *APP*, IV, 709, 730-735.

Prussia a "glorious peace" Vienna would win for herself "not a province, to be sure, but the Prussian army." To Count Chotek, the Austrian *chargé*, he spoke of the "inauguration of a policy of mutual compensation." In view of Rechberg's distaste for Augustenburg, he seems to have thought that the Austrians might actually accept.[42]

But in this he erred. His own policy ruined by the obstinacy of the Danes, Rechberg was compelled to choose the least harmful of two undesirable alternatives. He chose Augustenburg. Although probably caught by surprise, Bismarck was quick to squeeze advantage out of necessity. With Austrian help it was now possible at least to wrench the duchies conclusively away from Denmark. On May 28 the dual powers astonished Europe by announcing to the London conference their support of the "complete separation" of the duchies from Denmark "and their union in a single state" under the prince of Augustenburg, who "in the eyes of Germany" had "the greatest right to the succession."[43]

The Austrian decision drove Bismarck into a corner, but as usual he had a door of escape. Previously he had gotten Austrian agreement to an impressive list of conditions which were to be forced upon the Danes if they agreed to "personal union." Now they were applied to Augustenburg—only the list was longer.

Rebuffed in Berlin, Prince Frederick had hoped to ride to power on the ground-swell of popular sentiment in Germany. No sooner had the confederate troops entered Holstein than he established his headquarters in Kiel, which became a center of agitation for his cause in the duchies. To prove his liberalism he proclaimed his support of the revolutionary constitution of 1848, which provided for parliamentary government. Nevertheless, he grasped that Prussian support was indispensable and that it would have to be bought, if it was to be had at all. In April he assured William of his willingness to accept inclusion of the duchies in the Zollverein, construction of a peninsular canal and a Prussian naval base at Kiel, erection of a confederate fortress in Rendsburg garrisoned by Prussia, and the organization and training of the ducal armed forces on Prussian lines.[44] Three days after the joint dec-

42 *DPO*, III, 621; IV, 80, 120; *APP*, IV, 734, 742-743.

43 Ludwig Aegidi and Alfred Klauhold, eds., *Das Staatsarchiv, Sammlung der officiellen Aktenstücke zur Geschichte der Gegenwart*, VII, 23-24.

44 Jansen-Samwer, *Schleswig-Holsteins Befreiung*, pp. 116, 163 ff., 200 ff., 320 ff., 717-719; C. Boysen, "Ein Brief Bismarcks an Herzog Friedrich," *Zeitschrift der*

laration in London in his favor he arrived in Berlin for the interview with Bismarck which proved decisive for his cause.

Even before they met, the minister had made known to the prince that Prussia would require "guarantees of a conservative system of government" in the duchies. In effect, this meant repudiation of the 1848 constitution. During their three-hour interview he also brought up the subject of territorial compensation for Prussia. But the prince refused to bargain away land and peoples without consent of the ducal estates, or for that matter to enter into any written agreement with Prussia. By doing so he would have damaged his own position in the duchies. In his report to the king, Bismarck made the prince out to be an ingrate who, far from being thankful for Prussian aid, thought to reduce her just demands by appealing to Austria and the ducal estates. So black did he paint him that William, who before the interview had thought the issue settled, now began to turn against the Augustenburg cause.[45] Later Bismarck boasted that at London he had "hitched" the Augustenburg "ox" to the plough. "As soon as the plough was in motion he unhitched the ox."[46]

The Austro-Prussian declaration for Augustenburg left the London conference with nothing to discuss but the partition of Schleswig. In accord with Napoleon, Bismarck was willing to accept a division based on nationality, but the British proposed the line of the Dannevirke far to the south of the language frontier between Dane and German. Still hopeful of British aid, the Danes held to this line, and on June 25 the conference broke up without decision. Although Palmerston and Russell were belligerent, Queen Victoria was horrified at the thought of war against Germany, and the cabinet voted it down. After months of bluster and threat the British abandoned the Danes to their fate. They "recoiled with vigor," sneered Drouyn.[47]

On June 26 the armistice, which had halted the fighting during the conference, expired. Three days later Prussian forces crossed the narrow channel from the mainland to the island of Alsen, which the Danes were compelled to evacuate. This defeat shattered Danish confidence in the inaccessibility of Zealand. On July

---

Gesellschaft für Schleswig-Holsteinische Geschichte, Vol. 62 (1934), pp. 349-351.
[45] *Ibid.*, pp. 330 ff., 730-736; *GW*, IV, 448-450.
[46] Steefel, *Schleswig-Holstein*, p. 256.
[47] *Ibid.*, pp. 240 ff., 253.

8 a new cabinet took office in Copenhagen, which immediately offered to treat. In the preliminary peace of August 1 and in the final one signed on October 30 Christian ceded forever his rights in the duchies to Austria and Prussia. The Danish phase of the Schleswig-Holstein problem was over, but the question of who would ultimately possess the duchies remained.

5. SCHÖNBRUNN AND RECHBERG'S FALL

With the successful detachment of Schleswig-Holstein from Denmark, the purpose of Bismarck's alliance with Austria would seem to have been fulfilled. In fact, Vienna was now the one major obstacle in the way of his next objectives: annexation and the expansion of Prussian power in Germany. Recent experiences had shown that neither Britain nor Russia would intervene, and from France came positive encouragement. For a year and a half, nevertheless, Bismarck clung to the Austrian alliance, and even after the final separation began in January 1866 he left open the possibility of return. "Many paths" had to be explored, "the most dangerous at the end."[48]

Bismarck's aim was to extract from the Hofburg an ever higher price for the continuation of an alliance which the Austrians were reluctant to sever. Without it they would be isolated and exposed in Europe. To Rechberg and Franz Joseph it was also the necessary bulwark against France and the forces of revolution in Europe. By careful exploitation of the frictions arising from condominium over the duchies, Prussia could make the Austrians, plagued by internal difficulties and worried about their Italian frontier, long for a settlement—any settlement to get rid of the affair. A prolonged occupation would enable Berlin to suppress the Augustenburg movement and foster annexation sentiment in the duchies. Obligated by the peace treaty to pay the cost of the war and assume their share of the Danish national debt, the ducal taxpayers would soon see the wisdom of shifting the burden to Prussia. From the nearly bankrupt Austrian treasury there was no prospect of succor.[49]

In late August, 1864, soon after the fighting ended in Denmark, Bismarck had an opportunity to probe once more the minds and intentions of Franz Joseph and his ministers. On the twenty-first he accompanied William to Vienna on a state visit. Precisely what

[48] GW, IX, 50.   [49] GW, V, 95; OD, VI, 214-215.

transpired at the famous Schönbrunn conference has long been the subject of dispute.[50] Did Bismarck actually offer Rechberg an alliance against France and Italy for the defense of Venetia and the recovery of Lombardy, in return for Prussian annexation of Schleswig-Holstein and dual solidarity against the middle states? Such an offer would have been most unlike him, for his system of strategy depended upon the avoidance of such a choice. Apparently what he did was to dangle once more, as so often in the past, the enticing *possibility* of such a bargain. What he wanted was to acquire the duchies in return for a vague, verbal promise that at some future date, which might never arrive, Prussia would not object to Austrian reconquest of Milan, a war she could scarcely undertake without active Prussian support, which need never be forthcoming.

But Rechberg took him literally. On the morning of the 24th he suddenly presented to the assembled monarchs and ministers the draft of an agreement which stated with uncomfortable exactness that Prussia would receive the duchies if Lombardy were reconquered. Bismarck got rid of the document in typical fashion. Without opposing the proposition himself, he let it trip and fall over the obstacle of William's conscience. The critical moment came when Franz Joseph bluntly asked William whether he really desired to annex the duchies or whether he was satisfied merely to acquire certain rights in them. There was a tense pause. While William groped for a reply, Bismarck had a chance to ward off the question. But instead he encouraged it by declaring that he too wished to learn the king's will. Slowly and in some embarrassment William replied that "he had no right to the duchies and hence could lay no claim to them." In his memoirs Bismarck maintained that this placed him "out of action." But in reality it was Rechberg's draft which fell by the wayside. All that the Schönbrunn conferences produced was a meaningless promise of mutual cooperation in the affairs of the confederation.[51]

Rechberg and Franz Joseph continued their erratic course. They wanted to preserve the alliance with Prussia as well as that

[50] See Walter Lipgens, "Bismarcks Österreich-Politik vor 1866," *Die Welt als Geschichte*, x (1950), 240-262; Heinrich Ritter von Srbik, "Die Schönbrunner Konferenzen vom August 1864," *Historische Zeitschrift*, Vol. 153 (1935-1936), pp. 43-88; Rudolf Stadelmann, *Das Jahr 1865 und das Problem von Bismarcks Deutscher Politik, Beihefte der Historischen Zeitschrift*, Vol. 29 (Munich, 1933).
[51] Lipgens, "Bismarcks Österreich-Politik," pp. 244 ff.

with the medium states. Suspicious of Prussian ambition, they were still hopeful of keeping Berlin upon the narrow path of conservative virtue. Schmerling, Biegeleben, and their followers were sharply critical of the fluctuations which rose from the incompatibility of these objectives. In October Biegeleben presented to Franz Joseph a memorandum which bluntly asserted the necessity of either a definite alliance with Prussia or an agreement with France. There being no acceptable ground for the former, Austria must choose the latter. But the Kaiser was unconvinced. He accepted Rechberg's counterplan: no firm alliance with any power, but rapprochement with Britain and Russia and improved relations with France. By this policy of the "middle line" he hoped to halt Prussian aggression in Germany.[52]

Rechberg's days, however, were numbered. In August his opponents had challenged him to prove his policy toward Prussia by just one success, if only in the field of economic affairs. During the Danish crisis the Austrians had suspended their struggle against renewal of the Zollverein on the basis of the Franco-Prussian treaty.[53] Discouraged by Austrian collaboration with Prussia and coerced by the economic advantages of free trade, the lesser states had reluctantly re-entered the Prussian economic fold. All that Rechberg could now demand was a sop to Austrian prestige in the form of a Prussian promise, similar to that given in the treaty of 1853, to commence on request negotiations with Vienna concerning the terms of a customs treaty before 1872.[54] But even this was denied him.

The concession was comparatively harmless and Bismarck would have readily granted it in order to save the useful Rechberg. But he was opposed, on technical rather than political grounds, by the ministers of trade and finance and by the economic counsellor Rudolf von Delbrück. When the issue came to a head, the minister-president was on vacation in the south of France, and his written protests were disregarded. By the time he succeeded in getting his way it was too late. Rechberg, undermined within the

[52] *DPO*, IV, 330-340; Srbik, *Deutsche Einheit*, IV, 193, 211.
[53] See pp. 151-52, 182 ff.
[54] Chester W. Clark, *Franz Joseph and Bismarck, The Diplomacy of Austria before the War of 1866* (Cambridge, 1934), p. 91; W. O. Henderson, *The Zollverein* (Cambridge, 1939), pp. 296 ff.; Eugen Franz, *Der Entscheidungskampf um die wirtschaftspolitische Führung Deutschlands (1856-1867)*, *Schriftenreihe zur bayerischen Landesgeschichte*, Vol. 12 (Munich, 1933), pp. 341 ff.

government and severely attacked in the public press (partly directed by Schmerling), had no other choice than to resign (October 27, 1864).[55]

The consequences of his fall were not as severe as Bismarck feared. The actual author of Austrian foreign policy was not the foreign minister, but the Kaiser, to whom the Biegeleben policy of rapprochement with France and resumption of the offensive against Prussia in the confederation was as uncongenial as ever. As Rechberg's successor he chose Count Mensdorff, likewise dedicated to a policy of the "middle line." Nevertheless, Mensdorff was a general with no experience in diplomacy and thus more dependent upon Biegeleben's counsel than his predecessor. Gradually Austria drifted back toward cooperation with the medium states, and the alliance with Prussia began to loosen.[56] Within weeks after assuming office, Mensdorff found himself deeply involved in the first of a series of sharp crises which were to trouble the German Confederation with increasing intensity until the climax of 1866.

6. THE GASTEIN CONVENTION

Once the fighting was over, Bismarck resolved to liquidate the confederation's share in the occupation of Schleswig-Holstein; Austria had to be deprived of all support in the coming struggle over the disposition of the duchies. In July 1864 Rechberg had given him a start by agreeing—once more without gaining any real equivalent for Austria—to exclude the diet from the peace negotiations and to provide in the treaty for the cession of sovereignty over the duchies to the dual powers alone. During the same month Prussian troops rudely expelled the Hanoverian forces from the fortress of Rendsburg and Bismarck harshly protested agreements between the confederate commissioners and the Hanseatic cities on the use of telegraph lines in Holstein. On November 14 he followed this up by pressing Vienna for a joint demand that Hanover and Saxony withdraw their troops and offi-

---

[55] *GW*, IV, 544-575; V, 1-3; XIV, 678, 683-684; Waldemar von Roon, *Denkwürdigkeiten aus dem Leben des General-Feldmarschalls Kriegsministers Grafen von Roon* (4th ed., Breslau, 1897), II, 290-291. The actual figure behind Rechberg's fall may have been Count Moritz Esterhazy, rather than Biegeleben or Schmerling, and the issue one of domestic rather than Zollverein politics. See Clark, *Franz Joseph and Bismarck*, pp. 146 ff., 240-241.

[56] Srbik, *Deutsche Einheit*, IV, 215.

cials. Confederate law, he pointed out, did not permit continued occupation after the successful completion of an execution. Since Austria and Prussia were now sovereign in the duchies, their troops alone might legally remain.[57]

As the atmosphere grew cloudy, Prussia and the medium states began to deploy troops in the expectation of violence. From Vienna came the counterdemand that Berlin join in presenting the peace treaty to the diet along with the proposal that confederate troops be withdrawn after sovereignty had been granted to Augustenburg. In late November the affair was settled by a "compromise," which gave Bismarck the essence of what he wanted. He dropped the demand that the dual powers disregard the diet; Mensdorff gave up the demand for Augustenburg, and both powers joined in getting the diet to vote, nine to six, for the withdrawal of the confederate troops and commissioners.[58]

Now the question of disposition became more acute than ever. None of the Austrian statesmen was interested in the duchies for their own sake. By his Schönbrunn proposal Rechberg had shown that he was not opposed in principle even to Prussian annexation. What he, Mensdorff, and the Schmerling-Biegeleben faction desired was a settlement which would not disturb the power balance in the confederation to Prussia's advantage. Shortly after assuming office, Mensdorff had asked Prussia to choose between two alternatives: (1) creation of a new principality under Augustenburg rule, or (2) Prussian annexation accompanied by compensation to Austria (the Hohenzollern enclaves in Württemberg and certain border districts in Silesia). Although the message was heavily lathered with conservative principle, Austria had now made clear that, however reluctantly, she was willing to settle the fate of the duchies on the basis of mutual gain.[59]

While Mensdorff pressed for quick decision, Bismarck answered with a mixture of double-talk and delay. William would never agree to the cession of Hohenzollern soil, but Prussia might offer financial rather than territorial compensation. A possible solution was temporary partition of the duchies between the dual powers; someday Austria might grant Holstein to Prussia in return for her assistance in Italy. As for Augustenburg, the legal claims of

[57] *GW*, v, 4 ff.
[58] *GW*, v, 18-19, 29 ff.; xiv, 689-690; *DPO*, iv, 429 ff.
[59] *DPO*, iv, 371 ff.

the Grand Duke of Oldenburg also had to be considered, and likewise those of the Prussian king as ruler of Brandenburg! Prussia would have to wait upon the opinion of a crown tribunal summoned to judge the legal aspects of the case. In any event, Prussia's willingness to give up annexation would depend upon the extent of the special rights granted her in the duchies.[60]

Previously Bismarck had always avoided being very precise about the nature of these special rights, but now the Austrians pressed for the bill. Week after week Bismarck dallied with his reply, to the increasing irritation of the men in the Ballplatz. When it finally arrived, the content was startling. For all practical purposes the army and navy of Schleswig-Holstein were to be absorbed by Prussia; servicemen were even to swear allegiance to the king of Prussia. Other demands were the cession to Prussia of certain key coastal positions, Prussian construction and control over an isthmian canal, a Prussian garrison in a confederate fortress, and the entry of the duchies into the Zollverein.[61] Mensdorff found these "February conditions," as they came to be called, "without precedent in all history." To the astonished Franz Joseph they were "quite unacceptable."[62]

The Austrians had no other choice than to continue the existing condominium in Schleswig-Holstein. Under cover of this policy, however, they strove to construct a firmer defense against the annexation movement. The matter was urgent. By buying up the press and appealing to material interests, Bismarck was making a vigorous effort to win the inhabitants; Zedlitz, the Prussian commissioner, ruled Schleswig as though it were already a Prussian province. In Count Halbhuber Vienna finally found a commissioner tough enough to block Zedlitz's encroachment and protect the Augustenburg movement, which now began to bloom. Turning again to the middle states, Mensdorff encouraged Bavaria to submit a resolution to the diet recommending that the dual powers hand over the administration of Holstein to Augustenburg. After a sharp contest for votes it passed, nine to six (April 6, 1865). On the day before, Roon had announced in the Prussian Landtag the government's intent to establish a naval base at Kiel. The Austrians protested sharply. Ominously Bis-

[60] *DPO*, IV, 387 ff.; *GW*, v, 43-47, 59-66, 77-81.
[61] *GW*, v, 96-103.
[62] Clark, *Franz Joseph and Bismarck*, p. 197.

marck wrote, "We are reaching a bifurcation. . . . Unfortunately our tickets are on diverging lines."[63]

The *dénouement* appeared close. In the duchies Bismarck redoubled his efforts to cripple the Augustenburg movement. By March 1865 William had been fully won to the idea of annexation. The army, he was assured, demanded it. In fact, the pressure for annexation at the cost of war waxed even stronger than Bismarck desired. On May 29 a crown council was summoned to consider the matter. "Sooner or later," the minister-president admitted, the war would come; at the moment the international situation was favorable. Nevertheless, the wisest course was to eliminate from the February conditions the two points which had met the greatest objection: the oath of allegiance and the "amalgamation" of the Prussian and ducal armed forces.[64]

Why this moderation? Those who believe in the "blood and iron" Bismarck, whether critics or admirers, have always stumbled over this question. From his remarks on May 29 it is clear that he regarded the February conditions, even without the above points, as tantamount to annexation. The difference between open and camouflaged incorporation was not great enough to fight about, especially since in time the latter was likely to lead to the former. If war came, it must be fought for a "higher aim"—the "creation of a constitutional relationship between Prussia and the German medium and small states."[65] Bismarck was not yet ready to abandon his double course; he was not convinced that the Austrians had reached the end of the long road of compromise and concession; and he needed time to prepare the alternative of violence.[66] His assumption about the Ballplatz was soon proved correct.

During June and July the tension rose. Despite Bismarck's recommendation, William refused to surrender any of the February conditions. Austrian counterproposals were judged insuffi-

63 *Ibid.*, pp. 198 ff.; *GW*, v, 136 ff., 158 ff.; *DPO*, iv, 641 ff.
64 Clark, *Franz Joseph and Bismarck*, pp. 542-547; *GW*, v, 189-190.
65 Clark, *Franz Joseph and Bismarck*, pp. 545, 547; *OD*, vi, 213; Arnold O. Meyer, "Der preussische Kronrat vom 29. Mai 1865," in *Festgabe für Heinrich Ritter von Srbik* (Munich, 1938), pp. 308-318. While aware of the anti-Prussian views of Schmerling and Biegeleben, he banked on the conservatism and "good will" of Mensdorff and Franz Joseph. *GW*, v, 75. He may have been influenced by the fact that on May 23 Werther had reported Mensdorff's willingness to allow Prussian annexation of Lauenburg in return for a reduction in Austria's war costs. Stadelmann, *Das Jahr 1865*, p. 39.
66 *GW*, v, 271.

cient. Bismarck pressed for the "restoration of order" in the duchies, meaning the suppression of Augustenburg agitation and public criticism of the Prussian occupation. Both sides began to calculate the ponderabilities of war. Bismarck hurried his diplomatic preparations in Turin and Paris. Whether he was satisfied with the results is uncertain.[67] Although Roon believed Prussia financially ready for mobilization and war, Bismarck doubted it.[68] Austria, on the other hand, was almost bankrupt. The crisis came at a moment when the credit of the state was in peril; essential government services were being curtailed. It was no time for war.

As usual, the Austrians retreated. In a last attempt Franz Joseph sent Count Blome to confer with the Prussians in Bad Gastein, where William had gone for the cure. In outlook Blome stood much closer to Rechberg than to Mensdorff and Biegeleben. He feared that a second Olmütz would bring another new-era cabinet to power in Berlin with a foreign policy still more hazardous for Vienna than Bismarck's. On August 1 he returned with a proposal which stemmed from Bismarck, although he represented it as his own: the dual powers would divide the duchies, Austria assuming sovereignty in Holstein, Prussia in Schleswig. But the cabinet in Vienna restricted the agreement to the "administration" of the duchies, leaving joint sovereignty nominally intact. Lauenburg was to be sold to Prussia outright. On August 20 the agreement was signed in the episcopal palace in Salzburg.[69]

Blome miscalculated badly. He judged Bismarck to be more a "party man" than statesman, interested primarily in the suppression of "democracy" at home rather than in warring against Austria. He expected Berlin to find in Schleswig her Venetia, a constant source of discontent which would lame her foreign policy. While Mensdorff was inclined toward war, Franz Joseph thought he saw in the draft a way to save the peace and the conservative front by avoiding a final choice between the German Confederation and the Prussian alliance. Nevertheless, it meant the division of the "indivisible duchies," the abandonment of

---

[67] *GW*, v, 223 ff., 242 ff., 282 ff. Srbik follows the older view of Sybel that Bismarck had no certainty of the intentions of Italy and France, while Stadelmann argues with force that there was no reason for him to doubt Italian aid and French neutrality. Srbik, *Deutsche Einheit*, iv, 280 ff.; Stadelmann, *Das Jahr 1865*, pp 57 ff.

[68] Roon, *Denkwürdigkeiten*, ii, 354; *GW*, v, 271, 275.

[69] Stadelmann, *Das Jahr 1865*, pp. 43 ff.; *DPO*, iv, 811 ff.; v/1, 1-5.

Augustenburg, and a sharp loss of Austrian prestige among the medium states.[70]

For Bismarck the treaty was one more step along the rocky road of expansion. The question of Prussian annexation was only "adjourned."[71] Again the Austrians had failed to obtain any commitment closing the door to such an outcome. By preserving the principle of joint sovereignty, they foolishly handed Prussia a pretext for future intervention in Holstein. The special rights Prussia obtained in that duchy (naval base at Kiel, a garrison in Rendsburg, construction of a canal, and rights of access to Schleswig) presented ample opportunity to infiltrate the southern duchy and plenty of combustible material with which to ignite future difficulties.

7. THE PARTING OF WAYS

Throughout the period of fluctuating crisis which followed the end of the Danish war Bismarck continued to observe his fundamental rule that Prussia must hold the pivotal position between France and Austria, using the threat of a firm settlement with Vienna to moderate Napoleon's demands on Berlin and close relations with France to weaken Austrian resistance to Prussian importunity in the duchies.[72] Continually he held out to the French the prospect that both their selfish and idealistic motives might be realized. In Schleswig, he stressed, Prussia was favorable to a new frontier which would separate the Danish- and German-speaking peoples, and in Italy Prussia had no thought of guaranteeing Austrian possession of Venetia. While seeking to divert Napoleon's imperial ambition toward Belgium and Luxemburg, he carefully left open the possibility of his acquiring German soil as well. It would be folly for Paris to launch an aggressive war for the Rhineland. "The one who can give the Rhenish provinces to France is the one who possesses them."[73]

The most critical moments in this policy came at the time of Schönbrunn and Gastein. Immediately after both conferences Bismarck hastened to calm French suspicion. During Rechberg's formal dinner at the conclusion of Schönbrunn, he drew Gramont, the French ambassador, aside and assured him that no

[70] *DPO*, v/1, 5 ff.   [71] *GW*, v, 276.
[72] See his instructions to Goltz. *GW*, v, 72-76, 92-95, 266-273.
[73] *OD*, iv, 62.

final settlement had been reached and that for the time being "plenty of ink" would be spilled, but no blood.[74] A year later the Gastein treaty produced a serious reaction in Paris. But again Bismarck warned that French hostility could only compel Prussia to reconstruct the eastern alliance of conservative monarchies, while French encouragement could only strengthen the anti-Hapsburg front. The division of the duchies was "provisional and to be regarded as but the first step" toward Prussian annexation of both and the "triumph" of Prussian "hegemony" in the regions north of the Main. In return for her support France might expand "everywhere in the world where French is spoken."[75]

Early in October 1865 Bismarck went to Biarritz, ostensibly on vacation, but actually to confer with Napoleon and his chief advisers. Exactly what was said on the terrace of Eugénie's oceanside villa and later in Paris and St. Cloud is still in doubt. Some believe that the Junker actually sought agreement on the cost of France's benevolent neutrality in the event of war.[76] That he did not report it later to William is, of course, no proof to the contrary.[77] But the conjecture is improbable. Bismarck was not yet ready to part with Austria, and it was unlike him to make commitments so far in advance of their necessity. In all probability he wished to allay French anxiety over Gastein and reassure William concerning Napoleon's intentions in Germany. It may also be that he used the occasion to suggest again that France seek her compensation in French-speaking Europe, rather than on the Rhine.[78] In his major purpose at least he was successful. Napoleon was ready to forget Gastein, he reported, and "dance the cotillion with us, without knowing in advance when it will begin or what figures it will include."[79]

[74] OD, IV, 58 ff.

[75] RKN, I, 67; OD, VI, 267, 453-454; VII, 64, 91; GW, V, 285 ff., 300-302.

[76] In general, this view has been taken by Fester, Frahm, and Eyck. Richard Fester, "Biarritz, eine Bismarck-Studie," Deutsche Rundschau, Vol. 113 (1902), pp. 212-236; Friedrich Frahm, "Biarritz," Historische Vierteljahrschrift, Vol. 15 (1912), pp. 337-361; Eyck, Bismarck, II, 98-99.

[77] GW, V, 307-311. See also his relation to Goltz in Otto Graf zu Stolberg-Wernigerode, Robert Heinrich Graf von der Goltz (Oldenburg, 1941), pp. 403-408.

[78] Erich Brandenburg, Untersuchungen und Aktenstücke zur Geschichte der Reichsgründung (Leipzig, 1916), pp. 451-453. Geuss's view that the purpose of the journey lay in Bismarck's relationship to William rather than to Napoleon appears distorted. Geuss, Bismarck und Napoleon, p. 145.

[79] GW, XIV, 707.

The French did not have long to wait for proof that Gastein did not mean peace between the dual powers. While still in Biarritz Bismarck began yet another test of Austria's will to continue the alliance with Prussia at any cost. On October 1 deputies of the German parliaments had convened in Frankfurt to challenge the legality of the Gastein treaty, and on October 29 a congress of the Nationalverein was expected to take a similar stand. At Bismarck's urging the dual powers delivered sharp protests to the senate of the free city for permitting such demonstrations. But the burghers firmly rejected this interference in their sovereign rights.[80]

Bismarck forced the issue. In Vienna he proposed that the dual powers proceed against the senate through the confederate diet and, if voted down, act on their own authority. He recognized that the convention of deputies had been a failure and admitted that the gathering of the Nationalverein was not in itself a "misfortune" for Prussia. Nevertheless, he harbored an intense antipathy toward the liberal mecca on the Main. By resolute action against it he hoped to intimidate the Prussian liberals at home.[81] Yet his major purpose was to force Vienna to choose once more between the Prussian alliance and the lesser states and to undermine the confederation further by demonstrating the joint dictatorship of the dual powers in Germany.

But Mensdorff had finally resolved that the concessions must end. He parried with the proposition that the two powers be content to push through the diet a motion calling for stricter observance of confederate rules for the suppression of "revolutionary" associations and assemblies. Bismarck's reaction was severe. In the Prussian press and in talks with Chotek he declared that there could be no "half-relationship" between the dual powers. The Hofburg must choose between an "upright alliance" and war "to the knife."[82]

The refusal of Mensdorff and colleagues to join in chastizing Frankfurt seems to have convinced Bismarck that the usefulness of the Austrian alliance was about over. The course of events in the duchies offered further proof. At Gastein he had calculated that within months Vienna would agree to some kind of monetary

---

[80] *GW*, v, 312-315; *Staatsarchiv*, ix, 312 ff.; Richard Schwemer, *Geschichte der freien Stadt Frankfurt a. M., 1814-1866* (Frankfurt, 1918), iii/2, 221 ff.

[81] *GW*, v, 301, 312-313, 315. See also Johannes Schultze, ed., *Kaiser Wilhelms I. Weimarer Briefe* (Berlin, 1924), ii, 62-68.

[82] *DPO*, v/1, 59 ff., 90-93, 97 ff., 118; *GW*, v, 332-333, 338-345.

compensation for Holstein.[83] But French assistance eased the Hapsburg financial crisis, and Franz Joseph was against further concessions to Prussia. Edwin Manteuffel, newly installed as Prussian governor of Schleswig, systematically exploited the principle of joint sovereignty to interfere in the Austrian administration of Holstein. Much to Bismarck's irritation he also contributed, by his authoritarian acts, to the growing popularity of the Augustenburg movement.[84] When Ludwig von Gablenz, the Austrian governor, unwisely permitted a demonstration for the prince in Altona on January 23, 1866, a harsh note left the Wilhelmstrasse for Vienna. It had the sound of an ultimatum.

Complaining of Austrian "aggression," the note demanded that Vienna suppress "democratic" and "revolutionary" agitation in the duchies. "A negative or devious answer" would compel Prussia to consider the alliance at an end and to assume "complete freedom for our *entire* policy." While apologetic over the Altona incident, the Austrian reply (February 7) was indeed negative. A few days later Karolyi reported an "ominous stillness" in the Wilhelmstrasse. After weeks of voluble irritation the Junker was suddenly silent. "The polemic between Vienna and Berlin," he was reported as saying, "is now at an end."[85]

For more than two years Bismarck had exploited the Austrian desire for cooperation with Prussia, repeatedly tricking and forcing Vienna into abandoning its vital interests, while he steadily advanced, step by measured step, those of Berlin. Constantly aggressive, he invariably depicted himself as on the defensive; always injuring, he continually assumed the role of the injured; ever working for the upset of the *status quo*, he steadily posed as a genuine conservative. For Austria it was a long story of futility and frustration. Her protests were met by declarations of innocence and indignation, her attempts to temporize and delay by the threat that Prussia would act alone, her efforts to halt Prussian encroachments by the charge that they endangered the monarchical cause. But at last in the winter of 1865-1866 Bismarck reached the line of hard resistance. What he could not achieve through popular will in the duchies and further capitulation in Vienna, he now resolved to acquire through violence.

[83] *GW*, v, 309.

[84] Clark, *Franz Joseph and Bismarck*, pp. 317 ff.; *GW*, v, 342 ff., 346-349; *DPO*, v/1, 164 ff.

[85] *GW*, v, 365-368; *DPO*, v/1, 181-182, 196.

CHAPTER TWELVE

THE MAGNETISM OF POWER

1. UNITY OR FREEDOM?

ISMARCK'S successes in foreign policy during the years 1863-1865 created new problems for the Prussian opposition. In November-December 1863 the Landtag parties were thrown into confusion by the deepening crisis over the duchies. Acting for the moderates, the deputies Friedrich Stavenhagen and Rudolf Virchow moved a resolution urging the king to recognize Augustenburg and give "effective support" to his cause. They were emphatically opposed by Waldeck and his democratic faction of thirty-five deputies. Completely ignorant of Bismarck's secret intention, Waldeck favored annexation to Prussia as a step toward the development of German naval power. But he was against backing the government in any aggressive action against Denmark, for it would morally commit the chamber to grant the hated Bismarck cabinet the means with which to fight a war. Patriotic excitement, it was feared, would drain off energies needed in the constitutional conflict.[1]

Here again was the basic dilemma of German liberalism. For Waldeck and his followers freedom took precedence over unity; the victory of parliament over the crown was more important than a German triumph over Denmark. The moderates were of the opposite opinion. "We value freedom at home very highly," declared Loewe, "but independence abroad above all." What mattered was the "glory and greatness of Germany." Many deputies were torn between these extremes. "It was pitiful," wrote Twesten, "to see how most sought to weasel through: don't spoil matters with the Nationalverein and the rest of Germany, therefore forward despite the cabinet; don't spoil matters with the radicals and abstainers, hence no cooperation with the cabinet. No one could bring himself to be quiet."[2]

[1] *SBHA* (1863-1864), I, 114-115, 209-214; III, 37-38; *HW*, I, 182-183; Friedrich von Bernhardi, ed., *Aus dem Leben Theodor von Bernhardis* (Leipzig, 1893-1906), v, 156-157, 159, 161-162; Ludolf Parisius, *Leopold Freiherr von Hoverbeck* (Berlin, 1897-1900), II/2, 19-21.
[2] *SBHA* (1863-1864), I, 232; *HW*, I, 195-196.

Both factions were agreed that the reactionary cabinet would never follow the recommendations of the house. By clinging to the London protocol, Bismarck appeared to prove once more the liberal axiom that a conservative government could do nothing for the national cause. Waldeck feared that war would merely fortify the cabinet's position, but his opponents confidently asserted that it would never survive such a crisis. "With the first blow of a real storm we will be free of this bad government," orated Loewe, while Bismarck listened from the ministers' bench. War was to be the midwife of freedom. When the debate ended, the petition passed by a large majority.[3]

Now the situation foreseen by Waldeck actually arose. On December 9 Bodelschwingh presented a bill authorizing a credit of twelve million *Thaler* to finance Prussian support of the confederate execution against Denmark. Since the treasury had no need of the money, the government's purpose was to heighten the confusion among the deputies and alienate their public support in the event of refusal. For days they could not make up their minds. Waldeck made progress with his plea for outright rejection. Outside Prussia leading German nationalists pressed for acceptance, even at the cost of the liberal position in the constitutional conflict. In the end the moderates moved a resolution stating the readiness of the chamber to adjourn the internal conflict, if only the cabinet would adopt a "national policy" against Denmark.[4]

Bitterly Virchow reproached Bismarck for giving precedence to the "European" over the "German" aspect of the Schleswig-Holstein question. The Junker had shifted from one standpoint to another so often that "no one can define his actual position." He had no program or "guiding principle," was "anti-national" and devoid of any understanding of the national interest. Bismarck's reply was equally sharp. "As long as we live in Europe we must place ourselves on the European standpoint." Being a scientist, Virchow (an eminent pathologist) should understand that some things were difficult for the expert to explain to laymen. "Politics is not an exact science"; as the situation changes, so must the

[3] *SBHA* (1863-1864), I, 232, 242, 248, 258; *HW*, I, 204-205. Members of the old-liberal faction were busy drawing up a list of ministers for the next cabinet. Johannes Schultze, ed., *Max Duncker: Politischer Briefwechsel aus seinem Nachlass* (Stuttgart, 1923), pp. 369-371.

[4] *SBHA* (1863-1864), I, 508-509; *HW*, I, 203-204; Parisius, *Hoverbeck*, II/2, 195-197.

method of its exploitation. "I really believe, gentlemen, that without exaggeration I understand these matters better." The resolution passed, 207 to 107, the Waldeck faction voting with the conservatives in the negative.[5]

During January 1864 Bismarck continued his patronizing pedagogy in the debate on the authorization bill. Foreign policies, he explained, were based on the interest of state. Without a German state there could be no German interest. Prussia's departure from the London treaty was a matter of "opportunity rather than law." To be effective legal opinions must be backed by power. Should the house refuse the requested funds, "we must take them where we find them." Ultimately the government would "conquer." "I believe that you too are no longer stranger to the feeling that it will turn out this way." The deputies laughed. On January 22 they rejected, 275 to 50, the requested authorization.[6]

Only Waldeck seems to have believed that rejection would seriously hamper the government. What the rest apparently hoped to accomplish was Bismarck's dismissal. William was known to be sympathetic to Augustenburg, and Berlin was rife with rumors of a cabinet crisis. Through indirect channels Twesten "stormed" the king with promises that the chamber would support "any other minister," even a conservative, if only his policy were national.[7] As the session neared its end and Bismarck was still in the saddle, the liberals became desperate. Since the ministers had violated the constitution for two years, Twesten declared, the deputies were no longer bound to observe it. "In this case every means is justified which can lead to the fall of such a government." The choice of means was no longer a question of law, but policy. Parliament, asserted Rudolf Gneist, had reached the end of the path of legal resistance.[8]

On January 25 the chamber resolved to condemn the expenditure of public funds without parliamentary approval as a breach

<hr>

[5] *SBHA* (1863-1864), i, 481-492, 504-507.

[6] Horst Kohl, ed., *Die politischen Reden des Fürsten Bismarck* (Stuttgart, 1892-1905), ii, 247 ff.

[7] H. B. Oppenheim, *Benedikt Franz Leo Waldeck* (Berlin, 1880), p. 185; *Aus dem Leben Bernhardis*, v, 224-225; *HW*, i, 203-204.

[8] *SBHA* (1863-1864), ii, 715-717, 924. The context shows that what Twesten had in mind was not revolution, but a flat rejection of the budget bill without amendment, to be followed by a tax boycott. While he felt it justified, he opposed such a drastic step because he doubted its success. See also *HW*, i, 215.

of the constitution; on the same day a royal decree prorogued the
Landtag. Once more the Prussian liberals had the chance to determine whether there was indeed any other "means" at their disposal than parliamentary protest. Was the German national cause
any more capable of arousing a genuine popular movement than
the constitutional conflict?

Even in January leaders of the Nationalverein were complaining, "Nowhere is the movement and agitation for Schleswig-Holstein further behind (Austria naturally excepted) than in Prussia. They do not assemble, do not press, do not contribute." Sybel
too found the mood of the people "lamentable." Two centuries of
absolutism had lamed the capacity for popular initiative. No one
was willing to sacrifice for the cause, not even financially. On January 29 Theodor Mommsen wrote to Gustav Freytag, ". . . I have
completely given up the idea that the nation will interfere with
real energy." A few days later he commented, "What calls itself
the German Progressive Party is on the whole but a negative
mass. . . ."[9] Although there was again talk of a tax boycott, those
who may have taken it seriously were soon disabused. On returning home one of Waldeck's supporters, Saucken-Tarputschen,
wrote, ". . . the feudal party is fast gaining ground among all
those who are in any way dependent, and a large part of the
farmers are like soft wax, to be molded by anyone who knows how
to approach them. The Berliners have no conception how things
actually are in the country."[10]

Into this political vacuum now rushed the first great achievement of the Bismarck cabinet and the reorganized army. On January 30 Johann Gustav Droysen reported that the army was
jubilant over the prospect of war. After the opening battle he
expected a similar mood among the public. "Bets are being made
that with the first successes Herr von Bismarck will become popular." Indeed the dramatic victory at Düppel filled army and
nation with pride. For the first time in half a century Prussian
troops had tasted victory. In April and May, Bernhardi, a supporter of Augustenburg, detected a "very perceptible reversal of
public opinion" in Bismarck's favor. "If he should now dissolve

9 *HW*, I, 210-216.
10 Parisius, *Hoverbeck*, II/2, 1-2, 19.

the chamber, he would gain 100 seats."[11] The magnetism of national power had begun to exert its compulsive pull.

2. POWER OR RIGHT?

During January Bismarck had commenced to stir up Prussian national sentiment in preparation for annexation. Accused of "wanting to ignore Germany," he charged in turn that the deputies "wanted to ignore Prussia." They wished Prussia to exist "as the domain of the Nationalverein or not at all. To gain their confidence the cabinet would have to "depart from the Prussian constitution . . . from Prussia's traditions, from Prussia's history, from Prussian popular feeling." Repeatedly he harped upon this theme. "An open profession of the Prussian interest, of Prussian nationalism is not to be found on your side. . . . You reject the Prussian *Volksgeist*. . . . You reject the glorious traditions of our past, for you disavow the position, the great power position, of Prussia acquired through heavy sacrifice in the people's blood and property."[12]

In May 1864 came the petition of Arnim-Boitzenburg for annexation. Within weeks it had accumulated 70,000 signatures, chiefly from conservatives and right-wing liberals. While leaving open the possibility of either Prussian annexation or a protectorate, the document leaned toward the former. Many conservatives who in the beginning had favored Augustenburg and been repelled by his alliance with the liberals found in annexation a welcome alternative. While a few of the romantic school, like Ludwig Gerlach, were morally outraged by the idea, most found the renewal of Prussian *Machtpolitik* "irresistibly attractive."[13] But the liberals too were affected by the prospect of territorial gain.

Before Düppel and the London conference, to be sure, the Augustenburg phalanx remained fairly intact. In April 1864 the "thirty-six committee" drafted a declaration affirming that the

[11] R. Hübner, ed., *Johann Gustav Droysen: Briefwechsel* (Stuttgart, 1928), II, 830; *Aus dem Leben Bernhardis*, VI, 89, 102, 110-111, 116. Some cabinet members wished to exploit the victory by dissolving parliament, but Bismarck and Roon decided otherwise. Nearly a year passed between the end of the 1863-1864 session and the beginning of that of 1865. *GW*, XIV, 670; Roon, *Denkwürdigkeiten*, II, 257-258. Horst Kohl, "Aus der Korrespondenz des Grafen Friedrich Eulenburg mit dem Fürsten Bismarck," *Deutsche Revue*, Vol. 25/1 (1900), pp. 43-44.

[12] Kohl, *Reden*, II, 264-283. "I wouldn't mind," he lamented to Below-Hohendorf in May 1864, "if our nation were so strongly inflated by Prussian pride that the government would have to moderate, rather than vivify it." *GW*, XIV, 667.

[13] Ritter, *Konservativen*, pp. 100 ff.

duchies belonged to the prince both by inheritance and popular will and denying the right of an international conference to decide otherwise. Ultimately the document was signed by 1,362 deputies of various parliaments, of whom 186 were members of the Prussian Left Center and Progressive Parties. Scornfully Waldeck denied their right to speak for the German nation or to dispose of what had been gained through the "independent military and diplomatic action" of Prussia. Nevertheless, eighteen of his thirty-five supporters, made uncertain by the conservative campaign for annexation, now switched to Augustenburg.[14]

As the news of victory sped over the telegraph wires, the liberal front began to dissolve. The *Preussische Jahrbücher*, which in November 1863 had come out for Augustenburg, concluded in May 1864 that annexation would be a "more national goal than the creation of a small state" and in September that Prussian self-interest alone was adequate reason for demanding the duchies.[15] In December Wilhelm Wehrenpfennig, editor since Haym's retirement in June, accepted an article by Ludwig Häusser opposing annexation, but immediately engaged Treitschke to write a reply. Earlier an ardent supporter of Augustenburg, the volatile historian had completely reversed himself. He reveled in the display of military power at Düppel and returned to his earlier conviction that only Prussian expansion could create the unity capable of ending German particularism and the political impotence which was its consequence. According to Wehrenpfennig, the Treitschke article, a good example of his fiery eloquence, had considerable impact upon the deputies in Berlin.[16]

On November 9, 1864, Bennigsen reported, "The Bismarck course (that is, the worship of military power and diplomatic success) is growing in a shocking way." Soon afterward Wehrenpfennig wrote that the question of annexation had "wrought havoc among all political parties." While most old liberals had been won over, the Left Center and Progressive Parties were deeply

[14] Parisius, *Hoverbeck*, II/2, 4-7, 21-22.

[15] Friedrich C. Sell, *Die Tragödie des deutschen Liberalismus* (Stuttgart, 1953), pp. 211 ff.; *Preussische Jahrbücher*, XII (1863), 540 ff.; XIII (1864), 661 ff.; XIV (1864), 456 ff.

[16] *HW*, I, 223-234, 237, 243; *Preussische Jahrbücher*, XV (1865), 84 ff., 169 ff. Bennigsen's friend, Victor Böhmert, thought the article had "an enormous effect." Hermann Oncken, *Rudolf von Bennigsen* (Stuttgart, 1910), I, 655. On Treitschke's shift in viewpoint see Andreas Dorpalen, *Heinrich von Treitschke* (New Haven, 1957), pp. 88-89, 98-99, and Katsch, *Treitschke*, pp. 64 ff.

split. Of the progressive leaders only Virchow, Rönne, Franz Duncker, and Schulze-Delitzsch held to their original position, while Mommsen and Twesten (both natives of Schleswig-Holstein) led the fight for annexation. An eminent historian and liberal of unquestioned integrity, Mommsen's views carried considerable weight. Like Treitschke, he believed that Germany's primary problem was unity and that it could be achieved only through the expansion of Prussian power and creation of a strong executive. Despite all his difficulties with the existing government, Twesten again followed the course dictated by his conscience. He deplored the attitude of unconditional opposition which gripped many of the deputies and was willing to support the cause of a greater Prussia even if it strengthened the Bismarck cabinet.[17]

Nevertheless, the annexationists were troubled by a basic dilemma. Their case against Denmark had always been based upon the liberal principle of national self-determination. Yet it was evident that most inhabitants of the duchies favored Augustenburg. Wehrenpfennig got over the difficulty by believing that pride in the power and prestige of the state—"the most valuable possession of the citizen"—would surely win them to Prussian rule. In his article Treitschke argued that the Schleswig-Holsteiners could not be permitted to decide an issue affecting the whole of Germany. A small independent principality would have much less prospect of Germanizing the Danes in northern Schleswig. Even Mommsen, a man of firmer liberal conviction than Treitschke, maintained that the right of self-determination, while basic to the liberal creed, must be limited where the general interest of the German nation was concerned.[18]

But many found these arguments unconvincing. So deep was the division of opinion that the chamber of deputies was unable to adopt anything more than a "passive" attitude during the session of 1865. It was an "evil situation."[19] To go on record for annexation meant capitulation to the principle of "power over right," violation of the principle of self-determination, and sur-

17 Oncken, *Bennigsen*, I, 647; Duncker, *Briefwechsel*, pp. 380-381; *HW*, I, 234, 246-249, 251. Concerning Mommsen's views on the Schleswig-Holstein question see Alfred Heuss, *Theodor Mommsen und das 19. Jahrhundert* (Kiel, 1956), pp. 172 ff., and Albert Wucher, *Theodor Mommsen, Geschichtsschreibung und Politik* (Göttingen, 1956), pp. 151 ff.

18 *HW*, I, 236, 253-255; *Preussische Jahrbücher*, Vol. 15 (1865), pp. 179 ff.; Wucher, *Mommsen*, pp. 181-182.

19 *HW*, I, 186, 243.

render to the Bismarck cabinet on a vital issue. To reject annexation was to deny Prussia her reward for military success, increase the number of small states, sacrifice the prospect of Prussian naval power, and lose the chance for progress toward German unity through the expansion of Prussia. The liberals divided according to which of these considerations they gave the greater value.

Upon one point, nevertheless, there was little disagreement: if Augustenburg were to rule the duchies, their sovereignty must be sharply limited in favor of Prussia. Journals of all political viewpoints adopted Bismarck's February conditions as the minimum program acceptable to Prussia. Remembering the humiliating fate of the navy of 1848, the liberals were enticed by the prospect of Prussian naval power.[20] With the approval of Augustenburg leading members of the thirty-six committee and Nationalverein assembled in Berlin in March 1865 to accept most of the conditions.[21]

Yet the Augustenburg cause continued to wither. At Bismarck's request, the Prussian "crown syndicate" (a tribunal composed of members of the house of lords) had been asked for a judgment on the prince's claims. After solemn deliberation the lords ruled that the lawful heir to the duchies was the King of Denmark! William at least was convinced. Bismarck's next gambit was to publish his one-sided account of the talk with Frederick in June 1864. Fearing to be "trapped" by a lawsuit, the prince issued no public denial. The consequence was that many deputies came to believe the charge of his ingratitude and deserted his cause.[22]

The drift in Prussia toward annexation created new tensions within the German liberal-national movement. There had long been a precarious balance between the advocates of a federal and a centralistic German union, but also between the moderates, who were willing to compromise with an authoritarian Prussia, and the democrats (particularly in south Germany), who wished a more decisive stand against the regime in Berlin. Bismarck's policy

[20] Oncken, *Bennigsen*, I, 657, 672-674; Otto Bandmann, *Die deutsche Presse und die nationale Frage, 1864-1866* (Leipzig, 1909), pp. 22 ff. The navy had been sold at auction during the reaction.

[21] This was the so-called "Berlin compromise." Not accepted were the oath to the Prussian flag, Prussian control of conscription, and Prussian administration of customs, post, and telegraph. Oncken, *Bennigsen*, I, 661.

[22] Eyck, *Bismarck*, II, 45-47; Parisius, *Hoverbeck*, II/2, 58.

of self-interest, the support it attracted in Prussia, and the revulsion it aroused among southerners threatened to split the national movement along the axis of the Main.[23]

In September 1865 the cleavage became glaringly evident in the response to the call of the "thirty-six committee" for another congress of German deputies to be held in Frankfurt. The purpose was to condemn the Gastein treaty. At a caucus in Berlin most of the Prussian deputies voted not to attend. In public letters Mommsen and Twesten explained that the majority regarded the rally as an attack upon the Prussian state itself, not merely upon its existing government. Only the Prussian state was capable of unifying Germany. From the south came public replies from Wilhelm Schaffrath and Julius Frese. "No German," warned the former, "wants a Germany without Prussia, but neither does any German want the absorption of Germany into Prussia." If the Prussian deputies must as a matter of duty support Bismarck's foreign policy, Frese continued, this meant the end of the constitutional conflict. They must choose between "the politics of power and the politics of right."[24]

But even the Augustenburg faction in Berlin felt compelled to stay away from Frankfurt. Schulze-Delitzsch explained that by attending they would "compromise" their position at home. They would "discredit" themselves with the electorate and drive the annexationist liberals into the arms of Bismarck. Unruh put it more bluntly, "We are ready to let ourselves be locked up, but not on account of a spectacle doomed in advance to failure." Edward Lasker, newly elected to parliament in a Berlin by-election, felt that the convention would only serve to reveal the cleavages within the national movement. "Schleswig-Holstein has taught me," he confessed, "that the feeling of unity is not yet sufficiently developed for an instinctive solution of the German question. For the present, German unity still cannot expect any adequate help from the masses."[25]

Months before its final trial German liberal nationalism had

[23] Oncken, *Bennigsen*, I, 644 ff.; Friedrich Thorwart, ed., *Hermann Schulze-Delitzschs Schriften und Reden* (Berlin, 1909-1913), III, 221 ff. Bandmann, *Deutsche Presse*, pp. 33 ff.; Schieder, *Kleindeutsche Partei*, pp. 41-92.

[24] *HW*, I, 253-262. Bennigsen, who did his best to bridge the fissures, felt that the summons to Frankfurt, the work of south German radicals, was "folly." Oncken, *Bennigsen*, I, 671.

[25] Oncken, *Bennigsen*, I, 672-674; Thorwart, *Schulze-Delitzsch*, III, 240-254; *HW*, I, 263.

been split apart by the Schleswig-Holstein question. But even now the first doubt had been raised whether it was supported any more in its nationalism than in its liberalism by the German people as a whole.

3. PARLIAMENT IN 1865

The victory over Denmark also embarrassed the liberals on the issue of military reform. In January 1864 Sybel wrote that in the Rhineland many were saying, "Apparently the reorganization has proved itself militarily after all." Following Düppel, Hermann Baumgarten reported that in Karlsruhe the military reform was considered a *"fait accompli,"* and Karl Mathy, a Baden minister, advised the progressives to surrender on this point, lest "the idea of the state" be lost. Both proposed compromise: the military bill for recognition of parliament's budget rights. But Mathy's soundings showed that the mood of the progressives was unchanged. Sybel reported that not even twenty votes were to be had for such a bargain; the king, moreover, would just "laugh" at the idea. On December 16 twenty-five leading deputies caucused to consider their strategy in the coming session. They resolved to stand fast on the military issue and be "as passive as possible" on foreign policy.[26]

When the term commenced in January 1865, nevertheless, many deputies yearned for a settlement. According to Georg von Seydlitz, the conviction was growing that "the general public is weary of this dispute." Should it last much longer, the country would learn to accept the policies of the government and bask in the reflection of its military achievements. A few months before, Twesten had observed with bitterness that "from day to day" both the officials and common citizens were becoming "more servile."[27]

Because of the imminence of war with Austria, Bismarck and Roon were also inclined toward compromise. The speech from the throne which opened parliament on January 14 expressed an "urgent wish" for the adjustment of differences. The military bill which the government presented soon afterward was the same as that previously rejected by the chamber, but the two ministers were willing to consider amendments. In the palace they broached

---

[26] *HW*, I, 217, 223-224, 229-230.

[27] Martin Philippson, *Max von Forckenbeck, Ein Lebensbild* (Dresden, 1898), pp. 124-125; *HW*, I, 228, 231, 240-241.

once more the scheme William had rejected in October 1862. The three-year service period was to be reduced and the size and financial support of the army geared to the increase in population. But again William was negative. Next they turned to the amendment introduced by Eduard von Bonin, an old liberal and former minister of war. The three-year period would be kept, but the standing army limited to 160,000 men. Such a limitation, William replied, was "nothing less than an expression of mistrust against me personally."[28] Nor was the chamber sympathetic to the idea. After a debate marked by an acrimonious exchange between Gneist and Roon the entire bill was rejected.[29]

Despite the doubts it raised in many minds, the Schleswig-Holstein affair had by no means stilled the spirit of opposition in the chamber. The few conciliatory words in the throne speech were lost in a vigorous reassertion of the crown's position. After re-election as speaker, Grabow delivered his usual scathing indictment of the government; "no power on earth" could budge the deputies in their "reverence for constitutional right." Against the arguments of Wehrenpfennig, Bockum-Dolffs maintained that even at the cost of abandoning Schleswig-Holstein the deputies must continue to uphold the constitution. The leader of the Left Center was supported in this view by many progressives. Despite some desertions, Schulze-Delitzsch declared, the "entire liberal party" was ready to continue the struggle against the "Bismarck system without regard for the victory swindle."[30]

The debate on the budget bill for 1865 took the usual course. Once more the motion of Hoverbeck, Virchow, and others for outright rejection without amendment was turned down. Forckenbeck voted against it because such a "dangerous demonstration" ought logically to be followed by a tax boycott, for which there was no public support. Once again the deputies struck from the budget, along with other items, the funds requested for military reorganization. But this year they were faced with a new problem. Collection of the real estate tax passed in 1861 was to begin in 1865. Its yield would reinforce the financial independence of the

[28] *SBHA* (1865), I, 1-4; *Aus dem Leben Bernhardis*, VI, 169-170, 177-178, 200, 209; Roon, *Denkwürdigkeiten*, II, 325-326, 331-334. There is evidence that as early as the summer of 1864 Roon had negotiated with the moderates on the terms of the Bonin amendment. *HW*, I, 238-239.

[29] *SBHA* (1865), II, 1196-1355; VI, 878-893.

[30] *HW*, I, 238-239, 242-243; *Aus dem Leben Bernhardis*, VI, 180; Oncken, *Bennigsen*, I, 657.

crown. Waldeck's proposal that the chamber simply strike the tax out of the budget on the grounds that the Landtag of 1861 had no power to legislate for 1865 was rejected. Instead the deputies futilely insisted that the yield from the tax be limited to the sum originally estimated.[31]

Aware of their weakened position, the deputies tried to advance a program of greater popular appeal. The "naked legal question" of constitutional rights, they realized, had little interest for the lower classes; it was necessary to state their case in terms of the "material" welfare of the public. The budget committee prepared a "general report" surveying the entire financial structure of the state and ending with the recommendation that the sums clipped from the military budget be used for "productive purposes" such as river improvement, road construction, land reclamation, science and education, with salary increases to teachers, lesser officials, soldiers, and non-commissioned officers.[32] Against power and patriotism the deputies raised the standard of financial self-interest.

But not even in this field were they able to assert themselves. The government presented a series of bills dealing with economic matters whose obvious purpose was to divide the chamber and, in the event of rejection, to discredit it. To be sure, the Zollverein treaties were readily accepted; economic unity and free trade were important chapters in the liberal textbook. Nevertheless, they were an uncomfortable reminder of a signal success in Bismarck's diplomacy. Other bills on state aid for railway construction threw the deputies into confusion. No issue, Hoverbeck observed, was more suited to split the majority into warring factions. Principle conflicted with local self-interest, and the latter conquered. The proposal of Michaelis, a progressive, that the chamber refuse even to consider the bills until a legal budget was in existence was voted down 178 to 108. Over the protests of the *laissez-faire* faction and democratic liberals, all but one of the measures was then accepted.[33] A government bill to extend the operations of the Bank of Prussia throughout Germany, on the

[31] Philippson, *Forckenbeck*, p. 132; Parisius, *Hoverbeck*, II/2, 47-48; Oppenheim, *Waldeck*, p. 199; *SBHA* (1865), I, 471 ff.; V, 466-467.

[32] Parisius, *Hoverbeck*, II/2, 28-29; *SBHA* (1865), V, 433-469; Philippson, *Forckenbeck*, pp. 122-129; Fritz Löwenthal, *Der preussische Verfassungsstreit, 1862-1866* (Munich, 1914), pp. 236-237.

[33] Parisius, *Hoverbeck*, II/2, 30-33; *SBHA* (1865), II, 779-796, 813-853, 1117-1133, 2141-2151. See also Werner Schunke, *Die preussischen Freihändler und die Entstehung der nationalliberalen Partei* (Leipzig, 1916), pp. 23 ff.

other hand, was rejected, despite the support of important commercial interests.[34]

The tactical purpose of two other bills was equally evident. Tongue in cheek, the minister of finance asked the chamber to approve the government's financing of the recent war: the expenditure of 1,300,000 *Thaler* withdrawn from the treasury and 12,-000,000 *Thaler* in surplus revenues piled up by a booming economy in 1863-1864. Despite Twesten's admission that Bismarck's diplomacy had been "bold, clever, successful," the deputies felt compelled to reject the request and with it an amendment from Wagener calling for annexation of the duchies. On that very day they had resolved to hold cabinet members liable for funds taken from the public treasury without parliamentary approval.[35] The naval construction bill was equally harassing. To build two armed frigates and a naval base at Kiel 19,600,000 *Thaler* were requested, of which 10,000,000 were to be borrowed. Since 1848 naval power had been a favorite cause of German liberal nationalism. The suitability of Kiel as a naval base was one of the motives behind the swing toward annexation in Prussia. In the budget bill of 1865 the finance committee had voluntarily increased by more than one million *Thaler* the amount of the naval appropriation. But now the deputies, laden with embarrassment, had to reject the naval bill on the ground that without a legal budget no new funds could be granted the government.[36]

His enemies were exposed, and Bismarck struck with malicious skill. Like the false mother in the judgment of Solomon, the liberals would rather condemn the child than lose it. For twenty years Germany had dreamed of a fleet. Now that it was within reach the chamber was "impotently negative." The deputies accused him of incompetence; yet he had achieved over their obstruction what they themselves had demanded: the reconstruction of the Zollverein and the separation of Schleswig-Holstein from Denmark. All that stood in the way of a settlement with Augustenburg was the validation of his claims and acceptance of the February conditions. To fight the policy of the government was

[34] *SBHA* (1865), ii, 856-909.

[35] *Ibid.*, vii, 1549-1593; iii, 2087-2139.

[36] *SBHA* (1865), iii, 1833-1903; viii, 1601-1615; Löwenthal, *Verfassungsstreit*, pp. 242-243. In April 1864 Gustav Droysen, previously a supporter of Augustenburg, wrote that Prussia's next task was *"dominium maris baltici."* Droysen, *Briefwechsel*, ii, 836.

to fight one's own country in league with its enemies.[37] On June 17 the Landtag was prorogued.

The parliamentary term of 1865, longest of the constitutional conflict, marked yet another stage in the deterioration of the Prussian opposition. Cloven in one direction by the issue of annexation, they were riven in another by that of the priority between external power and internal right. Still other fissures were opened up by the bank and railway bills. In mid-March a liberal editor, August Lammers, wrote of an "unbelievable disorganization" in the liberal majority. "Instead of a single united party, we have ten to twenty little factions." Although some, like Twesten and Mommsen, were impressed by Bismarck's parliamentary performance in June, the effect was marred by an unfortunate incident. For questioning Bismarck's veracity Virchow received a challenge. Although the affair was settled without bullets, the deputies regarded it as another assault upon parliamentary freedom. Mommsen reported, "The Bismarck-madness is spreading here with every passing day." Among the deputies there was now only a single issue: "for or against Bismarck."[38]

The strategy Bismarck had planned in 1862 was proving successful. Many deputies were weary of the struggle, worn out by endless friction and frustration. As the years passed, parliamentary life seemed less and less realistic. While the cabinet submitted bills which had no chance of becoming law, the opposition deliberated endlessly upon amendments which had no chance of acceptance by the crown. While the deputies resolved and petitioned, the ministers governed the country independent of every parliamentary influence. Most discouraging of all was the revelation that Bismarck had been right in declaring that the government could carry on war with or without parliament's consent. What did it achieve to declare ministers liable for the unconstitutional disposal of public funds, when the house possessed no means with which to bring them to account?

By two further acts, committed soon after parliament adjourned, the ministers showed how little impressed they were by the threat. On July 5, the cabinet published in the official *Staatsanzeiger* the budget approved by the king, including provisions for

[37] Kohl, *Reden*, II, 353 ff., 378 ff.; see also *GW*, v, 161.
[38] *HW*, I, 244-245, 250-251; *SBHA* (1865), VII, 1886, 1897-1903, 1956-1964; *GW*, XIV, 695.

the construction and arming of the fleet. It had the appearance of a royal decree. A month later, the cabinet approved, without consulting parliament, a contract by which the government sold its right to purchase the stock of the Cologne-Minden railway. In securing the measure Bismarck overrode the legal scruples of Bodelschwingh and Itzenplitz. By this fresh breach of the constitution the crown acquired thirteen million *Thaler* with which either to purchase Austrian rights in Schleswig-Holstein or finance a future mobilization against her.[39]

Some deputies took comfort in the belief that the house had at least scored a great "moral success" with the public by its unyielding stand. But Hoverbeck feared this an "illusion." On returning home in June he wrote, "Those circles of the population which read newspapers at all or concern themselves in some degree with politics have long ago taken their position on these questions." Many had been driven by official pressure either into silence or into changing their views. "All our deliberations," he confessed, "have had no influence upon the great masses of the people, that is, upon the voters of the third and, in part, the second classes, for they never hear anything about them." Those who work for popular freedom, he concluded, "do not stand on solid ground." A fresh election might easily bring Prussia back to "naked absolutism."[40]

4. PREPARATIONS FOR A ''COUP D'ÉTAT''

Hoverbeck was not alone in this thought. Many ultra-conservatives longed for an "inner Düppel," which would destroy the constitution and restore absolutism. After a talk with Alvensleben, Bernhardi concluded that the "camarilla" reactionaries wished to make Edwin Manteuffel minister-president to carry out the coup. Within the cabinet Bismarck's colleagues pressed for action, and William was similarly inclined. But the Junker believed the time was not yet ripe.[41] In a crown council on June 19, 1865, he confessed that for a long time it had been his conviction that Prussia could not be ruled under the existing constitution. The "blow"

39 *Staatsarchiv*, x, 74 ff.; Löwenthal, *Verfassungsstreit*, pp. 268-271; Schunke, *Freihändler*, pp. 26-27; *GW*, xiv, 697-698.
40 Parisius, *Hoverbeck*, ii/2, 53-56.
41 Ritter, *Konservativen*, pp. 116-118; *Aus dem Leben Bernhardis*, vi, 171-172; Duncker, *Briefwechsel*, p. 392; Heinrich O. Meisner, ed., *Kaiser Friedrich III., Tagebücher von 1848-1866* (Leipzig, 1929), pp. 530-533.

must come either during the coming winter or the following one. It must be prepared by more vigorous steps against liberal deputies and civil servants.[42]

Since 1863 the pressure upon opposition deputies and civil servants had been unrelenting. After the election of that year severe reprisals were carried out against liberal voters, electors, and candidates.[43] Jacoby, one of the few surviving radicals, was sentenced to six months in prison for lese majesty. Seventeen east Prussian deputies were prosecuted and fined because of an election broadside mildly critical of the cabinet. Similar cases were initiated against Deputies Möller, Leeden, Lüning, Frese, and Franz Duncker. Conscience itself, declared Waldeck, was on trial. After the Landtag's close in June 1865 the citizens of Cologne refused to commemorate the fiftieth anniversary of the Rhineland's union with Prussia and chose instead to honor the returning opposition deputies. Eighty deputies appeared, but they were repeatedly blocked by the police from convening. Newspapers critical of this interference with the right of free assembly were confiscated.[44]

Firms connected in some way with the opposition were passed over in the purchase of military supplies. Liberal physicians were ignored for positions in public health. Lottery collectors and bank agents lost their franchises. Masonic lodges were admonished to support the crown. Liberal mayors chosen by municipal parliaments were not confirmed by the government. After the same candidate had been repeatedly re-elected in Königsberg and rejected by Berlin, the government arbitrarily appointed a "commissar" to administer the city. Eight of nine members elected to the Berlin city council in 1865 were not confirmed, and one was arbitrarily replaced by a government agent. In May 1864 Bismarck succeeded in getting William to approve salary increases for judges on the basis of political conformity rather than seniority. Count Lippe, the minister of justice, objected that

[42] Stern, *Geschichte Europas*, ix, 587. See also Ludwig Gerlach, *Aufzeichnungen*, II, 273.

[43] See particularly the report of the investigating committee of the chamber of deputies. *SBHA* (1863-1864), IV, 624 ff.

[44] H. Schulthess, ed., *Europäischer Geschichtskalender* (1864), p. 168; (1865), pp. 172-175, 180; *SBHA* (1865), I, 374-381; (1866), I, 13-14, 34-35, 185-186; Parisius, *Hoverbeck*, II/2, 56-61. Of 253 deputies invited, only 160 accepted, of whom only half appeared. The east Prussian deputies declined on the grounds that there was nothing to celebrate.

"rule and right" ought to prevail, but Bismarck replied, "The government must reward its friends and punish its enemies."[45]

Within the judiciary there was constant conflict between liberal and conservative judges. While most lower courts were presided over by liberals, the higher tribunals were a near monopoly of the conservatives. The fate of cases brought against the treasury by officials who had been assessed the cost of substitutes while serving in parliament was typical. Most plaintiffs won in the courts of first instance, while only a few survived the second, and the rest lost in the supreme court. The liberal judges on the latter tribunal, of whom Waldeck was one, were outnumbered by a reactionary majority. Sitting as the "disciplinary senate" of the civil service, the supreme court issued two decisions in September 1863 and October 1864 which read political meaning into the law of 1851, under which judges might be punished for unbecoming conduct.[46] The courts were no longer inviolable.

"For those in disfavor," lamented Hoverbeck, "there is no justice any more in Prussia!" He feared that this "very systematic" attack would silence the bureaucratic opposition in the next election with disastrous consequences for the liberal cause. "Are our people independent and perspicacious enough to find out by themselves what is right and especially in the face of such pressure? One could doubt it. It is very possible that through intimidation the reaction will conquer." Weary of "ineffectual opposition," the progressive leader was even inclined to hope for a government coup which would end the struggle. Open absolutism was better than the existing state of affairs. At the end he foresaw the dread possibility—after a "terrible deterioration in the entire character of the people"—of popular revolution.[47]

Not all civil servants were easy to silence. On May 20, 1865, Twesten delivered in the chamber of deputies a blistering indictment of Lippe and the government for converting the courts into instruments of political oppression. The treasured Prussian tradition of an independent judiciary was now only an "illusion." Decisions of the supreme court were no longer based upon law, but upon the "interests and prejudices of the ruling party." As a county judge Twesten was well acquainted with conditions in

---

[45] Parisius, *Hoverbeck*, II/2, 15; Schulthess, *Geschichtskalender* (1865), pp. 170, 174, 176, 180; *Aus dem Leben Bernhardis*, v, 160-161; vi, 118; *HW*, i, 231.
[46] Parisius, *Hoverbeck*, II/2, 23-24.   [47] *Ibid.*, pp. 15-16.

the judiciary and had himself been repeatedly "disciplined" for political activities. On June 2 Deputy Frentzel, previously the victim of two months' imprisonment for lese majesty, also attacked the government for destroying the Prussian tradition of the *Rechtsstaat*. Two weeks later the house of lords called upon the government to prosecute "defamatory and other criminal utterances" in the lower chamber. In the crown council of the 19th Bismarck advocated the prosecution of Twesten and Frentzel. Now he was ready to pursue the opposition into the sacred sanctuary of parliament itself.[48]

But still he had no intention of resorting to open absolutism. As before he was well aware that repression must be accompanied by positive efforts to attract the support of the masses. Roon hinted to Bernhardi that "appropriate liberal arrangements" were being considered, not a relapse into "Caesarism."[49] On June 17 Bismarck had informed Max Duncker that, should the next session of the Landtag turn out like the last, there were but two choices: either a convention to revise the constitution or "simply the re-establishment of direct and universal suffrage."[50]

Nevertheless, the old difficulties remained. Equal suffrage could not in itself supply the answer to the government's need. There had to be some assurance that, when given the vote, the masses would actually use it to elect deputies favorable to the government. While aware that the lower classes were not behind the liberals, Bismarck could not be sure that they were behind the government. What seemed more likely was that, at least where the artisan and factory workers were concerned, there existed a political void which could be filled by the crown only through concrete steps to care for their material wants.

5. AN EXPERIMENT IN SOCIAL REFORM

Despite his absorption in foreign affairs, Bismarck did not lose sight of the problem of social reform during 1864-1866. Again

---

[48] *SBHA* (1865), I, 284-299; *SBHH* (1865), I, 299.

[49] *Aus dem Leben Bernhardis*, VI, 209; see also Roon, *Denkwürdigkeiten*, II, 337, 346, 348-350.

[50] He added significantly, "It is also possible that foreign affairs may give public opinion a different direction." Friedrich III, *Tagebücher 1848-1866*, pp. 532-533. In the crown council of June 19 Eulenburg stated that the electoral law could only be changed in the direction of universal suffrage, but expressed serious doubts about the wisdom of such a step; once taken, it could never be recalled. Stern, *Geschichte Europas*, IX, 587.

his colleagues were hostile to his ideas and probably resentful of his interference. In May 1863 he pressed Itzenplitz to draft a bill legalizing trade unions. But the minister was doubtful and dilatory; not until December 1864 did the matter reach the cabinet. Before the ministers could act, such a bill was introduced in the lower chamber by a group of deputies headed by Schulze-Delitzsch. Speaking for the cabinet, Itzenplitz favored legalization, but only in combination with "positive measures," such as workers' cooperatives, for the amelioration of social distress. Wagener taunted the liberal deputies with the specter of universal suffrage, state-supported cooperatives, and a proletariat hostile to the bourgeoisie. Nevertheless, the bill presented to parliament in February 1866 and finally passed in 1869 granted the right to unionize, but made no mention of cooperatives. Bismarck's retreat on this point was partly owing to the failure of his model cooperative in Silesia.[51]

By halting the flow of raw cotton, the American civil war had plunged the Silesian textile industry into depression. In October 1862 the factory owners of Reichenbach county, including Leonor Reichenheim, a liberal member of parliament, had proposed construction of a work-house. They were infuriated by the way in which the local *Landrat*, Olearius, rejected the idea in a report which came to Bismarck's attention. "It is purely a question of saving from hunger a large number of people," Olearius declared, "who have fallen into need through no fault of their own, who have scarcely ever had the chance to save a penny for such a situation, and through whose effort others have become rich. For them a work-house?"[52]

In May 1864 a delegation of three weavers, sent by 200 workers of the Reichenheim works in Wüstegiersdorf, appeared in Berlin. Through Olearius and Wagener they reached Bismarck who, over the opposition of Eulenburg and the provincial governor, saw to it that they were sympathetically received by the

---

[51] Adolf Richter, *Bismarck und die Arbeiterfrage im preussischen Verfassungskonflikt* (Stuttgart, 1935), pp. 252-257; *SBHA* (1865), i, 119-202; iv, 208, 312-316. The motives of the liberals were mixed. Freedom to organize was regarded as a fundamental right like industrial freedom. Being the weaker party, labor had greater need of that right than capital. As long as the prohibition was in effect, the workers would suffer from the delusion that what held down their wages was the law of the state, not the "natural law" of supply and demand in the labor market.

[52] Richter, *Arbeiterfrage*, pp. 37-47; *SBHA* (1863), i, 23-28; iii, 1-2.

king. But a committee of inquiry, appointed to investigate the matter, delivered a report favorable to the owners. Adopted without essential change by the ministries of interior and commerce, it reached Bismarck in the summer of 1865.[53] A few days after Gastein, he took time out from diplomacy to write a devastating, fifty-seven page critique of its contents. The bias of the committee, he charged, was evident from its procedure. While justifying successive reductions in wages, it had made no investigation of business profits. The problem was one of actual conditions, not doctrines. He rejected the argument that, since the state could not make a general practice of alleviating social distress, it could not help the Silesian weavers. "Ought it therefore to help no one? *Der Staat kann.*"[54]

Meanwhile, Bismarck had directed Olearius to found and subsidize a model producers' cooperative in Wüstegiersdorf, employing the workers discharged by Reichenheim for petitioning the king. From the outset the experiment was plagued with difficulties. Although eleven weavers joined the project, the *Landrat* had trouble locating materials and quarters. The men were accustomed to cotton yarn, but all Olearius could supply was linen. The quality of the product was poor, and no regular market could be found. An attempt to get soldiers to buy it failed. Itzenplitz bought a few bolts, and Eulenburg tried vainly to get his friends to buy. Two weavers were sent with merchandise to the Frankfurt fair, but sold below cost. When the American conflict ended, the value of the yarn in stock fell precipitously. The weavers quarreled and intrigued against each other; Olearius concluded that they had always regarded the project as a "milk cow." Finally he was compelled to liquidate the venture.[55]

Bismarck was very disappointed. In February 1865 he had defended the experiment in the Landtag against the attacks of

---

[53] Heinrich von Poschinger, ed., *Aktenstücke zur Wirtschaftspolitik des Fürsten Bismarck* (Berlin, 1890), I, 20-25, 30-33, 49; *GW*, IV, 442; Richter, *Arbeiterfrage*, pp. 53 ff.

[54] *Ibid.*, pp. 92-117, 235 ff. Unfortunately this document was never published in full. See the excerpts in Hans Rothfels, ed., *Otto von Bismarck: Deutscher Staat* (Munich, 1925), pp. 353-360, and Poschinger, *Aktenstücke zur Wirtschaftspolitik*, I, 62-65. The ministers accepted many changes proposed by Bismarck, but the final report was not completed until July 1867. At that time its publication was decided against on the grounds that the issue was no longer so important "since the events of last summer." Richter, *Arbeiterfrage*, pp. 247-248.

[55] Richter, *Arbeiterfrage*, pp. 63-91.

Reichenheim and others with the ringing words, "The kings of Prussia have never been exclusively the kings of the rich." He had hoped Wüstegiersdorf would serve as the model for a large-scale program for the founding of artisan cooperatives. After its failure he limited state aid to existing organizations. During 1865-1866 he repeatedly intervened in behalf of cooperative banks and producers' associations threatened with bankruptcy. His aim was admittedly to demonstrate to the workers the inadequacy of the private support advocated by Schulze-Delitzsch and the liberals. To the same end he backed a plan to found a home for invalided workers and a proposal to shift the tax burden imposed on the lower classes during the new era to the merchants and manufacturers.[56]

As in the 1880's, these experiments in social reform were accompanied by acts of repression against the proletarian movement. After his death Lassalle's workers' association had continued to grow, despite the squabbling of its leaders. In January 1865 the first party journal, *Der Sozialdemokrat*, edited by J. B. von Schweitzer, began publication in Berlin. The early issues carried an evaluation of Bismarck's "Caesarism" in foreign and social policy so favorable that Marx, Engels, and Liebknecht severed relations with the journal. Through Countess Hatzfeld the bearded Zeus of proletarian radicalism had learned of Lassalle's talks with Bismarck. There were rumors that Schweitzer was in the pay of the government. In July, however, the *Sozialdemokrat* attacked the government for suppressing the Cologne festival and called for mass meetings of protest. The government's reaction was severe. Issues of the journal were repeatedly confiscated; the Berlin branch of the workers' association was dissolved by police order; Liebknecht and Bernhard Becker, Lassalle's successor, were given twenty-four hours to leave the country; Schweitzer, a naturalized citizen, was sentenced to sixteen months and the loss of his civic rights for a year.[57]

[56] Kohl, *Reden*, ii, 317; Poschinger, *Aktenstücke zur Wirtschaftspolitik*, i, 32-33, 54, 68-70, 76, 78-83; *GW*, v, 335, 384-385; xiv, 691; Karl Thieme, "Bismarcks Sozialpolitik," *Archiv für Politik und Geschichte*, ix (1927), 386.

[57] Gustav Mayer, *Johann Baptist von Schweitzer und die Sozialdemokratie* (Jena, 1909), pp. 110-142; Franz Mehring, *Geschichte der deutschen Sozialdemokratie* (Stuttgart, 1903), iii, 195 ff.; Schulthess, *Geschichtskalender* (1865), p. 175. That there was a connection early in 1865 between the government and the *Sozialdemokrat* is confirmed by the fact that Eugen Dühring was commissioned by Bis-

Time was to show that in the 1860's Bismarck had a far better chance to win the German working class for the monarchy than two decades later. As yet the party founded by Lassalle was not pledged to the uncompromising, revolutionary doctrine of the communist manifesto. Nor could it truthfully claim to represent the whole proletarian class, which was largely uncommitted politically. But Bismarck was far too busy with foreign affairs to give more than off-hand attention to the problem, and, despite his prodding, no one else in the cabinet would assume the burden. Although Wagener saw the need, his views were vague and impractical and at court he was *persona non grata*. When Bismarck finally secured his appointment to the civil service in March 1866, the chance for social reform was gone.

During that fateful spring Bismarck moved to fill the political void in Prussia with German nationalism rather than state socialism. The gap in the liberal armor which he chose to penetrate was not its unwillingness to attract the support of labor, but its proclivity for national power.

---

marck to write certain articles for the publication. Richter, *Arbeiterfrage*, pp. 57, 259. In October Lothar Bucher, now Bismarck's aide, offered employment to Karl Marx on the official Prussian *Staatsanzeiger* as a columnist on financial matters. Marx refused. Franz Mehring, *Karl Marx, The Story of His Life* (London, 1936), pp. 342-344.

CHAPTER THIRTEEN

THE CONQUEST OF NORTHERN GERMANY

1. ON THE RAZOR'S EDGE

RRIVING in Berlin on February 15, 1866, Lord Loftus, the British ambassador, found the political atmosphere "loaded." "It smelled of powder."[1] On the 28th a crown council assembled in the Wilhelmstrasse. The diplomatic corps noted uneasily that the list of participants was unusual. In addition to the king, crown prince, and cabinet ministers, Generals Moltke and Alvensleben were present, as were Ambassador Goltz, who had been summoned from Paris, and Edwin Manteuffel, who came from Schleswig. The diplomats had reason to be nervous. Behind the closed doors of the foreign office the subject of discussion was war.

William's opening remarks show how well he had learned the lessons Bismarck had drilled into him. Since August, he charged, Austria had steadily sabotaged the Gastein agreement. She was playing the old game: "il faut avilir la Prusse, pour la détruire." Prussia's mission, Bismarck added, was to lead Germany. An envious Austria had consistently blocked this "natural and very justified" ambition. A decisive struggle was only a matter of time. At the moment conditions in Germany and Europe were favorable for Prussia. Out of the conflict would come the solution of the German question. Another result, Eulenburg pointed out, would be the conquest of the Prussian opposition. This could not be the motive for war, Bismarck replied, but only its by-product. Of those present only the crown prince spoke for the avoidance of hostilities.[2]

What William desired was not an immediate decision for military action, but preparation for its eventual necessity. Nor had

[1] Lord Augustus Loftus, *Diplomatic Reminiscences*, 2nd series (London, 1894), I, 39.

[2] *APP*, VI, 611-619; Friedrich III, *Tagebücher 1848-1866*, pp. 541-544; Walter Reichle, *Zwischen Staat und Kirche, Das Leben und Wirken des preussischen Kultusministers Heinrich von Mühler* (Berlin, 1938), pp. 170-171.

Bismarck abandoned his double course. He was never one to confuse probability with inevitability. During the months ahead many things could happen. French policy might shift; the Italian alliance might not develop; William's final scruples might not be overcome; the Austrians, isolated in Europe and nearly bankrupt at home, might compromise once more.

Like two boxers, Bismarck and Mensdorff circled warily, the one aggressive, the other defensive. The Junker's task was to find, the general's to avoid, a *casus belli* which would place Austria in the wrong. In the age of the newspaper press and popular interest in public affairs it had become important to unload the burden of blame on someone else's back. Bismarck had yet another motive. Under the Prussian constitution the king alone tipped the scales for peace or war, and William was a man of stubborn conscience. He judged political questions more in terms of right and wrong than of power and possibility. If persuaded that his rights were being violated or his authority disputed (so Bismarck told Benedetti), William could be brought to take the most "energetic measures" and even to think of them as stemming from his own initiative. For months Bismarck flooded the Ballplatz with recriminatory messages whose actual purpose was to convince William of the righteousness of his cause. Like a clock, it was said in Berlin, the king had to be wound up each morning by his minister-president.[3]

Mensdorff's problem was different. In the Austrian government his voice, reinforced by that of Moritz Esterhazy, was that of moderation. He favored gradual concessions to Prussia in northern Germany, but was determined not to yield to the threat of force. Although he had advocated military resistance during the Gastein crisis, he now realized that Austria's position had deteriorated. Isolated and internally weak, she was unequal to a two-front war. Consequently Mensdorff wished to avoid any overt act which would furnish Bismarck with the pretext he sought. But Franz Joseph and his generals feared that this policy would place the Austrian army at a disadvantage. The Austrian mobilization system was an ox compared to the Prussian race horse. Given an equal start, the Hapsburg army would be left at the post. A premature mobilization would destroy the delicate web of

[3] *GW*, v, 396, 399; vii, 123; *OD*, vii, 214, 222-223, 257-258.

285

Mensdorff's peace efforts, but a delayed one might mean loss of the war itself.[4]

On March 14 the generals convinced Franz Joseph, over the protests of Mensdorff and Esterhazy, of the necessity of assembling a few regiments to strengthen the Bohemian defenses.[5] Reports of the Austrian movement soon reached Berlin and, properly exaggerated, gave Bismarck the weapon he sought. Now he could play before Germany and Europe his favorite role of the injured party. In dispatch after dispatch he accused the Austrians of warlike intentions. The Austrian measure also enabled him to wind up the royal clock once more. On March 29 the king signed an order to strengthen the frontier regiments and fortresses. Up to the last minute Bismarck feared he might back down. It was Maundy Thursday and William's mood was pious![6]

In desperation Mensdorff strove to counter the Prussian offensive. Bluntly he asked whether it was Berlin's intention to tear up the Gastein treaty. But it did little good to try to embarrass Bismarck with such a question. "No," the Junker replied and added sardonically that up to the eve of an attack no other answer could be expected from any power. Mensdorff's next *démarche* was more effective. On March 31 he informed Europe that Austria's intentions were peaceful and he challenged Prussia to say the same.[7] Behind the scenes he helped mobilize a formidable array of forces to weaken William's will to war: the Duke of Coburg, Queen Victoria, "Vicky" and the crown prince, Queen Augusta, the dowager queen, and the king's sister, Alexandrine. All were convinced of Bismarck's folly and the necessity of his fall. Others who wished him ill were Counts Goltz and Bernstorff (his two most influential subordinates), Baron Schleinitz, now

[4] *DPO*, v/1, 202, 427; Heinrich Ritter von Srbik, *Deutsche Einheit, Idee und Wirklichkeit vom Heiligen Reich bis Königgrätz* (Munich, 1935-1942), IV, 327-328 Chester W. Clark, *Franz Joseph and Bismarck, The Diplomacy of Austria before the War of 1866* (Cambridge, 1934), pp. 239 ff.

[5] The Austrian step was prompted by the warlike temper of the Prussian official press, an unusual practice mobilization in Berlin, and rumors of the Prussian intent to occupy Saxony immediately on the outbreak of war. Clark, *Franz Joseph and Bismarck*, pp. 363 ff.; 562-563. Since November the French military attaché had been reporting abnormal military preparations in Prussia. *OD*, VII, 171 ff.

[6] *APP*, VI, 707 ff.; *GW*, V, 416 ff.; XIV, 710.

[7] *DPO*, v/1, 298-299, 302-323, 306-309; *GW*, V, 410-411; Ludwig Aegidi and Alfred Klauhold eds., *Das Staatsarchiv, Sammlung der officiellen Aktenstücke zur Geschichte der Gegenwart*, x, 352-353.

Hohenzollern "house minister," and Justus Gruner, former state secretary in the foreign office.[8]

The "Coburg intrigue," as it was called, had some effect. William found Bismarck's reply to Mensdorff's challenge "very cold and abrupt" and insisted on moderating the tone. Nevertheless, the note of April 6 was still barbed enough to arouse Vienna. Within twenty-four hours a hasty and ill-considered rebuttal, drafted by the acid pen of Biegeleben, was dispatched to Berlin. Instantly Bismarck recognized it as a "crude and clumsy error."[9] Its caustic phrases provided a fresh irritant to rub into William's wounded feelings. Now the Prussian moves came in quick succession. On April 8 a military alliance was concluded with Italy; next day Berlin called for a confederate reform, including a German parliament based on universal suffrage.

In the crown council of February 28 Moltke had given his professional opinion that Italian participation in a war against Austria was indispensable. Only if Austria were squeezed in the vise of a two-front attack was Prussian superiority certain. In 1865 the Gastein agreement had disappointed the government in Florence. Consequently La Marmora, the premier, was now determined to bind Prussia to a definite time-table for war on Austria. But this was impossible for Bismarck. William was not yet ready for the final step, and Napoleon's position was still uncertain. Hence Bismarck had to leave open the alternative of a settlement with Austria. On March 14 an Italian general, Giuseppe Govone, arrived in Berlin to reconcile these differences. While Karolyi watched suspiciously from his window across the street, the Italians came and went at Wilhelmstrasse 76, until finally, with customary skill, Bismarck got his way. He achieved a secret treaty which left the exact timing of the war up to Prussia. But the Italians were committed to join only if the attack were begun within three months.[10]

The crisis of 1866 sharply revealed for the last time the fundamental dilemma of Austrian foreign policy. The Hapsburg mon-

8 *DPO*, v/1, 240, 292 ff., 312, 380-395; *GW*, xiv, 710-711; Srbik, *Deutsche Einheit*, iv, 335 ff.; Clark, *Franz Joseph and Bismarck*, pp. 374 ff.; Otto Graf zu Stolberg-Wernigerode, *Robert Heinrich Graf von der Goltz* (Oldenburg, 1941), pp. 146 ff.

9 *Staatsarchiv*, x, 356-357, 362-364; Horst Kohl, ed., *Anhang zu den Gedanken und Erinnerungen von Otto Fürst von Bismarck* (Stuttgart, 1901), i, 127 ff.; *GW*, v, 452.

10 *APP*, vi, 599-604, 626-627, 653 ff., 709-711; *GW*, v, 395 ff., 412-413; *DPO*, v/1, 337. See also Friedrich Beiche, *Bismarck und Italien, Ein Beitrag zur Vorgeschichte des Krieges 1866, Historische Studien*, Vol. 208 (Berlin, 1931).

archy was faced with the necessity of choosing between its positions in Germany and Italy. Lacking the power for both, the empire had either to come to terms with Prussia in order to concentrate on Italy, or voluntarily cede Venetia in order to assert itself in Germany. After Gastein, La Marmora made a last attempt to obtain the province by purchase and the promise of an alliance. Told that the Italians had offered 500,000,000 francs, Bismarck exclaimed, "Oh what folly! A war would cost only 300,000,000!"[11] In January he hinted again that Austria, by surrendering her primacy in Germany, might receive Prussian aid in the reconquest of Lombardy.[12] For Franz Joseph, however, it was an abiding principle, ultimately fatal for the empire, not to surrender except under duress any fragment of his inherited power either at home or abroad. He deluded himself that Austria was equal to a two-front war as long as France or Russia did not intervene on the opposing side.

During the latter part of April, Mensdorff made yet another valiant attempt to influence William and undercut Bismarck. For the moment the voices of the war party in Vienna were muffled by the desperate financial condition of the monarchy. It was estimated that the enormous expense of arming could be met only by manipulating the currency.[13] Mensdorff found his opportunity in the Prussian note of April 15 which, while rejecting Biegeleben's demand for Prussian disarmament, offered to follow suit if Austria herself disarmed. In a conciliatory reply Mensdorff now declared that the Hapsburg troops in Bohemia would be ordered back to their original stations on April 25, if the Prussians would do likewise "on the same or even the following day."[14]

Disarmament proposals have little realism unless coupled with the easing of political tensions. Nevertheless, the note had a strong effect upon William. The prospect of war was not popular in Prussia, and the influence of the "Coburg intrigue" lingered in his mind. On his insistence the Prussian reply of April 21 was also moderate. Vienna must take the initiative in ordering a return to the *status quo ante*, but Prussia would "keep in step."[15] The

---

[11] Srbik, *Deutsche Einheit*, iv, 296-297. *DPO*, v/1, 209, also 201; *OD*, vii, 299.
[12] *DPO*, v/1, 153.
[13] *DPO*, v/1, 443; Srbik, *Deutsche Einheit*, iv, 354.
[14] *GW*, v, 452-454; *Staatsarchiv*, x, 366. See also the protocol of the ministerial council in which the Austrian reply was discussed. *DPO*, v/1, 498 ff.
[15] *GW*, v, 460; vii, 109-110.

gap between the Prussian and Austrian views was narrowing, and the possibility loomed that it might actually close. Only a matter of etiquette seemed to stand in the way.

Desperately Bismarck struggled to control the king's mind. As often happened when he met such opposition, he fell ill with a "nervous rheumatic" disorder. To Roon he complained that he could "no longer bear this awful friction." Like a wounded boar, wrote Karolyi, he lay on a divan nursing his lame leg and looking more like a conspirator than a triumphator. Edwin Manteuffel came to his aid with a letter warning William of the dangers of a "second Olmütz." The old man reacted with a "magnificent display of anger" against Austria. Roon followed up with a "most sharp and cutting discourse on what we want and what we decidedly do not want." Bismarck's health began to improve. But it was the Austrians who made him well.[16]

On April 20 alarming reports reached Vienna from the south. Along the Venetian frontier, it was said, the Italians were busily assembling men and supplies. On the advice of his generals, and with Mensdorff's reluctant approval, the Kaiser hastily ordered, only a day later, the mobilization of the southern army. The reports were exaggerated. Karolyi suspected Bismarck was the source. At any rate Victor Emmanuel now made them a reality by openly mobilizing the entire Italian army. On May 1 Franz Joseph concluded that war was "unavoidable." Orders went out to strengthen further the northern army, and the treasury resorted to a dubious currency conversion to raise the necessary funds. News of the Austrian decision reached Berlin on the evening of May 3, and William, swollen with indignation, ordered mobilization.[17]

The natural fruit of mobilization is war. So great are the expenses and dislocations that both sides feel the pressure to act lest the sacrifice appear in vain. And yet even now, while troops and cannon rumbled toward their stations, Bismarck found a way to continue his double course. The opportunity came in the plan of the brothers Ludwig and Anton von Gablenz for a compromise peace.

[16] DPO, v/1, 486; GW, v, 461; xiv, 712; Waldemar von Roon, Denkwürdigkeiten aus dem Leben des General-Feldmarschalls Kriegsministers Grafen von Roon (4th ed., Breslau, 1897), ii, 400 ff., 421.

[17] DPO, v/1, 523 ff., 553; Srbik, Deutsche Einheit, iv, 363-364; Ernst Berner, ed., Kaiser Wilhelms des Grossen Briefe, Reden und Schriften (Berlin, 1906), ii, 124.

By heritage and interests the Gablenz brothers had a better chance than most to view the German quarrel objectively. They belonged to a family of imperial knights: Ludwig was Austrian proconsul in Holstein; Anton was a Prussian landowner and Landtag deputy (old liberal). On April 20 Anton departed from Kiel for Vienna with the draft of an agreement which the brothers hoped would avert the threatening conflict. One clause provided for an independent Schleswig-Holstein ruled by a Hohenzollern prince. While Prussia would be granted the most important of the special rights she had demanded, Austria would receive from the duchies the defrayment of her war costs. Germany was to be divided into two military units along the river Main; Berlin would command the north, Vienna the south. Backed by Germany, Austria would be able to protect her trans-Alpine possessions against Italy and France.

In Vienna and Berlin, Anton succeeded in gaining direct and secret access to the foreign ministers. For more than a month he shuttled back and forth between the Spree and the Danube bearing proposals and counterproposals. From the start he received only encouragement from Bismarck, who accepted the plan, with a few minor changes, as a "basis for negotiation." At Bismarck's direction a subordinate, Rudolf Hepke, worked out a more detailed plan, which sought to "square the circle" by combining a dual organization of Germany with the national parliament demanded on April 9. At the end of May, however, Anton heard from Mensdorff that Franz Joseph would consent to the Gablenz plan only if it were backed by one or more medium states. This ended the matter, for such consent was not to be had.[18]

There were several possible motives for Bismarck's encouragement of Gablenz.[19] As at Gastein, Prussia stood to gain the most from the agreement: Austria would have to accept Prussia's equal status in Germany; the lesser states would again feel betrayed by Vienna; even with the provision for *itio in partes* a confederate parliament based on universal suffrage would be more likely to support Prussian than Hapsburg interests. An Austrian rejec-

[18] *DPO*, v/1, 521-523, 560; *GW*, v, 479; Otto Becker, *Bismarcks Ringen um Deutschlands Gestaltung* (Heidelberg, 1958), pp. 121 ff.

[19] For a review of the widely diverging judgments on the significance of Bismarck's handling of the Gablenz plan see Otto Becker, "Der Sinn der dualistischen Verständigungsversuche Bismarcks," *Historische Zeitschrift*, Vol. 169 (1949), pp. 264 ff.

tion, on the other hand, would further help in convincing William of her perfidy. Most important of all, the back-door negotiation through Gablenz enabled Bismarck to leave open a line of retreat. In it he saw the means of continuing, up to the threshold of war, the basic strategy of alternatives which was his best security in the treacherous game of politics. During the weeks which remained before the shooting began, it was his only insurance against outside intervention.

The possibility that London or Petersburg would intervene was slight. The Russian government was still largely absorbed with internal problems. After her failure in Schleswig-Holstein and the death of Palmerston in 1865 Britain had withdrawn from continental politics. Bismarck's main concern was France.

2. CAESAR ON THE SEINE

Bismarck had no difficulty in recognizing Napoleon's basic strategy. It was the same as his own: a "double policy," seeking "to preserve the possibility of stepping at the right moment to one side or the other."[20] But Napoleon lacked the acute sense of timing, certainty of purpose, and sureness of maneuver of the German genius. While reasonably successful in foreign affairs until 1859, he had since consistently fumbled. His loss of control over Italian unification, his equivocations in the Polish affair, the folly of the Mexican adventure, and the collapse of the British entente showed increasing ineptitude. In the German question he steered a zigzag course which has left his intentions open to dispute.

Certainly he was pleased at the prospect of a German war and helped foster it by promoting the Italian alliance with Prussia. Some of the advantages which he expected to derive are equally apparent. He aimed to detach Venetia from Austria and fulfill the long-standing promise to the Italians which troubled his conscience. The grant of Venetia might also be a useful lever with which to limit the Italian union in a way favorable to France. Similarly he wished to restrict Prussian expansion to the region north of the Main and to replace Austrian with French influence among the southern states. Out of the coming cataclysm, moreover, would emerge the chance, probably even the necessity, of further territorial gains for France. He wavered between many

20 *GW*, v, 95.

temptations: the frontier of 1814, Bavarian Palatinate, Belgium, Luxemburg, French Switzerland, and a buffer state on the Rhine. Gerhard Ritter's thesis that his sole aim was the first of these possibilities[21] is refuted by the fact that the buffer state was both demanded and promised in the agreement reached with Austria in June 1866.

As the German conflict reached the critical stage, Mensdorff and Franz Joseph became convinced of the need for a compact with France. Originally their purpose was to use the French leash to check Italy. But Napoleon would only make recommendations in Florence, and La Marmora had already committed his country to Prussia. Now the Austrians were compelled to pay the price of procrastination. In March they might still have bought peace with Italy by ceding Venetia; in June they agreed to surrender it, not to avoid a two-front war, but to secure Napoleon's neutrality and his approval of Austria's war aims in Germany. Napoleon, they indicated, could acquire Belgium, and the Rhineland would become a buffer state.[22] The Caesar on the Seine drove a hard bargain. He would not commit France to support Austrian acquisition of Silesia and agreed to Hapsburg expansion in Germany only if it did not upset the European equilibrium. The contract was a poor one, but on June 12 the Austrians signed in the belief that it was the only way to assure French neutrality. Napoleon's knife, said Metternich, was at the Austrian throat.[23]

Logically the double policy should have dictated a like agreement with Prussia. In the crown council of February 28 Bismarck explained the necessity of obtaining "more definite guarantees" from France; returning to Paris in early March, Goltz carried to Napoleon a personal letter from William requesting an *entente plus intime*. But the emperor evaded Bismarck's effort to "fix" the French position in advance of the war. France would remain

[21] Gerhard Ritter, "Bismarck und die Rheinpolitik Napoleons III.," *Rheinische Vierteljahrsblätter*, xv-xvi (1950-1951), 340. It seems unlikely that such an important provision could have been included by Drouyn in the agreement with Austria without Napoleon's approval, as Ritter maintains. *Ibid.*, p. 363.

[22] *DPO*, v/1, 61, 185-186, 527 ff., 549; *RKN*, i, 144, 160, 164-165, 180, 202 ff., 227 ff. While the buffer state was not mentioned in the treaty, it was verbally agreed that this was to be France's compensation. *RKN*, i, 268; *OD*, x, 145; *GW*, vib, 108 (n. 3). See also Heinrich Ritter von Srbik, "Der Geheimvertrag Österreichs und Frankreichs vom 12. Juni 1866," *Historisches Jahrbuch*, Vol. 57 (1937), pp. 454-507.

[23] *RKN*, i, 247 ff., 264 ff., 290; *OD*, x, 114 ff., 147 ff., 164 ff.

neutral, he declared, but would seek agreement with Prussia if the European balance were threatened and she were compelled to secure her interests.[24] For four years he had refused to snatch at the bait Bismarck dangled with his talk of the Rhine and French-speaking Europe. He was surrounded by chauvinists—Eugénie, Drouyn, Persigny, and Prince Napoleon—who favored the ruthless exploitation of the German crisis.[25] Less rash than they, he undoubtedly feared to arouse the whole of Europe by a policy of expansion toward the Rhine.

Fluctuating between the poles of caution and ambition, Napoleon was unable to follow a resolute policy. Hence that aspect of the Austrian agreement dealing with the Rhineland was verbal, not written. For the same reason he sought to entice from Bismarck a concrete offer without raising a concrete demand. In response to soundings from Goltz in March, he spoke vaguely of Luxemburg and the Bavarian Rhineland. But in late April he became bolder. One evening at a court ball, which fairly vibrated with politics, he drew Goltz aside to say that France was tempted by far-reaching offers from Vienna. Lacking counteroffers from Berlin, he might have to accept. France could not stand idly by while other powers aggrandized themselves. "The eyes of the entire country are on the Rhine." On May 6 at Auxerre he publicly condemned the treaties of 1815.[26]

But then, as though shocked by his own extravagance, he suddenly recoiled.[27] Was it owing to the adverse reaction of the French public?[28] Did he fear to drive Bismarck into a settlement with Austria? Was he afraid of creating a hostile European coalition? Or did he rely on the estimate of his generals that Austria would be the victor? Whatever the motives, he now resisted Drouyn's desire to extort from Berlin a secret agreement equivalent to that with Vienna. It may be that in proposing a European congress in May his aim was to delay the war and put Prussia, as well as Aus-

24 *APP*, vi, 615; *GW*, v, 286-287; *OD*, vii, 293; *RKN*, i, 89-90, 98-99, 108.

25 Gerhard Ritter sees him as more the "shoved than the shover." "Rheinpolitik Napoleons III.," pp. 339-370; also "Die Politik Napoleons III. und das System der Mainlinie," *Korrespondenzblatt des Gesamtvereins der deutschen Geschichts- und Altertumsvereine*, lxxx (1932), 178-182.

26 *RKN*, i, 147, 165, 167 ff.   27 *RKN*, i, 170 ff., 180 ff.

28 This is the view of Lynn M. Case, "French Opinion and Napoleon III's Decision after Sadowa," *Public Opinion Quarterly*, xiii (1949-1950), 441-461, and *French Opinion during the Second Empire* (Philadelphia, 1954), pp. 196 ff.

tria, under pressure to come to terms. Perhaps he approved of the proposal of Prince Napoleon (conveyed to Berlin by a Hungarian colonel, Kiss de Nemesker) for a treaty in which France was to receive the triangle between the Moselle and the Rhine in return for joining the war against Austria.[29] At any rate he made no further official claims upon Prussia.

Bismarck was surprised by the extent and timing of Napoleon's demands in late April. They compelled him to leave open through the Gablenz plan the last door to a compromise settlement with Austria.[30] But the day was fast approaching when Prussia would have to make the final option for war. Then Napoleon would in all probability have to be bought. What did Bismarck expect to pay? Some German historians have taken comfort in the fact that Bismarck, in contrast to the Austrians, made it clear from the outset that William would never tolerate the cession of German soil.[31] His critics, on the other hand, can point to two highly suspicious documents, recording audiences with General Govone, the Italian agent, on June 2 and Count Benedetti, the French ambassador, on June 4.[32] According to the former, Bismarck confessed that, being "much less German than Prussian," he was willing to cede the region between the Rhine and Moselle, but the king would never agree to it.[33] The latter quotes him as saying that William preferred to see Napoleon find his compensation in French-speaking areas. Nevertheless, the Hohenzoller might possibly be persuaded to grant the region of the upper Moselle, which, with Luxemburg, would nicely round out the French frontiers. As for the lower Rhine (Mainz, Bonn, Cologne), Bismarck asserted that he would sooner quit politics than consent to its surrender.[34]

Years later, after the publication of the first document, Bismarck angrily denied its accuracy. His ablest defenders have explained away the second as an offer he knew Napoleon could not accept, extended in order to smoke out the terms being offered Paris by Austria. Can there be any doubt, asks Ritter, of Bis-

[29] RKN, I, 241 ff.   [30] GW, v, 482 ff.

[31] GW, v, 389, 394. See Ritter, "Rheinpolitik Napoleons III.," p. 366; Erich Brandenburg, Untersuchungen und Aktenstücke zur Geschichte der Reichsgründung (Leipzig, 1916), p. 409, and the editorial comments of Oncken and Thimme, RKN, I, 245, and GW, v, 518.

[32] See Erich Eyck, Bismarck, Leben und Werk (Zurich, 1941-1944), II, 218 ff.

[33] U. Govone, ed., General Govone, Mémoires (1848-1870) (Paris, 1905), pp. vii-viii, 206-207.

[34] RKN, x, 31.

marck's determination not to sacrifice one single inch of German soil to France?[35] But again the facts are obstinate. On April 30, the minister-president proposed to the Prussian cabinet that the state-owned mines of the Saar be sold to private investors in order to prevent financial loss to the government should the exigencies of war require ceding the region to France.[36] He foresaw, in other words, the likelihood of having to sacrifice at least the frontier of 1814. In an extremity it is probable that he would have surrendered even more. Unlike his historians, Bismarck was never one to dogmatize political possibilities.

As usual, Bismarck saw the problem of dealing with France as one of alternatives. The "easier way," he wrote on May 7, was to show Napoleon that "what Austria could offer him at our expense is more readily obtainable from us." The harder way was to threaten Napoleon with the anger of the German nation. As early as March 24 he had written Goltz that French ambitions made it all the more imperative to establish for Prussia "a firm and national foundation" by opening the "German question."[37] Before Europe the great advocate of national self-determination would be forced to choose between his principles and his interests. If he should choose the latter, Prussia would fall back, as in 1812, upon the volcanic passions of national hatred.

3. THE WAR BEGINS

Meanwhile, the dual powers were engaged in a hard contest for the loyalty of the medium states. "We appeal to the noble sentiments: patriotism, honor, principles of law, energy, courage,

---

[35] Ritter, "Rheinpolitik Napoleons III.," p. 367.

[36] *GW*, v, 474 ff. Fritz Hellwig, an Oncken student, has asserted that Bismarck's aim in the memorial of April 30 was financial rather than diplomatic, but he ignored the vital passage which refutes his thesis. See his *Der Kampf um die Saar 1860-1870, Beiträge zur Rheinpolitik Napoleons III.*, in Hermann Oncken, ed., *Forschungen zur neueren und neuesten Geschichte*, Part 3 (Leipzig, 1934), pp. 172-173. As Ritter himself points out, the project was dropped because of the opposition it aroused in the Saar and not, as he argues in another place, because of a sudden surge of confidence on Bismarck's part in the success of Prussian arms. Had Napoleon responded to William's March request for a "more intimate entente," the promise of the 1814 frontier would have been unavoidable, not as the result of a "catastrophic war development," as Ritter asserts, but in advance of the actual hostilities. "Rheinpolitik Napoleons III.," pp. 360, 367. According to Johannes Haller, Bismarck ordered a map showing the frontier brought to Nikolsburg during the intervention crisis of late July. Otto Scheel, *Bismarcks Wille zu Deutschland in den Friedensschlüssen 1866, Veröffentlichungen der Schleswig-Holsteinischen Universitätsgesellschaft*, Vol. 44 (Breslau, 1934), p. 90 (n. 2).

[37] *GW*, v, 357-358, 414-415, 488-489.

decision, sense of independence, etc.," complained an Austrian diplomat. "*He* reckons on the lower motivations of human nature: avarice, cowardice, confusion, indolence, want of decision, and narrow-mindedness."[38] In Hanover, Kassel, and Dresden Bismarck promised expansion and in Munich hegemony over southern Germany. Those who opposed Prussia, he warned, might expect the lash of revenge. The result was failure. From the outset King John and Baron Beust placed Saxony securely in the Austrian camp. After months of wavering the rulers of Hanover and Hesse-Kassel staked their future at the last minute upon confederate law and Austrian power.[39]

In the south everything depended upon Bavaria. Barons Dalwigk, Varnbüler, and Edelsheim, the leading ministers of Hesse-Darmstadt, Württemberg, and Baden, were pro-Austrian, but without Bavaria their support was strategically ineffective. In Munich Baron von der Pfordten first declared Bavaria neutral and sought to mediate between the dual powers. Vain and self-important, he enjoyed being courted by both, but he was also fearful of French intervention in a German civil war. Louis II, a romantic dreamer absorbed in Wagnerian phantasies, was stubbornly insistent on peace whatever the issue, and the officer corps had serious doubts about Austrian military strength. Despite Bismarck's flattery and promises, Pfordten drifted steadily, almost unconsciously, into the harbor of the Austrian alliance. While Austria too appealed to their cupidity, the motive which dominated the thoughts of the rulers and statesmen of the lesser states was dread of Prussian hegemony.[40]

On May 9 the Frankfurt diet voted, ten to five, for a Saxon resolution calling upon Berlin to explain her mobilization. Three weeks later Austria forced the issue by formally placing the future of the duchies in the hands of the confederation. The aim was to compel Berlin to defy the diet and furnish the pretext for confederate mobilization. By formally breaking the Gastein treaty, however, the Austrian action enabled Bismarck to bring William into the home stretch.[41] On June 7 Edwin Manteuffel, following orders

---

38 *DPO*, v/1, 270.

39 *GW*, v, 390 ff., 419 ff., 430 ff., 443 ff., 466-467, 489 ff., 547 ff.

40 Srbik, *Deutsche Einheit*, iv, 337 ff., 367 ff.; Eugen Franz, *Ludwig Freiherr von der Pfordten, Schriftenreihe zur bayerischen Landesgeschichte*, Vol. 29 (Munich, 1938), pp. 353 ff.

41 *DPO*, v/2, 800 ff.; *GW*, v, 519 ff.

from Berlin, sent his forces over the Eider into Holstein. Tensely the men in the Ballplatz and Wilhelmstrasse waited for news of the first skirmish. To their mutual distress Gablenz withdrew over the Elbe into Hanover without being attacked. The *casus belli* was lacking![42]

The scene shifted back to Frankfurt and the German question. On June 10 a dispatch from Berlin presented the "outline" of Prussia's plan for a German union excluding Austria. Even now Bismarck lacked William's final consent for war. "I've led the horse to the ditch," he remarked, "Il faut, qu'il saute."[43] The final prod came from Vienna. On June 11 Baron Kübeck, the Austrian delegate, began to push through the diet, in defiance of its rules, a motion for immediate mobilization of all confederate forces (except the Prussian). It passed on the 14th, nine to five. Karl von Savigny answered for Prussia by declaring the confederation dissolved. Next day Berlin sent ultimatums to Dresden, Hanover, and Kassel. They were rejected. At midnight the Prussian columns began to move.

Bismarck had entered upon the greatest gamble of his life. Ludwig Gerlach noted something "restless, desperate in his attitude." On May 6 he had faced the assassin Blind on the avenue Unter den Linden. Bullets pierced his clothing, but he came away unharmed. To Gerlach he spoke of his escape as a matter of indifference; he had made his peace with God. On the night of June 15 he strolled with Lord Loftus in the garden behind the foreign office. As the clock tolled twelve he informed the ambassador of the Prussian attack. "If we are beaten, I shall not return here. I shall fall in the last charge. One can but die once; and if beaten, it is better to die."[44]

4. REVOLUTION FROM ABOVE

With the assault on Austria Bismarck commenced to reconstruct the foundations of the Hohenzollern monarchy. Previously its supporting pillars had been dynastic loyalty, Prussian patriotism, the Junker nobility, and the Prussian army and bureauc-

---

[42] *GW*, v, 526 ff.; xiv, 714.

[43] *GW*, v, 534-536; Eduard von Wertheimer, *Bismarck im politischen Kampf* (Berlin, 1930), p. 250.

[44] Ernst Ludwig von Gerlach, *Aufzeichnungen aus seinem Leben und Wirken, 1795-1877* (Schwerin, 1903), ii, 292; Loftus, *Reminiscences*, i, 60.

racy. To these were now added what was to become a new and massive column: German nationalism.

In a public message on March 24 he wrote that Prussia must seek "in Germany the security once provided by the Austrian alliance." This was her natural course because of "her position, her German character, and the German outlook of her princes." The interests of Prussia and Germany were identical. Experience had shown, Savigny told the Frankfurt diet on April 9, that neither the debates of an elected parliament (1848-1849) nor negotiations between governments (1863) were capable of overcoming the evil of German disunion. Only the two combined could give new institutions to Germany. Hence the diet should "summon an assembly chosen by direct election and universal suffrage from the entire nation" to deliberate upon a new constitution to be presented by the German governments. In May and early June Bismarck kept the opposition under pressure by gradually releasing the details of the constitution Prussia intended to propose. Included were a parliament equipped with extensive legislative authority, the electoral law of the Frankfurt constitution of 1849, a dual army under Prussia and Bavaria, and the exclusion of Austria.[45]

On June 16 William issued a manifesto, "To the German people," composed by Bismarck. The German Confederation, it declared, had lost the trust of the nation in a half-century of impotent existence. By mobilizing illegally against Prussia, the German states had destroyed it. Only the "living unity of the German nation" remained. Governments and peoples must "find for this unity a new, vital expression." Prussia's struggle was for the unrestricted "national development of Germany."[46]

In accord with the strategy planned since 1857, Bismarck set out to *exploit* the idea of nationalism and the yearning for national unity in the interest of Prussia. Hopefully it would provide the moral basis for the war and the means with which to arouse popular enthusiasm for the conflict. It was a terrain upon which Austria could not travel because of the multinational character of the empire. But it also provided a means with which to ward off French intervention. South of the Alps it helped to convince the suspicious Italians that Prussia did indeed plan the war of

45 *GW*, v, 418-419, 432-434, 447-449, 491, 514-515, 534-536.
46 *GW*, v, 550-551.

"major dimensions" they demanded. In Germany it might sow confusion among the medium states and weaken their war efforts. Within a new, federal union it would supply the centripetal pressure with which to counteract the habits of particularism. Finally it was a way to end the internal conflict in Prussia by reconciling liberal nationalists to authoritarian rule and by providing an electoral system which might produce majorities favorable to the government.

Although an early proponent, Bismarck was not the first to forge the idea of a national parliament for the arsenal of Prussian foreign policy. We have seen Bernstorff bare the weapon before Austria and the medium states in December 1861 and again in August of the following year to meet the first of Schmerling's plans for great-German reform. Bismarck's contribution was the addition of universal, direct, and equal suffrage. Originally he had advocated a parliament chosen by the legislatures of the states. But the Austrians incorporated this idea in their reform plan of 1862. Consequently Bismarck was compelled to go a step further. In January and September 1863 his counterattacks against Rechberg and Schmerling advocated "direct election" and hinted at universal suffrage. Early in 1866 Mensdorff, backed by Biegeleben, futilely urged Franz Joseph to regain the initiative by calling for a "German parliament."[47] But Bismarck outtrumped him in April with the electoral law of the Frankfurt parliament. This had been the most radical product of the Paulskirche. By resurrecting it the Junker alligned the Prussian monarchy with the revolutionary tradition.

At the time of his talks with Lassalle, Bismarck had doubts that universal suffrage would produce, unless modified by some conservative device, a chamber sympathetic to the government. Nor was the promise of April 1866 unhedged by conservative features. As yet the word "equal" was avoided, and there was no promise of secret suffrage. Privately Bismarck spoke of prohibiting the remuneration of deputies and the election of state officials.[48] Whatever his inner doubts and reservations, Bismarck defended the enfranchisement of the masses in Munich, Petersburg, and

[47] Otto von Völderndorff, "Deutsche Verfassungen und Verfassungsentwürfe," *Annalen des deutschen Reichs,* 1890, p. 402 (n. 2); Clark, *Franz Joseph and Bismarck,* pp. 350 ff.

[48] Becker, *Bismarcks Ringen,* p. 172.

London as a "conservative principle," offering "greater guarantees for the conservative conduct of parliament than any of the artificial electoral laws which are calculated to achieve manufactured majorities." The masses were more interested in political order than the leaders of the bourgeoisie. Through universal suffrage the monarchy could be brought into contact with the "healthy elements" in society. In Prussia nine-tenths of the population were loyal to the crown.[49]

German political leaders of most factions, from the ultra-conservatives deep into the ranks of the Progressive Party, were dismayed over this "plunge into the dark," this "crude and frivolous experiment." Only the democratic liberals and Lassallean socialists rejoiced.[50] In Paris the reaction was divided. Drouyn was upset, while Napoleon remarked that "henceforth the two countries would pay homage to the same political system." In London, according to Bernstorff, the move was regarded as "completely revolutionary"; politicians were "alarmed" over the influence it might have upon the debate over the moderate reform bill of Gladstone. Gorchakov and Czar Alexander considered it a grave attack upon the monarchical principle. Mensdorff protested it as "either revolutionary or an unworthy toying with the German reform question." From Frankfurt Kübeck denounced it to Mensdorff as both "perfidious" and "dangerous"; the delegates were unanimous in expressing "their abhorrence for the criminal gamble of the Prussian government with revolutionary elements." But neither Austria nor the medium states dared publicly oppose the measure, fearing the subterranean forces their satanic opponent wished to invoke. They chose the tactic of delay. Before a national parliament could assemble, they insisted, the German states must reach agreement on the proposals it might entertain. There the matter stood at the outbreak of war.[51]

For months Bismarck had talked and written the language of

[49] *GW*, v, 393, 421-422, 456-458; vi, 13; Robert von Keudell, *Fürst und Fürstin Bismarck, Erinnerungen 1846-1872* (Berlin, 1901), pp. 351-352; Heinrich von Poschinger, ed., *Bismarck und die Parlamentarier* (Breslau, 1894), i, 60-61.

[50] Philippson, *Forckenbeck*, pp. 158-159; Duncker, *Briefwechsel*, p. 437; Ludwig Dehio, "Die preussische Demokratie und der Krieg von 1866," *Forschungen zur brandenburgischen und preussischen Geschichte*, Vol. 39 (1927), pp. 258-259; Dorpalen, *Treitschke*, pp. 124 ff.; Mehring, *Sozialdemokratie*, iii, 239 ff.

[51] *RKN*, i, 125-127, 130; Richard Augst, *Bismarcks Stellung zum parlamentarischen Wahlrecht* (Leipzig, 1917), p. 78; *GW*, v, 455-456; *DPO*, v/1, 444, 446; Srbik, *Deutsche Einheit*, iv, 347 ff., 372-373.

monarchical conservatism. In Berlin, Vienna, and Petersburg he had constantly accused Austria of damaging the monarchical cause and promoting "democratic revolution" by backing Augustenburg. We have seen him pushing for reactionary measures against the Nationalverein and Frankfurt senate. But all the while he was anticipating with sardonic satisfaction the turn of events which might require a sudden about-face. After Gastein he was reported as saying, "They accuse me of being reactionary . . . but I would march if need be even with revolution." In Dresden he treated Beust to one of those frank talks which often produced "astonishment bordering on stupefaction" in his hearers. "For all your courage and spirit," he is said to have remarked, "you would not know how to place yourself at the head of the revolutionary party in Germany. As for me, I could at any time become its chief."[52]

Judging from what Bismarck told Govone, it was not an easy task to get William's approval for such a radical step as universal suffrage. "Why, that is revolution you're proposing to me," the king protested. "But there is no harm in that," the Junker replied. "Your majesty will be seated on a rock above the flood. All who don't wish to perish will have to seek safety there."[53] In all probability, however, his most telling argument was that of its conservative purpose. His skill in managing William during these months was everywhere the subject of wonder. In Berlin the wits were saying that Bismarck was "his last mistress, for only such a creature can wield so magic a power over an old man. . . ."[54]

Bismarck's exploitation of revolutionary forces in 1866 went far beyond his proposals for a national parliament and universal suffrage. Seven years before, Napoleon had started Italy on the way to national unity; except for Rome, Bismarck now brought her to the journey's end. To conservatives Victor Emmanuel was a "robber king," sitting on a revolutionary throne.[55] The Prussian alliance, while an act of expediency, gave a powerful boost to the radical principle of self-determination in Europe.

Even more startling were Bismarck's plans for the incitement

[52] *GW*, v, 42, 57-58, 68-69, 156-158, 296 ff., 301, 320, 363, 365, 369; *OD*, vii, 12-13, 72-73.
[53] Govone, *Mémoires*, p. 186.
[54] *DPO*, v/1, 313. Bismarck himself was not above such jokes. See Govone, *Mémoires*, p. 211.
[55] Ludwig Gerlach, *Aufzeichnungen*, p. 279, also 247, 282 ff.

of national uprisings within the Hapsburg empire. Of all its peoples the Hungarians had proved the most difficult to rule. The crushing of Kossuth's republic in 1849 and the years of repression which followed left undiminished the will to national autonomy. In 1862 Bismarck had made contact with the Hungarian underground through an *émigré*, Count Seherr-Thoss. In March 1866 Count Usedom, now Prussian minister at Florence, began to report the possibility of a "Hungarian-south Slav diversion" in the event of war. He was directed to keep in touch with the *émigré* colony in Italy without committing Prussia. For the present William had to be "spared" involvement with revolutionaries. In late May Bismarck conferred in Berlin with Kiss de Nemesker, an agent of Kossuth. On June 3 Count Czaky and Generals Türr and Klapka, veterans of 1848, were hurriedly summoned to Berlin. Preparations began for the recruitment in Prussia of a Magyar legion under Klapka. From Italy a second "free corps" under Garibaldi was to assault the Dalmatian coast.[56]

The operation became doubly urgent when it was learned that the Italians planned to limit their attack to the quadrilateral fortresses south of the Alps. Bernhardi, who had been sent to Florence for military liaison, reported that the Hungarian diversion appeared to be the "only means" by which La Marmora could be induced to undertake an invasion of Austria.[57] Certainly Usedom acted in accord with the spirit of his instructions in drafting the famous "stab-in-the-heart dispatch" of June 17, in which he urged the Italians to march on Vienna in support of the Hungarian and Slavic insurgents.[58]

In every quarter of the empire Bismarck sought to uncoil the springs of nationalistic discontent. The success of Garibaldi's legion was believed to depend on a rising of the southern Slavs. In Belgrade Captain Oreskovich, a former Austrian officer, had

[56] *GW*, vii, 65-67, 125-127; *APP*, vi, 719; *GW*, v, 423, 505-506, 536 ff., 549; Johann Reiswitz, *Belgrad-Berlin, Berlin-Belgrad, 1866-1871* (Munich, 1936), pp. 58 ff.; Wertheimer, *Bismarck im politischen Kampf*, pp. 235 ff. According to Arthur Brauer, Prussians were also recruited into the Klapka legion. *Im Dienste Bismarcks, Persönliche Erinnerungen* (Berlin, 1936), pp. 7-8.

[57] Reiswitz, *Belgrad-Berlin*, pp. 59-60.

[58] "Austria will lose in the same measure in which we win; the thrusts to be directed at Austria should strike at its heart, not its members." Max Straganz, *Zur Geschichte der "Stoss ins Herz-Depesche" des Grafen Usedom* (Innsbruck, 1922), p. 25. In 1868, when his policy toward Austria had radically changed, Bismarck repudiated the "linguistic crudity" of the dispatch (published by La Marmora), but not its basic purpose. *Ibid.*, pp. 42-43; *GW*, vi A, 401-409.

long been conspiring, with the approval of Prince Michael Obren-ovich, to effect an insurrection among the troops of the Hapsburg military frontier. On June 1 Bismarck telegraphed his approval of the recruitment of a "Slavic corps" in Serbia. Nine days later a Prussian envoy, Pfuel, was dispatched to Belgrade and Bucharest, followed by General Türr. On arriving in the Rumanian capital, Türr conferred in secret with Prince Charles, the ruler of the Danubian principalities, about the possibility of support for a Hungarian-Rumanian uprising. A Hohenzollern prince and Prussian officer, Charles had accepted the throne in April on Bismarck's secret urging. While sympathetic to the Prussian cause, he was far too insecure to engage in such a quixotic enterprise. Nor were the Prussians any more successful with the Czechs and Slovaks. On entering Bohemia the advancing troops distributed a proclamation: "If our cause is victorious, the moment may come when Bohemia and Moravia can, like Hungary, realize their national ambitions." But the response was limp.[59]

Before the Hungarian and south-Slav expeditions could get underway, the Prussian army struck a sledge-hammer blow, which for the time being rendered them unnecessary. On July 3 Moltke's converging columns attacked the Austrian position at König-grätz. That evening Benedek's shattered troops streamed back in disorder along the road to Vienna. Despite an earlier victory over Italy at Custozza, Franz Joseph was compelled to treat. Anticipating the disaster Mensdorff had already telegraphed on July 2 a request for French mediation.

5. INTERVENTION AND REVOLUTION

Throughout Europe the swiftness and finality of the Prussian victory caused consternation. This was particularly true in Paris. Napoleon had allowed for an Austrian victory or for a long war exhausting to both sides, but not for what came. For the first

[59] Hermann Wendel, *Bismarck und Serbien im Jahre 1866* (Berlin, 1937), pp. 19 ff., 45-56; Stefan Türr, "Fürst Bismarck und die Ungarn, Reminiscenzen aus dem Jahre 1866," *Deutsche Revue*, Vol. 25/1 (1900), pp. 313 ff.; *GW*, v, 431, 446-447, 516-518; vii, 107 ff., 111; xiv, 711; *Aus dem Leben König Karls von Rumanien* (Stuttgart, 1894-1900), i, 69-70, 89; T. W. Riker, *The Making of Roumania* (Oxford, 1931), pp. 557-558; Hans Raupach, *Bismarck und die Tschechen im Jahre 1866* (Berlin, 1936), p. 7. The incitement of the Czechs aroused protests in both Berlin and Petersburg. To the Czar Bismarck excused it as a mere gesture to keep the population friendly during the Prussian occupation. Had the war continued, however, he was prepared to grant Bohemia an "independent constitution." *GW*, vi, 58-60.

Königsberg

Rügen

Lübeck

Hamburg
Bremen
Oldenburg

Varzin

P r u s s i a

Berlin

Elbe

Oder

Vistula

Langensalza

Dresden

Ems
Hesse
Frankfurt

Thuringian
States

Saxony

Galicia

Sedan

Mainz

Darmstadt

Prague

Königgrätz

Palatinate

Moselle

Bavaria

Nikolsburg

Rastatt
Strassburg

Karlsruhe
Stuttgart
Württemberg
Ulm

Rhine

Vienna

Danube

Belfort

Baden

Sigmaringen

Munich

Buda
Pest

Austria-Hungary

Custozza

Luxemburg

Trier

Sedan

Moselle

Saar

Prussia

Verdun

Metz

Spichern

Mars la Tour
Gravelotte

2nd Army

Weissenburg
Wörth

3rd Army

Nancy

Strassburg

Boundary of
1871

France

Alsace

Rhine

Belfort

War of 1870-1871

GERMANY
1866-1870

North German Confederatio

time he became fully aware of the implications of the Prussian reform plan of June 10 and feared that the national parliament which it proposed meant that Berlin was bent on hegemony over the whole of Germany. Drouyn, seconded by Eugénie, urged him (July 5) to take command of the situation by mobilizing 80,000 men on the exposed Rhine frontier. Napoleon agreed, then quickly reversed himself, settling on a policy of "friendly mediation." It may be that he was influenced by reports that French public opinion was pacifistic. But he was also confronted by the arguments of his advisers Rouher and La Valette that he dare not repudiate the doctrine of national self-determination and face the terrors of an aroused German nationalism.[60]

At any rate, Bismarck preyed upon the latter possibility. French threats, he instructed Goltz, were to be countered by the menace of "a national uprising in Germany" on the basis of the Frankfurt constitution of 1849. Prussia would use "every means, regardless of party standpoint," to excite national resistance. "Progressives and democrats" were ready "for every sacrifice in a war against France." Prussia would bring about "the complete ignition of the national spirit."[61]

Simultaneously he again held out the tantalizing possibility of compensation. On July 26 he was quoted as saying that the 1814 frontier offered "no difficulty"—except the approval of William and the Landtag! On August 4 Drouyn finally demanded outright the frontier of 1814, the left bank of the Rhine as far as Mainz (that is, the Bavarian and Hessian Palatinates), and the severance of all connection between Prussia, Limburg, and Luxemburg.[62] But the French were too late, for the treaty of Nikols-

[60] *RKN*, I, 38, 213, 285 (n. 4) 328 ff.; Case, "French Opinion," pp. 458 ff.; Pierre Renouvin, *Le XIXe Siècle* (Paris, 1953-1955), I, 370-371.
[61] *GW*, VI, 45, 55.
[62] *RKN*, II, 21-22; *OD*, XI, 394 ff.; *GW*, VI, 101. On the 26th, Benedetti, acting on instructions from Drouyn, sounded out Bismarck on the possibility of a secret treaty granting the frontier of 1814 and Luxemburg. Bismarck's immediate reaction was bellicose, but then he quickly calmed down and gave the response recorded above. By his own account he refused Benedetti's suggestion that the King of the Netherlands be compensated for the loss of Luxemburg in east Friesland. Benedetti's version was that Bismarck mentioned the possibility of ceding the Bavarian Palatinate either to France or to the Dutch king. *RKN*, II, 4-7; *OD*, XI, 219-225. Oncken believes that the most he could have offered was the surrender to the latter of the crown lands in the Palatinate. *RKN*, II, 5-6. Otto Scheel indignantly rejects as "fantastic" the possibility that Bismarck could have considered cession of the Palatinate. *Bismarcks Wille*, p. 258. But on July 8 Bismarck mentioned such a possibility to the crown prince. Friedrich III, *Tage-*

burg had already been signed. With Austria at his feet, Bismarck refused all German soil. "If you want war, you shall have it. We shall arouse the entire German nation against you." Even the rehabilitation of the confederate diet and a military alliance with Austria were conceivable. In such a war, he declared, "revolutionary strokes" might occur, against which the German thrones were more secure than that of a Bonaparte. William himself now talked of "proclaiming a national war in all Germany" and of stopping at nothing in a conflict with France.[63]

Napoleon was not the only recipient of these warnings. On learning the Prussian peace terms, the Russian government took the view that such fundamental changes in Germany required the sanction of a European congress. Bismarck's reply was sharp. Outside interference would force Prussia "to unleash the full national strength of Germany and the bordering countries." This was a threat to exploit even the national ambitions of the Poles. When Czar Alexander complained of Prussia's revolutionary policy, the Junker became even more explicit. "Pressure from abroad will compel us to proclaim the German constitution of 1849 and to adopt truly revolutionary measures. If there is to be revolution, we would rather make it, than suffer it." If Napoleon came to terms with Austria or Russia, he told Govone on August 10, "we would conduct a war of revolution; we would incite rebellion in Hungary and organize provisional governments in Prague and Brünn."[64]

If we are to judge accurately this amazing man, it is imperative to determine to what lengths he would actually have gone in July and August 1866, the most critical moment of his career. No statesman was ever more conscious than he of the hazards of bluff. On this, as on most occasions his words were not idle. On July 8 he pressed Eulenburg to organize a "pre-parliament," using the title of the revolutionary body which preceded the Frankfurt parliament. "The proclamation of the Reich constitution [of 1849]

---

bücher, 1848-1866, p. 458. What he had been willing to grant under the duress of war, however, he certainly had no intention of conceding in the moment of victory. In this he was aided by Benedetti's admission that a refusal would result, not in war, but only in diplomatic hostility. *RKN*, II, 36. According to one report, the "characterless people" of the Palatinate might easily have accepted French rule, Friedrich Curtius, ed., *Denkwürdigkeiten des Fürsten Chlodwig zu Hohenlohe-Schillingsfürst* (Stuttgart, 1907), I, 161.

[63] *GW*, v, 106-111; vii, 148-149; *RKN*, II, 45; *OD*, xii, 22-25.
[64] *GW*, vi, 93, 120; vii, 156; Mosse, *European Powers*, pp. 243-247.

can be useful to us as a final means in an extremity against France." He admitted, nevertheless, that "really it is serviceable to us only after a fundamental revision." As a war measure he was prepared to resurrect from the gloom of a decade the document which embodied the highest hopes of German liberal nationalism. The struggle won, he would have broken the compact by "purifying" the document of its most liberal features.[65]

The threat to disintegrate the Hapsburg empire poses an even greater problem. In 1859 Napoleon had also conspired with Kossuth and Klapka to produce an uprising in Hungary. What came naturally for Bonaparte, however, seems grotesque in the mind of a Prussian Junker. Would Bismarck knowingly have touched off mines of nationalistic discontent which might have destroyed one of the bulwarks of the conservative order in Europe? Had the interest of state triumphed so completely over conservative principle? Or did he have in reserve, as in the case of the Frankfurt constitution, some means by which the revolutionary character of the step could be blunted in the conservative interest?

As the intervention crisis reached its zenith at the end of July, Bismarck called for an Italian plenipotentiary empowered to negotiate "new agreements with further concealed aims." The preparations for Magyar and Serbian insurrections, relaxed after Königgrätz, were renewed. The recruitment and arming of the Hungarian legion was resumed. Another Hungarian *émigré* officer, General Eber, was dispatched to Bucharest to confer with Prince Charles. In Belgrade Stephen Türr was ordered to keep his "organization" intact.[66] Eighteen months later Bismarck told Carl Schurz that, if France and Austria had joined hands, "we would have been forced to explode every mine" in Germany, Serbia, and Hungary. "If this primer had been ignited, of course, retreat would no longer have been possible. To treat with Austria would have been out of the question. Her destruction would have been unavoidable. A great empty space would have been opened between Germany and Turkey. It would have been necessary to create something to fill this vacuum. We could not have left our

[65] *GW*, vi, 59; xv, 285 ff.; v, 397-398. See also Becker, *Bismarcks Ringen*, pp. 189-191.

[66] *GW*, vi, 93, 103, 114; Reiswitz, *Belgrad-Berlin*, pp. 70 ff.; *Aus dem Leben König Karls*, i, 94-95. Disappointed by the armistice of July 26, Klapka and his 1,500 men invaded Hungary after August 1 on their own. But the public received them coldly, and they were forced to retreat. A. Kienast, *Die Legion Klapka* (Vienna, 1900), pp. 199 ff.

Hungarian friends in the lurch." In an extremity Bismarck was prepared in 1866 to unleash forces which he recognized were beyond his power to control. He stood poised, match in hand, over the powder keg of national revolution.

Nevertheless, he did everything possible to avoid having to set it off. "Such eccentric means," he told Schurz, were to be used only as a last resort. He preferred to avoid war with France at such a cost. The existence of Austria was "necessary for Europe." "New creations in this area," he wrote in his memoirs, "could only be of a continually revolutionary character."[67] If possible, he was prepared to buy Austrian neutrality and even her alliance. But the threat of French intervention was not the only reason for his desire to give Austria an easy peace. By inflicting unnecessary wounds he feared to incur her enduring hostility. He remembered Frederick the Great's long feud with Maria Theresa. The relationship with Vienna must not be permitted to become an organic fault in Prussian foreign policy.[68]

William, whom he had dragged into the conflict, became most immoderate in his rage against Austria and in the demands to be made on her. His generals regarded with contempt the efforts of the diplomat to limit the war and were outraged by his interference in military operations. They wished to march on Vienna and dictate a conqueror's peace. At Nikolsburg on July 24-25 Bismarck's insistence on a preliminary peace treaty without loss of territory by Austria led to the most severe personal conflict monarch and minister were to experience in their long relationship. At one point Bismarck fled the room, burst into tears, thought of leaping to his death through an open window, and, in a calmer moment, of resignation. He was saved only by the intervention of the crown prince, whom he had recently striven to conciliate and who was convinced by his arguments. After listening to his son, the old man still complained about having to "bite into this sour apple." But bite he did.[69]

Bismarck's most revolutionary act in 1866, however, was not the plan for the disintegration of the Hapsburg monarchy, which proved unnecessary, or his attempt to arouse the sleepy giant of German nationalism, which failed, but the destruction of thrones

[67] *GW*, VII, 234-235, 242; XV, 278. See also *The Reminiscences of Carl Schurz* (New York, 1907-1908), III, 272.

[68] *GW*, XV, 272-273.

[69] *GW*, VI, 78-81; Friedrich III, *Tagebücher 1848-1866*, pp. 470-473.

and sovereignties which came with the expansion of Prussia's frontiers and the establishment of her hegemony over northern Germany.

Immediately after Königgrätz king and minister were apparently in agreement that the northern enemy states were to be greatly reduced in size, but not liquidated. Soon William was busy with fantastic plans for recarving German frontiers without butchering the principle of legitimacy. One called for a Prussian gerrymander reaching into the south to reclaim the traditional Hohenzollern lands of Ansbach-Bayreuth. Back home there was some public pressure for the complete annexation of Saxony, Hanover, and Hesse-Kassel. To his wife Bismarck wrote on July 9 that he had the "thankless task of pouring water into the bubbling wine and making clear that we do not live alone in Europe." On the same day he wrote to Goltz that the annexations were not worth "gambling anew with the fate of the monarchy." Nevertheless, he instructed the ambassador to sound out the French on the possibility of Prussia's acquiring most of the northern states *in toto*. Within hours it became apparent that Napoleon would object only to the inclusion of Saxony. Instantly Bismarck shifted to the principle of complete incorporation: "every full annexation, which can be attained without the cession of Prussian territory, is better than the half by way of reform."[70]

He convinced William that, rather than create *irredenta*, it was better either to take entire states or leave them intact. By the former policy he hoped to speed assimilation of the conquered peoples, by the latter the reconciliation of the defeated rulers. What he sacrificed was the principle of legitimacy. Only under Napoleon I had Europe experienced such a ruthless destruction of sovereignties. To genuine conservatives Prussia appeared to have taken the perilous path of Caesarism. "The monarchical principle," Czar Alexander indignantly complained to William, "has suffered a rude shock," not at all mitigated by the fact that it came from royal rather than revolutionary hands.[71]

[70] *GW*, vi, 40-47. Thimme's editorial note to these documents supersedes the earlier accounts of Brandenburg, *Untersuchungen*, pp. 558-569, and G. Roloff, "Brünn und Nikolsburg: nicht Bismarck, sondern der König isoliert," *Historische Zeitschrift*, Vol. 136 (1927), pp. 457-501. Nevertheless, it is unlikely that Bismarck's shift to full annexation was owing, as Thimme asserts, to the pressure of public opinion. As usual, he judged the matter in terms of alternative possibilities, with the final decision dependent upon the danger of foreign intervention. See Johannes Petrich, *Bismarck und die Annexionen 1866* (Hamburg, 1933), pp. 9 ff.

[71] *GW*, xv, 278-279; vii, 147; *APP*, viii, 42-43.

On July 26 at Nikolsburg and on August 23 at Prague the treaties were signed which ended the "seven weeks war." While granted a peace without annexation, Franz Joseph was compelled to concede the dissolution of the German Confederation and the reorganization of Germany into two new federations north and south of the Main. Except for Saxony, Prussia might make such territorial changes as she wished in Germany. In separate treaties Bismarck left Baden, Württemberg, and Bavaria intact; Hesse-Darmstadt lost some segments of territory. Indemnities were imposed on all the defeated states. On September 20, 1866 Prussia annexed Hanover, Hesse-Kassel, Nassau, and the city of Frankfurt. Toward the old confederate capital on the Main, isolated and helpless, Bismarck could vent all the vindictive hatred which he denied himself in "die grosse Politik." Under the threat of plunder and hunger twenty-five million *Gulden* were demanded of the hapless burghers, whose sole offense was their liberal reputation and dislike of Prussia.[72]

Napoleon too was among the losers. Had he insisted, he might have prevented Prussia's territorial expansion. What he did receive was the limitation of Prussian hegemony to the region north of the Main and the possibility of French influence in the south. By claiming his reward much earlier he might have attained the border of 1814, perhaps even the Bavarian Palatinate. But during these vital weeks he was physically ill and mentally indecisive. Later he claimed that Drouyn, not he, was the author of the formal demands presented at Nikolsburg. When Bismarck refused, he repudiated the foreign minister, who resigned. With much of her army committed in Algeria and Mexico, France was in no condition to fight a European war.[73]

Pounding his fist on the table, Bismarck exulted: "I have beaten them all! All!"[74] Not the least of the defeated were the Prussian liberals.

[72] The city had never declared war on Prussia and had already paid a levy of six million *Gulden*. Despite Edwin Manteuffel's brutal twenty-four-hour ultimatum, the senate successfully delayed paying the ruinous sum. After the city had been officially annexed, its collection was more difficult. Through the intervention of Queen Augusta the indemnity demand was dropped. But this was too late to save the life of the mayor, who in despair hanged himself. Eyck, *Bismarck*, II, 268 ff.; Richard Schwemer, *Geschichte der freien Stadt Frankfurt a. M., 1814-1866* (Frankfurt, 1918), III/2, 317 ff.

[73] *RKN*, II, 125 ff.; Henry Salomon, "Napoléon III à la veille et au lendemain de Sadowa," *Le Monde Slave*, Nouvelle Série, II (1925), 168-212.

[74] *GW*, VII, 140.

CHAPTER FOURTEEN

THE CONQUEST OF PRUSSIA

1. ABSOLUTISM RESTORED

ON January 15, 1866 the Prussian Landtag met for the last time prior to the Austrian war. Before convening, the liberals desperately tried to close ranks. "We are able to unite only in negation or on phrases!" lamented Unruh. "If that were only the case!" Hoverbeck replied, "But we can't even do that!"[1] Although the Schleswig-Holstein controversy had receded, the deputies divided again on the question of tactics in the coming session. Once more the issue was whether to go through the long process of amending the government's budget or to reject it outright without debate. By a bold action many hoped to force a *dénouement* in the long drama of the constitutional conflict.

Without being aware of it, the more decisive party leaders neared the position of Lassalle, so contemptuously rejected three years before. Twesten asserted, "We ought not to maintain any longer the appearance that the constitution is still in effect." Lasker wished to show that "in almost every respect the country is being governed absolutely in the true sense of the word." Hoverbeck concluded that despotism was better than "sham constitutionalism." The world must know that "force has destroyed law." For once the opposition must "speak the full truth and then be silent until called upon to act." Nevertheless, he was not at all certain that the summons would actually come. In the event of a dissolution he foresaw that "by an energetic application of all bureaucratic screws" the government might very well bring about the defeat of the liberals. Many battles, he concluded, would have to be fought before the ultimate triumph of liberty. Freedom would always be in danger until "an absurd loyalty" had been erased from "the feelings of the people."[2]

At the beginning of the session the issue of tactics was raised

[1] Ludolf Parisius, *Leopold Freiherr von Hoverbeck* (Berlin, 1897-1900), II/2, 64-65; *HW*, I, 267.

[2] Parisius, *Hoverbeck*, II/2, 55-56, 64 ff.; *HW*, I, 265-269.

in a caucus of the Progressive and Left Center (Bockum-Dolffs) Parties. As expected, the extremist faction was in the minority. Included in it, however, were most of the prominent names among the progressives: Twesten, Hoverbeck, Lasker, Schulze-Delitzsch, Forckenbeck, Virchow, and Loewe. Supported by Rudolf Gneist, Waldeck stubbornly took his customary stand on the necessity of fulfilling the parliamentary function, come what might. His group was joined by the moderates of the Left Center, who deplored the constitutional conflict and would do nothing to intensify it. To the delight of the conservatives the dispute erupted in the liberal press and on the floor of the chamber when the budget bill was introduced. With the support of conservatives, left centrists, and Waldeck progressives, the extremists were voted down. The bill was referred to committee.[3]

But here the defeated faction had the upper hand. On February 21, the committee completed a "preliminary report" composed by Virchow. After recapitulating the history of the constitutional conflict and listing the abuses of the government, the report concluded: ". . . it is clear as day that absolutism has been restored in Prussia and indeed absolutism without the self-imposed limitations of the pre-March period. There is no longer any control over finances or any legal budget; the *Staatsanzeiger* has replaced the statute books; the superior accounting office no longer has any function; the treasury and property of the state are at the free disposal of the government. One point alone has not been attacked. It is that upon which the old absolutism failed and constitutionalism was won in Prussia. Still in effect is the clause in article 103 of the constitution reading: 'loans for the treasury may be raised only on the basis of a law.' On June 2, 1865 the chamber of deputies resolved, 'The house is not in position to grant loans to the present cabinet. . . .' "[4]

The point was futile. Bismarck was quite willing if necessary to violate article 103.[5] But the need did not arise. Later, when war came, August von der Heydt, who replaced Bodelschwingh at the ministry of finance, raised the necessary funds from the treasury reserve and the sale of state-owned railway shares through the Prussian *Seehandlung*. While the deputies hotly pro-

---

[3] Parisius, *Hoverbeck*, II/2, 67 ff.; *HW*, I, 269; Biermann, *Waldeck*, p. 299; *SBHA* (1866), I, 19-29.
[4] Parisius, *Hoverbeck*, II/2, 68-70.   [5] *GW*, XIV, 697-698.

tested the constitutionality of these actions,[6] they were helpless to stop them. No more than in 1864 had they the power to cripple Bismarck's foreign policy.

The debates of January and February 1866 bristled with constitutional issues. The deputies voted to condemn the government's violation of the right of free assembly through the suppression of the Cologne festival. They took note of the prosecution of Leeden, Frese, Lüning, Jacoby, and Franz Duncker for utterances critical of the cabinet. By acquiring Lauenburg without consent of parliament, they charged, the government had violated no less than three articles in the basic law. In a clever speech, sparkling with irony, Bismarck demonstrated once more the rubbery character of Frederick William IV's constitution.[7]

It was the judicial persecution of Twesten and Frentzel, however, which produced the greatest outburst of indignation in the chamber and provided a climax for the constitutional conflict itself. The prosecution of deputies for speeches delivered on the floor of the chamber was not only a breach of the constitution (article 84), but an assault upon the parliamentary process itself. While the courts of first and second instance had declared the charge inadmissible, the judges of the supreme court ruled (January 29) the contrary by a majority of one. In doing so, the court reversed decisions of 1853 and 1865. The desired result was achieved only by packing the court with two "relief judges" of conservative views.[8] Three days after the verdict Hoverbeck introduced a motion that the chamber declare the action of the court, both in its procedure and decision, to be illegal and invalid. In succession the best speakers of the opposition mounted the rostrum to blast the perversion of the courts by the government. Lippe and Bismarck replied lamely that the chamber itself was guilty of illegal action in attempting to interfere with the courts. The minister-president flatly denied that the deputies had any greater freedom in than out of parliament. Hoverbeck's resolution passed, 263 to 35. In the major cities protest meetings were held, two of which (Berlin and Königsberg) were dispersed by the police.[9]

[6] Fritz Löwenthal, *Der preussische Verfassungsstreit, 1862-1866* (Munich, 1914), pp. 278 ff.; *SBHA* (1866), II, 162-177.

[7] *SBHA* (1866), I, 58-83, 222-250.

[8] *HW*, I, 270-275; Parisius, *Hoverbeck*, II/2, 70-72.

[9] *SBHA* (1866), I, 110-181; II, 54. Over 200 deputies signed the motion in order, by virtue of their number, to escape prosecution. Parisius, *Hoverbeck*, II/2, 70-71.

On February 22 the chamber received the refusal of the cabinet to accept the censures on Lauenburg, the Cologne festival, and the Twesten-Frentzel case. The charges of unconstitutionality were themselves rejected as unconstitutional. In the tangle of legal claims and counterclaims Bismarck could hope to blunt the public effect of parliamentary criticism. On the same day he climbed the rostrum to read, before the surprised and angered deputies, a royal decree proroguing the Landtag. The session had lasted but forty days and eleven sittings, the shortest in the history of the Prussian parliament. Immediately afterward, agents of the government seized the papers and documents of the house. When the *Rheinische Zeitung* published Virchow's critical report, the edition was confiscated by the police.[10]

The liberal deputies had assembled quarreling, but departed in harmony, welded once more into a solid front by the tyranny of the government. On February 23 none attended the closing ceremony in the palace, where Bismarck read the royal message. The days of their new-found unanimity, however, were numbered.

2. BALKY LIBERALS AND OBEDIENT MASSES

By seizing the initiative in the national cause Bismarck hoped in April 1866 "to put the German people in motion."[11] His aim was to convert the conflict with Austria from a civil into a national war, to mobilize the peoples of Germany against pro-Austrian rulers and governments, and to add the *élan* of national sentiment to the striking power of the Prussian army. This he believed attainable within weeks after the Twesten-Frentzel case, the abrupt closing of the Landtag, and the seizure of its papers had brought the liberals to a new height of indignation. To one who had witnessed the migration of the moderates from Frankfurt via Gotha to Erfurt in 1849-1850 the possibility seemed far from absurd. But his cynicism was not entirely justified. When it came, the great reversal in German liberal opinion was produced less by the appeal to German nationalism than by the demonstration of Prussian military power.

As the conflict neared, the mood of vocal public opinion was

9 *SBHA* (1866), I, 110-181; II, 54. Over 200 deputies signed the motion in order, ed., *Europäischer Geschichtskalender* (1866), p. 164. The abrupt adjournment of the Landtag had prevented presentation of Virchow's report to the house and hence it did not become part of the formal record of the session.

11 *GW*, VII, 110.

nearly the opposite of what Bismarck hoped. In Austria there was considerable support and even enthusiasm for the conflict. In the southern states the small-German nationalists voted apathetically for the necessary war credits on the grounds that Prussia was the aggressor.[12] In Prussia itself popular agitation against war reached a dimension which William termed "very unpleasant." From Solingen, where an anti-war rally was held on March 25, a wave of protest meetings spread through the monarchy. A torrent of resolutions and addresses descended on Berlin. Nor did the critical attitude change generally after Prussia came out for national reform on April 9. Within a few days the liberal press ran the gamut of "excitement, clamor, astonishment, laughter." *Kladderadatsch*, the famed humor magazine, announced it would cease publication: "We have been dealt a hard blow. . . . The Bismarck cabinet appeals to the German nation and supports itself upon the people! Hahahaha! Who's laughing? All Europe and adjacent parts of the world! We aren't up to such competition." The sudden switch from Hyde to Jekyll was far too swift to carry conviction. That no details of the plan were given until June 10 prevented many from taking it seriously. It had the appearance of a mere gambit on the chessboard of German politics, a momentary tactical stroke destined for oblivion once the game was won.[13]

During the first months of 1866 the Prussian opposition actually seemed to be leading a genuine mass movement. Indignation against the arbitrary actions of the government in January and February, followed by general antagonism toward war in March and April, gave the opposition for a time the popular foundation it had previously lacked. But the voices of protest were not wholly in unison. In the Rhineland the influence of non-Prussian Germany was greater; Catholics feared the growth of Protestant power; businessmen dreaded the disruption of commerce. In the east, stronghold of Prussianism, many were less opposed to war

[12] Otto Bandmann, *Die deutsche Presse und die nationale Frage, 1864-1866* (Leipzig, 1909), pp. 106 ff.; Clark, *Franz Joseph and Bismarck*, pp. 381, 470; Theodor Schieder, *Die kleindeutsche Partei in Bayern, Münchener historische Abhandlungen*, Vol. 12 (Munich, 1936), pp. 95 ff.; Hans Ruider, *Bismarck und die öffentliche Meinung in Bayern, 1862-1866, Deutsche Geschichtsbücherei*, Vol. 1 (Munich, 1924), pp. 128 ff.

[13] Kohl, *Anhang*, ɪ, 135; Schulthess, *Geschichtskalender* (1866), p. 51; *DPO*, v/1, 511-512; Bandmann, *Deutsche Presse*, pp. 126, 142-143; Ursula Schultz, *Die Politik Bismarcks in den Jahren 1862-1866 im Spiegel der rheinischen Presse* (Zella-Mehlis, Thür., 1933), pp. 120 ff.

than to the regime which presumed to conduct it. "For this cabinet not a penny!" was the battle cry.[14]

The liberal leadership was similarly divided. In a manifesto the Progressive Party pledged itself anew to the twin ideals of unity and freedom and blamed the war on the lack of parliamentary influence in Prussia. Once more Schulze-Delitzsch and others were buoyed by the assumption that a reactionary government could not possibly survive the stresses and strains of a major conflict. But Waldeck and his clique refused to take part in the protest movement. Every Prussian conquest was a step toward their ideal of a German unitary state. Among the moderates, voices were already heard demanding that the issues of liberty be postponed for the duration. Twesten and Lasker were by no means convinced that the party could make good its position of unconditional opposition. Differences of opinion were also evident among the old-liberals. A few—Schwerin, Patow, Gruner, and Bethmann—regarded the war as "frivolous." But most supported it. Max Duncker and Bernhardi had for years wanted war as the best way out of the internal conflict. Others—Sybel, Haym, Treitschke, and Wehrenpfennig—rated a Prussian victory over Austria as more important than the internal conflict. While granting the indispensability of Bismarck and Roon, they wished to replace the most reactionary ministers: Eulenburg, Bodelschwingh, and Lippe.[15]

Nor were opinions about the Prussian reform plan harmonious. The progressives were not opposed to the reform itself, but to the unclean hands which offered it. Summoned by Loewe, Schulze-Delitzsch, and Franz Duncker, members of the Nationalverein in Berlin crowded the Tonhalle on April 11 to approve unanimously a resolution refusing support for the reform until constitutional government was restored in Prussia. Only a liberal government, it was confidently believed, could marshall popular support in a war for such an objective.[16] But others were not so

14 Clark, *Franz Joseph and Bismarck*, p. 512; Martin Spahn, "Zur Entstehung der nationalliberalen Partei," *Zeitschrift für Politik*, I (1907-1908), 365 ff.

15 Felix Salomon, *Die deutschen Parteiprogramme* (3rd ed., Berlin, 1920-1924), I, 127-129; Ludwig Dehio, "Die Taktik der Opposition während des Konflikts," *Historische Zeitschrift*, Vol. 140 (1929), pp. 335 ff.; Bandmann, *Deutsche Presse*, pp. 92-94; Rudolf Haym, *Das Leben Max Dunckers* (Berlin, 1891), p. 380; *HW*, I, 280, 284-287, 292-293, 299, 303.

16 Bandmann, *Deutsche Presse*, pp. 101-102, 135 ff.; Spahn, "Entstehung," pp. 383 ff.; Hermann Oncken, *Rudolf von Bennigsen* (Stuttgart, 1910), I, 693; Fried-

sure that the reform should be rejected because of its origin. Impressed by the endurance of the Bismarck cabinet, Twesten, Lasker, and associates longed for a reversal of its internal policies which would enable them to support it on the national issue. In Halle a group of old-liberals led by Rudolf Haym resolved that the question of power took precedence over that of freedom. While condemning the war, a "democratic" branch of the Nationalverein in the same city resolved to agitate for the parliament plan. In Bremen a right-wing branch of the Nationalverein also announced its support, although "without enthusiasm." If forced to wait on a more acceptable minister-president in Berlin, the liberals might never attain their goal. They trusted in the "overwhelming power" of the parliamentary idea to secure the ultimate aims of liberty.[17]

In January Bismarck had boasted to Benedetti that Prussia could with equal ease "fight the Nationalverein or make a compact with it." Undoubtedly the general reaction to the Prussian reform plan was a keen disappointment. Nevertheless, he perceived and sought to exploit the cleavages of opinion in the liberal camp. From mid-April until late June he conferred successively with Max Duncker, Bernhardi, Roggenbach, Bennigsen, Miquel, and Duke Ernst of Coburg. On Bismarck's request the latter made a reconnaissance of the liberal parties and factions in southern Germany. Through these leaders and the popular forces they represented the Junker hoped to undermine the wavering governments of the medium states. He also sought to infiltrate the Prussian opposition by talking with Twesten, Unruh, and probably others of like opinion. Should battles be lost, the support of these moderates might become indispensable to the regime. It was necessary to learn their terms.[18]

The available records of these conferences show a consistent line of attack. Bismarck usually began by "confessing" that he might have to resign. Smiling ironically, he asked, "Is a liberal cabinet possible at this moment? Who would be foreign minister?" Progressives and old-liberals alike admitted the utter poverty of their talent. Since 1849 the reaction had been so successful, Unruh

rich Thorwart, ed., *Hermann Schulze-Delitzschs Schriften und Reden* (Berlin, 1909-1913), iii, 254-262; v, 255-256, 281-282, 295-298.

[17] Spahn, "Entstehung," pp. 370 ff.; Oncken, *Bennigsen*, i, 696-697; Hans Rosenberg, ed., *Ausgewählter Briefwechsel Rudolf Hayms* (Stuttgart, 1930), pp. 244-246.

[18] *OD*, vii, 243; *GW*, vii, 110, 130; Becker, *Bismarcks Ringen*, pp. 159 ff.

wearily conceded, that there were no longer "in high official circles" any liberals who possessed "the necessary energy, endurance, and general trust."[19] That only trained officials came into question is highly significant. Having never experienced power, the Progressive Party had no reservoir of trained talent upon which to draw for the state's most sensitive position. The system did not provide for it.

In these talks Bismarck began to construct his own myth, one which patriotic Germans have ever since been only too glad to believe. Since Frankfurt days, he told Bernhardi and Bennigsen, his "program" had been confederate reform and a German parliament. To Unruh he spoke of national unity as "the great goal of his efforts for sixteen years."[20] Having chosen the alternative of national reform, he now had to describe it as his sole objective from the start. The mold of his personal history had to be reshaped, the statue recast, the popular image reformed. To his contemporaries and to posterity he must appear in the pose of a German nationalist.

But the leaders of the Nationalverein were cautious and mistrustful. Bennigsen refused to commit himself to the Prussian reform plan without knowledge of its details and assurances that Bismarck would make concessions in the constitutional conflict. Roggenbach concluded that the parliament plan had to be supported, for a defeated Prussia could never "fulfill its future mission." But then the Badenser, frightened by premature publicity, abruptly left Berlin. He feared to jeopardize his political future by dealing with the hated minister. Nor was Miquel impressed by the argument that to support Prussia was his "national duty." Like Bennigsen, he found the constitutional conflict an insurmountable obstacle. Bismarck also failed in his effort to recruit Treitschke to draft nationalistic manifestos for the Prussian government. While sympathetic to the Prussian cause, the Freiburg professor feared to compromise himself.[21]

As the resolutions in Bremen and Halle showed, the views of Bennigsen were not those of the entire Nationalverein. Anxiously

19 *GW*, vii, 109-110, 112-113, 131.
20 *GW*, vii, 113, 130.
21 Oncken, *Bennigsen*, i, 702 ff.; Friedrich von Bernhardi, ed., *Aus dem Leben Theodor von Bernhardis* (Leipzig, 1893-1906), vi, 298 ff., 306 ff.; *GW*, v, 463, 481-482; vii, 118-119; *HW*, i, 278 ff.; Andreas Dorpalen, *Heinrich von Treitschke* (New Haven, 1957), pp. 105-107.

the Hanoverian queried his agents throughout Germany. Should the organization support the Prussian plan or sit on the fence for the time being? The answers were inconclusive. Only one-eighth replied, of whom thirty-one advocated immediate agitation for the plan and eight a reserved attitude. Meeting in Berlin on May 13-14, the central committee condemned the prospect of civil war and avoided commitment to the parliament proposal. Six days later a congress of German deputies, with Bennigsen serving as vice-president, met in Frankfurt and "damned the threatening conflict as a cabinet war serving only dynastic interests." The rulers and ministers responsible for such an "unnatural war" would be guilty of a "terrible crime against the nation."[22]

The conferences with Twesten and Unruh were also unsatisfactory. Already burdened by a sense of defeat, the former restricted his price to the confirmation of the chamber's budget rights. This, he insisted, was the only way the crown could make it "legally and morally possible" for the deputies to cooperate in the war. At the minister's request he drafted a passage on this point for the next "throne speech."[23] It is questionable whether, as Bismarck asserted to Unruh, the Twesten draft actually reached the king after being accepted by the cabinet. At any rate Unruh refused to weaken the passage in order to meet William's reputed objections. Nor did Bismarck get anywhere by reminding the deputy of his willingness in 1859 to accept a "temporary military despotism" for the sake of national unity. Internal peace, Unruh insisted, was to be had only by a return to the constitution.[24]

As yet Bismarck had little to offer for what he asked. He had no real intention of taking any liberal into the cabinet, unless compelled to do so by the fortunes of war. Contrary to what Bernhardi thought, he carefully avoided the subject in talking to Roggenbach. When Twesten's name was mentioned as a possible candidate, he merely laughed. Nor was he ready to fulfill Bennigsen's two requirements. The liberals should have no cares, they were told, "about the little bit of liberalism" they might sacrifice by

[22] Oncken, *Bennigsen*, I, 708-709; Thorwart, *Schulze-Delitzsch*, III, 282-295.

[23] *HW*, I, 307, 312-313, 497-499; Heinrich von Poschinger, ed., *Erinnerungen aus dem Leben von Hans Viktor von Unruh* (Stuttgart, 1895), p. 251. What Twesten understood by "budget rights," however, was rather far-reaching. See Spahn, "Entstehung," pp. 393-394.

[24] *GW*, VII, 128-130; Gerhard Ritter, "Die Entstehung der Indemnitätsvorlage von 1866," *Historische Zeitschrift*, Vol. 114 (1915), p. 24.

supporting his government. "You will later be able to recoup that within six weeks under the first good liberal cabinet, and in any case a new government will take office under the crown prince." If the delegates to the coming parliament would "take the initiative and begin with a revision of the constitution of 1849, I'll accept that with a kiss." "Don't bother yourselves about the constitution now; later, when we have conquered, you should have constitution enough." But his hearers resisted these blandishments. They wanted proof of his sincerity in the form of a detailed program and concrete acts.[25]

On the extreme left he had better luck. Through an assistant, Lothar Bucher, the turn-coat revolutionary of 1848, he was in touch with what remained of the old radical liberal movement. There is reason to believe that Bismarck instigated the impassioned war speech which Franz Ziegler, friend and adviser of Waldeck, delivered in Breslau. The result was a widely publicized resolution of the Breslau city council favoring the war. Karl Rodbertus—radical politician, social theorist, and admirer of Bismarck's "Caesarism"—also became a propagandist for the government. Count Oscar von Reichenbach, proscribed radical of 1848, ended his long exile in England. Acting on secret instructions from Robert von Keudell, another trusted Bismarck assistant, he traveled through southern Germany encouraging resistance to war. Two other veteran radicals, Arnold Ruge and Gottfried Kinkel, were also enlisted in the Prussian cause.[26]

With the socialists too Bismarck had some success. Three days after the Prussian commitment on German reform he lent 2,500 *Thaler* without interest to keep Schweitzer's *Sozialdemokrat* from bankruptcy. On May 9 the editor was prematurely released from prison. Immediately he set out to re-invigorate the faltering workers' association. At a convention held in Leipzig on June 17 the party, on his urging, resolved to commence general agitation for universal suffrage and a national parliament.[27]

[25] *Aus dem Leben Bernhardis*, v, 303; Oncken, *Bennigsen*, I, 705 (n. 3); Dehio, "Preussische Demokratie," p. 254; *GW*, VII, 112, 115, 119.

[26] Dehio, "Preussische Demokratie," pp. 230 ff.; Ludwig Dehio, "Beiträge zu Bismarcks Politik im Sommer 1866 unter Benutzung der Papiere Robert von Keudells," *Forschungen zur brandenburgischen und preussischen Geschichte*, Vol. 46 (1934), pp. 155 ff.; Hans Neumann, "Franz Ziegler und die Politik der liberalen oppositionsparteien von 1848 bis 1866," *ibid.*, Vol. 37 (1925), pp. 286-288; Becker, *Bismarcks Ringen*, p. 162.

[27] Gustav Mayer, "Der allgemeine deutsche Arbeiterverein und die Krisis 1866," *Archiv für Sozialwissenschaft und Sozialpolitik*, Vol. 57 (1927), pp. 170-171.

But these results were meager. The predominant "movement" among the German people in April-June 1866 was anti-war and anti-Bismarck. The Junker would have been amused, however, by Karolyi's judgment that popular opinion would prevent him from going to war. "One doesn't shoot at the enemy with public opinion," he told Bernhardi, "but with powder and lead." "We don't need you at all," were his parting words to Miquel. The agitation against war, he wrote Goltz, was the "superficial" creation of the bourgeoisie, unsupported by the masses. "At the moment of decision the masses will stand by the monarchy, whether or not it follows the liberal or conservative stream." The king had but to command; they would obey.[28]

The mobilization in May was not unaffected by the public mood. The militiamen resented the rude interruption of their private lives for purposes not wholly clear. "Scandals" occurred at some assembly points. Nevertheless, the traditional Prussian discipline prevailed. As the troops massed on the Austrian frontier, the war-spirit rose. To one observer the militia now appeared even more bellicose than the line. In the minor battles of the west and south and in the decisive clash at Königgrätz Prussian troops struck down their fellow Germans with the same efficiency, if without the same degree of enthusiasm, shown earlier against the Danes and later against the French. Back home, Schulze-Delitzsch noted, the public followed the news reports with an increasing sense of involvement. Because of military conscription almost every family had a member under arms. Prussia's isolation and the proximity of her foes heightened the feeling of common danger. The good citizens shuddered at the reputed savagery of the "Austrian hordes." The necessity of winning the war became more important than the issue of its origin.[29] Bismarck's confidence was thoroughly vindicated.

3. THE INTOXICATION OF THE CONQUEST

"Every Prussian," wrote Benedetti in March 1866, "has some-

Schweitzer und die Sozialdemokratie, pp. 161 ff., "Die Lösung der deutschen Frage im Jahre 1866 und die Arbeiterbewegung," in Festgaben für Wilhelm Lexis (Jena, 1907), pp. 221-268; Franz Mehring, Geschichte der deutschen Sozialdemokratie (Stuttgart, 1903), III, 250-251.

[28] DPO, v/1, 243, 269; GW, v, 429-430; VII, 119, 121.

[29] Schulthess, Geschichtskalender (1866), p. 506; Johannes Schultze, ed., Max Duncker: Politischer Briefwechsel aus seinem Nachlass (Stuttgart, 1923), p. 413; Thorwart, Schulze-Delitzsch, III, 299 ff.

thing of Frederick the Great in him, whatever his views on the issues of liberty." Bismarck would readily have agreed. In recommending draconian measures against the Frankfurt senate in October 1865, he wrote, "In my opinion every development of will power and might which we accomplish in Germany will be of substantial help in overcoming our inner conflict." If carried out in defiance of the views of the liberals, this would be all the more true, provided that the action were taken "decisively" and not as a "half-measure."[30] The ruthless use of power, he judged, commands respect regardless of its purpose.

Certainly this was true of Germany in 1866. The remarkable display of will and energy with which Bismarck carried the country into war against great popular opposition, the crushing power with which Prussia, supported by no other German state and opposed by most, swept all before her soon had their effect. What ceaseless propaganda from the government press and the bold exploitation of liberal and national ideals had been unable to accomplish in the preceding months was achieved within days by powder, smoke, and the intoxication of conquest.

On May 9 the Landtag had been dissolved, and, as the war neared, the voting dates were set for June 25 and July 3. It was what the British call a "khaki election." "For or against the soldiers" was the official slogan. On June 17, 18, and 19 Prussian troops occupied successively Hanover, Dresden, and Kassel. "Already," reported *Das Deutsche Museum* on June 20, "[Bismarck] is followed by rejoicing crowds whenever he appears in the street."[31] On June 22-23 the invasion of Bohemia was begun without resistance. Two days later the shift to the conservatives commenced in the voting for the electoral college. Hoverbeck, Forckenbeck, Grabow, and Waldeck were defeated and forced to seek safer districts for the final election. On June 26-29 came the first victories of the invading Prussian armies in Bohemia and on the 28th the capitulation of the Hanoverian army at Langensalza. While Prussian troops were storming the heights of Chlum on July 3, the electors cast their ballots at home. The conservatives captured 142 seats in contrast to their previous 28, while the left centrists sank from 110 to 65, the progressives from 143 to 83.[32]

30 *OD*, vii, 392; *GW*, v, 315.
31 Quoted in Spahn, "Entstehung," p. 388.
32 Johannes Ziekursch, *Politische Geschichte des neuen deutschen Kaiserreiches*

Had the election been held a few days later, after arrival of the news from Bohemia, the conservative victory would undoubtedly have been still greater. Even so, by allying with the old-liberal faction of nine members, the conservatives could now control the chamber.

But the conservative victory and the liberal defeat were not as clear-cut as first appeared, for the dramatic events of July 1866 had produced an incredible confusion in all parties. No longer were the conservatives unanimous in support of the Bismarck cabinet. Nor were the liberals any longer united against it. Out of the chaos soon emerged an astonishing realignment of political forces. The catalyst which dissolved the old compounds and combined the new was the indemnity bill.

4. THE ''GOLDEN BRIDGE''

In the exultation of victory the ultra-conservatives naturally expected the government to make the liberal defeat conclusive by suspending or revising the constitution. Yet on July 4 Bismarck agreed with the crown prince on the necessity of settling the internal conflict. Having chosen the path of national reform, he recognized the impossibility of basing his government on the "anti-German particularists" of the *Kreuzzeitung* party. "The power of the monarchy in Prussia must be supported by a powerful army," he was even reported as saying, "But it must go with the opinion of the nation. It is the duty of every Prussian minister to regard the will of the king as authoritative, but at the same time to let the will of the king be saturated with the opinion of the nation."[33]

To endure, revolutionary political constructions require a popular base. While the war had been fought without public support, the peace he planned could not be made secure without it. Inside Prussia the incorporated masses had to be reconciled to their new situation, their loyalties to the deposed dynasties erased. A creation of Prussian *Machtpolitik*, the North German Confederation could not subsist in the mass age without popular legitimation. These needs were to be met by German nationalism. It

(Frankfort a. M., 1925-1930), I, 192. Defeated in East Prussia, the liberals did best in the Catholic Rhineland, where some aversion for the war remained. Parisius, *Hoverbeck*, II/2, 93-95.

[33] *GW*, VII, 137, 141, 147; XV, 282 ff.; Friedrich III, *Tagebücher 1848-1866*, p. 454.

was the centripetal force with which to overcome the centrifugal habits of particularism. A continuation of the constitutional conflict would have driven German nationalists, north and south, into the opposing camp. By identifying its cause with that of the nation, Prussia could cut off all hope of revenge on the part of the defeated states and undermine their resistance to the future completion of German unification under Prussian hegemony. As early as July 4 Bismarck spoke of the coming North German Confederation as but a "stage" toward German unity.[34] Such an undertaking required that Prussia have the support of an aroused nation, for it would involve, in all probability, war with France.

To break off the internal struggle was also for Bismarck a matter of personal insurance. Given William's advanced age, he had to reckon that Frederick William might soon ascend the throne. Under him the quarrel, if still in progress, would most certainly be ended—but by another cabinet.[35] In any case Bismarck had never believed in the viability of naked absolutism in Prussia over a long period of time. Since he accepted parliament as a necessity, he had to face the task of building up within it a majority to support his policies. Despite the conservative victory at the polls, the liberals were still a political force. They would be re-inforced by voters in the annexed lands. The populations of Hanover, Hesse-Kassel, Nassau, and Frankfurt could be expected to vote more like the liberal Rhineland, with which they were socially akin, than the conservative east. Only in Mecklenburg could the conservatives expect political reinforcement. But in the other federal states of northern Germany—not to speak of those to be added in the south—Prussian conservatism would stand little chance at the polls.

To form a government majority, therefore, it was essential to attract the moderate liberals. Certainly Bismarck was aware that, despite all the clamor of the constitutional conflict, they were not fundamentally hostile to monarchical institutions or to the type of "mixed constitution" which he intended for Germany. He knew that their alliance with the democratic liberals was an uneasy one, the unnatural child of their common cause in the con-

---

[34] *GW*, VII, 137; xv, 293.

[35] Since 1863 the crown prince had retained his bitterness over the "fox" in the Wilhelmstrasse, but he too was affected by the grandeur of the victory and by Bismarck's efforts after Königgrätz at reconciliation. Friedrich III, *Tagebücher 1848-1866*, pp. xlvii-li.

stitutional conflict. In 1862 he had sought to split it apart as his first maneuver in domestic politics. In the succeeding years he had witnessed the inner cleavages of the liberal movement and observed their weariness and insecurity, their longing for a settlement. By giving in on the budget issue he could meet their conception of the *Rechtsstaat*. By taking up the cause of German unity he could bring them to support an essentially conservative order. This was the "golden bridge" over which he hoped to lead the moderates.[36]

His interviews with Twesten and Lasker apparently convinced him that the opposition could be reconciled only by a sweeping concession. Further evidence was the unwillingness of Bennigsen, Miquel, and others in mid-July to cooperate in summoning a "pre-parliament," despite the pressure of French intervention.[37] After Königgrätz, moreover, Bismarck could afford to grant what he had previously withheld. No longer could the liberals dispute the military reorganization. Without their financial help the government had fought and won two wars. Concessions on the constitutional issue now had the appearance of a royal benevolence rather than of a government defeat.

In Berlin the issue produced a major cabinet crisis. While all the ministers recognized the wisdom of ending the conflict, most thought this could be done by shadow concessions. Only Heydt, the new minister of finance, wished a "bill of indemnity" by which the government would ask parliament's approval of expenditures made during the last four years without its consent. The other ministers were surprised and shocked when word came from Bohemia that both Bismarck and William agreed with this judgment. They strove to have the decision revoked. Never was Bismarck to forget or forgive the "desertion" of his conservative colleagues on this issue. He had, however, a geographical advantage; they were in Berlin, he at the king's side in Bohemia. During the journey homeward on August 4 he talked William into holding to the original decision. The next day, Heydt's draft, with only minor changes, was read from the throne in the speech which opened the special session of the new Prussian Landtag.[38]

36 *GW*, xv, 294.
37 Dehio, "Beiträge," pp. 149-155.
38 *Ibid.*, pp. 147 ff.; Gerhard Ritter, "Entstehung der Indemnitätsvorlage," pp. 17 ff.

5. THE LIBERALS DIVIDE

On August 5, 1866 the white hall of the palace, so empty on February 23, was crowded with deputies, the political atmosphere completely changed. Popular support, for which the opposition had angled so long, was now overwhelmingly on the side of the monarchy. The army, whose reorganization they had opposed and whose financial support they had denied, was brilliantly victorious. Its officers were the Junkers against whose power they had striven in vain. Its commander-in-chief was the king whose ministers had violated the constitution and frustrated the parliamentary will. Back of the whole conservative order, furthermore, loomed the sentiment of German nationalism. In seven weeks dynasty, ministers, army, and Junkers had taken a mighty step toward the realization of the liberal dream of half a century. Achievement of the rest was assumed to be but a matter of time. Now the government announced its willingness to come halfway toward the settlement of the constitutional conflict.

The situation was powerfully persuasive. That the liberals were so strongly affected by it, however, was not merely owing to the dramatic events of June and July 1866. Their capitulation had been prepared for more than a century in the development of the German liberal tradition. Its origin lay in the delayed growth of the German middle class, the peculiar coupling of freedom and authority, the dualism of Kantian thought, the Hegelian deification of the state, and the romantic glorification of force. The liberals were the victims of their own limited ends, their lack of genuine popular support, and their lust for national power. What they had desired was not a fundamental change of the existing political structure, but merely the validation of the "mixed constitution." Never had they aimed at full responsibility for the management of public affairs. Theirs had been a purely defensive action, for the *Rechtsstaat* against the encroachments of arbitrary government. As in 1848 they feared the masses, and as in 1848 the masses were not behind them.

As early as 1864 they had displayed a fatal hunger for military success and foreign expansion; now they found this but an appetizer for the main course. Theirs had been the illusion that wars for great objectives could be fought only with their own support. But the unbelievable had happened. The supposed spokesman of reactionary conservatism had not only steered the country into a major war, but had summoned the nation to accomplish its unity under the protective umbrella of Prussian power. Again the Prussian state had stolen the most vital planks of the liberal platform. Bureaucratic liberalism had preempted once more the program of moderate liberalism. To most there now appeared no other place to stand than upon or under the inviting new structure Bismarck was busily building with stolen materials.

For many the conversion was not difficult. Wehrenpfennig concluded, "Bismarck is, except for Stein, the greatest statesman Prussia has ever had; it appears that he is luckier and perhaps even bolder than the latter." Rudolf Ihering, Göttingen professor of law, who earlier had denounced the war as an act of "frightful frivolity," now bowed down before the "genius of a Bismarck," declaring that for such a man of deeds he would give one hundred of impotent honesty. Almost overnight the Bismarck cult was born. Its devotees began to re-interpret their hero's actions during the preceding four years. They excused his infringements of the constitution in view of what was presumed to have been his hidden purpose. Impatiently the liberal press, so bitterly hostile from March to June, now pressed the deputies not to hinder the government in the fulfillment of its "duty" toward the rest of Germany. In view of the "glorious" work ahead, the issues of the constitutional conflict were declared petty and insignificant.[39]

The classic conversions were those of Gustav Mevissen and Hermann Baumgarten. After watching the victorious columns march down Unter den Linden through the Brandenburger Tor, Mevissen, who had headed the revolutionary cabinet of 1848, described in unforgettable words the emotions which gripped him: "I cannot shake off the impression of this hour. I am no devotee of Mars; I feel more attached to the goddess of beauty and the mother of graces than to the powerful god of war, but the trophies of war exercise a magic charm upon the child of peace. One's view is involuntarily chained and one's spirit goes along with the boundless rows of men who acclaim the god of the moment—success."[40] Baumgarten—student of Gervinus, press official of the new era,

[39] Duncker, *Briefwechsel*, p. 428; Eyck, *Bismarck*, II, 318; Spahn, "Entstehung," pp. 405 ff.
[40] Quoted in Ziekursch, *Politische Geschichte*, I, 189; the translation is from Koppel S. Pinson, *Modern Germany* (New York, 1955), pp. 139-140.

professor of history at Karlsruhe—remorsefully criticized his earlier convictions in the *Preussische Jahrbücher*. Theoretical and doctrinaire, the German liberals had placed their faith in words and ideals rather than in deeds. The middle class was incapable of political leadership. For the solution of its political tasks, he concluded, every people needs the help of an aristocracy.[41]

With care Bismarck nourished the plant of liberal capitulation. Soon after the Landtag opened he fed the deputies a series of bills designed to appeal to every segment of the former opposition. For men of principle there was a bill of indemnity, for Prussian chauvinists a bill of annexation, for German nationalists a Reichstag suffrage bill. He appeared in person to defend and explain them before the committees; in private talks he spun the web of personal charm and sweet reason which had snared so many diplomatic opponents. When the situation called for it, the master of scorn and contempt was equally adept at deference and consideration. He enjoyed the game intensely. A visitor reported that his face, while pale and ill, was radiant with laughter. The man was beyond all exaggeration.[42]

After Königgrätz the liberal deputies were greatly relieved to learn that the triumphant Junker did not intend a coup against the constitution and that he was still serious about a national parliament. Their first chance to respond to his overtures was in the election of a speaker. Since 1862 Grabow had annually been reelected to that office and his bitter opening speeches had been the first demonstration in each parliamentary session of the continued intransigeance of the opposition. But now the deputies chose Forckenbeck, a moderate noted for tact and parliamentary skill. When the reply to the throne speech was drafted, the moderates allowed amendments which made it acceptable even to the conservatives. They argued that the message must demonstrate that the German people were entirely united behind the German policy of the government. Only twenty-five deputies voted against it, including the veteran radical Jacoby, who once more condemned the war as a blow to freedom.[43]

Already there were signs of dissolution in the liberal ranks. In

---

[41] Hermann Baumgarten, "Der deutsche Liberalismus, Eine Selbstkritik," *Preussische Jahrbücher*, Vol. 18 (1866), 455 ff., 575 ff.

[42] Spahn, "Entstehung," p. 404.

[43] *Ibid.*, pp. 413 ff.; *SBHA* (1866-1867), I, 70-83.

mid-August a left centrist, Kannegiesser, reported to his constituents, "The world-historical events of the last months are having a powerful effect upon men's minds." He detected two currents in both of the major liberal parties: one placed the major emphasis on the German question, the other upon Prussian constitutional law.[44] Relieved of the pressure of the constitutional conflict and presented with the possibility of national unity under authoritarian auspices, the liberal deputies began to divide once more into the two traditional segments of moderate right and democratic left. The unnatural alliance of 1861 broke apart over the issue of the relative importance of national unity and the rule of law.

Both camps, to be sure, were inclined toward settlement. But the moderates considered the constitutional conflict irretrievably lost and wished to get rid of it on the terms offered by the government, while the democrats were inclined to seek as firm a guarantee as possible for the future respect of parliament's budget rights. The men of the left found it difficult to join the general jubilation. They had not forgotten that the last breach of the constitution—the creation by decree of a system of credit banks—had occurred but two months before the indemnity bill. They noted that even now the minister of interior continued his "disciplinary" measures against liberal officials and his refusal to confirm liberal city councillors; the minister of justice persisted in his prosecution of the liberal press and opposition deputies (including Twesten). Finally, they observed that the government's indemnity bill contained no guarantee against budgetless rule in the future.[45] When Forckenbeck officially presented the chamber's address, William declared belligerently, "I had to act that way, and I shall do so again, if the same circumstances recur."[46]

In the great debate on the indemnity bill the leaders of the left —Waldeck, Gneist, Ziegler, Virchow, Hoverbeck, Jacoby, Frentzel, and Schulze-Delitzsch—maintained that its passage would

44 Spahn, "Entstehung," p. 422.

45 Thorwart, *Schulze-Delitzsch*, v, 267; Duncker, *Briefwechsel*, p. 429; *SBHA* (1866-1867), I, 149-207.

46 For both Bismarck and Forckenbeck the utterance was an embarrassment. Since no minister was present, the speaker chose to interpret it as unofficial and hence not to be formally reported to the chamber. In a cabinet meeting Bismarck got the ministers to take a similar view. *SBHA* (1866-1867), I, 115; Martin Philippson, *Max von Forckenbeck, Ein Lebensbild* (Dresden, 1898), pp. 154-155; Eyck, *Bismarck*, II, 305.

legitimize the "gap theory" and pardon four years of unconstitutional behavior on the part of the cabinet. The deputies should postpone the bill pending passage of a legal budget and a law fixing ministerial responsibility. Military victory and respect for law must not be confused with each other. Whatever its successes abroad, the government must stay within the law at home. But the leaders of the right—Twesten, Forckenbeck, Lasker, and Michaelis—feared that, if the liberals remained in opposition, the flight of the voters to the conservatives would continue. By supporting the Bismarck cabinet, on the other hand, they might sever it from its conservative base and influence the future constitutional structure of Germany. In summing up the moderate position, Twesten declared that two issues were fundamental to every state: those of freedom and power. "No one may be criticized for giving precedence to the issue of power at this time and maintaining that the issues of freedom can wait, provided that nothing happens which can permanently prejudice them." From Bismarck the deputies heard of the dangers of French intervention and Austrian resurgence. Only a united people could succeed in Germany's mission against an injured and envious Europe. On September 3 the indemnity bill passed by a vote of 230 to 75.[47]

The constitutional conflict was over, but so also was the unity of the liberal movement. During August and September the caucuses of the Progressive Party became increasingly heated. The exodus of the moderates began with Michaelis, followed by Twesten, Lasker, and many others. By a number of concessions Bismarck gave the secessionists the chance to feel at last the exhilaration of being in harmony with the ruling power. They were permitted to redraft the indemnity bill to make it correspond with the budget clauses of the constitution. Instead of "personal union," Bismarck accepted the actual incorporation of the conquered lands into Prussia, but the introduction of the Prussian constitution was to be delayed one year. A bill presented by Heydt to legalize the government-sponsored credit banks was passed, but only after an amendment which soon put them out of business. A serious clash over the government's request for a credit of sixty million *Thaler* was settled by a compromise which limited the size and purpose of the reserves accumulated by the treasury. Prodded

[47] *SBHA* (1866-1867), I, 149-207; Spahn, "Entstehung," pp. 423 ff.; Löwenthal, *Verfassungsstreit*, pp. 302 ff.

by Lasker and Forckenbeck, the crown issued a general amnesty on September 21, the day of the victory celebration in Berlin. William's request for a dotation of one and a half million *Thaler* for the victorious generals was voluntarily amended by the chamber to include the name of Bismarck![48]

Originally the secessionists did not intend to found a new party. Their aim was to convince the majority in the Left Center and Progressive Parties of the validity of a new strategy. By supporting the Bismarck cabinet in foreign affairs, they hoped to bring it step by step along the road of domestic compromise. But their former comrades remained unconvinced that such a procedure would result in any fundamental changes in the existing order. In the expanded Landtag and constituent Reichstag of 1867 the secessionists found the non-Prussian liberals more sympathetic to their cause. Never personally involved in the Prussian conflict, the latter were untainted by its passions and less concerned about its issues. They too regarded the struggle as lost and relatively unimportant compared to the great task ahead. Out of this union of forces came the National Liberal Party. In numbers the non-Prussians predominated, and the leadership fell to two Hanoverians, Bennigsen and Miquel.[49]

The liberal movement had divided between a Progressive Party, largely Prussian and preserving the tradition of the conflict years, and a National Liberal Party, largely non-Prussian and more national than liberal. To the democratic left the cleavage was between "opportunists" and "men of principle"; to the moderate right it was between "practical statesmen" and "naïve idealists." The moderates had taken the road which ultimately led to unconditional surrender, the democrats that which finally ended in frustration and impotence.

6. THE CONSERVATIVES DIVIDE

In the heat of the constitutional conflict most conservatives failed to notice that the pied piper in the Wilhelmstrasse was leading them farther and farther away from the party's principles. The vigor and fearlessness of his struggle against parliament, the

---

[48] Spahn, "Entstehung," pp. 443 ff. Otto Michaelis belonged to a group of free traders, whose liberalism was primarily economic. They were attracted by the free trade policy of the Prussian government and had always been cool toward the constitutional conflict. See Schunke, *Freihändler*, p. 50.

[49] Spahn, "Entstehung," pp. 439 ff., 469.

Alvensleben convention, and the Austrian alliance seemed convincing evidence of his conservative orthodoxy. While Ludwig Gerlach was shocked by the "Godless and lawless greed" of the annexation policy, most conservatives soon convinced themselves that the duchies were Prussia's just reward for the glorious deeds of the army. Nevertheless, they welcomed the Gastein treaty, for cooperation with Russia and Austria was still a primary tenet in conservative political dogma. For the same reason the renewal of the diplomatic struggle in January 1866 was deeply disturbing. By an intensive campaign in the official and conservative press, however, Bismarck was able to propagate the view that his policy was purely defensive.[50]

In April the news of the Prussian reform plan, rumors of the Italian alliance, and the general drift toward war threw the conservatives into confusion. Wagener strove to convince the readers of the *Kreuzzeitung* of the virtue of the government's policy. But Ludwig Gerlach, as one of its columnists, severely censured the Bismarckian course. Through his contacts he sought to influence the court and cabinet. Finally he ventured into the "lion's den"! In a "lacerating interview" the two men severed a lifelong friendship. To Gerlach the attack on Austria was like "the fratricide of Cain, the betrayal of Judas, and the crucifixion of the Lord."[51]

But the elderly romantic was unable to carry the party as a whole. Among the cabinet members only Bodelschwingh could not square the Bismarck policy with his conscience. He resigned.[52] Most conservatives were not inclined to take the parliament plan seriously; the violent reaction of the liberals seemed proof of its inconsequence. Furthermore, the prospect of Prussian aggrandizement, nourished by the earlier propaganda for annexation, had its appeal. When the climactic moment came, Prussian patriotism and fear of a "second Olmütz" triumphed over the doubts of the conservatives. The astonishing electoral victory of July 3 was their reward for constancy. The "small but mighty party" was no longer small.[53]

[50] Gerhard Ritter, *Die preussischen Konservativen und Bismarcks deutsche Politik, 1858-1875* (Heidelberg, 1913), pp. 89 ff., 131 ff.

[51] Ludwig Gerlach, *Aufzeichnungen*, II, 281-293, 300.

[52] The minister of finance had long been concerned over Bismarck's readiness to violate the constitution in the struggle with parliament. *Ibid.*, II, 273, 277.

[53] Ritter, *Konservativen*, pp. 131 ff.

In late July the first report of Bismarck's intention to reconcile the opposition exploded in the conservative camp. The ultras, even as they gloated over their triumph and the final reckoning they presumed was to come, suddenly found themselves deserted by their own leader. Beginning on July 25, the *Kreuzzeitung* sounded the alarm. Through the indiscretion of a cabinet minister, the reactionary Hans von Kleist-Retzow learned the content of the coming throne speech. Frantically he sought to mobilize a camarilla of influential conservatives. Bismarck was bitter. "The little people don't have enough to do; they see no further than their own noses and like to swim on the stormy sea of phrases. With the enemy one can cope, but the friends!"[54]

The indemnity bill was a wedge which penetrated the conservatives as well as the progressives. Led by Count Bethusy-Huc, about fifteen deputies caucused at the end of July and agreed to support the policy of reconciliation. At the time it was not their intention to form a new party. They wished merely to find a basis for collaboration with the small remaining faction of old liberals, without whom the conservatives could not control the chamber. But as the session progressed, the cleavage widened, and the Free Conservative Party was born.[55]

Outwardly solid, the monolith of the Conservative Party had always had an internal fault. Whereas the "old conservatives" were Prussian particularists, the free conservatives were open-minded on the subject of national unity. In religious matters the former were solidly Lutheran, pietistic, and orthodox, while the latter were either Catholic or non-religious. The cleavage was also geographical and occupational. While the strength of the old conservatives lay among the feudal gentry of the Prussian heartland (East Prussia, Pomerania, Brandenburg), the free conservatives were strongest in the annexed regions of Silesia and the Rhineland. A party of *Bildung und Besitz*, its deputies were high nobility, officials, generals, professors, and (later) great industrialists. Never was the party to cultivate or attract a mass following. Its strength lay in the favor of the government, which it uncondition-

---

[54] *GW*, xiv, 720.

[55] Ritter, *Konservativen*, pp. 179 ff.; August Wolfstieg, "Die Anfänge der freikonservativen Partei," in Emil Daniels and others, eds., *Delbrück-Festschrift* (Berlin, 1908), pp. 317 ff.; Kurd Viebig, *Die Entstehung und Entwicklung der Freikonservativen und der Reichspartei* (Weimar, 1920), pp. 14 ff.

ally supported at home and abroad. It was the "Bismarck party *sans phrase*."[56]

In the debates on the annexation of Hanover and Hesse-Kassel, the effect of four years of Bismarckian leadership was evident on both conservative parties. In the two houses of the Landtag the conservatives, feudal as well as free, voted solidly for incorporation. "Thou shalt not steal," thundered Gerlach, but even Kleist-Retzow rejoiced at such a handsome expansion for Prussia.[57] In the society of states successful larceny is legitimized by time. Under Bismarck's tutelage the politics of power triumphed over the doctrinaire idealism of romantic conservatism, the appeal of Prussian patriotism over the sense of universal right. One day he would also succeed in the greater task of convincing the conservatives as a whole that German nationalism was a potential friend, not the irreconcilable foe of the aristocratic-monarchical order.

7. THE SOCIALISTS EMERGE

The war of 1866 had yet another consequence of importance for German social and political development. By choosing the path of national reform and the conversion of the moderate liberals, Bismarck began the welding of a political union between the land-owning aristocracy and the capitalistic bourgeoisie. Shut out by an alliance of the propertied classes, labor had no other choice than to find a leadership and ideology of its own.

At first Schweitzer, now the virtual dictator of the German Workingmen's Association, saw in the war an opportunity to resume Lassalle's negotiations with the extreme right. His premature release from prison and Bismarck's subsidy of the *Sozialdemokrat* pointed to the possibility of success. In December he sought contact with the minister-president, but no summons came from the Wilhelmstrasse and no help from the conservatives in the Reichstag election of February 12, 1867. In Elberfeld Schweitzer polled 4,668 votes, but lost the seat to Bismarck himself. Since the progressives also refused their cooperation, his party was unable to elect a single candidate in Germany's first major election under universal, direct, and equal suffrage.[58]

The Lassalleans no longer monopolized the independent labor

---

[56] See Siegfried von Kardorff, *Wilhelm von Kardorff* (Berlin, 1936), pp. 32 ff.
[57] Ritter, *Konservativen*, pp. 184 ff.
[58] Mayer, *Schweitzer*, pp. 180 ff.

movement. In Saxony a competing organization had appeared under the formidable leadership of August Bebel and Wilhelm Liebknecht. A disciple of Marx and emissary of the socialist international, Liebknecht had enjoyed no success as a proletarian agitator until his expulsion from Prussia in August 1865. Migrating to Leipzig, he found in the youthful Bebel a ready convert to the doctrine of proletarian socialism. A wood turner by profession, Bebel was the most important figure in the chain of Saxon educational associations (*Arbeiterbildungsvereine*) founded under liberal auspices for the cultural elevation of the working class. As late as 1865 Bebel had appealed to the Nationalverein for financial aid in combating the Lassallean socialists. In 1866 he opposed, with Liebknecht, the civil war produced by Prussian imperialism. Unlike Schweitzer and the Lassalleans, both remained unreconciled to the Prussian, little-German solution of the problem of national unity. They were convinced that Schweitzer had sold out to the Prussian government.[59]

But Bebel was also appalled at the readiness with which the liberals came to terms with Hohenzollern autocracy. With Liebknecht he founded in August 1866 the Saxon People's Party, which succeeded in electing two deputies (one of whom was Bebel himself) to the constituent Reichstag. The first party program was democratic rather than socialistic, for its founders realized that most proletarians were unprepared for the doctrine of the class struggle. At rallies in Nürnberg in 1868 and Eisenach in 1869, however, they commenced the conversion of their followers to the radical program of the socialist international. The outcome was the Social Democratic Labor Party founded at Eisenach for the "emancipation of the working class."[60]

In February 1867 Schulze-Delitzsch wrote that he was considering retirement from politics to devote his entire energy to the social question. "The agitation among the workers is becoming

[59] Ernst Schraepler, "Linksliberalismus und Arbeiterschaft in der preussischen Konfliktszeit," in Richard Dietrich and Gerhard Oestreich, eds., *Forschungen zu Staat und Verfassung, Festgabe für Fritz Hartung* (Berlin, 1958), pp. 398 ff.; August Bebel, *Aus Meinem Leben* (Stuttgart, 1910), I, 89-90, 126 ff. Two eminent students of the problem have denied that Schweitzer lost his independence through his dealings with Bismarck. Mehring, *Sozialdemokratie*, III, 248 ff.; Mayer, "Arbeiterverein," pp. 170-171.

[60] Bebel, *Leben*, I, 164 ff.; II, 86 ff.; Gustav Mayer, "Die Trennung der proletarischen von der bürgerlichen Demokratie in Deutschland, 1863-1870," *Archiv für die Geschichte des Sozialismus und der Arbeiterbewegung*, II (1912), 24 ff.

ever more serious and threatens our political and economic development in a dangerous way. Our political leaders do not yet see it. . . . It often seems to me that I am the only seeing person among the blind!"[61] The refusal of the liberals to accept the political equality of labor through universal suffrage, their unwillingness to face the social issue by questioning the dogma of *laissez-faire*, and, finally, their betrayal in 1866 of their own highest ideals, convinced a growing number of proletarians of the validity of the concept of the class struggle. The crack which had opened in the German social structure in 1863 began to widen.

[61] Thorwart, *Schulze-Delitzsch*, v, 268.

CHAPTER FIFTEEN

THE GERMAN BALANCE OF POWER

1. DRAFTING THE CONSTITUTION

NE of the early myths of the Bismarck cult was that the man of genius, assisted by Lothar Bucher, drafted the north German constitution in two days of intensive effort after his return to Berlin on December 1, 1866. Supporting this assumption was the fact that for two months prior to that date he had convalesced at Putbus on the Baltic from a serious illness brought on by the exertions and frictions of the preceding summer. According to his wife, the very thought of politics made him depressed and irate during much of that time.[1] The archives show, nevertheless, that the December draft had a lengthy ancestry, beginning with the "outline" presented to the Frankfurt diet on June 10. From such politically disparate persons as Max Duncker, Reichenbach, Wagener, and Savigny, preliminary drafts were received from which features were taken. The ministries of war and commerce supplied the military and economic clauses. Still, the basic structure of the document was entirely Bismarck's work. Only after more than six months of careful calculation and frequent change did the final version mature. Throughout the complicated process of adoption thereafter it retained the basic imprint he gave it. Seldom in history has a constitution been so clearly the product of the thought and will of a single individual.[2]

Controversy still rages over the interpretation of this document and the purposes of its author. For almost a century historians and political scientists have debated whether it was the outgrowth of a "German or great-Prussian" policy, whether his intention was to create a German national government or merely a federal mask for Prussian hegemony.[3] The issue, however, is

[1] Robert von Keudell, *Fürst und Fürstin Bismarck, Erinnerungen 1846-1872* (Berlin, 1901), pp. 313 ff.

[2] For a detailed study of the evolution of the Bismarck draft see Otto Becker, *Bismarcks Ringen um Deutschlands Gestaltung* (Heidelberg, 1958), pp. 211 ff.

[3] For a review of this controversy, see *ibid.*, pp. 17 ff., 834 ff.

falsely conceived. In all probability Bismarck's chief concern in drafting the constitution was simply the problem of political control. He wished to repeat in the North German Confederation the basic power arrangement of the Prussian state and thereby perpetuate the conservative order in the larger political context created by Prussian conquest. But he also had a personal problem: that of circumventing the collegial structure of the Prussian cabinet in order to build up his own authority as the chief minister of the crown.

Bismarck's constitution has long been celebrated as a masterpiece of political realism. Not an artificial design based on abstract party doctrine, it was a practical instrument which combined existing forces and sought their harmonious development. It united the forces of German nationalism and particularism, and solved the problem of uniting states of disproportionate size. Planned as the first stage toward little-German unity, its national features were intended to attract southern peoples and its federal ones to reassure their governments. While all this is true, German authors usually fail to recognize the additional fact that the constitution was designed primarily to serve a particular social and political interest. The essence of the Bismarckian constitution was its conservation, by the use of revolutionary means, of the Prussian aristocratic-monarchical order in a century of increasingly dynamic economic and social change.

2. THE PRUSSIAN CROWN

With the annexations of 1866 the Prussian state embraced over four-fifths of the population of the North German Confederation and two-thirds of that of the future German Reich. The great majority of the German people were now governed under the constitution which had produced the conflict of 1862-1866 and which the indemnity bill had left unchanged. Bismarck's December draft proposed a similar system for the rest of Germany.[4] Actually it gave even greater powers to the Hohenzollern crown than did the Prussian constitution of 1850.

To preserve the fiction that the new confederation was simply a reformed version of the old, the King of Prussia was granted the "presidency," an office previously held by the Hapsburg mon-

[4] For the December draft see *GW*, VI, 187-196.

archy. But the presidency of the North German Confederation was a position of real authority. It received full control over foreign affairs, including the right to declare war and make peace and to negotiate treaties and alliances. Furthermore, it might appoint and dismiss the chancellor and any officials of the confederation. It was empowered to publish the laws of the confederation and oversee their execution. Although parliament was to meet yearly, the presidency was authorized to summon, open, prorogue, and close it. On the motion of the upper chamber (Bundesrat) the presidency might also dissolve the lower chamber (Reichstag). No provision was made either for new elections or for reconvening that body within a definite time limit.

Among the most detailed articles were those dealing with military affairs. Here some nominal concessions were made to the states and their rulers. The confederate army was to be composed of state "contingents," whose "chiefs" were the reigning princes. To the latter belonged the authority to appoint all officers below the rank of contingent commander and to employ for police purposes the troops of the contingent and such confederate troops as were located within the borders of the states. The administration of routine military affairs was also apparently left to the state governments.

Yet these concessions to particularism were largely superficial. The draft provided the King of Prussia with most of the powers of military hegemony for which William had so long yearned and striven. It left no doubt that the army was a unitary force under his personal command. Its highest officers, including the contingent commanders, were appointed by him and swore allegiance to his person. All confederate troops swore a similar oath of unconditional obedience. He could mobilize all or any part of the army at will. The provisions dealing with the navy were similar, except that there were no contingents, and officers of all ranks were sworn to the King of Prussia. To quell internal disturbances he could declare martial law. In an emergency the king, as commander-in-chief, could order an "execution" against a rebellious state, even to the point of "sequestering" it. Normally, however, such an action required the approval of the Bundesrat.

Bismarck's draft extended the Prussian military system over the whole of the confederate army and consolidated the government's victory over parliament in the matter of military reform.

By establishing the peacetime strength of each contingent at one percent of the population and the obligation of every able-bodied citizen to serve three years in the line, four in the reserve, and five in the militia, it placed these matters beyond the reach of both the Reichstag and the chamber of deputies. To the commander-in-chief was given the authority to enforce uniformity in weapons, command, training, organization, and general preparedness. The Prussianization of the lesser contingents, moreover, was assured by a clause which made all Prussian military laws, regulations, instructions, and ordinances valid for the whole army. Such matters were to be beyond the control of the states and the Reichstag.

As though to obscure their import and reduce their vulnerability to attack, the articles dealing with public finance were scattered throughout the draft. They made a mockery of parliamentary budget rights. No provision was made for an annual budget, or a periodic budget of any duration. While the financial support of the armed forces was transferred to the confederation, the Reichstag did not gain the power lost by the Prussian chamber of deputies. The "iron budget," as it was subsequently called, set the yearly appropriations for the army at 225 *Thaler* per soldier for the indefinite future. Another clause obviously envisioned the establishment, though in agreement with the Reichstag, of a similar "iron budget" for the navy. Only military and naval expenditures in excess of the amounts thus determined were to be subject to regular legislative approval. Even under normal circumstances the armed forces consumed almost the whole of the confederate revenues; in 1868 the army received 88.8 percent and the navy 10.7 percent.[5]

Furthermore, parliamentary control over the sources of this income was to be just as scant. The confederation was given power to levy only indirect taxes. Since their yield increases with the development of the economy, taxes of this kind meant a constant growth in income without additional legislative approval. It was obvious, nevertheless, that the needs of the armed forces could not be fully met from such sources. Hence the draft provided for quotas to be levied on the states in ratio to their populations. In the case of the army the amount of these payments was to be determined by the presidency alone according to its estimate

[5] Karl Zuchardt, *Die Finanzpolitik Bismarcks und die Parteien im Norddeutschen Bunde, Leipziger Historische Abhandlungen*, Vol. 16 (Leipzig, 1910), p. 33.

of the "need." Because of the overwhelming size of the military budget, this last provision barred the Reichstag from any effective control over confederate income. Should parliament refuse new taxes, the presidency had only to increase the state quotas to make up the difference.

The power of the Reichstag and the freedom of its members was checked in still other ways. The draft made no express provision for the rights of interpellation and petition. Immunity was granted the deputies for speeches made in the chamber, but not to the press which reported them. The article dealing with libel and defamation of the confederation, its institutions and officials, was taken from the Prussian penal code, where it had been used to silence the opposition press during the constitutional conflict. Officials were declared ineligible for election. The remuneration of deputies for parliamentary service was expressly forbidden. The working man was given the right to vote, but only for his betters. Finally, there was no bill of rights stating the fundamental freedoms of the citizenry.

In Bismarck's draft the fundamental dilemma of his constitutional thinking is again apparent. While hoping to generate mass support for conservative institutions, he distrusted the lower classes and, despite his recent experiences, saw in men of property the best guarantee of political stability. He believed in the necessity of parliament to criticize and check unwise acts of the crown and bureaucracy, but he was reluctant to invest it with a power adequate to make such control effective.

3. THE EQUILIBRIUM

Bismarck's German constitution was not, however, a mere copy of the Prussian. His experiences in the recent conflict had demonstrated the inflexibility of the latter. When crown and parliament were in disagreement there was no alternative to the sort of deadlock which had occurred during the previous four years. In the multiple forces and institutions of a united Germany he saw the opportunity for a system of checks and balances which would provide the means of escape. Bismarck's system was not derived from the theory of Montesquieu or the constitutional practice of the American or any other government, but from those techniques of political strategy which he had developed in the diplomatic quarrels of the 1850's and applied with devastating success in the coups of the 1860's. The pattern was not one of three co-equal, mutually balanced forces, but of an equilibrium controlled from the pivotal position of the fulcrum with its enduring possibility of choice between opposed interests.

With this insight the old problem of Bismarck's "Germanism" or "Prussianism" loses its actuality. What interested him was not the supremacy of Germany or Prussia, but their duality and the advantages it offered for political control. Centralistic and particularistic institutions were to be played off against each other. A bid for power by the Prussian chamber of deputies could be countered through the Reichstag and vice versa. Based upon different suffrage laws, the two parliaments would very likely have different political compositions. After July 1867 there was still a third parliament, that of the Zollverein, chosen by universal suffrage and embracing the whole of Germany.

The structure of balanced forces in Bismarck's draft is also to be seen in the division of powers between the confederate and state governments. The former received legislative authority over: customs and commerce; the important means of transportation and communication (navigation, railroads, the post and telegraph); certain financial matters (banking, coinage, and currency); certain types of justice (code of civil procedure, bankruptcy procedure, commercial and exchange law); and several miscellaneous affairs vitally important to the business community (weights, measures, patents, copyrights, the consular services, and the rights of domicile, migration, and choice of occupation). To the confederation was given the right to levy tariffs and certain consumption taxes (sugar, spirits, salt, beer, and tobacco) and to receive the surplus income of the post and telegraph systems.

While the draft did not specifically say so, it was apparently intended that the state governments would retain the right to legislate on all other matters. The most important of the powers remaining to the states was that of executing most of the laws passed by the central government. The confederation was limited to the right of "supervising" this administration as to its conformity to the law. This applied even to the collection of customs and consumption taxes and to the local administration of the post and telegraph. Judicial matters, furthermore, were left within the jurisdiction of the state courts, even where offenses against confederate law were concerned. Although the constitution established a national citizenship, it permitted concurrent state citizenship. The phrasing of this article actually made the latter appear more important by requiring the states to grant to all residents the same rights enjoyed by their own citizens. The states might retain their consuls where none were stationed by the confederation.

Within the confederate government power was divided between the Reichstag and Bundesrat. Reichstag deputies were to be elected by universal and direct suffrage for a three-year legislative period and were to be regarded as "representatives of the whole population." The Bundesrat was modelled after the old Frankfurt diet.[6] Its delegates were representatives of the state governments, which instructed their votes. One clause even obliged the presidency to provide them with "diplomatic protection"! To become a law, a bill had to pass by simple majority through both houses. Constitutional amendments required a two-thirds majority in the Bundesrat. Both houses possessed the right of legislative initiative.

The two chambers were unequal. As conceived in the draft, the Bundesrat was not the upper house of a bicameral legislature, but a "cabinet" equipped with both legislative and executive power. Its executive functions were to be performed through certain committees which were established in the constitution itself. In accordance with their ministerial status, members of the Bundesrat were given the privilege of being heard at will on the floor of the Reichstag. The Bundesrat might convene without the Reichstag, but never the latter without the former. Finally, the delegates of the Bundesrat were paid officials of the state governments, while Reichstag deputies were expressly forbidden remuneration.

Bismarck's draft made no provision for a central judiciary. The only higher court mentioned was the superior court of the Hanseatic cities (Bremen, Hamburg, and Lübeck), which received jurisdiction over cases of treason (*Hochverrat* as well as *Landesverrat*). Disputes between states were to be settled by the Bundesrat and constitutional conflicts within states by way of confed-

[6] The draft of December 9 actually preserved the terms "Bundestag" and "Gesandte" from the nomenclature of the old diet. On the insistence of the crown prince, who found them "abhorrent," they were changed to "Bundesrat" and "Bevollmächtigte." Becker, *Bismarcks Ringen*, pp. 287-288.

erate legislation. In other words, constitutional issues in Prussia might be transferred from the Landtag to the Reichstag, which, having a different political composition, might accept the crown's position. Concerning disagreements over the interpretation of the confederate constitution itself, however, Bismarck's draft was significantly silent. The German constitution, like the Prussian, was to have its "gap."

Here then was Bismarck's mechanism of the balance. The institutions and powers of the confederation were to be in equilibrium with those of Prussia and the states. The former would receive more legislative, the latter more administrative authority. Within the central government a second division was to take place between two organs, one of which had only legislative, the other both legislative and executive functions. Pressure would be met by counterpressure: the nation against the dynasties, the confederation against Prussia, Reichstag against Bundesrat, parliament against parliament, centralism against particularism, the centripetal against the centrifugal. But how was the balance to be controlled?

4. THE FULCRUM

The privileged position of Prussia in the Bundesrat is usually taken as proof of her hegemony. Of forty-three votes she received seventeen. The number was derived by adding the votes of Prussia and the annexed states in the Frankfurt diet.[7] In addition, Prussia was given representation on all committees and the right to name the entire membership of those on military and naval affairs. Although small in ratio to her population, seventeen votes gave her an absolute veto over constitutional changes. Theoretically, Prussia could be outvoted on ordinary legislation, since the other states together possessed four more than a majority. But it was not difficult to hold enough of the smaller states in line to stave off revolt. Furthermore, the issue might always be taken to the Reichstag, where members of the Bundesrat had the right to present their views.

But the "hegemony of Prussia" was in Bismarck's draft actually that of the Prussian minister of foreign affairs. Through the fiction that the Bundesrat was but the reformed version of the diet, Bismarck retained the power to instruct the Prussian dele-

[7] *GW*, VI, 168-169.

gates, including the chancellor. In the original plan the latter was to have been merely the presiding officer of the Bundesrat. The position was consciously modelled after that of the "presidential envoy" in Frankfurt, who had acted only on orders from the Ballplatz. Ostensibly it was destined for Savigny, Berlin's last delegate in the diet. Through the power to instruct the chancellor and Prussian delegates Bismarck would have had, as foreign minister, the decisive voice in the affairs of a government in which he held no official post. Camouflaged by the Bundesrat, he would have presented the least possible target for the attacks of opposition deputies in the Reichstag.

But could he have escaped the restraint of his own colleagues in the Prussian cabinet? During the constitutional conflict they had repeatedly opposed him on domestic issues—sometimes with success. Most recently their opposition on the indemnity bill had excited his wrath and scorn.[8] Like the minister of war, the foreign minister had direct access to the king and was an exception to the collegial rule. But once he commenced to handle internal matters such as finance, commerce, and the like, friction with other ministers was certain. To assist in coordinating the affairs of Prussia and the confederation, Bismarck planned to appoint high officials (below the ministerial level) as Prussian delegates to the Bundesrat, where they were to head the "different branches" of confederate administration. But obviously this would have created conflicting loyalties. Bismarck admitted to the constituent Reichstag that he would not be able to ignore the wishes of the other cabinet members on matters of confederate policy. In cases of disagreement he would either have to concede or seek new colleagues.[9] Neither choice was attractive.

There are indications that from the beginning Bismarck secretly intended to assume the chancellorship and create under that office an executive organ capable of overshadowing his colleagues in the Prussian cabinet. His substitution of the more exalted title "chancellor" for "presidential envoy" is suspicious. Certainly he did not intend this as a favor to Savigny. In fact, he looked upon this diplomat as a talented, ambitious man with dangerously good connections at court. During October he became alarmed over what his old friend "Charles" wanted to make out of the chancellorship on his own account. He suspected him of intending to de-

8 Becker, *Bismarcks Ringen*, p. 243.   9 *GW*, x, 351-353.

mand the right of immediate access to the king. This surmise was enough to put an end, we may be sure, to whatever chance Savigny may still have had of becoming chancellor.[10]

Other signs indicate that Bismarck expected the development on the confederate level of a fairly extensive administrative apparatus. His draft assumed the existence of officials to perform the functions and wield the powers of the presidency in the administration of customs, indirect taxes, the post and telegraph systems, and the regulation of railways. It was not difficult to foresee that the use by the Reichstag and Bundesrat of confederate legislative power would soon create the need for numerous officials dealing with other matters. How was this civil service to be organized, and who was to direct it? Upon this subject the draft was suspiciously silent. Passages, unknown until recently, in his October 30 "dictation" to Keudell show that he expected the appearance of confederate "ministries" and foresaw the evolution of the Bundesrat into a purely legislative "upper house" chosen by the state governments in ratio to their populations. By "ministries" Bismarck actually meant "departments," for he intended them to develop, as they ultimately did, under his own direct authority as chancellor.[11]

But if this was his intention, why did he not openly provide for it? Like all that came from his pen, the constitutional draft was a diplomatic document. To have made clear his ultimate purpose would have excited the suspicion and jealousy of his fellow ministers and created a dangerous and time-consuming quarrel within the cabinet. So centralistic a feature, moreover, would have increased the difficulties of gaining the approval of the governments of the medium states, particularly those in the south, which were as yet outside the confederation. For these reasons it was prudent to conceal his aim until the time came for its achievement.[12] To progress by stages, attempting at any one stage only what circumstances would allow, while leaving open the avenue toward the next, was typical of his political procedure.

[10] Becker, *Bismarcks Ringen*, pp. 274-276, 236 ff., 257-264, 361-362.

[11] *Ibid.*, pp. 241-242, 255-256, 270-271 (n. 28); *GW*, vi, 167-169. See also his remarks to Grand Duke Frederick of Baden in 1870 about the necessity of "simplifying the mechanism for handling affairs in the uppermost regions." Hermann Oncken, ed., *Grossherzog Friedrich I. von Baden und die deutsche Politik von 1854-1871* (Stuttgart, 1927), ii, 234.

[12] Becker, *Bismarcks Ringen*, pp. 273-274.

As in the Schleswig-Holstein and German questions, each preliminary stage was a potential halting place, if the higher one should be unachievable. Had the construction of an independent confederate executive proved impossible, the chancellorship could have been left to a subordinate and its "business" (a word carefully chosen for ambiguity) restricted to presiding over the Bundesrat. In this event his personal force and political genius would have sufficed to make of the Prussian foreign ministry the dominant organ in the constitutional structures of both Prussia and the confederation.[13]

Yet the most secure lever of power was neither the chancellorship nor the Prussian foreign ministry alone, but the two in conjunction with each other. That Bismarck later relinquished for a time the minister-presidency shows that he believed this position—inaccurately as it proved—less important than the other two. Only by linking these positions of control was it possible to hold on to the many arms of the balance. Together they provided him with the pivotal situation from which were possible the many alternative combinations which were his constant quest in the uncertain game of politics. In possession of them he had some hope of avoiding in the future the kind of head-on clash with parliament which he had experienced during the last four years.

5. KING AND CABINET

Bismarck's virtuosity as a political tactician was never more brilliantly demonstrated than in the process by which he obtained the adoption, without crippling amendments, of his constitutional draft as the basic law of the North German Confederation, ultimately the German Reich. Each of the political forces which he intended to harness to the common chariot through the constitution had a voice in its adoption: the Prussian cabinet, the dynasties and governments of the free cities, the nation (represented by the constituent Reichstag), and the Prussian Landtag. None desired the solution he devised. Using the familiar technique, he proceeded by stages, nullifying each force in turn by the strategy of balanced alternatives. Every attempt to alter the fundamental arrangements of his plan was countered by evoking the opposing interest which stood to lose by the change. Again he occupied that strategic middle position between conflicting forces which enabled

[13] *Ibid.*, pp. 276-277.

him to exploit their mutual rivalry. The first obstacles thus surmounted were the king and cabinet.

Bismarck's illness in October-November 1866 was a misfortune from which he, as usual, knew how to squeeze an advantage. It removed him from Berlin and William's presence at a critical moment, but at the same time placed him conveniently out of reach of the ministers and Savigny, freeing him from the necessity of dealing with their views. In the seclusion of Putbus he made his decisions, and between December 1 and 8 he completed the draft in Berlin. On the ninth the king, crown prince, and ministers saw it for the first time. They had but five days to consider and amend it (two of which were taken up by a royal hunt) before its presentation on the fifteenth to a council of ministers representing the states.

In so brief an interval none were able to grasp the real meaning of this document, with its complicated relationships, or to penetrate the hidden purposes of its author. Undoubtedly Bismarck stressed the features which most appealed to their conservative hearts: the hegemonial authority of the presidency and the commander-in-chief, the limited power of the Reichstag in military and financial matters, and the safeguards against repetition of the constitutional conflict. To increase the prerogatives of Prussia, as the king and other ministers wished, or to accentuate the unitary element, as the crown prince desired, would simply make it more difficult for the lesser dynasties and free cities to accept the plan. Bismarck's arguments and the haste with which the matter was considered sufficed to prevent anything more than peripheral amendments.[14] The fundamental structure of the original draft remained unaltered.

6. THE COUNCIL OF MINISTERS

Even in the midst of war the first steps had been taken to bind the states of northern Germany to Prussia. An ultimatum on June 16 compelled nineteen petty principalities and free cities to ally with her, place their military forces under her command, and agree to a "new, more vital union." On August 4 Prussia demanded that they agree to cooperate with a popularly elected parliament in the establishment of a federal constitution.[15] By

14 See *ibid.*, pp. 284-289 and the footnotes in *GW*, vi, 187-196.
15 *GW*, vi, 1-3, 29-30.

August 18 fifteen had signed. The last, Meiningen, capitulated on October 8 under the duress of a Prussian occupation. The two enemy states of the north which escaped annexation, Hesse-Darmstadt and Saxony, were incorporated in the confederation through their peace treaties, September 3 and October 21.

Prussia was the victor and the lesser states were compelled to yield. Nevertheless, they were not utterly powerless to resist the terms of the constitution or to effect its amendment. In the south the remaining medium states were watching the fate of Prussia's new "allies," particularly Saxony, for clues to their own future. Furthermore, Bismarck wished to preserve the states as a vital political force. He needed their support against the demands of the liberal parties in the constituent Reichstag. Thereafter they were to be one of the important weights in the constitutional equilibrium.

The potential leader of the dynastic opposition was Saxony, after Prussia the largest in land, population, and wealth. At Nikolsburg Austria had insisted on the maintenance of Saxony's territorial integrity as a condition of peace. Frustrated in his lust for annexation, William was determined to insist upon military terms which would have ended the existence of the Saxon army. When the venerable King John resisted Prussia's threats and was supported by France, Bismarck moderated his terms to allow for a Saxon contingent under Prussian command. At this point the Junker fell ill and withdrew from the negotiation. In October he was "depressed" by the news that William, unwilling to accept even this concession, had permitted a peace treaty to be signed which left to a later date the settlement of the military question. Bismarck recognized instantly that Saxony would be able to use Prussia's need of a military convention as a lever with which to attempt constitutional amendments favorable to her interests and damaging to his basic constitutional plan.[16]

On receiving the Prussian draft (December 15), the members of the council of ministers were shocked. It had the appearance of a makeshift plan, a bundle of expedients, without the unity and harmony of a basic conception. Saxony, Hesse, and Braunschweig were alarmed because of its inroads into their military sovereignty, the feudal Mecklenburgs because of the powers

---

[16] Becker, *Bismarcks Ringen*, pp. 201-210. See also Fritz Dickmann, *Militärpolitische Beziehungen zwischen Preussen und Sachsen, 1866-1870* (Munich, 1929), pp. 12 ff.

granted a popularly elected Reichstag, Hamburg because of the loss of its commercial independence, Lübeck and the petty states because of the heavy financial burden assessed by population rather than wealth. Some Thuringian princes considered abdication and cession of their lands to Prussia. The nationalistic rulers of Oldenburg, Weimar and Coburg, on the other hand, objected to the Prussian-hegemonial features. Only Bremen, a stronghold of the Nationalverein, and tiny Meiningen, now ruled by a pro-Prussian prince, were relatively satisfied.[17]

Although their motives were disparate, the opposition soon found common ground in the counterproposals of Oldenburg for a hereditary Kaiser, house of princes, and confederate cabinet. Thirteen states were attracted to the plan in the belief that it would weaken Prussia's voice in the confederation and provide a more effective barrier to the ambitions of the Reichstag. The proposal was a serious threat to Bismarck's whole constitutional scheme. It endangered the duality of Prussia and the confederation. By displacing the Bundesrat, it would have destroyed the finely calculated system of control in the hands of the Prussian foreign minister. The substitution of "Kaiser" for "presidency" would at this point have given Napoleon obvious grounds to challenge the sincerity of the Prussian commitment to stop at the Main. Such centralistic features, moreover, were unacceptable to the Prussian cabinet and would have made more difficult the ultimate adherence of the south.[18]

But Bismarck divided the opposition and quelled the incipient revolt. Delaying the sessions of the council, he won time to conduct private negotiations with individual states. The petty princes were conceded the right to apply the financial burden of the "iron budget" gradually over a period of seven years. Bremen was encouraged with financial concessions and a strip of Hanoverian soil. The Mecklenburgs were led on by the prospect of financial and military concessions. Hesse was teased with the hope of a special status for that half of its army which lay inside the confederation. Hamburg was frightened into silence by a harsh note and a heavy barrage from the government press. But the most serious task was Saxony. Kings John and William, and their generals as well, were obstinate about their prerogatives. Finally

17 Becker, *Bismarcks Ringen*, pp. 292 ff.
18 *GW*, vɪʙ, 214-216; Becker, *Bismarcks Ringen*, p. 320.

Bismarck hammered out an agreement under which the Saxon king was left the right to nominate, the Hohenzoller to appoint, the commander of the Saxon contingent. For eight years, moreover, the confederation was to compensate Saxony for the loss of its postal revenues.[19]

Bismarck's most effective weapon, however, was the threat of the approaching Reichstag. Its election had been set for February 12. The ministers deliberated with the knowledge that by that date they must reach agreement with Prussia or suffer the consequences of their division. During the electoral campaign in January, Bismarck ordered Prussian officials, to whom all-out support of conservative candidates had become a habit, not to oppose the election of moderate liberals. Without them the Reichstag would not exert "sufficient pressure against recalcitrant governments."[20]

If abandoned by her "allies," Bismarck warned, Prussia would turn to the revolutionary forces of liberal nationalism. He was no friend of liberal doctrine, he told the Saxon envoy, and his actual aim was "to overthrow parliamentarianism with parliamentarianism." He preferred to establish the confederation in collaboration with the dynasties. But if they failed to support him, he would without qualm or hesitation unite with the radical liberals and establish a constitution in accord with their views. "Yes!" he emphasized repeatedly, "Flectere si nequeo superos, Acheronta movebo."[21] Should the attempt miscarry, he warned Oldenburg, Prussia would have no other recourse than the "currents of the national movement and the combinations of European politics."[22]

His divisive tactics prevented the ministers from making a concerted attack upon the Prussian draft and his threat of a revolutionary alternative kept them from rejecting it outright. The amendments[23] they achieved were those Bismarck was willing to

[19] Becker, *Bismarcks Ringen*, pp. 326 ff.; Dickmann, *Militärpolitische Beziehungen*, pp. 55 ff.

[20] *GW*, vi, 237-238.

[21] *GW*, vii, 176. See also Helmut Klocke, "Die sächsische Politik und der Norddeutsche Bund," *Neues Archiv für Sächsische Geschichte und Altertumskunde*, Vol. 48 (1927), pp. 127-129, 135-136.

[22] *GW*, vi, 251-252. A similar warning was delivered to Hamburg. *GW*, vi, 211.

[23] The successive drafts completed by the council of ministers and Constituent Reichstag are in Karl Binding, ed., *Deutsche Staatsgrundgesetze in diplomatisch genauem Abdrucke* (2nd ed., Leipzig, 1901), v, 75 ff. See also Otto von Völlendorff, ed., "Deutsche Verfassungen und Verfassungsentwürfe," *Annalen des deutschen Reichs*, Vol. 23, pp. 241-401.

accept because they did not alter the basic structure of his system. As was to be expected, many were intended to build up the power of the Bundesrat at the expense of the presidency, the commander-in-chief, and the Reichstag. Its approval was now required before the presidency might bring bills before the Reichstag. Should the commander-in-chief exercise his power of "execution" against a member of the confederation, the Bundesrat was to be informed without delay of the grounds for the action. Two of its committees were given consultative power in connection with the right of the presidency to appoint consuls and to oversee the collection of confederate revenues. All treaties affecting matters within the legislative competence of parliament had to be approved by the Bundesrat.

On the insistence of Baron Friesen, the Saxon delegate, the scattered clauses dealing with financial matters were assembled in a single section.[24] A new article was inserted providing for legislative enactment of a three-year budget covering all expenditures except those of the armed forces. The excess of expenses for all purposes over income from tax revenue was to be covered by quotas levied by the presidency alone on the states. The presidency was charged with the necessity of transmitting to the Bundesrat and Reichstag, though at no established interval, a statement of confederate expenses.

The provision for settlement of disputes between states and of constitutional conflicts within states met serious objection. The judicial power of the Bundesrat in the former instance was limited to questions of public law, and it was stipulated that the Bundesrat might enter the case only on the appeal of one of the disputants. That the confederation could by legislative action interfere in the internal disputes of states was too much for the feudal Mecklenburgs and reactionary Hesse. Instead, it was provided that constitutional conflicts could be settled by a competent authority within the state. If none existed, one of the parties might appeal to the Bundesrat. If that procedure were unsuccessful, the case might be settled by confederate legislation. This still left open for Bismarck the possibility of altering the Prussian constitution through the Reichstag and Bundesrat. Such was

[24] Becker, *Bismarcks Ringen*, pp. 357-358.

the meaning of his threat to conquer parliament through parliament.[25]

Despite their fears of the unitary features of the constitution, the ministers saw the wisdom of widening the legislative competence of the confederation. They included insurance, the condition of interstate waterways, the accreditation of public documents, the reciprocal execution of judicial decisions, and the fulfillment of judicial "requisitions." While still under Prussian command, the navy was renamed the "confederate navy." Although William was adamant in refusing any major concessions in military affairs, other than those granted Saxony, it was agreed that contingent commanders would be permitted to determine uniform insignia. On William's insistence, however, the title *Oberfeldherr* was shortened to *Feldherr* to emphasize the point that there was but one commander on the level of the confederation.[26]

Bismarck's difficulties were not limited to the states alone. The Prussian ministers had now had some weeks to consider the document they had so hurriedly ratified in December. They were alarmed over its invasion of Prussian sovereignty and its potential infringement of their own authority. This was useful to Bismarck in convincing the lesser states that it was impossible to get the cabinet to accept further amendments of a unitary character. But the reverse was also true. The impressive show of opposition in the council enabled him to insist that the states must be appeased by the cabinet on less vital issues. In some cases this enabled him to push through the cabinet changes which he himself evidently desired.[27] One such amendment concerned the chancellorship.

Throughout the sessions of the council Bismarck had evaded all efforts to clarify the status of this office. Defeated in the attempt to create a confederate cabinet, the Hessian minister, Hofmann, had proposed that ordinances issued by the presidency for the execution of confederate laws bear the "countersignature of the confederate chancellor." Such a signature implied the assumption of responsibility for the measure concerned. If the chancellor, in other words, was not to be a minister, he at least should have an attribute of one. In conference with Hofmann, Bismarck ap-

[25] *Ibid.*, pp. 367-368; Klocke, "Die sächsische Politik," pp. 138-140.
[26] Becker, *Bismarcks Ringen*, pp. 356 ff.
[27] *Ibid.*, p. 348.

parently substituted for *Kontrasignatur* the verb *mitunterzeichnen*. The original had the effect of exalting the chancellorship in relationship to the Prussian cabinet, including the foreign minister. But the substitution enabled him as foreign minister to assume the right of co-signature *with* the chancellor. If unable to assume that office, he could at least keep its incumbent in check. Savigny had begun to suspect the truth. "Bismarck is wrapped in silence. Apparently he wishes himself to be confederate chancellor."[28]

Only Bremen was satisfied with the final draft achieved on February 7, 1867. The more resolute ministers were disheartened by the general scramble, particularly on the part of Saxony, for special concessions. Everyone resented the heavy hand of Savigny, who presided over the body for Prussia. In drawing up the protocol which announced the results of their secret deliberations, the ministers angrily struck out the statement that the draft had been "agreed upon," substituting the phrase "definitively established."[29] But Bismarck was never one to quarrel over phrases when he had secured the substance of what he wanted.

7. THE CONSTITUENT REICHSTAG

On February 12, 1867, the voters of northern Germany went to the polls to elect the constituent Reichstag. Popular interest was high, and in many districts over seventy percent of the eligible voted; in some the percentage was over ninety. The results seemed to confirm Bismarck's confidence in the masses. Almost half of the 297 deputies chosen were noblemen and most of the rest were men of means. Among the former were 1 royal prince, 4 non-royal princes, 2 dukes, 27 counts, and 21 barons. The election of several high officers, including Roon and Moltke, testified to the lingering halo of victory. Bismarck was chosen in two constituencies, one of them with the aid of Schweitzer's socialists. The conservatives conquered 59 seats, the free conservatives 39, and the old liberals 27. The National Liberal Party was largest with 79 members, while the progressives were but 19. The remaining seats were shared by splinter parties, some of which—Danes,

---

28 *Ibid.*, pp. 359-363.
29 *Ibid.*, pp. 349-354. For the protocol see Ludwig Aegidi and Alfred Klauhold, eds., *Das Staatsarchiv, Sammlung der officiellen Aktenstücke zur Geschichte der Gegenwart*, XII (1867), 359-366.

Poles, ultramontanists, Schleswig-Holsteiners, and Hanoverian particularists—were bitterly opposed to the confederation.[30]

Despite the rebellion of the previous summer the conservatives could be depended upon to support the draft against liberal amendments. By February many had found solace in the fact that the new confederation meant an expansion in Prussian power. Again their Prussian pride triumphed over their sense of legitimist right. The free conservatives and old liberals were unconditional supporters of Bismarckian policy. On the opposite side of the chamber the progressives were equally adamant in opposition. They decried the general willingness to sacrifice liberty for unity, insisted on full budget rights for the Reichstag, and demanded a cabinet of responsible ministers. Between these extremes the national liberals held the decisive position. By participating in the work of national unification, they hoped to influence its political structure. They were out to see how far they could go in adding liberal features to the draft without endangering its acceptance by Bismarck and the state governments.[31]

In one hand Bismarck held the carrot, in the other the stick. While pleased by the victory of the moderate liberals, for the effect it would have on the governments, he now mobilized the latter to prevent the Reichstag from upsetting the basic features of his draft. The states were asked to defend jointly with Prussia what they had so reluctantly "established." On the floor of the Reichstag, places were prepared for more than forty "commissars," who were "to present a common front of the allied governments toward the Reichstag." But the states were averse to participating in this comedy. "For us," Bismarck warned Dresden, "there are always these alternatives: either to count completely and forever upon the governments now temporarily allied with us, or to face the necessity of seeking our center of gravity in parliament." In the latter case Prussia's conduct in parliament would have to assume a "more German-national character." Saxony was playing a "dangerous game." Confronted with these threats, King John and his ministers capitulated, and after Saxony the other states.[32]

---

[30] Becker, *Bismarcks Ringen*, pp. 371-372; Fritz Specht, *Die Reichstags-Wahlen von 1867 bis 1897* (Berlin, 1898), p. 104.

[31] Becker, *Bismarcks Ringen*, pp. 373-375; Ritter, *Konservativen*, pp. 204 ff.; Oncken, *Bennigsen*, II, 13.

[32] *GW*, VI, 273-274, 289-290; Becker, *Bismarcks Ringen*, p. 383.

But Bismarck also had to be prepared for the possibility that the Reichstag, despite the impressive array of commissars, might insist upon amendments unacceptable to him. On February 19 he invited the governments of Saxony, Darmstadt, Weimar, Oldenburg, and the two Mecklenburgs to appoint plenipotentiaries empowered to negotiate a secret treaty providing that in such a situation the governments would dissolve the Reichstag and decree their own version of the constitution. When friction with parliament increased in late March, he summoned the governments to sign the prepared text. As the conflict reached a dangerous climax during the second week of April, he secured the necessary ratifications. In this way he utilized the objections of the Reichstag liberals to force the governments to drop their reservations with regard to the draft of February 7. But he also got them to accept through the treaty some of the liberal amendments which he himself desired or found harmless.[33] Rare was the ill wind which failed to blow Bismarck some good.

In the constituent Reichstag, whose debates began on March 4, he made the deputies in turn feel the pressure of the allied governments. His first speech pointed out that the Reichstag (like the council of ministers) must work under a deadline. The treaties of alliance which obligated the states to consider the constitution were scheduled to expire on August 18, 1867. Since the treaties also reserved to the states the right of final approval, the Reichstag must finish its work in time for them to deliberate upon the amended draft. Hence the deputies must make haste, avoid acrimony, and steer clear of amendments unacceptable to the governments. Although the agreement of February 7 remained secret, the deputies were given reason to suspect its existence. In his opening address on February 24 William spoke of the "grave responsibility" of the deputies for the "peaceful and lawful execution" of the projected union.[34]

Naturally one of the major objectives of the liberals was to strengthen the unitary and national aspect of the draft by extending the legislative competence of the confederation at the

---

[33] *GW*, vi, 272-273, 312-315; Becker, *Bismarcks Ringen*, pp. 384-387, 445. The text of the treaty is in Egmont Zechlin, *Staatsstreichpläne Bismarcks und Wilhelms II, 1890-1894* (Stuttgart, 1929), pp. 175-176. It was signed by Prussia, Saxony, Hesse, and Saxe-Weimar on March 31 and ratified on April 9 and 11. The two Mecklenburgs signed on April 9 and ratified on April 14.

[34] *SBR*, i (1867), ii, 41-42.

cost of the states. Amendments were passed giving the confederation power to legislate on citizenship, passports, the regulation of aliens, army and navy affairs, the enforcement of medical and veterinary standards, certain aspects of transportation, judicial procedure, and corporation and criminal law. Another new clause required parliament to authorize credits and financial guarantees for the confederation.[35]

None of these amendments aroused serious conflict. Apparently Bismarck had deliberately limited the legislative power of the confederate government in order to ease the passage of his draft through the cabinet and council. His positive attitude on the subject of *Kompetenz-Kompetenz* (as it was later to be called) shows furthermore that he anticipated and approved the future growth of central legislative authority. During the debates he took the view that Bundesrat and Reichstag possessed the competence to extend their own competence. Their right of constitutional amendment carried with it the right to increase the range of their own legislative power.[36]

The most centralistic of the amendments offered by the liberals aimed at the creation of an independent executive. Both the progressives and national liberals desired to remove the obscurity which enveloped the executive features of the draft. Waldeck confessed that his goal was a unitary state, headed by a "constitutionally responsible cabinet." While accepting the federal system, the moderates desired a confederate cabinet whose responsibility would be "regulated" in a future law. In answer to the charges of the conservatives, both factions defined "responsibility" as legal rather than political. Their aim was not parliamentary government, but realization of a *Rechtsstaat*, the venerable dream of the moderates, a government of laws rather than men.[37]

Certainly "responsibility" in this form was no hindrance to autocratic government. A similar provision in the Prussian constitution had had no effect upon the recent conflict. Since no regulatory law had ever been passed, there was no way to bring min-

[35] The amendments introduced by the constituent Reichstag and accepted by the governments are italicized in J. C. Glaser, ed., *Archiv des Norddeutschen Bundes* (Berlin, 1867), III, 23-38. For the proposed amendments see *ibid.*, IV, 30-115. The official version of the completed constitution may be found in *Bundes-Gesetzblatt des Norddeutschen Bundes* (1867), pp. 1-23.

[36] *SBR*, I (1867), 316 ff., 324; Becker, *Bismarcks Ringen*, pp. 435 ff.

[37] *SBR*, I (1867), 331 ff., 359 ff., 374 ff., 383 ff.

isters to account for illegal actions in Prussia. What Bismarck objected to was not the idea itself, but one of the features of the amendment introduced by Bennigsen and the national liberals. By providing that the "heads of administrative branches," as well as the chancellor, might countersign the "orders and ordinances" of the presidency in execution of confederate laws, "thereby assuming the responsibility," the amendment opened up the prospect of a collegial executive like the Prussian cabinet. Bismarck found this intolerable, for the independence of the Prussian ministers had hampered execution of his domestic policies during the constitutional conflict. Hence he informed the liberals that Bennigsen's amendment was unacceptable to the governments. The liberals capitulated. The final version gave the chancellor the sole right of countersignature bearing a responsibility undivided and undefined. This Bismarck did not oppose, which raises the suspicion that it conformed to his hidden aim of becoming chancellor.[38]

Other amendments had the purpose of strengthening the Reichstag and the principle of parliamentary immunity. No one could be prosecuted for repeating or reprinting a true report of the public proceedings of the Reichstag. During a legislative session, members might not be imprisoned or prosecuted without the Reichstag's consent. Officials were no longer prohibited from election to the chamber. In order to deter the corruption of deputies by the government, it was provided that, on the acceptance of a state office or of a promotion in the civil service, a deputy must resign and seek re-election. In the event of dissolution an election must be held within sixty days, and the new Reichstag must convene within ninety. Without approval from the Reichstag the presidency could prorogue that body for only one period of thirty days in each session. Petitions directed to the Reichstag could be forwarded to the Bundesrat and presidency. Treaties involving matters within the legislative competence of the confederation must be ratified by the Reichstag.

These amendments removed some of the basic deficiencies of the Bismarck draft and gave the Reichstag many of the essential attributes of a modern parliamentary body. Two other amendments tampered with the conservative safeguards in the election

[38] Becker, *Bismarcks Ringen*, pp. 388 ff. Becker believes Bismarck may have been in collusion with the old liberal deputy, Sänger, who proposed the version of the amendment finally accepted under Bennigsen's name. *Ibid.*, p. 391.

laws. While opposed to universal suffrage, the national liberals dared not say so publicly. By adding the secret ballot, they hoped to prevent its exploitation for dictatorial ends in the style of Louis Napoleon.[39] This Bismarck accepted. But he firmly rejected their request for the remuneration of deputies. In his view the prohibition of per diem payments was necessary to reduce the dangers of universal suffrage. Only the well-to-do (noblemen, landowners, merchants, and industrialists) could afford to serve. The press of their personal affairs would insure short sessions, and their interests would presumably be more economic than political. He wished to prevent the appearance of professional politicians, who, being dependent upon parliament for livelihood, would have a selfish concern for the extension of its powers. When the vote came on March 30, he declared that under "no circumstances" would the governments accept the amendment. But it passed by a slim majority of six.[40]

Naturally the liberals subjected the articles dealing with parliament's financial powers to close scrutiny. The clause allowing only indirect taxes was stricken from the draft. An amendment provided that all revenues and expenditures of the confederation must be established annually "before the beginning of the budget year." Another change permitted the levying of state quotas only until parliament should provide the needed revenue. The amount levied, moreover, was restricted to that established in the budget. Surpluses might not accumulate, but must be used to defray current expenses of the confederation. These amendments plugged very serious holes in the financial power of the Reichstag. There remained, nevertheless, the yawning chasm of the iron budget.

As long as the peacetime strength of the army and the amount of its financial support were fixed in the constitution in ratio to the population, the budget rights of parliament were fictional. The power lost by the chamber of deputies with the transfer of the military budget from Prussia to the confederation would accrue, not to the Reichstag, but to the crown. While unwilling to accept such a retreat, the progressives and national liberals disagreed on what was to be demanded. The former wanted the right to determine yearly the strength of the army through the budget, but

39 *Ibid.*, p. 437.
40 *SBR*, I (1867), 474 ff.; Becker, *Bismarcks Ringen*, pp. 441-442. To make it more difficult for journalists to engage in political careers, Bismarck would have liked to locate parliament in some provincial city distant from Berlin. *Ibid.*, p. 365.

the latter, vitally impressed by the recent victories, were willing to accept the iron budget until 1870, when it would be subject to legislative approval for an additional period of years. Even this was unacceptable to William and his generals.[41]

The iron budget was the climactic issue which in early April threatened the whole constitutional settlement. In precarious negotiations behind the scenes, Bismarck arrived at a compromise with the national liberals. The peacetime size of the army was fixed at one percent of the population until December 31, 1871. Thereafter the ratio would be subject to legislation. The army's financial support was fixed at 225 *Thaler* per soldier until the same date, but with the additional proviso that the states must continue thereafter to provide money at the same rate and for the same size army until the size should be changed by law. It was further stipulated that parliament could not use its power to approve military appropriations (after 1871) to alter the organization of the army as established under the constitution.

From the standpoint of popular liberties the German constitution represented a retreat from the Prussian. One of the final actions of the constituent Reichstag was to vote down a progressive motion for incorporation of the Prussian bill of rights.[42] Bismarck's constitution was the first in the history of constitutionalism not to include such a bill. While the grant of control over revenues as well as expenditures was an advance, it was largely robbed of its significance by the exclusion of the military budget. Only by challenging the constitution itself could the parliamentary opposition attack the basic structure of the army. For this reason Bismarck judged that the government need not fear renewal of the constitutional conflict in 1871.[43] Even so, the final compromise contained yet another sacrifice for the liberals. They were compelled to surrender the amendment providing for the remuneration of deputies.[44]

On April 16 the Reichstag accepted, 230 to 53, the amended constitution. In the negative was the remnant of the progressives, led by Waldeck and Schulze-Delitzsch, supported by the Polish and Catholic factions and the chamber's only socialist, August Bebel. On May 31 the Prussian Landtag likewise accepted it, 227

41 Becker, *Bismarcks Ringen*, pp. 439-441.
42 *SBR*, I (1867), 726.   43 *GW*, VIB, 217-218.
44 Becker, *Bismarcks Ringen*, pp. 448 ff.

to 93, with the same determined group in the minority. Valiantly the democratic liberals clung to the position they had defended since 1861. Without secure budget rights, a judicially responsible cabinet, remuneration of deputies, and a bill of rights, they could not come to terms with the Hohenzollern monarchy. Obstinately they rejected the argument of the moderates that what was sacrificed today might be regained in the parliamentary battles of tomorrow. Unity they refused at the cost of freedom. From the start, however, their cause was doomed. Had they carried the day, Bismarck would have promulgated the north German constitution even without their approval. If necessary, he would have "thrown the entire Prussian constitution overboard."[45] Unity over freedom and power over law—this was the constellation under which the German Reich was born.

8. THE DUALISM OF POLITICAL AND MILITARY AUTHORITY

The institutional arrangements which Bismarck designed for Germany contained yet another vital deficiency of which the deputies in the constituent Reichstag were hardly conscious. No barrier was provided against the future growth of an unfortunate dualism in political and military authority.

We have seen that during the constitutional conflict one of the major objectives of Edwin Manteuffel was to depreciate the authority of the minister of war, who was subject to the interpellation of parliament, and to exalt that of the military cabinet, which was beyond the range of parliamentary attack. In pursuit of this objective he naturally came into conflict with Roon. The minister objected sharply to the attempt of the adjutant general to withhold from his cognizance not only William's orders to his commanding generals, but even information on such matters as the selection and promotion of officers which Manteuffel handled as head of the personnel division of the ministry of war. Both Roon and Bismarck, furthermore, were angered by Manteuffel's success in getting William to reject the compromise of 1865,[46] which might have ended the constitutional conflict. Soon after-

---

[45] *SBR*, I (1867), 729; *SBHA* (1867), 167-186. Klocke, "Die sächsische Politik," pp. 132-134, 139. In typical fashion Becker justifies Bismarck's intention on the grounds that it stemmed from a national rather than a reactionary purpose. *Bismarcks Ringen*, p. 368.

[46] See pp. 271-272.

ward they insisted that he was the only person who could be entrusted with the delicate task of governing Schleswig. The "fanatic corporal" was removed from Berlin.[47]

The issue, however, was personal, not constitutional. The absolutistic authority of the Hohenzollern crown in military matters, which was the basis of the military cabinet's power, was far greater under the north German than under the Prussian constitution. Being granted to the king of Prussia rather than the presidency, the authority of the confederate commander-in-chief was outside the constitutional sphere of the chancellor. For the same reason there was no confederate ministry of war. The Prussian ministry of war assumed the routine functions of confederate military administration, but the military cabinet was the agency which assisted the king in the exercise of his new powers of appointment, promotion, supervision, and command in the confederate army. Even without intrigue on the part of Manteuffel's successor, Hermann von Tresckow, its emancipation from the control of the Prussian ministry proceeded with "giant steps" after 1867.[48]

With the rise of Helmuth von Moltke, yet another military agency, the Prussian general staff, began its escape from the same orbit. Charged with war planning, the general staff was until the 1860's one of the subordinate departments of the ministry of war. When the Danish war commenced, Moltke, its chief since 1857, had no direct contact with or authority over Wrangel, the field commander. But he finished the war as chief of staff to Wrangel's successor, Prince Frederick Charles, and was generally recognized as the architect of victory. Later he participated in the crucial crown councils which led to war against Austria. A few days before the outbreak of war (June 2, 1866) a royal order provided for the communication of commands directly from the general staff to the troops, rather than through the ministry of war. When peace came, the general staff again became subordi-

[47] Gordon A. Craig, *The Politics of the Prussian Army, 1640-1945* (Oxford, 1955), pp. 172-173; Rudolf Schmidt-Bückeburg, *Das Militärkabinett der preussischen Könige und deutschen Kaiser* (Berlin, 1933), pp. 84 ff.; Heinrich O. Meisner, *Der Kriegsminister, 1815-1914* (Berlin, 1940), pp. 21 ff. Bismarck's feud with Manteuffel went back to 1857, when the general in effect ordered him out of Berlin and back to Frankfurt in order to keep him from influencing Frederick William IV. Wilhelm Gradmann, *Die politischen Ideen Edwin von Manteuffels und ihre Auswirkungen in seiner Laufbahn* (Dusseldorf, 1932), pp. 79-80.

[48] Schmidt-Bückeburg, *Militärkabinett*, pp. 96 ff.

nate to the ministry. Nevertheless, the first step had been taken which would one day lead to its complete liberation from all ministerial authority.[49]

Behind the scenes two military agencies were quietly gathering in the reins of power left dangling under the Prussian and north German constitutions. Both were beyond the reach of the Landtag and Reichstag. Their chiefs were to be immediate to the king and independent of the civil executive, whether chancellor or minister-president. As long as Bismarck was in office they were to fail in their efforts to usurp the political function. But even the Titan finally fell from Olympus.

[49] Craig, *Prussian Army*, pp. 193 ff.; Meisner, *Kriegsminister*, pp. 47 ff.

BOOK FOUR

THE YEARS OF FULFILLMENT

1867-1871

"*Bismarck was the one man who could juggle five balls, of which at least two were always in the air.*"—WILLIAM I

"*I was convinced that the gulf which in the course of history had opened between north and south in our country because of differences in ways of life and dynastic and tribal loyalties could not be more effectively bridged than through a common national war against the traditionally aggressive neighbor.*"—BISMARCK in *Erinnerung und Gedanke*

CHAPTER SIXTEEN

BRIDGES OVER THE MAIN

1. THE MILITARY ALLIANCES

O MANY German nationalists the peace settlement with Austria was a keen disappointment. The triumph of Königgrätz had reconciled them to the idea of a national union under conservative leadership. But now they read in Article II of the preliminary peace signed at Nikolsburg on July 26 that Germany was to be divided into two spheres along the river Main. The south, like the north, was to be allowed to federate. The "national bond" between them was to be the subject of a "closer understanding." The settlement appeared to create for Germany a new dualism, which would again frustrate the demand for national self-determination.[1]

The reasons for this decision have long been a subject of quandary and dispute. Nationalistic writers have found it difficult to believe that Bismarck willingly accepted such a limitation upon German unity. The original Prussian reform plan, it is pointed out, included the whole of small-Germany. One view has it that the "outline" of June 10 was sheer propaganda, another that the halt at the Main was dictated by the danger of French intervention. Recently Otto Becker even maintained that the Main line was "created" by the refusal of German liberals to cooperate in summoning the "pre-parliament" proposed to them by Bismarck through Eulenburg. In the crown council of February 26, however, King William had already given as Prussia's objective the establishment of a "decisive political preponderance" in *northern* Germany.[2]

Certainly a major reason for this limitation was diplomatic. From the beginning Napoleon's encouragement of Prussian ex-

[1] Otto Scheel, *Bismarcks Wille zu Deutschland in den Friedenschlüssen 1866*, *Veröffentlichungen der Schleswig-Holsteinischen Universitätsgesellschaft*, Vol. 44 (Breslau, 1934), pp. 1-7, 76. For the text of the treaty see *Staatsarchiv*, XI (1866), 166-168.

[2] Becker, *Bismarcks Ringen*, p. 180; *APP*, VI, 613. For a review of the older literature on this controversy see Bruno Gebhardt, *Handbuch der deutschen Geschichte* (7th ed., Stuttgart, 1931), II, 415-416.

THE YEARS OF FULFILLMENT, 1867-1871

pansion had been restricted to the region north of the Main. For all his talk of national self-determination as a general principle for the reorganization of Europe, Napoleon was enough of a realist to appreciate that the unification of Germany would produce on the French frontier a powerful competitor. Bismarck, the soul of realism, understood full well that, if his policy toward France was to be successful, it must be based on the premise that the Main frontier was for Napoleon a vital interest. In Paris he had constantly reiterated that hegemony over northern Germany was Prussia's sole ambition.[3] Since France's claim for compensation went begging, the limitation of the Main was the one visible success of Napoleon's efforts in 1866.

But the French danger was not the only reason for the halt at the Main. In years past Bismarck had regarded northern Germany as the natural area of Prussian domination because of the cultural homogeneity of its population. He had argued against German unification in 1848 on the grounds that southern lassitude would corrupt the Prussian virtues of industry and discipline.[4] From Frankfurt he wrote to Leopold Gerlach in 1854 that the struggle against ultramontanism was one of his most difficult tasks: "It is not a Christian creed, but a hypocritical, idolatrous papism full of hate and cunning, which conducts an unrelenting struggle with the most infamous weapons against the Protestant governments, and especially against Prussia, the worldly bulwark of the evangelical faith. The struggle goes on in practical affairs from the cabinets of the princes and their ministers to the feather-bed mysteries of the married set. Here in the city and diet, and at nearby courts, 'Catholic' and 'enemy of Prussia' are identical in meaning."[5] With Catholicism, he wrote, there could be no peace short of complete subjugation. Ultramontanes were more dangerous than democrats.[6]

His suspicion of a Catholic conspiracy affected his political judgments. Schwarzenberg's "favorite plan," he told Leopold Gerlach, was a coalition of France, Austria, and Russia "to suppress England and Prussia, and with them Protestantism and political freedom, the 'revolution in church and state.'" To coun-

[3] GW, v, 436; RKN, i, 329, 344; OD, viii, 264-266; x, 70-73.
[4] GW, vii, 13; x, 40; Günther Franz, Bismarcks Nationalgefühl (Leipzig, 1926), pp. 77-78.
[5] GW, xiv, 340.
[6] GW, i, 257-258, 265, 393; ii, 54; xiv, 544; Franz, Nationalgefühl, p. 52.

ter it he advocated alliances with the Protestant states of northern Europe (England, Holland, Denmark, and Sweden). "Southern Germany is alien to us and the German interest is without foundation." His proposal for a northern league of armed neutrals during the Crimean war had a confessional as well as a political basis.[7]

Despite these cultural differences, the ultimate completion of German unification became a necessity for Bismarck from the moment that war with Austria was certain. Yet this may not be taken as proof of his "will to Germany,"[8] that is, of his German national sentiment. We have seen that Bismarck's political thought was primarily concerned with problems of power, rather than ideology or sentiment. In German nationalism he had found the moral force with which to expand and buttress the power of the Hohenzollern monarchy against the hazards of European politics and the pressures of social change. Once the path of its exploitation had been taken in 1866, it was obvious that the Main could not be a permanent frontier. The disappointment of the nationalists would have cost the Prussian throne the halo so recently acquired.

Bismarck's decision to accomplish unification in stages was, however, a requirement of German as well as European politics. It arose as much from the continued strength of particularism in Germany as from the danger of French intervention. In July 1866 he wrote that inclusion of the "south-German, Catholic, Bavarian element" would make it impossible for Prussia to consolidate what she had gained. "For a long time" the south would not willingly consent to be ruled from Berlin. To conquer it would simply create a source of weakness, like Naples in united Italy. At Nikolsburg he remarked to Foreign Minister Varnbüler of Württemberg that Munich and Stuttgart could not "now" be digested by Berlin.[9] During the following months the difficulties encountered in integrating Saxony into the North German Confederation confirmed the wisdom of temporarily excluding the

---

[7] *GW*, xiv, 405; Leopold von Gerlach, *Denkwürdigkeiten* (Berlin, 1891), ii, 642; Egmont Zechlin, *Bismarck und die Grundlegung der deutschen Grossmacht* (Stuttgart, 1930), pp. 137 ff. See also *GW*, i, 503; ii, 42; xiv, 335.

[8] See Scheel, *Bismarcks Wille*.

[9] *GW*, vi, 44; Wilhelm Busch, "Bismarck und die Entstehung des Norddeutschen Bundes," *Historische Zeitschrift*, Vol. 103 (1909), pp. 73-74; Ulrich v. Stosch, ed., *Denkwürdigkeiten des Generals und Admirals Albrecht v. Stosch* (Stuttgart, 1904), pp. 94-95.

southern medium states. Before they could be added, the confederation had to be made a going concern, its institutional relationships firmly established.

After the expulsion of Austria the south was a political vacuum predestined to be filled by the power of France, Prussia, or a resurgent Austria. Even at Nikolsburg the conflict between French and Prussian interests was evident. A clause in Bismarck's treaty draft allowed for a union between the North German Confederation and the southern states on the basis of the "outline" of June 10, 1866, which provided for a national parliament with extensive authority over economic affairs. But Bavaria refused to cooperate, and Napoleon's mediation plan guaranteed the south "an independent international existence." Bismarck tried to evade the issue by deleting both clauses, leaving the matter open. But Napoleon protested, and the French clause was reinserted in the final peace signed at Prague on August 23.[10] If adhered to, it meant that the "national bond" between north and south could be only diplomatic, not constitutional.

The possibility that French influence might replace Austria's in southern Germany was by no means remote. During the peace negotiations with Prussia in July and August, Dalwigk, Varnbüler, and Pfordten repeatedly turned to Paris for protection against Bismarck's demands. On August 10 Lefebvre de Béhaine, a French diplomat, was told by Dalwigk that in the event of war with Prussia French troops would be welcome in southern Germany. Their immediate appearance in the Palatinate would encourage resistance to a Prussian invasion.[11] But French policy foundered on its own inconsistency. The wooing of the southern

[10] Erich Brandenburg, *Untersuchungen und Aktenstücke zur Geschichte der Reichsgründung* (Leipzig, 1916), pp. 555-556; Wilhelm Schüssler, *Bismarcks Kampf um Süddeutschland 1867* (Berlin, 1929), pp. 16 ff.; Scheel, *Bismarcks Wille*, pp. 45 ff.; Johannes Petrich, "Der erste preussische Präliminarentwurf in Nikolsburg 1866," *Historische Vierteljahrschrift*, xxx (1930), 593-599. For the text of Napoleon's proposal, which Goltz helped draft, see *GW*, vi, 64.

[11] *OD*, xi, 367-369, 377-379, 386; xii, 35-36, 49, 61-64. Naturally Dalwigk did not record this advice in his diary or in his report to the grand duke. Wilhelm Schüssler, ed., *Die Tagebücher des Freiherrn Reinhard von Dalwigk zu Lichtenfels aus den Jahren 1860-71, Deutsche Geschichtsquellen des 19. Jahrhunderts*, Vol. 2 (Stuttgart, 1920), 248-249, 293. For years the Hessian statesman had looked to France for protection against Prussian imperialism. Until 1870 he actively encouraged French intervention in German affairs. See Walter Vogel, *Die Tagebücher des Freiherrn Reinhard von Dalwigk zu Lichtenfels als Geschichtsquelle, Historische Studien*, Vol. 234 (Berlin, 1933), and Ernst Götz, *Die Stellung Hessen-Darmstadts zur deutschen Einigungsfrage in den Jahren 1866-1871* (Darmstadt, 1914), pp. 12 ff.

medium states was not compatible with the demand for German soil. In early August Drouyn's request for the frontier of 1814 and the Palatinate helped Bismarck to build his first bridge across the Main.

During the peace negotiations with the southern states, he demanded treaties of alliance placing their railways and troops under Prussian command during wartime. For such a price, he indicated, Prussia would relinquish her demand for large annexations and crushing indemnities. The representatives of Baden and Württemberg quickly agreed (August 9-10). Bavaria was more difficult, but Bismarck handled Pfordten with masterly finesse. In their initial interview he presented voracious demands for money and territory without mentioning an alliance. The shocked Pfordten hurried to the French embassy in search of support, but Paris was silent, for Drouyn had just demanded the Bavarian Palatinate. At the next meeting Bismarck stressed the completeness of Bavaria's isolation. Then, having plunged Pfordten to the depths of despair, he sent down a rope: in return for an alliance the Prussian demands would be sharply reduced. Greatly relieved, Pfordten gave his consent.[12]

The three treaties were identical and were labeled "offensive-defensive alliances." Later Bismarck insisted that this designation was purely "technical" and without aggressive intent. The contracting parties mutually guaranteed their respective territories and agreed in the event of war to accept the supreme command of the King of Prussia. For Bismarck the documents were a significant achievement. At the moment of the expiration of the German Confederation he succeeded in creating the strongest bond which had ever existed between northern and southern Germany. It was the fruit of military victory and French rapacity, of southern isolation and the threat of a Draconian peace. He valued it not only for its military reinforcement, but for the "national basis" it gave for resistance against France.[13]

[12] Johannes Petrich, "Die Friedensverhandlungen mit den Süddeutschen 1866," *Forschungen zur brandenburgischen und preussischen Geschichte*, Vol. 46 (1934), pp. 321-351; Gustav Roloff, "Bismarcks Friedenschlüsse mit den Süddeutschen im Jahre 1866," *Historische Zeitschrift*, Vol. 146 (1932), pp. 1-70. In order to offer these terms Bismarck had to overcome William's lust for Bavarian territory by threatening to resign. Prussia took only a small strip of land desired for a railway connection. *Ibid.*, p. 62.

[13] *GW*, vi, 255. For the texts of the treaties see Glaser, *Archiv*, iii, 39-42.

2 . DECISION ON FRANCE

The cult of the nation requires devils as well as gods. If Bismarck was the Washington of the German revolution, Napoleon was its George III. While Americans regard the British stamp act as pure villany, Germans have a similar view of the compensation demands of Napoleon III. It is difficult for them to recognize that any French interest was damaged by the consolidation of the German Reich on her northern frontier.[14] The reports of Goltz show, however, that Prussian success in the war against Austria and the progress of German unification produced in Paris an anxiety bordering on panic.

Napoleon had already commenced to doubt the tenability of the Main barrier. Prussian annexation of all the lesser states, he feared, was but a "matter of time."[15] His ministers and advisers reproached him for having encouraged Prussian preponderance in Germany. From the public arose those murmurs of dissatisfaction for which his ear was ever cocked. Emperor and empress, and those dependent upon them for power and influence, were again besieged, as so often in the past, by apprehension over the future of the dynasty. The unification of Germany would mean a fundamental shift in the European balance, which France dared not permit without compensation in the form of land, population, and a better military frontier.[16] This was the compulsion behind the demands which the Tuileries now raised for Prussian aid in annexing Belgium and Luxemburg.

In the past Bismarck had given the French reason to expect Prussian approval. Twice during the previous year he had suggested that France seek compensation in French-speaking Europe. According to Benedetti, he specifically mentioned Belgium in the interview of July 26, 1866. On the same occasion, moreover, the only objection he raised to the acquisition of Luxemburg was the difficulty of finding compensation for its ruler, the King of the Netherlands. In rejecting the demands of August 4, he told Benedetti that Prussia was willing to make "important sacrifices" in order to preserve good relations with France.[17]

14 In 1934 Otto Scheel could still ask indignantly, "Who threatened the security of France? Not Prussia and Germany." *Bismarcks Wille*, p. 92.

15 *OD*, XII, 194. Benedetti and Drouyn were of the same conviction. *Ibid.*, p. 171; *RKN*, II, 42.

16 *RKN*, I, 331, 340, 353; II, 72, 93, 173-174; Lynn M. Case, *French Opinion on War and Diplomacy during the Second Empire* (Philadelphia, 1954), pp. 205 ff.

17 *OD*, XI, 219-225; XII, 24.

The Grand Duchy of Luxemburg had been granted to the house of Orange in 1815 as compensation for the loss of Nassau. Its only connection with Holland was that of "personal union" under King-Grand Duke William III. Previously the principality had belonged to the German Confederation and possessed a confederate fortress manned by a Prussian garrison. The demise of the confederation had dissolved the link with Germany and placed in question the status of the garrison. While French was the predominant language of government, the populace spoke a German dialect with an admixture of French words. Some were pro-French and some pro-German, but most apparently wanted to preserve their country's independence.[18]

In mid-August Napoleon, acting on Rouher's advice, launched a final attempt at understanding with Prussia. Benedetti was instructed to propose two agreements: a public treaty conceding to France the frontiers of 1814 and the right to Luxemburg; and a secret treaty containing an "offensive and defensive alliance" and granting France the right eventually to annex Belgium. Immediately Bismarck objected to the 1814 frontier, and Benedetti let it drop, as Rouher had authorized. Concerning Belgium and Luxemburg, the Junker indicated that their annexation was consonant with Prussia's interests, if Berlin were granted a "free hand in Germany." On August 29 Benedetti actually handed over a draft agreement, in which France assented, in return for Belgium and Luxemburg, to a "federal union" between the North German Confederation and the southern states, which would respect "in just measure" the sovereignty of the latter.[19]

Agreement with France on such a basis offered several tempting advantages for Prussia. It would eliminate the possibility of French interference in the creation of the North German Confederation, and a constitutional union with the south could be achieved without risk of war. In the future, moreover, the French might be brought to sacrifice their interest in the southern states. Perhaps Bismarck's only purpose in listening to the overture was to prolong French hopes for an agreement.[20] But it is more likely

---

[18] Becker, *Bismarcks Ringen*, p. 400; Alexander Matschoss, *Die Luxemburger Frage von 1867* (Breslau, 1867), pp. 40 ff.

[19] *RKN*, II, 82-83, 87-89, 94-96, 166, 182; *OD*, XII, 116-117, 170-175.

[20] This point of view is supported by Bismarck's comment on a document seized during the campaign of 1870. In a report to Drouyn from Nikolsburg on July 26, Benedetti had written of Bismarck as "the only person in the whole kingdom who

that a delimitation of spheres between Berlin and Paris, as earlier between Berlin and Vienna, was one of the courses which entered for a time into his calculations.[21]

The draft which Benedetti suddenly drew out of his pocket, like that of Rechberg at Schönbrunn, was in any case much too precise and far-reaching. On August 17 Bismarck had told the ambassador that such a treaty would be difficult to obtain from William, although he would seek to dispose him in its favor. On September 7 he informed Paris that the king was not opposed to the growth of the empire "in the area of French nationality," but France must take the initiative. As for the alliance, the two nations should agree to consult for common defense, if dangers arose. This was a circumspect refusal. Bismarck and William had no intention of getting involved in war with Britain for a purely French interest.[22]

Concerning Luxemburg he expressed on August 17 his desire to be "obliging." While declining to initiate any action, he did offer to assist the French by giving the Dutch a fright. At the Hague, he promised, Prussia would make a "peremptory demand" for the inclusion of Luxemburg and Limburg in the North German Confederation. Simultaneously the French should stimulate "manifestations in her favor" among influential circles in Luxemburg. To save the Dutch population of Limburg, William III would probably let Luxemburg go,[23] a neat finesse by two expert bridge players.

Only one day after Benedetti presented his treaty draft, Bismarck actually raised the "peremptory demand" at the Hague.[24] This may not in itself be proof of a willingness to assist French annexation. But neither can it be assumed, as has been asserted, that his actual aim was the elevation of Prince Henry, the pro-German governor of the duchy, to the status of an independent

---

understands what an advantage there would be for Prussia in forming with France an intimate and lasting alliance at the price of a territorial sacrifice." In the margin the Junker commented, "So he honestly believed it." *RKN*, II, 7.

21 Later he maintained that, had the French not been so "foolish," they could have had Luxemburg. *GW*, VII, 199-200, 310.

22 *RKN*, II, 88, 100-109, 185-186; *OD*, XII, 215.

23 *RKN*, II, 87-89; *OD*, XII, 213-214. Like Luxemburg, Limburg had been part of the German Confederation.

24 From Perponcher, Prussian minister at the Hague, he already knew that neither William III, nor his government, was very interested in retaining Luxemburg. *GW*, VI, 91-92, 144-145, 154-155; *APP*, VIII, 44-47, 54.

ruler closely allied to Berlin.[25] It is more likely that, as in the Schleswig-Holstein question, he wished to leave open two courses of action. Should the French press with vigor and skill on the Luxemburg issue, the wiser course might be to withdraw the Prussian garrison and permit the duchy's annexation rather than suffer French hostility and interference at a critical time in the reorganization of Germany. But if the matter could be dragged out until after the formation of the North German Confederation, it might become highly useful to Berlin.[26]

French handling of the problem was neither vigorous nor skillful. Benedetti failed even to report Bismarck's suggestion that France incite "manifestations" in the duchy. In quest of the unattainable, Napoleon and Rouher risked the attainable. They pressed for the compensation of William III on Prussian soil, which was refused. Instead of concentrating on Luxemburg, they sought from Berlin a secret agreement on Belgium as well. At the end of August Benedetti determined that his health "imperatively" required a two-week vacation at Karlsbad. When he returned on September 15, Bismarck was reported too ill to receive him; on the 26th he learned that the minister had left for the country and that nothing could be done during his absence.[27]

Not until December 1 was the Junker back in Berlin. In an interview he told Benedetti that he still favored the project—but the king had to be "converted." On calling again, the ambassador was informed that the minister-president was too weak and too busy with internal affairs to see him. Acidly Bismarck complained to Paris of Benedetti's importunity in pressing the matter. But his procrastination was deliberate. "The French," he had written on October 22, "must retain hope and especially faith in our good will without our giving them definite commitments." Every delay was an advantage, he instructed Goltz on February 15, "for we shall win time thereby for the consolidation of our relationships in northern Germany and with southern Germany." In six months Berlin would be in a better position to meet the challenge.[28]

[25] Becker, *Bismarcks Ringen*, pp. 405 ff.

[26] This dual purpose is particularly evident in the instruction to Goltz on February 15, 1867. *GW*, vi, 264-269.

[27] *OD*, xii, 172, 193-196, 213-216, 311, 334-335; *APP*, viii, 110, 121, 133-135, 139-140.

[28] *OD*, xiii, 200-202, 226-227, 281; Becker, *Bismarcks Ringen*, p. 903; *RKN*, ii, 201.

But the vital question concerning the Luxemburg crisis is why he wished to provoke the challenge at all. Certainly he did not regard the grand duchy itself as vital to Germany. "The population of the country is hardly homogeneous with ours," he wrote on July 31, 1866. "In the judgment of military experts, moreover, the fortress is not of such strategic importance that its possession ought to be bought at the cost of other advantages and couldn't be compensated for by other strategically more important points in our adjacent area." He had no interest in acquiring the duchy for Prussia or the North German Confederation. To the Dutch envoy he even admitted that the population was "anti-Prussian."[29]

Not until his return from Putbus did Bismarck begin to refer to Luxemburg as "German" and to its fate as a matter of national concern.[30] On December 6 he instructed Goltz to express doubt that possession of the duchy would compensate France for the animosity which its seizure would "certainly" arouse "in all Germany." On December 19 and 20 he pointed out that Prussia could hardly be expected to take the initiative in ceding "German land" or accept the "odium" of delivering "Germans against their will and for no apparent cause to France." "If we must purchase the alliance with France by a humiliating injury to German national feeling," he told Goltz, "it is too dearly bought."[31]

Certainly Bismarck feared that involvement in the rape of Luxemburg would compromise his liaison with German nationalism. But he also calculated that to pose as the champion of the nation in the affair would help to consummate that alliance. Goltz assumed that Prussia's next objectives could best be achieved in harmony with France; Bismarck, in conflict with her. "Through the excitement of national feeling" he expected, "the quick consolidation of our relationships in Germany."[32] What spontaneous love of nation or trust in Hohenzollern leadership could not accomplish might better be achieved by fear and hatred of a foreign foe.

[29] *GW*, vi, 91-92, 155; *APP*, viii, 344, 471. The expert opinion was that of the ministry of war. In mid-January 1867 a judgment was requested of Moltke, who took a contrary view. *RKN*, ii, 188.

[30] On October 26 he even ordered August Brass not to publish "any teutonizing articles concerning Luxemburg." Keudel, *Fürst und Fürstin Bismarck*, p. 325.

[31] *RKN*, ii, 130, 143, 183, 203.

[32] *RKN*, ii, 155; *GW*, vi, 263-264, 303.

3. CRISIS OVER LUXEMBURG

Week after week Benedetti called at Wilhelmstrasse 76, but in vain. Usually so voluble and available, the Junker was now "silent and inaccessible." In the past so "fecund of resources and expedients," he could now see nothing but obstacles in the path of a French alliance. Bismarck, however, struck the pose of an injured friend. "From the beginning of my ministry," he complained, "I have regarded and handled this alliance as the natural expression of the enduring harmony of interests of both countries." By their "precipitate urgency" the French were endangering it. They must appreciate the difficulties he faced in persuading William, as well as the German public, to accept it. By their earlier demand for Rhenish territory the French had complicated his task. They wished to gather the fruits of a Prussian victory to which they had contributed nothing.[33] The tone was strikingly similar to that toward Austria in the years before the *dénouement* of 1866.

At Paris there was mounting anxiety and embarrassment. In a circular published on September 17 La Valette had alluded to the French demands. Now the suspicion began to spread that the government had been rebuffed. The point of political gravity in Europe appeared to be shifting from Paris to Berlin. The emperor and his ministers feared attacks in the coming session of the *corps législatif*. In desperation they decided to concentrate on Luxemburg, dropping for the time being the demands for Belgium and an alliance.[34] But Bismarck refused either to join in a *démarche* at the Hague or withdraw Prussia's garrison from Luxemburg without apparent cause. The French, he insisted, could furnish the cause, if they would but stimulate a demand for withdrawal on the part of influential Luxemburgers. But Napoleon feared to excite a popular reaction in Germany by such a move[35]—precisely the reason why Bismarck advised it!

On February 14, 1867, Napoleon opened the French parliament with a speech in which he strove to cover up the fiasco of his foreign policy during the past year. His words were boastful, but his delivery was uncertain and his manner melancholic. On

33 *OD*, xiii, 273 ff., 322-323, 367 ff.; *RKN*, ii, 143-150; *APP*, viii, 212.

34 Case, *French Opinion on War and Diplomacy*, pp. 221 ff.; *RKN*, ii, 157-158, 161, 172-178, 188-190, 194-196, 216.

35 *RKN*, ii, 151, 161, 165-168, 173, 210, 224; *APP*, viii, 246-247.

St. Helena, he recalled, Napoleon I had predicted the future agglomeration of peoples into national states. Hence the recent developments were only natural and no cause for alarm. Without calling up a single soldier or moving a regiment, France had halted the victorious Prussian army before the gates of Vienna. "Prussia seeks to avoid everything which might irritate our national sensitivity and is in agreement with us on the major European issues." But the opposition was unappeased. In mid-March the feared Adolphe Thiers delivered a devastating attack. Rejecting the concept of national self-determination, he upheld that of the balance of power, which required the restraint of Prussia. With biting sarcasm he contrasted the vision and boldness of Bismarck's operations with the pitiful oscillations of the French. His closing sentence combined threat with accusation: "There is not another single mistake to commit."[36]

The debate was barely over when Bismarck revealed that the roster of Napoleon's failures was even longer than Thiers assumed. On March 19 the texts of the treaties of alliance with the southern states were released to the press with their consent. In the constituent Reichstag the chancellor expected heavy criticism of the decision to stop at the Main. He needed an answer to the reproach that the treaty of Nikolsburg had left open the possibility of alliances between the southern states and foreign powers against the north. In Paris the revelation was the greatest sensation in the public press since Königgrätz. For Napoleon and his ministers it was a bitter blow. Bismarck had already acquired what they proposed to sell. The German nationalists were also impressed. "He is as smart as a snake," wrote Bennigsen, "but hardly lacking in deceit like the dove."[37]

Meanwhile, the French had taken the one path left to them. On March 16 they opened unilateral negotiations with the Netherlands. In return for Luxemburg, Napoleon offered to guarantee the frontiers of the Netherlands and Limburg. At the Hague neither William III nor his government had much interest in retaining Luxemburg, and they feared that Bismarck's aim was to obtain a frontier on the Meuse including the fortress of Maasstricht. Nevertheless, they were leary of entering into an agree-

[36] Case, *French Opinion on War and Diplomacy*, pp. 228-229; Émile Ollivier, *l'Empire libéral* (Paris, 1895-1912), IX, 231-237, 270 ff.; *APP*, VIII, 397.

[37] *GW*, VI, 272, 296; X, 328, 347; *APP*, VIII, 409 ff.; *RKN*, II, 235, 240-243, 257-260; Hermann Oncken, *Rudolf von Bennigsen* (Stuttgart, 1910), II, 33.

ment with France without consulting Berlin. On March 19 William III consented to cede Luxemburg for an indemnity of five million *Gulden*, but insisted on the approval of the King of Prussia. Simultaneously he informed Berlin of the proposition and offered to assist in bringing about a Franco-Prussian understanding. Meanwhile, French agents were active in the city of Luxemburg with petitions and placards. Those wishing to escape the "hated domination of Prussia" were urged to assemble in the Wilhelmsplatz every noon to shout: "Vive la France! Vive Napoléon!"[38]

The timing of these actions could hardly have been more convenient for Bismarck. The French maneuver reached fruition just as his constitutional draft entered the crisis stage in the constituent Reichstag. On March 26-27 occurred the crucial debates on ministerial responsibility, on March 30 the vote on the remuneration of deputies, in early April the critical debates and negotiations over the iron budget. Deliberately Bismarck exploited the Luxemburg issue to speed the deliberations of the constituent Reichstag to a favorable conclusion.

Prussia, he complained to Paris, was badly abused. The conditions he had stipulated for her tacit permission in the Luxemburg affair had not been followed. By seeking Prussian approval, William III had involved Berlin in the negotiation and hence in the responsibility for the duchy's loss to Germany. Furthermore, the street demonstrations in Luxemburg were far different from the decorous petitions of bankers and merchants that he had suggested. French clumsiness, he telegraphed to Goltz on March 30, had aroused public animosity throughout Germany. "Stoked by our opponents, the excitement is growing to critical dimensions. . . . Interpellation imminent in the Reichstag from the uttermost left."[39]

On April 1 Bennigsen delivered the interpellation. Did the Prussian government and its allies intend to make secure, "against every danger," the union of Luxemburg ("an old German land") with the "rest of Germany" and "particularly the Prussian right of garrison in the fortress of Luxemburg"? With passion the Hanoverian denounced the prince of "German descent" on the

[38] *OD*, xv, 80, 99 ff.; *RKN*, ii, 260; *GW*, vi, 320; *APP*, viii, 381-382, 441-442, 494-495, 509 ff.

[39] *GW*, vi, 320-323; *APP*, viii, 539-541. For the reaction in southern Germany see *APP*, viii, 531, 557.

Dutch throne for his willingness to sell to France a land which had "at all times been German" and wished now to remain so. Regardless of party, he declared, the nation would stand united behind the "strong policy" of the government. The applause seemed unending.[40]

The chief "stoker" of this demonstration was Bismarck himself. In all probability he had even agreed with Bennigsen upon the wording of the interpellation.[41] Openly he warned the French that their action would "make it easier to bring about the swift completion of the North German Confederation." Indeed it did. During the following days a sense of urgency pervaded the chamber and committee rooms of the constituent Reichstag. It heightened the spirit of compromise and encouraged the liberals to sacrifice the vital powers of parliament over the army and military budget. In this way the momentary crisis over Luxemburg left a permanent mark upon the institutional relationships of the second Reich.[42]

At the Hague, meanwhile, Napoleon and Moustier, who had replaced Drouyn as foreign minister, were heading down the home stretch in the race for the Luxemburg treaty, scheduled for signing on April 1. But Bismarck shoved one obstacle after another on to the track. On receiving the Dutch king's request for Prussian approval, he replied that William wished first to know the opinions of the other treaty powers of 1839, the German governments, and even the north German Reichstag. Had the agnates, moreover, been consulted?[43] Three days later he refused, for Prussia, any responsibility for the treaty. William III must decide what he owed himself and Europe. Prussia would look after her own interests "at the right time." The ominous clamor of public protest, he declared, made it impossible for Prussia to withdraw her garrison from Luxemburg. The man who for four years had contemptuously defied the attacks of press and parliament now pictured himself as helpless before the people's fury. "As things stand in Germany we must in my opinion dare the war rather than yield, despite the fact that the object, Luxemburg, is in itself hardly worth a war." The nation's "sense of honor," he actually declared, was the "decisive" factor. On April 3 he

40 *SBR*, I (1867), 487 ff.; II, 62; Oncken, *Bennigsen*, II, 35-40.
41 "He gladly lets himself be pressed," the Hanoverian wrote. *Ibid.*, II, 34.
42 *GW*, VI, 322-323, 356-357; Oncken, *Bennigsen*, II, 45-46.
43 *RKN*, II, 260; *APP*, VIII, 514-515.

telegraphed to the Hague, "After the incitement of public opinion war would scarcely be avoidable if the affair proceeds."[44]

In Paris there was anger and confusion. Moustier complained that France had held to the procedure suggested by Bismarck himself; it looked as though Berlin had set a "trap" for the French. But then he calmed down and added hastily that he had not meant to be comminatory. Napoleon was indignant and determined to go through with the affair if William III would sign. In talking to Goltz, however, he was careful to keep his manner "hearty" and emphasized that he desired peace, if it could be had with honor.[45] France, he knew, was in no condition to fight. The reorganization and strengthening of the army had barely begun; the infantry was not yet fully armed with breech-loaders; the forces being withdrawn from Mexico had not yet arrived in France; the empire had no dependable allies. Furthermore, Napoleon had just opened in Paris a great international exposition, which he hoped would brighten the tarnished luster of his regime and add to the prosperity of French industry. Both William I and Alexander II had accepted invitations. War would have wrecked the exhibition and the chance for Bonaparte to play host to Romanov and Hohenzoller.[46]

Bismarck likewise had no desire to fight over Luxemburg. His reply to Bennigsen's interpellation was moderate, though firm, and his warning to the Hague on April 3 was intended to keep William III from the final act which would make war almost certain. But if the Dutch should sign, the Junker had in mind a possible compromise with which to avert the struggle. Even while pushing the crisis to its climax on March 30, he instructed Goltz to inquire "cautiously" whether the French would be willing, in return for Luxemburg, to release Prussia from her Nikolsburg commitment ultimately to divide Schleswig on lines of nationality. After listening to Bennigsen on April 1, he telegraphed the ambassador not to bring the matter up "as yet."[47] The cynicism of such a bargain would have been highly damaging to the national

---

[44] *GW*, vi, 323-324, 331-333; *APP*, viii, 615-617.

[45] *RKN*, ii, 270-281.

[46] *RKN*, ii, 231, 268, 278. It was certainly no accident that during the weeks in which the Luxemburg crisis developed, Bismarck solicited invitations for the simultaneous visit of William and Alexander and that William's acceptance was dispatched on March 30, the day before Bennigsen's interpellation.

[47] *GW*, vi, 321; *RKN*, ii, 274; *APP*, viii, 549, 693.

posture of the government. With typical elasticity, however, he held the idea in reserve.

Meanwhile, he had sought to mobilize the support of the European powers. Beginning on March 30, he urged Britain and Russia to intervene at the Hague to prevent the king's signature. Although Gorchakov and the czar were critical of Napoleon's actions, they chose to let Britain take the lead. In London, the new foreign secretary, Lord Stanley, took the view that "so small a rearrangement of territory" would not disturb the European balance. Nor was he impressed by Bismarck's argument that Luxemburg was covered by the treaty of 1839 guaranteeing Belgian independence.[48] On April 2 Bismarck ordered Bernstorff to find out "how far we may count on England" in the event of war with France. Lacking her support, he bluffed, Prussia had the alternative of "shifting from the alliance with German public opinion to an alliance with France" at the cost of Belgium. But the answer was disappointing. Although disturbed about Belgium, Stanley replied that Britain would not take sides.[49]

On April 5, after days of uncertainty, William III finally declined to sign. This gave both sides the opportunity to find a way out of the affair. Soon Bismarck indicated to the British his willingness to accept an international conference. After some hesitation the French, shocked by the extent of their defeat, also declared their readiness to waive the claim to Luxemburg, if Prussia would withdraw her garrison and accept neutralization of the duchy. But Bismarck refused to enter into such an arrangement "now." To break with German national sentiment, he declared, would be more dangerous for the German governments than war with France.[50] He had not yet reaped, in other words, all the benefits he expected for his German policy from the Luxemburg crisis. The constituent Reichstag was still in session and negotiations with the south were still under way.

In Berlin there were those who in April advocated mobilization and war. French military preparations made the generals nervous. Convinced of the inevitability of conflict, Moltke wished to strike

[48] *RKN*, II, 269; *GW*, VI, 320, 324-325, 330-332; *APP*, VIII, 550, 627-629; Werner E. Mosse, *The European Powers and the German Question, 1848-1871* (Cambridge, 1958), pp. 263-264.

[49] *GW*, VI, 330, 332-333; *APP*, VIII, 575-576, 601, 624-625; Mosse, *European Powers*, pp. 264.

[50] *Ibid.*, pp. 265-267; *GW*, VI, 349; *APP*, VIII, 649.

before her rearmament was complete. Bismarck was also concerned. He feared that Napoleon, while peacefully inclined, might be pushed into an attack by his more belligerent advisers. While ready to meet the challenge, he had no intention of precipitating a conflict. "The chance of success," he remarked, "is not a just cause for beginning a great war."[51] Until the path of peace had been fully explored and found without exit, he was not ready to try the more hazardous one of violence. For the time being he hoped that mere friction with France would generate the heat with which to weld the nation together under the Prussian system.[52]

4. ALTERNATIVE PLANS

The Main line, Bismarck boasted, was not a wall but a paling which could never hold back the national stream. After Königgrätz there actually were signs of movement in the south. At Nikolsburg the governments of Hesse and Württemberg applied for admission to the North German Confederation. By volunteering, they hoped to exact better terms. In Munich the lower chamber voted (August 30, 1866), 124 to 11, for cooperation with Prussia in the formation of a German union. The next day Prince Hohenlohe-Schillingsfürst judged that, while court and government were opposed, the great majority of the Bavarian people were for "union with Prussia." In Karlsruhe a nationalistic cabinet under Karl Mathy, Rudolf von Freydorf, and Julius Jolly assumed office in July, and in October the Baden parliament voted for unconditional union with the north.[53]

But this mood soon evaporated. Wholesale annexations in the north gave the confederation the appearance of an enlarged Prussia. The governments feared the domination of this colossus, and liberal nationalists disliked its political system. Nor was either reassured by the constitution Bismarck designed and

---

[51] *Aus dem Leben Bernhardis*, vii, 358, 369 ff., 375-378; *GW*, vi, 362, 366-369, also 333 (footnote).

[52] *GW*, vi, 303, 322, 333.

[53] *GW*, vi, 303; *APP*, viii, 261-262; Brandenburg, *Untersuchungen*, p. 699; Adolf Rapp, *Die Württemberger und die nationale Frage, 1863-1871, Darstellungen aus der Württembergischen Geschichte*, Vol. 4 (Stuttgart, 1910), pp. 219 ff.; Friedrich Curtius, ed., *Denkwürdigkeiten des Fürsten Chlodwig zu Hohenlohe-Schillingsfürst* (Stuttgart, 1907), i, 174-175; Theodor Schieder, *Die kleindeutsche Partei in Bayern, Münchener historische Abhandlungen*, Vol. 12 (Munich, 1936), pp. 120 ff.; Georg Meyer, "Die Reichsgründung und das Grossherzogtum Baden," *Festgabe für Grossherzog Friedrich von Baden* (Heidelberg, 1896), pp. 147 ff., 178 ff.

pushed through to adoption. Despite his concessions to federalism, the governments were disappointed by the degree of centralism which remained. His concessions to the constituent Reichstag, moreover, were not sufficient to allay the suspicions of southern liberals. German national feeling in the south was chiefly the property of middle-class liberals who were prejudiced against the aristocratic-authoritarian regime in Berlin. Only in Baden did the sentiment for union still prevail. His anticipation of these reactions was precisely the reason why Bismarck had chosen to halt temporarily at the Main in the first place. The south's "indigestibility" was owing to its liberalism and particularism, as well as its Catholicism.[54]

Bismarck faced these difficulties in typical fashion. As in the Schleswig-Holstein affair he regarded the problem in terms of several possibilities, ranging from the desired maximum to the acceptable minimum. The maximum was simply the extension of the northern constitution over the south with no further concessions of either a liberal or decentralistic nature. For the time being, however, this was impractical both because of southern attitudes and the foreign complications which would arise from the open violation of the treaty of Prague. The minimum consisted of the military alliances with the south already achieved, supplemented by a Zollverein parliament with power to legislate in matters of customs and commerce.

Between these extremes lay a medium course, upon which Bismarck evidently placed his greatest immediate hopes: a "wider confederation" or "constitutional alliance." The constitution of the North German Confederation would be extended over the south in all but military and naval affairs. Legislative power would be exercised by an enlarged Bundesrat and Reichstag. The virtue of such an arrangement was that it left the southern governments in possession of the most important attribute of their cherished sovereignty (control over the army and its finances) and at the same time prevented the reinforcement of northern liberals by the liberal south in any future attempts to overthrow the iron budget. The constitutional union, moreover, would have

---

[54] Schüssler, *Bismarcks Kampf*, pp. 19-20, 35-36; Schieder, *Kleindeutsche Partei*, pp. 136-139; Karl Alexander von Müller, *Bayern im Jahre 1866 und die Berufung des Fürsten Hohenlohe, Historische Bibliothek*, Vol. xx (Munich, 1909), pp. 160 ff.; Götz, *Die Stellung Hessen-Darmstadts*, pp. 32 ff.

made it virtually impossible for southern states to carry on an independent foreign policy.[55]

As so often in the past, Bismarck's goals were not mutually exclusive. They were steps leading upward from the least to the most desirable outcome. If the Zollverein parliament were immediately attainable, the gradual expansion of its legislative competence might eventually create the "wider confederation." In turn, the latter might evolve into a fully sovereign state. The expansion of the Prussian system over Germany might well be achieved by evolutionary rather than revolutionary means, by the organic development of governmental institutions rather than through war with France.

5. FAILURE OF THE MEDIUM AND MAXIMUM

Bismarck's plan for a wider confederation had some support. Grand Duke Frederick of Baden and his ministers were still intent on union with the north, even under Bismarck's constitution. While King Charles of Württemberg was jealous of his sovereignty—and his Russian wife, Queen Olga, even more so—Foreign Minister Varnbüler was a realist who quickly reconciled himself to the prospect of Prussian supremacy after the defeat of 1866. Although determined to preserve as far as possible Württemberg's independence in military and political affairs, he recognized the necessity of union with the north in economic matters. In Bavaria the replacement (December 31, 1866) of Pfordten by Hohenlohe-Schillingsfürst as minister-president opened the prospect of a new era of cooperation between Berlin and Munich. Whereas Pfordten had distrusted Prussia and dreamed of a southern union under Bavarian leadership, Prince Hohenlohe believed that Bavaria could escape the dangers of isolation only by joining, under advantageous terms, a federal union led by Prussia. He was one of four members of the upper chamber who had voted in favor of the August resolution for union with the north. Nevertheless, he too was disappointed by the centralistic features of the northern constitution; his cabinet colleagues were particularistic; so likewise was King Louis, who eyed suspiciously any proposal which threatened Bavarian sovereignty. Hohenlohe, moreover, was not a strong personality of decisive political will.[56]

[55] Schüssler, *Bismarcks Kampf*, pp. 66-69.
[56] *Ibid.*, pp. 34 ff., 57 ff.; Hohenlohe, *Denkwürdigkeiten*, I, 171-175, 184 ff., 194 ff.;

With utmost care Bismarck sought to draw the prince, and with him the Bavarian state, into a "constitutional alliance." On January 31, 1867 he outlined his plan to Baron Spitzemberg, the Württemberg minister at Berlin. After reading the minister's report, Varnbüler was favorable. Through him Bismarck hoped to put pressure on Hohenlohe. But the particularistic current in Munich was swift, and, while personally inclined toward such an arrangement, Hohenlohe was compelled to reject it. Nor did the persuasion of Grand Duke Frederick have any effect. Hohenlohe did not have the power to commit Bavaria to the wider confederation of Bismarck's hopes.[57]

Thus far the treaties of alliance signed in August-September 1866 were Bismarck's only success in snaring the south. But now, as the Luxemburg crisis reached its peak, even these instruments appeared insecure. While his main purpose in publishing them (March 19, 1867) was to answer his critics in the constituent Reichstag, he also wished "to make it easier for the southern states to come to an understanding with each other over union with the North German Confederation and to accomplish this union itself." Knowledge of the treaties, however, served only to heighten the tension between pro- and anti-Prussians throughout the south. The latter could now claim that they had been misled and betrayed by their own governments. In Stuttgart Varnbüler consented to publication only under protest and requested a public declaration from Berlin to the effect that the treaty was purely defensive in character. Bismarck's reply was an irritated refusal. He feared what might be transpiring between Stuttgart and Paris.[58]

Instead of furnishing the needed impetus for a national union, the Luxemburg crisis even threatened to destroy what had already been accomplished. Both Varnbüler and Hohenlohe were alarmed over the prospect of being dragged into war. Generally it was

---

Müller, *Bayern im Jahre 1866*, pp. 89 ff., and "Die Tauffkirchensche Mission nach Berlin und Wien," in Karl A. von Müller, ed., *Riezler-Festschrift, Beiträge zur Bayerischen Geschichte* (Gotha, 1913), pp. 352 ff.; Ernst Salzer, "Fürst Chlodwig zu Hohenlohe-Schillingsfürst und die deutsche Frage," *Historische Vierteljahrschrift*, xi (1908), 40-74.

[57] *APP*, viii, 353-357, 373, 428-429; *GW*, vi, 239-241; Schüssler, *Bismarcks Kampf*, pp. 62 ff., 73 ff., 120 ff., 297-302; Hohenlohe, *Denkwürdigkeiten*, i, 198 ff.; Müller, *Bayern im Jahre 1866*, pp. 183 ff.

[58] *GW*, vi, 301, 316-317; *APP*, viii, 460, 507-508, 515-516; George G. Windell, *The Catholics and German Unity, 1866-1871* (Minneapolis, 1954), pp. 103 ff.

feared that the south would be the first victim of a war against France, allied with Austria and Italy. In Stuttgart there was talk of neutrality, and in Munich, according to Werthern, Hohenlohe faced the possibility of being outvoted or dismissed, if he stood by the alliance.[59] On April 8 Bismarck warned Bavaria that, if deserted, the north would be compelled to seek its allies elsewhere and to consider only its own interests in any constitutional arrangements. Even above the Main, however, Bismarck apparently had grounds for dissatisfaction. In notes dispatched on April 12 to all German capitals, north and south, he maintained that Prussia's sole interest in the Luxemburg affair was the obligation to satisfy German national pride. "If a people feels its honor injured, then it is injured and must be dealt with accordingly. National feeling and national honor are potencies which do not lend themselves to logical measurement." Were those who refused their support ready to defend their refusal and the loss of Luxemburg before the bar of public opinion?[60]

This attempt to whip the southern states into line by the threat of the nation's rage had only limited success. Karlsruhe and Darmstadt, to be sure, gave clear declarations of support, but the replies from Munich and Stuttgart were equivocal. In both capitals it was feared that Bismarck's aim was actually to unload on the backs of the southern governments the blame for a coming surrender of Luxemburg. While affirming their loyalty to the alliance, Varnbüler and Hohenlohe stressed their hopes that peace would be maintained. The former refused to take a stand on whether the *casus foederis* was applicable "at this moment," and the latter pointed to the uncertainty of Austrian policy as an "urgent" reason for peace.[61]

In February Hohenlohe had begun to insist that for Berlin the key to the south lay in Vienna, both with regard to Bavarian acceptance of the wider confederation and her support in the Luxemburg crisis. The general fear of Prussian hegemony and of a Franco-Austrian alliance would be allayed only by an agree-

---

[59] *APP*, VIII, 567, 574, 581-584, 599, 619, 655-656; IX, 35; Schüssler, *Bismarcks Kampf*, pp. 151 ff.;Veit Valentin, *Bismarcks Reichsgründung im Urteil englischer Diplomaten* (Amsterdam, 1937), pp. 353 ff.

[60] *GW*, VI, 347-348, 350-352.

[61] *APP*, VIII, 640-642, 662-664, 707-712, 717-718, 730-731; Hohenlohe, *Denkwürdigkeiten*, I, 230-231. Later Varnbüler asserted in parliament that Bismarck's question demonstrated that it lay in Württemberg's power to decide whether the *casus foederis* applied. *APP*, IX, 375-376, 408-411, 532-533.

ment between Hapsburg and Hohenzoller. Happily for Bismarck this suggestion coincided with his own intentions. In granting Austria an easy peace his aim had been to restore her to the list of Berlin's potential allies.[62]

Immediately on returning from Putbus in December 1866 he stressed to Count Wimpffen, Karolyi's successor, the need for an "intimate understanding" with Austria. Such a combination was only natural in view of the German character of the Hapsburg dynasty and many of its subjects. The amazed diplomat heard him deplore the failure of the Gablenz mission and regret that the two countries had not formed a common front against France and "shot the deer together." On April 12 Bismarck outlined the details of his plan to Count Tauffkirchen, Hohenlohe's intimate adviser and emissary. The "organic" connection he desired was not a "constitutional alliance," but the revival of the German Confederation without a diet. This would guarantee indefinitely the security of the German provinces of Austria. The rest of the Hapsburg empire would be guaranteed in a defensive alliance limited to periods of three years. Russia too was to be brought into the system. He hoped for a revival of the holy alliance.[63]

The man to whom fell the duty of responding to these overtures was none other than Baron Beust. By refusing to deal with him in negotiating peace with Saxony, Bismarck had brought about his dismissal in Dresden, only to make him available for a more dangerous post! In October 1866 Franz Joseph chose him to replace Mensdorff as Austrian foreign minister. As his memoirs reveal, Beust was a vain and self-important man, who never forgot a witticism or compliment. He was certain that, had his advice been followed, none of the disasters which Austria had suffered since 1859 would have occurred. Nevertheless, he understood that Bismarck's "cynical" offer of an alliance was actually designed to facilitate Berlin's absorption of the south. He was not deceived by the Junker's assurance that this would be a "misfortune" for Prussia, nor shaken by his threat that, failing an Austrian alliance, Berlin would have to seek allies in Paris and Petersburg. Beust's refusal made it impossible for Hohenlohe to

---

62 Hohenlohe, *Denkwürdigkeiten*, I, 202, 206 ff., 224 ff.; *APP*, VIII, 428; Stosch, *Denkwürdigkeiten*, p. 102.

63 *APP*, VIII, 190-191, 505-506, 652 ff., 671; Walter Platzhoff, "Die Anfänge des Dreikaiserbundes, 1867-1871," *Preussische Jahrbücher*, Vol. 188 (1922), pp. 283 ff.; Müller, "Die Tauffkirchensche Mission," pp. 392 ff.

accept the plan of the wider confederation. Russia was also negative. Vigorously Gorchakov pointed out that the conflict of Austrian and Russian interests in the Balkans made impossible a renewal of the holy alliance.[64] But these were not the only disappointments Bismarck suffered in the spring of 1867.

As usual he was attempting to move simultaneously on more than one front. While striving for the constitutional alliance, he sought to make headway toward his higher goal as well. The time had come, he determined, to cross the Main by bringing southern Hesse into the North German Confederation. Since Baden would surely follow, it was possible that Württemberg and Bavaria would ultimately find it difficult to stay out. Should the French take up his suggestion for a deal on Luxemburg and northern Schleswig, progress toward German unity would make the bargain more palatable in Germany. Should the French seek to frustrate a seemingly spontaneous Hessian demand for union with the north, Berlin would acquire, in addition to the Luxemburg issue, yet another cause with which to belabor the patriotic feelings of the German nation.[65]

Again there was some prospect of success. The desire of the Hessian government for a military convention to end the divided condition of its armed forces provided a convenient lever. But the project had an able and determined foe in the Hessian minister Baron Dalwigk. An old personal enemy of Bismarck, Dalwigk was irreconcilably opposed to a Prussian dominated Germany. In order to get around him, the chancellor instigated an effort by the Prussian crown prince and his brother-in-law, Prince Ludwig of Hesse, to arouse sentiment in Darmstadt for the inclusion of the southern province. On Dalwigk's advice, the grand duke replied that he would wait to see what kind of military convention Berlin would grant. In view of the crisis with France, Bismarck agreed to the signing of a convention on April 7, followed by a military alliance on April 11. The lever was lost, and thereafter Dalwigk remained unmoved.[66]

[64] Friedrich Ferdinand Graf von Beust, *Aus drei Viertel-Jahrhunderten* (2 vols., Stuttgart, 1887); *APP*, VIII, 683 ff., 809; Schüssler, *Bismarcks Kampf*, pp. 180 ff.; Becker, *Bismarcks Ringen*, pp. 419 ff.; Müller, "Die Tauffkirchensche Mission," pp. 415 ff.

[65] Schüssler, *Bismarcks Kampf*, pp. 89 ff.

[66] Dalwigk, *Tagebücher*, 315 ff., 351 ff.; *APP*, VIII, 416-417, 438-439, 443-444, 463-464, 487-488, 497-498, 599-603, 671-672. For the texts of the military agreements see Glaser, *Archiv*, III, 53-57.

Bismarck's defeat was all the more humiliating in view of the fact that he had meanwhile made public his aim. Through Prince Ludwig he brought about an interpellation in the constituent Reichstag on April 9 by a nationalist Hessian deputy, Solms-Laubach. After describing the divided condition of the Hessian state as intolerable, the deputy expressed confidence that the union of the southern segment to the north would provide a "bridge" for the completion of German unity. In reply Bismarck also emphasized the evils of Hesse's divided condition and the advantages of *Anschluss*. Should Darmstadt request such a step, Berlin would consult with the southern governments and with Vienna, whose opposition was not expected. But this obvious appeal to public pressure had no effect upon Dalwigk, who found in Beust, and even Hohenlohe, diplomatic support for the preservation of the *status quo*. The only lasting mark of Bismarck's effort was a hopeful amendment to article 71 of the northern constitution, which the liberals passed with his approval: "The entry of the south German states or of one of the same into the confederation shall take place on the proposal of the confederate presidency by way of confederate legislation."[67]

The Luxemburg crisis had failed to provide the needed steam for the engine of Bismarck's German policy. Neither the medium nor maximum alternatives had been achieved. In fact, the crisis revealed more glaringly than ever the depth of the fissures which still divided Germany. Having squeezed all possible benefit from the affair, Bismarck gave up the pretense of trembling before the terrors of German public opinion. On April 26 he agreed to an international conference to negotiate a compromise. At the conference, held May 7-11 in London, the sovereignty of William III was confirmed; the duchy was neutralized under the guarantee of the great powers; the Prussian right of garrison was withdrawn; and the fortress was consigned to demolition.

For Napoleon this compromise was a harsh defeat. Withdrawal of the Prussian garrison was the only achievement to which he could point in a year of disaster. The retreat from Mexico under the threats of the United States, coupled with the failure to derive for France any benefit from the German civil war, starkly revealed the debility of his regime precisely in that area in which a Bonaparte was expected to excel. Many Germans were also dis-

---

[67] *SBR*, I (1867), 638-639; Schüssler, *Bismarcks Kampf*, pp. 138 ff.

satisfied. To William the settlement was a "slap" from France, an inglorious "sacrifice" on the altar of peace.[68] German nationalists looked upon it as "almost a defeat." But in May-July agents of the Nationalverein reported from Luxemburg that, if compelled to choose between Prussia and France, nine-tenths of the inhabitants would prefer the latter. The pro-German party hardly dared show its face in the grand duchy.[69] Bismarck had known it all along.

6. SUCCESS OF THE MINIMUM

In his struggle for a favorable relationship with the south, Bismarck held in reserve a weapon of considerable power. While the economic unity of northern Germany was assured, the Zollverein was still indispensable for the welfare of the south. But the events of 1866 had rendered the Zollverein treaties obsolete. In the peace treaties Bismarck had provided that they might be abrogated on six months' notice. This was a sword suspended over the heads of the southern statesmen. For the time being, however, he made no motion to cut the thread. If neither the medium nor maximum goals could be achieved through the national pressure generated by the Luxemburg crisis, the menace of abrogation would suffice to achieve the minimum.

On February 15, 1867, while mounting his campaign for the higher alternatives, he approached the southern states for an informal exchange of views on the subject of Zollverein reform. Prussia favored, he declared, either a Zollparlament or the addition of southern deputies to the Reichstag when matters of customs and commerce were under consideration. On March 11 he brought the plan before the public in a speech to the constituent Reichstag.[70] But even this proposal, more modest than that of the wider confederation, was opposed by Bavarian particularists. To Bismarck's annoyance, Hohenlohe was compelled to reject for the time being any kind of parliamentary union with the north.[71]

---

[68] *APP*, viii. 829.

[69] Oncken, *Bennigsen*, ii, 43-45. For those who take the cultural view of the nation, however, the revelation is meaningless. Recently Otto Becker wrote of the settlement as "a painful, national loss." *Bismarcks Ringen*, p. 425.

[70] *GW*, vi, 269-270; *SBR*, i (1867), 138; Hohenlohe, *Denkwürdigkeiten*, i, 205.

[71] Walter Schübelin, *Das Zollparlament und die Politik von Baden, Bayern und Württemberg 1866-1870* (Berlin, 1935), pp. 18 ff.; Schüssler, *Bismarcks Kampf*, pp. 233 ff. Because of the Luxemburg crisis Bismarck failed to dispatch the reply he dictated on March 29. *GW*, vi, 317-319.

In May Bismarck commenced to tighten the screw. He rejected the Bavarian-Württemberg counterproposal for a loose confederation with a Bundesrat composed of state envoys whose legislation would be subject to the approval of the northern Reichstag and the southern parliaments.[72] While disclaiming any desire to coerce, he declared that the common parliament was the "indispensable prerequisite" for the Zollverein renewal. Should no agreement be reached by July 1, Berlin would serve notice of her intention to abrogate. Varnbüler fully understood the necessity of the Zollverein and he feared further opposition would enable Bismarck to increase still further the price of its renewal. The forthcoming visit of William to Paris, furthermore, raised the prospect of a French-Prussian understanding at the cost of southern Germany. On May 23 he suggested that Berlin grasp the initiative in summoning the southern states to a general conference. Bismarck speedily complied.[73]

On assembling in Berlin, June 3, the southern ministers were presented with a Prussian proposal. Drafted by Rudolf Delbrück, it had been extensively revised by Bismarck and was essentially his handiwork. Like the northern constitution, its revolutionary character was concealed by the fiction of continuity with older forms. While the existing treaties remained in effect, Zollverein affairs were to be decided in the future by a "common organ of the contracting states" and a "common representation of their peoples." The former was to be organized like the Frankfurt diet, with Prussia occupying the presidency and authorized to negotiate with foreign powers, while the latter was to be composed of the deputies of the northern Reichstag and deputies elected from the southern states. In a subtly worded clause Prussia was granted the right of veto. Varnbüler and Freydorf accepted immediately for Württemberg and Baden; Dalwigk declared his agreement, while reserving the final decision for Darmstadt.[74]

Hohenlohe was also favorable, but at home he faced a formid-

[72] Hohenlohe, *Denkwürdigkeiten*, I, 232 ff.; *APP*, IX, 45-48; Schübelin, *Zollparlament*, pp. 34 ff.; Schüssler, *Bismarcks Kampf*, pp. 212 ff.

[73] *APP*, IX, 59, 69 ff., 91-92; *GW*, VI, 393-394; Schüssler, *Bismarcks Kampf*, pp. 231, 237 ff.; Becker, *Bismarcks Ringen*, pp. 572-574; Schübelin, *Zollparlament*, pp. 38 ff.

[74] Becker, *Bismarcks Ringen*, pp. 576-577; Schübelin, *Zollparlament*, pp. 44 ff. Delbrück's draft has never been published. For the agreement signed on June 4 and the protocol ultimately signed by Bavaria see Ludwig Hahn, *Zwei Jahre preussisch-deutscher Politik 1866-1867* (Berlin, 1868), pp. 622-624.

able task. In messages to Munich he frightened king and ministers with the prospect that refusal would mean dissolution of the Zollverein. First the cabinet and then Louis, though painfully reluctant, came around. Nevertheless, the Bavarians exacted concessions. While accepting the titles *Bundesrat des Zollvereins* and *Zollparlament*, they saw to it that these bodies were differentiated as clearly as possible from the legislative organs of the North German Confederation. In the Bundesrat they achieved for Bavaria six votes, as against four in the Frankfurt diet. The legislative competence of the Zollverein, moreover, was expressly limited to tariffs, their collection, and the taxation of domestic sugar, salt, and tobacco. Bismarck, on the other hand, clung to the Prussian veto and the provision that the southern deputies were to be unsalaried and elected on the same basis as those of the Reichstag. In the requirement for renewal at twelve-year intervals he retained a means with which to effect future changes. The final treaty was signed on July 8.[75]

The last word belonged to the southern parliaments. As in the case of the constituent Reichstag, Bismarck had taken care that they should work under pressure of a deadline (October 31). In Baden and Hesse there was no difficulty, and in Munich the lower chamber voted (October 22) for acceptance, 117 to 17. But the great majority of the Bavarian upper chamber was fiercely opposed. Aristocratic particularists, ultramontanes, and pro-Austrian great-Germanists were determined to preserve for Bavaria at least the right of *liberum veto*. Only after Hohenlohe had personally escorted the speaker, Baron Thüngen, to Berlin for an interview with Bismarck could the members be convinced of its impossibility. Angry editorials in the liberal-nationalist press and swarms of telegrams and petitions from the urban public and commercial interests warned them that the Zollverein was indispensable. Finally, on October 31, the chamber voted with the greatest reluctance, 35 to 13, for acceptance.[76]

In Württemberg the major opposition developed in the chamber of deputies. Both the Zollverein treaty and military alliance were debated, the latter meeting even more antagonism than the

[75] Becker, *Bismarcks Ringen*, pp. 579 ff.; Schübelin, *Zollparlament*, pp. 48 ff.; Hohenlohe, *Denkwürdigkeiten*, I, 244 ff. For the final treaty see Hahn, *Zwei Jahre*, pp. 624-631.

[76] *APP*, IX, 310, 322 ff., Schieder, *Kleindeutsche Partei*, pp. 158 ff.; Schübelin, *Zollparlament*, pp. 59 ff.; *GW*, VIA, 92-93.

former. The democratic majority feared domination by the autocratic, militaristic north with its greater voting strength. But the commercial interests lobbied for acceptance of the customs parliament, and Bismarck warned that neither treaty was acceptable without the other. To his annoyance, however, Varnbüler eased the alliance through the chamber on October 30 by claiming Prussia's acceptance of Württemberg's right to approve the *casus foederis*.[77] Even now, however, the deputies hoped that an unfavorable vote in Munich would relieve them of the necessity of accepting the customs parliament. But on the 31st the telegraph reported the contrary. With heavy hearts the democratic majority capitulated.[78]

The customs parliament had been achieved, but the degree of opposition it met was inauspicious for Bismarck's further aims. In December 1867 Varnbüler voiced the prevailing mood of the south in a speech to the Württemberg parliament. With the Zollverein and alliance treaties, he asserted emphatically, the southern states had fulfilled their duty to the German nation. There would be no further sacrifice. "Württemberg wants to remain Württemberg as long as it has the power."[79]

[77] *GW*, VIA, 69-70, 110-111.

[78] Rapp, *Württemberger*, pp. 247 ff.; Schübelin, *Zollparlament,* pp. 62 ff. In the event of a negative vote the Prussian ministers in Bavaria and Württemberg were instructed to announce termination of the Zollverein in six months. *GW*, VIA, 84, 92, 96.

[79] Erich Brandenburg, *Die Reichsgründung* (2nd ed., Leipzig, 1922), II, 307; Schüssler, *Bismarcks Kampf*, pp. 281-282.

CHAPTER SEVENTEEN

FAILURE OF THE NATIONAL MOVEMENT

1. THE ZOLLVEREIN ELECTIONS

IS aim, Bismarck told the impatient Badenese, was to find the shortest path to the voluntary entry of all southern states into the North German Confederation. "Direct and immediate pressure" was to be avoided. To admit Baden alone would create a pressure upon Bavaria and Württemberg which would be resented, to the injury of the national cause. The simultaneous admission of Baden and Württemberg, on the other hand, might cause Bavaria to take a "regrettable course." It would supply the "pretext" for disunity at a time when Germany required the greatest solidarity.[1]

Through "patience" he hoped to save what would have to be sacrificed by the use of violence. "Force can be useful against a resistance which is to be broken by a single blow, but it can be justified only by necessity against a resistance which would have to be continually held down." The Badenese should be able to imagine for themselves what conditions would develop in Bavaria and Württemberg, "if in their present mood these two states were brought by force into the North German Confederation."[2] Instead he hoped to rely upon the pressure of common interests eventually to unite both sides of the Main under the northern constitution. "If Germany should attain its national goal in the nineteenth century," he remarked, "that would seem to me something great. Were it in ten or even five years, that would be something extraordinary, an unexpected gift of God."[3]

"Everything depends," he wrote to Karlsruhe, "on the direction and swiftness with which public opinion develops in southern Germany, and a fairly secure judgment about that will first become possible through the customs parliament." The next task was to elect and summon that body as soon as possible and then

[1] *GW*, VIA, 112-113, 133-136; also 127-128 and *APP*, IX, 289-293.
[2] *GW*, VIA, 329-330.   [3] *RKN*, I, 68; *APP*, IX, 474.

"to awaken and nourish" a demand for the extension of its powers. He expected it to adopt the laws of the North German Confederation in such matters as citizenship, passports, and civil law. In a few years—perhaps ten, at the most twenty—the organic growth of the Zollverein would create a little-German union on the northern pattern. Eagerly he waited to see what "temperament" the customs parliament would show.[4]

Throughout the south, the parties, politicians, and general public were similarly aware that what was being decided in the Zollverein elections was not merely the question of tariffs and taxes, but Germany's future. In August 1867 the leaders of the national parties convened in Stuttgart to agree on a common platform calling for the extension of the powers of the new parliament.[5] At home they entered into the campaign with vigor and confidence, advertising the election as a plebiscite of the national will. For the first time southerners were to vote under direct and equal suffrage. At last German nationalists had the chance to prove at the polls that their yearnings were those of the masses.

In Bavaria an opposition began to form during 1867. Whereas the old great-Germanist party, now defunct, had been bourgeois and aristocratic in composition, the new "Patriot Party" was composed of peasants, lower clergy, and petty bourgeoisie, supported by the high aristocracy and the democratic left. Motives were mixed. The democrats had split with the moderates of the Progressive Party. They opposed "dancing to Bismarck's fiddle" in a German parliament which appeared to have all the limitations of the northern Reichstag and Prussian chamber of deputies. But the bulk of the opposition was confessional and particularistic, rather than political. Catholics, both clergy and laymen, feared domination by the Protestant north. Conservative aristocrats were horrified by the prospect that the Wittelsbach dynasty, Germany's oldest, should be mediatized by a Hohenzoller. Bavarian nationalism, moreover, was a vital force for particularism, especially in "old Bavaria," the kingdom's nucleus.[6] "Be-

---

[4] *GW*, vɪᴀ, 113, 135, 153-155; Otto Becker, *Bismarcks Ringen um Deutschlands Gestaltung* (Heidelberg, 1958), pp. 583-584. At least since 1858 he had calculated on the possibility of a Zollverein parliament as a means with which to undermine particularistic governments. *GW*, xɪᴠ, 487; ɪᴠ, 31-32.

[5] Schübelin, *Zollparlament*, pp. 71-72.

[6] Schieder, *Kleindeutsche Partei*, pp. 156 ff., 173 ff.; Schübelin, *Zollparlament*, pp. 98 ff.; Windell, *Catholics and German Unity*, pp. 124 ff.

cause of her material importance, her definite tribal individuality, and the talents of her rulers," Bismarck had written in 1865, "Bavaria is perhaps the only German country which has succeeded in developing a real, harmonious national sentiment."[7] Even today the Bavarian sense of cultural individuality is a factor of importance in German political life.

Despite the activity of the Patriot Party, the German nationalists of the Progressive and Middle Parties went to the polls on February 10, 1868 confident of victory. But the result was devastating. The Patriot Party elected 26 of the 48 deputies, many by overwhelming majorities. In view of its minor strength in the Bavarian lower chamber it had been expected to capture only 4 or 5 seats. Together the two liberal parties brought in but 21. The greatest defeat was suffered by the Middle Party, largest in the lower chamber, which elected only 9. Formerly the party of the liberal great-Germanists, it had lost its following both to the left and the right.[8]

Of all southern states the nationalists had the greatest prospects in Baden. Ruler, ministers, and the dominant Progressive Party favored a united Germany. The campaign declaration of December 20, signed by ministers and deputies, described the customs parliament as but a "preliminary step" to German unity. Only those determined to further the "national union," it declared, should offer themselves as candidates. But the national issue became intertwined with domestic ones, and the opposition swelled to unexpected proportions. Catholic rights, Protestant conservatism, economic protectionism, and particularistic patriotism were the dominant motives. Beginning quietly and rationally, the campaign became bitter, fanatical, and demagogic on both sides. Nationalist strength lay in the urban middle class, while the particularists appealed to workers and peasants. The government intervened for the progressives, and the Catholic clergy did the same for the opposition during the final days of the campaign. On February 18 the nationalists succeeded in filling only 8 of 14 seats. The opposition actually polled the greater number of votes (90,078 to 86,890). Throughout Germany the result was seen as a severe setback for the national cause.[9]

In Württemberg the prospects of the nationalists were least.

7 *GW*, v, 56.   8 Schübelin, *Zollparlament*, pp. 100-101.
9 *Ibid.*, pp. 72 ff.; Windell, *Catholics and German Unity*, pp. 124 ff.

Only the German Party supported further unification. At first the People's Party, which in October had provided the core of the opposition to the treaty, voted to boycott the election. But after the defeat of the nationalists in Baden and Bavaria the populists leaped into the campaign. The government itself was their ally. "We want to prove to Germany and Europe," Varnbüler declared, "that . . . the North German Confederation has no appeal whatever for us." Here the issue was more political than confessional. Swabian democrats dreaded the "Caesarism" and "saber government" of the Prussian north. Their ideal was republican Switzerland and its citizen army. The northern constitution, it was joked, had only three clauses: (1) pay taxes; (2) be a soldier; (3) hold your tongue.[10]

In fighting back Bismarck chose the weapon of conservatism. The Prussian legation in Stuttgart sued the leading democratic journal, *Beobachter*, for slandering the king of Prussia and obtained a judgment. The anti-Prussian deputies replied by introducing a bill to require jury trial in such cases. Bismarck denounced it to Varnbüler as an attack upon the monarchical principle. After the bill passed, he turned to Dresden, Munich, and Karlsruhe for assistance in warning Stuttgart of the "revolutionary movement" being fostered by its policy in the Zollverein election. Then he took the matter up with Vienna, expressing fear that the Württemberg government would lose control to a revolutionary republican party whose aim, nourished by contacts with Switzerland and America, was a "united states of Europe." Finally he addressed his forebodings to London, Paris, and Petersburg with the accusation that Beust himself was playing with revolutionary fire by supporting the Swabian radicals.[11]

Yet on March 24 the candidates of the People's Party and the government polled three-quarters of the total vote and took all 17 seats in the customs parliament. The German Party (popularly called the "Prussian Party") had pleaded with the Swabians to consider themselves primarily as Germans and to find in German national institutions the objects of their loyalty and patriotism. For most, however, the issue was not whether they were German, but whether they were to be "Prussianized."[12]

[10] Schübelin, *Zollparlament*, pp. 86 ff.; Rapp, *Württemberger*, pp. 258 ff.; *APP*, IX, 774, 815.

[11] *GW*, VIA, 202-204, 214-215, 227-228, 234-235, 256-257.

[12] Schübelin, *Zollparlament*, pp. 95 ff.; Windell, *Catholics and German Unity*, pp. 131 ff.

Of the 6 deputies elected in southern Hesse, only 3 were nationalists. Hence 49 of the 85 deputies chosen by the southern states entered the customs parliament pledged to block every attempt to extend its authority. Direct and equal suffrage, so successful for Bismarck's purposes in the north, had proved to be the route to disaster in the south.

2. THE ZOLLPARLAMENT

"To attain with one blow a homogeneous structure for Germany," Bismarck wrote to Karlsruhe on February 28, 1868, "is only possible in the event of war. Aside from this eventuality, which we shall neither predict nor precipitate, the development will have to run through one or more transitional stages." He still hoped, despite the sharp rebuff from southern voters, that the customs parliament would provide such a stage. Once the deputies came to grips with practical problems, he told the demoralized government in Baden, they would find "no room for doctrinaire obstinacy, scholastic habits of thought, or religious bias." Their horizons would widen as they dealt with the problems of German and world commerce. "The satisfaction of each common need will make perceptible yet another and render easier its satisfaction." He expected that the elections at the end of each three-year parliamentary term would produce constantly more favorable results for the national cause.[13]

On April 27, 1868 the customs parliament assembled in Berlin. In a brief speech, composed by Bismarck, William traced the growth of the Zollverein and credited its success not only to the economic needs of the German people, but to "the power of the national idea." "Hold the common German interest firmly in view," he admonished at the end, ". . . and win the thanks of the nation." The German alliances "can with God's help always count on the united strength of the German people."[14] The Zollverein and military alliances, in other words, were inseparable links in a common chain. By emphasizing the national character of both he sought to soothe the fear of "Prussianization" and overcome resistance to the expansion of the parliament's powers.

Despite an abundance of official hospitality, the southern deputies felt out of place in Berlin. Behind the "studiously polite amiability" of their reception, the Swabian democrats detected

13 *GW*, VIA, 284-286.   14 *GW*, x, 464-465.

"something sly and pedagogical." "In every corner" of the capital they saw the monuments and memorials of the military state they dreaded. They huddled together in common living quarters and longed for the day of departure. In the chamber, particularists of all political views combined in a "South German Party" to fight for the common cause. Among the 297 north German deputies they gained some support from Poles, Hanoverian "Guelphs," Prussian conservatives, and the socialists Bebel and Liebknecht. Romantic conservatism made common cause with Swabian radicalism, Bavarian Catholicism, and Saxon socialism.[15]

During the three years of its existence the achievements of the customs parliament were considerable within the competence granted by the treaties. New trade agreements were reached with Austria and Switzerland; many new lands in Latin America and the Pacific opened their doors to German businessmen. Tariff reductions made possible the entry of Lübeck and Mecklenburg into the customs union. A uniform tax on sugar and tobacco was established for the whole of Germany. After some difficulty a general tariff law was finally passed in 1870.[16]

The South German Party, nevertheless, zealously guarded the bridges of the Main against every attempt to extend the competence of the assembly. The first foray in 1868 was a motion, introduced by the nationalists of Baden and Hesse, for an address to the King of Prussia expressing the hope that the "power of the national idea" would soon lead to complete unification. Even Bismarck thought it unwise to allow south German nationalists to defeat their particularistic colleagues with the help of northern votes. The address was rejected. During the deliberations which followed, the South German Party sought by vigilant interruptions to halt every attempt of nationalist speakers to enlarge the scope of the debates to general political matters.[17]

On May 18, however, one of their own number made a mistake which Bismarck exploited with lightning speed. The issue was the wine tariff and whether the parliament had the authority to take up the grievances of Hessian producers. In denying it, a Swabian deputy pointed obliquely to the threat of French inter-

---

[15] Rapp, *Württemberger*, pp. 289 ff.; Windell, *Catholics and German Unity*, pp. 135 ff.

[16] Becker, *Bismarcks Ringen*, pp. 590 ff.; Schübelin, *Zollparlament*, pp. 125 ff.

[17] *Ibid.*, pp. 111 ff.; Windell, *Catholics and German Unity*, pp. 137 ff.

vention. "Somewhere on a mountain hangs an avalanche, which the least disturbance can plunge into the chasm." Never, replied Bismarck, would the north German government seek to force its institutions on the south against the will of the majority. As for the avalanche, the deputies should know that "an appeal to fear never finds an echo in German hearts!" An ovation thundered through the hall. Not for nothing had the Junker been practicing for a decade the vocabulary of national sentiment. In succession the nationalist speakers followed his lead. "Now it is springtime in Germany," cried Josef Völk, deputy for Augsburg. "If some are still throwing snowballs, the advance of spring will soon put an end to the snow."[18]

Three springs came and went, but the frost remained. After May 18, 1868 the customs parliament produced no major political debates. Except for occasional allusions to the greater issue of unity, the deliberations were restricted to tariffs and taxes. While seeking to squeeze every possible advantage for the national cause by the full exercise of the parliament's legislative powers, the nationalists were deeply discouraged over its limitations. Southern particularists, on the other hand, felt triumphant. "The Bismarck machine," they reported home, "stands still."[19]

It has been asserted, nevertheless, that the customs parliament was psychologically of great value in preparing the German people for unity. Even southern particularists, like Baron Thüngen, felt compelled to stress to the parliament the depth of their German patriotism. They had no other choice, moreover, than to base their case for preservation of the *status quo* upon the very treaties they had previously condemned. To oppose further unity they had publicly to argue the adequacy of what had already been achieved. Contrary to their expectations, moreover, Bismarck did not seek openly to exploit the parliament for the extension of Prussian hegemony, and held to his avowal that the southerners themselves must decide whether they wished to join the north.[20]

[18] *Stenographische Berichte über die Verhandlungen des Deutschen Zoll-Parlaments* (1868), pp. 264-282.

[19] Rapp, *Württemberger*, p. 327; Schübelin, *Zollparlament*, pp. 124 ff.

[20] Rapp, *Württemberger*, p. 332; Schieder, *Kleindeutsche Partei*, p. 191; Becker, *Bismarcks Ringen*, pp. 591 ff. It is difficult to see how Becker intended to prove his undocumented assertion that "many returned home with changed views even if they didn't dare openly to say so."

Contemporary observers of nationalist viewpoint differed concerning what was taking place in the hidden recesses of the popular mind. Before the parliament's first session, Gustav Freytag wrote that it was an "error" to assume that "time and some kind of peaceful, cultural effort will bring the southern states into the confederation. On the contrary, they are becoming more alien to us every year, despite the Zollverein."[21] After the first adjournment Wehrenpfennig commented in the *Preussische Jahrbücher* that the parliament had been "the preparatory school for the entry of the south into the north German state." With Roggenbach he felt that even the cooperation of northern and southern particularists against the parliament was a gain.[22] But Treitschke judged otherwise. "All of those loyal German words" and "ardent expressions of affection" spoken by southerners, he growled, "cannot change the fact that the majority of cabinets and peoples in the south wish to continue undisturbed in their *vierthalbstaatlich* confusion." From Munich the Prussian secretary of legation, Radowitz, reported on September 1, 1868 that anti-Prussian forces were daily gaining in zeal and strength throughout the south. Ultramontane circles were openly pro-French, exulted in her growing military strength, and anticipated her coming victory over Prussia.[23]

The vital question, however, is how Bismarck himself judged the Zollparlament, its achievements, and its potentiality. Certainly it is significant that during the session of 1869 he appeared in the chamber only once for a brief speech. To Rudolf Delbrück was left the task of representing the Prussian government. When the nationalists complained of the chancellor's seeming indifference, he referred them to his doctor. But the register of his activities during the three-week period shows that he was not at all incapacitated and spent a good part of the time on an inspection tour of western Germany. It is evident that he no longer had much interest in the parliament and its deliberations.[24] His mind

21 *HW*, I, 408.
22 *Preussische Jahrbücher*, XXI (1868), 700-701; Julius Heyderhoff, ed., *Im Ring der Gegner Bismarcks* (2nd ed., Leipzig, 1943), pp. 86-87; Rapp, *Württemberger*, p. 302; Becker, *Bismarcks Ringen*, pp. 591-592.
23 Heinrich von Treitschke, *Zehn Jahre Deutscher Kämpfe, Schriften zur Tagespolitik* (3rd ed., Berlin, 1897), I, 246-247; *APP*, X, 157-161.
24 *Verhandlungen des Zoll-Parlaments* (1869), pp. 220-222; Horst Kohl, ed., *Bismarck-Regesten* (Leipzig, 1891), I, 374-375. During the short session of May 1870 Bismarck was actually ill in Varzin. *Ibid.*, p. 392. Schübelin (*Zollparlament*,

was busy with other possibilities in the German question—with the promotion of a south German parliament and the negotiation of military conventions with the southern states.

3. FAILURE OF THE SOUTHERN UNION

Another of the possible "transitional stages" which Bismarck foresaw on the way to national unity under the northern constitution was that of a southern confederation. We have seen that the treaties of Nikolsburg and Prague provided for such an organization. At the time both Varnbüler and Pfordten believed in the practicality of a *trias* arrangement as a lasting solution of the German problem. The former expected that a south-German union, if equipped with free institutions, would have sufficient popular appeal to provide a lasting barrier to Prussian domination. But in November 1866 the two statesmen concluded that Prussian annexation of Frankfurt and Nassau, the inclusion of upper Hesse in the northern confederation, and the German policy of the Baden government made achievement of a southern union most unlikely. Bavaria and Württemberg alone could not make it viable.[25]

During 1867, however, the project was revived under stimulation from Vienna and Paris. Bismarck's success in negotiating the military treaties and reorganizing the Zollverein showed that something had to be done to shore up the sagging line of the Main. In a south-German confederation Beust and Napoleon expected to find the needed reinforcement. Returning from a conference with Franz Joseph at Salzburg in late August, the emperor expressed to Hohenlohe his regret that the southern states had not united. Two months later, after accompanying Franz Joseph to Paris, Beust conferred with Varnbüler and Hohenlohe in a determined effort to launch the project. French concern over Berlin's intentions toward the south, he declared, endangered the peace. Only the creation of a southern union in some form or other would quiet these fears and prevent a conflict. Hohenlohe found the argument convincing. He was still under the illusion, moreover, that the "stream of public opinion" would swamp any

pp. 130-131) believes that in 1868 he had already ceased to regard the customs parliament as important for his aims. Becker (*Bismarcks Ringen*, p. 592) argues unconvincingly the contrary view.

[25] *APP*, VIII, 173-174; Becker, *Bismarcks Ringen*, pp. 629-630.

government which failed to show some initiative in the German question, even if it were merely a southern union.[26]

On November 9 he communicated his intention to Bismarck through Tauffkirchen. With customary flexibility the wily Prussian saw immediately that a southern union might be a help rather than a hazard to his own policy. What Beust and Napoleon had set in motion might be converted to their own undoing. At Nikolsburg, the chancellor declared, he had accepted the provision for such a union with the thought that, "should a south German and a north German parliament one day exist, they would soon link hands and find a way to unite." A southern parliament, he told Julius Fröbel, was a means with which to "break" southern particularism. What mattered was not the transitory stage, but the end. "Everything human is only provisional."[27]

Hohenlohe passed over his suggestion. The draft of a constitution for the "united states of southern Germany," which he forwarded to Varnbüler on November 30, provided only for a "union authority" composed of foreign ministers authorized to "regulate common affairs." In this body Bavaria was accorded 6 votes, Württemberg 4, Baden 3, and Hesse 2. Having no permanent location, the authority was to rotate yearly among the southern capitals, returning to each with a frequency proportionate to the voting strength of the state. "By way of treaties" it was to seek conformity in the laws of northern and southern Germany. The "common army" was to have no common commander in peacetime; Prussia was to be granted an advisory voice in military matters. Except for common consulates, the states were to retain their own foreign services.[28]

Varnbüler rejected the plan for the very possibilities which Bismarck saw in it. The greatest barrier to the expansion of the northern confederation, he wrote to Hohenlohe on December 15, was the enduring vitality of existing states. But nothing would sap this vitality more rapidly than a south-German confederation of "organic" character. Such a development would cause the traditional loyalties to deteriorate and open the way for the growth

---

[26] Hohenlohe, *Denkwürdigkeiten*, I, 259, 277-281; *APP*, IX, 188-189, 361-363, 368-369.

[27] *APP*, IX, 372, 401-405; *GW*, VIA, 113, 125-126; Julius Fröbel, *Ein Lebenslauf* (1890-1891), II, 544-546.

[28] Hohenlohe, *Denkwürdigkeiten*, I, 282 ff.; Otto von Völderndorff, "Deutsche Verfassungen und Verfassungsentwürfe," *Annalen des deutschen Reichs*, Vol. 23 (1890), pp. 282 ff.

of a "great national life." Addition of a parliament would greatly accelerate this process and lead either to a republic or the demand for union with the north. The consultative voice of Prussia in the military committee would very likely become the decisive one.[29]

In Karlsruhe, on the other hand, the nationalist government failed to recognize these potentialities. After transmitting the plan to Bismarck, Mathy and Freydorf were surprised by his positive reaction. Baden should avoid, he advised, the odium of a rejection. She should accept "in principle" and insist upon amendments which would either transform the project into "a bridge" for German unity, or cause it to collapse.[30] When Hohenlohe revived the plan in February after the disaster of the Zollverein elections, Bismarck advised the incredulous Badenese to demand a southern parliament as the price of approval: "The most difficult part of the task of national reconstruction is the removal of the existing. If what exists is breached, even though it be through a south-German confederation, a healthy national life will grow by itself out of the ruins. But this breach can be achieved only by such a far-reaching reconstruction as a common parliament, not by a mere confederation of governments."[31]

While accepting the argument in general, Freydorf still balked at the prospect of a southern parliament. He feared that the multiplication of parliaments and elections would result in fatigue and loss of interest by the voters. Bismarck countered with the sly suggestion that elections to the southern chamber might be synchronized with those to the customs parliament! To Freydorf's further objection that in a south-German parliament the nationalists would find themselves confronted by an "ultramontane-democratic-particularistic majority," he replied that such a coalition could not possibly hold together indefinitely. It must soon founder of its own contradictions.[32]

By March 1868 Bismarck was aware that the attitudes which prevailed in Munich and Stuttgart made the realization of Hohen-

---

[29] *APP*, IX, 546-549, 584-587. The idea of a southern confederation received considerable support in the People's Party and its organ, *Der Beobachter*, in 1868, and Varnbüler was compelled to take a public stand against it. Rapp, *Württemberger*, pp. 304 ff. In May 32 members of the South German Party of the customs parliament signed a declaration favoring such a confederation. Schübelin, *Zollparlament*, pp. 120-121.

[30] *GW*, VIA, 155-156; *APP*, IX, 472.

[31] *GW*, VIA, 284-286.

[32] *APP*, IX, 786-788, 828-830; *GW*, VIA, 328-330, 338-339.

lohe's project most unlikely.[33] In this he was utterly correct. On the insistence of King Louis it was presented to the Bavarian cabinet on February 22. All of the prince's colleagues, except the minister of war, were against it. They shared Varnbüler's premonitions. On March 28 Hohenlohe reluctantly told Louis that for the time being nothing more could be done. In July he confessed to Werthern, the Prussian minister, that the plan was unachievable.[34]

Since they had provided the impulse, Hohenlohe's failure looks like another defeat for Beust and Napoleon.[35] In view of the possibilities Bismarck saw in the plan, however, the defeat has to be regarded as chiefly his. To be sure, he had never positively engaged Prussian foreign policy for its achievement and had instructed his envoys to handle the matter as one of "indifference" to Prussia.[36] Its collapse, nevertheless, removed from the scene one more of those "stages" through which he might have advanced toward German unification under the northern constitution. The alternatives of peace were diminishing.

4. THE PROGRESS OF MILITARY ASSIMILATION

During the years 1866-1870 the most tangible progress toward the integration of Germany under Prussian leadership came in the area of military affairs. By providing for the supreme command of the King of Prussia, the military alliances had made possible the assimilation by the southern states of the Prussian military system at a time of great popular and governmental resistance to Berlin's political control. Their own miserable record in the fighting of 1866 and the remarkable efficiency of the Prussian military machine had had a considerable impact upon southern officers and statesmen. Naturally German nationalists were now eager to accept the Prussian system, but many particularists were similarly inclined. If but to re-inforce their own independence, it behooved the southern states to copy the seeming virtues of Prussian militarism.

One of Hohenlohe's first acts upon assuming office in January 1867 was to propose a conference to coordinate military reform throughout the south. At the time Baden and Hesse were seeking

[33] *GW*, VIA, 330.
[34] Becker, *Bismarcks Ringen*, p. 642.
[35] Thus *ibid.*, p. 642.
[36] *GW*, VIB, 7, 35-36, 46-47.

military conventions with Prussia, the former for nationalistic reasons and the latter because of the divided condition of her forces. The Bavarian minister of war, Baron Pranckh, desired to emulate the Prussian system, although for particularistic reasons. But in Württemberg his counterpart, Oskar von Hardegg, wished to adopt the Swiss militia system. Hohenlohe's purpose was to arrive at a uniform policy based as nearly as possible on the Prussian model.[37]

Bismarck readily supported him. To be sure, he would have preferred military conventions with each of the southern states. By providing for common weapons, insignia, training, and the like, such conventions would have been a valuable supplement to the military alliances already achieved. One of the purposes of the concessions made to Saxony in the convention which integrated her forces into the north-German army was to entice the south into similar agreements. But it was now obvious that for the time being such treaties were impossible in Bavaria and Württemberg. Should the wishes of Baden be granted, these states would become concerned for their independence and might seek support abroad. Her size and divided status made Hesse an exception, and a convention was signed on April 11, 1867. In Hohenlohe's proposal, however, Bismarck saw the chance to achieve his end without the direct engagement of Prussian foreign policy. He urged Karlsruhe to participate in the conference and influence its outcome.[38]

Held in Stuttgart (February 3-5, 1867), the conference produced a protocol signed by Hohenlohe, Varnbüler, Freydorf, and Dalwigk. The southern states agreed to increase and reorganize their forces upon the principles of the Prussian system in order to make possible "the defense of the national integrity in common with the rest of Germany." Behind closed doors, however, the ministers disagreed sharply concerning the degree to which the Prussian system was to be adopted. No agreement was reached upon such important matters as length of service, military regulations and training, and types of armament and munitions.[39]

---

[37] Hohenlohe, *Denkwürdigkeiten*, I, 194-195; *APP*, VIII, 269-271, 279-281; Becker, *Bismarcks Ringen*, pp. 597 ff.

[38] *GW*, VI, 233-234, 239-243, 256-257.

[39] Max Leyh, *Die bayerische Heeresreform unter König Ludwig II., 1866-1870, Darstellungen aus der Bayerischen Kriegs- und Heeresgeschichte*, Vol. 23 (Munich, 1923), pp. 32-37. For the text of the agreement see J. C. Glaser, ed., *Archiv des Norddeutschen Bundes* (Berlin, 1867), III, 42-44.

In late April, as reports streamed into the Wilhelmstrasse of the menacing preparations of the French army, Bismarck complained to Munich, Stuttgart, and Karlsruhe that the south had made no improvements in its military preparedness since the preceding year. He urged the governments to summon their parliaments and demand cooperation in remedying the "evils" of their military establishments. In this way they could demonstrate the solidarity of the nation in the Luxemburg affair. But the replies were negative and even the Baden government was offended by the criticism. Nor did he have much better luck in exploiting the French threat to get military conventions. On May 2 he proposed to Hohenlohe that Berlin negotiate such agreements with individual states "on different levels" commencing with Baden. Hohenlohe approved the convention with Baden, provided it remained secret and was limited to the current crisis.[40] Although drafted, it remained unsigned, for the London conference assured the peace. In any case the episode showed that conventions with Württemberg and Bavaria were still unattainable. Both Kings Charles and Louis rejected the idea. It was his duty, the former declared, to demonstrate to Prussia that he was an independent sovereign and would remain so.[41]

The implementation of the Stuttgart agreement met considerable opposition in all three southern states. In Baden even the nationalists disliked the three-year service period, the cost involved in doubling the size of the army, and the importation of Prussian militarism. Ultimately the military reform bill was passed only through compromise and the promise of liberal reforms. Naturally in Bavaria, remote from the French frontier, the antagonism was even greater. Particularists, ultramontanes, and democrats assailed the reform as the first step in Bavaria's domination by Prussia. The Swiss militia system was extolled and standing armies decried as the scourge of freedom and culture. From the press, however, the public learned on March 17 that Pfordten had already committed the Bavarian army to Prussian command in wartime. After an initial failure, the bill finally passed at the end of January 1868. But the dissatisfaction was still intense. "We don't want to be Prussian," conscripts yelled

40 *GW*, vi, 366-369, 374.
41 *APP*, ix, 80, 104-105, 150.

at their officers. Firm measures were necessary to establish discipline.[42]

In Württemberg the difficulties were greatest. Minister of War Hardegg still regarded the Prussian system as "barbaric and un-German." Instead he advocated a citizen militia of twelve months' training distributed over a period of six years. But the officer corps had become increasingly pro-Prussian and nationalistic. When his views were attacked by a leading officer, Major Albert von Suckow, Hardegg resigned and was replaced by Colonel Wagner von Frommenhausen. As the latter's adjutant, Suckow pushed the military laws through parliament over severe opposition. His only major concession was reduction of the length of service from three to two years. In this parliamentary struggle the government had to abandon its liaison with the radicals of the People's Party and accept the support of the German Party, which it had helped to defeat in the Zollverein election.[43]

The pace of Prussianization in the south was speeded by an exchange of military personnel. In Karlsruhe two Prussian officers were appointed chief of the general staff and minister of war. Officer candidates of the Baden army were trained in Prussian academies. By treaty, citizens of Baden and Hesse were allowed to discharge their military service in Prussia, and vice versa. Southern armies took over the Prussian system of drilling, communication, command, and battle organization. Except for Bavaria, they adopted the same breech-loading "needle-gun" which had slaughtered their troops in 1866. Even in outward appearance—knapsack, uniform, and spiked helmet—their soldiers began to resemble the Prussian. Younger officers began to imitate the speech, gait, and mustache of their Prussian counterparts. For the troops there was more discipline, spit and polish, and physical duress. "Cadaver obedience" had its insidious appeal to the southern military mind, and began through conscription to influence civilian attitudes as well.[44] The school which Roon and

---

[42] Hermann Baumgarten, *Staatsminister Jolly* (Tübingen, 1897), pp. 88 ff., 169-170; Schieder, *Kleindeutsche Partei*, pp. 149 ff., 168 ff.; Leyh, *Bayerische Heeresreform*, pp. 37 ff., 52-63.

[43] Becker, *Bismarcks Ringen*, pp. 598-600; Wilhelm Busch, ed., *Rückschau von Albert von Suckow* (Tübingen, 1909), pp. 111 ff. ⠂

[44] Becker, *Bismarcks Ringen*, p. 600; Rapp, *Württemberger*, pp. 333-337; Georg Meyer, "Die Reichsgründung und das Grossherzogtum Baden," *Festgabe für Grossherzog Friedrich von Baden* (Heidelberg, 1896), pp. 176-177; Baumgarten, *Jolly*, pp. 83, 121 ff.

William designed for Prussia had opened its classrooms to the whole of Germany.

The problem of what to do with the equipment of the old confederate fortresses offered Bismarck still another opportunity to penetrate the military independence of the south. While the fortress of Mainz had been acquired by Prussia, three others (Ulm, Rastatt, and Landau) were located on southern soil. Soon after the conclusion of peace Bismarck directed that Prussia's share in them be upheld as a means with which to develop "new common relationships." Beginning in April 1868 Hohenlohe promoted the creation of an exclusively "south-German military committee" to administrate the three southern fortresses and coordinate the southern military effort. But Baden forced a compromise which required a prior settlement with Prussia.[45]

In January 1869 Bismarck explained to William how he intended to exploit this opportunity. Prussia's share in the common property gave her the chance to insist upon the principle of joint inspection and control over its use. Once established on even a periodic basis, a commission for this purpose would of necessity become a standing one. Beginning with a "civilian physiognomy," it could gradually be given a military one. Ultimately he expected the growth of a common organ for national defence under Prussian leadership.[46] From the seed would come the sprout, and from the sprout a flourishing plant. A typical example of Bismarckian statecraft!

Hohenlohe and Varnbüler, however, were reluctant to enter into the arrangement. They suspected his ulterior aim and were concerned over the possible reaction of France and Austria. Only after vigorous notes from Berlin did the two men agree to a conference, which convened in Munich, April 4, 1869. After much contention an agreement was finally reached (July 6) which conceded the essence of the Prussian program.[47] The seed had been planted, but the squabbling at Munich placed in doubt the fertility of the soil. From his estate in Varzin, whence he had retired with ailing body and frazzled nerves, Bismarck growled at those southern "phrase makers," who deluded themselves by thinking

---

[45] *APP*, viii, 104–106; ix, 872, 903; x, 111, 119–120, 179–181, 198–200; Hohenlohe, *Denkwürdigkeiten*, i, 320 ff.; *GW*, via, 413–414.

[46] *GW*, via, 531–533, also 495–496.

[47] *GW*, via, 527–530, 539–542; vib, 2–5, 8; Leyh, *Bayerische Heeresreform*, pp. 77–86.

they were more important to the north than the north to them. He would like now, à la Hannibal Fischer, to auction off everything.[48]

Meanwhile, French military preparations had actually enabled the Prussian general staff to commit the south to a common plan of mobilization. In late April 1867, as the Luxemburg affair reached its final and most dangerous stage, Bismarck negotiated an exchange of "military plenipotentiaries" with southern states. Early in 1868 the pace of French armament and the belligerent tone of its press aroused a fresh war scare. While reports from Paris indicated that no attack was in the offing, it behooved Moltke to confer with Suckow, now chief of the Württemberg general staff, and Freyberg, the Bavarian military plenipotentiary. In these talks (May 1868) he explained his plan for an "indirect defence" of southern Germany. Southern troops were to assemble in the Palatinate to form the left wing of a general assault upon the flank of any force seeking to invade across the upper Rhine. Soon the details, including the use of railways and communications, had been decided upon. For the first time German sovereigns committed themselves during peacetime to a common plan of deployment for the eventuality of war.[49] If ineffective on other levels, the Luxemburg affair at least produced a greater degree of national cohesion in military planning than had ever before existed in Germany.

5. A YEAR OF DISAPPOINTMENT

Mobilization plans are, of course, state secrets. As far as the public was concerned, the year immediately preceding the outbreak of war in July 1870 was one of decay and even retrogression in the cause of national unity. It was marked in Bavaria by electoral victories of the particularists and the fall of the Hohenlohe cabinet, and in Württemberg by a rousing campaign to end the Prussianization of the Swabian army.

During his three years in office Prince Hohenlohe had the uncomfortable task of balancing the mutual hostilities of a particularistic cabinet, the liberal-national majority in the chamber, and

48 *GW*, viii, 104, 118; Becker, *Bismarcks Ringen*, pp. 602-603. In 1852 Fischer, an Oldenburg official, was commissioned to auction off the German fleet assembled during the revolution.

49 *GW*, vi, 354, 374-375; viiA, 340-342, 362, 383; *APP*, x, 96-97. Becker, *Bismarcks Ringen*, p. 603.

a voting public which was rapidly turning conservative and particularistic. The issues concerned the internal reforms of the Hohenlohe regime, as well as its foreign policy. In February 1869 the cabinet, supported by liberal deputies, pushed through the lower chamber a bill which nearly eliminated clerical supervision of the schools. The Bavarian quarrel over clerical influence in education was part of a general conflict between church and state which developed throughout Europe in the 1860's. The steady progress of the autonomous state since the French revolution, culminating in Italian unification and the loss of papal sovereignty, had made Catholics everywhere extremely sensitive to any curtailment of the authority of the church. To Hohenlohe and his supporters, on the other hand, the school law was a defensive act intended to protect the "cultural state" from an aggressive ultramontanism.[50]

Under the impact of this dispute the Patriot Party began in the winter of 1868-1869 to take on form and organization. In the general election of May 1869 the contrasts were even starker than in the Zollverein election of the preceding year: German nationalism against Bavarian particularism, the autonomous state against the international hierarchy of the church, liberalism against Catholic romantic conservatism, the urban middle class against feudal agrarianism. When the votes were counted, the Patriot Party had won another significant victory. Although the progressives picked up some seats, the continuing deterioration of the center chiefly benefited the right.[51]

What they had not been able to achieve at the polls, the progressives now sought to attain through political manipulation. By challenging the count in a number of constituencies, they managed to cut back the patriot majority until the house was evenly divided, 71 to 71. This hopeless parliamentary situation required a fresh dissolution on October 6. In order to improve their chances, the liberals now demanded that the electoral districts be redrawn. The cabinet complied. Given a new issue, the Patriot Party entered the campaign with redoubled vigor and on

[50] Schieder, *Kleindeutsche Partei*, pp. 193 ff. On the general issue of church and state see Georg Franz, *Kulturkampf, Staat und katholische Kirche in Mitteleuropa von der Säkularisation bis zum Abschluss des preussischen Kulturkampfes* (Munich, 1954).

[51] Schieder, *Kleindeutsche Partei*, pp. 197 ff. Windell, *Catholics and German Unity*, pp. 176 ff.

November 25 captured 80 seats to take control of the chamber.[52]

When parliament met after January 17, the patriots opened their attack. While no one openly denounced the military alliance, its "offensive" feature met heavy criticism. But the most effective assault was upon Hohenlohe's sincerity. Quite accurately the deputies pointed out that, while constantly proclaiming his intention to preserve Bavarian sovereignty, the prince pursued a foreign policy which must end in its destruction. Bavaria had no desire, they averred, to participate in a "great-Prussian" union; never would she enter the "palace of the North German Confederation, whose walls are cemented with blood—fraternal blood." By 77 to 62 the deputies voted their lack of confidence in the government. Technically Hohenlohe was not responsible to the chamber and under no obligation to resign. From Berlin, Bismarck telegraphed to keep him from such a "dangerous political mistake." But on February 18 King Louis accepted his resignation.[53]

The consequence of this event, however, was the enhancement of royal authority in Munich, rather than the inauguration of parliamentary government. Since the opposition majority was weak, Louis was able to appoint a professional cabinet with no political connections. His choice for minister-president fell on Count von Bray-Steinberg, Bavarian minister at Vienna and a close friend of Beust. While not a doctrinaire particularist, Bray was a thorough Bavarian with no feeling for the German national cause. He wished to hold fast to the military alliance with Prussia, but recognized it only as a "defensive" instrument.[54]

During the first six months of 1870 agitation increased in the south against the alliance treaties and the "Prussianization" of the armed forces. In the Bavarian parliament an attempt was launched, with the support of the left wings of both the Patriot and Progressive Parties, to substitute for the Prussian system adopted in 1868 a militia of eight months' service on the Swiss pattern. In Württemberg popular discontent and parliamentary pressure for a reduction in military expenditures led to the resig-

---

[52] Schieder, *Kleindeutsche Partei*, pp. 213 ff.

[53] *Ibid.*, pp. 223 ff.; *GW*, vɪɪɪ, 243-245.

[54] Schieder, *Kleindeutsche Partei*, pp. 234 ff.; Becker, *Bismarcks Ringen*, p. 607. Bismarck recognized that the Bray cabinet was at least better for his purposes than an ultramontane one and assured the new minister-president of his "complete trust." *GW*, vɪɪɪ, 259.

nation of Wagner as minister of war in late March. During 1869 the People's Party had begun a general campaign to liberate the country from the "slavery of the barracks." Mass meetings protested the harshness of the new drill and discipline, which transformed free citizens into automatons. A monster petition was launched demanding repeal of the military service law of 1868. Ultimately the signatures reached 150,000, about three-quarters of the usual Württemberg electorate. By comparison the pilgrimage of 1,400 persons which the German Party organized to visit the Zollerburg, ancestral castle of the Hohenzollern, was a minor effort.[55]

The Zollverein elections of 1868, the Bavarian elections of 1869, and the Württemberg petition of 1870 constituted a popular referendum whose meaning was plain to the most ardent German nationalists.[56] After the first of these catastrophes Julius Weizsäcker concluded, "The German question will make little progress until the great conflagration." "We aren't allowed to pick unripe fruit," observed Wehrenpfennig, "but a violent storm could dislodge it into our laps." A year later Werthern, the Prussian minister in Munich, wrote, "From the short period in early 1867 when it was powerfully agitated and capable of exploitation German national feeling has steadily declined, and I see no end to this process without a new crisis. . . . No one believes any more that Germany can move forward upon the chosen path."[57] In 1870 Roggenbach, who had earlier been more optimistic, reached a similar opinion: "At the time of the Luxemburg strife there were still signs of a national movement capable of resisting attempts at outside intervention in the struggle for complete independence and free self-determination in German internal questions. At this hour the situation is no longer so favorable. Division and partisanship of every kind have erased the last traces of the movement for national unity and given the upper hand for

[55] Schieder, *Kleindeutsche Partei*, pp. 237 ff.; Eugen Schneider, "Württembergs Beitritt zum Deutschen Reich 1870," *Württembergische Vierteljahrshefte für Landesgeschichte*, xxix (1920), 123-124; Rapp, *Württemberger*, pp. 333 ff., 361. The replacement of Wagner by Suckow came about not because, but in spite of, the latter's nationalistic sentiments. There was no other suitable replacement; he was not given ministerial rank until the war began; and the government retained its particularistic course. Suckow, *Rückschau*, pp. 154 ff.; Freiherr von Mittnacht, *Rückblicke* (Stuttgart, 1909), pp. 2 ff.

[56] See Treitschke, *Zehn Jahre*, i, 266, and Andreas Dorpalen, *Heinrich von Treitschke* (New Haven, 1957), pp. 134 ff.

[57] *HW*, i, 419, 421; *APP*, x, 553.

a long time to come to centrifugal currents." A Prussian initiative in the national question, he concluded, would arouse little support in Germany, even if it involved her in a European war. Only in the event of an "unjustified attack" would Germany rally to her defense. Speaking to the downcast Rudolf Haym, Treitschke, the most impassioned nationalist of them all, placed his hopes upon "a sudden, unforeseeable upset . . . like that of 1866."[58] In their discouragement German patriots returned, as so often in the past, to the conviction that the German nation could be welded together only by the torch of a great popular war.

6. THE KAISER PROJECT

The victory of particularism in the two southern kingdoms had at least one favorable by-product for Bismarck. Their governments would now have to lean increasingly upon Berlin for support against the domestic opposition. Neither was willing to concede to the demands of the democrats that the Prussian military system be abandoned. In late March 1870 Bismarck even offered Stuttgart military assistance in the event of a revolutionary uprising.[59] Nevertheless, his satisfaction over this development could not have been very great. His plans for acquisition of the south depended on the conversion of peoples as well as governments. In 1870 popular resistance appeared to be hardening. While Bavaria had a large minority favoring union with the north and Württemberg a small, if growing national party, the great majority of voters in both countries were increasingly fanatical in their opposition to it.

The waxing vigor of south-German particularism was not the only problem which Bismarck faced. He also had to deal with the criticisms of nationalists in the Reichstag over the seeming stagnation of the government's policy on the national issue. In February 1870 Edward Lasker introduced a measure calling for the inclusion of Baden in the North German Confederation. Bismarck objected bitterly to this incursion into his special province of foreign policy. In a speech on the 24th he argued that such an act might easily strengthen the forces of particularism and stifle the emergent national movements in Bavaria and Württemberg.

[58] Becker, *Bismarcks Ringen*, pp. 591-592; *HW*, I, 450; Hans Rosenberg, ed., *Ausgewählter Briefwechsel Rudolf Hayms* (Stuttgart, 1930), p. 281.
[59] *APP*, x, 114-116, 125-126; *GW*, vIB, 317.

Rather than use coercion, it was preferable to wait "another generation." Pointing to what had been accomplished thus far—the customs parliament, military treaties, and Prussian command in wartime—he asked, "Have we not attained with regard to the south a valuable piece of national unity?" "Does not the presidency of the North German Confederation exercise in southern Germany a degree of imperial power such as German Kaisers have not possessed for 500 years?"[60]

This was no mere oratorical arabesque. For nearly two months Bismarck had secretly been working to make William "Kaiser of Germany" or at least "Kaiser of the North German Confederation." At a royal hunt in Potsdam on January 7, he had broached the matter to the crown prince. As the future bearer of the title, the prince might be useful in persuading the king. Bismarck pointed out that in 1870 elections were due both for the Reichstag and chamber of deputies. Majorities favorable to the government were vitally necessary, for after December 31, 1871 the Reichstag would gain the right under the constitution to review the iron budget. The proclamation of a German Kaiser would provide a winning slogan for those supporting the government and avoid recurrence of the constitutional conflict. The approaching transformation of the "Royal Prussian Ministry for Foreign Affairs" into the "Foreign Office of the North German Confederation" (January 10) provided a plausible excuse for the change. In diplomatic intercourse the neuter *Präsidium* was exceedingly awkward.[61]

To succeed, the scheme required not only William's approval, but that of the lesser states (north and south), the European great powers, and the Reichstag. William would most certainly object, but he could be managed. The national liberals to whom Bismarck broached the matter showed a disposition to bargain, but there was no reason to doubt that, when actually presented with the proposition, the Reichstag majority would accept.[62] If

---

[60] *SBR* (1870), I, 58-77. Lasker withdrew the motion, which was an amendment to a treaty with Baden on judicial reciprocity.

[61] *GW*, VIII, 212 ff. See also his note to Eulenburg, March 8, 1870, pp. 265-266. Gustav Roloff believes the purpose of the Kaiser project was to counteract a French attempt, through a disarmament proposal, to "encircle" and weaken Prussia, but the argument admittedly rests on a "timing coincidence." See his "Abrüstung und Kaiserplan vor dem Kriege von 1870," *Preussische Jahrbücher*, Vol. 214 (1928), pp. 189 ff.

[62] According to one source the national liberals demanded as *quid pro quo* the

Bismarck's calculation were correct, the idea would, in fact, generate considerable enthusiasm. In 1866-1867 the lesser states of the north had themselves proposed the Kaiser title as a protection against Prussianization.

In the south, Baden could be expected to give wholehearted support, particularly if the title chosen were "Kaiser of Germany." Their increasing dependence upon Berlin for support against subversion at home might be exploited to get the approval of Stuttgart and Munich. Without knowledge of Bismarck's intentions, leaders of the Bavarian Patriot Party had advocated reviving the imperial title. They were even willing to accept a Hohenzollern Kaiser, but insisted on the inclusion of Austria, location of the capitol in Frankfurt, and acceptance of the black-red-gold colors of the revolution. Werthern saw a glimmer of hope that southern particularists would find it much easier to subject themselves to a German Kaiser than to the feared and hated Prussia. "A lot lies in a name. . . ."[63]

Most important for Bismarck's purposes was the reaction in London and Paris. This came much quicker than expected. Through the indiscretion of a leading progressive, Franz Duncker, Loftus was able to report the plan to Clarendon on January 8. Three days later the new foreign secretary brought the subject up in a talk with Bernstorff. He claimed to be favorable and said that he would even seek to induce Paris to take a similar view. While pleased at Clarendon's response, Bismarck quickly denied that an expected struggle over the military budget had prompted the idea. The sole purpose of the Kaiser project, he insisted, was to overcome particularism, especially in Prussia. In passing up the title in 1867 he had "underestimated the importance which externals have in the opinion of my countrymen."[64]

But his words were wasted in London, for Clarendon had not carried out his promise to Bernstorff. Far from intervening in

---

inclusion of Baden and southern Hesse, while another has it that the demand was for the creation of "responsible confederate ministries." *GW*, vɪɪʙ, 280.

[63] *GW*, vɪɪʙ, 260, 279; Becker, *Bismarcks Ringen*, p. 616.

[64] *GW*, vɪɪʙ, 214-218. Veit Valentin has corrected the assumption of Walter Platzhoff that the news of the Kaiser plan reached London first through an indiscretion of Frederick William. Valentin, *Bismarcks Reichsgründung*, pp. 404-405; Walter Platzhoff, "England und der Kaiserplan vom Frühjahr 1870," *Historische Zeitschrift*, Vol. 127 (1923), pp. 454-475. A year earlier Clarendon had volunteered the suggestion that it would have been better had William taken the title "Kaiser or King of Germany" in 1867. *APP*, ɪx, 862.

Paris in behalf of the new title, he disparaged it in his talk with La Valette on January 26. On the following day he informed Bernstorff of his fears that such a coup would excite the French and produce a new crisis. Surely it was not worth risking the peace of Europe to attain that which must come in the natural course of events. For William's benefit Bismarck commented in the margin: "right." At the end he remarked that the matter had not gone very far and there was no need for haste.[65]

In March, nevertheless, the chancellor began to push the project again. On a visit to Berlin, Julius Fröbel, an influential Bavarian publicist subsidized by Prussia, was told by Keudell that the chancellor was "busy day and night with the Kaiser idea." The crown prince recorded in his diary, "Bismarck is working in union with Roon and Moltke on a regulation of the national question by taking up seriously the Kaiser question." About this time the chancellor discussed the matter with Grand Duke Frederick of Baden. From Konstantin Rössler, editor of the official *Preussischer Staatsanzeiger*, Fröbel learned of a proposal to offer Louis a sort of vice-emperorship with the title "German King." No official *démarche* appears to have been made in Munich, but British informants reported that the two southern kings, on being approached indirectly, reacted negatively and thereby put an end to the matter.[66]

The Kaiser project reveals that during the early months of 1870 Bismarck was on the hunt for a national issue capable of outflanking southern particularism and overcoming liberal opposition to renewal of the iron budget. Albrecht von Stosch, an intimate of the crown prince, detected a certain "restlessness" in his attitude. To avoid further compromise with the liberals he had to make progress in the national question. Southern rulers, Stosch believed, would never accept a Hohenzollern Kaiser, "unless they be coerced into it by an external impetus."[67] German affairs had reached an impasse from which, as so often in the past, the only possible egress appeared to be a crisis or war with France.

[65] *GW*, vııı, 217; *OD*, xxvı, 233-234.
[66] Fröbel, *Ein Lebenslauf* (Stuttgart, 1890-1891), ıı, 546-547; *APP*, x, 94-96; *GW*, vııı, 279-281; Oncken, *Grossherzog Friedrich I*, ıı, 137, 162; M. Doeberl, *Bayern und die Bismarckische Reichsgründung* (Munich, 1925), pp. 301-302; Schneider, "Württembergs Beitritt," pp. 126-127; Valentin, *Bismarcks Reichsgründung*, pp. 410-413. Political and diplomatic circles were full of rumors about the plan. See Erich Brandenburg, "Die Verhandlungen über die Gründung des deutschen Reiches 1870," *Historische Vierteljahrschrift*, xv (1912), 494 ff.
[67] Stosch, *Denkwürdigkeiten*, pp. 181-182.

CHAPTER EIGHTEEN

DIPLOMATIC PRELUDE

1. RENEWAL OF THE RUSSO-PRUSSIAN ENTENTE

HE years following the Luxemburg crisis were marked by mounting tension in Europe. It was generally believed that another war was in the offing. The German military machine was kept well oiled, ready for motion on short notice. Across the Rhine, French rearmament got underway in 1868. The failures of 1866-1867 had revealed a stark imbalance between military preparedness and the commitments of foreign policy. On the Danube the Hapsburg Monarchy strove to arm within the narrow limits of its financial capability. European chancelleries were full of plans, rumors, and anxieties. Where would the conflict break out—on the Rhine or in the Balkans? How would Europe divide?

The potential combinations were many. The Luxemburg affair had ended French speculation on the possibility of agreement with Berlin. But Russia's need for support in the Balkans caused Gorchakov to revive for a time his perennial hope of alliance with France. Both Vienna and Paris were aware of a common interest in preventing the further expansion of Prussian power and of undoing the settlement of Prague. Austria required French help in frustrating Russian penetration of the Balkans. Other possible members of their entente were Italy and Britain. What Bismarck feared most was the combination of French land power and British sea power. In each of these potential alliances the common partner was France. Had any one of them materialized, Bismarck's plans for the future would have been gravely jeopardized.

The source of greatest danger was Beust. "From oxen," the Junker once remarked, "one can expect nothing but beef; from Beust nothing but an ambitious, intriguing Saxon *Hauspolitik*."[1] The success of his old opponent in gaining the confidence of Franz Joseph alarmed and angered him. In February 1867 the Saxon was appointed Austrian minister-president, in June imperial

[1] *GW*, XIV, 332.

419

chancellor, in December 1868 he was dignified with the hereditary title of count. His primary objective was revenge for the defeat of 1866 and restoration of Austrian power in Germany. In preparation for such a move he pushed through the settlement with Hungary which created the "dual monarchy." At whatever cost, the Hapsburg house had to be set in order at home for the reassertion of its power abroad. By granting a constitution he hoped to outstrip Berlin in attracting the liberals of southern Germany.

In his German policy, however, ~Beust had a serious handicap. There was no adequate support in the dual monarchy for a policy of direct action. The Hungarians were not interested in the restoration of Hapsburg authority in Germany; its loss had been the means of their own advancement. In Austria there was a small war party composed of influential nobles, officers, and clergymen, but the dominant sentiment was against conspiring with France for war on Germany. Instead Vienna should wait, it was believed, upon a Franco-Prussian conflict and exploit her neutrality to dictate her desires in Germany. Unable to undertake a bold policy in Germany, Beust determined to involve Berlin in a European war over eastern issues.[2]

In 1866 a rebellion in Crete had reopened the "eastern question," the most persistent problem in nineteenth-century politics. The success of Prince Charles in Rumania and friction with Serbia had shaken the Turkish regime. Now the Cretan revolt, actively supported by Greece, threatened its collapse. Digging into the archives, the Russian government discovered that in 1829 the Porte had made commitments on the treatment of the Christian population which it had failed to keep. In London and Paris Gorchakov proposed (August 30, 1866) a joint remonstrance in Constantinople.[3]

From Vienna, however, came the depressing news that Petersburg had a new competitor in the game of protecting Balkan Christians. Abandoning the previous Hapsburg policy of supporting the Turks, Beust sought to outdistance Gorchakov by organizing the western powers in a common front in the Balkans. His aim was to embroil Europe in an eastern conflict in which

[2] Werner E. Mosse, *The European Powers and the German Question, 1848-1871* (Cambridge, 1958), pp. 253 ff.

[3] Otto Becker, *Bismarcks Ringen um Deutschlands Gestaltung* (Heidelberg, 1958), pp. 625 ff.

Berlin would feel compelled to support Russia, her only major ally. A war of eastern origin had none of the disadvantages of one over western issues. Hungarians would support it with enthusiasm. Germans, accustomed to Austrian leadership in Balkan affairs, would be sympathetic. Out of the eastern embroglio would come the chance for Austria's revenge against Prussia and the restoration of her power in Germany.[4]

The internal limitations on his German policy, nevertheless, compelled Beust to pass up the opportunity for a far-reaching compact with France. In the final days of the Luxemburg crisis Gramont, the French ambassador, arrived from Paris with a "lot of rather indiscreet, but characteristic questions." Would the Hofburg be interested in an "offensive and defensive alliance"? Napoleon wished to acquire the left bank of the Rhine, but would leave Belgium untouched. Austria might have Silesia and disposition over southern Germany, except for Baden, which would be reserved for France. But Beust had to reply that such a conspiracy would be ill received in the empire by Slavs, Hungarians, and Germans alike. Nothing would be more repugnant to the latter than a war whose avowed end was to bring part of Germany under alien rule. If the main object of the alliance were the eastern question, on the other hand, Beust confessed that he would "not recoil from any of its possible consequences, not even from an aggrandizement of France in Germany." But this could be only the by-product rather than the principal purpose of the conflict.[5]

During the summer Bismarck's success in reorganizing the Zollverein produced a fresh wave of alarm on the Seine. On August 18, 1867 Napoleon called upon Franz Joseph in Salzburg. Ostensibly his purpose was to condole the Kaiser over the execution of his brother, Archduke Maximilian, in Mexico. In the secrecy of the archiepiscopal palace, however, there was talk of the future as well as of the past. Gramont presented an ambitious

---

[4] *RKN*, III, 60-61, 68-70; *APP*, VIII, 208; Friedrich Ferdinand Graf von Beust, *Aus drei Viertel-Jahrhunderten* (Stuttgart, 1887), II, 337 ff.; Walter Vogel, *Die Tagebücher des Freiherrn Reinhard von Dalwigk zu Lichtenfels als Geschichtsquelle Historische Studien*, Vol. 234 (Berlin, 1933), pp. 61-62; Eduard von Werthheimer, "Zur Vorgeschichte des Krieges von 1870," *Deutsche Rundschau*, Vol. 185 (1920), pp. 1-26.

[5] *RKN*, II, 338, 362-365. Gramont's presentation may have been more blunt than Napoleon intended. At the outset he admitted that he was authorized only to "sound out the terrain," but added that he preferred to talk "frankly."

plan for an ultimatum to Berlin, demanding dissolution of the ties with southern Germany. But Napoleon himself discarded it and instead accepted a draft submitted by Beust. In Germany the two powers were to impress upon the southern states the necessity of a "reserved and independent attitude" toward the north. But they would avoid any action which could be exploited by Prussia as "a menace or provocation" and which might excite a German national reaction. In the east the French agree to a joint *démarche* in Petersburg on the Cretan problem, which the British were to be invited to join. Although London refused, Paris and Vienna entered in the fall of 1867 on a period of cooperation in Turkish affairs.[6]

Beust's success was Gorchakov's failure. Following the rejection of his proposal for a joint remonstrance with Britain and France in the Cretan question, the Russian vice-chancellor had gyrated from one European capital to another in search of support for his Turkish policy. His greatest hopes were placed on Paris. But Napoleon and Moustier refused to be explicit concerning their eastern plans and requested Russian support for their objectives (undefined) in the west. Although his reaction to the French attempt to grab Luxemburg was unfavorable, Gorchakov assisted in bringing about the London conference and hoped for French gratitude. To his annoyance, Napoleon avoided all serious political discussion during the czar's visit to Paris in early July 1867. Moustier was cold, moreover, to Gorchakov's plan for uniting Crete with Greece. Nor did the unfriendliness of the public and the two shots fired at Alexander by a Pole help matters. Already it was evident that Gorchakov's hopes were vain. In the fall the first signs of Austro-French collaboration in Turkey confirmed their futility.[7]

Depressed in one direction, the rubber ball of international politics inflates in another. After rebuffs in Paris, Vienna, and London, the Russians had no other choice than to turn to Berlin. They expected war in the spring, both in western Europe and the Balkans, and dared not be without an ally.[8] Between a con-

[6] *RKN*, ii, 454-458; *APP*, ix, 136 ff., 342-344; Joseph Redlich, "L'entrevue de l'empereur François-Joseph et de l'empereur Napoléon à Salzbourg le 18 août 1867," *Le Monde Slave*, Nouvelle Serie, iii (1926), 143-151; Mosse, *European Powers*, pp. 280 ff.

[7] *Ibid.*, pp. 254 ff.

[8] *Ibid.*, p. 280; Walter Platzhoff, "Die Anfänge des Dreikaiserbundes, 1867-

cert and hunt on February 4, 1868, Czar Alexander had a long and intimate talk with Prince Reuss, the Prussian ambassador. Expressing fears that Austria might exploit the Balkan crisis to occupy Bosnia and Herzegovina, the monarch declared: "Let us hope that this will not occur. Let us hope also that France will not attack Germany. But should, contrary to expectations, both events occur, the king can count on me to paralyze Austria, just as I would rely on his aid. In both cases the deployment of an army on the Austrian border would suffice to achieve this end." In March Alexander became more explicit. Should Prussia become involved in war with France, Russia would mobilize 100,000 men on the Austrian border, while Prussia would do the same in the event of an Austro-Russian conflict.[9]

Bismarck, however, was cautious. Verbally he assured Oubril, the Russian ambassador, on March 20: "We believe ourselves equal to a war against France and have no need to expand it into a general conflict, if Russia covers our rear against Austria. We assume the same of Russia, if she became involved in war with Austria and we granted her security against French support of the latter. But the minute one of us—whether it be Russia or Prussia—is attacked by a coalition of two powers, common interests necessitate that each support the other." By slight shifts in terrain he had established several crucial points. Common interests rather than a written agreement were to be the foundation of the alliance. Unless the European balance were threatened by French participation, Prussia was not committed to go to war to rescue Russia's Balkan interests against Austria. In event of an Austro-Russian conflict, north German troops would be deployed chiefly on the French, rather than the Austrian frontier.[10]

The czar was satisfied and Bismarck doubly so. In a Franco-German war the Russians would help to neutralize Austria, while without French support Austria was unlikely to move in the Balkans. The vital question was whether Beust would actually succeed in embroiling all four powers in a war over eastern issues.

1871," *Preussische Jahrbücher*, Vol. 188 (1922), pp. 287 ff.; Gerhard Heinze, *Bismarck und Russland bis zur Reichsgründung* (Würzburg, 1939), pp. 74 ff.

9 *APP*, ix, 671, 706-707, 759-760, 844.

10 *GW*, via, 321. Fearing Gorchakov's jealousy over direct negotiations with the czar, Bismarck had earlier avoided all but the most general response to Alexander's proposals. *GW*, via, 262, 306-307. On the character of the agreement see Walter Ebel, *Bismarck und Russland vom Prager Frieden bis zum Ausbruch des Krieges von 1870* (Gelnhausen, 1936), pp. 48-57.

During 1868 there were rumors of such a plan in the newspaper press, and Bismarck was well aware of the danger. As winter approached, Beust thought his moment had arrived. In Rumania irredentist agitation, led by Minister Bratianu, mounted against Hungary, and the smoldering feud between Greece and Turkey over Crete flared up once more. But Bismarck saw to it that Prince Charles dismissed the troublesome Bratianu and promoted an international conference in Paris which ordered Athens to cease her aid to the Cretan insurgents. Had his efforts failed, the Junker was ready with an alternative plan. Rather than go to war over a Balkan issue, he told the Russians in February 1869, he was prepared to provoke war with France over the German question. Nothing would be easier than to make France "assume the role of an aggressor."[11]

2. FAILURE OF THE AUSTRO-FRENCH ALLIANCE

Napoleon, complained Metternich in mid-November 1867, was not frank. He would say neither what he thought, what he had done, nor what he intended to do. Even his own ministers were uninformed. The Austrian ambassador was inclined to see in his silence the sinister aim to come to terms with Berlin.[12] What the mask of silence concealed, however, was simply indecision. Naturally indolent, his mental processes slowed by ill health, Caesar was uncertain what to do. Previously he had played at the game of international politics—in the Crimea, Italy, and Mexico—without great hazard to himself. But now suddenly he was compelled to gamble for the highest stakes: crown, empire, and the judgment of history. He had to win.

Bismarck believed the emperor personally had no thought of going to war with Germany. "But conditions in France are incalculable."[13] No longer did the Junker think that the conduct of states was governed by self-interest alone: "In the case of alliances, traditions and personalities carry almost more weight than

11 *GW*, VIA, 322, 504-505; *APP*, X, 402, 523; Chester W. Clark, "Bismarck Russia, and the origins of the war of 1870," *Journal of Modern History*, XIV (1942), 198. See also Horst Michael, *Bismarck, England und Europa (vorwiegend von 1866-1870), Forschungen zur Mittelalterlichen und neueren Geschichte*, Vol. 5 (Munich, 1930), pp. 127 ff.

12 *RKN*, II, 477.

13 *GW*, VIA, 253. See also *GW*, VI, 369; VIB, 113, 166.

interests, emotions more than calculation. . . . The conduct of Russia and England in the Crimean war, that of France with regard to Poland, Italy, Mexico, and that of Austria in the Danish affair and in early 1866 hardly corresponded to the interests of these countries. Personalities and opinions took precedence over interests." Napoleon was not in command of the situation in France, but dependent upon "the streams of partisan passion."[14]

Indeed the currents of dissatisfaction in France were deep and swift. Repeated blunders in foreign policy had provided plenty of ammunition for the anti-dynastic opposition of Orleanists, legitimists, and republicans. But even those linked to the dynasty by careers and interests were demanding that something be done to halt the decline of imperial prestige. Evidently this was especially true of the officer corps, whose confidence increased as France rearmed her infantry with the new breech-loading *chassepots*. The approach of parliamentary elections added to the general nervousness.[15]

From Rouher, his most trusted adviser, Napoleon received the warning in late September 1867 that important circles of opinion, alarmed over the seeming "stagnation" of French policy, wanted an unequivocal decision on the German question. Would the government oppose or consent to the incorporation of the south into the North German Confederation? To declare the crossing of the Main a *casus belli* would lead precipitously to war with Germany. Was France prepared? On the other hand, a declaration of consent might momentarily appease some interests, but would anger the army, "of which we have need." It would also excite more of those "perfidious, cruel, and incessant attacks" from journalists who charged that "France has fallen to the third rank."[16]

During the following months the increasingly proprietary attitude of Berlin toward the south made it apparent that a policy had to be found. After Salzburg, Bismarck publicly warned that "German national feeling" would not bear the "tutelage of foreign intervention."[17] When Paris proposed a European conference to deal with the status of Rome, he objected not only to the invitation issued to Saxony (indeed an impertinence!), but to those sent to the sovereign states of southern Germany. In European questions, he made it known, Berlin alone could speak for

14 *GW*, via, 263.
16 *RKN*, ii, 468-469.
15 *RKN*, i, 64-66; ii, 511-512.
17 *RKN*, ii, 459-461.

Germany.[18] Although the results of the Zollverein election were reassuring, it was still possible that Bismarck might succeed in converting the customs parliament into an instrument of unification. After visiting Berlin in mid-March 1868, Prince Napoleon reported that the absorption of the south was only a matter of time. Benedetti was of the same opinion.[19]

Under these pressures Napoleon turned again to Vienna. On April 7, 1868 he asked Metternich to find out from Beust: (1) what would be done, should the peoples of southern Germany "throw themselves into the arms of Prussia"; (2) what would be done, if Prussia resorted to violence and committed "spontaneously" a serious infraction of the treaty of Prague; (3) what line of conduct was to be followed, if the Rumanian principalities revolted against Turkey and proclaimed their independence contrary to "our advice"; (4) whether another attempt should be made to bring Britain into an entente, despite the poor prospect of success. In the first eventuality (considered unlikely "if prudence is exercised") direct intervention would be difficult. As for the German problem in general, it was up to Austria to take the initiative in any "preventive diplomatic action or eventual protest." France would support her "in the second line" in order not to offend German national sentiment and precipitate a "cataclysm."[20]

Beust, however, was not to be enticed from his original position. Taking advantage of Napoleon's cautious words, he agreed that the first eventuality was unlikely and lauded the effect of his own "prudence" in building up southern resistance. He doubted, furthermore, that Bismarck would place Prussia in the wrong by an "act of despair." While praising Napoleon's desire to avoid a cataclysm, he left undecided whether France *or* Austria should "take the second line." The eastern question, he believed, was more important and ought to be "the ostensible basis of our entente." Confident of French support, Vienna awaited events on the lower Danube. As for Britain, Vienna was ready to support Paris in any *démarche*, but doubted that the London cabinet would bind itself in advance.[21]

18 *GW*, vɪa, 118, 130-131, 136-137, 140-141, 144-146, 177, 192-193.

19 *RKN*, ɪɪ, 542-543, 545, 547-548; *APP*, ɪx, 625, 834.

20 *RKN*, ɪɪ, 553-554. Gramont gave Bray, the Bavarian minister, a different account.

21 See his dispatch to Metternich, April 14, 1868. *RKN*, ɪɪ, 554-556. In a pre-

During the following months rumors spread through the diplomatic corps that the "war party" had gained the upper hand in the Tuileries. On July 20 Metternich telegraphed that the emperor wanted to know about the possibility of an "active alliance" for a "common and determined end." If impossible, would Vienna accept a "passive alliance" to summon a European congress to consecrate the *status quo* in Europe? As for the former, France would not demand "a priori" any territorial aggrandizement, but seek only the re-establishment of Austria's position in Germany. But again Beust pointed out that such an alliance with a foreign power would cost Vienna the sympathy of those Germans without whose support the restoration of Austria was impossible. Nothing would be more likely to make Prussia popular in Germany.[22]

Napoleon's second idea, however, suggested to Beust a magnificent opportunity. Neither England nor Russia could support a guarantee of the *status quo*, he argued, and in rejecting it Bismarck would win the applause of all Germany. But why not, he shrewdly submitted, achieve the same end by another route? By calling for general disarmament the emperor would electrify public opinion throughout Europe. North Germans would welcome the prospect of tax relief and south Germans the prospect of escape from the rigors of the Prussian drill. In France it would influence the voters in the approaching parliamentary elections. By approving, Prussia would accept in effect the *status quo* in Germany and destroy her alliance with German nationalism. By refusing she would invite the disfavor and suspicion of public opinion. In event of war, Berlin would bear the moral responsibility.[23]

At first Napoleon was enamored with Beust's suggestion. But the longer he considered it, the more he began to fear being

---

liminary statement to Gramont, however, he regarded the second possibility as "the real menace of the future." He would protest Prussian abandonment of the treaty of Prague, but it was less certain that he would act to prevent it. If France did so, Austria would be a benevolent neutral in the beginning, but thereafter do her duty as a "good ally." Warming to the subject, he declared that Prussian "intrigues and perfidious maneuvers" would ultimately compel him to "take some initiative in Berlin." An open war was better than a hidden one. *OD*, xxi, 165-168. See the more colorful version of the interview which Gramont related to Bray. *RKN*, ii, 556-559.

[22] *RKN*, iii, 12-16. For this and subsequent negotiations see Anton Lamberti, *Die Bündnisverhandlungen Napoleons III. gegen Preussen in den Jahren vor 1870* (Würzburg, 1939), pp. 26 ff.

[23] *RKN*, iii, 14-15, 19-22, 28-31, 33.

"duped." Their reserve system would enable Prussia to reassemble an army in three months, while France would require a full year. Hence the agreement would have to provide for the dissolution of the Prussian reserve organization. What would be done, furthermore, when Prussia refused as she certainly would? Beust, however, did not have to answer this embarrassing question which raised precisely the issue he wished to avoid. In mid-October Lord Clarendon, on the eve of his appointment to the British cabinet, told Napoleon that a disarmament manifesto "would only serve to render war more inevitable." After visiting the military camp at Châlons, moreover, Napoleon concluded that the word "disarmament" was hardly suitable for the ears of the army.[24]

The failure of Napoleon's proposal and Beust's counterproposal did not cool the ardor of either for an alliance. On the contrary, their mutual need to block Prussian expansion, their mutual ambition to assert themselves in Germany, and their mutual fear that the other might come to terms with Berlin now impelled both into serious negotiations.[25] On November 6 Beust launched the effort by instructing Metternich to state frankly what had often been "insinuated"; namely, that the eastern question provided a far more suitable *casus belli* against Prussia than the German. Although Napoleon in reply accepted the "eastern base as the point of departure of our entente," the problem of the relative importance of the two "terrains" remained the most difficult of the entire negotiation. Napoleon had no interest in getting into another Crimean war, while the Ballplatz was compelled to avoid involvement in a Franco-German war over the issues of German unity and French expansion.[26]

By January a compromise suggested itself. Should Austria go to war against Russia, France would deploy an observation force on the Prussian frontier, but remain neutral unless Prussia entered the conflict. Should France go to war against Prussia, on

---

[24] *RKN*, III, 19-24, 33-37, 53, 71-72.

[25] The failure of his attempt at economic penetration of Belgium in the winter of 1868-1869 reinforced Napoleon's desire to come to terms with Austria. See Kurt Rheindorf, "Der belgisch-französische Eisenbahnkonflikt und die grossen Mächte 1868/1869," *Deutsche Rundschau*, cxcv (1923), 113-136.

[26] *RKN*, III, 59-62, 71-74, 79. The chief source for the negotiation is the correspondence between Beust in Vienna and Metternich and Count Vitzthum in Paris. For Napoleon, Rouher and La Valette were the negotiators. Neither Moustier nor Gramont were brought into the secret.

the other hand, Austria would perform a similar service against Russia.[27] But still both powers were uneasy about the prospect of facing a major foe without active support from the other.[28] Finally Beust admitted his conviction that "force of circumstances" would "soon" make Austrian neutrality in a Franco-Prussian war impossible, while Napoleon expressed the view that France too would find itself "unable" to remain neutral in an Austro-Russian conflict.[29] Despite the avowals of peaceful intent with which they sprinkled the record, both parties foresaw that the likely consequence of the commitments they were making would be a general European war.

The reconstruction of Germany, naturally, was to be a fundamental purpose of the alliance. It was agreed that the victorious powers would establish a new German confederation based on states as nearly equal in size as possible. Concerning territorial gains and compensations, the evidence left in the files by the negotiators was intentionally scanty. "Littera scripta manet!" The Hungarians, wrote Metternich, were to find nothing in the treaty about the restoration of Austrian power in Germany and the Austrian Germans no mention of the Rhine.[30] In none of the preliminary drafts were the full intentions of the participants revealed.

Even so the final draft of May 10, 1869, was less menacing in appearance than the preliminary ones. Agreeing to follow a common policy in European affairs, the contracting powers reciprocally guaranteed the integrity of their respective territories "against every eventuality." Should "symptoms of war" appear, they would conclude an "offensive and defensive alliance." In event of war between Austria and Prussia, France would come to the aid of the former.[31] Of "neutrality" and "observation forces" there was no longer any mention. Franz Joseph had decided these clauses were too provocative; they were unlikely, furthermore, to be accepted by Italy.

The Austrians had finally learned the necessity of buying off

27 *RKN*, III, 111-113.

28 See Beust's warning to Metternich that a common diplomatic front in the eastern question was absolutely essential to the agreement and La Valette's objection that Austrian neutrality in a Franco-Prussian war was unreciprocal in view of France's commitment to aid in an Austro-Prussian conflict. *RKN*, III, 76-79, 160.

29 *RKN*, III, 158-159, 168-169.   30 *RKN*, III, 111-113, 119.

31 *RKN*, III, 185-188.

the government in Florence before undertaking a major war. In negotiations conducted by Paris, King Victor Emmanuel was asked to contribute an army of 200,000 men for the common defense, to aid France in a war with Prussia, and to assume the same obligations as France in any war involving Austria. After victory Italy was promised a "rectification" of the frontiers of Nice and the Tyrol, possession of the Swiss canton of Tessin (if Switzerland "violated" her neutrality), a naval base in Tunisia, repayment of war costs, and diplomatic support in certain Papal affairs. On May 15 Metternich telegraphed: "Definitive version reached with Italy. Mr. de Vimercati leaving for Florence. Acceptance almost certain."[32]

Metternich's ecstatic optimism proved unjustified. In Florence the price had risen. The Menabrea cabinet determined to exact, in addition to the concessions already promised, the frontier of the Isonzo from Austria and the evacuation of French forces from Rome.[33] In France, moreover, the treaty was delayed by other startling developments. On May 23 the parliamentary election went badly for the government. During June, five days of street rioting in Paris raised doubts about the stability of the regime. At the end of the month Rouher and La Valette were compelled to resign under the attack of the strengthened opposition in the new chamber. Napoleon was faced with the choice of returning to dictatorial methods or advancing on the road to parliamentary government. "The situation is grave," wrote the dejected Metternich. "It is a decisive crisis."[34]

The emperor chose the latter course. The period of transition, however, lasted six months. In the interim cabinet only the foreign minister, Prince de la Tour d'Auvergne, was told of the alliance project, and he refused to take further action because of his temporary status.[35] On August 20 Napoleon went to bed suffering from his old malady, a bladder ailment, and was incapacitated for a month. During this time all policy-making ceased in a regime still subject to his will. In September rumors of a triple

32 RKN, iii, 171-176, 185-188.

33 RKN, iii, 194-198, 208, 215-216, 228-229. See also F. Engel-Janosi, "The Roman question in the diplomatic negotiations of 1869-70," Review of Politics, iii (1941), 319-349.

34 RKN, iii, 216-218. Official candidates polled 4,467,720 votes against 3,258,777 for the opposition.

35 RKN, iii, 245-246, 253-254, 270-271.

alliance, launched apparently by the Italian government, excited the European press and alarmed the chancelleries. Lord Clarendon hurried off to Paris to learn the truth. Napoleon, pale and feeble, denied everything but *pourparlers* ending without result.[36]

Actually the emperor believed that something had been accomplished. Although the draft of May 10 remained unsigned, all three sovereigns considered themselves "morally" bound by it. From Victor Emmanuel the emperor received a letter in September in which the king adhered "to the idea of a triple alliance" and hoped for its "prompt" conclusion, but insisted that first the French must evacuate Rome. Hence Napoleon had reason to believe that the Italian alliance was attainable whenever the recall of French troops from Rome could be made palatable to French Catholic opinion.[37] On September 24 he wrote to his "good brother" Franz Joseph stating that, if Austria were menaced by any aggressor, "I shall not hesitate an instant to place all the forces of France at her side." Without prior agreement with Vienna, furthermore, he would not negotiate with any foreign power.[38]

Franz Joseph's reply has vanished. Apparently it contained a similar commitment to inform Paris prior to negotiations with a third power, but failed to give a reciprocal promise of military aid in event of war.[39] As the fatal year 1870 arrived, nevertheless, Napoleon persisted in the delusion that the Austrian alliance had been "morally" ratified.[40] Beust, however, had not budged from his insistence upon the necessity of neutrality at the beginning of a Franco-Prussian conflict. His strategy was the same as that of Napoleon in 1866 and was to prove just as futile. By intervening at the critical moment he expected to achieve maximum gain at minimum cost.[41]

Bismarck banked on identity of interests, rather than a con-

---

36 *RKN*, III, 226-227, 233-234, 251.

37 Émile Ollivier, *l'Empire libéral* (Paris, 1895-1912), XI, 611-612. See also the forthcoming article by S. William Halperin, "Napoleon III and Italy, the Crisis of July 1870."

38 *RKN*, III, 192-193, 224, 235-236.

39 *RKN*, III, 232, 253, 261.

40 *RKN*, III, 251, 268.

41 See his remarks to Dalwigk. *RKN*, III, 225 (n. 2). He regarded Napoleon's letter with satisfaction and informed Vitzthum (October 19, 1869) that it sufficed "for the moment to fix the state of our relations with France." Further negotiations, he feared, would enable the French to press the argument for making violation of the treaty of Prague a *casus belli*. *RKN*, III, 261.

tractual agreement, to secure the entente with Russia, but Napoleon chose to believe in the existence of an alliance with Austria secured neither by a signed treaty nor by actual solidarity of interests. Such were the circumstances as the most realistic political strategist of the century entered upon his final match with its most successful romantic adventurer.

CHAPTER NINETEEN

ORIGINS OF THE WAR OF 1870

1. THE PROBLEM OF "WAR GUILT"

N July 3, 1870 the news began to spread through the European press that the crown of Spain had been offered to a Hohenzollern prince. Two weeks later France and Germany plunged into the first truly "national war" which Europe had seen since 1815. No more than the participants have historians been able to agree on the responsibility for this conflict which poisoned the political atmosphere of Europe for generations. German scholars feel a compulsion to prove that the war of 1870 was the result of French imperialism and French unwillingness to grant to Germany the right of national self-determination. But beyond the Rhine the opposite view is equally obstinate. The war of 1870, we are told, was the result of a trap deliberately set and sprung by Bismarck in an effort to humiliate France.

Bismarck's defenders can point to an impressive array of utterances during 1869-1870 in which he, while admitting the probability of war with France, forswore its provocation. One of the most eloquent is the famous dispatch to Werthern of February 26, 1869.[1] As the Prussian minister in Munich, Werthern was deeply discouraged over the course of south-German development and critical of his superiors for not having marched on Vienna in 1866. In rebuttal Bismarck explained one of his fundamental convictions on the subject of politics:

"That German unity would be furthered by violent events I also hold probable. But it is quite another question to assume the mission of bringing about a violent catastrophe and the responsibility for the choice of timing. Arbitrary interference in the course of history, motivated on purely subjective grounds, has never had any other result than the shaking down of unripe fruit.

---

[1] *GW*, VIB, 1-2; VII, 235; Johannes Schultze, ed., *Max Duncker: Politischer Briefwechsel aus seinem Nachlass* (Stuttgart, 1923), pp. 436-437. See also Hajo Holborn, "Bismarck und Freiherr Georg von Werthern," *Archiv für Politik und Geschichte*, v (1925), 469 ff.

That German unity is not at the moment a ripe fruit is in my opinion obvious. . . . We can put the clocks forward, but time does not on that account move any faster, and the ability to wait, while the situation develops, is a prerequisite of practical politics."

In December he admitted to Keudell that the pressure for war was evident in German as well as French business circles. They wanted the "situation clarified."[2] "This attitude, however, is abominable. One must continue to remove the possible causes of war and trust to the quieting effect of time. No one can assume the responsibility for the outbreak of a struggle which would perhaps be but the first of a series of national wars (*Rassenkriegen*)." Even Benedetti was convinced, according to his report of January 14, of the "pacific views" of king and chancellor and their determination not to provoke "any regrettable incident."[3]

Another argument for Bismarck's innocence is the absence of any impelling motive. There is no reason to believe, we are told, that Bismarck had abandoned "the path of peaceful organic development."[4] To Werthern he wrote that in view of the progress made toward unity since 1740, and especially since 1840, "we can look forward to the future with repose and leave to our successors what remains to be done."[5] In a memorial to the king on November 20 he described German unity as the "further and greater" goal of Prussian policy. "We can with certainty expect its achievement in the course of time through the natural development of the nation, which makes progress every year." In the margin William wrote: "Agreed."

His "nearer goal," however, was to prevent Bavaria from becoming "a base for Austrian-French-ultramontane efforts against us." He feared the prospect of "calamity" in Munich: namely, the replacement of Hohenlohe by a "Catholic-Austrian minister" and a reverse for the national cause in the Bavarian parliament.[6] How did he react when the calamity actually occurred? Was this the turning point in his attitude on war with France?

If so, his utterances in late February 1870 do not show it. On the 23rd, he confidently remarked to Benedetti that the forward

2 *GW*, VII, 302.

3 Le Comte Benedetti, *Ma Mission en Prusse* (Paris, 1871), pp. 284-285; *GW*, VIB, 203 (n. 3).

4 Becker, *Bismarcks Ringen*, pp. 669, 682.

5 *GW*, VIB, 2.

6 *GW*, VIB, 166-167; also p. 180.

current of German development was inexorable.[7] In the Reichstag on the following day he maintained that the national cause was making "steady, moderate progress" in Bavaria and Württemberg, "despite everything we hear from there."[8] A few hours later he told Moritz Busch: "The question of German unity is making good progress, but it requires time—one year perhaps, or five, or indeed possibly even ten years. I cannot make it go any faster, nor can these gentlemen either. But they have no patience to wait."[9] In a dispatch to Karlsruhe on March 12, his air was a little less confident: "I can leave it undecided whether the policy of deference and consideration has furthered the national cause in Bavaria and Württemberg." At a recent conference of national liberal deputies, he pointed out, the Württemberg delegates had stressed that the national cause in their country "is not going backward."[10]

The Kaiser project shows, nevertheless, that Bismarck felt compelled to move *forward* in the national question during the year 1870. In view of the coming elections the Hohenzollern monarchy required a fresh baptism of national sentiment with which to ward off the liberal attack upon the iron budget. The policy of deference, moreover, was under heavy attack. The seeming stagnation of Prussian policy was discouraging to the Badenese as well as to the impatient deputies of the Reichstag. In the fall of 1869 William came home highly disturbed from a visit with his son-in-law in Karlsruhe. Continued frustration of their desire for union with the north, he feared, would alienate Prussia's "friends" in the south. Bismarck also expressed concern over the "fatigue" of the national movement. Clarendon was probably wrong, however, in assuming he intended to use the Kaiser project to precipitate war with France.[11] During the early months of 1870 he apparently believed that the completion of German unification depended less upon his own plans than upon the opportunities, and even necessities, which might emerge from the political situation in France.

[7] Benedetti, *Ma mission en Prusse*, p. 289.   [8] *GW*, XI, 101.

[9] Moritz Busch, *Bismarck: Some Secret Pages of His History* (New York, 1898), I, 3.

[10] *GW*, VIB, 277.

[11] *GW*, VIB, 163-164, 168, 265, 281. For the influence of the coming struggle over the iron budget on Bismarck's search for a national issue in the spring of 1870, see Rosslyn Wemyss, ed., *Memoirs and Letters of Sir Robert Morier* (London, 1911), II, 150-153.

His first reaction to the election of May 23, 1869 was that it meant greater stability for the regime, and hence peace. The powerful showing of the radical opposition, he judged, would compel the propertied class to rally to Napoleon's support; it showed that the immense majority of the French nation desired peace. Fortified by this support, Napoleon, of whose personal disinclination for war there was no doubt, would be able to resist the pressure of the relatively small war party of "Arcadians" led by Rouher.[12]

Within a few months he had reason to change his mind. In early November Napoleon again took up the issue of the fulfillment of article v of the treaty of Prague by the return of northern Schleswig to Denmark. One of his trusted men, Count Fleury, was sent to Petersburg with instructions to enlist Russian assistance. Bismarck returned to the conviction that "Parisian policy is bewildered and hence incalculable." He feared that an exchange of notes on the issue between Berlin and Paris might lead to war. To prevent it he took a "firm and hard" line in Petersburg, and the incident passed.[13]

On December 27 Napoleon took the final plunge into parliamentary government by summoning Ollivier, leader of the opposition, to form a cabinet. In this development Bismarck saw a number of possibilities. To Friesen, the Saxon foreign minister, he spoke of "early war with France as an unavoidable necessity"— for Napoleon, because his regime was unstable, and for Germany, because the uncertainty of French policy hampered German development.[14] He believed, nevertheless, that the parliamentary regime might also mean the chance for German unity without war. At the end of February he told Busch: "The French Arcadians are watching the course of events in Germany and waiting their opportunity. Napoleon is now well disposed to us, but he is very changeable. We could now fight France and beat her too, but that war would give rise to five or six others; and while we can gain our ends by peaceful means, it would be foolish, if not criminal, to take such a course. Events in France may take a warlike or revolutionary turn, which would render the present brittle metal there

[12] *GW*, vib, 111, 117.   [13] *GW*, vib, 163, 166.
[14] *GW*, vii, 301. Thimme dates this interview in early 1870, rather than late 1869. *GW*, vib, 203 (n. 3).

more malleable."[15] His Reichstag speech of February 24 had been intended to strengthen the new government in Paris which "signifies peace for us." The constitutional regime, he explained to Karlsruhe, was developing "not unsatisfactorily" for Germany. Should the experiment succeed, it would give a peaceful direction to French development favorable to the independence of her neighbors.[16]

These judgments, at first sight confused and contradictory, reveal once more the elasticity of Bismarck's mind. Unclear about what might come of Napoleon's experiment, he resolved to wait and see. Publicly Ollivier was committed to a policy of peace, which could mean that the new cabinet would end French opposition to the voluntary completion of German unity. But there was also a chance that the constitutional reforms would sap the regime and lead to revolution. Internal chaos would diminish France's external power and distract her attention from Germany. If his hold on the army weakened, furthermore, it was possible that Napoleon would seek to divert the dissatisfied into foreign adventures. Issues elsewhere in Europe might embroil the other great powers and give Germany the freedom and the compulsion to complete her unification.[17]

Once more the effort to dogmatize Bismarck ends in failure—for eulogists and critics alike. His favorite garment was never the straitjacket, but the reversible overcoat. Never did he commit himself irrevocably to a specific course of action long in advance of the necessity for decision. On the contrary, it was his custom to approach major problems with more than one potential solution. The year 1870 was no exception. He had not abandoned the prospect of evolutionary unification, a process which might be greatly speeded up by the internal difficulties in France. But at the same time he did not lose sight of the fact that in the past (1813-1815, 1840, 1858, and 1866) fear of France had most effectively aroused the awareness of a single nationality among the governments and peoples of Germany. Hatred of a foreign foe, rather than spontaneous devotion to Germany, had proved to be the force most capable of defeating the sentiment of separatism. War with France

<hr>

[15] Busch, *Bismarck*, I, 6, also 9-10. See also H. E. Brockhaus, *Stunden mit Bismarck, 1871-1878* (Leipzig, 1929), pp. 34, 46.

[16] *GW*, VIB, 262; see also p. 206.

[17] See *GW*, VIB, 166; H. O. Meisner, ed., *Denkwürdigkeiten des General-Feldmarschalls Alfred Grafen von Waldersee* (Stuttgart, 1923), I, 49.

could accomplish "with one blow" what normally would require a generation.[18]

2. THE HOHENZOLLERN CANDIDATURE

Fundamentally the origin of the war of 1870 lay in a collision of interests. For the sake of Prussian expansion Bismarck had taken up the cause of German national self-determination whose fulfillment was possible only at the cost of France. Since 1866 the French had dreaded the consolidation of a powerful state on their northern frontier, at least without compensation sufficient to preserve their own relative weight in the European balance. These were the ingredients of an explosive compound. The catalyst which brought them together was the abrupt announcement in the summer of 1870 that a Hohenzollern prince was to be king of Spain.

In September 1868 a long-expected revolution had driven Queen Isabel II from the throne in Madrid. A provisional government came to power, headed by Marshals Serrano and Prim as regent and prime minister. Weary of Bourbon misrule, the two statesmen began the hunt for a new dynasty. In the interest of Iberian unity they preferred the ruling house of Portugal, but were refused; two Italian princes likewise declined. Next the Spaniards turned to Germany, the traditional market for European royalty. Prince Leopold of Hohenzollern-Sigmaringen was an obvious choice, being the son of Prince Charles Anthony, head of the southern and Catholic branch of the Prussian ruling house. His wife was Donha Antonia, sister of King Louis of Portugal. Someday she or her children might inherit the Portuguese crown. Only recently his brother, Charles, had been chosen to rule Rumania.[19]

For the French his candidacy was a serious concern. Although but distantly related, the two branches of the Hohenzollern family had in recent years been closely associated. During the new era Charles Anthony had been minister-president of Prussia; at the

---

[18] In a recent defense of Bismarck's innocence, Dittrich maintains that the sources show "without exception" that he "rejected a military solution of the German question." What he positively rejected, however, was the use of violence against the south German states. Dittrich himself admits that the candidature was a "diplomatic stroke" which counted on the possibility of war as *ultima ratio* "in accordance with the political method of that time." Jochen Dittrich, "Bismarck, Frankreich und die Hohenzollernkandidatur," *Die Welt als Geschichte*, XII (1953), 44-46.

[19] Robert H. Lord, *The Origins of the War of 1870* (Cambridge, 1924), pp. 13 ff.

moment he was military governor of the Rhineland and West-phalia. In Prussia he was addressed as "royal highness" and his sons were treated as royal princes. Leopold was a Prussian officer and had served in the war of 1866. The Sigmaringen Hohenzollern were for all practical purposes members of the Prussian ruling house. Under the family law Leopold could not accept a crown without William's consent. To be sure, the Sigmaringen branch was even more closely related to the Bonapartes. One of Leopold's grandmothers was a Murat, another a Beauharnais! But this did not count. "I am," he wrote William, "to the innermost fibre of my heart a Prussian and a German."[20]

Even before Leopold's candidature arose, Bismarck regarded the Spanish situation with considerable satisfaction. In contrast to Isabel, the provisional government was expected to be anti-French and pro-Prussian. He saw the issue of the succession as a "peace-fontanel" which would distract the French from an attack upon Germany. "A solution agreeable to Napoleon is hardly useful to us."[21] In December 1868 the Prince of Putbus and a general staff officer, Colonel Strantz, were in Madrid and in May Theodor Bernhardi arrived. Apparently their function was to report, not negotiate.[22] But soon rumors appeared in the European press that Leopold was under consideration. In some alarm Napoleon, recognizing that the French would never tolerate his election, ordered Benedetti to make inquiries in Berlin. In an interview on May 8 Bismarck indicated that the Hohenzollern family had indeed been sounded out and that the prince had declined, but he teased the ambassador by evading his attempt to find out if William had vetoed the idea. He reported having handled the matter "jestingly."[23]

Before the Reichstag and in his memoirs in later years Bismarck consistently maintained that until July 1870 Leopold's candidacy had been strictly a family affair with which he as chancellor and minister-president had nothing to do.[24] But this was

[20] *Ibid.*, pp. 14-16; Georges Bonnin, ed., *Bismarck and the Hohenzollern Candidature for the Spanish Throne* (London, 1957), p. 67.

[21] *GW*, VIA, 412-413, 422-423, 426-427, 429. According to Forckenbeck, he even remarked that "the Spanish revolution rescued us from war." *GW*, VIA, 474.

[22] Lord, *Origins*, p. 17. This part of Bernhardi's story was censored from his diary by his son at the request of the German foreign office. Bonnin, *Candidature*, p. 19.

[23] Benedetti, *Ma Mission en Prusse*, pp. 306 ff.; *GW*, VIB, 78-82; Bonnin, *Candidature*, p. 286.

[24] *GW*, XI, 129 ff.; XV, 302 ff.

true apparently only until February 1870 when the Spanish offer was actually made. From then on he was deeply involved in the negotiation. At a crucial point he even promoted it without the knowledge and contrary to the desires of the king. Since 1900 a steady trickle of information has revealed this hidden page of his history. But the full extent of his involvement was until recently a closely guarded secret of the German foreign office and certain patriotic historians.[25]

In late February Prim's agent, Don Salazar, called at Charles Anthony's residence in Düsseldorf equipped with plenary power to offer Leopold the Spanish crown. The prince, who dominated his son, found the prospect dazzling: "a dynasty which represents the center of gravity of central Europe and whose scions flourish by the Black Sea and beyond the Pyrenees . . . a dynasty such as that has not been known to history since Charles V. . . ." Nevertheless, he was realistic enough to appreciate its dangers. In response to earlier soundings he had insisted on the approval of both William and Napoleon in the interest of European "peace and tranquillity." But now he dropped the stipulation of French consent, which was tantamount to refusal. He anticipated, however, that "a Hohenzoller in Spain would give rise to a wild outcry in anti-Prussian Europe and either precipitate or defer the solution of many pending questions."[26] To counteract it, his son would need the full backing of the Prussian government. To this end he apparently determined to extract from William a command that the crown be accepted in the interest of the Prussian state. This tactic was made all the more necessary by the fact that Leopold himself genuinely did not want the offered throne.

In letters to William and Bismarck on February 25 Charles Anthony expressed the hope that the king would "command an unqualified refusal . . . may spare me all that is necessarily inherent in an acceptance so pregnant with consequences." But "should the interests of Prussian power demand" acceptance, he and his son would, as loyal patriots, accede. On March 2, Leopold wrote of his "repugnance" for the job. He lacked, he confessed, both the ambition and experience to rule that turbulent land. But if "higher political considerations and the expansion of the power and luster

---

[25] See Bonnin, *Candidature*, pp. 13 ff.; also Rudolf Morsey, "Geschichtsschreibung und amtliche Zensur," *Historische Zeitschrift*, Vol. 184 (1957), pp. 555-572.
[26] Bonnin, *Candidature*, pp. 62-65.

of our house as a whole so demand," he would do his duty as a "Hohenzoller, soldier, and subject."[27]

For William, Charles Anthony's letter was a "bolt of lightning out of a clear sky"; he dashed off a note to Bismarck saying that he was "utterly against the affair." His chancellor closed the door to all visitors and sat down to think the matter through.[28] In a memorial, dated March 9, he assaulted the king's mind with a barrage of reasons for supporting the candidature. "French peaceableness towards Germany will always wax or wane in proportion to the dangers of a war with Germany." To guard the Spanish frontier in war would cost Napoleon one or two army corps. If Leopold declined, the crown would probably go to the Wittelsbach dynasty, raising the danger that both Madrid and Munich would fall under French, Austrian, and Roman influence. There was also the chance that Spain would turn republican and become a source of revolutionary agitation throughout Europe. Friendly relations between Spain and Germany would improve trade. But the most eloquent argument concerned the effect of acceptance upon Hohenzollern prestige: "The repute of the Hohenzollern dynasty, the justifiable pride with which not only Prussia regards its royal house but Germany too tends more and more to glory in that name as a common national possession, a symbol of German fame and German prestige abroad; all this forms an important element in political self-confidence, the fostering and strengthening of which would be of benefit to national feeling in general and to monarchist sentiment in particular. It is therefore to Germany's political interest that the House of Hohenzollern should gain an esteem and an exalted position in the world such as does not find its analogy in the past record of the Hapsburgs since Charles V. This element of pride in the dynasty is not to be estimated lightly as a force operating in favor of the contentment of our people and the consolidation of conditions."

William was totally unconvinced. In razor-sharp marginal comments he hacked his minister's arguments to pieces. He doubted that the unruly land would tolerate for long any foreign dynasty, and its fall would be a harsh blow for Hohenzollern prestige. Con-

[27] *Ibid.*, pp. 62-67.

[28] Horst Kohl, ed., *Anhang zu den Gedanken und Erinnerungen von Otto Fürst von Bismarck* (Stuttgart, 1901), I, 207; Robert von Keudell, *Fürst und Fürstin Bismarck, Erinnerungen 1846-1872* (Berlin, 1901), pp. 430 ff.

cerning the possibility of Spanish military assistance against France, he asked, "What potentate in Spain would be in a position to *guarantee* such a policy?"[29] Although Bismarck marshalled Roon, Moltke, and Delbrück to support his view in a conference on March 15, William, weakly seconded by the crown prince, persisted in the negative. He had "strong scruples" against acceptance and would consent only if Leopold himself heard the call of duty.[30]

The issue, however, refused to die; there were too many interested parties. In Leopold's place Charles Anthony proposed his third son, Frederick. But "Fritz" was traveling abroad incognito. When located, he declined on the same grounds as Leopold. Again William refused to over-ride the rejection. He was still unconvinced that the question came "within the interests of the Prussian state." Meanwhile, Bismarck had sent Lothar Bucher and a staff officer, Major von Versen, to Spain to report on conditions affecting the prince's decision. In mid-April, however, the chancellor fell ill of jaundice at Varzin and for nearly five weeks was *hors de combat*. The enthusiastic reports of Bucher and Versen had no effect on William. The two envoys were recalled, and a telegram to Madrid on May 4 seemingly ended the affair. "The Spanish affair," Bismarck complained to Delbrück, "has taken a wretched turn." The interest of state was being sacrificed to princely selfishness and "feminine-ultramontane influences." The Junker was angry and his nerves were frayed.[31]

But again the candidature refused to expire. Prim had staked all on a Hohenzollern king. On Bucher's advice he ignored the telegram and waited anxiously for Bismarck's return to health.[32] Meanwhile, the persuasive Versen painted for the Sigmaringen princes a rosy picture of monarchist sentiment in Spain. On May 24 he could report to Bismarck, who had returned to Berlin, that Charles Anthony was willing to reconsider—"in the interest of state." In a letter to the prince on May 28 the chancellor willingly supplied the missing motive. "Today no less than before I feel no doubt that Germany has a vital interest here, and that at critical moments the pointer on the scales might well register differently according as we know Madrid to be a friend or an enemy." Wil-

29 Bonnin, *Candidature*, pp. 68-73.   30 *Ibid.*, pp. 291-294.
31 *Ibid.*, pp. 80 ff., 101-150; *GW*, xiv, 776.
32 Bonnin, *Candidature*, pp. 135-137, 153 ff.

liam was indignant; he had thought the matter "dead and buried." Consistent with his previous position, nevertheless, he declared he would not oppose the inclination of "any" Hohenzollern prince to accept. This time Leopold heard the call of duty and destiny.[33]

This accomplished, Bismarck withdrew (June 8) to Varzin to take a "drastic cure" with bottles of Karlsbad water. To all further appeals he replied that he was without a code book, separated from "all departmental resources," and unable to attend to state business. Completion of the negotiation was up to the participants themselves, for it was a family matter in which the Prussian government had "no say."[34] This was the posture he was soon to assume toward France, Europe, and history.

It was entirely false. From the outset the aim of Charles Anthony had been to make sure that the venture had the backing of the Prussian government. He would have preferred a command from William to Leopold, but lacking that he accepted Bismarck's assurance that the Prussian interest dictated acceptance. Without that assurance the project would have lapsed. After Bismarck's withdrawal, furthermore, his subordinates under his orders provided liaison between the negotiating parties. Bucher dashed off once more to Spain and Versen to Leopold in Bad Reichenhall. By telegraph and courier Thile, Bismarck's principal aide in the foreign office, held together the threads and periodically reported to his master in Varzin.

Leopold was vexed when Versen appeared. He wanted to enjoy a leisurely cure at the Bavarian spa and a final summer free of royal protocol before assuming his new dignity. But the major insisted that the matter was pressing. In Madrid the new king had to be legally chosen by the Cortes, which could not be held in session much longer. Intrigues were rife in behalf of other candidates. Before the Cortes could act, the terms of acceptance had to be negotiated with the Spaniards. Under Hohenzollern family law, moreover, William's approval had to be formally requested and given. On June 16, the two men hastened to Charles Anthony in Sigmaringen to draft the letter of request. Here they were soon joined by Bucher and Salazar, who arrived from Spain with word that the situation was critical and no time was to be lost. On June

[33] *Ibid.*, pp. 295 ff., 158, 162-164, 261 ff.; *GW*, vɪɪɪ, 321-325.
[34] Bonnin, *Candidature*, pp. 178-180, 201 (n. 6).

19, Bucher hurried off with Leopold's letter to Bad Ems, where William was taking his summer cure.[35]

That same day Thile had to report to Bismarck that William was highly annoyed.[36] The crown prince, now a convert to the candidature, had "let slip" the fact that Bucher was in Spain, Salazar en route to Germany, Versen "travelling about" contrary to William's own order to return to his post in Posen. The king found it "very extraordinary that this sort of thing was going on without his authorization." While anxious not to "irritate your nerves," Thile reported, the king wished to be informed "of everything that Salazar brings either by word of mouth or in writing before any action is taken." The chancellor's nerves were quite irritated. In the margin of the message he ejaculated:

"That beats everything!

"So his majesty wants the affair treated with *official royal interference?!*

"The whole affair is possible only if it remains the limited concern of the Hohenzollern princes, it must not turn into a Prussian concern, the king must be able to say without lying: I know nothing about it."

What transpired in Ems on the twenty-first, however, demonstrates again how great a fiction was the posture of non-involvement. Bucher succeeded "not without difficulty" in getting the royal assent. But William's exasperation is evident in his reply to Leopold:

"You have taken a decision which you previously, and in my opinion rightly, with full consciousness refused to entertain. Now you regard the political views put forward in the winter of this year by Minister Count Bismarck as justified and incontrovertible from the statesman's point of view. Had that been my own view originally I should not so decidedly have approved of your rejection at that time of the Spanish crown."[37]

Between quaffs of mineral water, meanwhile, Bismarck had written to absolve himself from acting behind William's back. Bucher and Versen, he declared, had been instructed to tell Prim and Leopold that the affair was entirely theirs and nothing more could be expected from the Prussian government. In Ems, Abeken, counsellor of the foreign office, did his best to defend his chief. On

35 *Ibid.*, pp. 191-192, 271 ff.   36 *Ibid.*, pp. 190-191.
37 *Ibid.*, pp. 197, 201.

444

the twenty-second he could report that William resented only the "shillyshallying" of his Sigmaringen relatives.[38]

Sheer chance ultimately prevented Leopold from becoming king of Spain. On June 21st, the elated Salazar telegraphed through the Prussian foreign service to Zorrilla, president of the Cortes, the news that he would arrive in Madrid "about the twenty-sixth" bearing Leopold's acceptance and terms. A clerk in the Madrid embassy inexplicably decoded it as "about the ninth."[39] The consequence was disastrous. On June 23 Zorrilla prorogued the Cortes. Madrid was sweltering, the deputies idle and impatient. He sent them home until November. But the secret could not be kept until then. By July 2 it had reached Paris. The fat was in the fire.

3. THE PROBLEM OF MOTIVATION

What did Bismarck intend to achieve with the Hohenzollern candidature? The concentric problems of the origin of the war of 1870 lead inward to this central question. The known evidence does not present a conclusive answer. This is true even of the recently published files of top secret documents. In none is there any direct proof that the chancellor expected war to develop out of the Spanish affair.[40] Nor do the documents show absolutely what he expected to achieve if his end were not war. The answer must be reasoned from the general situation, his actions, and what we know of his political technique.

Those who maintain that his purpose was pacific point out that his first *démarche* in the question came on March 9 at a time when he apparently expected progress toward national unity through the proclamation of a German Kaiser and the internal decay of the French government. Friedrich Thimme maintained that the candidature was but a "detour" toward the goal of the imperial title. Elevation of the prestige of the dynasty would have

---

[38] *GW*, xiv, 778-779. This is the letter of June 20, which Bonnin could not locate "in the files." Bonnin, *Candidature*, pp. 201-202, 204-206.

[39] *Ibid.*, p. 196.

[40] *Ibid.*, p. 42; see also Rudolf Morsey, "Die Hohenzollernsche Thronkandidatur in Spanien," *Historische Zeitschrift*, Vol. 186 (1958), pp. 573-588. That the documents published by Bonnin have merely stirred up, not resolved, the controversy is evident in the opposing views of Erich Eyck, "Bismarck, Wilhelm I. und die spanische Thronkandidatur," *Deutsche Rundschau*, Vol. 84 (1958), pp. 723-734, and Leonhard von Muralt, "Der Ausbruch des Krieges 1870/71," *Jahrbuch des Ostdeutschen Kulturrates*, v (1958), 348-376.

eased its acceptance by king, crown prince, and the German public.[41] Other writers have taken seriously Bismarck's own argument
that the purpose of the candidature was purely defensive. With a
hostile power in her rear France would be less likely to risk war
with Germany.

These explanations make the lion of European diplomacy look
like a house cat. To argue that Bismarck was unable to anticipate
the consequences of the candidature in France is to depict the
most skillful and realistic tactician of modern diplomacy as a
third-rate chess player shoving his pieces guilelessly about the
board of European politics. It would place him even behind such
an amateur as Charles Anthony, who from the outset predicted
a "wild outcry in anti-Prussian Europe." At the moment of final
decision on June 19, as the letter to William was being drafted in
Sigmaringen, the prince still could not rid himself of anxiety on
this score. Versen has recorded the conversation:

"Then came various scruples on Prince Charles Anthony's part.
What would France say about it? Would it not give rise to complications? I said: 'Bismarck says that is just what he is looking
for.' Charles Anthony: 'Yes, Count Bismarck may want it, but is
it really in the interests of the state?' Myself: 'Yes, Bismarck's
interests and those of the state are the same thing.' Bucher: 'I can
only say what Bismarck has often said to me: If in these last years
Napoleon had wanted war he could have found plenty of grounds
for it.' "[42]

Versen was hardly privy to Bismarck's inner thoughts. Nevertheless, it is evident that he, Bucher, and Charles Anthony were
fully aware of the possible outcome of their actions. Surely the
puppeteer understood as much as his puppets.

It has been argued that the severity of the "complication" to
which the candidature gave rise was owing not to his design, but
to the chance of a code clerk's error. He had expected to present
France with a *fait accompli* beyond the power of public protest
and diplomatic intervention to change. In reply to the uproar he
would simply have stated that the affair was the sole concern of
the Spanish government and a private individual. The French
would find no object for their hostility.[43] But did Bismarck really

41 *GW*, vɪɪв, 270.　　　　　　　　　　42 Bonnin, *Candidature*, p. 278.
43 In 1876 a Spanish historian, Antonio Pirala, published a document allegedly
from the Spanish archives in which Bismarck is supposed to have instructed

believe in the effectiveness of this subterfuge? For two years reports from France had constantly stressed the excitable state of French opinion, the fears and anxieties arising from the decline in French power and prestige. He himself had often emphasized the "incalculability" of French policy because of these pressures. Clearly he expected a severe reaction in France from the diplomatic coup he was preparing.

Did he, however, expect it to lead to war or merely the collapse of the regime? Again it is safe to say that he had more than one possibility in view. Whatever the result it would bring egress from the impasse of the German question and triumph in the coming debates on the military budget. In the Reichstag on the day after his return from Varzin (May 23) he had the chance to ascertain once more the power of the national idea for the achievement of his political ends. The newly drafted code of penal law was threatened with defeat. In two forceful speeches during its final reading he called upon the deputies to sacrifice partisanship in the interest of the "holy cause of our national unity" and to accept the code as a "promising pledge" of Germany's future. The bill passed.[44]

Recent events in France may have influenced his decision to press the candidature. On May 8, Napoleon had resorted for the first time in eighteen years to the device of a plebiscite. The result

---

Bucher and through him the Madrid government concerning the tactic he intended to adopt when Leopold's election became known in France. "It is possible that we may see a passing fermentation in France, and, without doubt, it is necessary to avoid anything that might provoke or increase it." That being the case, he wished as a Prussian minister to avoid all appearance of involvement in the candidature. "Thus we shall have an unassailable position before the European public. If there is an outburst in France, we shall simply ask: What do you want? Do you wish to dictate the decisions of the Spanish nation and of a German private citizen? . . . Undoubtedly they will cry 'intrigue,' they will be furious against me, but without finding any point of attack." Lord, *Origins*, pp. 23-24. While this is the only known document in which Bismarck dealt with the problem of the French reaction, no one since Pirala has been able to locate it in the Spanish archives and it has been the subject of considerable controversy. Recently Lawrence Steefel has argued forcefully that the probable author was Bucher himself rather than Bismarck or Salazar. See his "Bismarck and Bucher: The 'Letter of Instructions' of June 1870," in A. O. Sarkissian, ed., *Studies in Diplomatic History and Historiography in Honour of G. P. Gooch, C. H.* (London, 1961), pp. 217-224. Whoever the author, the thoughts were certainly Bismarck's. But it may not be used as proof that he actually expected the French to be frustrated by his posture of non-involvement. No one understood better than he the volatile and unreasoning nature of popular passion. The purpose of the document was to calm fears of the Spanish government that the election of a Hohenzoller would trigger a European war.

44 *SBR* (1870), ii, 1120 ff.

was an impressive vote of approval for the "liberal empire" and a fresh legitimation for the regime. Bismarck's anticipation that it would soon collapse because of its internal contradictions appeared in error. What followed, however, was even more alarming. On May 15, Daru resigned as foreign minister. He was replaced by Gramont, the volatile advocate of alliance with Austria. Bismarck regarded the appointment itself as a "most warlike symptom." On the margins of three reports dealing with the policy of the new minister he penned the awesome comment: "War!"[45] It was during this period that he relaunched the torpedo of Leopold's candidature.

Before it reached its mark, however, his view of the French situation apparently changed. At the end of May he persuaded William to visit Czar Alexander, who was vacationing at Ems. On June 5 he returned to Berlin, evidently confident of the continued solidarity of the Russian entente. Two days later he dispatched a lengthy reply to a note from Bernstorff, in which he denied that Napoleon might soon be driven to discharge the mounting current of domestic discontent by the lightning rod of foreign adventure. For the last time he reiterated the view that the emperor feared an attack on the Rhine would unite the whole of Europe against him. Failure in war meant revolution at home and the end of his regime. Both Napoleon and France had need of peace and the maintenance of the *status quo*. The danger of a French attack was no greater now than at any time since 1866—recognizing "naturally the incalculability of European conditions."[46] With this judgment he returned to Varzin next day to resume his interrupted cure.

Clearly the Hohenzollern candidacy was an offensive, not a defensive act. It is false to argue that his aim in May was to gain an ally for the coming crisis.[47] Unlike the Italians in 1866, the Spaniards had no grievance against France. Leopold could scarcely commence his rule by insisting upon war for German interests. Still unanswered was William's query: "What potentate in Spain would be in a position to *guarantee* such a policy?" But the best proof is that Bismarck's first promotion of the candidacy predated his alarm of May by many months and that after that alarm subsided in early June he made no effort to extinguish the fuse he had reignited. He departed for Varzin and let it burn.

[45] *GW*, vɪʙ, 321.   [46] *GW*, vɪʙ, 326-329.   [47] *GW*, vɪʙ, 324.

Bismarck's goal was not an ally, but a crisis with France. He deliberately set sail on a collision course with the intent of provoking either war or a French internal collapse. The partisans of his innocence ask us to believe a most improbable case: that the shrewdest diplomatic mind of recent history permitted Germany to be drawn into a war which he was eager to avoid. The man who in 1863, 1865, and 1867 had known how to approach the brink and yet save the peace, when it was wise to do so, found it impossible to maneuver his way out of a situation of his own making in the summer of 1870 without resort to violence. We are asked to believe that this tremendous talent, ordinarily so richly inventive, so inexhaustible of resource, suddenly and briefly became barren and impotent to prevent what, it is declared, he did not seek and did not want.[48] The proposition, to be believed, requires an act of faith.

4. TO THE EMS DISPATCH

The person to whom fell the duty of meeting Bismarck's offensive was unequal to the task. The situation required in the Quai d'Orsay a personality self-possessed, sober in outlook, without illusion concerning the strength of France and its chances in war with Germany. It called for the deft unmasking of the Hohenzollern intrigue and the maintenance of French prestige without peril to the peace. But the Duke of Gramont was a career diplomat of the high nobility who had lived for years abroad. His image of France was that of another era, that of French dominance in Europe. He was an ardent patriot, inclined to be rash and reckless where the honor of France was at stake. As a diplomat he was often a shrewd and able reporter, but brash in executing his instructions. He was without experience in the formulation of high policy and poorly suited for the tasks of a constitutional minister required to lead a volatile parliament along the narrow path of *raison d'état*. During recent years, moreover, he had associated in Vienna with that circle in court and government which dreamed of revenge for the humiliation of Sadowa. He arrived in Paris burdened with a belief in the dependability of the Austrian alliance.[49]

On hearing the news from Madrid on the afternoon of July 3,

---

[48] See Becker, *Bismarcks Ringen*, pp. 669, 682, and Muralt, "Ausbruch des Krieges," pp. 364 ff.

[49] Pierre de la Gorce, *Histoire du Second Empire* (Paris, 1894-1905), VI, 216-217.

this proud and irritable man reacted according to form. He took no time to reflect or consult. Instead of shrewdly asking for Prussia's good offices in terminating the candidature, he swiftly drafted a comminatory telegram to Berlin. Was the Prussian government, he demanded to know, "a stranger to this intrigue"? As he knew, the Prussian capital was practically empty of responsible officials. It was the time of year for travel and mineral water. Bismarck was in Varzin, William in Bad Ems, Benedetti in Wildbad. Hence the first thrust and parry in the great duel were executed by two underlings: Le Sourd, French chargé d'affaires, and Thile, under secretary in the foreign office. Showing embarrassment, Thile answered, as Bismarck wished, "that the Prussian government knew absolutely nothing about this affair and that for it the affair did not exist." When their reports arrived in Varzin and Paris, Bismarck found the question "impudent," Gramont the reply "derisory."[50]

The position which Thile assumed for Prussia was the one Bismarck had planned and which, if he had had his way, would have been consistently maintained throughout the affair. His intention was simply to refuse to discuss the matter with the French except to refer them to Madrid and Sigmaringen; the candidacy was an affair of the Spanish government and a private individual, with which the Prussian government and William had nothing to do. Hardly had Thile given his reply, however, when a cleavage appeared in the Prussian front which, had it been properly exploited by Gramont, could have brought the affair to a close with a French diplomatic victory. It arose because of Bismarck's failure to instruct Werther, his ambassador in Paris, and because of his geographical separation from William in Ems.

Goltz's successor in Paris had no advance knowledge either of the candidature or of the attitude he was supposed to take toward it. On July 4, he was preparing for a trip to see the king at Ems and called on Gramont. Far from refusing to discuss the matter, he listened considerately to the remonstrance of his colleague of Vienna days. News of the candidature, the minister said, had produced a "painful impression" in France and threatened the peace. Werther promised to convey the complaint personally to William. Early on the morning of the sixth he arrived in the Hessian

50 Lord, *Origins*, pp. 30-31, 121-122.

spa. To Count Waldersee, who met him at the station, he burst out, "The devil is loose at Paris: it looks very much like war."[51]

Bismarck was highly alarmed. In a flood of messages from Varzin he strove to re-establish his broken front and to prevent Werther from "worrying" William. After the ambassador's trip to Ems, however, it was scarcely possible to continue refusing to discuss the matter. But the French should at least be told, he wrote, that William, while knowing of the Spanish offer, had exercised no influence on the outcome and until recently had believed Leopold would refuse. Legally he could do no more than advise rejection, which he had in fact already done. Prussia had no primary interest in the matter and was surprised that France wished to intervene in Spain's internal affairs, considering the usual fate of such interventions. The French reaction was also surprising since the prince was by ancestry more Bonaparte than Hohenzoller! Werther should display only "cool astonishment." Above all the impression had to be avoided that Prussia could be intimidated: "The firm and fearless attitude which we have always hitherto adopted in the face of every disturbance at Paris, is the most essential factor to which we owe the preservation of peace. France, in my opinion, fears a serious breach more than we; but if we give grounds for the belief that we are the more afraid, French insolence will soon leave us no other choice than war."[52]

Bismarck was determined, in brief, to force the issue; France must either bend or be broken. In Paris a like mood prevailed.

After the disaster Ollivier, Gramont, and Napoleon blamed the pressure of public opinion for the bellicose posture they assumed in the Hohenzollern affair. But the public reaction was, in part, stimulated by the cabinet itself. On the morning of July 4 the first protests, dictated by Gramont, appeared in the pro-government journals. The opposition, however, did not join in the chorus.[53] On the sixth, a deputy sought to restrain the government through an interpellation. But Gramont, with the approval

---

[51] *Ibid.*, pp. 32 ff. Bismarck's failure to instruct Werther argues, of course, for the innocence of his intentions. The most damaging aspect of the incident, however, he could not have foreseen. It arose from the accident that Werther was, at the moment the crisis broke, on the verge of a trip to Ems and in a position to take the French protest directly to William, rather than submit it through Thile and Bismarck. He proved very inept at interpreting his chief's purposes.

[52] *Ibid.*, pp. 129 ff.

[53] *OD*, xxviii, 22; E. Malcolm Carroll, *French Public Opinion and Foreign Affairs, 1870-1914* (New York, 1931), pp. 25-26.

of his colleagues, used the opportunity for an inflammatory challenge. By placing one of its princes on the throne of Charles V, a foreign power threatened the European equilibrium and imperilled the "interests and honor" of France: "To prevent it, we count both upon the wisdom of the German, and friendship of the Spanish people. But if it should be otherwise, strong in your support, gentlemen, and in that of the nation, we should know how to do our duty without hesitation and without weakness." Frantic applause filled the chamber and next day spilled over into the chauvinistic press. At the Quai d'Orsay Gramont ordered Benedetti to proceed to Ems and induce William "if not to order, at least to advise" Leopold to renounce his candidacy. Should he refuse, "c'est la guerre."[54]

At breakfast in Varzin on the morning of the eighth Bismarck received the text of Gramont's speech. According to an assistant, he was surprised at its bellicosity. "Gramont could not have spoken so recklessly," he remarked, "if war had not been decided upon." He talked of mobilizing immediately and falling upon the French. But then he reflected that this would hardly do. Before the bar of William's conscience and European opinion, France had to appear the aggressor. Instead he ordered mobilization of the German press. "The newspapers . . . must be very rough and as many of them as possible."[55]

In Ems, meanwhile, there was confusion and uncertainty. Honest William was not without a sense of guilt, and Werther warned that war would be the consequence of Leopold's failure to withdraw. News of Gramont's speech stiffened the monarch's back, but did not end his hope for peace. He decided to receive Benedetti, but promised Bismarck he would speak "very sternly," using the arguments supplied from Varzin. Subterfuges, however, were contrary to William's nature. On July 9 he admitted to the ambassador having approved Leopold's acceptance and even of having informed Bismarck of "these various incidents." While insisting he had no authority to make Leopold withdraw, he revealed that he was even then asking his Sigmaringen relatives to state their intentions. During the next four days, William—for once—

[54] Lord, *Origins*, pp. 42, 48; Ollivier, *l'Empire libéral*, xiv, 92-110.

[55] Keudell, *Fürst und Fürstin Bismarck*, p. 429; Lord, *Origins*, pp. 46, 155. For Bismarck's instructions to the press in this critical period see Busch, *Bismarck*, I, 28 ff., and Eduard Schulz, *Bismarcks Einfluss auf die deutsche Presse* (Juli 1870) (Halle, 1910).

followed an independent policy. He kept Bismarck in the dark about the extent of his admissions to Benedetti and of his interpellation in Sigmaringen.[56]

The beginning was unpropitious. On July 10 reports arrived from Paris that the war fever was raging in the French capital. Military preparations were underway. Should the candidacy continue, the cabinet was determined to strike. That same evening came Charles Anthony's letter refusing a renunciation except on William's express command. Leopold himself was off on an Alpine excursion and could not be reached. Still William did not give up. While he and Werther staved off Benedetti, a trusted emissary, Colonel Strantz, was dispatched to Sigmaringen. His train missed connections, and he arrived twelve hours late. In a tense audience at noon on the eleventh, William again put off the impatient ambassador. At Paris, emperor and ministers wavered on the brink, averse to war, yet fearful of diplomatic humiliation and the public temper. In the Alps Leopold enjoyed the scenery blissfully unaware that the peace of Europe hung by a thread from his name. On the morning of the twelfth, Charles Anthony, under attack from both Paris and Ems, withdrew his son's candidacy on his own authority. William felt as though a stone had been lifted from his heart.[57]

Bismarck felt differently. While William, unknown to him, had been mediating between Paris and Sigmaringen, the telegrams from Varzin had directed a policy of stern intransigence. He had opposed suggestions from the king that a royal letter be sent to Napoleon and the mediation of neutrals invoked. He advised against William's continued dealings with Benedetti. To keep control of the situation he set out on the morning of the twelfth, uncommonly silent, for Berlin en route to Ems. In the late afternoon his carriage halted in the Wilhelmstrasse and a sheaf of telegrams was shoved into his hand. Sitting there in the street he learned for the first time of Charles Anthony's decision and the extent of William's involvement in his renunciation. Other messages from Paris told of "vaunts and taunts" in the Paris press. Descending to the sidewalk, he thought of resigning. Prussia, he judged, had suffered a humiliation worse than Olmütz.[58]

[56] Lord, *Origins*, pp. 49 ff.
[57] Bonnin, *Candidature*, pp. 242 ff.
[58] Lord, *Origins*, pp. 68 ff.; *GW*, xv, 305 ff.

Once at his desk in the chancellery, however, he began to grapple with the problem of salvaging as much as possible from the wreckage. He wanted war, but William's appeasement had left no way for Prussia to begin it without appearing the aggressor. Hence all he could do for the time being was to minimize and disguise the extent of the catastrophe. With Roon and Eulenberg he sent a telegram to William entreating him not to make the mistake of announcing Leopold's renunciation to Benedetti and hence to the world. If the word came from Madrid or Sigmaringen, the tarnished fiction of his non-involvement might still be upheld. A message from Paris helped. Werther reported that the Spanish ambassador had informed Gramont of an "official telegram" from Charles Anthony renouncing the throne for his son. Quickly Bismarck transmitted this news to the press and to Prussian legations in Germany and Europe. In conferences with the crown prince, Ambassador de Launay of Italy, and Gorchakov, who happened to be in Berlin, he spoke of the crisis as settled and of his intention to return to Varzin.[59]

But the truth was that he was even then searching for a way to renew the conflict on more advantageous grounds. Public opinion, he telegraphed to Ems, had been "injured" by Gramont's threats and demanded satisfaction; the king should react by granting Werther an indefinite leave and making the reason known. His directives to the press, however, reveal that he himself was stirring up public resentment over Gramont's "offensive tone." To Werther in Paris he telegraphed early on the afternoon of the 13th that, if "a completely satisfying statement as to the intentions of France" were not soon received, he would recommend to the king that the Reichstag be convened and consulted upon what course to take. His aim was to keep the affair alive by demanding an explanation of Gramont's conduct, by chauvinistic demonstrations from the Reichstag, and the menace of mobilization.[60]

[59] Lord, *Origins*, pp. 201-204, 215, 261-262; Heinrich O. Meisner, ed., *Kaiser Friedrich III., Das Kriegstagebuch von 1870/71* (Berlin, 1926), p. 2; Clark, "Bismarck, Russia, and the War of 1870," pp. 200-201; S. William Halperin, "Bismarck and the Italian Envoy in Berlin on the Eve of the Franco-Prussian War," *Journal of Modern History*, XXXIII (1961), 35-36. For Bismarck's actions on July 12 and 13 see particularly Lawrence Steefel, *Bismarck, the Hohenzollern Candidacy, and the Origins of the Franco-German War of 1870* (Cambridge, 1962), pp. 165 ff.

[60] Lord, *Origins*, pp. 205, 219-220; Ernst Walder, *Die Emser Depesche, Quellen zur neueren Geschichte herausgegeben vom Historischen Seminar der Universität*

That same day, however, their plan was made superfluous by the folly of Gramont. The duke failed to recognize the extent of his victory. He was disturbed over the failure to receive from William himself word of the Sigmaringen decision and an admission of his own participation in it. There was also the feeling that something more was owed, some act of expiation on William's part for what appeared to have been a Prussian conspiracy against France. Both in parliament and among the public there were ominous rumblings of dissatisfaction over this "insufficient and almost derisory concession."[61] With the approval of Ollivier, Gramont asked Werther to convey to William the request for a letter of apology to Napoleon which would appease the French public. Still the duke did not feel right about the matter. Had Leopold, whose whereabouts were still unknown, slipped off, like his brother in 1866, to claim his crown in Spain? With Napoleon's assent, but without the knowledge of Ollivier and the rest of the Cabinet, he dispatched that evening the fatal telegram to Benedetti demanding that William associate himself with Charles Anthony's renunciation and "give us assurance that he will not authorize a renewal of the candidacy." Without this, he urged, it was doubtful if the government could dominate popular unrest.[62]

On the morning of the thirteenth, Benedetti placed himself in William's path in the Kurgarten by the Lahn and obtained his famous audience. While promenaders watched from a respectful distance, he made his demand and was refused. The two men argued, Benedetti to the point of impertinence, until William tipped his hat and coldly withdrew saying that he had nothing further to add. Early that afternoon under the urging of Eulenberg and Abeken, he determined to call off a scheduled audience with the ambassador. In mid-afternoon the report of these events was telegraphed to Berlin.[63]

Since morning on that decisive day Bismarck had received a number of comforting dispatches. From Vienna Schweinitz reported that Austria, despite French wooing, would probably remain neutral in event of war. From Bavaria, Baden, and finally

---

Bern, Vols. 27-29 (Bern, 1959), pp. 62-68; Clark, "Bismarck, Russia, and the War of 1870," p. 201.

[61] Lynn M. Case, *French Opinion on War and Diplomacy during the Second Empire* (Philadelphia, 1954), pp. 251 ff.

[62] *OD,* Vol. 28, pp. 254-255.

[63] Walder, *Die Emser Depesche,* pp. 49 ff.

even Württemberg came assurances of support. Gorchakov appeared sympathetic. English neutrality was fairly certain. The situation favored war. The problem was how to bring it about on favorable grounds. For several hours vague reports trickled in from London, Munich, Stuttgart, and Gorchakov that Gramont had made new demands, but to Bismarck's growing irritation there was no confirmation from Werther. Then suddenly the dispatch from Ems supplied the missing provocation.[64]

When it arrived that evening Bismarck was at dinner with Roon and Moltke. At first sight the message was rather disappointing. Insulted by an outrageous demand, William had failed to dramatize his indignation. (As yet there was no word of Gramont's further request for an apology, whose receipt at Ems later in the afternoon terminated the king's last hope of appeasing the French.) Nevertheless, Abeken's dispatch was made to serve. After asking Moltke once more if the army was ready, the Junker drew out his pencil and went to work. By subtracting words, he gave the message a terse abruptness which altered its sense. Now it appeared that, in reply to a presumptuous demand, the king had closed the door to Benedetti and to all further negotiation. The generals read the revised version with relief. "Yes," they declared, "that will do."[65]

On the morning of the 14th Gramont, his face livid, rushed into the office of Ollivier with the news of the publication of the "Ems dispatch." It was, the trembling diplomat declared, a "slap in the face." The premier also recognized that Bismarck's action was openly provocative. That evening, as the news spread through Paris, a howling mob surged through the boulevards shouting, "To Berlin!" "Down with Prussia!" and singing the forbidden "Marseillaise." Within the court and cabinet, nevertheless, there was wavering indecision. Reports from Ems showed that William had remained courteous to the end, that even after the meeting in the Kurgarten he had sent Benedetti a message "approving"

[64] Lord, *Origins*, pp. 194 ff. Although Gorchakov dodged the opportunity to reaffirm the Russo-Prussian agreement concerning Austria, an appeal to the Czar through Oubril brought reassurance. Clark, "Bismarck, Russia, and the War of 1870," pp. 199 ff.; Platzhoff, "Anfänge des Dreikaiserbundes," p. 299.

[65] William L. Langer has cut away the embroidery of the tale which Bismarck so often told about the swift transition from despondency to exultation which the edited dispatch produced in Roon and Moltke. See his "Bismarck as a Dramatist," in Sarkissian, *Studies in Diplomatic History*, pp. 199-216. For the original and edited texts of the dispatch see Walder, *Die Emser Depesche*, pp. 13 ff.

Leopold's renunciation, and finally that he had received the ambassador again at the railway station before departing for Coblentz. But it was recognized that he had not complied fully with the French demands and that the "Ems Dispatch" was a deliberate challenge. The excitement in the streets, the impatience of nationalistic deputies in the chamber, the agitation of the war party at court constituted pressures which the new and uncertain parliamentary regime could not ignore. Napoleon too, dreading the consequences, felt the force of the hurricane. Gradually, as the hours progressed and one ministerial conference succeeded another on July 14 and 15 the decision congealed.[66]

In the end war came because Bismarck believed it necessary and opportune and because the French cabinet had neither the wisdom nor the firmness of will to avoid it.

[66] By emphasizing different aspects of the evidence, Carroll and Case come to diametrically opposed views on the origins of the French decision for war. The former believes that Gramont and Ollivier willed it, while the latter accepts their excuse that public anger required it. The truth probably lies somewhere in between. Carroll, *French Opinion*, pp. 25 ff.; Case, *French Opinion on War and Diplomacy*, pp. 256 ff. For the best account of the events in Paris on July 14 and 15 leading up to the declaration of war see Steefel, *Hohenzollern Candidacy*, pp. 195 ff.

CHAPTER TWENTY

A NATIONAL WAR

1. STRATEGY AND DIPLOMACY

OOKING backward from the perspective of the twentieth century, some historians have found much to admire in the way Bismarck's wars were conducted. In our day warfare has tended to become absolute under the influence of crusading national ideologies. The quest on moral grounds for total victory has exalted military over political policy. Statesmen and generals have been increasingly inclined to see as their primary objective the utter destruction of the foe rather than attainment of a stable peace. By contrast the conflicts of 1864, 1866, and 1870 appear to have been classic examples of Clausewitz's famous principle that war is properly but a continuation of policy by other means. They were fought for limited objectives on isolated battlefields. While they reconstructed, they did not destroy the European balance.[1]

This was achieved, however, only at considerable cost. The dualism of political and military authority in Prussia, which Bismarck himself perpetuated, made it increasingly difficult to establish the supremacy of political purpose over military strategy. During the Danish war he infuriated the generals by insisting that the invasion of Jutland be delayed. They could not accept his view that agreement with Austria and avoidance of foreign intervention took precedence over military expediency. Later Roon, Moltke, and others were distressed over the leniency shown the Danes in the armistice preceding the London conference. The army, wrote Roon, did not regard itself as "purely a political instrument, a lancet for the diplomatic surgeon."[2]

[1] The similarity of viewpoint between the chancellor and military philosopher was apparently accidental. In 1889 Bismarck observed, "To my shame I have to confess that I have never read Clausewitz and have known little more about him than that he was a meritorious general." Lucius von Ballhausen, *Bismarck-Erinnerungen* (Stuttgart, 1921), p. 502.

[2] Gordon A. Craig, *The Politics of the Prussian Army, 1640-1945* (Oxford, 1955), pp. 182-192; Anneliese Klein-Wuttig, *Politik und Kriegsführung in den deutschen Einigungskriegen 1864, 1866 und 1870/71, Abhandlungen zur Mittleren und Neueren Geschichte*, Vol. 75 (Berlin, 1934), pp. 5 ff.

The Austrian war produced frictions of even graver nature. To Moltke's irritation Bismarck meddled in the mobilization and deployment of the Prussian forces in the west during the first days of the conflict. But the great altercation came after Königgrätz, when the generals urged William to pursue the retreating forces of Benedek across the Danube and into Vienna. They wanted a conqueror's peace. "In eight days it will be all over," wrote General-adjutant von Boyen on July 19, "if the diplomats, who attach themselves to every honorable war like bugs to a bed, don't destroy the sport for us."[3] Only with the greatest difficulty did Bismarck succeed in limiting the conflict by gaining William's acceptance of French mediation. Although the generals were satisfied with the ultimate peace terms, the incident left behind a residue of resentment, which influenced the conduct of the war of 1870.

The potentiality of conflict was greatly increased by the rise of Moltke and the general staff. While Roon was usually open to Bismarck's arguments and willing to take into account the needs of foreign policy, Moltke believed it possible to draw a distinct boundary between politics and strategy. Until the outbreak of war, diplomacy was paramount; thereafter, military necessity. Nor did his experiences of 1864 and 1866 convince him of the error in such a division of functions. With the group of devoted "demi-gods" which surrounded him in the general staff, he entered the campaign against France firm in the conviction that the movement of German forces was the sole concern of the generals, whatever its effect upon the attitudes of European powers and the negotiation of peace.[4]

During the first month of hostilities there was little occasion for conflict between the statesman and military chiefs. The campaign went so quickly that it discouraged outside intervention. The German forces mobilized with machine-like precision, while beyond the Rhine all was chaos and confusion. When the German offensive began (August 4), the French were still unready. On that day Prussian and Bavarian troops struck at Weissenburg;

---

[3] Craig, *Prussian Army*, p. 202; Oberst von Haeften, "Bismarck und Moltke," *Preussische Jahrbücher*, Vol. 177 (1919), pp. 85 ff.; Hermann Gackenholz, "Der Kriegsrat von Czernahora vom 12. Juli 1866," *Historische Vierteljahrschrift*, xxvi (1931), 332-348.

[4] Craig, *Prussian Army*, pp. 195 ff.; Gerhard Ritter, *Staatskunst und Kriegshandwerk, Das Problem des "Militarismus" in Deutschland* (Munich, 1954), i, 247 ff.

two days later the double victories of Wörth and Spichern oc-curred. On the 16th and 18th came the bloody battles of Mars la Tour and Gravelotte which cut off the main French army under Bazaine and forced it to retire into the fortress of Metz. Unable to succor Bazaine, the remnant of the French forces under Mac-Mahon marched to Sedan, where on September 1, after fierce combat, it surrendered. Napoleon himself was one of the prisoners.

At the outset the French fully expected Austrian and Italian assistance. In March Archduke Albrecht, Austria's foremost gen-eral, had been in Paris to confer on military collaboration be-tween the three powers in event of war with Germany. Toward the end of May the French General Lebrun had continued the exchange of views in Vienna. But the triple entente remained a "moral" rather than a military commitment. On June 14 Franz Joseph told Lebrun that he would make common cause with France only "when Napoleon stands in south Germany with his army, not as an enemy, but as a liberator." Apparently Gramont, in-formed by Beust of the secret negotiations in Paris during the preceding year, assumed office in Paris under the impression that the alliance had practically been achieved. On July 8 he asserted in a cabinet meeting that Austria would station an observation corps on the frontier and "paralyze" part of the Prussian forces. But the next day Beust, in response to Napoleon's inquiry, prom-ised just diplomatic support. Only if Russia joined Prussia would the Hapsburg monarchy enter the conflict.[5]

Beust suspected an understanding between Berlin and Peters-burg, and in this he was absolutely correct. On July 16 Czar Alexander responded to an inquiry from Berlin by confirming his commitment of the previous year; should Austria go to war, Rus-sia would occupy Galicia with 300,000 men. In a crown council on July 18 Beust raised the question whether, in view of the Rus-sian threat, Austria should continue her "passive policy." Opin-ions were divided, but Franz Joseph decided on a declaration of official neutrality, coupled with some military preparations. In order to buttress this decision, Bismarck disclaimed any intention of detaching German Austria, and Alexander offered a guarantee of Austrian territorial integrity.[6]

[5] *RKN*, I, 94 ff.; III, 376 ff., 413 ff.

[6] *GW*, VIII, 389, 422-423; Werner E. Mosse, *The European Powers and the Ger-man Question, 1848-1871* (Cambridge, 1958), pp. 306-310; Eduard von Wertheimer,

Albrecht believed, however, that in early September a decisive battle would occur in Saxony, and Beust was tormented by the thought that Austria might not benefit from a French victory. Hence he let Gramont know *sub rosa* that neutrality was for the Hapsburg monarchy merely a means for gaining time in which to complete Austrian rearmament. He advised France to come to terms meanwhile with Italy by evacuating Rome. Through an agent Napoleon learned that Victor Emmanuel intended to go through with his commitment of the previous year to ally with France. While the emperor revealed his intention to recall the Roman garrison, the king declared that Italy would respect the independence of the papal state. But again Bonaparte was destined to disappointment, for Victor Emmanuel could not persuade the Italian cabinet to honor his "anterior promises." Throughout the diplomatic crisis Foreign Minister Visconti-Venosta worked for peace and, when war came, he kept Italy neutral.[7]

In England the belligerents engaged in a sharp contest for public and official favor. No sooner had Napoleon proclaimed his respect for Belgian neutrality, the point of chief interest in London, than Bismarck produced for British consumption a document of sensational content. It was the treaty draft, which Benedetti had so unwisely left in his hands in August 1866. On July 25 it appeared in the *London Times*. The impression was deliberately created that the document was of recent origin and that the Prussian refusal alone had prevented a Franco-Prussian alliance at the cost of Belgium and the German southern states. While skeptical, the British cabinet resolved to obtain a fresh guarantee of Belgian frontiers from both belligerents. After it was signed on August 9 and 11, the British sat back to watch the struggle in France, comfortable in the thought that, whatever the outcome, their interests were secure.[8]

These actions by the European powers in July and August

Graf Julius Andrassy (Stuttgart, 1910), I, 510-520. See also Ernst Erichsen, *Die deutsche Politik des Grafen Beust im Jahre 1870* (Kiel, 1927), pp. 14 ff.

[7] *RKN*, III, 464-467; *OD*, XXIX, 201 ff.; Friedrich Ferdinand Graf von Beust, *Aus drei Vierteljahrhunderten* (Stuttgart, 1887), II, 410-411, 437-438; S. William Halperin, "Visconti-Venosta and the Diplomatic Crisis of July 1870," *Journal of Modern History*, XXXI (1959), 295-309, and his forthcoming article, "Napoleon III and Italy, the Crisis of July 1870."

[8] Mosse, *European Powers*, pp. 312-317; Kurt Rheindorf, *England und der Deutsch-Französische Krieg 1870/71* (Bonn, 1923), pp. 47-56.

went as Bismarck had calculated they would and justified his assumption that war with France in the summer of 1870 was possible without outside intervention and hence without triggering a general European conflict. Austria was the critical point, and his judgment that Beust, for all his dreams of revenge, would be unable to ally with France proved entirely correct. But after the fall of Sedan difficulties began to appear which greatly complicated Bismarck's task and led to serious trouble with the generals over the most fundamental issues of state policy.

2. BISMARCK AND MOLTKE

On August 16, while the cannon thundered at Mars la Tour, Bismarck wrote to his wife that the campaign was "as good as ended, unless God should manifestly intervene for France, which I trust will not happen."[9] But the war of 1870 went differently than that of 1866. France's reaction to military disaster was not capitulation, but revolution and resistance. When the ominous news of Wörth and Spichern reached Paris on the sixth, there was general panic. Under attack from the assembly, Gramont and Ollivier resigned. Acting as regent, while her husband was in the field, Eugénie bravely tried to bolster the regime with ringing words of honor and valor. But after Sedan the flood could no longer be held back. The mob was in motion and the tottering empire collapsed. On September 4, following the traditional ritual of revolution in Paris, the republic was proclaimed at the Hotel de Ville. A "Government of National Defense" was organized, with General Trochu as president and Leon Gambetta as its leading figure. For the revolutionists the war was far from over; it had, in fact, just begun.

Napoleon had been defeated in one month; six more were required to conquer France. On September 18 the victors of Sedan appeared before the ramparts of Paris. Manning the forts and trenches was a motley army of soldiers, sailors, national guardsmen, and volunteers. Within days the city was enclosed in an iron ring. During the following weeks the great sieges of Metz and Paris (Strassburg capitulated on September 27) tied down the bulk of the German forces. Escaping from Paris by balloon, the fiery Gambetta galvanized the population of the south to further

9 *GW*, xiv, 785.

effort. While a new army was being formed on the Loire, the irregular *francs-tireurs* began their attacks upon German detachments and communications in the north.

Continued French resistance created a host of new problems at the Prussian headquarters in Versailles. For the general staff the transformation of the war from a professional into a popular struggle raised strategic problems which the generals had not foreseen. As long as the fighting lasted, moreover, so did the danger of foreign intervention. Bismarck had to find as soon as possible a French government capable of speaking for the nation and willing to accept the German terms. The impingement of these problems of strategy and politics upon each other led inevitably, under the dual structure of the Prussian system, to a test of strength between the chancellor and the chief of the general staff.

Apparently Moltke and his "demi-gods" had firmly determined to exclude Bismarck from the war councils in which the crucial issues of strategy were debated and decisions taken. This time, their ears were to be free of his biting sarcasm and his injection of political considerations into strategic problems. Before Sedan the chancellor does not appear to have objected to his exclusion. The campaign went largely according to plans already known to him. But after Sedan ignorance of the generals' intentions disrupted his efforts to end the war. Most irritating of all, he had no other source for what had taken place on the fighting front than the army communiqués in the German press, received five days after the event. Repeatedly he demanded at least to see these reports as they emanated from headquarters. Not until October 15 was a system set up for this purpose, and even then it was carried out in a grudging and haphazard way. In January Bismarck was still complaining over the inadequacy of his information.[10] A still more serious clash, however, came over the treatment of Napoleon.

After his surrender Napoleon was handled with the utmost chivalry and sent off to comfortable captivity in the palace on Wilhelmshöhe at Kassel. "Revenge," said Bismarck, "is God's affair." With the beleaguered army at Metz and thousands of

---

[10] Craig, *Prussian Army*, pp. 204 ff.; *GW*, vɪʙ, 590-592, 637-638, 658-660. Shortly after Sedan he also had a sharp altercation with Moltke over instructions he had issued to Dr. Stieber, chief of the *Feldpolizei*, who was officially subordinate to the general staff. *GW*, vɪʙ, 490-491. For the generals' side of the story see Haeften, "Bismarck und Moltke," pp. 87 ff., and Paul Bronsart von Schellendorff, *Geheimes Kriegstagebuch, 1870-1871* (Bonn, 1954), pp. 78-79, 82.

prisoners the fallen emperor was a valuable resource—"Tell's second arrow for the Gessler 'republic.' " "The French must remain uncertain whether they will get him again."[11] As usual, the Junker left open every door and every turning. For months after Sedan he held out to Louis and Eugénie the prospect of a return to power, while threatening the Government of National Defense with the nightmare of a resurgent Bonaparte. "It is a matter of indifference to us who rules France," he telegraphed to London, "whether Napoleon or a white or red republic." What mattered was that a government be found which would cede Alsace-Lorraine.[12]

If a restored empire were to be a real possibility, rapport had to be re-established between Bazaine at Metz, Napoleon at Kassel, and the demoralized Eugénie, who had escaped to England. The unilinear minds of the military could not comprehend this maneuver. Prince Frederick Charles, who commanded at Metz, regarded its capitulation as a purely military concern. When Bazaine's emissary, General Bourbaki, returned from a mission to emperor and empress, the stubborn prince protested his re-admission to the invested fortress, with the consequence that the impatient general made off for Tours and offered his services to the revolutionary government. Grimly Bismarck wrote that the unexpected failure of a single wheel to turn had rendered useless weeks of careful diplomacy. Warfare, he explained, was properly but a means to political ends.[13]

To Bismarck's disgust Louis and Eugénie could not make up their minds; they were reluctant to mortgage their return to France with the cession of French soil. The fall of Metz (October 27) increased the difficulty of the negotiation. Not even now, however, did Bismarck remove the Napoleonic ace from his deck. As late as January 14, he regarded Louis' return as "the most advantageous" solution for Germany. In the final negotiations with Favre and Thiers he used the threat of it to pry concessions from the revolutionary government.[14] Moltke was outraged at

11 *GW*, vIB, 469-470; vII, 344 ff.; xIV, 793, 814-815.
12 *GW*, vIB, 504; vII, 373. See Joachim Kühn, "Bismarck und der Bonapartismus im Winter 1870/71," *Preussische Jahrbücher*, Vol. 163 (1916), pp. 49-100.
13 *GW*, vIB, 551-553. Klein-Wuttig, *Politik und Kriegführung*, pp. 109 ff.
14 *GW*, vIB, 666-669; vII, 379, 393, 407; Hermann Oncken, ed., *Grossherzog Friedrich I. von Baden und die deutsche Politik von 1854-1871* (Stuttgart, 1927), II, 333-334.

the prospect and crossed Bismarck by prejudicing William against it. He hated France and despised the Napoleonic regime. Peace, he maintained, was inadmissible until the enemy had been utterly crushed.[15] But Bismarck saw that, with every passing day, the danger of foreign intervention increased.

For a time the seeming finality of the victory at Sedan had discouraged the European powers from any such thought. Alexander and Gorchakov abandoned their project for a joint effort by the neutrals to shorten the war and preserve the European balance. Gladstone reaffirmed the principle of non-intervention. Queen Victoria actually rejoiced at the triumph "of civilization, of liberty, of order and of unity . . . over despotism, corruption, immorality and aggression."[16] On September 4 Bismarck heard of the revolution in Paris with some satisfaction for the effect it would have on the neutrals. In Vienna and Petersburg he now argued that the best safeguard for "order and civilization" against "revolutionary and republican interests" was solidarity of the three eastern monarchies—and the cession to Germany of Alsace and Lorraine![17]

News of the German intention to annex was received with concern in both Russia and Britain. In August Alexander had expressed to Reuss, the Prussian ambassador, his fears that the lost provinces would become a source of constant friction in the future and urged moderation.[18] Gladstone was "much oppressed" by this "transfer of human beings like chattels." When Granville, who had replaced Clarendon at the foreign office, proposed (October 16) joint steps by the neutrals for an acceptable peace, he was rebuffed by Gorchakov.[19]

Very soon the British learned the real reason for Russian disinterest. On October 31, Czar Alexander issued a circular repudiating the Black Sea clauses of the treaty of Paris. The Russians had decided to exploit Europe's preoccupation with the war in France to rid themselves of the galling restrictions imposed after the defeat in the Crimea. For years Bismarck had curried favor in Petersburg by urging Gorchakov to take this step, and now he

---

[15] Craig, *Prussian Army*, pp. 208-209; Oncken, *Grossherzog Friedrich I*, II, 166-167.

[16] Mosse, *European Powers*, pp. 324 ff.

[17] *GW*, VIB, 448, 476, 486.

[18] *GW*, VIB, 456, 458-459, 476.

[19] Mosse, *European Powers*, pp. 338 ff.

was compelled to support it. Nevertheless, the timing was most unfortunate for Germany. In Britain public indignation threatened to push the cabinet into war. Austria too became "ominously hostile." But Bismarck managed to get agreement on a conference to be held in London. It opened on January 17 with a joint declaration on the sanctity of treaties and ended on March 13 with the revocation of the neutralization of the Black Sea. By this legerdemain principle was preserved and self-interest satisfied.[20]

The Black Sea issue was a source of anxiety to Bismarck because of its possible repercussions upon the conflict in the west. Had Russia gotten herself involved in war with Britain, the Franco-German struggle might easily have developed into a European cataclysm. During the conference, moreover, there was a chance that the neutrals might discuss intervention in France. Hence it was all the more important to end the war as quickly as possible.[21] His agitation upon this score brought him again into bitter conflict with the generals.

After Sedan the Junker grew increasingly critical of the way the general staff ran the war. He opposed the advance on Paris. It was better to "let the people there fry in their own fat for a time, while we set up house in the conquered provinces before going further." If left alone, he believed, the quarrelsome republic would fall apart of itself. But his advice was ignored. When the German forces reached the capital, he wanted an immediate assault instead of a siege. The investment, he complained, tied down the bulk of the army and left Gambetta free to raise new forces in the south and west. In the occupied regions German troops were so thinly spread that it was difficult to make the conquered population "feel" the war.[22]

During November and December the major issue was the bombardment of Paris. Most of the generals were skeptical about the effectiveness of their artillery and preferred the tedious course of starving out the inhabitants. Lack of conviction, bad planning, and poor transportation delayed the arrival of the siege guns and adequate munitions. Bismarck could not believe that honest disagreement and technical difficulties stood in the way. His let-

---

[20] *Ibid.*, p. 346. See Heinrich Mertz, *Die Schwarze Meerkonferenz von 1871* (Stuttgart, undated) and particularly Kurt Rheindorf, *Die Schwarze-Meer- (Pontus) Frage* (Berlin, 1925), pp. 75 ff.

[21] *GW*, vin, 602-606.

[22] *GW*, vin, 648-651; xiv, 791, 800.

ters home alluded darkly to "some kind of intrigue" spun by wives, archbishops, intellectuals, and free masons; the war was being prolonged by sentimental humanitarianism and fear of foreign reaction. He fell ill from wrath and jangled nerves; his old leg injury returned to plague him; and for days he lay in bed incommunicado. Finally, on December 27, the bombardment began. But the forts withstood the pounding and within the city the shells caused only limited damage. Bismarck's psychological warfare merely increased the will of the Parisians to resist, while the idea that non-combatants could be fired upon horrified Europe and left the Germans with a clinging reputation for brutality. Starvation alone brought about the capitulation of January 29.[23]

The generals were infuriated by Bismarck's "infantile counsels." They sneered at "the civilian in cuirrassier uniform" and his "ill-mannered," "domineering" ways. Having nothing else to do, it seemed, he meddled in their affairs and conspired to take over the military direction of the war. To Bismarck, on the other hand, it appeared that the generals were woefully ignorant of the political import of their decisions. During December and January he used whatever opportunities came his way to limit their influence. Letters sent by Moltke to General Trochu in Paris gave him occasion to demand the right to review such communications. On January 25 two royal orders curbed Moltke's power to communicate with the enemy and gave Bismarck the right to present his views on future military operations. Moltke was outraged. He drafted a sarcastic reply, suggesting that the chancellor be given responsibility for directing the war. But then he thought better of it and wrote a memorial justifying his position on the grounds that chancellor and chief of the general staff were two parallel, "mutually independent agencies under the direct command of your majesty."[24]

The conflict between Moltke and Bismarck is a classic example of the uneasy relationship between political and military leader-

[23] GW, vm, 570-571; vii, 390, 395, 409, 416, 419, 424; xiv, 797 ff.; Rudolf Stadelmann, Moltke und der Staat (Krefeld, 1950), pp. 232 ff.; Otto Bihler, Die Beschiessung von Paris 1870/71 und die Ursachen ihrer Verzögerung (Tübingen, 1932); Melvin Kranzberg, The Siege of Paris, 1870-1871 (Ithaca, 1950), pp. 133 ff.

[24] Craig, Prussian Army, p. 210 ff.; Klein-Wuttig, Politik und Kriegführung, pp. 135 ff. Schellendorff, Kriegstagebuch, pp. 185-186, 208 ff., 233-237, 249, 279-281, 303 ff.; Haeften, "Bismarck und Moltke," pp. 98-103; GW, vm, 615-617, 673.

ship in wartime. To the chancellor the fall of Paris meant the possibility of peace on German terms, but to the general it meant the release of troops for further military operations. After a futile attempt to reconcile the two men, Frederick William realized that Moltke was bent upon a "war of extermination." His aim was to extend the iron grip of German military might over the whole of France. But William was wise enough to know whose side to take. To the anger and mortification of the general staff, Bismarck alone conducted the talks with Jules Favre which produced an armistice. Without their advice he determined which Paris forts were to be surrendered. When the new French government in Bordeaux required an extension of the armistice, he decided for it over Moltke's strenuous opposition. The final terms of peace were essentially of his dictation. "Never," wrote General von Stosch, "have I witnessed such bitterness toward an individual as that at the moment toward Bismarck."[25]

The Junker had won his private struggle with the military at a crucial time in German history. But the institutional dualism of military and political authority which was its cause remained unaltered. One day, long after his death, the problem would rise again to plague his successors in a war of far greater dimensions.

3. ''FUROR TEUTONICUS''

By great effort Bismarck was able to limit the war of 1870 to the realization of rational political objectives in the tradition of *raison d'état*. Nevertheless, the conflict was not a *Kabinettskrieg* in the style of the eighteenth century, but a *Nationalkrieg* of modern character.[26] In this respect the Franco-German war was a link between the national wars of the French revolution and those of the twentieth century. In contrast to 1854, 1859,[27] 1864, and 1866, the war of 1870 was one of peoples, more than governments. By a quick peace after Königgrätz, the Hapsburg monarchy deliberately avoided the hazardous experiment of calling upon the peoples of the empire to resist invasion. After the de-

[25] Friedrich III, *Kriegstagebuch*, pp. 325-326; Oncken, *Grossherzog Friedrich I*, II, 260 ff., 279, 282, 290 ff., 313-315, 363-364; *GW*, VIB, 665 ff., 676 ff., 693-694; Ulrich von Stosch, ed., *Denkwürdigkeiten des Generals und Admirals Albrecht von Stosch* (Stuttgart, 1904), p. 227.

[26] This Moltke himself recognized. Ritter, *Staatskunst*, I, 252; Stadelmann, *Moltke und der Staat*, pp. 173 ff.

[27] Only Italy, the weakest of the three participants, regarded the conflict of 1859 as a national war.

struction of the imperial armies and the fall of the Napoleonic regime, however, the war with France continued far beyond the expectations of Bismarck and the Prussian generals. The catastrophe merely opened wider the Pandora's box of national feeling and the spirit of popular sacrifice. A war for the destruction of armies became a conflict for the exhaustion and dismemberment of a nation.

On both sides the war had the characteristics of a national crusade. As he confessed to Metternich on July 8, Gramont considered the Hohenzollern candidature a safe terrain for a crisis, precisely because it did not involve German national sentiment.[28] But this was a bad miscalculation. In editing the Ems dispatch Bismarck counted on the reality that any crisis with France, whatever the origin, was sufficient to arouse the *Furor Teutonicus.* The great revival of national feeling in 1840 had begun with a crisis in Egypt, that of 1859 with war in Italy. Germans of 1870 had been raised in the tradition of the war of 1812. Popular suspicion of France was as endemic in Germany as hostility toward Britain in the United States during the same period. In contrast to 1866, Bismarck's effort of 1870 to identify the Prussian cause with that of the German nation was an overwhelming success.

From the outset the war was popular on both sides of the Rhine. While patriotic crowds demonstrated in the streets of Paris, William received ovation after ovation on his journey from Ems to Berlin. In the capital thousands gathered spontaneously at the railway station to receive him. Afterward they massed in the square before the royal palace to cheer and applaud. In a Reichstag speech, composed by Bismarck, he stressed the national character of the coming struggle. France's leaders had used the Hohenzollern candidature as a "pretext" for war. In earlier centuries Germans had borne in silence foreign assaults upon their rights and honor. Since 1813, however, they had been bound ever more closely together by spiritual and legal ties. Now they possessed the will and strength to defend themselves. The governments, north and south, called upon the German people to show the patriotism and sacrifice of their forefathers in a struggle for "our freedom and our right against the brutality of foreign con-

[28] *RKN,* III, 405.

querors." His words were interrupted frequently by deafening applause.[29]

Addressing the Bundesrat on July 16, Bismarck gave a highly partial account of the negotiations which led to the "insult" at Ems, contrasting Prussian innocence with French malevolence. France, he declared, had left "Germany" no other choice than war and had committed a grievous sin against humanity. The general agitation of German national feeling was evidence that this was the conviction of the public. On the twentieth he read to the Reichstag his reply to England's offer to mediate. Berlin was willing to negotiate on any basis acceptable to the "honor and national consciousness of Germany." But she was unwilling to undertake any initiative to this end, for it "would be misunderstood by the national feelings of the German people," which were deeply wounded and agitated by the French threat. "Our strength lies in the national sentiment of the nation, in its sense of right and honor." Cries of "Bravo!" "Very Good!" and "Very Right!" echoed through the chamber.[30]

These declarations set the tone for official propaganda throughout the war. In two published diplomatic circulars (July 18-19) Bismarck traced French aggression to "instincts of hate and jealousy" and the desire to suppress freedom at home through involvement abroad. The size and power of the two countries and their "national embitterment" opened the prospect of a "titanic struggle" hazardous to national welfare and the peaceful development of civilization. The "criminal" actions of the French coerced "us to take up the struggle for the sake of the national honor and freedom of Germany." For victory he trusted in God and the "support of the entire German nation."[31]

While most of this was propaganda, it is nevertheless true that Bismarck himself felt in some degree the national character of the war. During the campaign he entertained his guests and associates at dinner with facile comparisons of the German and French character: "France is a nation of ciphers—a mere herd. The French are wealthy and elegant, but they have no individuality, no consciousness as individuals, but only as a mass. They are like thirty million obedient Kaffirs, each one of whom is in himself featureless and worthless, not fit to be compared with

29 Friedrich III., *Kriegstagebuch*, pp. 4 ff.; *GW*, xi, 134-135.
30 *GW*, xi, 129-133, 135-138.   31 *GW*, viB, 394-397, 401-402.

Russians and Italians, to say nothing of ourselves. It was an easy task to recruit out of this impersonal, invertebrate mass a phalanx ready to oppress the remainder of the country so long as it was not united."

By contrast the Germans were individualists, each with his own opinion. "But when once a large number of Germans come to hold the same opinion, great things can be done with them. If they were all agreed they would be all-powerful." In combat, he declared, the Germans were driven by a sense of duty imposed by religious conviction rather than obedience to the state. Unlike the French they were willing to die at lonely posts, unseen and unrewarded, without hope or fear. He believed in "a divine providence which has ordained this German nation to something good and great."[32]

The "nation of ciphers," the "herd" without individual self-reliance, produced after the fall of Sedan a spontaneous popular resistance which surprised and baffled the German leadership. Without an army at the moment of its birth, the republic resorted to a *levée en masse* in the areas still under its control. Most indicative of the transformed, popular character of the war were the *francs-tireurs*. In the German-occupied regions partisans began to appear. From behind hedges and buildings they sniped at passing troops; in guerrilla bands they fell upon isolated detachments and sabotaged communications. While neither universal nor always motivated by patriotism, partisan activity threatened to become a real hazard for the German forces. On the night of October 8 a band of *francs-tireurs* attacked with success a large German commando at Ablis and took away sixty-five prisoners; at Chateaudun on October 18 an eight-hour battle occurred; on January 23 a vital bridge in the Vosges was blasted, putting out of commission one of the two railway lines to the German frontier.[33]

The German reaction was harsh. Death was decreed for those found with weapons or caught in the act of sabotage. Heavy contributions were levied on communities suspected of sheltering or assisting *francs-tireurs*. Hostages were taken to insure payment. In extreme cases whole communities were pillaged and put to the

---

[32] Busch, *Bismarck*, I, 138, 162-163.
[33] Bertram Winterhalter, *Die Behandlung der französischen Zivilbevölkerung durch die deutschen Truppen im Kriege 1870/71* (manuscript dissertation on deposit in the library of Freiburg University), pp. 75 ff., 128-129, 229.

torch. At Chateaudun this meant a town of 7,000 inhabitants. Gustav Freytag, acting as a journalist at Prussian headquarters, estimated in late October that two months of partisan warfare had cost France about 3 million francs in contributions, 20 to 30 single houses destroyed, 20 to 30 villages burned down, 150 to 200 persons shot or burned to death (among them women and children guilty or presumed guilty of murderous attacks on German soldiers).[34]

For Bismarck, however, these measures were not severe enough. Repeatedly he complained that, because of the thin deployment of German occupation troops, it was difficult to make the civilian population "feel" the war by heavy exactions of money and material. He deplored the tendency of the military government to shield non-combatants from suffering.[35] One evening at dinner his views were reinforced by an expert witness, General Philip Sheridan, who summed up his experience in the American civil war: "The proper strategy consists in the first place in inflicting as telling blows as possible upon the enemy's army, and then in causing the inhabitants so much suffering that they must long for peace, and force their government to demand it. The people must be left nothing but their eyes to weep with over the war."

Even Sheridan must have been impressed by the way his pupil absorbed the lesson. Concerning the "treacherous *francs-tireurs*," the Junker remarked a few days later, "It will come to this: that we will shoot down every male inhabitant."[36] Such judgments were frequent. His wrath was aroused by reports that guerrillas were being taken prisoner rather than shot on the spot. This was also his view of uniformed prisoners taken in regular combat. On hearing of 1,600 captured in an engagement on the Loire, he remarked, "I should have been better pleased, if they had all been corpses. It is simply a disadvantage to us now to make prisoners." As the months advanced, he repeatedly deplored that prisoners were still being taken. Toward African troops he was particularly savage. "There should have been no question of making prisoners of these blacks. . . . If I had my way, every soldier who made a black man prisoner should be placed under arrest. They are

[34] *Ibid.*, pp. 94 ff.

[35] *GW*, xiv, 806, 808; vii, 378. See particularly his memorial to William of December 14. *GW*, viв, 632-637.

[36] Busch, *Bismarck*, i, 128, 167.

beasts of prey, and ought to be shot down." He accused them of torturing German soldiers.[37]

He thoroughly approved of burning villages out of reprisal, for "war is war." Concerning the incident at Ablis, he remarked that every male inhabitant ought to be hanged. In cases of sniping and sabotage he thought it would be a good idea to transport everyone in the area to camps in Germany. He favored firing on "French scamps" who spat at German troops from a bridge. Persons escaping from Paris by balloon ought to be treated as spies and shot immediately on capture. Starving women and children who came out of the beleaguered city to dig for potatoes in the fields between the lines must be fired upon. Soldiers who refused to press the trigger ought to be executed. "Brutality," concluded a listener, "is decidedly one of his instincts!"[38]

Most of these remarks were made, to be sure, in animated conversation. They show Bismarck's anxiety over Germany's inability to end the conflict. While capable of saying, "After all, war is, properly speaking, the natural condition of humanity,"[39] this was more in the nature of a psychological observation than moral approbation. On the contrary, he was highly affected by the carnage he saw on the battlefields of Bohemia and France and deeply conscious of the responsibility of the statesman who decides the issue of peace or war. It confirmed his prejudice against preventive war and his conviction that violence was a last resort, to be tried only when unavoidable or when every other means for the attainment of a necessary political objective had failed. Even when this has been said, however, it is still true that his attitude during the French campaign reveals what for that age was a "harsh and coarse" conception of war.[40]

4. ALSACE AND LORRAINE

The demand for Alsace and Lorraine was another factor which gave to the Franco-German struggle the character of a national war. The people of Alsace and part of Lorraine speak a German dialect; historically both provinces once belonged to the Holy

[37] *GW*, vii, 388, 404, 422; Busch, *Bismarck*, i, 246, 258.

[38] Busch, *Bismarck*, i, 190, 192-193; *GW*, vii, 396, 405; Ernst Feder, ed., *Bismarcks grosses Spiel, Die geheimen Tagebücher Ludwig Bambergers* (Frankfurt, 1932), pp. 153, 241.

[39] Busch, *Bismarck*, i, 210.

[40] Winterhalter, *Behandlung*, pp. 196 ff.

Roman Empire. During the reigns of Louis XIV and his successors, they had been gradually annexed to France. It was an era of dynastic politics when national feeling was but weakly developed and the wishes of the population of little concern. With the French revolution the final connection between the provinces and Germany was severed. Politically and economically the area was completely incorporated into the French state; psychologically its citizens became French through participation in the common experience of the revolution and its wars. By raising the demand for its annexation, Bismarck helped to make the war of 1870 a popular national crusade in Germany and inflicted upon the French nation a terrible wound, which nearly a century has failed to heal.

In Bismarck's defense it is usually pointed out that his motive for claiming the Vosges frontier for Germany was not blood relationship, common language and culture, or any of the usual justifications from the cult of nationalism. He dismissed such arguments contemptuously as "professorial ideas." In private conversation, diplomatic dispatches, and declarations of government policy the one justification which he consistently stressed was that of security. "We must have the two fortresses [Metz and Strassburg] in order to make difficult for France another aggressive war, not in order to bring Alsace and Lorraine back to Germany."[41] This consideration was, in fact, dominant at the Prussian headquarters. The two provinces formed a triangular wedge with the apex at Strassburg pointing toward the heart of Germany. To France they gave the benefit of interior lines of communication and to Germany the disadvantage of exterior ones. Only the greater speed of German mobilization, Moltke believed, had prevented French invasion of Baden at the beginning of the war. This belief was shared by Roon, William, and Frederick William.[42] Hence there is some support for the view that the annexation of Alsace and Lorraine was an act of *Staatsräson* rather than *Nationalpolitik*. Once again, however, the argument is but part of the truth.

[41] Busch, *Bismarck*, I, 124; *GW*, VII, 338-339.

[42] Martin Spahn, *Elsass-Lothringen* (Berlin, 1919), pp. 246-247; Waldemar von Roon, *Denkwürdigkeiten aus dem Leben des General-Feldmarschalls Kriegsministers Grafen von Roon* (4th ed., Breslau, 1897), II, 442; Erich Brandenburg, ed., *Briefe Kaiser Wilhelms des Ersten* (Leipzig, 1911), I, 244, 246; Friedrich III, *Kriegstagebuch*, pp. 115-116.

The necessity of justifying annexation compelled Bismarck to alter fundamentally the official German view of the war and reinforce its popular character. In the beginning the words which he placed in William's mouth distinguished between the French government, which desired war, and the French people, whom it misled. "I make war against soldiers," William proclaimed, "and not against French citizens." But soon after the first successes on the battlefield Bismarck began to shift the burden of culpability. In Petersburg he declared that, while the folly of Napoleon and his advisers was the cause of war, "everyone has recognized that the emperor was but the expression of the senseless and criminal desires of the French people. . . . It is not merely Napoleon. It is France herself whose quest for domination forms a permanent danger for her neighbors, with or without Napoleon at her head." In London he argued that during the last two centuries Germany had been attacked "twelve or fifteen times" by France. The source of these wars of conquest was "the incurable arrogance and desire to dominate which are peculiar to the character of the French people and are exploited by every ruler of the country." Nor was the new line limited to diplomatic dispatches. When the German press continued to blame Napoleon, he instructed Thile in Berlin to correct this "error." In two circular dispatches, released to the press, Bismarck publicly traced the origins of the conflict to the domineering pride and ambition of the French nation and described annexation as a national demand of the German people.[43]

During the first three weeks of war, there were many allusions in the German press to the justice and necessity of annexations. But the first open demand was voiced by the south German *Augsburger Allgemeine Zeitung* on July 21. Four days later *Die Neuesten Nachrichten* of Munich exhorted Germany not to lay down its arms "until Alsace and Lorraine are again German and the Rhine is Germany's river, not Germany's frontier." After the victories of August 4, 5, and 18 the trickle became a flood which swept the entire press.[44] The private correspondence of the lead-

[43] *GW*, vɪʙ, 443, 454-455, 492-494, 500-502.

[44] Hirth und Gosen, *Tagebuch des Deutsch-Französischen Krieges, 1870-1871* (Berlin, 1871), ɪ, 93, 399-400; E. Malcolm Carroll, *Germany and the Great Powers, 1866-1914* (New York, 1938), p. 75; Karl Jacob, *Bismarck und die Erwerbung Elsass-Lothringens 1870-1871* (Strassburg, 1905), p. 8; Gustav Körner, *Die norddeutsche Publizistik und die Annexionsfrage im Jahre 1870* (Hanover, 1907), pp. 17 ff., 38 ff.

ers of German liberal nationalism—Lasker, Sybel, Baumgarten, and others—shows the same swift progress of opinion. By August 20 they had agreed upon a program of agitation. Only among the progressives, according to Forckenbeck, were there any doubts about the wisdom of annexing a hostile population on the basis of its German past.[45]

The public pressure, before which Bismarck professed to tremble, was in part his own creation. On August 25 he telegraphed to Berlin: "Since the position of England and Russia on the dismemberment of France has been discussed in the *Independence Belge* and the *Journal de St. Petersbourg*, all papers accessible to us, namely all German ones, are to express the national indignation over the intervention of neutral powers inimical to us and the firm will of the German people to secure the south German frontier through annexations from France and to make easier the defense of our borders against repetition of predatory attacks like those which have occurred in the last two centuries."[46]

During the following days there was a perceptible increase in chauvinistic agitation throughout Germany. At a rally in Berlin on August 30, with the lord mayor presiding, prominent liberals of both the Progressive and National Liberal Parties drafted a resolution in favor of annexation; similar meetings followed in other major cities, north and south.[47] From headquarters in France, Bismarck added more fuel to the flames. At his direction Moritz Busch, a press secretary, wrote an article on annexation for the official *Provinzial-Korrespondenz*, which was quickly seconded by other prominent journals. The *Preussische Jahrbücher* provided the climax with a stirring essay by Treitschke: "What do we demand from France?"[48]

By no means was the German case for annexation limited to strategic necessity. Those who participated in the decision were hardly free from the influence of that "professorial idea" which excited Bismarck's contempt. Long ago during the crisis of 1840

---

[45] *HW*, I, 475 ff.; Duncker, *Briefwechsel*, 589; Ludwig Bamberger, *Gesammelte Schriften* (Berlin, 1894-1897), II, 123 ff.; Körner, *Publizistik und Annexionsfrage*, p. 9.

[46] *GW*, VIB, 460; see also pp. 454-455.

[47] Körner, *Publizistik und Annexionsfrage*, pp. 21 ff.; Jacob, *Bismarck und Elsass-Lothringen*, p. 31; Hirth und Gosen, *Tagebuch*, II, 1619-1623, 1633.

[48] *Ibid.*, pp. 1648-1651; Busch, *Bismarck*, I, 91-93; Körner, *Publizistik und Annexionsfrage*, pp. 33-34; *Preussische Jahrbücher*, XXVI (1870), 367-409; *HW*, I, 476-478.

Moltke had published an essay proving that Alsace and Lorraine belonged to Germany on grounds of nationality and historical right. "These fine provinces were severed like a sound limb from the living body of Germany." Thirty years later he still regarded the quarrel with France from the national standpoint. Nor was William free of this conception. To Augusta he wrote that for strategic reasons that area must be annexed "which was and is German."[49] Busch's article shows the same mixture of motives. While the emphasis was upon military security, he added, "Besides, it must not be forgotten that this territory which we now demand was originally German and in great part still remains German, and that its inhabitants will perhaps in time learn to feel that they belong to one race with ourselves." Bismarck too defended the annexation as a "return of German soil," of "her old Reichsland," and once he wrote of the "genuine German nationality" of Alsace. In delimiting the frontier, he wished to follow as closely as possible the linguistic boundary, on the theory that the German-speaking population would be easier to assimilate. Later he deplored that "the entire pro-French population" had not been deported from the annexed provinces.[50]

In the public mind the national motive was apparently as important as military security. At any rate both motives were stressed about equally in the flood of newspaper editorials and pamphlets over the issue, which, if they did not reflect public opinion, certainly helped to form it. In the past little attention had been given to Alsace-Lorraine as German *irredenta*, except in the crisis years of 1814-1815, 1840, and 1859. But now the great historical wrong was rediscovered that it might be righted, the German character of the inhabitants reaffirmed that they might be rescued from the contamination of French decadence. Treitschke's inflammatory article, reprinted as a pamphlet, stressed the rights of security and conquest, but his most powerful appeal was that of nationality: "These lands are ours by the right of the sword and we wish to have disposal over them by virtue of a higher right, the right of the German nation, which cannot permit its lost sons to alienate themselves forever from

[49] Helmuth von Moltke, *Gesammelte Schriften und Denkwürdigkeiten* (Berlin, 1892-1893), II, 175-228; Stadelmann, *Moltke und der Staat*, pp. 182 ff.; Brandenburg, *Briefe Kaiser Wilhelms*, p. 244.

[50] Busch, *Bismarck*, I, 93; *GW*, VIB, 453-454, 498; VII, 339; XIV, 816; Oncken, *Grossherzog Friedrich I*, II, 392-393; Brockhaus, *Stunden mit Bismarck*, pp. 80-81.

the German Reich. We Germans, since we know Germany and France, understand better what is good for the Alsacians than those unfortunate people themselves. . . . Against their own will we wish to give them back their true selves. . . . The spirit of a people embraces not merely contemporary, but successive generations. We invoke the will of those who were once there against the will of those who now live there."[51]

In diplomatic dispatches Bismarck was compelled to deny this viewpoint. He suspected attempts to arouse the anxiety of the Russians over future German demands for the Baltic provinces. On September 16 he telegraphed that such an idea was "laughable"; the case for Alsace and Lorraine was based on military security, rather than the return of an ancient possession. In Vienna and Budapest he repeatedly denied as "absurd" any ambition to dismember the Hapsburg empire through the annexation of "so-called" German Austria.[52] But Treitschke also disclaimed the need to recover "every clod of German soil" in Austria, Switzerland, and the Netherlands. What could not be tolerated was the "destruction of German nationality (*Volkstum*)" by French cultural imperialism.[53] While Bismarck disdained this viewpoint, his propaganda made use of it. What mattered to him at the moment was the greatest possible agitation of German opinion, whatever the justification.

The pressure for annexation within Germany was helpful in warding off intervention by the neutral powers. In Petersburg he maintained that a German government which failed to acquire the provinces would fall prey to revolution and republicanism. Annexation, he advised London, was the firm and unanimous will of the German people. When Granville advised moderation, he savagely replied that for the sake of a defensible frontier Germany would not shrink from a battle of extermination at Paris, from ten years of warfare, from the "most daring invocation of the national strength of Germany against neutral intervention," or from agreement with *any* French government.[54]

The demand for annexation lengthened the war. No other issue proved to be such a stumbling block. Because of it Louis and

[51] *Preussische Jahrbücher*, xxvi (1870), 371. See also Andreas Dorpalen, *Heinrich von Treitschke* (New Haven, 1957), pp. 164 ff.
[52] *GW*, viii, 422-423, 416-417, 499.
[53] *Preussische Jahrbücher*, xxvi (1870), 371-372.
[54] *GW*, viii, 454-459, 501, 503-504.

Eugénie were extremely reluctant to enter into serious negotiations and for months an armistice could not be achieved with the Government of National Defense. At Ferrières on September 20-21 Bismarck conferred with Jules Favre, and at Versailles on November 1-2 with Adolphe Thiers. Although the Frenchmen desired a cease-fire during which to elect a new government, the threat of annexations compelled them to demand terms which would have permitted a resumption of the fighting. Naturally this was unacceptable to Bismarck. Not until the fall of Paris on January 28 did the French face the bleak fact that the war was lost and with it Alsace-Lorraine.

When Thiers, chosen "chief of the executive power" by the new parliament at Bordeaux, reappeared at Versailles on February 21, the only questions remaining were the delimitation of the new frontier and the amount of the French indemnity. Bismarck believed that Lorraine, because of its French-speaking inhabitants, was politically undesirable. But back home its acquisition, as Grand Duke Frederick observed, had assumed "the character of a national demand." More important, William and his generals insisted that Metz was militarily indispensable. The officers at Versailles were in a savage mood. They talked of "destroying the enemy, laying waste the country, exhausting all sources of wealth and income."[55] To satisfy the military, Bismarck insisted on Metz, and Thiers had to capitulate. The Junker consoled him with the retention of Belfort and a reduction of the French indemnity from six to five billion francs.

Since August the warning had been frequently heard that loss of the two provinces would permanently embitter France toward Germany. But Bismarck was unimpressed. The bitterness, he argued, would be just as great even without annexations. France would never forget her humiliation. "An enemy, whose honest friendship can never be won, must at least be rendered somewhat less harmful. Under the circumstances this is the only correct policy."[56] There could scarcely be any better evidence of the national character of the war of 1870 than Bismarck's own admission that it would inaugurate an era of enduring antagonism between France and Germany.

[55] *GW*, xiv, 816; viii, 475; Oncken, *Grossherzog Friedrich I*, ii, 366-367, 387 ff.; Johannes Haller, *Bismarcks Friedensschlüsse* (Munich, 1916), pp. 82-83.
[56] *GW*, viii, 454-455, 457-458, 476-478

CHAPTER TWENTY-ONE

WINNING THE SOUTH

1. NEGOTIATING THE TREATIES

HE lasting hostility of France was the un-avoidable by-product of a war whose necessity arose from the incohesion of the German nation. Bismarck's major war aim was not the conquest of French soil, but the voluntary acceptance by the south of the north German constitution without essential change. Through a national crusade against France he expected to produce a flood of German sentiment which would overflow the barriers of southern particularism. From the palaces of Munich and Stuttgart to the palisades of Paris he propagated the view that the struggle against France was "a great national war," "a moral and national revolt against foreign attack and arrogance," whose only logical outcome would be the consolidation of "Germany's unity and power" under the northern system.[1]

At the onset of war the vital question was whether the south would recognize the *casus foederis*. Of Baden's complete loyalty there was never any doubt. Without summoning parliament, the government in Karlsruhe ordered mobilization and destroyed the bridges over the Rhine. Even the most fanatical anti-Prussians in Baden preferred to fight rather than suffer French occupation. In Darmstadt, on the other hand, Dalwigk and Grand Duke Louis tried desperately to evade the commitment to Berlin. In recent months the minister had repeatedly sought French and Austrian aid against Prussia's encroachments. Even now he hoped for the appearance of their troops in Germany. Twist and turn as he might, there was no other recourse than fulfillment of the alliance. Despondently he wrote, "We are completely in the talons of the eagle."[2]

[1] *GW*, xiv, 795, 799, 801; vib, 394-397.

[2] George G. Windell, *The Catholics and German Unity, 1866-1871* (Minneapolis, 1954), p. 249; Otto Becker, *Bismarcks Ringen um Deutschlands Gestaltung* (Heidelberg, 1958), pp. 691 ff.; Ernst Vogt, *Die Hessische Politik in der Zeit der Reichsgründung (1863-1871)*, Historische Bibliothek, Vol. 34 (Munich, 1914), pp. 188 ff.; Walter Vogel, *Die Tagebücher des Freiherrn Reinhard von Dalwigk zu*

When news arrived of the French demands, Württemberg was shaken by a patriotic tremor which abruptly put an end to the agitation of the People's Party against the Prussian military system. The sudden surge of popular anger and fear which swept the cities and towns overcame the lingering doubts of the extreme democrats, rural Catholics, and great-Germanists. On July 13 Varnbüler informed Berlin that Gramont's impudence had "deeply wounded" German national feeling in Württemberg. Four days later, the king ordered mobilization and on July 22 the Landtag voted, with only a single dissent, the necessary war credits. But many cast their ballots with heavy hearts. Thirty-nine deputies signed a declaration lamenting that 1866 had made it impossible for "all Germany" to stand against the foe.[3]

Again the major concern was Bavaria. However, Bray was much too realistic to follow his personal inclinations. He reasoned that, if she remained neutral or sided with France and were conquered, Bavaria would suffer the fate of Hanover. But if she sided with Prussia and lost, Napoleon would out of self-interest preserve Bavaria's independence. In parliament the sudden crisis interrupted the assault of the patriots and left progressives upon the "Prussianization" of the Bavarian army. On the fifteenth the deputies adjourned to await developments. The next day Bray extracted from King Louis the order to mobilize. In the cities, where German nationalists were strongest, popular excitement ran high. Parliament reconvened, but a special committee reduced the government's request for war credits by eighty percent and stipulated armed neutrality. Nevertheless, the particularists were unable to stem the tide. In the end the deputies granted, 101 to 47, nearly seventy percent of the sum requested and left the issue of belligerency up to the cabinet. On July 20 Bavaria entered the conflict without a formal declaration of war.[4]

In August German soldiers, north and south, underwent a common baptism of fire on the fields of France. At home every village

---

Lichtenfels als Geschichtsquelle, Historische Studien, Vol. 234 (Berlin, 1933), pp. 46 ff., 72 ff.

[3] *GW,* viB, 365; Adolf Rapp, *Die Württemberger und die nationale Frage, 1863-1871, Darstellungen aus der Württembergischen Geschichte,* Vol. 4 (Stuttgart, 1910), pp. 363-385; Freiherr von Mittnacht, *Rückblicke* (Stuttgart, 1909), pp. 51 ff.

[4] M. Doeberl, *Bayern und die Bismarckische Reichsgründung* (Munich, 1925), pp. 30 ff.; Windell, *Catholics and German Unity,* pp. 249 ff.; Theodor Schieder, *Die kleindeutsche Partei in Bayern, Münchener historische Abhandlungen,* Vol. 12 (Munich, 1936), pp. 251 ff.

and town joined in the general jubilation over their triumphs. As Bismarck anticipated, war with France produced an upsurge of German national feeling which helped to fill the chasm of time. In sharing the same dangers, experiences, and hatreds the Germans established a psychological bond which, if it did not extinguish, at least diminished, the significance of the tribal sentiments, dynastic loyalties, customs, and mores which had previously divided them.

From Karlsruhe came the first overture. On September 2 Minister-President Jolly forwarded to Bismarck a memorandum proposing the founding of a "German Reich." On the same day Varnbüler was replaced in Stuttgart by Baron von Mittnacht, formerly minister of justice. While in agreement with Varnbüler's policies in recent years, Mittnacht grasped that a turning point had been reached. Over dwindling opposition he launched a national policy in collaboration with Suckow. At Meaux on September 17 Bismarck informed Suckow, as he had Jolly by dispatch on the 12th, that the southern governments must take the initiative. Berlin would avoid every appearance of pressure, which could only arouse mistrust and antagonism. He was still in the dark, he declared, concerning the views of King Louis of Bavaria.[5]

Both Bray and Louis were suspicious of Bismarck's intent to use the war as a lever against southern sovereignty. Somehow the Bavarians had to be induced to volunteer what could not be openly demanded. In August Bismarck hinted through Thile at the possibility of territorial rewards in Alsace and Lorraine. Ultimately he decided that the two provinces should become the common property of Germany, to be called the "Reichsland." But even this solution was intended to precipitate a discussion of Germany's future. On September 1 Delbrück, Bismarck's trusted aide, was dispatched to Dresden to discuss the matter and urge the Saxons to take the initiative in Munich.[6] Perhaps by this back door a way could be found into the Wittelsbach castle.

5 GW, VIII, 488-489; Hermann Baumgarten, Staatsminister Jolly (Tübingen, 1897), pp. 175-176; Oncken, Grossherzog Friedrich I, II, 128 ff.; Wilhelm Busch, ed., Rückschau von Albert von Suckow (Tübingen, 1909), pp. 167-168; Mittnacht, Rückblicke, pp. 64 ff. On Mittnacht see Walter Seefried, Mittnacht und die deutsche Frage bis zur Reichsgründung, Darstellungen aus der Württembergischen Geschichte, Vol. 18 (Stuttgart, 1928), pp. 84 ff.

6 Erich Brandenburg, ed., Briefe und Aktenstücke zur Geschichte der Gründung des deutschen Reiches, 1870-1871 (Leipzig, 1911), I, 3 ff.; Doeberl, Bayern und Reichsgründung, pp. 43 ff.; Rudolf von Delbrück, Lebenserinnerungen, 1817-1867 (Berlin, 1905), II, 409 ff.

On the Isar the mighty victory at Sedan, and the outpouring of German patriotism which it produced, convinced Louis and his ministers that the *status quo* in Germany could not be preserved. The problem was no longer whether Bavaria would remain out of a German union, but under what conditions she would enter it. What they most desired was to dissolve and replace the North German Confederation with a "German confederation" of looser structure.[7] This, of course, Bismarck had no intention of conceding. While conscious of the necessity of concessions, he was fully resolved to preserve the basic structure of the northern constitution. Alterations might be made in the façade and trim, even new windows and doorways added, but the beams and joists which determined the shape and style must remain untouched.

At Bray's request Delbrück took the train for Munich and a series of conferences (September 22-26) in which the two southern kingdoms made known their views on Germany's future constitution. By evading the issue of dissolution, the Prussian succeeded in making the northern constitution the basis of the discussion. But the demands of Bray and Mittnacht for "special" and "reserved" rights in such matters as foreign policy, military affairs, and the veto power were so far-reaching that the cohesion of the proposed Reich was gravely threatened. Delbrück came away, however, feeling that much had been accomplished. Yet it was ominous that in their final audience Louis avoided every allusion to the German question and spoke only of papal affairs. In view of Bismarck's flat opposition to dissolution, Bray had in fact determined upon a final attempt to form with Württemberg a "wider confederation" whose link with the north was to be diplomatic rather than constitutional.[8]

From afar Bismarck strove to influence the deliberations in Munich with his usual mixture of threat, enticement, and blandishment. In Early September he let Count Tauffkirchen, now a prominent official of the military government in France, have a quick glimpse at his armory of alternatives. Should Bavaria's

[7] Otto von Bray-Steinburg, *Denkwürdigkeiten aus seinem Leben* (Leipzig, 1901), pp. 136 ff.; Doeberl, *Bayern und Reichsgründung*, pp. 69 ff., 85 ff.; Brandenburg, *Briefe und Aktenstücke*, I, 29-32.

[8] Becker, *Bismarcks Ringen*, pp. 715-716; Doeberl, *Bayern und Reichsgründung*, pp. 91 ff., 256 ff.; Delbrück, *Lebenserinnerungen*, II, 413 ff.; Wilhelm Stolze, "Zur Geschichte der Reichsgründung im Jahre 1870," *Preussische Jahrbücher*, Vol. 197 (1924), pp. 1-12.

demands be too extreme, the German question would simply be regulated without her, the Zollverein treaties might be permitted to lapse, and the Bavarian Palatinate would be included in the North German Confederation. While the conference was in session, however, he hinted at the possibility of generous concessions to bring Bavaria "over the Rubicon." The object was not to produce in six weeks a constitution for all time, but to build the foundation of a structure which might be completed in ten, twenty, or fifty years. Above all, William was eager to come to terms with Louis, from whose hands he hoped to receive the imperial title.[9]

On reading Delbrück's report of the Munich negotiations, Bismarck recognized immediately that much less had been achieved than his emissary assumed. Immediately he set in motion the system of pressures by which he hoped to pierce the barrier of southern particularism. On September 30 he dispatched to Karlsruhe the message for which the Badenese had waited so long and impatiently. A formal request for entry into the North German Confederation was "welcome at the moment both as a basis for negotiations with Bavaria and as a means of pressure on the same." The grand ducal government responded quickly, and the cabinet in Stuttgart followed suit. In mid-October delegations headed by Jolly and Mittnacht arrived in Versailles to negotiate the necessary treaties. Faced by the prospect of isolation, the Bavarians were compelled to treat.[10] On October 20 Bray and his delegation likewise took the train for France; four days later came the representatives of Hesse. The cast was complete and on stage; the final act in the long drama of German unification could begin.

Luckily for Bismarck, the southern delegations were unable to present a common front at Versailles. Their different goals and mutual frictions enabled him to negotiate separately with each and avoid having to grant the same concessions to all. Baden was willing, and Hesse compelled, to accept the northern constitution almost without reservation. The demands raised by Württemberg were not insuperable, and the negotiation with Mittnacht and

9 Karl A. von Müller, "Bismarck und Ludwig II. im September 1870," *Historische Zeitschrift*, Vol. 111 (1913), pp. 89-132, and "Aktenstücke aus den Papieren des Grafen Karl v. Tauffkirchen," *Forschungen zur brandenburgischen und preussischen Geschichte*, Vol. 27 (1914), pp. 572-592; *GW*, viii, 516.

10 *GW*, viii, 527-529, 538-540; Baumgarten, *Jolly*, pp. 177 ff.; Doeberl, *Bayern und Reichsgründung*, pp. 103 ff.

Suckow proceeded smoothly. But the Bavarians were difficult. Bray and his associates had not surrendered their desire for a "wider confederation." While willing to accept "Reich and Kaiser," they presented a long list of requirements which jeopardized the sovereignty of the national government. As at Munich they demanded (among other rights) an equal voice in foreign policy, a separate army (except in war), an independent military budget, the right of veto against constitutional changes, and surrender of the right to terminate the Zollverein.[11]

Bismarck pulled every wire in the effort to bring the Wittelsbach puppet into motion. He proposed a congress of princes to be held in Versailles, but King Louis could not be enticed from his Alpine retreat. He thought of mobilizing German opinion by summoning the north German Reichstag to convene in Versailles, but even the national liberals found the idea of a parliamentary session in the hall of mirrors too "baroque." Once again he refused to relinquish the right to terminate the Zollverein. To show the Bavarians their isolation, he accelerated negotiations with the other three states. In Germany his propaganda service worked full blast to build up public pressure for national unity. By November 8 these measures had their effect. Bray and his associates realized that they dare not return home empty-handed. They determined to surrender the "wider confederation" and seek the best possible terms for Bavarian entry into a federal union. For a few days it appeared as though the separate negotiations might be brought to simultaneous conclusion. Bismarck looked forward to a dramatic ceremony in which the representatives of north and south would sign the treaties and demonstrate to Germany and Europe their unanimity of purpose.[12]

On November 12 his hopes were rudely shattered. At the final conference with the Württemberger, after the last issues had been settled, Mittnacht unexpectedly declared that he had no power to sign. To Bismarck's consternation the delegation returned home for consultation. In Stuttgart King Charles had at the last minute resolved to make no greater concessions than Bavaria in joining the north. Concerned and wrathful, Bismarck saw that the time had come to unleash the forces of popular agitation

11 *Ibid.*, pp. 109 ff.; Becker, *Bismarcks Ringen*, p. 729.
12 *GW*, viii, 583-584; Doeberl, *Bayern und Reichsgründung*, pp. 113 ff.; Becker, *Bismarcks Ringen*, pp. 727 ff.

against the two southern kingdoms. "Unless a German storm intervenes," he wrote, "nothing will be accomplished with these diplomats and bureaucrats of the old school, at least not this year." To Grand Duke Frederick he announced his intention to mobilize a "pressure from below." "These governments appear to overlook entirely the dangerous elements which surround them." It was not his fault if a movement should now develop which jeopardized their very existence. To Berlin, Koblenz, Hanover, and Munich went instructions to incite the national liberal press against southern particularism.[13]

In Versailles the negotiations with Baden and Hesse were pressed to conclusion and signed on November 15. As usual Bismarck extracted advantage from calamity. No longer did he have to consider Stuttgart in negotiating with Munich. The concessions made to the latter need not be limited to those granted the former. On November 18 the conferences with Bray and his associates were resumed. Because of Roon's illness Bismarck was compelled to handle both the military and political negotiations. In hour-long talks the critical points were hammered out. On November 23 the treaty was signed. Meanwhile, Mittnacht and Suckow had succeeded in convincing King Charles of the futility of his position. Even during the final negotiations with Delbrück in Berlin, however, they had to struggle against the particularistic current in Stuttgart. On November 25 the treaty was finally signed.[14]

2. CONCESSIONS TO PARTICULARISM

Since 1866 Bismarck had insisted that the south must be won, not conquered. The system of checks and balances in the constitutional system he had designed for Germany depended upon the voluntary cooperation of the remaining German dynasties and governments. By using force, he would have weakened them and upset the balance in favor of the Reichstag and centralism. He was aware, moreover, that the expansion of the north German system over so many millions of people could be successful only if most approved. Coercion was not enough. To endure as the

[13] Suckow, *Rückschau*, pp. 176 ff.; Mittnacht, *Rückblicke*, pp. 136-138; Eugen Schneider, "Württembergs Beitritt zum Deutschen Reich 1870," *Württembergische Vierteljahrshefte für Landesgeschichte*, xxix (1920), pp. 138 ff.; *GW*, viii, 586-587; Hermann Oncken, *Rudolf von Bennigsen* (Stuttgart, 1910), ii, 196 ff., and *Grossherzog Friedrich I*, ii, 169-172.

[14] Doeberl, *Bayern und Reichsgründung*, pp. 125 ff.; Mittnacht, *Rückblicke*, pp. 139 ff.; Becker, *Bismarcks Ringen*, pp. 739 ff.

government of Germany, the Prussian system had to be based upon a moral consensus.

At least one important person in the Prussian camp disagreed. During October and November, the crown prince was filled with apprehension and mistrust by the difficulties of the negotiations with Bavaria and Württemberg. Bismarck's moderation made him question the Junker's German patriotism and his will to national unity. There seemed to be no awareness, he repeatedly complained, of Prussia's power to coerce. "We have them after all in our grasp." But the Junker replied that such tactics would reap a harvest of hate and suspicion for generations. He was confident that in the future the course of organic development would render unimportant whatever concessions were necessary to win the voluntary adhesion of the south.[15]

The list of concessions made in the treaties of November 1870 was long.[16] They fall into two categories: (1) those which heightened the power of the state governments in general, and (2) those "special" and "reserved" rights which benefited only Baden, Bavaria, and Württemberg. The federated states in general gained from the expanded authority of the Bundesrat. The approval of that body was now necessary for declarations of war, except in cases of foreign attack. Furthermore, the commander-in-chief must seek approval of the Bundesrat for an "execution" against a recalcitrant state. The supervisory power of the Kaiser was limited by the necessity of seeking Bundesrat approval before ordering the correction of deficiencies in the administration of imperial laws. The authority of the Kaiser to issue decrees for the execution of imperial laws was likewise made dependent upon Bundesrat approval, unless the law itself provided otherwise. The old rule that a two-thirds vote in the Bundesrat was necessary to pass a constitutional amendment was changed; henceforth, a negative vote of fourteen could block such an amendment. This placed the veto within reach of the combined votes of Bavaria, Saxony, and Württemberg, or of Bavaria, Württemberg, Baden, and Hesse, or of a combination of the small states. The principle of *itio in partes* was adopted by the provision that in matters not

---

[15] Becker, *Bismarcks Ringen*, pp. 747-749; Heinrich O. Meisner, ed., *Kaiser Friedrich III., Das Kriegstagebuch von 1870/71* (Berlin, 1926), pp. 200, 223-225.

[16] For the final version of the German constitution see *Reichs-Gesetzblatt* (1871), pp. 63-85; also Karl Binding, ed., *Deutsche Staatsgrundgesetze in diplomatisch genauem Abdrucke* (2nd ed., Leipzig, 1901), I, 2 ff.

common to the whole of the Reich, only the votes of the affected states would be counted in Bundesrat and Reichstag. Likewise, "reserved" and "special rights" of member states might be altered only with their approval.

The "special rights" granted to Bavaria were fresh evidence of Bismarck's genius for giving the appearance of concessions without the substance. Should a Prussian delegate be unable to preside over the Bundesrat, a Bavarian delegate might substitute for him. Bavaria was to possess a permanent seat on the Bundesrat committee for military affairs and the chairmanship of a new committee on foreign affairs, in which Saxony and Württemberg were likewise to have permanent seats. While member states surrendered their own consular services abroad, they might receive foreign consuls on their own soil. Should an envoy of the Reich be incapacitated, the Bavarian envoy could be authorized to substitute for him. In a special protocol, which remained secret until 1917, Bavaria was granted the right to be represented at peace negotiations.

Time was to show that these rights were purely decorative. They left to the states merely the symbols of sovereignty. As Mittnacht observed, the committee on foreign affairs was "stillborn"; neither Bismarck nor his successors permitted it any important role in the conduct of foreign affairs. The right to maintain a diplomatic corps was empty, since the envoys of the Reich were the actual agents of its foreign policy. The right of substitution was seldom used, while the Bavarian delegate at the peace conference of Brest-Litovsk was simply an observer. The foreign services of the lesser states withered on the uprooted vine.[17]

The "reserved rights" were of greater importance. Bavaria was given autonomy in matters of domicile and residence within her borders. She could regulate and maintain her own railway system, subject to Reich laws in matters of national defense. Bavaria and Württemberg retained their independent postal and telegraph systems, subject to regulation by the Reich in only a few respects. With Baden they might levy taxes on domestic beer and spirits, although they should "endeavor" to enact uniform

[17] Heinrich Triepel, *Unitarismus und Föderalismus im deutschen Reiche* (Tübingen, 1907), p. 46; Freiherr von Mittnacht, *Erinnerungen an Bismarck* (Stuttgart, 1904), i, 30 ff.; Ernst Deuerlein, *Der Bundesratsausschuss für die Auswärtigen Angelegenheiten 1870-1918* (Regensburg, 1955).

legislation. They were to receive no part of the Reich's revenue from such sources.

The military conventions with Württemberg and Bavaria[18] contained a number of reserved rights even more extensive than those granted Saxony in 1867. Whereas the commander of the Saxon contingent was appointed by the commander-in-chief on the nomination of the Saxon king, that of Württemberg was appointed by the Swabian king with the approval of the commander-in-chief. Whereas all general officers in the Saxon army had to be approved by the latter, this was not true in Württemberg. The King of Württemberg retained the right to determine uniforms and insignia. While his troops were actually under the authority of the commander-in-chief, to whom they swore allegiance, the king kept the ceremonial rights and privileges of a commanding general. To Württemberg it was also guaranteed that during peacetime the organization of the contingent would be undisturbed; none of its troops would be stationed outside Württemberg; and no other German troops would be stationed in the state without the king's approval (except for border garrisons). Unexpended surpluses of the military budget need not be returned to the Reich treasury at the end of the fiscal year.

Even greater concessions were granted Bavaria. Its "army" was to be "a self-contained unit of the German army with an independent administration and under the command of his majesty, the King of Bavaria." In other words, the Kaiser assumed command of the Bavarian army only on the inception of war. The Wittelsbach king retained, furthermore, the power to appoint all officers and the commanders of all fortresses located in Bavaria. While obligated to follow the standards of the Reich in such matters as organization, formation, training, and mobilization, the king could adopt Reich standards in equipment, armament, and rank insignia at his own discretion. Though the Kaiser was given the power of inspection, it was hedged by numerous restrictions. Bavaria retained a separate military budget, established by its own government, but according to the standards of the Reich constitution. It was not the Reich chancellor's responsibility to see that actual expenditures conformed to this budget, and the ac-

---

[18] While the agreements on military affairs were generally called "military conventions," only that with Württemberg was specifically designated as such. For the texts see *Bundes-Gesetzblatt des Norddeutschen Bundes* (1870), pp. 658-662 and *Reichs-Gesetzblatt* (1871), pp. 9-26.

counting was a purely Bavarian concern. Unexpended surpluses of the Bavarian military budget were to stay in the Bavarian treasury.

While the sacrifice was great, Bismarck had achieved his basic objective. The governmental system which he had devised for northern Germany had been accepted by the southern governments without fundamental change. There were even some gains for its centralistic side. On the proposal of Bavaria and Württemberg the legislative competence of the Reich was enlarged to include the publishing industry and the right of association (*Vereinswesen*). Twenty-four basic laws of the North German Confederation were accepted by the south along with the constitution. Psychologically speaking, however, the greatest gain was adoption of the title "German Kaiser."

3. KAISER AND REICH

To Bismarck the imperial title was a political necessity. The historical image which it aroused in German minds, he believed, would encourage "unity and centralization." German princes would accept in good grace from a German Kaiser what they would resent from a King of Prussia. Only the German title conveyed the idea that the rights associated with it had been "freely granted." National institutions must not appear to be mere extensions of the Prussian state.[19]

William disliked the idea for the very virtues which Bismarck saw in it. He was not free from the ambition to lord it over his fellow princes. Dynastic pride made it difficult for him to accept a crown whose authority had once oppressed the Great Elector and against which Frederick the Great had fought. "What do I want with that?" he asked contemptuously. "Certainly," Bismarck replied, "your majesty does not want to remain forever a neuter—*das Prasidium?*" But the thought of resurrecting "Kaiser and Reich" sent the imagination of Frederick William soaring. He busied himself with designs for crowns and coats of arms and dreamed of a "free German empire," which would lead civilization by realizing "all noble ideas of the modern world," by "humanizing" mankind and saving it from French frivolity. The German nation would be freed from bureaucratism, despotism,

19 *GW*, viii, 601-602.

Jesuitry, orthodoxy, and socialism. "The crown prince," sneered Bismarck, "is the dumbest and vainest of men; he's crazed again by the Kaiser madness."[20]

The key to the situation, the Junker realized, was again Bavaria. A Hohenzoller could hardly reject a crown offered by a Wittelsbach. But the strange man in the lonely Alpine castle of Hohenschwangau was likewise proud of his dynasty, which had borne the imperial title when the Hohenzollern were petty Swabian princes. In his negotiations with Tauffkirchen in September and later with Bray, Bismarck indicated that "Kaiser and Reich" were the price demanded for vital concessions to Bavarian particularism. Only these exciting symbols of past and future glory would make possible a general acceptance of the Bavarian treaty. Should Bavaria delay, the Reichstag might repeat the offer of April 1849. In the interest of monarchism, the matter could not be left to popular initiative.[21]

For months Louis had been vexed by the suggestion. Now his own ministers became its advocates. Grand Duke Frederick of Baden likewise pressed. While given to dream and fantasy, Louis was not without his practical side. He determined to sell what could apparently no longer be withheld. In addition to the special and reserved rights being negotiated in Versailles, he demanded as "compensation" a segment of territory and two million *Gulden* (approximately four million marks). Twice in November his equerry, Count Max von Holnstein, traveled to Versailles to discuss this delicate matter. Nothing came of the territorial demand, but the financial claim was successful. Until 1892 Louis apparently received a yearly income of about 300,000 marks from Bismarck's secret "Guelph fund"; Holnstein collected ten percent. Not until many years later, after Louis' tragic suicide and Bismarck's retirement, was anything publicly known of this transaction. The exact details will probably never be learned, for no records were kept. To himself Louis apparently represented

---

20 *GW*, xv, 324-325; Frederick III, *Kriegstagebuch*, pp. 103, 146-147, 180, 260, 265-266, 452; Bamberger, *Bismarcks grosses Spiel*, p. 243. Frederick William's diary contradicts Bismarck's memory that just before and after Sedan the prince desired the title "King of the Germans," and wished to degrade the kings of Saxony, Bavaria, and Württemberg to ducal status. According to one authority, he entertained this idea at Nikolsburg in 1866, but shifted to the imperial title at the beginning of the following year. Martin Philippson, *Friedrich III. als Kronprinz und Kaiser* (Berlin, 1893), p. 144.

21 Doeberl, *Bayern und Reichsgründung*, pp. 151 ff.; Bray, *Denkwürdigkeiten*, p. 172.

these payments as partial repayment of the war indemnity paid by Bavaria in 1866. But the sums went into his personal account, not the public treasury. German historians like to call it a "dotation"; but to outsiders it has more the appearance of a bribe.[22]

Bismarck himself was the author of the famous "Kaiser letter" in which Louis bid William "re-establish a German Reich and the German imperial dignity." On November 27 Holnstein carried the draft to Hohenschwangau and on December 2 he was back with a copy in Louis' own hand. When Prince Luitpold of Bavaria formally presented it on the following day, William was deeply annoyed. Once again he had been presented with a *fait accompli*. Only with the greatest reluctance did he consent to bear this "cross" which Bismarck had hewn for him. Immediately the chancellor telegraphed the text of the letter to Delbrück for use against the parliamentary opposition.[23]

On November 25 the Reichstag had convened in Berlin to consider the treaties with the south and the revised constitution. Led by Schulze-Delitzsch, the progressives objected to the whole procedure. They demanded an all-German parliament to draft a new constitution which would make good what had been surrendered in 1867. When this was refused, they introduced amendments to guarantee the fundamental civil rights and the remuneration of deputies. Again they failed. But the national liberals were also disgruntled. Like Lasker, many found the concessions to Bavarian particularism "shocking" and "dangerous"; the cohesion of the Reich appeared in jeopardy. Bebel of the tiny but noisy socialist faction irritated everyone by advocating a republic.[24]

Bismarck had anticipated these complaints. During the negotiations with Bray and Mittnacht he had invited leaders of the National Liberal, Free Conservative, and Conservative Parties to Versailles for consultation. Unable to return to Berlin for the session, he dispatched Delbrück to represent the government and mobilized as many emissaries as possible to convince the deputies that the treaties were the best obtainable. Jolly, Freydorf, and

[22] Becker, *Bismarcks Ringen*, pp. 790 ff.; Oncken, *Grossherzog Friedrich I*, II, 141 ff., 207 ff.; Wilhelm Schüssler, "Das Geheimnis des Kaiserbriefes Ludwigs II.," in Martin Göhring and Alexander Scharff, eds., *Geschichtliche Kräfte und Entscheidungen, Festschrift für Otto Becker* (Wiesbaden, 1954), pp. 206-209.

[23] Friedrich III, *Kriegstagebuch*, pp. 253-254; Brandenburg, *Briefe und Aktenstücke*, I, 112 ff.

[24] *SBR* (2nd extraordinary session, 1870), pp. 71 ff.

Roggenbach made the trip from Baden. Ludwig Bamberger, Hessian publicist and national liberal, was sent well stocked with arguments. The crown prince wrote to Edward Simson, the speaker of the chamber, in the interest of a favorable vote. When the situation looked critical, all deputies on duty with the armed forces were furloughed to Berlin.[25]

Boiling with wrath, Bismarck sent the deputies a potpourri of threats. Any essential change in the agreements, achieved with such great difficulty, would be equivalent to rejection. In that case there would be little prospect of union with the south in the immediate future. Louis was childless and in bad health; his brother and heir was "entirely in ultramontane hands." An outbreak of strife in Germany over such a vital issue would have "incalculable disadvantages for us in our relations with France and the neutrals." Bavarian nationalists would demonstrate; Beust would renew his attempts at intervention; Bismarck, moreover, would tender his resignation; the king would reject it and dissolve the Reichstag.[26]

Perhaps his most effective stroke, however, was the revelation that more had been achieved than the national liberals themselves originally thought possible. During September Bennigsen, Forckenbeck, and Lasker had visited the southern capitals to confer with political leaders and help galvanize a popular movement for national unity. In Munich, Lasker, impressed by the strength of particularistic sentiment, left behind a memorandum on the constitutional question which conceded much of what the Bavarians wanted. Taking it along to Versailles, Bray produced it when the Junker, following his usual technique, argued that the northern Reichstag would never yield to the Bavarian demands. But again Bismarck converted a handicap on one front into advantage on another. He sent the embarrassing document off to Delbrück for use against the dissatisfied deputies.[27]

Much was also expected of the announcement that the Wittelsbach king had offered William the imperial title. But the weapon

25 Oncken, *Bennigsen*, ii, 189-190; Friedrich III, *Kriegstagebuch*, pp. 258, 468-470; *GW*, vib, 607; vii, 431, 433; Oncken, *Grossherzog Friedrich I*, ii, 231, 233.

26 *GW*, vib, 598-601, 607-608, 611-614. Actually Bismarck expected that the expiration of the Zollverein treaties in 1878 would present another opportunity to make good a failure in 1870.

27 *GW*, vib, 594, 598-600; Doeberl, *Bayern und Reichsgründung*, pp. 247-248. Bamberger, *Bismarcks grosses Spiel*, pp. 227 ff. On Lasker's trip to southern Germany see *HW*, i, 457 ff., and Oncken, *Bennigsen*, ii, 180 ff.

nearly failed because of Delbrück's ineptitude as a parliamentary *regisseur*. In response to a staged inquiry during the debate on December 5, he rummaged through his briefcase and produced the letter, reading it in his usual dry manner without oratorical effect. This casual, seemingly accidental, communication of so important a document incited his hearers to amusement rather than enthusiasm. It was, lamented Frederick William, as though he had pulled the "poor German Kaiser crown" out of his pocket wrapped in an old newspaper. Bismarck also reacted in character. "The farce," he said, could have had a better "stage manager." Nevertheless, the deputies realized that they had no other recourse than to accept the despised treaty. "The maid is ugly," Lasker remarked, "but she has to be married anyhow." On December 9 the measure passed, 195 to 32. Even the progressives voted for it; in the minority were socialists, Hanoverian Guelphs, democratic liberals, and members of the Catholic faction. On the following day the necessary changes in the north German constitution were accepted, with only six socialist votes in the negative. Finally the Reichstag resolved to send a delegation to Versailles to bid William to accept the imperial crown.[28]

Again William was much upset. Even now he was unreconciled to the new dignity his chancellor had so skillfully thrust upon him. The actions of Reichstag and Bundesrat, he complained, were presumptuous. Neither he nor the German princes as a whole had accepted the titles "Kaiser and Reich" which the parliament had inserted in the constitution. Toward Bismarck his manner was frigid. He would not receive the Reichstag delegation until the other sovereigns had been heard from. Among the latter not all were happy over Louis' commitment. The Kings of Saxony and Württemberg were miffed over his failure to consult them beforehand. Once taken, however, the step was irrevocable. In the night of December 17 a telegram from Hohenschwangau reported that all rulers and free cities had given their consent. The next day William, flanked by princes and generals, listened to the Reichstag petition presented by the venerable Simson, who on April 3, 1849 had offered the Frankfurt crown to Frederick William IV. Haltingly the elderly Hohenzoller, near-sighted and

---

[28] *GW*, vib, 609-611; Friedrich III, *Kriegstagebuch*, p. 264; Busch, *Bismarck*, i, 292; Eduard von Wertheimer, *Bismarck im politischen Kampf* (Berlin, 1930), pp. 444-446.

choked with emotion, read the favorable reply Bismarck had composed for him.[29]

William's conduct in the Kaiser question is very indicative of his psychology and his relationship to Bismarck. About the sincerity of his revulsion there can be no doubt. Nevertheless, he could hardly have been unaware of the web Bismarck was spinning to entrap him. Yet he took no step to rip it asunder. This had also been true of Leopold's candidature, of the decision for war against Austria, and many other situations in preceding years. The minister had long since become completely indispensable. Bowing to his will had become a habit. It was as though a tacit understanding existed between them that, if Bismarck could make the step appear inescapable, William would take it—reluctantly, even angrily, but conclusively. Once done, he accepted the new situation completely, for he was not a brooder and his resentments were never lasting. A few days after receiving the Reichstag delegation he awarded his chancellor the iron cross, first class.

Even now the matter was not ended, for the last word lay with the southern parliaments. In Baden and Hesse there was no difficulty. In Württemberg the German party, which had scored a great victory at the polls on December 5, pushed the treaties through the lower chamber over dwindling opposition. But in Bavaria there was intense dissatisfaction. Not until January 11 did the debate begin. The irreconcilables of the Patriot Party denounced the mediatization of Bavaria and her subjection to Prussian autocracy and militarism. But there were also signs that Louis himself, disturbed by the criticisms of his family, was wavering.[30]

From Versailles Bismarck watched these developments with mounting concern. In Rome he sought to bring papal pressure to bear upon the ultramontanes. Through Werthern he secured Bray's agreement to dissolve the chamber immediately after an adverse vote. But he also warned that in any case the treaties with Baden, Hesse, and Württemberg would go into effect, as would the new constitution and the imperial title. "A painful tension" would arise in Germany which could only benefit the French. "The German nation would hold Bavaria accountable for the

29 Friedrich III, *Kriegstagebuch*, pp. 259, 268 ff., 279-281; Oncken, *Grossherzog Friedrich I*, II, 240 ff.

30 See Kläre Kraus, *Der Kampf in der bayerischen Abgeordnetenkammer um die Versailler-Verträge, 11. 21. Januar 1871* (Köln, 1935).

sacrifices made necessary by prolongation of the war." A separate peace between Bavaria and France would be equivalent to a declaration of war on Germany.[31] In the final vote on January 21 the division of the Patriot Party and the absence of three irreconcilables enabled the proponents of the treaties to achieve the necessary two-thirds majority. The margin of victory was two.

4. THE "GERMAN KAISER"

The final scene in the long drama of German unification, like most which preceded it, was taut with suspense. Once the imperial title had been accepted, a fresh quarrel arose over its phrasing. William preferred: "By the grace of God, King of Prussia, chosen Kaiser of Germany." But Bismarck insisted on: "By the grace of God, German Kaiser, King of Prussia." After some discussion the Hohenzoller accepted his view that the word "chosen" would make the title appear elective, like that of the Holy Roman Empire. Reluctantly he also acceded to the argument that the imperial must precede the royal title, if the intended political effect were to be achieved. But he stubbornly insisted upon the form, "Kaiser of Germany." He wanted no "pseudo-emperorship." If he had to bear the title, it must clearly express his authority. In the crown prince and the Grand Duke of Baden he found support.[32]

To Bismarck the issue was petty in itself. What did it matter in which form the imperial authority was clothed, as long as it existed? He had to point out, nevertheless, that commitments had already been made to the title in its weaker form. To abandon it now would jeopardize his entire work. During the treaty negotiations Bray had insisted upon "German Kaiser" and this was the form used in Louis' letter. When the issue came up in the Bundesrat, he had telegraphed to Delbrück, "Kaiser of Germany, if possible, but, if the others don't want it, German Kaiser will do."[33] Hence the constitutional amendments accepted by Bundesrat and Reichstag had used the latter form. If William could not be brought to change his mind, the amendments would have to be reworded, the agreement with Bavaria redrafted. All of the hazards so successfully surmounted would have to be faced again.

[31] *GW*, VIB, 643-646, 657, 672.
[32] *GW*, VIB, 654-656, 662-665; Oncken, *Grossherzog Friedrich I*, II, 308 ff.
[33] Becker, *Bismarcks Ringen*, p. 811; *GW*, VIB, 622.

January 18, birthday of the Prussian monarchy, was the date set for the ceremony in which the emperorship was to be proclaimed. In a three-hour conference on the preceding day William held to his position. With rising temper he insisted upon the more exalted title, yet wept that within a few hours he must "take leave of the old Prussia." Frederick William pointed out to his father that the house of Hohenzollern had repeatedly assumed new and higher titles as it rose in power and responsibility. Finally William broke off the discussion in fury, declaring he wanted to hear no more of tomorrow's celebration. He considered abdication; "Fritz" would know better than he how to adjust to the new situation.[34] But the mood passed.

The next day the celebration took place on schedule in the glistening hall of mirrors, where the kings of France once held court. As the prince of highest rank (the Kings of Saxony, Bavaria, and Württemberg not being present), Grand Duke Frederick of Baden had the honor of hailing William with the new title. While the company assembled, he conferred hastily with William and Bismarck. Neither had changed his mind. When the historic moment came, Frederick simply evaded the issue by crying out, "Long live his imperial and royal majesty, Kaiser William!" Descending from the dais to greet the assembled princes and generals, the indignant old man passed Bismarck by without a word or handshake.[35]

To no one else, however, belonged the credit for what was consummated that wintry day in Versailles. The imperial title, the glittering uniforms and regimental standards, and William's sonorous manifesto "To the German People"[36] symbolized the completed union of three traditions: Hohenzollern authoritarianism, Prussian militarism, and German nationalism. Onward rushed the stream of time down a new and potentially hazardous channel.

---

34 Friedrich III, *Kriegstagebuch*, pp. 334-338, 349 (note 3).
35 *GW*, xv, 328-329; Oncken, *Grossherzog Friedrich I*, ii, 320-329.
36 The document was composed and read by Bismarck. *GW*, viB, 671-672.

INDEX

Other Titles in European History
and International Affairs
Available in Princeton Paperback

73

PT 233

93